Fourth Edition

Sadlier-Oxford

Building an Enriched Vocabulary

Senior Consultant

John Heath, Ph.D.
Santa Clara University

Sadlier-Oxford
A Division of William H. Sadlier, Inc.

Reviewers

The publisher wishes to thank for their comments and suggestions the following teachers, who read portions of the book prior to publication.

Eileen Bacha
English Department Chair
Cardinal Mooney High School
Youngstown, Ohio

Carole Tatem
English Teacher
Paul VI High School
Haddonfield, New Jersey

Elizabeth Bradstreet
English Teacher
Lower Richland High School
Hopkins, South Carolina

Printed in the United States of America.
ISBN: 0-8215-7571-6
1 2 3 4 5 6 7 8 9/08 07 06 05 04 03

Contents

Learning Words

An Introduction for the Student

I. The Vocabulary of Vocabulary

Before you begin learning the words presented in this book, it might be useful to review what you know about the "vocabulary of vocabulary." Accordingly, a number of key concepts or technical terms relating to the study of words are discussed below. Some of these items—*synonyms*, for instance—will no doubt be familiar, but the discussion may help to bring their meaning and use into sharper focus. Others—*connotation*, for example—may be entirely new to you.

Denotation and Connotation. It would be fair to say that words basically convey meaning in two distinct ways, for which the terms *denotation* and *connotation* have been devised.

The **denotation** of a word is its specific meaning as given in a dictionary. For example, the denotation of the adjective *scholarly* is "learned." Similarly, the denotation of the adjective *grasping* is "overly eager for material gain," and the denotation of the verb *travel* is "make a journey." The verb corresponding to *denotation* is *denote*.

Connotation, on the other hand, relates to the tone of a word—that is, the emotions or associations that the word arouses in the listener or reader. If a word—*scholarly*, for instance—arouses positive emotions, its tone or connotation is said to be favorable or positive. If it arouses negative emotions (the way *grasping* does), its tone or connotation is said to be negative, unfavorable, or pejorative (pronounced pə-jôr′-ə-tĭv). A word that does not arouse any strong feeling, either good or bad, is said to be neutral. The verb *travel* is such a word. The verb corresponding to *connotation* is *connote*.

Literal and Figurative Meaning. It would also be fair to say that, generally speaking, words may be used on two quite distinct planes of meaning, which for convenience can be termed *literal* and *figurative* (or *metaphorical*).

When a word is being used in a **literal** sense, it is being employed in its strict or primary dictionary meaning in a situation (or context) that makes sense from a purely logical point of view. For example, if someone says that there are logs floating in the river, he or she is using the verb *float* literally because logs can actually float in water.

If, however, the person says that a famous actress "floated" into the room, he or she is using *float* in a nonliteral way and in a context that does not make sense from a purely logical point of view. People can't really float into a room except by artificial means. In other words, the person has applied the verb *float* to an unusual context in order to create a vivid and forceful image of the grace and elegance with which the actress *walked* into the room. Notice that now *float* no longer means "be buoyed up by" but, rather, something closer to "move gracefully or as if on air." We call this extended or nonliteral application of a word a **figurative** or **metaphorical** usage.

Another example may help clarify this distinction. If you read an old tale about a knight who slew a fire-breathing dragon, the word *fire-breathing* in this context is being used quite literally. Dragons were indeed believed to breathe real fire. If, however, your best friend says that her father rushed into the room "breathing fire," the expression *breathing fire* is being used figuratively or metaphorically in order to convey a vivid picture of the man's state of mind. In other words, your friend is simply saying that her father was very angry or upset, but she is saying it more colorfully and dramatically than the words "in a very angry/upset frame of mind" could possibly convey. It is this added dimension that makes the figurative use of language so striking and appealing.

One final note: Though all words, of course, have literal meanings and can be used literally, only a fraction of the vocabulary can normally be applied figuratively. Such words are often referred to as *resonant*. One must be careful, therefore, not to try to use nonresonant words in a figurative way.

Parts of Speech. Lexicographers (dictionary writers) and grammarians classify the words and other expressions that make up our language as different parts of speech, depending upon the function or functions they perform. Knowing what these classifications are and what they signify helps a person use a word correctly. For that reason, it might be well at this point to review some of the more common classifications that appear in this book.

A **noun** is a word or phrase that names a person, place, thing, or idea. Examples include *astronaut, library, trowel*, and *justice*. Nouns are usually divided into *common nouns* (e.g., *girl, day*) and *proper nouns* (e.g., *Jane, Wednesday*). All the nouns on the Basic Word List in this book (see pages 21–25) are common nouns.

An **adjective** is a word that is used to describe a noun (or pronoun). It changes (or modifies) the meaning of the word to which it refers by answering such questions as: How many? Which one? What kind? Examples include *yellow, old, first*, and *many*. As with nouns, adjectives are divided into *common adjectives* (e.g., *tall, earliest*) and *proper adjectives* (e.g., *Spanish, Elizabethan*). All the adjectives on the Basic Word List in this book (see pages 21–25) are common adjectives.

A **verb** is a word that expresses some kind of action or indicates some state of being. Examples include *run, think, enjoy, remain,* and *be.* Verbs are further subdivided into those that can take an object (*transitive* verbs) and those that cannot (*intransitive* verbs). *Shoot* is an example of a transitive verb; *sleep,* an illustration of one that is intransitive.

An **adverb** is a word that modifies a verb, an adjective, or another adverb. Adverbs usually answer such questions as: Where? When? How? How much? How long? Examples include *there, sometimes, badly, forever,* and *almost.*

One final note: Some words perform a number of different functions and are, therefore, classified as more than one part of speech. For example, *hope* is both a noun and a verb, *exact* is both a verb and an adjective, and *corporal* is both a noun and an adjective.

Synonyms and Antonyms. Over the centuries English has absorbed a great many words that mean more or less the same thing as other words in the language. Two words that are similar in meaning are called **synonyms**. For example, *fragile* and *delicate* are more or less synonyms. So are *thief* and *robber.* The adjective form of *synonym* is *synonymous.*

Of course, no two words in English ever really convey exactly the same meaning, have exactly the same tone or connotation, or apply to exactly the same situations. They may be very close to one another, but they are rarely identical twins. That is because usage over a long period of time has shaped and molded a special character for most words, and it is this character that makes a word unique. For example, *hate* and *detest* mean much the same thing except that *detest* conveys a stronger or more intense feeling of loathing than *hate* does. Accordingly, a person who says that he or she "detests" spinach is registering a stronger dislike of the vegetable than is the person who merely says that he or she "hates" it. Usually a dictionary provides much useful information about such fine distinctions of meaning and usage, but it cannot cover everything. For that reason, the student must often learn such subtleties by observation—that is, by noticing how and when other people use a given word, both in speaking and in writing.

Just as some words mean more or less the same thing, others indicate opposites. A word that means the opposite of another word is called its **antonym**. For example, the verbs *relish* and *detest* are antonyms. So are the adjectives *wet* and *dry.* The adjective form of *antonym* is *antonymous.*

Frequently, the term *antonym* is used not so much for the opposite of a given word as for its *counterpart.* For example, *doctor* doesn't really have an opposite, but it does have *counterparts*— *nurse* and *patient.* Similarly, *actor* doesn't have an opposite, but it does have a counterpart—*actress.* These are the items that people mean when they speak of the antonym of *doctor* or the antonym of *actor,* and the student should bear this in mind when dealing with antonym questions on various kinds of standardized tests.

The Parts of a Word. As you probably already know, words are made up of various parts or elements, for each of which a general name has been devised. The most important of these are:

prefix—a syllable or syllables placed at the beginning of a word. Examples include *in* (as in *inspect*), *pre* (as in *predict*), and *post* (as in *postpone*).

root or **base**—the main part of a word to which prefixes and suffixes (see below) are attached. Examples include *spect* (as in *inspector*), *dict* (as in *prediction*), and *pone* (as in *postponement*).

suffix—a syllable or syllables placed at the end of a word. Examples include *or* (as in *inspector*), *ion* (as in *prediction*), and *ment* (as in *postponement*).

Exercise

The following questions are designed to help you apply your knowledge of the vocabulary of vocabulary to real situations.

1. With or without the aid of a dictionary, supply the *denotation* of each of the following adjectives. Then indicate whether its *connotation* is favorable, unfavorable, or neutral. (There are two examples of each.)

    a. valiant   c. sudden   e. enchanting
    b. malevolent   d. puritanical   f. parallel

2. Indicate whether the connotation of the *italicized* word in each of the following sentences is *positive, negative* (*pejorative*), or *neutral.* (There is one example of each.)

    a. Though his answers are technically correct, they are invariably routine and *mechanical.*

    b. We are looking for students with outstanding *scholastic* records.

    c. The candidate's *rugged* honesty made a strong appeal to the voters.

3. Indicate whether the *italicized* word in each of the following sentences is being used in a *literal* or a *figurative* way. (There are two examples of each.)

    a. Dawn *tiptoed* silently across the meadow and drummed her rosy fingers on my windowpane.

    b. I *danced* with the most beautiful girl in the class last night.

    c. Stella *tiptoed* across the room so as not to disturb her sleeping brother.

    d. All kinds of delightful images *dance* across the pages of that wonderful novel.

4. In each of the following groups, select the *synonym* of the lettered word. Consult a dictionary, if necessary.

   a. petty
      unusual   slight   foreign   dry   visible

   b. neat
      sloppy   strong   tidy   foolish   loud

   c. rebellion
      failure   defeat   uprising   change   courtesy

   d. conceal
      burn   show   plunge   answer   hide

   e. quarrel
      doubt   work   order   excite   argue

5. In each of the following groups, select the *antonym* of the lettered word. Consult a dictionary, if necessary.

   a. cheerful
      noisy   soft   sad   pleasant   dangerous

   b. graceful
      awkward   polite   colorful   anxious   hard

   c. fix
      disturb   please   enjoy   reply   break

   d. bravery
      intelligence   cowardice   wealth   beauty   strength

   e. amateur
      beginner   pupil   farmer   professional   volunteer

6. With or without the aid of a dictionary, divide each of the following words into its component parts. Some of the words may lack one or more of these parts.

	Prefix	Root	Suffix
a. reporter			
b. interrupt			
c. confusion			
d. description			
e. mindful			

II. The Tools of Vocabulary Building

The Dictionary. The dictionary is the most important reference book and guide for the student who wishes to increase his or her vocabulary and acquire the ability to use words accurately and effectively. An entry in a good dictionary provides a wide range of information about the word being considered. Though the treatment is usually concise, the information is reliable. For that reason, you should regard the dictionary as your bible of the English language and its vocabulary.

Of course, most dictionaries come in two basic versions: a large *unabridged* edition designed for scholarly use and a smaller *compact* edition designed to meet everyday needs. The difference between the two lies not so much in the fact that words have been left out of the smaller book but, rather, in the fact that the entries are much briefer and more succinct in the compact edition.

Thus, a typical entry in an unabridged dictionary provides the reader with the following information:

- the spelling and syllabication of the word
- its pronunciation
- an indication of the part of speech of the word
- information regarding inflectional endings
- the etymology or origin of the word
- its definition or definitions, both past and present
- illustrative phrases utilizing the word
- idiomatic expressions involving the word (when applicable)
- special or technical uses of the word
- related or derivative forms of the word
- a selection of synonyms and antonyms, often with explanatory notes clarifying subtle distinctions of meaning, tone, or usage

Study the following example of a typical entry from an unabridged dictionary. It is taken from the Unabridged Edition of *The Random House Dictionary of the English Language* (New York: Random House, 1967). Try to determine where each of the items listed above appears in the entry.

a·bate (ə-bāt'), v., a·bat·ed, a·bat·ing. —v.t. 1. to reduce in amount, degree, intensity, worth, etc.; lessen; diminish: *to abate a tax; to abate one's enthusiasm.* 2. *Law.* a. to put an end to or suppress (a nuisance). b. to suspend or extinguish (an action). c. to annul (a writ). 3. to deduct or subtract: *to abate part of the cost.* 4. to omit: *to abate all mention of names.* 5. to remove, as in stone carving, or hammer down, as in metalwork, (a portion of a surface) in order to produce a figure or pattern in low relief. —v.i. 6. to decrease or diminish in intensity, violence, amount, worth, etc.: *The storm has abated. The pain in his shoulder finally abated.* [late ME ⟨ MF *abat(re)*, equiv. to *a*- A-⁵ + *batre* ⟨ LL *batere* for L *batuere* to beat] —a·bat'·a·ble, *adj.* —a·bat' er; *Law.* a·ba'tor, *n.*
—**Syn.** 6. subside. —**Ant.** 1, 6, increase, intensify.

Here is the way a compact dictionary treats the same word. The entry is taken from the College Edition of *The American Heritage Dictionary* (Boston: Houghton Mifflin Company, 1982). Which of the items listed above appear in both the unabridged and the compact dictionaries? Which appear only in the unabridged dictionary?

a·bate (ə-bāt') v. a·bat·ed, a·bat·ing, a·bates. —tr. 1. To reduce in amount, degree, or intensity; lessen. 2. To deduct from an amount; subtract. 3. *Law.* a. To put an end to. b. To make void. —intr. 1. To subside. 2. *Law.* To become void. [ME *abaten* ⟨ OFr. *abattre,* to beat: *a-,* to ⟨⟨ Lat. *ad-*) + *batre,* to beat ⟨ Lat. *battuere.*]

For the vast majority of the exercises in this vocabulary book, you will need to make use of a compact dictionary. Occasionally you will also need to consult an unabridged dictionary or another reference book, such as a thesaurus.

The Thesaurus.   Do you own a thesaurus? No student should be without this useful reference book.

The word *thesaurus* is derived from the Greek *thesauros,* meaning "treasure" or "treasury." Although the word is sometimes used in the general sense of "dictionary" or "encyclopedia" —as a "thesaurus of quotations"—it more commonly denotes a special kind of wordbook. The words are presented (not defined) in groups of related-idea categories according to a distinctive logical pattern. An index tells the reader, by a system of reference numbers, where a certain word, together with its associative words, is to be found in the main part of the thesaurus.

Writers have found this kind of reference book to be a valuable memory prodder. And the word *writer,* as used here, means not only a professional author or journalist but also anyone who is trying to use English with force and precision and who needs help in finding the right word.

How to Use a Thesaurus.   Before you can make effective use of the thesaurus, you will need to do the following things:

1. Read the Preface or Introduction. It discusses in detail the special principles on which the thesaurus is based.

2. Read the Synopsis of Categories, which will give you an idea of the order and general range of the various related categories.

3. Read the introductory section, "How to Use the Book," which tells the reader, among other things, how to find:

    a. the most fitting word for a given idea
    b. the correct word for something vaguely remembered in its associations
    c. words suggestive of new ideas on a given subject

4. Always *turn first* to the Index Guide, which lists alphabetically the words you are looking for in the book.

Exercise

The following activities have been designed to help you improve your ability to use a dictionary or thesaurus.

1. Using the unabridged dictionary entry for *abate* that is printed on page 6, answer the following questions.

    a. Define *abate.*
    b. Give one phrase that illustrates its meaning.
    c. Give the etymology of *abate.*
    d. Give three special meanings *abate* has when used as a legal term.
    e. Give one synonym and two antonyms for *abate.*
    f. Syllabicate *abate,* and place the major stress mark (') after the syllable that is accented when the word is pronounced.

2. Read the Preface (Introduction), Synopsis of Categories, and Index Guide in your thesaurus. Then answer the following questions.

   a. In what specific writing situations or problems can the thesaurus serve as a helpful reference book?
   b. In what respects is the thesaurus different from an ordinary dictionary?
   c. Name five different cleaning devices listed under "Cleanliness."
   d. Give five synonyms suggested in the category under the word *corrective*.
   e. From the sections captioned "Obedience" and "Disobedience," select three adjective synonyms for *revolt*, and three verb synonyms for *disobey*.
   f. The thesaurus lists more than twenty forms of government. Define five such terms.

III.   The Development of Our Vocabulary

Since many of the exercises contained in this book relate to the origins or sources of the vocabulary of present-day English, it might be wise at this point to review briefly the development of the language. Doing this will help you make sense out of much of the isolated information scattered throughout the pages of this book. It may even give you a few new insights into the character and history of the language.

The Family Tree of English.   English belongs to the Indo-European family of languages. **Indo-European** is thought to have developed 5000 or more years ago somewhere in central Europe or western Asia. Quite a few modern English words appear to have their origins in Indo-European. Examples include *wolf* and *snow*.

Eventually, the people who spoke this parent language or group of related languages split up and went off in different directions. From these separate groups of people, a number of related branches of Indo-European developed. These branches include Celtic (now chiefly represented by Welsh, Irish, and Scottish Gaelic), Hellenic (that is, Greek), Italic (Latin and its Romance offshoots—French, Italian, Spanish, Portuguese, etc.), and Germanic.

It is to the **Germanic** branch of Indo-European that English specifically belongs. Germanic, however, is divided into three large groups of related languages. These are North Germanic (that is, the Scandinavian languages except Finnish), East Germanic (which consists only of an extinct language called Gothic), and West Germanic (to which a number of languages, including English, belong).

The **West Germanic** group of languages is usually further subdivided into High and Low German. High German includes

Modern German and Yiddish. **Low German** (named for the relative lowness of the area in which it is spoken) consists of Frisian (spoken in parts of Holland), Dutch and Flemish (also spoken in the Low Countries), Plattdeutsch (spoken in northern Germany), and English. Note, however, that English and Frisian are sometimes grouped separately between High German and the other Low German languages.

Angles, Saxons, Jutes, and Old English. The history of the English language and its vocabulary can be said to start around A.D. 450. About then, a number of Germanic tribes (the Angles, the Saxons, the Jutes, and probably some Frisians) began to invade and conquer the island of Britain.[1] For more than a century, these peoples poured in from Denmark, north Germany, and the Low Countries. Eventually they occupied all of present-day England, a bit of Wales, and part of southern Scotland.

The newcomers brought with them a number of closely related West Germanic dialects, out of which **Old English** (sometimes called Anglo-Saxon) developed. Old English is the earliest form of English that can be documented. In use until perhaps 1150, Old English represents the basic Germanic foundation upon which Modern English has been built.

[1]Previously, Britain had been occupied by Celtic-speaking peoples (from ca. 900 B.C.). In A.D. 43, the Romans invaded the island and made it part of their empire. However, they withdrew in 410, before the first Germanic settlers arrived. Thus, the population that these settlers found in Britain was basically a mixture of romanized and unromanized Celts. From this population, however, the Germanic settlers picked up very little in the way of vocabulary, except for place-names (e.g., *Avon*).

Alfred the Great (849–899), the most famous Anglo-Saxon king of England, was an influential patron of the language and literature of the Old English period.

Many Old English words have survived into Modern English. For example, *man, wife, child, house, ship, sheep, wrath, mirth, strong, good, well, drink, fight, to, after, and, if, we, us,* and many other common words derive from Old English. Nonetheless, these survivors constitute only a fraction of the vocabulary of Modern English. That is because much of the Old English element has long since dropped out of the language in favor of words from other sources.

Christianity, Latin, and Greek. In 597, the Church of Rome began to convert the Anglo-Saxon peoples of England to Christianity. This was one of the most important events in English history for the development of vocabulary. The adoption of Christianity paved the way for the introduction of a good many **Latin** words into English.[2] Most of these borrowings related, of course, to religion (e.g., *altar, mass, creed*). However, others referred to household items (*candle*), clothing (*cap*), food (*radish*), medicine (*fever*), and a host of other things. These words and others like them represent the beginning of Latin's influence on English. It would be hard to overemphasize this influence. Modern English probably owes more of its vocabulary, either directly or indirectly, to Latin than to any other language.

[2]While still on the Continent, the Germanic peoples of England had already picked up a few Latin words. For the most part, these relate to military, commercial, or culinary matters (e.g., *wall, street, pound, cheap, kitchen, cup, wine, cheese*), though other areas of life are also represented. Before the advent of Christianity, a few Latin words may also have come into Old English via Celtic (e.g., *port* and the place-name element *-c(h)ester* or *-caster*).

The Christian missionary St. Augustine of Canterbury lands in Kent in southeast England in 597.

In addition, these naturalized Latin words represent the first installment in a long series of borrowings from many languages including French and Greek. Over the centuries, such borrowings (called **loan words**) have greatly altered and enriched the vocabulary of English. Indeed, without them, English would not be what it is today.

With the coming of Christianity, a number of words that Latin had borrowed from **Greek** also entered Old English, usually in their Latin forms. These include *monk, deacon, psalm, oyster, chest,* and *school.* Earlier, when the Germanic peoples of England were still on the continent, they had borrowed a few other Greek expressions via Latin. These include *bishop, anchor, dish, copper, chalk,* and *pepper.*

Vikings and Old Norse. In 787, Viking bands from Denmark, Norway, and other areas of Scandinavia began to raid Anglo-Saxon territory. This was the start of what proved to be a large-scale, long-term invasion. By 878, much of northern and eastern England (to say nothing of Scotland) had been overrun. In 1014, the king of Denmark seized the English throne, and Danish kings ruled the country until 1042.

The upshot of all this turmoil was the permanent settlement of large numbers of Scandinavians (mostly Danes and Norwegians) in Britain. These newcomers spoke Old Norse dialects—that is, early forms of the modern Scandinavian languages. **Old Norse** (sometimes called Scandinavian) was Germanic. For that reason, it was fairly closely related to Old English. Culturally, the Anglo-Saxons and the Vikings were also similar. Thus, it was almost a foregone conclusion that, as the two peoples fused, large numbers of Old Norse words should begin to filter into English. Of course, much of this borrowing can't actually be documented until somewhat later, in what is called the Middle English period (see page 15).

Surprisingly, most of the Old Norse vocabulary that entered English referred to everyday things for which there were usually Old English words already. Every part of speech in the language was affected. For example, the following nouns all derive from Old Norse: *axle, birth, dirt, egg, fellow, gap, girth, leg, loan, outlaw, rift, score, slaughter, snare, thrift, window.* The same is true of the following verbs: *call, cast, crawl, droop, gape, gasp, glitter, kindle, lift, nag, ransack, scare, sprint, thrust.* The same is also true about these adverbs or adjectives: *akimbo, aloft, athwart, both, flat, ill, loose, low, muggy, odd, rotten, rugged, same, weak.* The same is true of the conjunction *though* and the pronouns *they, their, them.* Even something as basic to the language as the verb *to be* was affected, since *are* derives from Old Norse.

In some instances, the Old Norse word drove the corresponding Old English word out of the language. For example, *take* displaced *niman,* and *sky* superseded *wolcen.* In other cases, the Old English word survived but took on the meaning of its Old Norse counterpart. Examples include *dream, dwell,* and *bread,* which in

Old English meant "joy," "lead or go astray," and "fragment," respectively. In still other cases, both words remained in the language, but with somewhat different meanings or uses. Examples include *craft* and *skill*, *hide* and *skin*, *rear* and *raise*, and *shirt* and *skirt*. Even a few mixed forms (or **hybrids**) were created—for example, *screech* and *shriek*, which technically should be something like *shreech* and *scriek*.

Normans and Old French.   Directly across the English Channel from Britain lies the French province of Normandy. In the 9th and 10th centuries, Vikings (called *Normanni*, or "Northmen," in Latin) occupied the area. Subsequently, these Scandinavians converted to Christianity and adopted an early form of French as their official language.

In 1066, William, Duke of Normandy, defeated Harold, the last Anglo-Saxon king of England, at the Battle of Hastings. As a result, Duke William became the first Norman king of England. Norman monarchs ruled the country until 1154, when they were succeeded by other French-speaking kings.

The Norman conquest of England was probably the most important event in English history for the development of the language. For one thing, Norman French became the official language of the royal court and upper classes. This state of affairs lasted for about 200 years, during which time English was pushed well into the background. (Of course, English remained the language of the common people and middle classes throughout the period.)

The Battle of Hastings, 1066.

In addition, the use of an early form of French at the upper levels of society led to the introduction of many **Old French** words into English. This was just the beginning of the tremendous influence that French has exerted on the language. This influence has subsequently been reinforced by later borrowings from Modern French. French and Old Norse are, after Latin, the two most important sources for the vocabulary of Modern English.

Old French altered almost every aspect of the vocabulary, and more of the Old English element dropped out of the language. For example, Old French words relating to the following broad topics entered the language during the Middle Ages:

Topic	Borrowed Word
government	*realm, royal, govern, mayor*
social rank	*prince, duchess, baron, peasant*
land and property	*manor, demesne, estate, chattels*
law	*justice, suit, jury, pardon*
religion	*saint, mercy, charity, preach*
defense	*war, peace, battle, lieutenant*
wearing apparel	*costume, robe, cape, lace, jewel*
food	*beef, gravy, cream, peach, jelly, vinegar, spice, mince, roast*
household	*chair, couch, chamber*
art and literature	*beauty, paint, treatise*

Of course, a great many other common words also derive from Old French. Here are some examples:

nouns	*city, courtesy, virtue, grace, joy, marriage, people, point, reason*
adjectives	*able, brief, chaste, debonair, fine, gay, petty, puny, rich*
verbs	*chafe, embrace, enjoy, force, pay, reply, trace*

Even the wording of many common idiomatic expressions was influenced by the corresponding French phrase—for example, *by heart* and *in vain.*

Finally, a number of hybrids were created. These "mixed" forms usually fused an Old English (that is, Germanic) suffix onto a French (or Latin) root. Examples include *courtship, faintness, dukedom, artless, princely,* and *powerful.*

Learning, Latin, and Greek. Old French is a Romance language derived from Latin. Thus, many of the words given above can be traced back beyond Old French to Latin. During the Middle Ages, Latin (in its medieval form) was the language of the university, the church, some types of law, and many official documents. So it shouldn't be surprising that between 1066 and 1485, many words entered English directly from Latin. Examples include *adjacent, genius, index, inferior, intellect, lucrative, limbo, minor, necessary, ornate, picture, prevent, stupor,* and *tract.* As these items indicate, many of the new Latin words were abstract or technical terms. Thus, they may have first been used by professionals and only later achieved a wider circulation.

More Greek words also came into English during the Middle Ages, usually through Latin or French. Examples include *tyrant, scepter, theology, schism,* and *heresy.* As with the new Latin words, many of these Greek borrowings were technical terms that educated people may have introduced.

The Crusades and Arabic.　In 1095, the First Crusade to recover the Holy Land from the Muslims got under way. Subsequently, eight other crusades were launched. These expeditions brought Europe into contact with the Arabs (who held Palestine) and Arabic civilization. The Arabs also held much of Spain during the Middle Ages.

As a result of these contacts, **Arabic** words began to make their way into English. Most of these words relate to science and mathematics (e.g., *alchemy, alkali, elixir, zenith, algebra, cipher, zero*). Others refer to food (e.g., *orange, sherbet, spinach, syrup*), clothing (e.g., *sash*), rooms and furniture (e.g., *alcove, sofa, mattress*), and many other things (e.g., *admiral, tariff, salaam*). Not all of these words, of course, came into the language during the Middle Ages; some appeared later. Also, none of them entered English directly from Arabic; instead, they came through intermediary sources (*e.g.,* Spanish, French, Medieval Latin). Some of these words can be recognized by the presence of the Arabic definite article *al* ("the") at the beginning of the English form.

The launching of the First Crusade, 1095.

Trade and the Low German Languages. During the Middle Ages, England traded extensively with the Low Countries and north Germany, especially in wool. These commercial relations continued to be close until well into the 18th century.

As a result, a good many **Dutch, Flemish,** and other **Low German** words filtered into English, either during the Middle Ages or later. Some of these words relate to shipping (e.g., *yacht, schooner, sloop, cruise, skipper, mate, swab, deck, dock*), commerce (e.g., *freight, smuggle, roster, dollar*), and textiles (e.g., *nap, ravel, cambric*). Others refer to military matters (e.g., *furlough, tattoo, plunder, beleaguer*), painting (e.g., *easel, sketch, etching, stipple, landscape*), and a good many other things (e.g., *measles, pickle, plump, poppycock, rant, slurp, snoop, spook, sputter, squirt, tattle, wiseacre, wriggle*). The Dutch settlers of North America were also responsible for some new terms (e.g., *cookie, cruller, patroon, Yankee*). And, much later, *veldt, trek,* and *apartheid* were contributed by **Afrikaans,** the form of Dutch spoken in South Africa.

Synonyms and Middle English. By the end of the Middle Ages, the process of word acquisition had provided English with a rich and varied assortment of synonyms. Often there were three or more words for the same thing. Each of these words had entered the language from a different source and at a different time. Usually the elements involved were Germanic, French, and Latin (or Greek). Here are a few examples: *kingly—royal—regal; climb—mount—ascend;* and *ask—question—interrogate.*

The vocabulary developments since 1066 and some technical changes relating to sounds and grammar resulted in the creation of **Middle English.** Roughly in use from 1150 to 1500, Middle English is the earliest form of the language that is unmistakably English. Accordingly, a speaker of Modern English can read many

A sample of Middle English. A page from *The Vision of Piers Plowman,* probably by William Langland (ca. 1330–ca. 1400), one of the greatest works of Middle English literature.

Middle English texts, especially those written in the 1400s, without a great deal of difficulty. For example, college students frequently study the poems of Geoffrey Chaucer (died 1400) in the original language. To do this, they receive relatively little special training.

During the early years of its existence, Middle English was not the dominant language in England. Norman French held that position and kept it for about 200 years after 1066. Still, Middle English made steady advances during this period and by the mid-1300s was well on its way to becoming the dominant language of the country, a position it finally secured in the 1400s.

Neither Old nor Middle English was a single, monolithic language; each was a group of related dialects. For that reason, there was nothing in either period that could be considered standard English. Toward the end of the Middle Ages, however, London English had moved a long way in this direction, but a standard form of the language wasn't completely achieved until later.

Early Modern English, 1500–1660. The 16th and 17th centuries were an eventful period in the history of English. The invention of printing from movable type, the tremendous revival of interest in classical Greece and Rome that occurred during the Renaissance, the Protestant Reformation, and other developments helped to introduce the use of English into fields of learning where Latin had formerly reigned supreme and also did much to establish a more uniform spelling of the language. The great voyages of discovery and the creation of British colonies in North America and elsewhere spread the language beyond the confines of England and enriched it by introducing new words from all sorts of faraway places.

As a result of these developments, together with a number of technical changes relating to the sounds and grammar of the language, **Modern English** was born. Modern English, of course, is the form of the language that is used today throughout the English-speaking world. It is with this form of the language that this vocabulary book is concerned and in which it is written.

The creative genius that shaped events during the early modern period also affected the vocabulary of English. During the 16th and 17th centuries, thousands of new words entered the language. Most of them were from Latin (e.g., *create, dexterity, notorious, transition, vindicate*), but others came from Greek (e.g., *atmosphere, anachronism*), French (e.g., *essay*), Italian (e.g., *argosy, charlatan, gala*), and Spanish or Portuguese (e.g., *palisade, desperado, armada*). Purely English resources were also called on in the coining of new words—for example, *freshman*.

Some of the new words that entered the language at this time retained their original form (e.g., *climax, epitome*); others underwent some modification or simplification. Often this took the form of dropping a foreign ending—for example, *consult* from the Latin *consultare*. Sometimes a word that had already been borrowed was borrowed a second time with a slightly different form or meaning. Examples include *dish* and *disc.*

Since so many strange new words were entering English, the first dictionaries began to appear. These were usually very modest publications that confined themselves to the hard new words in the language. For example, *The Table Alphabeticall of Hard Words,* by Robert Cawdry, published in 1604, contained only about 3000 entries and did not deal with everyday words that even a child would understand. Also, most early dictionaries only defined the words they included and did not contain the other useful information that a modern dictionary provides.

Finally, it was during this period that **American English,** the particular brand of Modern English used in the United States, had its beginnings. While this was happening, a number of words from the languages used by the Native Americans began to filter into English. Examples include *hickory, moccasin, opossum, powwow, skunk, tomahawk, totem,* and *wigwam.*

The language of the early English settlers in America also absorbed a good many words from the languages used by other colonizing nations, notably Dutch (e.g., *cookie, waffle, boss, Yankee*), French (e.g., *chowder, prairie, buccaneer*), and Spanish (e.g., *banana, cockroach*). Words from the African languages used by the slaves who were brought to America from 1619 on also probably began to enter American English at this time, though most of these contributions (e.g., *voodoo, gumbo, cooter*) cannot be documented until much later. The foregoing examples and others like them reflect the English colonists' need for new words to describe what was unfamiliar to them.

The founding of Philadelphia by William Penn, 1681.

Developments Between 1660 and 1800. Between 1660 and 1800, the spirit of creativity that had marked the early modern period gave way to a desire for system, regularity, and conformity to a standard based upon reason and buttressed by authoritative example from the classical past. This led to efforts to standardize, refine, and fix the English language. Thus, for the first time grammar books laying down rules for the proper use of English (*e.g.*, William Loughton's *Practical Grammar of the English Language* [1734]), style manuals (*e.g.*, George Campbell's *Philosophy of Rhetoric* [1776]), and a dictionary in the modern sense of the word (Dr. Samuel Johnson's *A Dictionary of the English Language* [1755]) began to appear.

Despite somewhat misguided attempts to purify and control the language during the 18th century, the vocabulary of English continued to grow. Since France was at the height of her power as a cultural force, more French expressions came into the language. Examples include *ballet, champagne, coiffure, connoisseur,* and a host of other familiar words.

At the same time, Great Britain was building up a vast overseas empire in such places as North America, Australia, and India. This development not only led to an expansion of the use of English

A scene from Tchaikovsky's ballet *Swan Lake. Ballet* is one of the words that English has borrowed without change from French. French, of course, had originally borrowed the word from Italian.

throughout the world but also encouraged many exotic words to enter the language. For example, India contributed such items as *bungalow, cashmere, jungle, thug,* and *verandah*; the West Indies supplied *barbecue, hurricane,* and *tobacco*; and Australia provided *boomerang* and *wombat.* The influence of Great Britain's overseas territories continued through the 19th century, when some of the items listed above came into the language, and it is still felt today.

The period also saw significant developments in American English. All kinds of new expressions were being introduced to fill the needs of life in colonial America and later the United States. Examples include *bullfrog* (which appeared around 1705), *buckshot* (1775), *sidewalk* (1765), *cent* (coined by Thomas Jefferson around 1785), *harmonica* (invented by Benjamin Franklin about 1765), and a huge number of other familiar terms. Noah Webster's *American Spelling Book* appeared toward the end of this period, and his *American Dictionary of the English Language* somewhat later.

From 1800 to 2000. The 19th and 20th centuries witnessed the rise of an industrialized society in both Europe and America. The various technological advances that accompanied this development contributed greatly to the enrichment of our vocabulary. Scarcely any phase of life or language was untouched. Not only were new words and phrases relating to technological progress invented (e.g., *automobile, telephone, television, computer*), but a good many old expressions took on new meanings (e.g., *park* a car, a radio *broadcast*).

The growth of science during the 19th and 20th centuries also had a tremendous impact on the vocabulary. Thousands of new technical or scientific terms entered the language (e.g., *stethoscope, carbohydrate, psychoanalysis, cyberspace*), and new concepts appeared on the scene (e.g., *relativity, evolution, automation*). Though much of this new scientific vocabulary was used only by specialists, a good part of it filtered into the everyday language, usually as the result of popularization by our greatly improved means of mass communication. Startling new scientific developments, such as the exploration of space, also channeled some of the vocabulary of science into the popular language (e.g., *countdown, astronaut*).

A new science devoted to the study of language appeared on the scene during the 19th century. It is called **linguistics** (or sometimes **philology**). The contributions of philologists greatly increased our knowledge of language and also furnished new and improved tools for its study—for example, the multivolume *New (Oxford) English Dictionary.* As a result, popular interest in language continued to grow.

New social, political, or economic philosophies (*e.g.,* communism) left their mark on our language, and the two great world wars of the 20th century also enriched it (e.g., *blitzkrieg, camouflage, Iron Curtain*). The same is true of countless social, political, economic, and cultural developments in our country (e.g., *consumerism, environmentalist, integration*).

Finally, the tremendous influx of immigrants to our shores beginning in the late 19th and early 20th centuries also made our language richer. Certainly it would be hard to do without the contributions of these new Americans—for example, the yiddishisms listed on page 85 of this book.

Into the Future. English will certainly continue to grow in the 21st century. New developments, new problems, new needs, and new interests will require new terminology. Keep your eyes peeled for new expressions. It is a rewarding experience.

Exercise

The following questions will help you review what you have learned about the development of our vocabulary.

1. To which branch of the Indo-European family of languages does English belong?

2. Define each of the following terms relating to the development of English, and state when this phase of our language was in use.

   a. Old English   b. Middle English   c. Modern English

3. Give **one** example of a word or phrase that English has borrowed from each of the following foreign languages. Then define your example, and use it in a short illustrative sentence.

   a. Latin   c. Old Norse   e. Arabic
   b. Greek   d. Dutch   f. French

4. Explain how each of the following historical events contributed to the growth of the vocabulary of English.

   a. conversion to   c. Norman conquest of
      Christianity   England
   b. Viking invasions of   d. colonization of North
      England   America

5. Briefly explain the impact of each of the following on the growth of our vocabulary.

   a. industrialization   b. science

Basic Word List

Lesson 7

61. bleak
62. blight
63. blithe
64. boisterous
65. bombastic
66. boorish
67. boycott
68. brash
69. bravado
70. brusque

Lesson 8

71. bungle
72. bureaucracy
73. buttress
74. cajole
75. callous
76. calumny
77. candid
78. cantankerous
79. captious
80. catholic

Lesson 9

81. caustic
82. censor
83. censure
84. chagrin
85. charlatan
86. chronic
87. circuitous
88. circumspect
89. circumvent
90. clandestine

Lesson 10

91. coerce
92. cogent
93. cohere
94. collaborate
95. compatible
96. complacent
97. concise
98. condone
99. confrontation
100. conjecture

Lesson 11

101. connoisseur
102. consensus
103. construe
104. consummate
105. copious
106. corpulent
107. corroborate
108. counsel
109. credibility
110. criterion
111. crucial
112. culpable
113. cursory
114. curtail
115. cynical

Lesson 12

116. dapper
117. defect
118. defer
119. dejected
120. delete
121. delineate
122. delinquent
123. delude
124. demure
125. denouement
126. desultory
127. deviate
128. devoid
129. devout
130. dexterous

Lesson 13

131. dilapidated
132. dilatory
133. diligent
134. dire
135. discomfit
136. discourse
137. discriminate
138. disparage
139. disparity
140. distraught
141. divulge
142. docile
143. dormant
144. drastic
145. duplicity

Lesson 14

146. **eclectic**	151. **elite**	156. **empathy**
147. **effete**	152. **emaciated**	157. **emulate**
148. **efficacious**	153. **emanate**	158. **enclave**
149. **effrontery**	154. **embellish**	159. **endemic**
150. **elicit**	155. **eminent**	160. **enigma**

Lesson 15

161. **entice**	166. **equitable**	171. **euphemism**
162. **entreat**	167. **erudite**	172. **exacerbate**
163. **envisage**	168. **esoteric**	173. **exalt**
164. **epithet**	169. **ethical**	174. **exemplary**
165. **equanimity**	170. **ethnic**	175. **exigency**

Lesson 16

176. **exodus**	181. **fabricate**	186. **fatuous**
177. **exotic**	182. **facetious**	187. **feasible**
178. **expedient**	183. **facsimile**	188. **feign**
179. **exploit**	184. **fallacy**	189. **felicitous**
180. **expound**	185. **fathom**	190. **fetish**

Lesson 17

191. **fiasco**	196. **flaunt**	201. **formidable**
192. **fickle**	197. **flout**	202. **fortuitous**
193. **filch**	198. **fluctuate**	203. **frugal**
194. **finesse**	199. **foible**	204. **fulsome**
195. **flagrant**	200. **forestall**	205. **futile**

Lesson 18

206. **gape**	211. **gratuitous**	216. **gruesome**
207. **garble**	212. **gregarious**	217. **gullible**
208. **gloat**	213. **grimace**	218. **haggard**
209. **goad**	214. **grope**	219. **harangue**
210. **graphic**	215. **grueling**	220. **harbinger**

Lesson 19

221. **haughty**	226. **immunity**	231. **implacable**
222. **heinous**	227. **immutable**	232. **implicit**
223. **ignominy**	228. **impasse**	233. **impugn**
224. **illicit**	229. **impediment**	234. **incarcerate**
225. **immaculate**	230. **impervious**	235. **incense**

Lesson 20

236. inception
237. indigent
238. ingenious
239. inherent
240. innovation
241. instigate
242. insuperable
243. intervene
244. intrepid
245. inveigh
246. irony
247. jeopardize
248. jettison
249. judicious
250. justify

Lesson 21

251. kudos
252. lackadaisical
253. legacy
254. liability
255. libel
256. litigation
257. lucid
258. lucrative
259. lurk
260. lush
261. malapropism
262. malice
263. mammoth
264. mandatory
265. medium

Lesson 22

266. mercenary
267. moot
268. morass
269. motley
270. mundane
271. myriad
272. narcissistic
273. nebulous
274. negligible
275. nepotism
276. nomadic
277. nominal
278. nostalgia
279. novice
280. nuance

Lesson 23

281. obscene
282. obsequious
283. obsession
284. obsolete
285. officious
286. ominous
287. opportune
288. ostensible
289. ostracize
290. pandemonium
291. paradox
292. paraphrase
293. parochial
294. parody
295. pensive

Lesson 24

296. peremptory
297. perjure
298. permeate
299. pernicious
300. persevere
301. phobia
302. plagiarism
303. plaintive
304. plethora
305. poignant
306. precarious
307. precocious
308. predatory
309. prelude
310. premise

Lesson 25

311. prerogative
312. probity
313. procrastinate
314. prodigious
315. proliferate
316. promulgate
317. propensity
318. propitiate
319. protracted
320. prowess
321. pseudonym
322. purge
323. pusillanimous
324. quell
325. quixotic

Lesson 26

326. raze	331. redundant	336. repercussion
327. recalcitrant	332. relent	337. replenish
328. recant	333. reminiscence	338. reprisal
329. reciprocate	334. remorse	339. rescind
330. recrimination	335. renegade	340. resilient

Lesson 27

341. reticent	346. ritual	351. sacrilegious
342. retribution	347. rudiment	352. salient
343. retroactive	348. ruminate	353. sanctimonious
344. reverberate	349. ruse	354. sanguine
345. revere	350. sabotage	355. satellite

Lesson 28

356. scapegoat	361. solace	366. stipulate
357. schism	362. sordid	367. strategy
358. scrutinize	363. stamina	368. strident
359. secular	364. stereotype	369. surveillance
360. senile	365. stigmatize	370. syndrome

Lesson 29

371. tacit	376. thwart	381. ubiquitous
372. taciturn	377. tranquil	382. urbane
373. tangible	378. traumatic	383. usurp
374. tenable	379. trenchant	384. vagary
375. tentative	380. turbulent	385. venal

Lesson 30

386. veneer	391. vie	396. wrath
387. venerable	392. vindictive	397. yoke
388. veracity	393. vitiate	398. zany
389. versatile	394. volatile	399. zeal
390. veto	395. wane	400. zenith

Pronunciation Key

The authorities used for the pronunciation of words in the Basic Word List include the *Random House Dictionary, Webster's Third New International Dictionary,* and the *American Heritage Dictionary.* In the relatively few cases where these authorities are not in agreement, the editors have chosen the pronunciation that appears to be representative of the actual preference of most educated people in the American speech community. In some instances, several equally acceptable pronunciations are given.

Diacritical Marks. The following diacritical marks are used in this book to indicate the pronunciation of all the vowel sounds and one consonant in the words of the Basic Word List:

ā as in f*a*ce
ă as in m*a*t
ä as in f*a*ther
â as in c*a*re

ē as in f*e*ver
ĕ as in s*e*nd
ē as in p*e*rfect
ə as in *a*lone

ī as in b*i*te
ĭ as in b*i*ll
î as in p*i*er

ō as in c*o*de
ŏ as in c*o*d
ô as in f*o*r
ōō as in sp*oo*n
ŏŏ as in l*oo*k
ou as in *ou*t or c*ow*

yōō as in p*u*re
ŭ as in *u*p
û as in l*u*rk

<u>th</u> as in clo*the*
th as in clo*th*

The Schwa. In a great many English words, the vowel sounds of unstressed syllables are faint or indistinct. These neutral vowel sounds, for all practical purposes, are identical, regardless of the letter that may be used to represent them. In most modern dictionaries, the pronunciation of such vowel sounds is indicated by the symbol ə (an inverted *e*). This is designated by the term *schwa*—pronounced *shwa* or *shva.*

The schwa should be used to indicate the pronunciation of the unstressed vowel sound (*italicized*) in each of the following words: form*a*l, p*a*rtner, vis*i*ble, hum*o*r, circ*u*s, par*a*lysis. A schwa is usually pronounced as the *a* in *a*lone or the *u* in *u*p.

Lesson 1

[handwritten: abdicate – resign, relinquish, renounce, resign from job, relinquish a right, renounce a claim or title]

1. abdicate — 10. addiction[1]

---

1. **ab-di-cate**   *verb*   ăb'-dĭ-kāt

[handwritten notes in margin]

[*ab* (Latin), "away" + *dicare, dicatus* (Latin), "proclaim"]

Definition: To give up formally, as an office, duty, power, or claim.

The first Romanov czar of Russia was crowned in 1613; the last was forced to **abdicate** in 1917.

However heavy the burden may be, you cannot **abdicate** your responsibilities as the head of this household.

Related Form: (*noun*) abdication

Synonyms: (*verbs*) resign, renounce, relinquish, divest oneself of; (*nouns*) resignation, renunciation, relinquishment

Antonyms: (*verbs*) retain, hold on to

Related Phrases: renounce a claim or title, relinquish (or waive) a right, resign from a job, divest oneself of power

Usage Note:
Abdicate is usually used of a *crowned* head of state; *resign* is used of an *elected* official. Thus, Edward VIII *abdicated*, but Richard Nixon *resigned*.

2. **a-bet**   *verb*   ə-bĕt'

[*a*, from *ad* (Latin), "to" + *beter* (Germanic), "bait or incite"]

Definition: To encourage or assist, especially in wrongdoing.

In Shakespeare's *Richard III* Buckingham knowingly **abets** Gloucester's plans to seize the throne.

At that memorable concert the great singer's efforts were ably **abetted** by her accompanist.

Phrase: to aid and abet

Synonyms: (*verbs*) egg on; promote, further, advance, help, aid

Antonyms: (*verbs*) dissuade, discourage, deter, restrain, curb, inhibit, hinder, block, frustrate, thwart (Word 376)

Related Phrases: with the connivance of, in league with

[handwritten: abet = to encourage on a shot]

---

[1]For a full listing of the basic words in each lesson, see the Basic Word List, pages 21–25.

3. ab-hor   *verb*   ăb-hôr′

[*ab* (Latin), "from; at" + *horrere* (Latin), "shiver, shudder"]

Definition: To regard with horror and loathing; to hate intensely.

Religious prejudice is something decent people **abhor.**

Related Forms: (*adjective*) abhorrent; (*noun*) abhorrence

Usage Note:
Because *abhor* implies strong *moral* condemnation, it should properly be reserved for attitudes or actions that really do offend a person's sense of right and wrong (*e.g.*, racism, child abuse). This, of course, is not to say that the word *cannot* be applied to other things. On the contrary, it is frequently used of trifling matters that normally would not be thought to grate on one's *moral* sensibilities—for example, spinach or TV game shows.

Synonyms: (*verbs*) loathe, despise, detest, abominate; (*noun*) aversion

Antonyms: (*verbs*) like, fancy, relish, love, cherish, delight in, be fond of, dote on

Related Phases: look askance at, make a wry face at, turn up one's nose at, turn thumbs down at

Usage Note:
Do not confuse the verb *loathe*, meaning "dislike intensely," and the adjective *loath*, meaning "reluctant, disinclined." Note the following pair of sentences:

The human vice I *loathe* most deeply is insincerity.

I am *loath* to sign your petition.

4. ab-ject   *adjective*   ăb′-jĕkt   *or*   ăb-jĕkt′

[*ab* (Latin), "down; from" + *jacere, jactus* (Latin), "throw"]

Definition:
   a.   Wretched, miserable; degrading, humiliating.

     Many people around the world live in such **abject** poverty that they cannot afford even the most essential items of food and clothing.

   b.   Mean-spirited, base; despicable, contemptible.

     Only an **abject** coward would stand idly by as a defenseless person was mugged.

   c.   Complete and unrelieved.

     At the slightest sound of thunder, my dog dives under the bed in a state of **abject** terror.

Phrases: an abject flatterer, an abject liar, an abject imitator, abject surrender, abject apologies

Synonyms: (*adjectives*) disheartening, debasing, hopeless, helpless; vile, shameless, ignoble, craven; utter, sheer, downright, thoroughgoing *abhor = detest, abominate, despise.*

5. ab-solve   *verb*   ăb-sŏlv′

[*ab* (Latin), "from" + *solvere* (Latin), "loosen; release"]

Definition: To clear of guilt or blame.

"The evidence I will present," the lawyer told the jury, "clearly **absolves** my client of any complicity in the crime."

The most effective way we can **absolve** our society of the charges of racism and prejudice is to remedy the injustices of the past.

Related Form: (*noun*) absolution

Usage Note:

In a religious sense, *absolve* and *absolution* refer to granting a pardon, especially for a sin.

Synonyms: (*verbs*) acquit, exonerate, exculpate, vindicate; (*nouns*) acquittal, exoneration, vindication

Antonyms: (*verbs*) incriminate, inculpate; indict, impeach; convict, condemn; (*nouns*) indictment; conviction, condemnation

6. ab-stain   *verb*   ăb-stān′

[*abs*, a form of *ab* (Latin), "from" + *tenere* (Latin), "hold; keep"]

Definition: To refrain completely and voluntarily.

Only ten members of the Security Council voted on the resolution; the others **abstained**.

If you want to lose some weight, you'll have to **abstain** from eating those rich desserts you love so much.

Related Forms: (*nouns*) abstinence, abstention; (*adjective*) abstinent

Usage Note:

Abstain and *abstinence* are often used in reference to strong drink, with the meaning "refrain completely from drinking." A common synonym for *abstinence* in this sense is *temperance*. Persons who never drink intoxicating beverages are sometimes referred to as *teetotalers*.

Synonyms: (*verbs*) forgo, forbear, avoid, shun, eschew; (*nouns*) self-restraint, self-denial, forbearance, abstemiousness; (*adjectives*) abstemious, forbearing, temperate, sparing, moderate; ascetic

Antonyms: (*verbs*) indulge (in), partake (of); (*noun*) indulgence; (*adjectives*) self-indulgent, intemperate, immoderate

Usage Notes:

a.   *Abstemious, forbearing, temperate,* and *sparing* all indicate moderation in indulging one's appetites. *Abstinent,* on the other hand, indicates a total avoidance of the thing in question.

b.   Be careful not to confuse the verb *forbear,* meaning "to restrain oneself," with the noun *forebear,* meaning "ancestor." The noun, which is usually plural, has a slightly different pronunciation, with the accent on the *first* syllable (fôr′-bâr).

7. ac·a·dem·ic   *adjective*   ăk-ə-děm'-ĭk

[From *Akademia*, the name of the ancient Greek philosopher Plato's school outside Athens. It was located in a grove or park dedicated to the hero Akademos.]

Definition:
- a. Pertaining to a college or other institution of learning; scholarly.

    The role of a scholar in modern society is a subject of abiding concern in **academic** circles everywhere.
- b. Theoretical rather than practical; unrealistic.

    What we need to do is develop a solid plan of action, not engage in **academic** debates over purely theoretical questions.

Related Forms: (*nouns*) academy, academician; (*adverb*) academically

Phrases: academic freedom, the halls of academe; an academic question

Synonyms: (*adjectives*) scholastic; speculative

An academic procession during the graduation exercises at an American university.

From the Halls of Academe

Academy applies to institutions of higher learning, secondary schools, or any place where special subjects, arts, and skills are taught (*e.g.*, military academies, riding academies). The word is also used to refer to societies of learned individuals who have united to advance learning, literature, the arts, and the sciences (*e.g.*, the National Academy of Sciences, the Academy of Motion Picture Arts and Sciences).

The phrase *academic freedom* refers to the freedom of a teacher or student to discuss or express his or her views on political, social, or economic issues without interference from public or school officials.

An *academician* is a member of a learned society.

An *academic question* is one that is purely theoretical and has little or no bearing on practical problems or real situations.

8. **ac·cede**   *verb*   ăk-sēd′

[*ad* (Latin), "to" + *cedere* (Latin), "go; yield"]

Definition:
   a. To yield to; to agree to.
       It took no little persuasion to get my parents to **accede** to my plan for a trip to California on my own.
   b. To enter upon an office or dignity.
       Queen Elizabeth II **acceded** to the throne of Great Britain upon the death of her father, George VI, in 1952.

Related Forms: (*nouns*) access, accession, accessory; (*adjective*) accessible

Synonyms: (*verbs*) agree, assent, consent, concur, acquiesce, comply

Antonyms: (*verbs*) dissent, demur, balk at

9. **ac·cli·mate**   *verb*   ə-klī′-mĭt   *or*   ăk′-lə-māt

[*acclimater* (French), "get used to"]

Definition: To get used to (usually an environment or situation).

Coming from the Pacific Northwest, we found it difficult to **acclimate** ourselves to the heat and humidity of a New York summer.

Related Forms: (*verb*) acclimatize; (*nouns*) acclimation, acclimatization

Synonyms: (*verbs*) adjust, adapt, orient, orientate, familiarize, accustom, habituate; (*noun*) orientation

10. **ad·dic·tion**   *noun*   ă-dĭk′-shən

[*addictus* (Latin), "given over to"; from *ad* (Latin), "to" + *dicere, dictus* (Latin),"say"]

Definition: A habit-forming practice or pursuit, usually one that is bad for a person's health or morally objectionable; habitual use of, or devotion to, something.

Cigarette smoking is an **addiction** that may prove difficult to overcome.

The speaker at last Thursday's assembly discussed a number of problems relating to young people, including drug **addiction**.

Related Forms: (*noun*) an addict; (*adjectives*) addictive, addicted to

Usage Note:

Addiction and *addicted to* are much used today in connection with drugs, but neither expression is limited to that area alone. One may, for example, be addicted to gambling, television, or coffee. In addition, both terms may be employed semihumorously, as in "addicted to detective stories" or "an addiction to chocolate marshmallow sundaes."

Using the Words

Exercise I.   Syllabication and Pronunciation

Syllabicate the following words correctly, and place the major stress mark (') after the syllable that is accented when the word is pronounced. Two answers are correct in some instances.

Example: a-bet'

1. addiction
2. abject
3. academic
4. acclimate
5. accede
6. absolve

Exercise II.   Words Out of Context

In each of the following groups, select the item that best expresses the meaning of the numbered word at the left.

1. abstain
   a. transfer   b. refrain   c. indulge
   d. vote

2. abhor
   a. relish   b. release   c. frustrate
   d. detest

3. abet
   a. encourage   b. initiate   c. deplore
   d. hamper

4. accede
   a. offer   b. renew   c. demur
   d. yield

5. abject
   a. proud   b. temperate   c. wretched
   d. scholarly

Exercise III.   Completing Sentences

Complete each of the following sentences by selecting the most appropriate word from the group of words given below. Make whatever adjustments are necessary to fit the words into the sentences properly.

absolve	academic	acclimate
abject	addiction	abdicate

1. I chose an _____ career rather than business because I felt that I was better suited to the life of a teacher and scholar.

2. Convinced by the evidence presented by the defense, the jury _____ the defendant of all wrongdoing.

3. Long accustomed to their own traditional way of life, the refugees found it difficult to _____ themselves to a new language and strange customs.

4. Many a crime is committed by someone who has developed an _____ to drugs and must have large sums of money to support this habit.

5. "I'd rather resign from my job," Professor Harris declared, "than _____ my right to speak out publicly on such an important social problem."

Exercise IV. Synonyms and Antonyms

Classify each of the following pairs of words as **S** for **synonyms** or **A** for **antonyms**.

1. absolve—convict
2. familiarize—acclimate
3. relinquish—retain
4. accede—consent
5. abet—encourage
6. relish—abhor

Exercise V. Word Roundup

1. What is the difference between an *abstemious* person and a person who is *abstinent?* Complete each of the following with one of these words.

   a. Henry takes a drink once in a long while. He is _____.
   b. Henry never touches liquor. He is _____.

2. Define each of the following phrases. Consult a dictionary or other reference book if necessary.

   a. academic robes
   b. a riding academy
   c. academic freedom
   d. an academic question

3. Explain the difference in meaning between the terms in each of the following word pairs.

   a. forbear—forebear
   b. loathe—loath

Exercise VI. Framing Sentences

A. Use each of the following words in a short illustrative sentence.

1. abet
2. abject
3. accede
4. addiction

B. Give a **noun** form of each of the following words, and use it in a short illustrative sentence.

1. abdicate
2. abhor
3. absolve
4. abstain
5. academic
6. acclimate

Dissecting the Words

At this point in half the lessons in this book, there is a section devoted to etymology. **Etymology** is the study of where words come from and how they are formed or change. Accordingly, each of these sections focuses attention on some of the prefixes, roots, and suffixes that make up the bulk of the words on the Basic Word List. The reason for studying these word elements is simple: They form the backbone of a substantial proportion of the English words in current use. For that reason, one effective way to expand your word power is to learn the meanings of such word elements and to use them as "keys" to a wider understanding of new words that crop up in your reading and school studies.

Prefix

The Latin prefix **ab**, **abs**, meaning "away from, off," is found in numerous English words. A few of them, including *abdicate* and *abject*, appeared in this lesson. Here are some more:

abduct (literally, "to lead away")—to take away by force

abscond—to depart secretly

abrupt—(literally, "broken off")—sudden or hasty

abstract—to draw from. The noun *abstract* means "a brief summary or a shorter form of the original."

Other English words containing this prefix include *abrasion, absent, abrogate,* and *absurd.*

Sir James A. Murray (1837–1915), the editor of the multivolume *New (Oxford) English Dictionary,* probably the most authoritative and certainly the most complete English dictionary in existence.

1. **Ced** is a Latin root meaning "go" or "yield." It provides the core meaning of many English words, including *accede*, studied in this lesson. (Note that this root appears as **ceed** in some English words.) Here are some other words from the same root:

concede—to grant or admit. Noun: *concession*

secede—to break away from; to withdraw from membership in. Noun: *secession*

exceed—to go beyond what is necessary or proper. Noun: *excess*; adjective: *excessive*; adverbs: *exceedingly, excessively*

recede—to go back, to withdraw. Noun: *recession*

proceed—to go forward. Noun: *procession*

antecedent—going before. A person's *antecedents* are his ancestors or forerunners.

procedure—the regular, definite order by which something is done.

Other words from this root are *intercede, precedent, cession*.

2. The root **dic, dict**, which is found in the Latin verb *dicere*, "to say," and in the related verbs *dicare*, "to indicate, consecrate, devote, dedicate," and *dictare*, "to declare; to order," is the basis of the words *abdicate* and *addiction*, studied in this lesson. Note the following English words also formed from this root:

contradict (literally, "to speak against")—to oppose, to deny

valedictory (literally, "saying *be well*")—farewell

indict (literally, "to declare against")—to charge with guilt

interdict (literally, "to say between")—to prohibit

dictum (literally, "a thing said")—an authoritative statement

Other English words containing this root include *edict, dedicate, benediction, predict, malediction* (a curse), *predicament, indicate, dictionary*, and *dictator*.

Exercise

1. Select the word that does not contain the prefix *ab*.

    a. abhor **b.** abscond **c.** abide **d.** abject

2. Give **three** English words that are derived from the same root as *accede*. Use each in a short illustrative sentence.

3. Explain the origin of each of the following words: *indict, dictum, contradict, benediction.*

4. Explain the meaning of each of the following phrases, with particular reference to the etymology of the word in *italics*. Consult a dictionary or other reference book if necessary.

    a. the class *valedictorian*   **c.** *abstract* art
    b. a *receding* hairline   **d.** the *antecedent* of a pronoun

Enriching the Lesson

This lesson includes a number of legal terms, such as *absolve* and *accessory*. The following exercise may help you widen your knowledge of the language of the law. Consult a dictionary or other reference book for the meanings of the words indicated; then do the exercises.

A. Match the legal term in Column A with the phrase that defines it in Column B.

Column A	*Column B*
1. indictment	a. a law passed by a duly authorized law-making body
2. subpoena	b. one who is guilty of a crime
3. statute	c. a formal written accusation of a crime
4. culprit	d. a temporary delay in carrying out a sentence
5. affidavit	e. a written order summoning a person to a court to give testimony
6. plaintiff	f. to call before a court to answer a formal charge
7. reprieve	g. to expel from the practice of law
8. arraign	h. a written statement made under oath
9. contraband	i. the person who makes the complaint in a lawsuit
10. disbar	j. smuggled goods

B. Now complete each of the following.

1. What is the difference between an *accessory before the fact* and an *accessory after the fact*?

2. What is a *quitclaim*? Show how *quit* in this word is related etymologically to *acquit*.

3. Why would a respected lawyer object to being called a *shyster*? In which country is the term *barrister* used?

4. What is a *writ*? Define *writ of habeas corpus* and *writ of mandamus*.

5. What is the difference between *impeach* and *convict*? Which branch of Congress has the power to *impeach* a president of the United States? Which is authorized to *try and judge* him?

6. What is a *plea*? Define *plea bargaining* and *to cop a plea.*

7. Legally speaking, what is a *misdemeanor?* a *felony?* What is the difference between the two? Define *tort.*

8. If the defendant in a criminal case is seeking a *change of venue*, what is he or she asking for? Why might a judge grant such a request?

9. Define the following: *petit jury, grand jury, hung jury.*

10. What principle of constitutional law is usually referred to by the phrase *double jeopardy?*

Exercise II.   Place Names in Common Use

A fair number of common English words—for example, *academic*, studied in this lesson—are derived from the names of places. Some of these expressions are listed below. With or without the aid of a dictionary, define each as it is used in present-day English. Then give the place name from which the word is derived. Finally, choose any **five** of the items, and for each compose an original sentence that clearly illustrates the expression's meaning.

1. limerick	6. hackneyed	11. blarney
2. varnish	7. limousine	12. mayonnaise
3. mecca	8. bedlam	13. gasconade
4. cologne	9. sybaritic	14. tawdry
5. bunkum	10. donnybrook	15. sardonic

Exercise III.   Expanding Your Word Power

The words listed below are not on the Basic Word List, but they were mentioned in passing in Lesson 1. All of them would make useful additions to your working vocabulary. Define each, give its etymology, list **two** synonyms and **two** antonyms (where possible), and use in a short sentence that clearly illustrates its meaning.

1. waive	5. connive	9. acquiesce
2. deter	6. incriminate	10. orientation
3. aversion	7. ascetic	11. indulge
4. ignoble	8. eschew	12. demur

Lesson 2

11. adjourn — 20. agile

---

11. ad·journ   *verb*   ə-jûrn'

[*a*, from *ad* (Latin), "to" + *diurnum* (Late Latin), "day"]

Definition:
   a. To close formally.

   Congress is scheduled to **adjourn** in two days, but pressing business will probably delay its closing for at least a week.

   b. To put off to another time; to move to another place.

   "This meeting is **adjourned** until ten o'clock tomorrow morning," the chairwoman declared, rapping her gavel smartly on the table.

   In view of clear community prejudice against the defendant, the judge **adjourned** the trial to another county.

   After dinner we **adjourned** to the living room for a quiet chat.

Related Form: (*noun*) adjournment

Synonyms: (*verbs*) conclude, terminate; defer (Word 118), postpone; suspend; transfer

12. ad·verse   *adjective*   ăd'-vûrs   *or*   ăd-vûrs'

[*ad* (Latin), "to; against" + *vertere, versus* (Latin), "turn"]

Definition: Hostile in purpose or effect; unfavorable.

Although the novel received much **adverse** criticism in the press, it became a national best-seller.

Related Forms: (*adverb*) adversely; (*nouns*) adversary, adversity

Usage Note:
Do not confuse *adverse* with the related adjective *averse*, meaning "opposed" or "disinclined." *Adverse* (with the *d*) is used of things to indicate that they have gone contrary to a person's wishes. *Averse* (without the *d*), on the other hand, indicates opposition on the part of the person himself or herself. Note the following pair of sentences:

   The Supreme Court handed down an *adverse* decision on censorship.

   The Supreme Court showed itself *averse* to censorship laws.

Synonyms: (*adjectives*) unfavorable, unfriendly, negative, antagonistic, antipathetic, inimical

Antonyms: (*adjectives*) favorable, friendly, propitious

13. **ad·vo·cate**   *verb:* ăd'-və-kāt   *noun:* ăd'-və-kĭt

[*ad* (Latin), "to" + *vocare, vocatus* (Latin), "call"]

Definition:

a.   (*verb*) To speak or argue in favor of; to give active public support to.

In his TV address to the nation, the president **advocated** a series of measures that he believed would stimulate the economy.

b.   (*noun*) A person who pleads in the interest of a cause or individual.

I have become her **advocate** because I honestly believe in her ideas.

Related Form: (*noun*) advocacy

Synonyms: (*verbs*) champion, support, espouse, uphold, recommend; (*nouns*) proponent, backer, defender, spokesman

Antonyms: (*verbs*) denounce, condemn, oppose, attack; (*nouns*) critic, opponent, adversary, antagonist

A scene from *The Devil's Disciple* (1897), a play about the advocates and opponents of the American Revolution by George Bernard Shaw (*inset*).

Devil's Advocate

In the Roman Catholic procedure of canonization, by which a person is elevated to sainthood, arguments are heard pro and con regarding the proposed measure. A church official is selected to pick flaws in the record or character of the candidate—to present arguments against the canonization. This official is given the title *advocatus diaboli*, "devil's advocate." The idea is that any candidate who can survive the onslaughts of a skilled devil's advocate probably does have authentic credentials for sainthood.

The expression has been widened to embrace anyone who expresses the opposition point of view as a means of arriving at the truth, even though, in fact, he may not be in disagreement with his opponent. Thus one might say: "I am not necessarily in disagreement with your plan, but I am going to serve as a *devil's advocate* and point out its possible flaws."

14. aes·thet·ic   *adjective*   ĕs-thĕt'-ĭk

[*aisthetikos* (Greek), "perceptible to the senses"]

Definition: Pertaining to a sense of beauty; artistic.

Though the picture did not have much **aesthetic** appeal, it had considerable commercial value.

In 1756 the English philosopher Edmund Burke wrote an influential book on **aesthetic** theory.

Related Forms: (*adverb*) aesthetically; (*nouns*) aesthete, aesthetics

Usage Notes:

a.   *Aesthetic* is sometimes spelled *esthetic*. Do not confuse the word with *ascetic*.

b.   An *aesthete* is a person who is sensitive to, or has a love of, the beautiful in art or nature. However, the term is often used with an unfavorable tone to indicate someone who makes overmuch of his or her sensitivity to beauty.

c.   *Aesthetics* is a branch of philosophy dealing with theories and principles of beauty in art and literature.

15. af·fa·ble   *adjective*   ăf'-ə-bəl

[*ad* (Latin), "to" + *fari* (Latin), "speak" + *abilis, abile* (Latin), "able to"]

Definition: Courteous and agreeable in manner; easy to talk to or approach.

It's fun to spend an hour or two chatting with my next-door neighbor because she is one of the most **affable** people I know.

Related Forms: (*adverb*) affably; (*nouns*) affableness, affability

Synonyms: (*adjectives*) sociable, genial, amiable, friendly, good-natured

Antonyms: (*adjectives*) unsociable, surly, testy, ill-tempered

16. af·fec·ta·tion   *noun*   ăf-ĕk-tā'-shən

[*affectare, affectatus* (Latin), "strive after"]

Definition: A pretentious display of manners or sentiments that are not genuine; a peculiar habit of dress or behavior that has been adopted to impress others.

Beneath his **affectation** of elegance and refinement, I could easily recognize the crude and awkward youth I had known years before.

Related Forms: (*adjective*) affected: (*verb*) affect

Phrases: an affected style of speaking; to affect an air of sophistication

Synonyms: (*nouns*) pose, pretense; mannerism

Related Phrase: to put on airs

40

17. af-flu-ent   *adjective*   ăf'-loo-ənt

[*ad* (Latin), "to" + *fluens*, *fluentis* (Latin), "flowing," from *fluere* (Latin, "flow")]

Definition: Prosperous, wealthy.

A good friend of mine is constantly borrowing money from his more **affluent** relatives.

The German writer Thomas Mann's novel *Buddenbrooks* details the lives of generations of **affluent** Hamburg merchants.

Related Forms: (*noun*) affluence; (*adverb*) affluently

Synonyms: (*adjectives*) flourishing, well-to-do, opulent

Antonyms: (*adjectives*) indigent (Word 237), destitute, penniless, poverty-stricken

Related Phrases:

living high off the hog — This phrase of rural American origin suggests that a person is in good circumstances because he or she is eating the more desirable cuts of meat from a slaughtered hog.

as rich as Croesus — This phrase goes back to Croesus, king of Lydia, an ancient country in western Turkey. Croesus had a reputation among the Greeks for being extremely rich, and he became the personification of limitless wealth.

to serve Mammon — The word *mammon* means "riches" in Aramaic, an ancient Semitic language related to Hebrew. Among the Hebrews of biblical times, *mammon* was personified as the god Mammon, who represented not merely wealth but materialism and an excessive concern with acquiring riches.

well-heeled — In the old days only wealthy people could afford shoes with heels on them. Since they were wealthy, they could also afford to keep those heels in good condition. Hence, to be *well-heeled* came to mean "to be wealthy or affluent." The opposite is *down-at-heel*, meaning "poor" because run-down heels were a sign of poverty. As Shakespeare says in *King Lear*: "A good man's fortune may grow out at heel."

A depiction of Croesus (*top right*) displaying his wealth to the Greek philosopher Solon. Solon admonished Croesus by pointing out that happiness was based on good fortune, not great wealth.

18. **a·gen·da**   *noun*   ə-jĕn′-də

[*agere* (Latin), "do"]

Definition: A list or program of things to be done or acted upon.

"Have you any idea what is on the **agenda** for today's meeting?" she asked.

Poland had top priority on Adolf Hitler's **agenda** of military conquest in the fall of 1939.

Usage Note:

Agenda was originally a Latin plural noun meaning "things to be done" (singular, *agendum*). However, it is generally treated in English today as a collective noun taking a singular verb, as in the following example:

The *agenda* includes the question of raising money for the dance.

On the other hand, it is certainly not wrong—although it may seem a bit pedantic—to treat *agenda* as a plural form. In that case, the Latin singular form *agendum* may be used to indicate one particular item among several included in the agenda.

Synonyms: (*nouns*) schedule, docket

Usage Note:

A *docket* is literally a list of cases awaiting action in a court of law, but the word is often used figuratively of any list of things to be done.

"Winter Carnival is the next item on today's *docket*," the head of the planning committee announced.

19. **ag·gre·gate**   *noun and adjective:* ăg′-rə-gĭt
                                verb: ăg′-rə-gāt

[*ad* (Latin), "to" + *grex, gregis* (Latin), "herd"]

Definition:

    a.   (*noun*) The total amount or sum total of the individual parts.

       The United Nations is no more than a loose **aggregate** of nations, each of which retains full sovereignty.

    b.   (*verb*) To gather or merge into a single whole; to amount to.

       The merger of the two great banks **aggregated** working capital totaling several trillion dollars.

    c.   (*adjective*) Total, collective.

       The **aggregate** effect of misguided monetary policies is usually financial chaos.

Related Form: (*noun*) aggregation

Usage Note:

Perhaps the widest current use of *aggregate* as a noun occurs in the prepositional phrase *in the aggregate*, meaning "collectively."

Synonyms: (*nouns*) mass, assemblage, amalgamation, conglomeration, cluster; (*verbs*) amalgamate, consolidate; (*adjectives*) net, composite

20. ag·ile   *adjective*   ăj'-əl

[*agilis* (Latin), "busy; active," from *agere* (Latin), "do")

Definition: Swift and light in action, movement, or thought.

Despite his sixty-odd years, the circus clown was as energetic and **agile** as any of the younger members of the troupe.

It certainly takes a very **agile** mind to do some kinds of crossword puzzles.

Related Form: (*noun*) agility

Synonyms: (*adjectives*) nimble, limber, alert, brisk, supple, lithe, spry

Antonyms: (*adjectives*) torpid, sluggish, lethargic; awkward, clumsy

Related Phrases: to limber up one's muscles, to look chipper

Usage Note:

Some distinctions should be drawn among the synonyms listed above: *alert* refers to quickness of mind; *brisk* suggests liveliness; *supple* means "pliant" or "bending and twisting easily"; and *spry* indicates agility despite age or infirmity.

Using the Words

Exercise I.   Parts of Speech

Indicate the part of speech of each of the following words. Two answers are possible in one instance; three in another.

1. agenda	3. advocate	5. affluent
2. adjourn	4. agile	6. aggregate

Exercise II.   Words in Phrases

In each of the following groups, select the item that best expresses the meaning of the *italicized* word in the introductory phrase.

1. *adjourned* the meeting promptly at three o'clock
    a. planned   b. opened   c. suspended   d. attended

2. very *agile* for her age
    a. ignorant   b. clumsy   c. popular   d. spry

3. *advocated* changes in the tax laws
    a. considered   b. rejected   c. supported   d. ignored

4. came from a very *affluent* family
    a. obscure   b. poverty-stricken   c. brilliant   d. wealthy

5. the *aggregate* opinion of the jury
    a. collective   b. informed   c. far-reaching   d. mistaken

Exercise III.   Completing Sentences

Complete each of the following sentences by selecting the most appropriate word from the group of words given below.

aesthetic	advocate	agenda
affectation	adverse	affable

1. We are determined to succeed in spite of all the _____ conditions affecting this project.

2. The first item on the _____ at the convention was the selection of a temporary chairperson.

3. Our personnel manager is a very _____ woman whose friendly, informal manner immediately puts a person at ease.

4. While the Romans were essentially practical in their approach to building design, the Greeks were deeply concerned with beauty for its own sake and worked hard to produce structures of high _____ appeal.

5. Throwing an obscure French expression into the middle of an English sentence just to show that you've been to Paris is an _____ that really irritates me.

Exercise IV.   Synonyms and Antonyms

A. Match each word in Column A with its **synonym** in Column B.

Column A	Column B
1. terminate	a. amiable
2. nimble	b. consolidate
3. opulent	c. pretense
4. pose	d. conclude
5. fuse	e. luxurious
	f. spry

Now indicate which of the basic words taught in this lesson (Words 11–20) is most nearly **synonymous** with each of the words in Column A.

B. In each of the following groups, select the two words that are most nearly **antonyms**.

1. a. agile   b. filthy   c. hostile   d. sincere   e. awkward

2. a. civilian   b. opponent   c. foreigner   d. advocate
    e. aesthete

3. a. ascetic   b. sluggish   c. propitious   d. adverse   e. neat

4. a. artificial   b. testy   c. penniless   d. aesthetic   e. affable

5. a. wealthy   b. insincere   c. indigent   d. lithe   e. illegal

Exercise V.　Word Roundup

1. Explain the derivation of *agenda*. Give the singular form of the word. How do you explain the fact that *agenda* itself may be used as a singular form?

2. Define each of the following phrases.

   a. a devil's advocate
   b. living high off the hog
   c. the affluent society
   d. to put on airs
   e. to serve Mammon
   f. in the aggregate

Exercise VI.　Framing Sentences

Use each of the following words in an original sentence that clearly illustrates its meaning.

1. adjourn
2. adverse
3. advocate
4. affable
5. affluent
6. agenda
7. agile
8. affectation
9. aesthetic

Completing Verbal Analogies

What Is a Verbal Analogy?　Today, practically every standardized test in vocabulary contains at least one section dealing with verbal analogies. A **verbal analogy** is a kind of equation that uses words rather than numbers. This equation indicates that the relationship between two words or expressions is the **same** as the relationship between two other words or expressions.

　Here is a simple verbal analogy:

$$\text{boy : man = girl : woman}$$

This is to be read, "The word *boy* is to the word *man* as the word *girl* is to the word *woman*"—or, simply, "*Boy* is to *man* as *girl* is to *woman*." What the analogy is saying is that the relationship between the word *boy* and the word *man* is the same as the relationship between the word *girl* and the word *woman*.

　And what is that relationship? Well, a boy grows into a man. In other words, the word *boy* refers to the immature version of the male human being, while the word *man* indicates the fully adult specimen.

　In the same way, a girl grows into a woman. In other words, the word *girl* refers to the immature version of the female human being, and the word *woman* indicates the adult.

　Now, if the four words in the original analogy are replaced by what they mean (as indicated above), the new analogy will read:

$$\text{immature male : adult male = immature female : adult female}$$

This makes it clear that the relationship between the pair of words on each side of the equals sign is the same. That relationship can be expressed as "A boy becomes a man, just as a girl becomes a woman." This is essentially what the analogy is saying.

In the analogy sections of standardized tests, students are asked to complete analogies just like the one given above. They are to do this by selecting one or two (or a group of two) items from a possible four or five choices. The format varies a bit from test to test, and, of course, the number of word relationships involved is as infinite as a human being's capacity to manipulate words and ideas.

Exercise I

Three common word relationships that occur in analogy questions on standardized tests are listed below. (In this list, *A* means the first word or expression in the analogy, *B* the second, and so forth.)

  a. *A* means the same as *B*; *C* means the same as *D*.
  b. *A* means the opposite of *B*; *C* means the opposite of *D*.
  c. *A* is an example of *B*; *C* is an example of *D*.

And here are five complete analogies taken from typical standardized tests. The four expressions that make up each have been marked A, *B*, *C*, and *D*. Look at each analogy carefully. Then indicate which of the three word relationships on the list it illustrates.

         A   *B*   *C*   *D*
1. gigantic : tiny = wet : dry

      A   *B*   *C*   *D*
2. oak : tree = rose : flower

      A   *B*   *C*   *D*
3. stop : halt = rest : relax

           A   *B*   *C*   *D*
4. Rembrandt : painter = Beethoven : composer

        A   *B*   *C*   *D*
5. abet : aid = fuse : merge

Exercise II

Below are five complete analogies. Three of them are correctly constructed; the other two are not. Read each analogy carefully. Then indicate which **three** are correctly constructed. Explain why the other two are not.

1. affluent : indigent = wealthy : poor

2. advocate : support = accede : dissent

3. Asia : continent = Sri Lanka : island

4. fire : hot = ice : cold

5. renounce : retain = abhor : loathe

Enriching the Lesson

Exercise I.   Specialized Knowledge

There are many terms in English that indicate specialized skills or knowledge and the people who possess them—for example, *academician* (studied in Lesson 1) and *aesthete* (studied in Lesson 2). A number of these terms are listed below. With or without the aid of a dictionary, define each. Then choose any **five**, and for each compose an original illustrative sentence.

1. conjurer
2. chiropractor
3. disc jockey
4. therapist
5. environmentalist
6. consumer advocate
7. spin doctor
8. podiatrist
9. comptroller
10. programmer
11. anthropologist
12. sociologist
13. pediatrician
14. obstetrician
15. ophthalmologist
16. veterinarian
17. optometrist
18. acrobat
19. neurosurgeon
20. meteorologist

Exercise II.   Portmanteau Words

A **portmanteau word** (sometimes called a **blend**) is a word that has been coined by combining elements of two other words. For example, the portmanteau word *brunch* is made up of *breakfast* and *lunch*.

Read the following excerpt from Lewis Carroll's *Through the Looking-Glass*. It deals with portmanteau words.

"You seem very clever at explaining words, Sir," said Alice to Humpty Dumpty. "Would you kindly tell me the meaning of the poem called 'Jabberwocky'?"

> 'Twas brillig, and the slithy toves
> Did gyre and gimble in the wabe;
> All mimsy were the borogoves,
> And the mome raths outgrabe.

"That's enough to begin with," Humpty Dumpty interrupted. "There are plenty of hard words there. *Brillig* means four o'clock in the afternoon—the time when you begin broiling things for dinner."
"That's very well," said Alice—"and *slithy*?"
"Well, *slithy* means *lithe* and *slimy*. *Lithe* is the same as *active*. You see, it's like a portmanteau [a kind of large suitcase]—there are two meanings packed up into one word."

Below are a number of portmanteau words. Define each, and indicate the elements that went into its formation.

1. chortle
2. splatter
3. simulcast
4. happenstance
5. squawk
6. infomercial
7. telecast
8. smog
9. motel
10. guesstimate
11. advertorial
12. cablegram
13. telethon
14. sitcom
15. heliport

Exercise III. Exploring the Dictionary

1. What is a business *conglomerate*? How does it differ from an ordinary business organization?

2. Consult a dictionary or other reference book for the specific meaning of each of the following "group" words. Then use each in a sentence that clearly illustrates its meaning.

    a. federation
    b. confederation
    c. cabal
    d. bloc
    e. cartel
    f. coalition
    g. consortium
    h. alliance
    i. junta

3. Define *federalism*. What does the term *world federalism* mean?

4. Explain the meaning of each of the following expressions involving the word *devil*.

    a. in a devil-may-care mood
    b. giving the devil his due
    c. deviled eggs
    d. between the devil and the deep blue sea
    e. a devilish expression
    f. a printer's devil
    g. a devil's food cake
    h. bedeviled by misfortune

Exercise IV. Expanding Your Word Power

The words listed below are not on the Basic Word List, but they were mentioned in passing in Lesson 2. All of them would make useful additions to your working vocabulary. Define each, give its etymology, list **two** synonyms and **two** antonyms (where possible), and use in a short sentence that clearly illustrates its meaning.

1. adversary
2. adversity
3. inimical
4. espouse
5. surly
6. genial
7. destitute
8. amalgamate
9. composite
10. lethargic
11. antipathetic
12. nimble

Related Forms in Context

Beneath each sentence below are four words introduced in Lesson 1 or 2. Review the related forms for these words, and choose the one that best completes the sentence. Write that related form in the space provided.

1. The _____ of King Edward VIII in December 1936 stunned the British people.

    a. advocate   b. absolve   c. abdicate   d. aggregate

2. Thanks to translations provided in the form of subtitles, foreign-language films are _____ to a wide audience.

    a. acclimate   b. adjourn   c. aggregate   d. accede

3. Prejudice in all its forms is _____ to those who believe in a just and democratic society.

   a. abhor   b. accede   c. abdicate   d. advocate

4. Someone who is very fashion conscious is likely to devote a great deal of attention to choosing the perfect _____ to complete an outfit.

   a. adjourn   b. aggregate   c. accede   d. acclimate

5. The determined _____ of many groups lobbying for equal opportunities for the disabled led to the enactment of the Americans with Disabilities Act of 1990.

   a. addiction   b. agenda   c. affectation   d. advocate

6. The U.S. Census Bureau offers numerous options for the _____ of data — for example, making it possible for a researcher to access totals by region, country, or year.

   a. aggregate   b. agenda   c. advocate   d. addiction

7. Each year the National _____ of Sciences honors eminent scientists and engineers for their significant original research.

   a. abject   b. affluent   c. academic   d. adverse

8. On June 22, 1937, African Americans cheered as Joe Louis, great-grandson of a slave, knocked out his _____ to win the World Heavyweight Championship, which he held until 1949.

   a. affable   b. adverse   c. affluent   d. academic

9. Although tai chi was developed as a martial art, it improves posture, mental focus, balance, and _____.

   a. affluent   b. aggregate   c. agile   d. aesthetic

10. At Pilgrim Hall Museum, we could see evidence of the _____ of some colonial families—works by local silver-smiths and artists and luxury goods imported from England.

    a. affable   b. adverse   c. affluent   d. agile

11. A strict vegan diet requires _____ from all animal foods and dairy products.

    a. accede   b. absolve   c. adjourn   d. abstain

12. Many travelers to Denver, the Mile High City, find that it takes them a day or two to _____ to the altitude.

    a. accede   b. acclimate   c. abet   d. abhor

13. People who owe a great deal of money may seek _____ from their debts by declaring bankruptcy.

    a. abstain   b. accede   c. acclimate   d. absolve

14. Mrs. Young complains that the Internet is definitely _____, for Soo Mee spends most of her waking hours on-line, frequently forgetting to eat or do her homework.

    a. advocate   b. addiction   c. aggregate   d. agenda

15. Whenever he returns from visiting his family in Atlanta, Georgia, my Boston cousin Ron _____ a southern accent.

    a. affectation   b. aggregate   c. addiction   d. advocate

16. My anger quickly faded as the customer service representative politely and _____ responded to my complaints.

    a. affluent   b. adverse   c. academic   d. affable

17. Which of these portraits by the seventeenth-century Dutch artist Jan Vermeer do you find more _____ pleasing— *The Milkmaid* or *Girl with a Pearl Earring?*

    a. academic   b. affable   c. aesthetic   d. affluent

18. Despite a backlog of bills waiting to be dealt with, the state legislature refuses to postpone its _____, which is scheduled for Friday of next week.

    a. abstain   b. absolve   c. abdicate   d. adjourn

19. During the Great Depression of the 1930s, a time of economic _____, people flocked to the movies, seeking a respite from their troubles.

    a. affluence   b. adverse   c. affable   d. aggregate

20. The controversial bill narrowly squeaked past the Senate with forty-nine votes in favor, forty-eight against, and three _____.

    a. absolve   b. abstain   c. adjourn   d. abdicate

Lesson 3

21. **alienate** — 30. **anecdote**

---

21. **al-ien-ate**   *verb*   āl'-yə-nāt   *or*   ā'-lē-ə-nāt
[*alienare, alienatus* (Latin), "estrange," from *alius* (Latin), "other"]

Definition: To cause hostility or indifference where love, friendliness, or interest formerly existed.

During the years before the Russian Revolution, the increasingly rigid and oppressive policies of the czarist government **alienated** many of those who formerly supported it.

Related Forms: (*noun*) alienation; (*noun and adjective*) alien; (*adjectives*) alienable, inalienable

Usage Note:
Alienation denotes a state of estrangement, disaffection, or isolation. In psychology, the word is used in a special sense to indicate a state of estrangement between a person and the outside world or between the different parts of the personality.

Synonyms: (*verbs*) estrange, disaffect, antagonize

Antonyms: (*verbs*) befriend; captivate

Related Phrases: sever (or break off) relations with; the generation gap; catch someone's fancy, ingratiate oneself with

22. **al-lege**   *verb*   ə-lĕj'
[*ad* (Latin), "to; toward" + *legare* (Latin), "depute, grant, bequeath"]

Definition: To claim that something is true but without offering any proof.

The men now being held in police custody are **alleged** to have robbed eight supermarkets in the past year.

As an excuse for refusing to lend me the money, she **alleged** that she had financial troubles of her own.

Related Forms: (*noun*) allegation; (*adjective*) alleged

Usage Note:
The use of the word *allege* often implies that there is some doubt about the truth of a statement—for example, in the second sentence above. At other times, the word *allege* is used because the speaker wishes to disclaim all responsibility for the truth of whatever follows—for example, in the phrases "an alleged miracle" or "the alleged visitor from Mars."

Synonyms: (*verbs*) claim, contend; declare, assert, affirm, avow, asseverate, aver

23. al·lude   *verb*   ə-lo͞od′ *or* ăl-yo͞od′
[*ad* (Latin), "to" + *ludere* (Latin), "play"]

Definition: To refer to indirectly.

During the course of the evening, he **alluded** to the fact that he had attended Harvard.

Related Forms: (*noun*) allusion; (*adjective*) allusive

Usage Note:
Take care not to confuse the following words:

allude (refer indirectly to) and *elude* (evade, escape)
allusion (an indirect reference) and *illusion* (a false perception or impression)
allusive (containing allusions; suggestive) and *illusory* (tending to deceive) or *elusive* (difficult to find or grasp)

Synonyms: (*verbs*) hint at, suggest, insinuate, intimate

24. am·bi·ence   *noun*   ăm′-bē-əns
[*ambi* (Latin), "around" + *iens* (Latin), "going," from *ire* (Latin), "go"]

Definition: The surrounding or pervading atmosphere; the tone and spirit of an environment.

In the 1920s, the literary and artistic **ambience** of the Latin Quarter in Paris attracted many young American writers, such as Ernest Hemingway and F. Scott Fitzgerald.

Related Form: (*adjective*) ambient

Synonyms: (*nouns*) surroundings, milieu, setting; character, flavor

25. am·biv·a·lent   *adjective*   ăm-bĭv′-ə-lĕnt
[*Ambivalenz*, a German word coined by Sigmund Freud from *ambi* (Latin), "both" + *valens, valentis* (Latin), "worth"]

Definition: Wavering or uncertain because of an inability to make a choice between two contradictory feelings or viewpoints in regard to a person, a thing, or a course of action.

My parents have **ambivalent** feelings about the college I have chosen. On the one hand, they are favorably impressed by its academic standards; on the other, they are unhappy about its great distance from our home.

Related Form: (*noun*) ambivalence

Phrases: ambivalent emotions, an ambivalent position

Synonyms: (*adjectives*) contradictory, opposing, conflicting, equivocal; vacillating

Antonyms: (*adjectives*) definite, firm, unwavering, steady; clear-cut, unequivocal

26. am-nes-ty   *noun*   ăm'-nəs-tē
[*a* (Greek), "not" + *mnasthai* (Greek), "remember"]

Definition: An official pardon granted to offenders against the government, especially for political offenses.

A new government, seeking to restore normal conditions after a bitter civil war, may grant an **amnesty** to all who had been guilty of political offenses.

Synonyms: (*nouns*) forgiveness, immunity (Word 226), remission (of punishment), absolution (of sin)

27. a-nach-ro-nism   *noun*   ə-năk'-rə-nĭz-əm
[*ana* (Greek), "backwards" + *chronos* (Greek), "time"]

Definition: The misplacing of an object or event in a period to which it cannot possibly belong; anything out of its proper time frame.

Cassius's reference to mechanical clocks in Shakespeare's *Julius Caeser* is an **anachronism** because such devices were unknown in Roman times.

Someone who lives too much in the past is bound to be considered something of an **anachronism** by her or his contemporaries.

Related Forms: (*adjective*) anachronistic

Synonyms: (*nouns*) incongruity, inconsistency, contradiction; throwback

28. an-ar-chy   *noun*   ăn'-ər-kē
[*anarchia* (Greek), "anarchy," from *an* (Greek), "without" + *archos* (Greek), "ruler"]

Definition: Absence of governmental authority; general political and social disorder.

During the famous Year of the Four Emperors (A.D. 69), the Roman Empire was thrown into a state of almost total **anarchy**.

A sloppy clerk can easily reduce a filing system to complete **anarchy** in no time at all.

Related Forms: (*nouns*) anarchism, anarchist

Usage Note:

Anarchism is a political doctrine that advocates the abolition of all forms of government as being oppressive and undesirable. The word is also used in an extended sense to indicate active resistance to the state, including terrorism and guerrilla warfare. An *anarchist* is a person who favors the ideas of anarchism or engages in activities aimed at the violent overthrow of an existing government.

Synonyms: (*nouns*) disorder, chaos, lawlessness, pandemonium (Word 290), turmoil

29. a-nath-e-ma   *noun*   ə-năth′-ə-mə
[*anathema* (Late Latin), "a curse," from *anathema* (Greek), "a votive offering"]

Definition:
   a. A curse or strong denunciation.

      Many an Old Testament prophet did not hesitate to hurl stinging **anathemas** at the wayward children of Israel.

   b. The person or thing cursed; more generally, any object of intense dislike.

      Red meat is usually **anathema** to a vegetarian.

Usage Note:
When *anathema* occurs without modification after the verb *to be* (as in the second example above), it functions more as an adjective than as a noun. For that reason, it may properly be replaced by such adjectives as *repugnant* or *abhorrent*, rather than by the corresponding nouns (*repugnance, abhorrence*). Thus, the second example above could also read:

      Red meat is usually *repugnant/abhorrent* to a vegetarian.

One of the few nouns that can replace *anathema* in this situation is *abomination* (with the indefinite article).

      Red meat is usually *an abomination* to a vegetarian.

Related Forms: (*verb*) anathematize; (*noun*) anathematization

Synonyms: (*nouns*) malediction, execration, imprecation; abomination

Antonyms: (*nouns*) blessing, benediction, eulogy, encomium; (*verbs*) bless, glorify, praise, extol, cherish

30. an-ec-dote   *noun*   ăn′-ĭk-dōt
[*anekdota* (Greek), "unpublished things," from *an* (Greek), "not" + *ek* (Greek), "out" + *dotos* (Greek), "given"]

Definition: A brief account of some interesting or amusing incident, especially one containing biographical or historical details.

      The *Oxford Book of Royal **Anecdotes*** contains amusing true-life stories about the men and women who have worn the English crown.

Related Forms: (*adjective*) anecdotal; (*nouns*) anecdotist, anecdotage

Usage Note:
Anecdotal means "containing anecdotes." An *anecdotist* is a person who tells anecdotes, especially as a hobby or profession. *Anecdotage*, a blend of *anecdote* and *dotage*, indicates the kind of old age that is accompanied by a tendency to ramble on endlessly about the past.

Synonyms: (*nouns*) tale, story, vignette, sketch, narrative, reminiscence, memoir; episode; storyteller, raconteur

An Amusing Anecdote

Louis Armstrong (1901–1971), known familiarly as "Satchmo," was one of this nation's great jazz musicians. As a bandleader and soloist, he did much to popularize jazz across America during his long career. He also starred in several films and was noted for his sense of humor.

Many amusing anecdotes are told about this colorful figure. Once, for instance, he was asked if he objected to his fellow performers imitating his exuberantly extroverted musical style. "No," he replied. "A lot of cats copy the Mona Lisa, but people still stand in line to see the original!"

Louis Armstrong

Using the Words

Exercise I. Syllabication and Pronunciation

Syllabicate the following words correctly, and place the major stress mark (') after the syllable that is accented when the word is pronounced.

Example: al-lege'

1. amnesty
2. allude
3. ambience
4. alienate
5. anarchy
6. anecdote

Exercise II. Words Out of Context

In each of the following groups, select the item that best expresses the meaning of the numbered word at the left.

1. ambience   a. formula   b. concern   c. atmosphere   d. schedule

2. ambivalent   a. discourteous   b. imaginary   c. wealthy   d. conflicting

3. anathema   a. a throwback   b. an abomination   c. a champion   d. an illusion

4. anarchy   a. chaos   b. poverty   c. fear   d. danger

5. amnesty   a. assemblage   b. gap   c. mannerism   d. pardon

Exercise III. Completing Sentences

Complete each of the following sentences by selecting the most appropriate word from the group of words given below. Make whatever adjustments are necessary to fit the words into the sentences properly.

allege   anachronism   alienate

anecdote   allude   anarchy

1. During a speech a politician may repeatedly _____ to "pressing economic problems" without actually specifying what he or she has in mind.

2. A modern-dress production of one of Shakespeare's tragedies may be full of the most absurd _____ but still be quite convincing.

3. The people now being held in police custody are _____ to have committed a series of spectacular bank heists over the past year.

4. The English writer Fanny Burney's diaries and journals are full of the most interesting stories and _____ involving people who were prominent in her lifetime.

5. A supervisor who treats the members of his or her staff with contempt or indifference will soon _____ each and every one of them.

Exercise IV. Synonyms and Antonyms

Classify each of the following pairs of words or phrases as **S** for **synonyms** or **A** for **antonyms**.

1. alienate—antagonize
2. milieu—ambience
3. anathema—blessing
4. anecdote—yarn
5. claim—allege
6. unequivocal—ambiguous
7. allude to—hint at
8. order—anarchy
9. anachronism—throwback
10. immunity—amnesty

Exercise V. Framing Sentences

A. Use each of the following words in an original sentence that clearly illustrates its meaning.

1. alienate
2. allude
3. amnesty
4. ambivalent

B. Give an **adjective** form of each of the following words, and use it in an original sentence that clearly illustrates its meaning.

5. anecdote
6. anarchy
7. anachronism
8. allege

Exercise VI.   Word Roundup

Explain the difference in meaning between the words in each of the following groups.

1. allude—refer
2. allusion—illusion

3. allusive—elusive
4. elusive—illusory

Dissecting the Words

Prefixes

1. The Latin prefix **ad**, meaning "to, toward," appears in countless English words. Sometimes it is disguised when it precedes a root beginning with a consonant. In such cases, the *d* in *ad* is often dropped, and the following consonant doubles. For example, *affluent*, meaning "prosperous," studied in Lesson 2, comes from *ad* and the Latin verb *fluere*, meaning "flow." When the two parts are joined, the *d* of *ad* is replaced by an *f* (because *fluere* begins with an *f*). Similarly, *ad* and *knowledge* merge to become *acknowledge*; *ad* and *grandize* become *aggrandize*, meaning "to increase in power or rank."

Thus, *ad* may appear in an English word as **ac-, af-, ag-, al-, an-, ap-, ar-, as-,** or **at-**. This merging, or fusion, of consonants is technically called **assimilation**.

2. The Greek prefix **a, an,** meaning "not," "without," or "opposed to," is found in two words studied in this lesson: *anarchy* and *anecdote*. (Note that the prefix takes the form **an** before a root beginning with a vowel and usually before *h*.) Other words derived from this prefix include:

anonymous (from *an*, "without" + *onuma*, "name")—of unknown authorship

atypical—not typical

amorphous (from *a*, "without" + *morphe* "form")—shapeless, formless

asymmetrical—not symmetrical

amoral—without moral quality (that is, neither moral nor immoral); lacking a sense of morals

Roots

1. The Greek root **arch** (the *ch* is pronounced as a *k*) has a variety of meanings. One of them is "government" or "ruler." It appears in *anarchy*, studied in this lesson. Other English words containing *arch* with the same meaning include:

monarchy (from *monos*, "sole" + *archos*, "ruler")—a government in which one person is the sole and absolute ruler

oligarchy (from *oligos*, "few" + *arche*, "rule")—a government which is entirely in the hands of a small group of people or families

patriarch (from *pater*, "father" + *archos*, "ruler")—a father who is the head of a family or tribe

As a prefix, **arch** (here the *ch* is pronounced *tch*) means "principal" or "of the highest rank." English words in which this meaning of **arch** appears include:

archbishop—bishop of the highest rank

archenemy—chief enemy

archduke—a nobleman whose ceremonial or social status is the same as that of a reigning monarch

archfiend—chief fiend (a name for the devil)

Be careful not to confuse the Greek prefix/root **arch** with the English word *arch*, which means "*sly*" or "mischievous" (as in "an *arch* smile").

2. The Latin root **voc, voke,** meaning "call," forms the basis of the word *advocate* (Word 13). Other words containing this root include:

vocation—a profession, trade, or calling

avocation—a hobby (that is, something that a person pursues for pleasure in addition to his or her regular job)

revoke (literally "to call back")—to withdraw. Noun form: *revocation*

convoke (literally "to call together")—to assemble. Noun form: *convocation*

invoke—to call upon ("*invoke* God's blessing") or ask for ("*invoke* aid"). Noun form: *invocation*

provoke—to stir up or cause. Noun form: *provocation;* adjective form: *provocative*. An *agent provocateur* is a person who deliberately stirs up trouble or dissension.

vociferous—loud-voiced

evoke—to call forth or elicit

A sample of Old English. A page from the only surviving manuscript of the great Anglo-Saxon epic poem *Beowulf*, which was probably written in the 8th century. (The manuscript, however, only dates from around A.D. 1000.) *Beowulf*, which blends both Christian and pagan elements, gives a remarkable picture of the life and customs of the early Germanic peoples.

Exercise

1. How does the prefix *ad* change when added to a root beginning with a consonant? What is the technical name for this phenomenon? Give **six** words studied in Lessons 1–3 that illustrate it.

2. Complete the following activities relating to *arch*.

   a. What is an *archdiocese*? What church official resides in an archdiocese? Give the adjective form of *archdiocese*.

   b. What is a *patriarch*? Name the three patriarchs mentioned in the Bible.

   c. What does the word *arch* mean in such phrases as *an arch smile*? What does the prefix *arch* mean in such phrases as *an archenemy*?

   d. Add *arch* to each of the following, and explain how the addition adds stature or dimension to the original word: *angel, duke, duchess, priest, deacon*.

   e. Match the word in Column A with its meaning in Column B.

Column A	*Column B*
1. monarchy	a. government by the few
2. hierarchy	b. rule by a single sovereign
3. oligarchy	c. a ruling body arranged into series of grades

3. In place of the blank space in each of the following sentences, supply a word or phrase that clearly shows that you know the meaning of the Latin root *voc, voke*.

   a. To deliver the *invocation* at the beginning of your school's graduation exercises is to _____ upon God for divine favor.

   b. If something you have done has *provoked* an argument with your kid brother, it has _____.

   c. If your bus pass has been *revoked*, it has been _____.

   d. If a statement by the president of the United States has *evoked* a lot of comment, it has _____.

   e. If you attended a *vocational* school, you would expect the school to prepare you for your _____ in life.

4. For each of the following definitions, supply a word beginning with the Greek prefix *a, an*.

   a. shapeless or formless
   b. the condition of a country without an effective government
   c. of unknown authorship
   d. lacking a sense of morals
   e. a short narrative, often containing biographical details

5. Occasionally *ad* appears in a Latin phrase that English has borrowed without change. A few such phrases are listed below. Define each.

a. ad libitum (*or* ad lib, *for short*)
b. ad hoc
c. ad hominem
d. ad nauseam
e. ad infinitum
f. ad valorem

Enriching the Lesson

Exercise I. Parlez-Vous Français?

The word *milieu*, mentioned in this lesson, is taken wholly and without change from French. English has many other such words and phrases. A few of them are listed in Column A below. With or without the aid of a dictionary, match each of these expressions with its meaning in Column B.

Column A	*Column B*
1. carte blanche	a. appetizers
2. fait accompli	b. an object of strong dislike
3. savoir-faire	c. a meeting or meeting place
4. chef d'oeuvre	d. a small specialty shop
5. bête noire	e. full power to act as one sees fit
6. faux pas	f. knowing the right or proper thing to do
7. hors d'oeuvres	g. something that cannot be reversed
8. boutique	h. a blind alley or dead end
9. rendezvous	i. a social blunder
10. cul-de-sac	j. a masterpiece

Exercise II. Stating the Case

1. Lesson 3 contains two words, *allege* and *allude*, that indicate particular ways of giving information in speech or writing. A number of other such terms are listed below. With or without the help of a dictionary, define each in such a way as to bring out its distinctive meaning.

a. intimate (*verb*)
b. expatiate
c. avow
d. insinuate
e. assert
f. declaim
g. enunciate
h. asseverate
i. avouch
j. aver
k. cite
l. imply

2. What is the distinction between a *soliloquy* and a *colloquy*? What is a *colloquium*? a *monologist*? *dialogue*?

3. Each of the following colloquial expressions has to do with talking or keeping silent. Define each.

a. rap
b. chew the fat
c. clam up
d. talk back
e. spiel
f. gab
g. badmouth
h. talk big
i. blurt out

Exercise III.   Telling a Story

1. What is a *fable*? How does it differ from an *anecdote*? an *allegory*? Give the names of two authors who are famous for writing fables. In a short paragraph, retell a fable by one of these authors. Why do you think these stories are called fables?

2. Define the following: *tall story, memoir, yarn, parable.* How does each differ from the other? Recount a *yarn* you have heard; a *parable* from the Bible; a *tall story.*

3. What is a *quip? retort? bon mot?* Define each of these words, and, if possible, supply an anecdotal illustration of the definition.

4. The noted American painter James McNeill Whistler is as famous for his witty retorts as for his artistic achievement. The following anecdote shows Whistler in top form:

   At a dinner attended by Oscar Wilde and Whistler, Whistler is said to have remarked: "People will forgive anything but beauty and talent. So I am doubly unpardonable." Everybody roared at this observation except Wilde. Wilde, a noted wit in his own right, looked rather chagrined at Whistler's "score" and muttered, "I wish I'd said that." To this, Whistler retorted, "You will, Oscar—you will!"

   Now recount an anecdote by Benjamin Franklin; a witticism by James Thurber; an example of repartee by Dorothy Parker; an anecdote about Will Rogers. To do this, you will probably have to consult biographies and other books dealing with these witty writers.

5. What does the Latin word *fabula* mean? How does the Latin word contribute to the meaning of the English word *fabulous*? Explain what *fabulous* means in the following phrases: *a man of fabulous wealth, fabulous exploits, a fabulous party.*

Exercise IV.   Expanding Your Word Power

The words listed below are not on the Basic Word List, but they were mentioned in passing in Lesson 3. All of them would make useful additions to your working vocabulary. Define each, give its etymology, list **two** synonyms and **two** antonyms (where possible), and use in a short sentence that clearly illustrates its meaning.

1. alien	5. chaos	9. episode
2. estrange	6. encomium	10. extol
3. vacillate	7. affirm	
4. contend	8. vignette	

Lesson 4

31. anomaly — 40. assimilate

---

31. **a-nom-a-ly** *noun* ə-nŏm'-ə-lē
[*an* (Greek), "not" + *homalos* (Greek), "even," from *homos* (Greek), "same"]

Definition: A deviation from what is normal or expected.
Charles Darwin wrote that there was no greater **anomaly** in nature than a bird that could not fly.

Related Form: (*adjective*) anomalous

Phrases: an anomalous situation, in an anomalous position; an anomaly in the world of politics

Synonyms: (*nouns*) abnormality, peculiarity, oddity, freak, misfit; incongruity; (*adjectives*) abnormal, irregular, freakish, deviant, atypical; incongruous

Antonyms: (*noun*) the norm; (*adjectives*) normal, usual, commonplace, ordinary, regular, typical; congruous

---

32. **ap-a-thy** *noun* ăp'-ə-thē
[*a* (Greek), "without" + *pathos* (Greek), "feeling; suffering"]

Definition: Lack of feeling, emotion, or interest.
I hoped that my idea for the class project would be greeted with some enthusiasm. Instead, it met with complete **apathy.**
Fewer people turned out to vote this year. This is indicative of the growing **apathy** with which the general public seems to regard political campaigns.

Related Forms: (*adjective*) apathetic; (*adverb*) apathetically

Synonyms: (*nouns*) indifference, unconcern, aloofness, detachment, impassivity; (*adjectives*) indifferent, uninterested, aloof, detached, stolid, impassive, unfeeling, emotionless

Antonyms: (*nouns*) enthusiasm, ardor, fervor, zeal (Word 399); concern, interest; (*adjectives*) interested, concerned; ardent, fervent, keen, zealous, passionate

Usage Note:
Be careful not to confuse *uninterested* and *disinterested.* A person is said to be *uninterested* when he or she takes no interest in something; a person is said to be *disinterested,* however, when he or she has no self-interest involved in the matter. Thus, *uninterested* is a synonym of *apathetic,* but *disinterested* means the same as *impartial.*

33. **ap-pall**   *verb*   ə-pôl'

[*ap(p)alir,* (Old French), "grow pale," from *ad* (Latin), "at" + *pallere* (Latin), "be pale"]

Definition: To fill with intense horror, fear, or dismay.

The huge number of soldiers killed during the bloody battle of Antietam **appalled** the entire nation, both North and South.

I was **appalled** to learn that a fistfight had broken out on the floor of the State Senate yesterday.

Related Form: (*adjective*) appalling

Phrases: an appalling sight; appalling disclosures

Usage Note:
Appall, also spelled *appal,* implies a strong sense of helplessness in the face of something truly enormous or monstrous.

Synonyms: (*verbs*) horrify, shock, astound, stupefy, stun, dismay; (*adjectives*) horrifying, shocking, stunning, horrific, frightful, dreadful, fearful

Antonyms: (*verbs*) please, cheer, gladden, exhilarate, elate; (*adjectives*) cheering, gratifying, exhilarating

Related Phrase: be aghast at

34. **ap-pre-hend**   *verb*   ăp-rĭ-hĕnd'

[*ad* (Latin), "to" + *prehendere* (Latin), "seize"]

Definition:
   a.   To arrest or take into custody.

     The police **apprehended** the escaped convict about three blocks from the prison.

   b.   To perceive or understand the meaning of.

     One cannot fully **apprehend** the principles of our Constitution without studying the Federalist Papers.

   c.   To look forward to with fear or anxiety.

     The doctor assured his patient that there was nothing to **apprehend** in the forthcoming operation.

Related Forms: (*nouns*) apprehension, apprehensiveness; (*adjective*) apprehensive; (*adverb*) apprehensively

Usage Notes:
   a.   The noun *apprehension* has several meanings: (*1*) anxiety about the future; (*2*) an arrest; (*3*) understanding. *Apprehensiveness,* on the other hand, indicates merely uneasiness about the future.

   b.   *Apprehensive* means "fearful of what may be coming."

Synonyms: (*verbs*) seize, capture, nab, collar; grasp, comprehend, discern, fathom (Word 185); dread, fear, have misgivings about, anticipate the worst, have a foreboding of; (*noun*) discernment

35. ar-bi-trar-y   *adjective*   är'-bə-trĕr-ē *or* är'-bĭ-trâr-ē

[*arbiter* (Latin), "judge" + *-arius* (Latin), "connected with"]

Definition:

   a.   Subject to or determined by one's judgment; random.

       "The example I have used is purely **arbitrary**," the speaker told her audience. "I'm sure all of you could come up with others that would be just as illuminating."

   b.   Arrived at by an exercise of the will, personal preference, or whim, as opposed to being based on reason or justice.

       The sentence a judge hands down should be based firmly on - accepted principles of law and justice. It should not be a purely **arbitrary** decision.

   c.   Given to willful decisions or demands; tyrannical or dictatorial.

       He wouldn't make a good supervisor because he is so **arbitrary** and overbearing in his dealings with others.

       During the reign of Czar Nicholas I (1825–1855), the Russian government became increasingly **arbitrary** and repressive.

Related Forms: (*adverb*) arbitrarily; (*noun*) arbitrariness

Synonyms: (*adjectives*) judgmental, discretionary; capricious, irrational; prejudiced, partial; unreasonable; high-handed, overbearing, despotic, autocratic, authoritarian

Antonyms: (*adjectives*) objective, fair, just, equitable (Word 166)

Related Phrase: a judgment call

36. ar-bi-trate   *verb*   är'-bə-trāt

[*arbitrari, arbitratus* (Latin), "give judgment," from *arbiter* (Latin), "judge"]

Definition: To act as an impartial judge in a dispute; to settle.

       Both the union and the employer have confidence in Mr. Donelli's fair-mindedness and knowledge of the industry. That is why he was chosen to **arbitrate** the contract dispute.

Related Forms: (*nouns*) arbitration, arbitrament; arbitrator, arbiter; (*adjectives*) arbitrational, arbitrable

Phrases: submit to arbitration, binding arbitration; an arbiter of taste, *arbiter elegantiae* (or *elegantiarum*)

Usage Note:

An *arbitrator* (or *arbiter*) is the person who is chosen to settle a dispute. *Arbitration* is the process by which a settlement is reached. *Arbitrament* is the act of settling the dispute or the settlement that is finally made. *Arbitrable* means "open to arbitration." For example, if the president of a union says that certain demands are not arbitrable, he/she means that they are not negotiable. An *arbiter elegantiae* is a judge of what's tasteful and what isn't.

Synonyms: (*verbs*) adjudicate, mediate

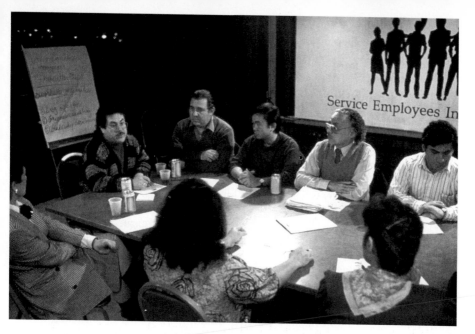

A collective bargaining session under the direction of a mediator.

37. **ar-ray**   *verb and noun*   ə-rā′
[*arayer* (Old French), "arrange," possibly from *arredare* (Vulgar Latin), "arrange"]

Definition:
a. (*verb*) To line up; to dress up.

Scouts first brought the general news that the entire enemy force was **arrayed** along a series of hills not two miles distant.

The various crews and contingents participating in the Mardi Gras parade were **arrayed** in the most fantastic and elaborate outfits.

b. (*noun*) An imposing grouping; rich and beautiful attire.

The defendant entered the courtroom accompanied by an impressive **array** of lawyers and other legal advisers.

Soldiers in full battle **array** patiently awaited inspection by their commanding officer.

Usage Note:
Originally *array* meant "to ready for battle," though the word is rarely used in this sense today. Nonetheless, something of this association with the military still clings to the word's more modern usages. A careful inspection of the examples given above will reveal this.

Synonyms: (*verbs*) align; assemble, draw up, marshal, muster; deploy; adorn, deck out, doll up, gussy up; equip, outfit, accoutre; (*nouns*) alignment, lineup; finery; equipment, accoutrements

Antonyms: (*verbs*) disperse, disband, dismiss

38. ar-tic-u-late   verb: är-tĭk'-yə-lāt   adjective: är-tĭk'-yə-lĭt

[articulare, articulatus (Latin), "say clearly," from articulus (Latin), "division; part"]

Definition:
a. (verb) To pronounce distinctly; to express well in words.

The speaker couldn't be understood because he slurred and mumbled his words instead of **articulating** them clearly.

One of the duties of a president is to **articulate** the policies and programs of his administration in a forceful and convincing way.

b. (adjective) Expressed clearly and forcefully; able to employ language easily and fluently.

The president's statement in defense of his economic program was unusually **articulate** and effective.

Helen was chosen to present our petition to the mayor because she is the most **articulate** speaker in the class.

Related Forms: (nouns) articulation, articulateness

Synonyms: (verbs) enunciate; clarify, expound (Word 180), elucidate, explicate; (adjectives) fluent, eloquent, silver-tongued, glib

Antonyms: (verbs) mumble, mutter, maunder, swallow one's words; (adjectives) slurred, unintelligible, garbled; inarticulate, incoherent

39. a-skew   adjective and adverb   ə-skyōō'

[Derivation uncertain but probably a (Middle English), "on" + skew]

Definition:
a. (adjective and adverb) Out of line or position; turned to one side.

The drawers had been pulled out of the bureau, the lamps had been knocked over, and every picture on the wall was **askew.**

b. (adverb) Disapprovingly; scornfully.

"Why is the principal looking **askew** at me?" I wondered. "Do I have my shirt on backwards or something?"

Synonyms: (adjectives) crooked, cockeyed, uneven, unsymmetrical, awry; (adverbs) disdainfully, contemptuously, askance, derisively

Antonyms: (adjectives) straight, symmetrical; (adverbs) approvingly, benignly

Usage Notes:
a. Note the somewhat subtle difference in the use of askew and awry (pronounced ə-rī'). Askew is usually reserved for concrete objects such as lampposts and hats. Awry, on the other hand, is generally used for more abstract things such as plans, arrangements, or actions.

b. Also note the distinction between askew and askance, meaning "sideways" or "oblique(ly)." Askew usually implies simple disapproval or scorn. Askance (variant, askant), however, implies mistrust and suspicion as well as disapproval.

40. **as-sim-i-late**   *verb*   ə-sĭm′-ə-lāt

[*ad* (Latin), "to" + *similis* (Latin), "like; same"]

Definition:

a. To absorb fully or make one's own; to adopt as one's own.

Some children **assimilate** new information more quickly than others.

The body may **assimilate** some foods more easily than others.

America has **assimilated** the cultural traditions of many different peoples, and this process has greatly enriched our national life.

b. To adapt fully or to make like.

High school students are often under a great deal of pressure to **assimilate** their manner of dressing to that of their peers.

Related Form: (*noun*) assimilation

Usage Note:

The word *assimilation* is much used by sociologists to indicate the process by which individuals belonging to a minority group adopt the living habits and standards of the dominant group in the society. The process is also called *acculturation*. (For the use of *assimilation* in linguistics, see page 57.)

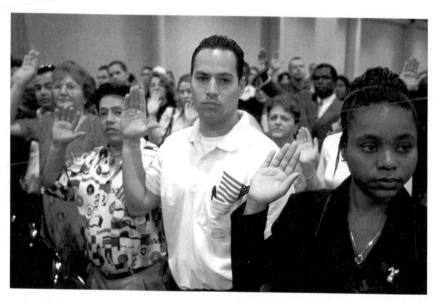

Every year thousands of immigrants from all over the world become naturalized citizens of our country.

Synonyms: (*verbs*) integrate, homogenize; fuse, merge; naturalize, acculturate; digest; incorporate, appropriate; adjust, transform

Antonyms: (*verbs*) segregate, isolate, insulate

Related Phrases: a process of naturalization; in the mainstream; a separatist movement, a standoffish attitude

Using the Words

Exercise I.   Parts of Speech

Indicate the part of speech of each of the following words. Two answers are possible in some instances.

1. apathy
2. askew

3. array
4. arbitrary

5. apprehend
6. articulate

Exercise II.   Words in Phrases

In each of the following groups, select the item that best expresses the meaning of the *italicized* word in the introductory phrase.

1. *apprehended* the suspect
   a. accused   b. protected   c. caught   d. released   e. tried

2. an *articulate* proponent of the plan
   a. long-standing   b. unexpected   c. well-known
   d. eloquent   e. self-appointed

3. an *anomaly* in today's world
   a. adage   b. issue   c. element   d. ideal   e. abnormality

4. with the bedclothes all *askew*
   a. crooked   b. faded   c. clean   d. torn   e. neat

5. a totally *arbitrary* group of numbers
   a. meaningless   b. random   c. unlikely   d. useful
   e. unworkable

Exercise III.   Completing Sentences

Complete each of the following sentences or pairs of sentences by selecting the most appropriate word from the group of words given below. Make whatever adjustments are necessary to fit the words into the sentences properly.

appall	apathy	arbitrate
assimilate	anomaly	array

1. "Randy must be totally uninterested in politics," Tony observed. "Lately I've noticed that an expression of profound _____ and boredom comes over his face every time the subject comes up."

2. In the face of my opponent's formidable _____ of facts and figures, I was forced to concede that I was wrong.

3. "The only practical way to settle this dispute," the attorney remarked, "is to call in an impartial third party to _____ it."

4. It may take long hours of hard work to _____ all the technical data you need to become a computer programmer.

5. The devastation and suffering wrought by the meteorological phenomenon called *El Niño* _____ the entire country.

Exercise IV. Synonyms and Antonyms

A. Match each word in Column A with its **synonym** in Column B.

Column A	*Column B*
1. comprehend	a. askance
2. mediate	b. horrify
3. disapprovingly	c. despotic
4. dismay	d. referee
5. tyrannical	e. grasp

Indicate which of the basic words taught in this lesson (Words 31–40) is **synonymous** with each of the words in Column A.

B. In each of the following groups, select the two words that are most nearly **antonyms**.

1. a. adorn   b. mediate   c. muster   d. instill   e. disperse

2. a. inarticulate   b. ordinary   c. objective   d. eloquent   e. scornful

3. a. boredom   b. oddity   c. process   d. norm   e. umpire

4. a. keen   b. dreadful   c. apathetic   d. partial   e. straight

5. a. equip   b. appall   c. manage   d. elate   e. capture

Exercise V. Word Roundup

1. Explain the difference in meaning between *disinterested* and *uninterested*.

2. What special meaning does the word *assimilation* have for a sociologist? for a linguist? Give a synonym for *assimilation* as used in sociology and one for the word as used in linguistics.

3. What is an *arbiter*? an *arbiter elegantiae* (or *elegantiarum*)?

Exercise VI. Framing Sentences

Use each of the following words in an original sentence that clearly illustrates the word's meaning.

1. anomalous
2. apathetic
3. appall
4. apprehensive
5. arbitrary
6. arbitration
7. array
8. articulate
9. askew

Completing Verbal Analogies

Analogy Question Type I. Perhaps the simplest type of analogy question used on standardized tests (and also the easiest word relationship met with) is shown below. For convenience, the four elements involved in this sample have been labeled *A, B, C,* and *D.*

Type 1

A   B   C   D

absolve : exonerate = abstain : (*indulge, acquit, forgo, impeach, abet*)

What the student is being asked to do in this type of question is complete an analogy that is three-quarters finished. The student is to do this by selecting one of the five choices offered under *D*. Note that these choices are italicized within a pair of parentheses.

Completing Type-I Analogy Questions Correctly. There are three basic steps involved in the correct completion of Type-I analogy questions.

Step 1: Look at items *A* and *B*, and determine the relationship between them. *A* and *B* represent the two words that are in the **key** or **given relationship.** The key or given relationship usually comes before the equals sign (or before the word *as*) in an analogy question. It indicates which word relationship is being used on both sides of the equals sign in the particular analogy under consideration. (In this book the words in the key or given relationship are printed in **boldface type** so they can be spotted easily.)

In the sample analogy given above, the relationship between *A* and *B* (*absolve, exonerate*) is clearly sameness. *Absolve* and *exonerate*, as indicated in Lesson 1 (page 29), are synonyms; they mean the same thing.

This means that the relationship between *C* and *D* must also be one of sameness. In other words, the answer selected from the group of five choices given under *D* must mean the same as *C*.

Step 2: Now look at *C*, and determine what it means. In the sample, *C* is *abstain*, which, as indicated in Lesson 1 (page 29), means "refrain."

Step 3: Finally, look at the group of choices offered under *D*, and select the word that means the same as *abstain*. This is the item that is needed to complete the analogy correctly.

And what is the word wanted? It is *forgo*, which was listed as a synonym of *abstain* on page 29.

The other choices offered under *D* are clearly wrong. *Indulge* means the opposite of *abstain*, and the other words (*acquit, impeach,* and *abet*) bear no relation to it whatsoever. (Note, however, that *acquit* is a synonym of *absolve* and *exonerate*, while *impeach* means the opposite of these two words. These items were intentionally included in the group in order to confuse the student. When doing analogy questions, always keep an eye out for such traps.)

"A Means the Same as B." Thus, the complete analogy reads:

absolve : exonerate = abstain : *forgo*

Note that the word relationship involved in this sample is *sameness*. We can express this relationship in abstract terms as *"A means the same as B; C means the same as D."* This relationship is one of the most frequently used on standardized tests.

Exercise I

Complete, the following analogies.

1. **agenda : schedule** = affectation : (*sincerity, adversity, mannerism, conclusion, aesthetics*)

2. **ambivalent : uncertain** = equivocal : (*illusory, abominable, eventful, ambiguous, unanimous*)

3. **advocate : champion** = critic : (*accessory, opponent, teetotaler, flatterer, bystander*)

4. **anomaly : misfit** = anarchy : (*setting, freak, chaos, denunciation, yarn*)

5. **academic : theoretical** = opulent : (*civil, destitute, natural, unsociable, luxurious*)

Exercise II

Write **three** complete analogies of your own to illustrate the word relationship "*A* means the same as *B*; *C* means the same as *D*." In **two** of your original analogies, use at least **one** of the basic words studied in Lessons 3–4 (Words 21–40).

Noah Webster

In 1828, Noah Webster (1758–1843), America's first scientific lexicographer, published a two–volume *American Dictionary of the English Language.* This work and its successors down through the years have made the name Webster synonymous with dictionary in American households. What got Webster started on the dictionary project was his profound dismay over the continued use of British textbooks and dictionaries in American schools after the United States had become independent from Great Britain. Thus, Webster began his great work in a spirit of national pride. When he was finished, his dictionary contained more than 12,000 words that were not listed in any other dictionary then available. Many of these new items were "Americanisms"—that is, expressions coined and used by Americans. Sales of the dictionary were tremendous, and the work did much to shape and standardize the spelling and pronunciation of American English. Webster produced a second edition of his dictionary in 1840, and the work has been revised and updated many times since then. Indeed, Webster's dictionary (in its revised form) is still a staple item in libraries and households in the United States.

Enriching the Lesson

Exercise I.   Our Greek Heritage

The words *apathy* (Word 32) and *anarchy* (Word 28) are but two of the numerous English words based on Greek originals. Some other words of the same type are listed below. With or without the aid of a dictionary, define each, and indicate what the original Greek word or word elements meant.

1. archaic	8. philanthropy	15. cataclysm
2. cacophony	9. dogmatic	16. dynasty
3. neophyte	10. dynamic	17. pedantic
4. paragon	11. epidemic	18. pedagogy
5. phobia	12. panegyric	19. didactic
6. stratagem	13. sophistry	20. orthodox
7. misanthropic	14. monopoly	

Exercise II.   Order and Chaos

1. In Lesson 3 you learned that *anarchy* denotes the chaos resulting from a lack of effective government. The following words indicate different types of government. (An anarchist is opposed to them all.) Define each term in such a way as to bring out the distinctive characteristics of the type of government involved.

   a. democracy   c. socialism   e. fascism
   b. theocracy   d. communism   f. oligarchy

2. Answer the following questions, or supply the information requested.

   a. What is a *nihilist*? *nihilism*?

   b. What is a *subversive* interested in doing? Give a verb related to this word, and tell what it means.

   c. What is meant by *sedition*? Give an adjective related to this word, and tell what it means.

Exercise III.   Expanding Your Word Power

The words listed below are not on the Basic Word List, but they were mentioned in passing in Lesson 4. All of them would make useful additions to your working vocabulary. Define each, give its etymology, list **two** synonyms and **two** antonyms (where possible), and use in a short sentence that clearly illustrates the word's meaning.

1. stolid	4. elate	7. capricious
2. indifference	5. discern	8. adjudicate
3. aghast	6. misgiving	9. deploy

Related Forms in Context

Beneath each sentence below are four words introduced in Lesson 3 or 4. Review the related forms for these words, and choose the one that best completes the sentence. Write that related form in the space provided.

1. Can you explain why the striking clock in Act II, scene i, of Shakespeare's *Julius Caesar* is _____?

   a. amnesty   **b.** anecdote   **c.** anachronism   **d.** ambience

2. Filled with _____, I let the six-inch black snake coiled on Shoshi's outstretched hand slither onto my arm.

   a. allude   **b.** alienate   **c.** articulate   **d.** apprehend

3. Supporters of Nicola Sacco and Bartolomeo Vanzetti, Italian immigrants executed in 1927, claimed they did not receive a fair trial because they were _____.

   a. amnesty   **b.** anarchy   **c.** anecdote   **d.** anomaly

4. Doctors caution that exposure to _____ sound greater than 120 decibels may result in hearing loss caused by damage to sensitive hair cells in the inner ear.

   a. apathy   **b.** ambience   **c.** anachronism   **d.** anathema

5. The researcher could offer only _____ evidence from several interviews to support her claim.

   a. anecdote   **b.** array   **c.** anathema   **d.** anomaly

6. In Arthur Miller's *The Crucible*, based on the Salem witch trials of 1692, ordinary citizens are _____ and tried as witches.

   a anarchy   **b.** anachronism   **c.** amnesty   **d.** anathema

7. The _____ demanded that both parties listen respectfully, without interrupting, as each side stated its case.

   a. assimilate   **b.** apprehend   **c.** arbitrate   **d.** alienate

8. Next week several local political groups will sponsor a symposium on what can be done to combat the _____ voter turnout in local elections.

   a. anarchy   **b.** apathy   **c.** anomaly   **d.** anecdote

9. A grand jury is investigating an _____ money-laundering scheme involving ten banks in three countries.

   a. allege   **b.** allude   **c.** arbitrate   **d.** apprehend

10. At the lecture, we learned of the _____ events of December 29, 1890, at Wounded Kneé, South Dakota, when 29 U.S. soldiers and about 200 Sioux men, women, and children were killed.

    a. alienate   b. allude   c. assimilate   d. appall

11. If your goal is the _____ of a vast store of knowledge, you must read extensively about a wide range of subjects.

    a. alienate   b. allude   c. assimilate   d. appall

12. The Universal Declaration of Human Rights, passed by the U.N. General Assembly in December 1948, lists the _____ rights of all human beings.

    a. allude   b. alienate   c. assimilate   d. apprehend

13. Compared with animals born in the wild, zoo-bred animals may exhibit _____ patterns of behavior.

    a. anomaly   b. anarchy   c. amnesty   d. anathema

14. Jed claims it will take _____ to decide whether his family will visit the Pro Football Hall of Fame (his choice) or the National Baseball Hall of Fame and Museum (his sister's choice).

    a. alienate   b. arbitrate   c. assimilate   d. articulate

15. In his three-minute Gettysburg Address, President Lincoln presented a brief, eloquent _____ of the Union's goals.

    a. allude   b. assimilate   c. articulate   d. allege

16. *My Favorite Martian*, a 1960s TV sitcom, featured a human-looking _____ with retractable antennae at the back of his head.

    a. array   b. arbitrate   c. assimilate   d. alienate

17. Can you identify any of the literary _____ in T.S. Eliot's poem "The Hollow Men"?

    a. allege   b. allude   c. apprehend   d. appall

18. The lead story in today's paper is about two whistle-blowers' _____ of waste and outright theft in the city administration.

    a. apprehend   b. assimilate   c. allege   d. allude

19. We waited _____ for the latest forecast on where and when the hurricane would make landfall.

    a. apprehend   b. appall   c. articulate   d. arbitrate

20. Whenever his mother nags him about cleaning his room, Jim looks up at her _____ and then continues reading.

    a. anecdote   b. anarchy   c. ambience   d. apathy

Lesson 5

41. astute — 50. authentic

---

41.   a-stute   *adjective*   ə-stoot' *or* ə-styoot'
[*astutus* (Latin), "cunning," from *astus* (Latin), "craftiness"]

Definition: Keen of mind and judgment, especially in practical ma
cunning.

> The novelist Jane Austen was an **astute** observer of life and mar
> in the English countryside at the beginning of the 19th century
>
> More than one clever money manager has been able to ama
> tremendous fortune by **astute** speculation in the stock market.

Related Forms: (*noun*) astuteness; (*adverb*) astutely

Phrases: an astute analysis, an astute criticism; astute advertising

Synonyms: (*adjectives*) shrewd, perceptive, sharp, acute; sagaci
judicious (Word 249); farsighted, perspicacious; quick-witted, cle
wily, cagey; (*nouns*) perceptiveness, discernment, acumen, sagacity

Antonyms: (*adjectives*) obtuse, unperceptive, undiscerning; em
headed, stupid, foolish, doltish, vacuous, inane

Related Phrases: sharp practice; acute perceptions; cunning as a
shrewd insights into human nature; a shrewd investor

42.   a-sy-lum   *noun*   ə-sī'-ləm
[*asylon* (Greek), "place of refuge," from *a* (Greek), "without" + *sylon* (Gre
"right of seizure"]

Definition:

a.   An institution that shelters and cares for mentally unbalance
aged, or homeless persons.

> The eighteenth-century poet Christopher Smart spent a goc
> deal of his life in the infamous London insane **asylum** common
> called Bedlam.

b.   Any place offering protection or security.

> Ever since early colonial days, the United States has served a
> an **asylum** for the oppressed and downtrodden of the world.

c.   Protection against a legal or social penalty.

> Many Cubans escaping from the oppressive regime of Fidel Castro
> have been granted political **asylum** in the United States.

Synonyms: (*nouns*) sanctuary, refuge, haven

Related Phrases: seek sanctuary; take refuge; protective custody;
a safe house

Sanctuary

Literally, the word *sanctuary* (from *sanctus* [Latin], "sacred") denotes a holy place, usually the most sacred part in a church, often referred to as "the holy of holies" In biblical times, the sanctuary sheltered the Ark of the Covenant.

The word *sanctuary* is imbedded in historical tradition. In ancient and medieval times, churches and monasteries served as a place of asylum or sanctuary for persons fleeing violence or penalties of the law. Once inside such a refuge, a fugitive would claim "the right of sanctuary"—that is, immunity from arrest or injury. To injure such a protected person or to remove him by force was regarded as a sacrilege. Eventually the abuse of the privilege led to its general abolition, though it survives in modern times in certain situations.

---

a-tone   *verb*   ə-tōn′

[from the English phrase "to be *at one* with," the idea being that a person who atones for a misdeed is brought back together with God and made whole (or one with himself) in conscience]

Definition: To make up for or repent.

"You made an honest mistake," Wanda said. "Don't feel that you have to **atone** for it."

The plot of the novel is awfully contrived, but the wonderfully vivid descriptions of the setting do much to **atone** for this weakness.

Related Form: (*noun*) atonement

Usage Note:

The *Day of Atonement* (from the Hebrew *Yom Kippur*) is a day set aside by Jews for fasting and prayer as penance for sins and misdeeds committed during the year just past.

Synonyms: (*verbs*) expiate, redeem, offset; (*nouns*) penance, expiation; compensation, reparation, restitution, redress

Related Phrases: make amends for; do penance for

44. a-troc-i-ty   *noun*   ə-trŏs′-ə-tē
[*atrox, atrocis* (Latin), "cruel" + *-ox, -oc-* (Latin), "looking"]

Definition: A savagely cruel, brutal, or inhuman deed; a monstrosity.

For days after the city had fallen to the enemy, bands of drunken soldiers wandered the streets, committing one **atrocity** after another on the helpless and terrified population.

"*You* may call that thing a hat," Al exclaimed. "*I* call it an **atrocity**."

Related Forms: (*adjective*) atrocious; (*noun*) atrociousness

Usage Note:
Atrocious (pronounced ə-trō′-shəs) means not only "extremely cruel or brutal" (as in the phrase "an atrocious crime") but also "extremely poor or bad" (as in the phrases "atrocious behavior" and "atrocious taste"). *Atrociousness*, the noun form, is used in exactly the same way.

Synonyms: (*nouns*) enormity, outrage; (*adjectives*) barbarous, barbaric, sadistic; grisly, gruesome (Word 216), ghastly; heinous (Word 222), outrageous; horrible, dreadful, abominable

Antonyms: (*nouns*) kindness, good deed, act of charity; (*adjectives*) clement, benevolent, kindhearted, merciful, humane; impeccable, flawless, irreproachable, unimpeachable

Related Phrases: war crimes, a crime against humanity

45. at-ro-phy   *noun and verb*   ă′-trə-fē
[*a* (Greek), "without" + *trophe* (Greek), "nourishment"]

Definition:
a.   (*noun*) A failure to develop normally; a progressive wasting away or decline.

    Medical experts state that almost every case of muscle and tissue **atrophy** is the result of changes in cell nutrition, disease, or prolonged disuse.

    The tremendous influx of wealth, luxuries, and slaves that resulted from the acquisition of foreign lands was in part responsible for the moral **atrophy** of the Roman ruling class.

b.   (*verb*) To waste away.

    "Well, here I am," Mr. Kravitz thought to himself sadly on the morning of his 40th birthday, "a middle-aged man whose talents are beginning to **atrophy**."

Related Form: (*adjective*) atrophic

Synonyms: (*nouns*) deterioration, degeneration, decay; (*verbs*) decay, deteriorate, degenerate, shrivel, wither, shrink, rot, stunt

Antonyms: (*nouns*) growth, development, maturation; (*verbs*) grow, develop, mature, flourish, prosper

46. at-tri-tion   *noun*   ə-trĭsh′-ən

[*attritio, attritionis* (Latin), "a rubbing against," from *ad* (Latin), "against" + *terere* (Latin), "rub"]

Definition:

  a. A gradual wearing down or weakening of resistance resulting from constant friction, pressure, or harassment.

      Guerrilla warfare achieves its ends through a slow but steady process of **attrition**, rather than by victory in a quick, winner-take-all campaign.

      "A heavyweight boxing match is not so much a pitched battle as a war of **attrition**," the sportscaster observed. "For that reason, the winner is usually the fighter who is not too battered and exhausted to go on."

  b. A gradual, often natural decrease in size, strength, or number as a result of resignation, retirement, death, or the like.

      "The sales department is a bit overstaffed," the firm's personnel manager remarked. "However, the normal rate of **attrition** around here should solve that problem fairly quickly."

Synonyms: (*nouns*) abrasion, erosion; exhaustion, enervation; reduction, diminution

Antonyms: (*nouns*) increase, augmentation, expansion, enlargement

47. aug-ment   *verb*   ôg-mĕnt′

[*augmentum* (Latin), "an increase," from *augere* (Latin), "to increase"]

Definition: To make greater; to become greater.

If we are to contend with the population explosion, we must **augment** the world's food supply.

Traffic noises in the street outside my window **augment** appreciably during rush hour.

Related Form: (*noun*) augmentation

Synonyms: (*verbs*) increase, enlarge, expand, extend, magnify

Antonyms: (*verbs*) decrease, lessen, reduce, curtail (Word 114), diminish; contract, shrink, shrivel, abate, slacken, dwindle

48. au-gur   *noun and verb*   ô′-gûr

[*augur* (Latin), "soothsayer, diviner"]

Definition:

  a. (*noun*) Someone who can forecast the future by spotting various signs or indications of what is to come.

      "I know you claim to be a reliable **augur** of future trends and developments in the economy," Mike remarked. "Still, your predictions are usually no more accurate than other people's."

b. (*verb*) To predict or foretell through signs; to point to or be an omen of.

> The Aztecs of Mexico believed that comets **augured** impending disaster, even the end of the world.

> The enthusiasm with which our candidate has been greeted all over the country certainly **augurs** well for success in the upcoming election.

Related Form: (*noun*) augury

Usage Note:

The noun *augury* (pronounced ô'-gyə-rē) means a number of things: (1) "the art of forecasting the future," (2) "a prophecy," and (3) "a sign or omen." Accordingly, words that mean the same thing include both *divination* and *prediction*, as well as *portent, premonition,* and *harbinger.*

Synonyms: (*nouns*) soothsayer, diviner, prophet, seer; (*verbs*) prophesy, divine, prognosticate; portend, forebode, presage, bode, foreshadow

The second inauguration of Abraham Lincoln, January 1, 1865.

Augur

In ancient Rome, the *augurs* were a group of priests who sought to discover, by observing certain signs, whether or not the gods approved of a proposed policy or action. The sign most often used for this purpose was the flight of birds, although the augurs also depended on such phenomena as lightning, comets, and the appearance of the entrails of animals. The "taking of the auguries" preceded every important public action, and especially in the early days of Rome, was widely used by private individuals.

From *augur,* we get the word *inaugurate,* meaning "to begin formally; to induct into office," and the corresponding noun, *inauguration.* The hope is, of course, that the omens will be favorable for such an important beginning.

A specialist among soothsayers or diviners in ancient Rome was the *auspex,* who depended specifically on the flight of birds. From this title, we get the word *auspicious,* meaning "favorable, under good omens," and its opposite, *inauspicious.*

49. aus-tere   *adjective*   ô-stēr'
[*austeros* (Greek), "harsh, rough, bitter, unadorned"]

Definition: Rigidly severe; severely simple or bare.

My grandfather was an **austere** man whom I never knew to laugh or smile.

During World War II, living conditions in England were extremely **austere** because of severe shortages of food, fuel, and consumer goods.

The Puritans practiced an **austere**, cheerless form of religion.

Caesar's simple, even **austere**, style of writing contrasts greatly with the complicated and ornate manner of Cicero.

Related Forms: (*nouns*) austereness, austerity, austerities; (*adverb*) austerely

Phrases: austere surroundings, an austere manner, an austere diet; a life of austerity; the austerities imposed by want

Synonyms: (*adjectives*) stern, strict, straitlaced; abstemious, sober, puritanical, ascetic; solemn; harsh, forbidding; somber, gloomy; plain, unadorned, undecorated

Antonyms: (*adjectives*) gentle, mild, kindly; affable (Word 15), tolerant; self-indulgent; elaborate, involved; orotund, florid; gaudy, flamboyant

50. au-then-tic   *adjective*   ô-thĕn'-tĭk
[*authentikos* (Greek), "genuine"]

Definition: Genuine, trustworthy.

"The painting the salesman showed you has to be a fake," Vera informed me. "You can't buy an **authentic** Rembrandt for five dollars."

Related Forms: (*noun*) authenticity; (*verb*) authenticate

Phrases: an authentic record, an authentic document, an authentic account

Synonyms: (*adjectives*) real, true, actual, veritable, bona fide, legitimate, kosher; indisputable, indubitable

Antonyms: (*adjectives*) counterfeit, fraudulent, fake, forged, spurious, phony, bogus, apocryphal; dubious, untrustworthy, fishy

Usage Notes:

a. The synonyms and antonyms listed above include a number of colloquial or slang terms, including *fake, phony, bogus,* and *fishy. Kosher,* a colloquial term meaning "legitimate or proper," has come into English (via Yiddish) from the Hebrew word *kasher,* meaning "in accordance with Jewish dietary laws and, therefore, clean or proper."

b. *Bona fide,* literally meaning "in good faith," is one of a large group of words and phrases that English has borrowed without change from Latin. In English it means "genuine" or "sincere."

Using the Words

Exercise I.   Syllabication and Pronunciation

Syllabicate the following words correctly, and place the major stress mark (') after the syllable that is accented when the word is pronounced.

1. astute
2. atone
3. atrocity
4. attrition
5. augment
6. authentic

Exercise II.   Words Out of Context

In each of the following groups, select the item that best expresses the meaning of the numbered word at the left.

1. asylum
   a. prison   b. booth   c. arena   d. haven
   e. office

2. atrocity
   a. natural talent   b. inhuman act
   c. outstanding accomplishment
   d. grievous fault   e. kind deed

3. augment
   a. imagine   b. solidify   c. belittle
   d. curtail   e. enlarge

4. augur
   a. accumulate   b. bode   c. expiate
   d. compensate   e. refine

5. authentic
   a. phony   b. gross   c. kosher   d. cagey
   e. rotten

Exercise III.   Completing Sentences

Complete each of the following sentences by selecting the most appropriate word from the group of words given below. Make whatever adjustments are necessary to fit the words into the sentences properly.

| atone | attrition | austere |
| astute | atrophy | augment |

1. The reason why premed programs have such a high rate of _____ is simple: A great many students find the course of study too demanding and turn to something easier.

2. Protestant churches in New England tend to be _____ structures with little or no architectural adornment.

3. It was never clear whether the defendants had been acquitted because they were innocent or because they had an _____ lawyer who found a clever way to get them off the hook.

4. I have heard it said that many people no longer know right from wrong and have, in effect, sunk into a profound state of moral _____ .

5. Paying for the repairs that are necessary seems to be an effective way to _____ for the damage you have done.

Exercise IV. Synonyms and Antonyms

Classify each of the following pairs of expressions as **S** for **synonyms** or **A** for **antonyms**.

1. erosion—attrition
2. gaudy—flamboyant
3. perceptive—dense
4. seer—prophet
5. bona fide—bogus
6. sanctuary—refuge
7. flourish—wither
8. magnify—minimize
9. impeccable—flawless
10. humane—barbaric

Exercise V. Framing Sentences

A. Use each of the following words in an original sentence that clearly illustrates its meaning.

1. asylum
2. atrocity
3. atrophy
4. attrition
5. augment
6. augur

B. Give a **noun** form of each of the following words, and use it in an original sentence that clearly illustrates its meaning.

1. astute
2. atone
3. authentic
4. austere

Dissecting the Words

Roots

1. The Greek root **auto(s)**, meaning "self" or "same," is found in numerous English words, including *authentic*, studied in this lesson. Here are some other words in which this root appears:

autocrat (literally "self-ruling")—a ruler with unlimited or unrestricted power; a tyrant or despot. Noun: *autocracy*; adjective: *autocratic*

autopsy (literally "seeing with one's own eyes")—the examination of a dead body to determine the cause of death

autonomy—independence; self-government. Adjective: *autonomous*

autograph—a person's own signature or handwriting

autodidact—a person who is self-taught

automatic—self-operating; running or working by itself

2. The Latin root **ag, act** (as in the Latin verb *agere, egi, actus*) means "act, drive." It occurs in such words as *agenda* (Word 18) and *agile* (Word 20). Other words derived from the same root include:

exigency—a driving need

agitate—to stir up

coagulate—to form into a compact mass; to congeal

enact—to make into law; to act out on the stage. Noun: *enactment*

cogent—forceful; convincing

cogitate (literally "drive about in one's mind")—to ponder or consider intently

Suffix

The suffix **-ize** (British variant, **-ise**) has the general meaning of "make or make into." It has proved to be a handy tool for making a verb out of a noun or an adjective. For example:

popular + ize = *popularize*—to make popular

deputy + ize = *deputize*—to make into a deputy

Sometimes, of course, the spelling of the form to which *-ize* is attached is modified in some way in the new word. For example:

pole + ize = *polarize* (not *polize*!)—to concentrate around two conflicting or contrasting positions

fraternity + ize = *fraternize* (not *fraternitize*!)—to be sociable with

Exercise

1. Answer the following questions regarding words containing the root *auto(s)*.

   a. The word *autointoxication* may be used in both a physical and a psychological sense. Explain the two senses in which the word may properly be used.

   b. Explain the italicized word in this sentence: "The remaining colonies in Africa demanded *autonomy*."

   c. What part of the human nervous system is referred to as *autonomic*? Why is this word appropriate?

   d. What does *autosuggestion* mean? Explain its origin.

2. With or without the aid of a dictionary, define each of the nouns or adjectives listed below, and convert it into a related verb form by adding *-ize*. (Make any spelling changes that are necessary.)

a. victim	f. eulogy	k. social
b. dogma	g. civil	l. plagiarism
c. politics	h. legitimate	m. theory
d. trauma	i. proselyte	n. radical
e. deputy	j. tyranny	o. normal

Enriching the Lesson

Exercise I.   Latin Phrases in English

As indicated earlier in this lesson, *bona fide* is just one of a large group of phrases that English has borrowed without change from Latin. Some other examples are listed below. What does each mean in present-day English? What is its literal meaning in Latin?

1. alter ego
2. quid pro quo
3. de facto
4. persona non grata
5. obiter dictum
6. amicus curiae
7. de jure
8. status quo
9. pro tempore *(often shortened to* pro tem)
10. prima facie
11. modus operandi (*often shortened to* MO)
12. ex officio
13. alma mater
14. sub rosa
15. in absentia
16. vice versa
17. casus belli
18. non sequitur
19. sine qua non
20. deus ex machina

Exercise II.   "Newsworthies"

A number of the basic words studied in this lesson, including *atrocity, attrition,* and *asylum,* frequently crop up in newspaper and magazine articles and on radio-TV news programs. Each gained a currency that made it newsworthy. A number of other examples of newsworthy expressions are listed below. With or without the aid of a dictionary, explain what each of these items means. Then use it in a phrase or sentence of your own.

1. détente
2. an activist
3. deficit spending
4. elitist
5. a police state
6. dumb down
7. a pluralistic society
8. a welfare state
9. a civil libertarian
10. permissiveness
11. a status symbol
12. urban renewal
13. disinformation
14. a reactionary
15. sexist
16. the establishment
17. gentrification
18. insider trading
19. rapprochement
20. a conservative
21. downsizing
22. neoconservative
23. a grass-roots movement
24. open diplomacy
25. software
26. a third-world nation
27. the feminist movement
28. a liberal
29. the inner city
30. human rights

Can you think of any others to add to this list?

Exercise III.   Yiddish in English—Is It Kosher?

Yes, today it certainly is kosher (a Yiddish word meaning "clean" or "proper") to use the word *kosher* colloquially. All dictionaries sanction such usage. A word or phrase that is Yiddish in origin and has been assimilated into our daily language is called a **yiddishism**.

Many of us use yiddishisms without being aware of their origin. Here are a few familiar expressions that are actually translations from Yiddish: *O.K. by me! How come? He knows from nothing. It shouldn't happen to a dog. What's with the jokes?*

It should be noted that since many of these adopted expressions are identified as either *slang* or *informal* by the dictionaries, they must be handled with care. One should not use them in formal writing. Some of the words fill a language need. For example, we have no equivalent English word or phrase to pinpoint the kind of annoying meddler that the yiddishism *kibitzer* denotes.

The American writer Leo Rosten (1908–1997) made a comprehensive study of Yiddish in English. Two of the words that he analyzes in detail are *chutzpah* ("unbelievable gall") and *megillah* ("a long, boring, overdetailed account"). The yiddishism *shtik*—meaning "a stylized or arch piece of acting overused by a performer"—is widely used, especially among actors and theater people generally.

The yiddishisms listed below are in common use. How many of them can you define?

1. yenta	5. schlock	9. schmaltz
2. mensch	6. kvetch	10. nosh
3. kvell	7. schlemiel	11. schlepp
4. klutz	8. schmooze	12. maven

Can you suggest any other words or phrases that would be appropriate for a lexicon of yiddishisms?

Exercise IV.   Expanding Your Word Power

The words listed below are not on the Basic Word List, but they were mentioned in passing in Lesson 5. All of them would make useful additions to your working vocabulary. Define each, give its etymology, list **two** synonyms and **two** antonyms (where possible), and use in a short sentence that clearly illustrates the word's meaning.

1. acumen	5. redress	9. clement
2. obtuse	6. impeccable	10. foreshadow
3. enormity	7. deteriorate	11. flamboyant
4. grisly	8. enhance	12. spurious

Lesson 6

51. avarice — 60. bland

---

51. **av·a·rice**   *noun*   ăv′-ə-rĭs
[*avarus* (Latin), "greedy," from *avere* (Latin), "desire"]

Definition: An excessive desire to acquire and possess wealth; a combination of greed and stinginess.
Few novels portray the dehumanizing effects of avarice as vividly and forcefully as George Eliot's *Silas Marner*.

Related Forms: (*adjective*) avaricious; (*noun*) avariciousness

Synonyms: (*nouns*) acquisitiveness, cupidity, covetousness, rapacity; miserliness, parsimony, niggardliness; (*adjectives*) acquisitive, greedy, covetous, rapacious, grasping; stingy, miserly, niggardly, tightfisted

Antonyms: (for the miserly side of *avarice*): (*nouns*) generosity, liberality, openhandedness; (*adjectives*) generous, liberal, openhanded

52. **av·id**   *adjective*   ăv′-ĭd
[*avidus* (Latin), "craving; greedy," from *avere* (Latin), "desire"]

Definition: Extremely eager, anxious, or enthusiastic.
Your mom and dad may be **avid** readers of spy novels.
Your little brother may be an **avid** baseball fan.

Related Forms: (*noun*) avidity; (*adverb*) avidly

Phrases: an avid sportsman, an avid moviegoer, avid for adventure

Synonyms: (*adjectives*) zealous, ardent, keen, fervent, fervid, voracious, insatiable, rabid, fanatical, passionate, gung ho

Antonyms: (*adjectives*) indifferent, apathetic, unresponsive; (*nouns*) apathy (Word 32), indifference

53. **bad·ger**   *verb*   băj′-ēr
[Origin uncertain, possibly from the name of the animal]

Definition: To tease; to annoy with a constant string of petty torments.
A curious child may **badger** his or her parents with an endless string of almost unanswerable questions.
A judge may reprimand an overly aggressive attorney for **badgering** a witness.

Synonyms: (*verbs*) harass, torment, pester, plague, vex, irritate, hassle, bait, harry

Antonyms: (*verbs*) leave in peace; soothe, calm, pacify

---

54. **baf·fle**   *verb*   băf'-əl
[Origin uncertain]

Definition:
   a. To puzzle completely.

      "How you manage to do well on tests when you never seem to crack a book completely **baffles** me," Jerry remarked.

   b. To prevent from achieving a goal.

      Despite several clues that at first seemed promising, the police were eventually **baffled** in their attempt to solve the murder.

Related Forms: (*adjective*) baffling; (*noun*) bafflement

Synonyms: (*verbs*) perplex, mystify, bewilder, nonplus, confound; thwart (Word 376), foil, balk, frustrate, stymie, stump; (*adjectives*) mystifying, bewildering, enigmatic; perplexed, mystified, quizzical

Antonyms: (verbs) understand, comprehend, fathom (Word 185); help, aid, assist

---

55. **ba·nal**   *adjective*   bə-näl' *or* bā'-nəl
[*banal* (French), "commonplace," from *ban* (Old French), "summons to military service"]

Definition: Made stale by constant use or repetition.

      I expected dialogue by such a well-known writer to sparkle with wit. Unfortunately, it proved to be **banal** and flat.

Related Forms: (*noun*) banality; (*adverb*) banally

Synonyms: (*adjectives*) trite, hackneyed, stereotyped, prosaic, commonplace, pedestrian, insipid, vapid, fatuous (Word 186), jejune, corny; (*nouns*) triteness, insipidity; cliché, platitude, bromide

Antonyms: (*adjectives*) novel, fresh, original, innovative, provocative, striking, sparkling, scintillating, piquant; (*nouns*) novelty, originality

Usage Note:
   a. *Trite* and *hackneyed* indicate staleness or dullness due to overuse. *Stereotyped* suggests a lack of originality and an overheavy reliance on conventional ideas, images, or forms. *Pedestrian* and *prosaic* simply indicate that something is quite ordinary. *Vapid* and *fatuous* suggest a lack of substance or perceptivity. *Jejune* adds to this the idea of childishness. *Corny* is a slang expression that can designate anything from triteness to oversentimentality.

   b. Do not confuse *banal* with *baneful*, which means "harmful" or "destructive."

56. bel·lig·er·ent   *adjective and noun*   bə-lĭj′-ər-ĕnt

[*bellum* (Latin), "war" + *gerens* (Latin), "waging," from *gerere* (Latin), "wage"]

Definition:

a. (*adjective*) Warring, actually engaged in a war; warlike or hostile.

   Between 1915 and 1917, Italy, Bulgaria, Romania, Greece, Turkey, and the U.S.A. all entered World War I. This increased the total number of **belligerent** nations to a dozen, though that many were never involved in the conflict simultaneously.

   How can we hope to arrive at a fair settlement or even discuss the situation calmly when your attitude is so **belligerent**?

b. (*noun*) A party (for example, a nation or organization) engaged in a war.

   The Security Council called upon the **belligerents** to halt all military operations and send representatives to an emergency peace conference.

Related Forms: (*nouns*) belligerence, belligerency; (*adverb*) belligerently

Synonyms: (*adjectives*) martial, combative, bellicose, quarrelsome, contentious, militant, pugnacious, hawkish

Antonyms: (*adjectives*) pacific, peaceable, conciliatory, dovish

Usage Note:
Though *belligerent* and *bellicose* are often used interchangeably, they are really quite different. Both words of course mean "warlike or hostile," but only *belligerent* also means "warring" or "actually engaged in a war." In addition, *bellicose* tends to be used of a natural or inborn inclination toward aggressiveness, whereas *belligerent* tends to be reserved for a hostile attitude that is not innate but, rather, the result of some quite specific external cause.

Mars and Martial

Mars was the Roman god of war. His name is the source of our word *martial*, meaning "warlike" or "military," and also of the name of the month of March, during which the chief festivals of Mars occurred. The planet Mars is also named after this deity.

57. **be·nign**   *adjective*   bǐ-nīn′
[*bene* (Latin), "well" + *genus* (Latin), "birth; race"]

Definition:
   a. Gentle and kindly.

      Though a bear cub may look friendly and **benign**, it is still dangerous.

   b. Wholesome or favorable.

      On the whole, the years she spent abroad had a **benign** effect on the development of her personality.

Related Forms: (*noun*) benignity (pronounced bǐ-nǐg′-nə-tē); (*adjective*) benignant (pronounced bǐ-nǐg′-nĕnt); (*adverb*) benignly

Usage Note:
In medicine, *benign* means "not a threat to a person's health or life" — for example, in the phrase "a benign tumor." Its opposite is *malignant.*

Synonyms: (*adjectives*) benevolent; favorable, auspicious, beneficial, salutary, salubrious

Antonyms: (*adjectives*) malevolent; pernicious (Word 299), deleterious, injurious, inimical, noxious, detrimental

58. **bick·er**   *verb*   bǐk′-ĕr
[*bikeren* (Middle English), "thrust; attack"]

Definition: To engage in petty quarreling.

The conference soon degenerated into an ugly dispute as the participants began to **bicker** over minor details of procedure.

Related Form: (*noun*) bickering

Synonyms: (*verbs*) squabble, wrangle, haggle, dicker

Antonyms: (*verbs*) agree, concur

59. **bi·zarre**   *adjective*   bǐ-zär′
[*bizarre* (French), "strange," originally "gallant": from *bizarro* (Spanish), "handsome, manly"; from *bizar* (Basque), "beard"]

Definition: Weird or fantastic.

Wearing **bizarre** masks and costumes on Halloween is a tradition that goes back many centuries.

The emperor Caligula's behavior was so **bizarre** that many Romans doubted his sanity.

Related Form: (*noun*) bizarreness

Synonyms: (*adjectives*) grotesque, outlandish, freakish, odd, queer, singular, far-out, unconventional, eccentric

Antonyms: (*adjectives*) normal, conventional, orthodox, straight, square; sedate, conservative, sober, staid

60. **bland**   *adjective*   blănd

[*blandus* (Latin), "smooth; soft-spoken"]

Definition:
   a. Mild or gentle. (When used in this sense, the word is usually neutral in tone.)

   > The doctor prescribed a **bland** diet for the patient suffering from ulcers.

   b. Lacking interest or liveliness; flat. (When used in this sense, the word is distinctly pejorative.)

   > He expressed his opinion in language so ordinary and **bland** that he made little or no impression on his audience.

Related Forms: (*noun*) blandness; (*adverb*) blandly

Phrases: bland food, a bland personality, a bland smile, a bland style

Synonyms: (*adjectives*) calming, soothing, nonirritating; dull, boring, unexciting, insipid, vapid, lifeless; nondescript, mediocre, run-of-the-mill

Antonyms: (*adjectives*) irritating, harsh; spicy, pungent, piquant, racy, colorful, florid, scintillating, lively, sprightly

Using the Words

Exercise I.   Parts of Speech

Indicate the part of speech of each of the following words. In one case, two answers are correct.

1. benign	3. avid	5. avarice
2. bicker	4. belligerent	6. bizarre

Exercise II.   Words in Phrases

In each of the following groups, select the item that best expresses the meaning of the *italicized* word in the introductory phrase.

1. a *benign* countenance
   a. beautiful   b. scarred   c. kindly   d. surly

2. motivated by *avarice*
   a. vengeance   b. fear   c. greed   d. ambition

3. *bizarre* behavior
   a. weird   b. aggressive   c. laudable   d. ordinary

4. a *bland* writing style
   a. curious   b. nondescript   c. florid   d. original

5. *badgered* me with questions
   a. thrilled   b. puzzled   c. flattered   d. pestered

Exercise III. Completing Sentences

Complete each of the following sentences by selecting the most appropriate word from the group of words given below.

banal avarice belligerent

baffle bicker avid

1. Though Queen Victoria sympathized deeply with the Southern cause, she had no intention of allowing Great Britain to become a(n) _____ in the American Civil War.

2. "We will never be able to present a united front in the upcoming election if we continue to _____ among ourselves about matters of no importance," the politician warned.

3. Ordinary detectives are often unable to solve the crimes they're investigating, but no mystery—no matter how complicated or puzzling—ever seems to _____ the great Sherlock Holmes.

4. "I've been a(n) _____ sportsman all my life," the movie star told the reporter, "and I rarely miss a day on the golf links or the tennis court."

5. Some of the incidental ideas expressed in the film are novel and interesting, but the overall handling of the theme is terribly _____ and flat.

Exercise IV. Synonyms and Antonyms

A. Match each of the words in Column A with its synonym in Column B.

Column A	Column B
1. mediocre	a. harass
2. beneficial	b. fantastic
3. pester	c. run-of-the-mill
4. foil	d. salutary
5. outlandish	e. frustrate

Now indicate which of the basic words in this lesson (Words 51–60) is **synonymous** with each of the words in Column A.

B. In each of the following groups, select the two words that are most nearly **antonyms**.

1. a. terminate b. squabble c. concur d. atrophy

2. a. triteness b. bafflement c. miserliness d. generosity

3. a. piquant b. freakish c. swift d. vapid

4. a. quarrelsome b. conciliatory c. typical d. inane

5. a. fervent b. peaceful c. orderly d. apathetic

Exercise V. Word Roundup

1. Explain the difference in meaning and usage between *bellicose* and *belligerent*. Use each in an original sentence that clearly shows its meaning.

2. By means of illustrative sentences, show how *bizarre* may be applied to each of the following.

   a. human behavior
   b. physical objects
   c. ideas or points of view

3. What is a *benign* tumor? Give an antonym for *benign* in the medical sense.

4. A number of the expressions mentioned in the Synonyms and Antonyms sections of the word entries in this lesson are *slang*. Make a list of these items.

Exercise VI. Framing Sentences

Use each of the following words in an original sentence that clearly illustrates its meaning.

1. avaricious
2. avidity
3. badger
4. baffling
5. banality
6. belligerence
7. benignly
8. bickering
9. bizarre
10. blandness

Completing Verbal Analogies

"*A Means the Opposite of* B." Analogy questions involving opposites (antonyms) occur frequently on standardized vocabulary tests. This type of analogy can be expressed in abstract terms as "*A* means the opposite of *B*; *C* means the opposite of *D*." Look at the following example of such an analogy question, and try to figure out the answer.

   A   *B*   *C*   *D*

affluent : indigent = equitable : (*florid, destitute, arbitrary, opulent, bland*)

The answer is *arbitrary*. Here's why: The words in the key relationship (*A, B*) are *affluent* and *indigent*. They are opposites or antonyms. So, an antonym for *C*, *equitable*, is needed to complete the analogy correctly. The only word available for this purpose from among the five choices given is *arbitrary*. Hence, *arbitrary* is the correct answer.

Note, however, that *destitute* is both an antonym of *affluent* and a synonym of *indigent*. Similarly, *opulent* is both an antonym of *indigent* and a synonym of *affluent*. In addition, *florid* is something of an antonym of *bland*. All these words were included among the five choices in order to confuse the student and make selecting the right answer more difficult.

Note also that in analogy questions involving opposites (antonyms), the positive or desirable quality often comes first.

Whoopi Goldberg (born 1949) has been performing since the age of eight. Her many Hollywood roles have highlighted her skill as both an accomplished dramatic actress and a talented comedian. She has also appeared on the Broadway stage, in nightclubs, and on television. Her one-woman stand-up comedy act has become legendary.

An ability to use words well, combined with a well-developed sense of humor, has catapulted many an American into fame and fortune in this country's ever-growing entertainment industry.

Whoopi Goldberg

Exercise I

Complete each of the following analogies.

1. **augment : decrease** = wax : (*polish, wane, declare, frustrate, accelerate*)

2. **piquant : bland** = generous : (*ardent, dull, amiable, miserly, liberal*)

3. **absolve : incriminate** = acquit : (*liberate, mystify, convict, resolve, exclude*)

4. **conciliatory : belligerent** = astute : (*passionate, sagacious, indifferent, bellicose, obtuse*)

5. **authentic : spurious** = austere : (*flamboyant, bogus, puritanical, reliable, wily*)

6. **relish : abhor** = agile : (*lithe, contradictory, clumsy, zealous, commonplace*)

Exercise II

Write **three** original analogies involving opposites (antonyms). In your analogies use at least **three** of the basic words presented in Lessons 1–6 (Words 1–60).

Exercise III

The following items review what you have so far learned about analogy questions. Complete each.

1. **anarchy : chaos** = avarice : (*indulgence, mannerism, provocation, cupidity, encouragement*)

2. **hackneyed : innovative** = pedestrian : (*original, quarrelsome, auspicious, prosaic, grisly*)

3. **badger : harass** = abstain : (*pester, indulge, pacify, champion, forbear*)

4. **haven : sanctuary** = aggregate : (*anomaly, pretense, cluster, refuge, misdemeanor*)

5. **malevolent : benign** = adverse : (*noxious, weird, mediocre, favorable, covetous*)

6. **assiduous : indolent** = diligent : (*inconsolable, lethargic, abstemious, charitable, rapacious*)

Enriching the Lesson

Exercise I. Fighting Words

With or without the aid of an unabridged dictionary, complete the following exercises.

1. Define the following expressions.

a. war of nerves	i. mobilization
b. amphibious operation	j. guerrilla
c. blitzkrieg	k. armistice
d. pacification	l. skirmish
e. preemptive strike	m. hostage
f. pacifist	n. ordnance
g. hostilities	o. broadside
h. maneuvers	p. hold out the olive branch

2. What is an *Armageddon?* Explain the story behind this word, and indicate where it comes from.

3. What is a *Pyrrhic victory?* Explain the story behind this phrase.

4. What is *martial law?* When is it usually imposed? What are *martial arts?* Name a movie star or other celebrity who is a noted *martial artist.*

5. The Latin word *bellum* means "war." What does *antebellum* mean? In what connection is this Latin phrase used in American history?

Exercise II. Clichés

A **cliché** is simply an expression that has grown stale and flat as a result of overuse. Some good examples of clichés are *enjoy the fruits of one's labor, wolf down one's food, go like a house afire,* and similar hand-me-down metaphors and similes. Every cliché was presumably once fresh and original, but such expressions have been so overworked that today they strike us as being trite and corny.

This, however, is not to say that clichés should be avoided altogether. Countless clichés, such as *bend over backwards, cut corners,* and *turn a new leaf,* are still serviceable, even if they are overly familiar. In fact, it would be hard, if not impossible, to carry on a conversation or otherwise communicate without calling on clichés.

For that reason, a sound principle to follow in regard to clichés is this: Don't be a fanatic about avoiding them, but don't overuse them either. Also, bear in mind the literal meaning of the cliché, and try to use it only where it will be appropriate and effective. For example, a 12th grader who has just mailed out a batch of college applications might sum up his or her hopes for them by using a familiar cliché in this novel way: "Well, I've cast my bread upon the waters," the student might observe. "Now all I can do is pray that some of it comes back sandwiches!"

Now complete the following group of exercises involving clichés.

1. Some of the sentences below contain clichés; others have a measure of freshness and originality in them. Write the identifying letter of each sentence containing a cliché. Then replace the cliché with language that is more distinctive and effective.

   a. On that hot summer afternoon, the garden sizzled with bees.

   b. When we arrived back at camp, we were as hungry as bears.

   c. Her mere presence on the platform turned a routine gathering into a once-in-a-lifetime event.

   d. She left no stone unturned in her search for the missing papers.

   e. The news we received this morning was like a bolt from the blue.

   f. The fullback drove through the line like a knife going through soft cheese.

2. Substitute a fresher, more original expression for each of the clichés listed below.

   a. worked like a Trojan
   b. a sumptuous repast
   c. slept like a log

   d. prostrate with grief
   e. lost his shirt at the track
   f. paint the town red

3. Draw up a list of **twenty** clichés that you have heard or seen in the last week.

4. Complete each of the following comparisons with a word or phrase that is not a cliché.
   a. as fat as _____
   b. as mad as _____
   c. as old as _____
   d. as pretty as _____
   e. as quiet as _____
   f. as big as _____

Exercise III.   A Verbal Diversion

Modern English is rich in colloquial expressions involving the names of members of the animal kingdom. Two such expressions are *chicken feed* (meaning "a woefully insufficient sum of money") and to *smell a rat* (meaning "to suspect that something is not quite as it should be"). A number of similar items, all of them widely used today in informal speech and writing, are listed below. With or without the aid of a dictionary or other reference book, define each. Then choose any **five**, and use each in a short sentence that clearly illustrates the expression's meaning.

1. a red herring
2. a round-robin
3. a stool pigeon
4. a loan shark
5. an eager beaver
6. to dovetail
7. to play possum
8. a white elephant
9. to handle with kid gloves
10. a dark-horse candidate
11. a kangaroo court
12. a lame-duck session of Congress
13. a bookworm
14. to let the cat out of the bag
15. to go to the dogs
16. a harebrained scheme
17. to throw to the wolves
18. a paper tiger
19. to take the bull by the horns
20. a sacred cow
21. to get one's goat
22. a wild-goose chase
23. a sheepish grin
24. to have a frog in one's throat

Can you add to this list from your own knowledge?

Exercise IV.   Expanding Your Word Power

The following words are not on the Basic Word List, but they were mentioned in passing in Lesson 6. All of them would make useful additions to your working vocabulary. Define each, give its etymology, list **two** synonyms and **two** antonyms (where possible), and use in a short sentence that clearly illustrates the word's meaning.

1. niggardly
2. voracious
3. bait
4. quizzical
5. platitude
6. insipid
7. grotesque
8. foil
9. haggle
10. militant
11. sedate
12. eccentric

Related Forms in Context

Beneath each sentence below are four words introduced in Lesson 5 or 6. Review the related forms for these words, and choose the one that best completes the sentence. Write that related form in the space provided.

1. The county commission authorized the purchase of six new school buses, a significant _____ of the current fleet.

    a. augur   b. atrophy   c. augment   d. baffle

2. According to Greek mythology, _____ King Midas, when granted a single wish, made the mistake of wishing that everything he touched would turn into gold.

    a. atrophy   b. avarice   c. augur   d. attrition

3. To collect data on the movements of schools of fish, biologists use different kinds of tags that _____ identify individual fish.

    a. bizarre   b. benign   c. austere   d. banal

4. The world was appalled to learn of the _____ conditions in the refugee camps.

    a. avarice   b. atrocity   c. asylum   d. attrition

5. To Anya's astonishment, the expert _____ her copy of the Declaration of Independence, which she bought at a garage sale for a few dollars.

    a. astute   b. authentic   c. avid   d. bizarre

6. Before conducting public or private business, ancient Romans consulted _____ such as thunder and lightning or the songs and flight of birds.

    a. augur   b. avarice   c. atrophy   d. atrocity

7. Ninety-two-year-old Uncle Albert complains about age-related _____ changes in his body that make it difficult for him to get around.

    a. avarice   b. belligerent   c. asylum   d. atrophy

8. Every stockbroker boasts of the _____ of his or her investment advice, but good results are never guaranteed.

    a. banal   b. avid   c. astute   d. belligerent

9. In Shirley Jackson's shocking story "The Lottery," each year one resident of a New England village is chosen by lottery as a scapegoat for the _____ of the other villagers' sins.

    a. augment   b. atone   c. bicker   d. baffle

10. The guest of honor's after-dinner speech perfectly matched the _____ of the meal, which was uninspired and tasteless.

    a. bland   b. benign   c. authentic   d. avid

11. Sir Arthur Conan Doyle's Sherlock Holmes, who easily solves the most _____ crimes, made his debut in the novel *A Study in Scarlet* in 1887.

    a. atrophy   b. bicker   c. baffle   d. badger

12. A panel of paleontologists was called in to assess the _____ of a fossil found in China that appeared to be the missing link between dinosaurs and birds.

    a. avid   b. astute   c. austere   d. authentic

13. The weekly magazine's TV critic frequently attacks the networks' programming for the _____ of most soap operas, talk shows, and daytime TV in general.

    a. banal   b. astute   c. avid   d. benign

14. To stop the constant _____ between Janie and her brothers, their parents have instituted a weekly family meeting at which they welcome suggestions from everyone.

    a. atone   b. augur   c. augment   d. bicker

15. An annual contest celebrates the complexity and _____ of Rube Goldberg's cartoon "inventions" by challenging students to draw complex contraptions that use everyday materials and involve at least 20 steps to accomplish a simple task.

    a. belligerent   b. bizarre   c. avid   d. bland

16. United Nations peacekeeping forces have been dispatched to countries all over the world to stop acts of _____ and protect civilians.

    a. austere   b. bizarre   c. benign   d. belligerent

17. Most years Marc, a veterinarian, _____ predicts the Best in Show in the Westminster Kennel Club show from among the winners of the seven categories of show dogs—herding, hound, nonsporting, sporting, terrier, toy, and working.

    a. astute   b. avid   c. bizarre   d. bland

18. Stranded for years on a desert island, Robinson Crusoe stoically endures his life of _____ and loneliness until he discovers human footprints that aren't his own.

    a. astute   b. authentic   c. austere   d. belligerent

19. Although my supervisor spoke _____, his words were shocking: "Pack up your things and turn in your key. You've been laid off, and today is your last day."

    a. authentic   b. bland   c. banal   d. avid

20. Teresa has been reading _____ since childhood and is never without a book.

    a. bizarre   b. avid   c. austere   d. benign

Lesson 7

61. bleak — 70. brusque

---

61. **bleak**   *adjective*   blēk
[*ble(i)kke* (Middle English), "pale," from *bleikr* (Old Norse), "white; pale"]

Definition:
a. Desolate, windswept, and bare.

Much of the coast of northern Alaska is **bleak** and uninviting.

b. Cold and gloomy; unpromising.

The funeral cortege moved off slowly and silently through the chill air of the **bleak** November day.

Unless we can raise fresh capital, the outlook for the survival of this company is exceedingly **bleak**.

Related Form: (*noun*) bleakness

Synonyms: (*adjectives*) barren; raw, harsh, chilling, forbidding; dour; dismal, dreary, drab, somber, grim, cheerless, depressing

Antonyms: (*adjectives*) lush (Word 260), verdant; balmy, mild, rosy, temperate; cheerful, blithe (Word 63), joyful, joyous; positive, upbeat; promising, encouraging, bright, sunny

---

62. **blight**   *verb and noun*   blīt
[Origin unknown]

Definition:
a. (*verb*) To check or destroy the growth of.

According to the paper, an unexpectedly early frost has **blighted** a sizable part of the Florida citrus crop.

High interest rates **blighted** the manufacturer's plans to borrow the capital he needed to modernize his operation.

b. (*noun*) Something that impairs growth or causes ruin.

A truly nationwide effort is needed if we are going to check the **blight** that is slowly destroying our inner cities.

Phrases: blighted hopes, urban blight

Synonyms: (*verbs*) nip, wither, shrivel; blast, ruin, devastate, efface; frustrate, foil, dash; (*nouns*) bane, scourge, plague; eyesore

Antonyms: (*verbs*) foster, nourish, promote, stimulate; (*nouns*) stimulus, stimulant

Related Phrases: dry rot; put a damper on; urban renewal

63. blithe   *adjective*   blī<u>th</u>   *or*   blīth

[*blithe* (Old English), "sweet; happy"]

Definition:
  a. Merry and carefree.

  The **blithe** and sunny personality that had made her so popular in school was unaffected by the passage of years.

  b. Overly unconcerned; reckless.

  Their **blithe** lack of concern for the safety of the children in their charge disturbed me greatly.

Related Forms: (*noun*) blitheness; (*adverb*) blithely

Synonyms: (*adjectives*) lighthearted, jolly, jocund, jovial, buoyant, sprightly, mirthful, happy-go-lucky; light-minded, heedless, indifferent, nonchalant, blasé

Antonyms: (*adjectives*) morose, saturnine, gloomy, despondent, morbid, melancholy; pensive (Word 295); solemn, dour

64. bois-ter-ous   *adjective*   boi'-stər-əs   *or*   boi'-strəs

[*boistres* or *boistous* (Middle English), "violent; fierce"]

Definition: Noisy and rowdy.

It is only natural to expect small children to be a bit **boisterous** and high-spirited.

Related Forms: (*noun*) boisterousness; (*adverb*) boisterously

Phrases: boisterous students, boisterous laughter

Synonyms: (*adjectives*) loud, obstreperous, vociferous, clamorous; unruly, disorderly, riotous, uproarious, disruptive, turbulent (Word 380), tempestuous

Antonyms: (*adjectives*) quiet, peaceful, tranquil (Word 377), halcyon; calm, orderly; muted, hushed, muffled, sedate

Halcyon

The adjective *halcyon* (hăl'-sē-ən), meaning "calm and peaceful" or "prosperous," has an interesting history. It comes from the Greek word *halkyon,* meaning "kingfisher" (a kind of seabird; see drawing). In Greek mythology, the kingfisher was reputed to have the power to calm the wind and the waves while it nested on the sea during the winter solstice (December 22). Accordingly, *halcyon days* are the days of fine weather that occur about that time and, by extension, any period of peace or tranquility.

65. bom-bas-tic   *adjective*   bŏm-băs'-tĭk

[*bombax* (Late Latin), "cotton (often used for padding)," related to *pambuk* (Turkish), "cotton"]

Definition: Pompous or inflated in language.

Lincoln's short, subdued address at Gettysburg is far more moving than Hale's lengthy and **bombastic** oration on the same occasion.

Related Form: (*noun*) bombast

Synonyms: (*adjectives*) grandiloquent, grandiose, hyperbolic, high-sounding, high-flown, highfalutin, extravagant; swollen, bloated, turgid; (*nouns*) fustian, rant, claptrap

Antonyms: (*adjectives*) plain, direct, straightforward; lean, spare; unvarnished, unembellished; artless, unpretentious; terse, succinct; muted

Usage Note:

Bombast indicates overly padded and pretentious language. *Fustian* applies to inflated language that is absurdly out of keeping with its quite ordinary content. *Rant* (also a verb) emphasizes the expression of strong emotions together with extravagance of language and violence of delivery. *Claptrap* is pretentious, insincere, or empty language designed to attract applause.

66. boor-ish   *adjective*   bŏŏr'-ĭsh

[*boer* (Dutch), "farmer"]

Definition: Rude or unrefined.

Fortunately, the loud and generally **boorish** behavior of a few of the guests did not spoil the party for the rest of us.

Related Forms: (*nouns*) boor, boorishness

Usage Notes:

a. Do not confuse a *boor* (that is, a rude or unrefined person) with a *bore* (that is, a dull or tedious person). An easy way to keep the two straight is to remember that *bore* is related to *boring* and *boredom.*

b. Also keep *boor* separate from the proper noun *Boer.* You may recall from your study of history that the Boers were South Africans of Dutch descent who engaged in an unsuccessful war with Great Britain from 1899 to 1902. Their descendants are the *Afrikaners* of today.

Synonyms: (*adjectives*) vulgar, uncouth, gauche, crude, crass, churlish, ill-bred, lowbred, ill-mannered, unmannerly; (*nouns*) vulgarian, lout, yahoo

Antonyms: (*adjectives*) urbane (Word 382), suave, polished; tactful, discreet, diplomatic; (*nouns*) savoir faire, social savvy, finesse (Word 194), class, style

67. **boy-cott** *verb and noun* boi'-kŏt

[After Charles C. Boycott, a land agent in County Mayo, Ireland, who was subjected to this form of treatment in 1880 for refusing to lower rents on the lands he managed]

Definition:

a. *(verb)* To refuse to buy, use, or deal with as a way to protest (or force acceptance of) some form of behavior.

During the civil rights movement of the 1950s and 1960s, both black and white Americans **boycotted** segregated lunch counters, bus depots, schools, and the like.

b. *(noun)* An instance of such treatment.

Many forms of nonviolent protest, including sit-ins, picket lines, and **boycotts**, have become common in today's United States.

Synonyms: *(verbs)* ban, proscribe, ostracize (Word 289), blacklist, blackball; *(nouns)* ban, embargo

Antonyms: *(verbs)* patronize, fraternize with, support; endorse, sanction, approve

Charles C. Boycott

In 1873, a retired English army officer, Captain Charles C. Boycott (1832–1897), became the rent collector on the estates of an aristocrat called Lord Erne. These estates were in Country Mayo, Ireland, and the tenants on them were Irish small farmers who paid an annual rent for the use of the land. Unfortunately, Captain Boycott took his job too seriously; and as a result, a new word, *boycott,* entered the language.

This is what happened. A series of poor harvests in the late 1870s caused widespread suffering among Lord Erne's tenants. Accordingly, in 1880 they asked for a 25% reduction in their rents. To these pleas Captain Boycott turned a deaf ear. As a matter of fact, he attempted to evict some of the tenants for nonpayment of their rent. In reply, the tenants and other people who sympathized with them decided to have nothing whatsoever to do with the captain. He was refused lodgings when he traveled, frequently did not receive his mail, and had to make special arrangements to get food and other necessities. These tactics worked so well that Captain Boycott was forced to give up his job and return to England. He left Ireland late in 1880, and shortly thereafter the verb *boycott,* meaning "to refuse to deal with as a means of protest," first appeared in English.

68. **brash** *adjective* brăsh

[Origin unknown, possibly *brisk* + *rash*]

Definition: Overly bold, hasty, and thoughtless.

Nature and experience have a way of turning a **brash** and tactless youngster into a thoughtful and considerate adult.

Related Form: (*noun*) brashness

Phrases: a brash comedian, brash behavior

Synonyms: (*adjectives*) rash, reckless, foolhardy, impetuous, precipitate; impudent, saucy, impertinent, brazen, shameless; tactless, gauche

Antonyms: (*adjectives*) cautious, prudent, circumspect (Word 88), wary; tactful, considerate

69. **bra·va·do** *noun* brǝ-vä'-dō

[*bravada* (Spanish), "boastfulness," from *bravo* (Spanish), "brave; boastful"]

Definition: A boastful or swaggering show of false bravery; false courage in general.

His challenge to fight was pure **bravado**; inwardly he hoped that no one would take him on.

Synonyms: (*nouns*) braggadocio, swagger, bluster, cockiness, bluff

Antonyms: (*nouns*) fearlessness, intrepidity, gallantry, audacity, bravery, valor, pluck, daring, stoutheartedness, dauntlessness

Related Phrases: put up a bold front; call someone's bluff

70. **brusque** *adjective* brŭsk

[*brusque* (French), "fierce; harsh," from *brusco* (Italian), "sharp; sour"]

Definition: Overly short or abrupt.

He is so courteous and affable that I was totally taken aback by his unaccountably **brusque** answer to my question.

Related Form: (*noun*) brusqueness

Phrases: a brusque reply, a brusque tone, a brusque manner

Usage Notes:
   a. *Brusque* is also spelled *brusk*. This applies to *brusqueness* as well.
   b. Do not confuse *brusque* (*brusk*) with *brisk,* meaning "lively or energetic."

Synonyms: (*adjectives*) curt, blunt, terse; gruff, rough, sharp, harsh; uncivil, impolite

Antonyms: (*adjectives*) civil, polite, cordial, affable (Word 15); voluble, effusive

Using the Words

Exercise I.   Syllabication and Pronunciation

Syllabicate the following words correctly, and place the major stress mark (') after the syllable that is accented when the word is pronounced.

Example: a-bet'

1. boycott
2. bombastic

3. bravado
4. brusque

5. boisterous
6. boorish

Exercise II.   Words Out of Context

In each of the following groups, select the item that best expresses the meaning of the numbered word at the left.

1. brusque
   a. pompous   b. curt   c. energetic
   d. obscure   e. unwieldy

2. bombastic
   a. fearful   b. reckless   c. mild
   d. sprightly   e. inflated

3. boisterous
   a. tranquil   b. bloated   c. dismal
   d. rowdy   e. exhausted

4. blight
   a. bluster   b. merriment   c. eyesore
   d. claptrap   e. curiosity

5. brash
   a. overly sensitive   b. overly forward
   c. overly critical   d. overly tired
   e. overly stingy

Exercise III.   Completing Sentences

Complete each of the following sentences by selecting the most appropriate word from the group of words given below. Use the words exactly as they are printed in this list.

bleak	blight	boorish
boycott	bravado	blithe

1. The speeches of both Hitler and Mussolini were full of the kind of overblown bluster and _____ that today strikes us as pathetic.

2. Her _____ and sunny disposition is clearly the product of a happy childhood spent amid pleasant surroundings and among caring relatives.

3. I know they think they're being suave and sophisticated, but I consider their conduct downright _____.

4. They are depressing people to be around because their attitude toward life is so _____ and cheerless.

5. Since most of the country continued to buy the product to which the small group of protesters objected, the _____ failed.

Exercise IV.   Synonyms and Antonyms

Classify each of the following pairs of words as **S** for **synonyms** or **A** for **antonyms**.

1. bleak—rosy
2. lighthearted—blithe
3. boycott—patronize
4. halcyon—tempestuous
5. reckless—brash
6. brusque—civil

Exercise V.   Word Roundup

1. Distinguish between the words in each of the following pairs.

   a. brusque—brisk
   b. boor—bore

2. Explain the meaning of the *italicized* element in each of the following phrases.

   a. *bleak* prospects
   b. urban *blight*
   c. *boisterous* laughter
   d. *blighted* hopes
   e. a *brash* comedian
   f. a *brusque* reply

3. Define each of the following terms.

   a. bombast
   b. claptrap
   c. rant
   d. fustian

   What do these words have in common?

4. Explain the story behind the phrase *halcyon days.* Then retell the myth of Alcyone and Ceyx, and relate it to the history of the phrase. (If you don't know the myth, look it up in Robert Graves's *The Greek Myths* or *Bulfinch's Mythology.*)

Exercise VI.   Framing Sentences

A. Use each of the following words in an original sentence that clearly illustrates its meaning.

1. blight
2. blithe
3. boycott
4. bravado

B. Give a **noun** form of each of the following words, and use it in an original sentence that clearly illustrates its meaning.

1. bleak
2. boisterous
3. bombastic
4. boorish
5. brash
6. brusque

Dissecting the Words

1. The Latin prefix **ambi** means "both" or "around." It occurs in *ambience* (Word 24) and *ambivalent* (Word 25). Other words using this prefix include:

ambidextrous (literally, "with a right hand on both sides")—able to use both hands equally well

ambient (literally, "going around")—surrounding or encompassing

ambiguous (literally, "going in both directions at once")—unclear or uncertain

ambition (literally, "a going around [to canvass for votes]")—a strong desire to achieve some goal

The corresponding Greek prefix is **amphi.** It occurs in the following English words:

amphitheater—a kind of theater or stadium that has seats going all around the stage or arena

amphibious (literally, "living both lives")—able to live or operate on land *and* in the water

2. The prefix **be**, meaning "thoroughly" or "completely," is of Germanic origin. It appears in many words that have come down to us from Old and Middle English. Today it is used for the following purposes:

a. To give greater force or thoroughness to an action.

   be + smirch = *besmirch*—to soil thoroughly

b. To make an intransitive verb (*i.e.*, one that cannot take a direct object) transitive.

   be + moan = *bemoan*—to moan and groan about

c. To form a verb or participial adjective from a noun.

   be + witch = *bewitch*—to enchant; *bewitching*—enchanting; *bewitched*—enchanted

Samuel Johnson

The eminent 18th-century writer and critic Samuel Johnson (1709–1784) published his two-volume *Dictionary of the English Language* in 1755. It surpassed earlier dictionaries in the precision of its definitions and the wealth of its examples of usage. Though the work had its flaws and revealed much about Johnson's personal prejudices, it soon became a staple item in most private libraries.

Root

The Latin root **vert**, **vers** means "turn." It is found in many English words, including *adverse* (Word 12). Here are a few other words from this root:

advert—to refer to

animadversion—a strong criticism; a hostile remark

averse—disinclined, reluctant, or opposed to

avert—to turn away from; to prevent. Noun: *aversion*

divers—several

diverse—varied. Another adjective with the same meaning is *diversified*.

invert—to turn over or in on itself. Noun: *inversion*

convert—to transform, exchange, or adopt. A *convert* is a person who adopts (turns to) a new religion or other doctrine. Noun: *conversion*

revert—to turn or go back to. Noun: *reversion*

subvert (literally, "turn from under") —to overthrow; to seek to undermine (as, for example, a government or institution). Adjective: *subversive;* noun: *subversion*

vertigo (literally, "a turning about") —a sensation of dizziness and a feeling that one is about to fall

Exercise

1. Define each of the following words using the prefix *be,* and use the word in a short sentence that clearly illustrates its meaning. Then give the etymology of the word, and explain the function that *be* performs.

a. beseech	f. betroth	k. bereave
b. bespeak	g. beguile	l. befall
c. bedizen	h. berate	m. belittle
d. belie	i. begrudge	n. befriend
e. beleaguer	j. behoove	o. belabor

2. Complete each of the following sentences by supplying a word or phrase which clearly shows that you know the meaning of the underscored root or prefix.

   a. To di<u>vert</u> a person is to _____ his or her mind aside from the business at hand.

   b. A sub<u>vers</u>ive movement is one that seeks to _____ the existing government or social order.

   c. An <u>amphi</u>bious military operation is one that will take place _____.

   d. In an <u>amphi</u>theater the seats go all _____ the stage or arena.

Enriching the Lesson

Exercise I.   Eponyms

A good many English words derive from the names of the people who were originally associated with the object, practice, or attitude that the word indicates. Such words are called **eponyms**. A good example of an eponym is *boycott*, studied in this lesson.

Below are listed a number of other useful eponyms. With or without the aid of a dictionary or other reference book, define each, and give the name of the person from whom the word comes. Then choose any **five** items on the list, and for each write a short sentence that clearly illustrates its meaning.

1. bowdlerize
2. quisling
3. shrapnel
4. mesmerize
5. lynch
6. maverick
7. sadistic
8. gerrymander
9. chauvinist
10. sandwich
11. silhouette
12. galvanize
13. martinet
14. nicotine
15. masochistic

Exercise II.   Classical Contributions to English

A. *"O Ye Immortal Gods!"*   Surprisingly, the names of a number of Roman (or sometimes Greek) gods live on in present-day English words. Some of these words are listed below in Column A. With or without the aid of a dictionary, match each with its meaning in Column B. Then give the name of the god from which the modern English word derives, and explain how the deity in question is connected with the current meaning of the word.

Column A

1. jovial
2. bacchanalian
3. mercurial
4. saturnine
5. martial

Column B

a. warlike or military
b. sullen and gloomy
c. jolly or merry
d. riotous and drunken
e. fickle or changeable

B. *Gifts from the Greeks.*   The geography, history, and mythology of ancient Greece have contributed much to the richness and variety of modern English. Below are listed a few samples of this remarkable heritage. Define the *italicized* item in each of the following phrases, and explain its connection with the ancient Greeks.

1. a *titanic* struggle
2. a *herculean* task
3. a *laconic* reply
4. to run in a *marathon*
5. a *colossal* mistake
6. an *Achilles' heel*
7. a *spartan* lifestyle
8. a *tantalizing* glimpse
9. an *atlas* of the world
10. to deliver a *philippic*

Exercise III.   Spanish Borrowings

Present-day English contains a number of words borrowed with little or no change from Spanish. *Bravado,* studied in this lesson, is a good example of such a word. A number of others are listed below. Define each as it is used in English today. Then use it in an original sentence that clearly illustrates its meaning.

1. aficionado
2. bonanza
3. peccadillo
4. macho
5. embargo
6. armada
7. desperado
8. cargo
9. incommunicado

Exercise IV.   Short, Sturdy Words

According to an old saying, "the shorter the word, the harder the push." This lesson has presented a number of short, sturdy words with a lot of "push" (e.g., *blight, bleak, blithe*). These items, of course, do not exhaust the list. On the contrary, English abounds in forceful one-syllable expressions. Many of them have come down to us from Old and Middle English; others are derived from Old Norse, the language of the Vikings.

1. With or without the aid of a thesaurus, list **ten** forceful, one-syllable synonyms for the humble and rather bland word *hit.* Then define each of your choices so as to bring out its distinctive qualities, and use it in an original sentence. (Hint: You might do well to start with *thwack* or *cuff.*)

2. With or without the aid of a dictionary, define the following words that were in use long before Chaucer died in 1400 and are still alive today. Then use each in an original sentence.

a. goad
b. bliss
c. meek
d. quake
e. throng
f. craft
g. wail
h. bleat
i. rend
j. grim
k. skulk
l. cram

Exercise V.   Expanding Your Word Power

The words listed below are not on the Basic Word List, but they were mentioned in passing, in one form or another, in Lesson 7. All of them would make useful additions to your working vocabulary. Define each, give its etymology, list **two** synonyms and **two** antonyms (where possible), and use in a short sentence that clearly illustrates the word's meaning.

1. dour
2. stimulus
3. blasé
4. obstreperous
5. hyperbole
6. turgid
7. sanction
8. impertinent
9. crass
10. jocund
11. efface
12. voluble

Lesson 8

71. bungle — 80. catholic

---

71. bun·gle   *verb*   bŭn'-gəl
[Origin unknown, perhaps from *bangla* (Swedish), "work poorly"]

Definition: To mismanage or make a mess of.
They **bungled** the job so badly that it took me days to straighten out the mess.

Related Form: (*noun*) bungler

Synonyms: (*verbs*) botch, butcher, mangle, mar, spoil, foul up, bollix up; (*nouns*) butcher, klutz; (*adjectives*) incompetent, inept; clumsy, awkward

Antonyms: (*nouns*) expert, whiz, ace; (*adjectives*) competent, workmanlike, skillful, adroit, deft, dexterous

Usage Note:
Some of the items included among the synonyms for *bungle*—for example, *bollix up* and *klutz*—are slang expressions that should be avoided in formal speech and writing. The same is true for the antonyms provided. For example, neither *ace* nor *whiz* would be considered appropriate in formal contexts.

72. bu·reauc·ra·cy   *noun*   byōō-rŏk'-rə-sē
[*bureau* (French), "desk; office" + *kratos* (Greek), "rule"]

Definition: A complicated system of administrative agencies and officials; the officials themselves.
"I don't know whether the people being helped by our federally funded social programs are eating up too much of the taxpayer's money," the senator remarked. "However, the **bureaucracy** that administers such programs may be."

Related Forms: (*noun*) bureaucrat; (*adjective*) bureaucratic

Usage Note:
Today *bureaucracy, bureaucrat,* and *bureaucratic* are used most frequently of government, especially the federal government, to suggest too much formalism or red tape. As a result, the terms are almost always pejorative (unless, of course, the context indicates otherwise). Note, too, that all three expressions may properly be used of nongovernmental institutions, since private organizations are run in much the same way as the government. Indeed, *bureaucracy* and its derivatives can justly be applied to any administrative setup that has become overgrown or that insists upon following complex rules and procedures that seem to hinder or stifle quick and effective action.

Charles Dickens

Thomas Carlyle

Red Tape

The term *red tape* is used critically to describe bureaucratic procedures that are considered unnecessarily rigid, complicated, and time-consuming. When we say that something "is tied up in red tape," we mean that there are so many regulations, so many papers to be filled out, so many technicalities to observe that it is difficult to get anything done.

The term is said to have been introduced by Charles Dickens and popularized by Thomas Carlyle, the English historian. It originated from the common use of pieces of red tape to tie together bundles of legal papers in English courts and governmental offices.

Today, official papers are more likely to be processed by a computer than tied together by a clerk, but people still complain about the delays and frustrations caused by too much red tape.

---

73. **but·tress**   *noun and verb*   bŭt'-rĭs

[*bo(u)terez* (Old French), "thrusting," from *bo(u)ter* (Old French), "strike against, butt"]

Definition:

   a. (*noun*) A support or reinforcement.

      The towering walls of many medieval cathedrals are prevented from falling down by huge flying **buttresses** on the outside of the building.

   b. (*verb*) To support or reinforce.

      The speaker **buttressed** her arguments with a solid presentation of relevant facts and figures.

      From time to time, Congress has considered a number of measures designed to **buttress** and protect the economy against the ravages of inflation.

Synonyms: (*nouns*) prop, brace; mainstay, cornerstone, pillar; (*verbs*) prop up, brace, bolster, shore up, strengthen

Antonyms: (*verbs*) weaken, impair, undermine

74. ca-jole *verb* kə-jōl′ *or* kă-jōl′

[*cajoler* (French), "chatter like a jay in a cage"]

Definition: To persuade or obtain by flattery or deceit.

Like most people, I enjoy flattery, but I can't be **cajoled** into doing something that I know in my heart is foolish.

He's so tight with his money that it's just about impossible to **cajole** a nickel out of him, no matter how worthy the cause.

Related Forms: (*nouns*) cajolery, cajoler

Synonyms: (*verbs*) wheedle, inveigle, coax, beguile, induce, flatter

Antonyms: (*verbs*) dissuade, deter, discourage

Related Phrases: soft-soap, sweet-talk; curry favor with; apple-polishing

75. cal-lous *adjective* kăl′-əs

[*callosus* (Latin), "thick-skinned," from *callus* (Latin), "hard skin"]

Definition: Unfeeling or insensitive.

The sight of children starving slowly and horribly to death brought tears of rage and indignation to the eyes of even the most **callous** and thick-skinned observer among us.

Related Forms: (*noun*) callousness; (*adverb*) callously

Usage Note:
Do not confuse the adjective *callous* with either the noun *callus*, meaning "a hardened or thickened part of the skin" (*e.g.*, "had a callus on his hand"), or the adjective *callow*, meaning "untried or inexperienced" (*e.g.*, "a callow youth").

Synonyms: (*adjectives*) indifferent, unresponsive, unsympathetic; thick-skinned, hard-hearted, hard-boiled, hard-nosed

Antonyms: (*adjectives*) compassionate, tenderhearted, softhearted, kindhearted; thin-skinned, sensitive

76. cal-um-ny *noun* kăl′-əm-nē

[*calumnia* (Latin), "trickery; slander"]

Definition: A false statement deliberately made up to injure a person.

"It is one thing to make honest criticisms of my administration and its methods," the president observed. "It is quite another to repeat **calumnies** and slanders that simply have no basis in fact."

Related Forms: (*verb*) calumniate; (*adjective*) calumnious

Synonyms: (*nouns*) lie, falsehood; slander, libel; slur, aspersion

Antonyms: (*nouns*) flattery, adulation

Related Phrases: do a hatchet job on, hurl brickbats at; mudslinging

112

77. **can-did**   *adjective*   kăn'-dĭd

[*candidus* (Latin), "white; pure," from *candere* (Latin), "glisten"]

Definition:

a. Fair and impartial.

"Only a disinterested observer of a traffic accident can give you a **candid** account of what actually happened," the officer told the reporter.

b. Frank or outspoken.

"You can't expect diplomats to be as **candid** and forthright as you might wish," she observed.

c. Informal or unposed.

"Why do I always look so awful in **candid** photos?" my little brother asked plaintively.

Phrases: a candid opinion, a candid interview, a candid critic

Related Forms: (*nouns*) candor, candidness; (*adverb*) candidly

Synonyms: (*adjectives*) objective, disinterested, unbiased, unprejudiced, balanced; forthright, unreserved, straight-from-the-shoulder; spontaneous, impromptu

Antonyms: (*adjectives*) partial, biased, prejudiced; reserved, reticent (Word 341); disingenuous, artful, evasive, equivocal, ambiguous

Candidate

In ancient Rome a man who wished to be elected to public office wore a white robe or toga while canvassing for votes. That way, he could be recognized more easily wherever he went. Since the Latin word for "white" is *candidus*, the would-be official came to be known as a *candidatus*, meaning "one clothed in white." From this we get our English word *candidate*.

78. can-tan-ker-ous   *adjective*   kăn-tăng′-kẽr-əs

[Probably *contekour* (Middle English), "brawler," from *contek* (Norman French), "strife"]

Definition: Foul-tempered and quarrelsome.

"Having to put up with a surly and **cantankerous** boss can sometimes make life pretty miserable," Betty Lou said. "Still, I like working in an office."

"When I was a young man I tried to be as agreeable as possible," Dad remarked. "But now that I'm getting on in years, I find that I have become surprisingly **cantankerous**."

Related Forms: (*noun*) cantankerousness; (*adverb*) cantankerously

Usage Note:

Though *cantankerous* is normally used of people who are determined to be nasty or disagreeable (*e.g.,* "the cantankerous leader of the opposition party"), the word may also be applied to animals or things. In that case, it means "irritating or difficult to deal with." Examples of such usage include "a cantankerous washing machine" and "a cantankerous camel."

Synonyms: (*adjectives*) peevish, contrary, cross-grained, irritable, irascible, perverse, choleric, bearish, testy, crabby, grouchy, cranky; intractable, unamenable, ornery; (*nouns*) curmudgeon, grouch

Antonyms: (*adjectives*) good-natured, sweet tempered, amiable, lovable, affable (Word 15), genial; even tempered, unexcitable, imperturbable, equable; docile (Word 142), tractable, amenable

79. cap-tious   *adjective*   kăp′-shəs

[*captieux* (French), "hypercritical," from *captio* (Latin), "seizure; deception"]

Definition:

  a. Quick to find petty faults or raise trifling objections; overly demanding or fussy.

     Though they found a lot to disagree with in my plan, most of their objections were **captious** and niggling.

  b. Intended to trap, confuse, or show up.

     "A president has to be pretty alert when talking to the press," the aide observed. "After all, a careless answer to a **captious** question could land him in a great deal of political hot water."

Phrase: a captious critic

Related Forms: (*noun*) captiousness; (*adverb*) captiously

Synonyms: (*adjectives*) hypercritical, caviling, carping, censorious; niggling, pettifogging, hairsplitting, picky, picayune, nit-picking; artful, tricky, loaded

Antonyms: (*adjectives*) unexacting, uncritical, undiscriminating; straightforward; laudatory, complimentary

80. cath-o-lic   *adjective*   kăth′-ə-lĭk   *or*   kăth′-lĭk

[*katholikos* (Greek), "general," from *kata* (Greek), "according to + *holos* (Greek), "(the) whole" + *ikos* (Greek), "pertaining to"]

Definition:

a. Broad or widely inclusive.

Painting and sculpture, architecture and engineering, mathematics and music—these were just a few of Leonardo da Vinci's truly **catholic** interests.

b. General or universal; worldwide.

Even though living standards in many parts of the world have noticeably improved since 1900, poverty, hunger, and unemployment are still **catholic** concerns for humankind more than one hundred years later.

Related Form: (*noun*) catholicity

Usage Note:

Be sure to distinguish carefully between *catholic* (with a *c*) and *Catholic* (with a *C*). The word with the capital letter is a proper adjective that refers to the ancient universal (that is, undivided) Christian church or to its present-day representatives. Frequently, of course, *Catholic* is used as an abbreviation for *Roman Catholic*—that is, in reference to the Church of Rome, its beliefs and practices, or its members.

Synonyms: (*adjectives*) comprehensive, wide, liberal; ecumenical, global

Antonyms: (*adjectives*) narrow, provincial, parochial (Word 293)

Using the Words

Exercise I. Parts of Speech

Indicate the part of speech of each of the following words. In one case, two answers are correct.

1. bungle
2. buttress
3. callous
4. cajole
5. calumny
6. catholic

Exercise II. Words in Phrases

In each of the following, select the item that best expresses the meaning of the *italicized* word in the introductory phrase.

1. nothing more than a blatant *calumny*

    a. trick b. crime c. mistake d. joke e. falsehood

2. a *cantankerous* lawn mower

    a. useful b. ornery c. complicated d. expensive e. new

3. unusually *candid* comments
   a. learned   b. tactful   c. sour   d. frank   e. amusing

4. *catholic* tastes in music
   a. broad   b. strange   c. ordinary   d. austere   e. narrow

5. tried to *buttress* her position at the office
   a. undermine   b. clarify   c. strengthen   d. eliminate
   e. utilize

Exercise III.   Completing Sentences

Complete each of the following sentences or pairs of sentences by selecting the most appropriate word from the group of words given below.

callous	captious	bureaucracy
buttress	bungle	cajole

1. If you focus your attention too single-mindedly on trifles, as some overly _____ critics do, you may lose sight of the more important aspects of the thing you are considering.

2. "I'd hoped that my proposal for reducing our overgrown federal _____ would have passed the House by now," the representative told the press. "Unfortunately, it is still all tied up in congressional red tape."

3. "If you keep telling your uncle what a superb driver he is," Marv advised me, "you may be able to _____ him into giving you driving lessons in his new car."

4. Anyone who can look at photos from Auschwitz or Buchenwald and not be moved deeply is indeed _____ and insensitive.

5. "Just how am I supposed to get quality work out of a staff that manages to _____ the simplest job?" the production chief asked ruefully.

Exercise IV.   Synonyms and Antonyms

A. In each of the following numbered groups, select the **two** words that are most nearly **synonyms**.

1. a. discourage   b. butcher   c. mangle   d. attend   e. retain

2. a. bolster   b. impair   c. pretend   d. brace   e. convene

3. a. patronize   b. magnify   c. inveigle   d. boycott
   e. wheedle

4. a. mannerism   b. libel   c. chaos   d. slander   e. order

5. a. objective   b. grisly   c. spurious   d. lethargic
   e. impartial

116

Now, for each of the pairs of synonyms that you have selected, supply a word from the Basic Word List for this lesson (Words 71–80) that means the **same** or **almost the same** thing.

B. In each of the following numbered groups, select the **two** words that are most nearly **antonyms**.

1. a. cantankerous   b. penniless   c. genial   d. authentic
   e. workmanlike

2. a. spry   b. captious   c. illegal   d. chipper   e. unexacting

3. a. deft   b. inept   c. academic   d. collective   e. inimical

4. a. illusory   b. atrocious   c. catholic   d. narrow   e. gaudy

5. a. smooth-talking   b. glib   c. brand-new   d. callous
   e. tenderhearted

Exercise V.   Word Roundup

1. Two groups of expressions with related meanings are given below. Indicate the items in each that would be classified as *slang* or *overly colloquial*.

A.   Ability

a. expert   c. competent   e. klutz
b. inept   d. ace   f. adroit

B.   Persuasion

a. coax   c. inveigle   e. wheedle
b. sweet-talk   d. cajole   f. soft-soap

2. Define *callous, callus,* and *callow.* Use each in an original illustrative sentence.

3. What is the difference between *catholic* and *Catholic?* Use each in a sentence that clearly illustrates its meaning.

4. Define *red tape,* and use the phrase in an original sentence.

5. Explain the story behind the word *candidate.* How is the word related to *candid?*

Exercise VI.   Framing Sentences

Use each of the following words in an original sentence that clearly illustrates its meaning.

1. bungle
2. bureaucrat
3. buttress
4. cajole
5. callously
6. calumniate
7. candor
8. cantankerous
9. captious
10. catholic

Completing Verbal Analogies

"A Denotes the Lack of B." Another word relationship frequently encountered on standardized vocabulary tests may conveniently be expressed as "A denotes the lack of B." An example of an analogy question utilizing this word relationship is given below. See if you can figure out the correct answer.

> *A*   *B*   *C*   ┌─────────────*D*─────────────┐
> **cowardly : courage** = awkward :(*fear, honor, grace, kindness, intelligence*)

The answer, of course, is *grace*. An *awkward* person lacks *grace* (or gracefulness), just as a *cowardly* person lacks courage.

Exercise I

Complete the following analogies based on the word relationship "A denotes the lack of B."

1. **biased : objectivity** = callous : (*ambition, experience, compassion, malice, humor*)

2. **boorish : manners** = blithe : (*skills, morals, funds, friends, cares*)

3. **indigent : money** = lethargic : (*wisdom, energy, talent, family, schooling*)

Exercise II   Answers will vary.

Write **three** original analogies based on the relationship "A denotes the lack of B." In your analogies use at least **one** of the basic words studied in Lessons 1–8 (Words 1–80).

Exercise III

The following items review what you have so far learned about analogy questions. Complete each.

1. **affable : cantankerous** = catholic : (*liberal, genial, critical, provincial, abnormal*)

2. **bungle : botch** = defame : (*flatter, slander, ignore, praise, persuade*)

3. **bleak : warmth** = brash : (*caution, frankness, pride, greed, enthusiasm*)

4. **grasping : rapacious** = generous : (*miserly, ardent, liberal, bellicose, grotesque*)

5. **buttress : undermine** = foster : (*sanction, foreshadow, promote, redress, blight*)

Enriching the Lesson

Exercise I.   The Language of Government and Politics

The word *bureaucracy,* studied in this lesson, often comes up in discussions of government and politics. A number of other words and phrases connected with the workings of our government or political system are listed below. Define each.

1. checks and balances	14. popular sovereignty
2. political machine	15. regulatory agency
3. revenue sharing	16. due process of law
4. civil rights	17. judicial review
5. merit system	18. civil service
6. pocket veto	19. bipartisan
7. executive privilege	20. franchise
8. separation of powers	21. eminent domain
9. lobby *or* interest group	22. senatorial courtesy
10. reapportionment	23. pork barrel
11. referendum	24. conflict of interest
12. party platform	25. filibuster
13. executive order	26. political patronage

Can you think of any others? List and define them.

Exercise II.   Gobbledygook

Gobbledygook is the name by which people commonly refer to the inflated, involved, and unnecessarily obscure language that is characteristic of bureaucratic pronouncements. The word was coined by Maury Maverick, chairman of the Smaller War Plants Corporation during World War II. As head of this government agency, Maverick was subjected to a seemingly endless flow of trite, tortured, or pompous language, for which he devised the name *gobblebygook.* Here is an example of the kind of writing (and speaking) that Maverick had in mind. It is taken from an administrative order issued by the federal Food and Drug Administration.

> References in this order to any order shall be construed as referring to that order as amended by any subsequent order, whether made before or after the making of this order, and if any order referred to in this order is replaced by any such subsequent order, the references shall be construed as referring to that subsequent order.

As you know, the purpose of language is to communicate ideas and information clearly and concisely. Needless to say, this sentence and the kind of writing it represents defeat that purpose. To begin with, the sentence is oppressively long (58 words) and involved. This makes it almost impossible for the reader to grasp what is being said without rereading the sentence several times.

(A simple way to begin correcting this problem would be to break the sentence in two just before the words *and if*.)

In addition, the phrasing is awkward and unnatural. Notice, for instance, the number of passive constructions, the use of the single word *order* to indicate several different sets of instructions issued at different times, and the presence of clumsy or tortured expressions (*e.g.*, "shall be construed as referring to," "the making of this order," "any such subsequent order"). These items add to the difficulties the reader already faces in trying to make something meaningful out of this muddle.

By now the point of this discussion should be clear to you: Write as clearly, simply, and concisely as you can. Don't let your sentences become unduly long and involved. Don't overload them with highfalutin expressions or bizarre turns of phrase. Use the active voice of the verb rather than the passive. And, finally, try not to string together too many Latinate words; such expressions tend to weigh down a sentence and produce a ponderous effect. As Maury Maverick wrote to his staff in a now-famous memo about writing style: "Say what you're talking about" as clearly and directly as possible.

One final note: Needless to say, gobbledygook is not the exclusive preserve of government. Indeed, anyone who has been in the armed forces, tried to make sense out of the fine print in an insurance policy, or had occasion to inspect business documents knows just how pervasive it can be.

1. Read the following statement from an official report issued by one of the administrative departments of the government of New Zealand. The statement concerns the possible use of a certain piece of land for recreational purposes. Then try your hand at rephrasing the statement in comprehensible English.

   > It is obvious from the difference in elevation with relation to the short depth of the property that the contour is such as to preclude any reasonable development potential for active recreation.

2. A federal agency that was considering the accuracy of a label used on a certain brand of bottled beer said that the label *"retained a tendency to mislead."* Rephrase the *italicized* words in intelligible English.

Exercise III.   Expanding Your Word Power

The words listed below are not on the Basic Word List, but they were mentioned in passing, in one form or another, in Lesson 8. All of them would make useful additions to your working vocabulary. Define each, give its etymology, list **two** synonyms and **two** antonyms (where possible), and use in a short sentence that clearly illustrates the word's meaning.

1. deft	4. adulation	7. irascible
2. impair	5. impromptu	8. amenable
3. cavil	6. disingenuous	9. curmudgeon

Related Forms in Context

Beneath each sentence below are four words introduced in Lesson 7 or 8. Review the related forms for these words, and choose the one that best completes the sentence. Write that related form in the space provided.

1. At the end of the second debate, which lasted an hour, one of the candidates observed that his opponent's remarks were all _____ and no substance.

   a. bleak   b. bombastic   c. captious   d. catholic

2. The tight end, a notorious _____, recovered the fumble and took off running—in the wrong direction.

   a. blight   b. boycott   c. bungle   d. cajole

3. In Act I, scene iii, of *Hamlet*, Polonius advises his son Laertes, "Virtue itself [e]scapes not _____ strokes."

   a. bravado   b. bureaucracy   c. buttress   d. calumny

4. The author was extremely upset by the _____ of the critic's review of her first novel.

   a. captious   b. bleak   c. catholic   d. blithe

5. In Guy de Maupassant's short story "The Necklace," Monsieur Loisel is a minor _____ in the Ministry of Education and cannot afford the luxuries his wife desires.

   a. boycott   b. bureaucracy   c. bravado   d. calumny

6. Despite the _____ of her mother and the photographer, the little girl refused to look at the camera and smile.

   a. bungle   b. cajole   c. boycott   d. buttress

7. In Anton Chekhov's one-act play *The Brute*, a rudely impatient landowner challenges a beautiful widow to a duel, but his _____ disappears when he suddenly falls in love with her.

   a. catholic   b. bombastic   c. boorish   d. candid

8. W. C. Fields, an American comic actor with a reputation for _____, wrote his own epitaph: "On the whole, I'd rather be in Philadelphia."

   a. cantankerous   b. blithe   c. bleak   d. candid

9. When we tried to collect on an insurance claim for flood damage to our house, we found ourselves caught in a _____ nightmare.

   a. boycott   b. blight   c. bureaucracy   d. calumny

10. We frequently have to complain to the police about the _____ of our neighbors' parties, which last until the small hours of the morning.

    a. bleak   b. blithe   c. callous   d. boisterous

11. The Brontë sisters—Charlotte, Anne, and Emily—must surely have been affected by the _____ of the dark, windy moors near their Yorkshire home, especially in winter.

    a. brash   b. bleak   c. brusque   d. bombastic

12. Hunters _____ slaughtered the great herds of American buffalo that were central to the lives of the Plains Indians.

    a. candid   b. cantankerous   c. callous   d. captious

13. During soccer matches fans _____ sing and chant, urging their teams to victory.

    a. boisterous   b. callous   c. cantankerous   d. candid

14. The _____ of her behavior suggests that when she gets her driver's license, she may be reckless behind the wheel.

    a. blithe   b. brusque   c. callous   d. brash

15. An elderly woman stepped to the mike at the city council meeting and pointedly announced, "We voters have a right to expect both _____ and responsibility from all our elected officials."

    a. boisterous   b. brash   c. candid   d. cantankerous

16. From the _____ of Marty's reply and the look on his face, I could tell that he had been deeply hurt by what was intended to be a humorous remark.

    a. boorish   b. brusque   c. blithe   d. captious

17. When her husband could no longer travel, Eleanor Roosevelt traveled for him; and in a daily newspaper column called "My Day," she _____ reported what she had observed and felt.

    a. candid   b. cantankerous   c. boisterous   d. callous

18. To win Prince Charming, Cinderella's stepsister _____ cut off her heel and tried to force her huge foot into the dainty glass slipper.

    a. candid   b. blithe   c. captious   d. boisterous

19. At the Morgan Library, which was once financier J. P. Morgan's home, we were impressed by the _____ of Morgan's taste in art and rare books.

    a. cantankerous   b. brusque   c. catholic   d. candid

20. African American slaves suffered greatly from the _____ of their owners and their overseers.

    a. blithe   b. callous   c. catholic   d. candid

Lesson 9

---

81. **caus·tic**   *adjective*   kôs'-tĭk
    [*kaustikos* (Greek), "burnt"]

    Definition:
    a. Able to dissolve or eat away by chemical action.

    Substances with highly **caustic** or corrosive properties are widely used in present-day commercial processes, such as the manufacture of cloth and yarn.
    b. Sharp and biting.

    Why is it that so many successful theater critics seem to possess sharp tongues and **caustic** wits?

    Phrases: a caustic substance, a caustic agent, a caustic reply

    Related Forms: (*noun*) causticity; (*adverb*) caustically

    Synonyms: (*adjectives*) corrosive; keen, cutting, stinging, tart, pungent, trenchant, mordant, astringent, acidulous, sarcastic, sardonic, acrimonious, venomous; (*nouns*) asperity, acrimony, mordancy, acerbity; sarcasm

    Antonyms: (*adjectives*) mild, bland (Word 60), amiable, good-natured, charitable; sweet, sugary, honeyed, saccharine

82. **cen·sor**   *noun and verb*   sĕn'-sər
    [*censor* (Latin), from *censere* (Latin), "estimate, assess"]

    Definition:
    a. (*noun*) An official who examines works of literature, films, and the like for things considered to be immoral, offensive, or dangerous and who is empowered to prohibit or remove this material; anyone who acts as an arbiter of morals or reading/viewing matter.

    "If it were always easy to distinguish art from obscenity," the official remarked, "the job of a **censor** wouldn't be so difficult."
    b. (*verb*) To examine for and remove objectionable material.

    Many parents believe that prime-time TV programs should be carefully **censored** in order to protect children from accidental exposure to "adult" material.

    Related Forms: (*adjectives*) censorial, censorious; (*noun*) censorship

    Synonyms: (*nouns*) expurgator, bowdlerizer; Comstockery, Grundyism; (*verbs*) expurgate, bowdlerize; excise, delete (Word 120), expunge

Anthony Comstock (*left*);
Cato the Censor (*above*)

Censors and Censorship

English has borrowed a good many words and phrases without change from Latin. One such word is *censor*. In ancient Rome there were two magistrates with this title. Their functions included taking the census of citizens (which was necessary for tax purposes), filling vacancies in the Senate (Rome's governing body), and supervising public morals and behavior. One Roman censor, Cato the Elder (234–149 B.C.), became especially well known for his stern and unyielding standards of behavior and for the overly aggressive way in which he sought to impose them on the Roman people.

The word *censor* and the powers connected with the office or the act have passed down to present-day society. Various public officials in the United States possess a limited power of censorship over moving pictures, written materials, TV programs, etc., although the word itself is likely to be avoided. Of course, censorship is limited by the First Amendment guarantees of freedom of expression.

English has a number of interesting expressions connected with censorship. One of these is *Grundyism*. Grundyism is a rigid insistence upon strict conformity to the accepted moral or social code. The word derives from Mrs. Grundy, an overly proper character in the English playwright Thomas Morton's comedy *Speed the Plough* (1798).

Another useful expression is *Comstockery*, which indicates zealous but narrow-minded (and often unfair) censorship of art, literature, or the like. The word is derived from Anthony Comstock (1844–1915), an American author and an aggressive, if somewhat bigoted, crusader against what he considered immorality.

124

83. **cen-sure**   *noun and verb*   sĕn'-shər
[*censura* (Latin), "censorship"]

Definition:

a. (*noun*) Open and strong criticism or disapproval (often taking the shape of a formal reprimand by someone in authority).

Perhaps my actions were hasty and ill-advised, but they certainly did not merit the kind of harsh public **censure** they received.

The 18th-century English satirist Jonathan Swift wrote that "**censure** is the tax a man pays to the public for being eminent."

What do you think Polonius means when he advises his son, Laertes, to "take each man's **censure** but withhold thy judgment"?

b. (*verb*) To criticize severely; to disapprove strongly.

I am very wary of anyone who is too quick to **censure** and too slow to forgive.

Phrases: a letter of censure, a vote of censure, a resolution of censure

Related Forms: (*noun*) censurer; (*adjective*) censurable

Synonyms: (*nouns*) rebuke, reprimand, reproof; (*verbs*) rebuke, reprimand, reprove, reprehend, condemn, upbraid, chastise; (*adjectives*) reprehensible, blameworthy

Antonyms: (*nouns*) praise, commendation; approval, approbation; (*verbs*) praise, commend, laud, extol, applaud; (*adjectives*) laudable, praiseworthy, meritorious, admirable, creditable

Related Phrases: (*expressing strong disapproval*) take to task, call on the carpet, dress down, bawl out; (*expressing mild disapproval*) let off with a slap on the wrist; (*expressing approval*) give a pat on the back

84. **cha-grin**   *noun and verb*   shə-grĭn'
[*chagrin* (French), "sadness"]

Definition:

a. (*noun*) Irritation, embarrassment, or humiliation caused by disappointment or frustration.

"I didn't particularly want to go to the party," Alex admitted. "Still, I felt a deep sense of **chagrin** when I realized that I wouldn't be invited."

b. (*verb*) To cause such a feeling.

Since Marsha prides herself on her skill as a politician, her failure to win election to the student council **chagrined** her deeply.

Synonyms: (*nouns*) vexation, annoyance, mortification; (*verbs*) vex, annoy, mortify, abash

Antonyms: (*nouns*) jubilation, exultation, delight, exhilaration, elation; (*verbs*) exult, delight, exhilarate, elate

85. char·la·tan *noun* shär′-lə-tən

[*ciarlatano* (Italian), a variant of *cerretano* (Italian), "an inhabitant of Cerreto," a village near Spoleto in central Italy. The place was famous for its quacks.]

Definition: Anyone who claims to have skills or knowledge that he or she doesn't possess.

"Don't be too eager to accept the claims of every fad diet that comes along," my physician warned me. "Some of these programs may have been concocted by **charlatans** whose recommendations could do you great harm."

Related Forms: (*nouns*) charlatanism, charlatanry

Synonyms: (*nouns*) impostor, quack, mountebank, humbug, fraud, faker

Two famous charlatans and their 20th-century impersonators: Burt Lancaster as Elmer Gantry and Fernando Corena as Dr. Dulcamara ("Sweet and Sour"), the quack doctor in Gaetano Donizetti's comic opera *The Elixir of Love* (*inset*).

Quacks and Other Charlatans

A *quack* (from *quacksalver*) is a person who makes false claims about the salves and other medications that he or she sells. By extension, the word indicates anyone who makes false or exaggerated claims about his or her medical knowledge, skills, or techniques. A *mountebank* (literally, a person who "climbs on a bench") is a charlatan who uses clownish or flamboyant techniques to sell his or her wares. By extension, the word is applied to any boastful or unscrupulous salesman. A *humbug* is a self-important fraud. An *impostor* is simply someone who assumes another person's identity for the purposes of fraud or deception.

86. chron-ic   *adjective*   krŏn'-ĭk

[*chronikos* (Greek), "pertaining to time," from *chronos* (Greek), "time"]

Definition: Continuing over a long period of time or recurring often.

The poor woman suffers terribly from **chronic** arthritis.

His inability to arrive anywhere on time, at first an amusing weakness, has become a **chronic** problem.

There have been long periods when our economy has been plagued by **chronic** inflation.

Phrases: chronic insomnia, chronic attacks of asthma, chronic financial problems, chronic unemployment, a chronic complainer

Related Form: (*adverb*) chronically

Usage Note:

When used as a medical term, *chronic* indicates the kind of ailment or disease that develops slowly over a very long period of time and only gradually becomes serious or fatal—for example, heart disease. The opposite is *acute*, which indicates the kind of medical problem that comes on a person suddenly or unexpectedly and takes only a short time to become critical— for example, appendicitis.

Synonyms: (*adjectives*) long lasting, prolonged, continual, constant; habitual, inveterate, confirmed, deep-rooted, ingrained; perennial, recurrent

Antonyms: (*adjectives*) transitory, transient, evanescent, ephemeral; sporadic, occasional

Related Phrases: a hardened criminal, a lingering illness, a confirmed bachelor, sporadic fighting

87. cir-cu-i-tous   *adjective*   sẽr-kyōō'-ĭ-təs

[*circu(m)* (Latin), "around" + *ire, itus* (Latin), "go"]

Definition: Indirect or roundabout; long-winded.

"If I have a little time on my hands after school, I take the long way home," Marta said. "It's a **circuitous** route, but the scenery is just beautiful!"

His style of writing is so **circuitous** and diffuse that I often get lost halfway through one of his paragraphs.

Phrases: circuitous logic or reasoning, circuitous procedures

Related Forms: (*nouns*) circuitousness, circuit

Synonyms: (*adjectives*) winding, meandering, rambling, sinuous, devious, oblique; circumlocutory, periphrastic, digressive

Antonyms: (*adjectives*) direct, undeviating, unswerving, straightforward, unveering

Related Phrases: veer off at a tangent, sidetrack a discussion, beat around the bush; as the crow flies

88. cir-cum-spect   *adjective*   sûr'-kəm-spĕkt

[*circum* (Latin), "around" + *specere, spectus* (Latin), "look"]

Definition: Cautious or prudent, especially in regard to the consequences of actions or statements; tactful.

Since you don't know most salespeople personally, always be as **circumspect** as possible in your dealings with them.

Phrases: a circumspect investor, circumspect behavior

Related Forms: (*noun*) circumspection; (*adverb*) circumspectly

Synonyms: (*adjectives*) careful, watchful, vigilant, guarded, wary, chary, leery; discreet, politic, diplomatic, judicious

Antonyms: (*adjectives*) careless, imprudent, incautious, heedless; rash, reckless, foolhardy; brash (Word 68), precipitate; indiscreet, tactless

89. cir-cum-vent   *verb*   sûr-kəm-vĕnt'

[*circum* (Latin), "around" + *venire, ventus* (Latin), "come"]

Definition: To get around or avoid, especially by trickery or deception.

We planned our route so as to **circumvent** heavily congested urban areas that might slow down our progress.

If people are not in agreement with a given law, they may attempt to ignore or **circumvent** it.

Related Form: (*noun*) circumvention

Synonyms: (*verbs*) bypass, skirt, evade, sidestep, dodge, duck

Antonyms: (*verbs*) obey, observe, comply with, respect, abide by

90. clan-des-tine   *adjective*   klăn-dĕs'-tĭn

[*clandestinus* (Latin), "secret," from *clam* (Latin), "in secret"]

Definition: Concealed from view so as to hide one's purpose.

Try as they might, federal agents were unable to locate the **clandestine** printing press that had turned out the counterfeit $100 bills.

Related Forms: (*noun*) clandestineness; (*adverb*) clandestinely

Phrases: a clandestine meeting, clandestine broadcasts, clandestine activities

Synonyms: (*adjectives*) surreptitious, covert, furtive, stealthy, underhand(ed)

Antonyms: (*adjectives*) open, undisguised, overt, manifest, obvious, avowed

Related Phrases: deep cover, behind closed doors, cloak-and-dagger, an undercover agent

Using the Words

Exercise I.   Syllabication and Pronunciation

Syllabicate the following words correctly, and place the major stress mark (') after the syllable that is accented when the word is pronounced.

Example: a-bet'

1. charlatan
2. circumspect
3. censor
4. chagrin
5. circuitous
6. circumvent

Exercise II.   Words Out of Context

In each of the following groups, select the item that best expresses the meaning of the numbered word at the left.

1. charlatan   a. officer   b. immigrant   c. fraud   d. critic

2. clandestine   a. sharp   b. secret   c. savage   d. sensible

3. censure   a. rebuke   b. remove   c. relax   d. restore

4. circuitous   a. electrical   b. collective   c. indirect   d. foolhardy

5. caustic   a. expensive   b. final   c. responsible   d. biting

Exercise III.   Completing Sentences

Complete each of the following sentences or pairs of sentences by selecting the appropriate word from the group of words given below. Use each word only once.

censor   chagrin   circumvent

charlatan   chronic   circumspect

1. The novelist felt a deep sense of _____ when the book he had worked on so long and hard received unfavorable reviews in the press.

2. "A person never knows where a friendship will lead," Mom observed. "That's why it's always best to be as _____ as possible in choosing one's companions."

3. Unemployment is a _____, rather than an occasional, problem for some members of our society.

4. I thought we should meet the problem head-on; Tom thought we should try to _____ it.

5. During a war, a government will often _____ all kinds of documents in order to keep sensitive or classified material from falling into the hands of the enemy.

Exercise IV. Synonyms and Antonyms

Classify each of the following pairs of words as **S** for **synonyms** or **A** for **antonyms.**

1. caustic—corrosive
2. bowdlerize—expurgate
3. commend—censure
4. chagrin—delight
5. charlatan—mountebank
6. covert—overt
7. habitual—chronic
8. circuitous—straightforward
9. imprudent—circumspect
10. circumvent—dodge

Exercise V. Word Roundup

1. Explain the difference between a *chronic* illness and an *acute* illness.

2. Give **two** colloquial phrases that mean "censure strongly." Use each in an original sentence.

3. Define each of the following.
   a. a humbug
   b. a quack
   c. a pat on the back
   d. cloak-and-dagger
   e. an undercover agent
   f. as the crow flies
   g. a hardened criminal
   h. a confirmed bachelor

4. What is the source of the term *Grundyism?* the word *Comstockery?* What does each of these words mean?

5. Give **three** synonyms for each of the following. Consult a thesaurus if necessary.

   a. praiseworthy
   b. blameworthy

Exercise VI. Framing Sentences

A. Use each of the following in an original sentence.

1. clandestine
2. censor
3. charlatan
4. chagrin
5. circuitous
6. censure
7. circumvent
8. caustic

B. Give an **adverb** form of each of the following, and use it in an original sentence.

1. chronic
2. circumspect

Dissecting the Words

The Latin prefix **circum**, meaning "around" or "about," occurs in a number of English words, including *circuitous, circumspect,* and *circumvent,* all of which were studied in this lesson. Here are some other examples:

circumference (literally "a carrying around")—the boundary of a circle

circumlocution—a roundabout way of saying something. Adjective: *circumlocutory*

circumnavigate—to sail around (for example, the globe)

circumscribe (literally, "to write around"—to encircle; to confine or restrict within limits

circumstance (literally, "a standing around")—a fact or condition that accompanies an event or has some bearing on it. The related adjective *circumstantial* means "relating to the circumstances involved" or, by extension, "incidental; nonessential."

In some English words *circum* loses its *m* and becomes **circu**. Good examples of this include *circuitous* and *circuit.*

Finally, note that *circum* itself comes from the Indo-European root **(s)ker**, which means "bend" or "turn." Words from this root include *circus, circle, circulate, curvature,* and, surprisingly, *search* and *crown.*

Roots

1. The Greek root **chron(o)** means "time." It is found in a small number of English words, including *chronic* and *anachronism.* Here are some other words using this root:

chronology—the arrangement of events in time; a list of events in the order that they happened. Adjective: *chronological*

chronicle—a year-by-year record of historical events; to record events in this way. Noun: *chronicler*

synchronize—to occur at the same time; to cause to coincide in time.

2. English words ending in *-cracy* are derived from the Greek root **kratos** meaning "rule" or "power." One such word is *bureaucracy* (Word 72). Here are a few more:

democracy (*demos* [Greek] "people" + *kratos,* "rule")—rule by the people

plutocracy (*ploutos,* [Greek] "wealth" + *kratos,* "rule")—rule by the wealthy class of society. Noun: *plutocrat;* adjective: *plutocratic*

aristocracy (*aristos* [Greek] "best" + *kratos,* "rule")—rule by the upper or privileged classes. Noun: *aristocrat;* adjective: *aristocratic*

theocracy (*theos* [Greek] "god" + *kratos,* "rule")—a government controlled solely by the religious authorities. Adjective: *theocratic*

ochlocracy (*ochlos* [Greek], "mob" + *kratos,* "rule")—mob rule

thalassocracy (*thalassa* [Greek], "sea" + *kratos,* "rule")—domination of the sea; naval supremacy. Noun: *thalassocrat*

Exercise

1. Define the following terms or phrases, and indicate what part the prefix *circum* plays in each.

   a. circumstantial evidence   c. a circuit court
   b. a circuit breaker   d. a circumlocution

2. Two of the books of the Bible are called *Chronicles.* Judging by this name and your knowledge of the meaning of the root *chron(o),* what do you think these books contain?

3. One of the most common forms of Elizabethan drama is called the *chronicle play.* Judging by this name and your knowledge of the root *chron(o),* what do you think such a play would be about, and how would it be organized?

4. What is a person's *chronological age? mental age?*

5. Name an example, past or present, of each of the following forms of government. For instance, *Great Britain* is a good example of a *constitutional monarchy.*

   a. aristocracy   c. autocracy
   b. democracy   d. theocracy

Enriching the Lesson

Exercise I. "Time on My Hands"

With or without the aid of a dictionary, define each of the following expressions involving the word *time.* Then choose any **five** of the items, and for each compose an original sentence that clearly illustrates the expression's meaning.

1. timeserver	6. time bomb	11. make time
2. timely	7. in good time	12. high time
3. time-honored	8. for the time being	13. timepiece
4. behind the times	9. time-out	14. time clock
5. time deposit	10. timetable	15. keep time

Now, using a thesaurus, supply the following information:

16. List and define **five nouns** that relate in one way or another to the concept of time. For instance, you might begin with *duration* or *infinity.*

17. List and define **five verbs** that have to do with time. For example, you might begin with *tarry* or *abide.*

18. List and define **five adjectives** involving the concept of time. For instance, you might begin with *retroactive* or *transient.*

19. List and define **five phrases** connected in some way with the concept of time. For instance, *the ravages of time* or *tide over* might top your list.

Exercise II.   Our Latin Heritage

A good number of words commonly used in modern English come with little or no change from Latin. One such word, *censor*, was studied in this lesson. Some other words of this kind are listed below. With or without the aid of a dictionary, define each. Then choose any **five**, and for each compose an original sentence.

1.	alias	6.	onus	11.	animus
2.	quorum	7.	affidavit	12.	caveat
3.	propaganda	8.	opprobrium	13.	ultimatum
4.	bonus	9.	consensus	14.	verbatim
5.	gratis	10.	alibi	15.	imprimatur

Can you think of any others? Make a list of them.

Exercise III.   Curious Compounds

The way English forms compound words is fascinating. **Compound words** are words that are made up of two (or more) separate words or word elements (e.g., *standoff, takeover, kingless, fearful*). One curious group of compound words is made up of a short, usually monosyllabic verb plus its object, usually a noun, in that order. A good example of this kind of compound is *scarecrow*, which, as you already know, is a dummy set up in a field to *scare* (the verb) off *crows* and other birds (the object) looking for food.

Below are listed a number of other compound words made up of a verb and its object. The first ten items are given out of context; the others are *italicized* in a representative phrase. Define each item, and indicate which part of the word is the verb and which its object. Then choose any **five**, and for each supply an original sentence that illustrates the word's meaning.

1.	scofflaw	6.	tattletale	11.	at a *breakneck* pace
2.	pickpocket	7.	scapegrace	12.	a *telltale* odor
3.	turncoat	8.	spoilsport	13.	a *makeshift* arrangement
4.	spendthrift	9.	daredevil	14.	a *lackluster* performance
5.	breakwater	10.	cutthroat	15.	a *stopgap* measure

Exercise IV.   Expanding Your Word Power

The words listed below are not on the Basic Word List, but they were mentioned in passing in Lesson 9. All of them would make useful additions to your working vocabulary. Define each, give its etymology, list **two** synonyms and **two** antonyms (where possible), and use in a short sentence that clearly illustrates the word's meaning.

1.	sarcasm	5.	manifest	9.	periphrastic
2.	saccharine	6.	inveterate	10.	diplomatic
3.	sporadic	7.	ephemeral	11.	approbation
4.	abash	8.	oblique	12.	trenchant

Lesson 10

---

91. **co-erce** *verb* kō-ûrs'
[*co*, a form of *cum* (Latin), "together" + *arcere* (Latin), "confine"]

Definition: To force someone to do something against his or her will by using undue pressure, threats, intimidation, or physical violence.

There are far more subtle ways of **coercing** a person into doing what you want than twisting his or her arm.

"Though my parents frequently advise me about how to act in a particular situation," Rhoda said, "they never try to **coerce** me into doing what they think best."

If you seek to impose your will on others by **coercing** them, you will make many enemies.

Related Forms: (*nouns*) coercion, coerciveness; (*adjectives*) coercive, coercible; (*adverb*) coercively

Synonyms: (*verbs*) constrain, compel, pressure, bulldoze, dragoon; hector, browbeat, cow

Related Phrases: strong-arm tactics; high-pressure someone, bring pressure to bear, railroad someone into; under duress

92. **co-gent** *adjective* kō'-jĕnt
[*cogens, cogentis* (Latin), "driving together"; from *co*, a form of *cum* (Latin), "together" + *agere* (Latin), "drive; force"]

Definition: Forceful and convincing; to the point.

"The objections that Gloria raised to my plan were not only **cogent**," Frank admitted candidly, "they were totally unanswerable!"

One of the articles in yesterday's paper had some **cogent** and perceptive things to say about our troubled economy.

Phrases: a cogent argument; a cogent criticism, a cogent account, a cogent description, a cogent analysis, at her most cogent and compelling

Related Forms: (*noun*) cogency; (*adverb*) cogently

Synonyms: (*adjectives*) powerful, potent, effective, telling; persuasive, compelling; valid, sound; relevant, pertinent, apposite, germane, apropos

Antonyms: (*adjectives*) weak, ineffective, unconvincing, frivolous, inane; invalid, untenable; irrelevant

93. co-here   *verb*   kō-hēr′
[*co*, a form of *cum* (Latin), "together" + *haerere* (Latin), "stick, cling"]

Definition: To hold or stick together; to fit together into an orderly, logical, and unified whole.

> Add just enough water to the mixture of sand and cement to produce a gritty substance that **coheres** like oatmeal.

> If all the elements in your essay don't **cohere** properly, you won't achieve a single overall effect.

Related Forms: (*nouns*) coherence, coherency, cohesion, cohesiveness; (*adjectives*) coherent, cohesive

Usage Note:
In spoken and written English, *coherence* is the principle that requires the parts of a sentence or a longer composition to be so worded and arranged that they stick together in an orderly, logical relationship. Errors that usually produce incoherence, especially in student writing, include dangling or misplaced modifiers, faulty pronoun references, lack of an overall focus, puzzling shifts in thought, the inclusion of irrelevant details, the illogical arrangement of facts or events, and the omission of essential information.

Synonyms: (*verbs*) coalesce, combine, gel

Antonyms: (*verbs*) separate, fall apart, come apart, come asunder; diverge, disperse, dissipate, diffuse, scatter; (*noun*) incoherence; (*adjectives*) incoherent, disjointed

94. col-lab-o-rate   *verb*   kə-lăb′-ə-rāt
[*col*, a form of *cum* (Latin), "together" + *laborare, laboratus* (Latin), "work"]

Definition:
   a.   To work together on some kind of joint project. (In this sense the tone of the word is neutral.)

> Though Shakespeare usually worked by himself, other Elizabethan dramatists frequently **collaborated** on plays.

   b.   To cooperate with the enemy in some kind of treasonable activity. (In this sense the tone of the word is definitely pejorative.)

> "Make no mistake," the leader of the resistance movement declared. "A frightful punishment awaits any citizen who willingly **collaborates** with the foreign power that has occupied our country."

Related Forms: (*nouns*) collaboration, collaborator

Synonyms: (*verbs*) cooperate, team up, join forces, pool one's efforts; intrigue, collude, conspire; (*nouns*) partner, colleague, coworker; quisling, fifth columnist, fellow traveler; partnership, team effort, joint effort

Antonyms: (*verbs*) work by oneself; dissociate oneself from, part company with, take leave of

Related Phrase: in cahoots with

Quisling

In the 1930s Vidkun Quisling (1887–1945) was a respected Norwegian serving in various political and diplomatic posts. By 1945 he had become Norway's most notorious turncoat, and his surname had supplied English with a new word for *traitor.*

Trained at Norway's only military academy, Quisling became a major in the Norwegian army. After that, he served as an official at the League of Nations and was responsible for the handling of refugees fleeing Stalin's Russia.

While acting as Norway's Minister of Defense from 1931 to 1933, Quisling developed a great admiration for the Germans. When World War II broke out, Quisling helped the German military plan the invasion of his native land; and when the Nazis arrived, he used his influence to hasten Norway's collapse. Somewhat later, the Nazis appointed Quisling Premier of Norway, a position he held until the war ended. In May 1945, Quisling was arrested, tried, and executed for high treason. Because of Quisling's part in the betrayal of Norway, his name became synonymous with treachery.

---

95. **com-pat-i-ble**   *adjective*   kəm-păt'-ə-bəl
[*com*, a form of *cum* (Latin), "together" + *pati* (Latin), "feel; endure" + *abilis* (Latin), "able to"]

Definition:
    a. Capable of use with some other brand or model.

        A particular software program that you have seen advertised on television or in the newspaper may or may not be **compatible** with the type of home computer you own.

    b. Capable of living or getting along together.

        The two people work well together despite the fact that their personalities don't seem at all **compatible**.

Related Forms: (*nouns*) compatibility, compatibleness; (*adverb*) compatibly

Synonyms: (*adjectives*) harmonious, agreeable, like-minded; consistent, congruous; parallel

Antonyms: (*adjectives*) incompatible, antagonistic; inconsistent, incongruous

Related Phrases: in sync, in keeping with, in line with

136

96. com·pla·cent   *adjective*   kəm-plā'-sĕnt

[*com*, a form of *cum* (Latin), "with; very" + *placens, placentis*, from *placere* (Latin), "please, be satisfied"]

Definition: Overly self-satisfied; smug.

"If you had achieved as much this year as he has," I replied, "you'd be a little **complacent,** too!"

Related Forms: (*nouns*) complacence, complacency; (*adverb*) complacently

Phrases: a complacent attitude, a complacent look

Usage Note:
Do not confuse the adjective *complacent,* meaning "self-satisfied," with the related adjective *complaisant,* meaning "eager to please" or "cheerfully obliging."

Synonyms: (*adjectives*) content(ed), self-content(ed)

Antonyms: (*adjectives*) dissatisfied, discontent(ed), malcontent

Related Phrases: to rest on one's laurels, pleased with oneself; displeased with oneself

97. con·cise   *adjective*   kən-sīs'

[*concidere, concisus* (Latin), "cut up"; from *con*, a form of *cum* (Latin), "very" + *caedere, caesus* (Latin), "cut"]

Definition: Saying a lot in a few words.

Since there is a charge for every word you use in a telegram, always make your message as **concise** as possible.

Phrases: a concise account, a concise statement

Related Forms: (*nouns*) conciseness, concision; (*adverb*) concisely

Synonyms: (*adjectives*) brief, compact, succinct, terse; laconic, summary; pithy

Antonyms: (*adjectives*) wordy, prolix, verbose, garrulous, loquacious, long-winded

98. con·done   *verb*   kən-dōn'

[*condonare* (Latin), "forgive"; from *con*, a form of *cum* (Latin), "completely" + *donare* (Latin), "give away"]

Definition: To overlook or disregard an offense, thereby implying forgiveness, acceptance, or possibly approval of it.

"I'm perfectly willing to wink at a harmless practical joke," Mom remarked, "but I refuse to **condone** outright vandalism."

Today it is considered permissible for children to behave in ways that earlier generations of parents would not have **condoned.**

Related Forms: (*nouns*) condonation, condoner

Synonyms: (*verbs*) ignore; accept, countenance, stomach, tolerate

Antonyms: (*verbs*) condemn, denounce, disapprove, deprecate, castigate, decry, revile

Related Phrases: close one's eyes to, turn a blind eye to; put up with

99. **con-fron-ta-tion**   *noun*   kŏn-frən-tā'-shən
[*confrontare, confrontatus* (Latin), "have a common border"; from *con*, a form of *cum* (Latin), "together" + *frons, frontis* (Latin), "forehead"]

Definition: A face-to-face encounter, usually (but not always) suggesting a hostile or defiant attitude.

"Our two countries must make every effort to settle our differences peacefully," the ambassador said. "An all-out **confrontation** might ruin us both."

Related Form: (*verb*) confront

Synonyms: (*nouns*) showdown, face-off, shoot-out

Related Phrases: stand up to, square off against, throw down the gauntlet, take up the gauntlet, on the brink

Maya Angelou

The African American poet and writer Maya Angelou (born 1928) is best known for her engaging series of autobiographical books dealing with problems and issues she confronted growing up black and female in 20th-century America. Beginning with I *Know Why the Caged Bird Sings* (1970), she has given her audience a series of memorable self-portraits designed to lay bare the black experience of life in these United States. The themes she evokes in her autobiographical writing also find expression in her numerous volumes of poetry. Angelou's writing combines a rich and flexible vocabulary with a deft ear for the cadences of ordinary, everyday speech.

100. con-jec-ture   *noun and verb*   kən-jĕk'-chər

[*conjectura* (Latin), "conclusion"; from *con*, a form of *cum* (Latin), "together" + *jacere, jactus* (Latin), "throw"]

Definition:
   a.   (*noun*) A conclusion based on inadequate evidence; a guess.

   Since the coroner's findings were inconclusive, the exact cause of the child's death remains for the present a matter of **conjecture**.

   b.   (*verb*) *To* conclude from inadequate evidence; to guess.

   "I haven't enough hard evidence at hand to say for sure," the detective declared. "I can only **conjecture**, based on past experience, that this was an inside job."

Related Forms: (*adjective*) conjectural

Synonyms: (*nouns*) surmise, supposition, presumption, suspicion, inference; speculation, theory; (*verbs*) surmise, suppose, presume, suspect, infer; speculate, theorize

Antonyms: (*nouns*) fact, certainty; (*verbs*) demonstrate, substantiate

Related Phrases: an educated guess, a shot in the dark, a ballpark estimate

Using the Words

Exercise I.   Parts of Speech

Indicate the part of speech of each of the following words. In one case, two answers are correct.

1. confrontation	3. conjecture	5. cogent
2. compatible	4. coerce	6. complacent

Exercise II.   Words in Phrases

In each of the following groups, select the item that best expresses the meaning of the *italicized* word in the introductory phrase.

1. a particularly *cogent* argument
   a. forceful   b. bizarre   c. elaborate   d. weak   e. silly

2. *compatible* interests
   a. unusual   b. conflicting   c. deep   d. parallel   e. scholarly

3. *condone* wrongdoing
   a. point at   b. flinch at   c. aim at   d. rail at   e. wink at

4. find someone with whom to *collaborate*
   a. chat   b. team up   c. disagree   d. sit down   e. sympathize

5. an interesting *conjecture*
   a. fact   b. situation   c. guess   d. development   e. history

Exercise III. Completing Sentences

Complete each of the following sentences or pairs of sentences by selecting the most appropriate word from the group of words given below.

concise	confrontation	cohere
coerce	conjecture	complacent

1. Though it omitted many details, her spare and _____ account of the accident left us in no doubt as to exactly what had happened.

2. Some chemical compounds _____ readily; others are highly unstable and separate easily.

3. "I don't understand why you are walking around with that _____ grin on your face," I exclaimed. "Exactly what have you done to make you so pleased with yourself?"

4. The bitter rivals for public office met in a dramatic _____ on TV to debate the issues of the campaign.

5. You should know better than to try to _____ me into doing something that goes against my principles.

Exercise IV. Synonyms and Antonyms

A. In each of the following numbered groups, select the **two** words that are most nearly **synonyms**.

1. a. gel   b. rebuke   c. separate   d. coalesce
2. a. disregard   b. overlook   c. redress   d. compel
3. a. circumvent   b. blight   c. pressure   d. bulldoze
4. a. put-on   b. showdown   c. time-out   d. shoot-out
5. a. terse   b. succinct   c. frivolous   d. incongruous

   Now, for each of the pairs of synonyms you have selected, supply a word from the Basic Word List for this lesson (Words 91–100) that means **the same** or **almost the same** thing.

B. In each of the following numbered groups, select the **two** words that are most nearly **antonyms**.

1. a. cogent   b. agreeable   c. unique   d. frivolous
2. a. campaign   b. conjecture   c. certainty   d. chagrin
3. a. awry   b. faulty   c. discontented   d. complacent
4. a. collaborate   b. border   c. dissociate   d. recognize
5. a. joyful   b. compatible   c. frequent   d. antagonistic

Exercise V. Word Roundup

1. With or without the aid of a dictionary, define or explain each of the following expressions.

   a. strong-arm tactics
   b. fifth columnist
   c. in cahoots with
   d. in sync
   e. rest on one's laurels
   f. throw down the gauntlet
   g. quisling
   h. a shot in the dark
   i. an educated guess
   j. turn a blind eye to

2. Explain what principle of good writing (and speaking) is indicated by the term *coherence*. What are some of the characteristics of *incoherent* writing?

3. Explain the difference between *complacent* and *complaisant*. Use each in a sentence that clearly illustrates the word's meaning.

Exercise VI. Framing Sentences

A. Use each of the following words in an original illustrative sentence.

   1. conjecture
   2. cogent
   3. collaborate
   4. compatible
   5. confrontation
   6. condone

B. Give an **adjective** form of each of the following, and use it in an original illustrative sentence.

   1. cohere
   2. conjecture
   3. coerce

C. Give an **adverb** form of each of these words, and use it in an original illustrative sentence.

   1. cogent
   2. complacent
   3. concise

William Safire

William Safire (born 1929) is a noted commentator on the American language. For over twenty years he has written a popular weekly column, "On Language," which investigates and spotlights development in our language. He has also written seven books on American English. An influential political columnist as well, Safire was awarded a Pulitzer Prize for political commentary.

Completing Verbal Analogies

"A Indicates the State of Being B." Another important word relationship that turns up on standardized vocabulary tests may conveniently be expressed as "*A* indicates the state of being *B*." An example of an analogy question involving this word relationship is given below. See if you can figure out the correct answer before you read the explanation of it given below.

$$A \qquad B \qquad C \qquad \qquad \qquad D$$
chagrin : mortified = candor : (*careless, vexed, frank, reserved, hungry*)

The answer, of course, is *frank. Candor* indicates the state of being *frank* or open about one's knowledge, thoughts, or feelings, just as *chagrin* indicates the state of being *mortified* or humiliated by some kind of disappointment or frustration.

Note that, as usual, the wrong choices offered under *D* include some traps for the unwary. For example, *vexed*, which is something of a synonym of *mortified*, indicates how a person feels when overcome with *chagrin*, but it has nothing to do with *candor*. Similarly, *reserved* indicates a trait that is the opposite of the one suggested by *candor*.

Exercise I

Complete the following analogies based on the word relationship "*A* indicates the state of being *B*."

1. **complacence : smug** = vigilance : (*sweet, quarrelsome, generous, watchful, jolly*)

2. **conciseness : brief** = cogency : (*terse, forceful, elaborate, bizarre, childish*)

3. **prudence : careful** = apathy : (*indecisive, indignant, indigent, indiscreet, indifferent*)

Exercise II

Write **three** original analogies based on the relationship "*A* indicates the state of being *B*." In your analogies use at least **two** of the basic words studied in Lessons 1–10 (Words 1–100).

Exercise III

The following items review what you have so far learned about analogy questions. Complete each.

1. **anarchy : order** = apathy : (*influence, ignorance, income, interest, intelligence*)

2. **callous : compassionate** = caustic : (*forthright, bland, callow, myopic, pungent*)

3. **clandestine : openness** = compatible : (*conflict, direction, sympathy, meaning, unity*)

4. **coerce : constrain** = cohere : (*circumvent, censure, compel, commend, coalesce*)

5. **affluence : rich** = captiousness : (*hypercritical, hyperbolic, hyperactive, hypothetical, hypocritical*)

Enriching the Lesson

Exercise I.   Look-Alikes

English has a great many duos or even trios of words that look alike but mean quite different things. Some of these items are paired off below. With or without the aid of a dictionary, explain the difference in meaning between the members of each pair.

1. abrogate—arrogate	11. affect—effect
2. human—humane	12. flaunt—flout
3. resound—redound	13. fallible—fallacious
4. envious—enviable	14. noisy—noisome
5. official—officious	15. founder—flounder
6. laudable—laudatory	16. ceremonious—ceremonial
7. judicial—judicious	17. fortunate—fortuitous
8. ferment—foment	18. contemptible—contemptuous
9. ingenious—ingenuous	19. progeny—prodigy
10. martial—marital	20. depredation—deprivation

Now, choose any **five** of the pairs of words listed above. For each, compose a set of **two** sentences, each of which illustrates the meaning and use of **one** of the words in the pair.

Exercise II.   By the Sweat of Your Brow

Some terms and expressions used in connection with working in general and labor-management relations are listed below. With or without the aid of a dictionary or other reference book, define each.

1. labor force	11. seniority
2. skilled worker	12. real wage
3. unskilled worker	13. minimum wage
4. blue-collar worker	14. cost-of-living increase
5. white-collar worker	15. craft union
6. journeyman	16. industrial union
7. apprentice	17. right-to-work laws
8. injunction	18. automation
9. collective bargaining	19. featherbedding
10. equal employment opportunity	20. productivity

Exercise III.   Ships That Have Never Seen the Sea

Below you will find a group of "ship" words. With or without the aid of a dictionary, define each. Then illustrate its meaning by using it in an original sentence or by telling an anecdote that conveys its basic idea.

1. statesmanship
2. gamesmanship
3. horsemanship
4. wordsmanship
5. sportsmanship
6. one-upmanship
7. leadership
8. lifemanship
9. guardianship

Exercise IV.   A Verbal Diversion

A. *Doublets*   A good many common English phrases are made up of two elements connected by the word *and* or the word *or* (or sometimes a preposition). Such phrases are often called **doublets**. A good example of a doublet is *aid and abet,* mentioned in Lesson 1. Below are listed a number of other doublets. Define each.

1. flotsam and jetsam
2. null and void
3. sackcloth and ashes
4. kith and kin
5. rank and file
6. spick and span
7. by hook or by crook
8. raise a hue and cry
9. cut and dried
10. in dribs and drabs

B. *Triplets*   There is also a small group of common phrases made up of three elements. Such phrases are sometimes called **triplets**. A good example of a triplet is the phrase *ready, willing, and able.*

Below you are given the first two elements of a number of other common triplets. Supply the missing third element. Also, define any of these phrases that is not immediately intelligible to you.

1. lock, stock, and _____
2. hook, line, and _____
3. bell, book, and _____
4. healthy, wealthy, and _____
5. tall, dark, and _____
6. any Tom, Dick, or_____
7. signed, sealed, and _____
8. beg, borrow, or _____
9. rag, tag, and _____
10. blood, sweat, and _____

Exercise V.   Expanding Your Word Power

The words listed below are not on the Basic Word List, but they were mentioned in passing in Lesson 10. All of them would make useful additions to your vocabulary. Define each, give its etymology, list **two** synonyms and **two** antonyms (where possible), and use in a short illustrative sentence.

1. potent
2. relevant
3. inane
4. valid
5. incongruous
6. diffuse
7. intrigue
8. malcontent
9. substantiate

Related Forms in Context

Beneath each sentence below are four words introduced in Lesson 9 or 10. Review the related forms for these words, and choose the one that best completes the sentence. Write that related form in the space provided.

1. The _____ of Richard Rodgers, composer, and Oscar Hammerstein, lyricist, produced such classics of the American musical theater as *Oklahoma!, Carousel, South Pacific,* and *The King and I.*

   a. censor   b. circumvent   c. coerce   d. collaborate

2. The federal government indicted two young men for the _____ of coding in software programs designed to protect copyrighted DVDs.

   a. censure   b. circumvent   c. cohere   d. condone

3. Did you see the movie based on a true story about the _____ of a young man without any credentials who passes himself off as a doctor and a pilot?

   a. censor   b. charlatan   c. confrontation   d. chagrin

4. During the Cuban Missile Crisis in October 1962, the two great superpowers—the United States and the USSR—_____ each other head-on over the Soviet installation of missiles in Cuba, only 90 miles from Florida.

   a. chagrin   b. conjecture   c. confrontation   d. charlatan

5. During World War II, when soldiers wrote home from the front, their letters were subject to military _____.

   a. censor   b. censure   c. conjecture   d. chagrin

6. How much of a role do you think American _____ played in the devastating attack on Pearl Harbor, which left more than two thousand dead and sank or damaged almost two dozen ships?

   a. compatible   b. concise   c. cogent   d. complacent

7. After a three-month investigation, the grand jury concluded that the city officials' actions were not only _____ but actually indictable as criminal offenses.

   a. conjecture   b. censor   c. censure   d. confrontation

8. When writing dictionary definitions, lexicographers aim for clarity and _____.

   a. circuitous   b. concise   c. complacent   d. compatible

9. Without evidence to support it, your intriguing theory remains purely _____.

   a. chagrin   b. conjecture   c. censure   d. censor

10. "Of course you're right," she said _____. "You always are, aren't you?"

   a. clandestine   b. compatible   c. complacent   d. caustic

11. The speaker explained Albert Einstein's general theory of relativity so _____ that even a layperson could understand its basic points.

   a. complacent   b. cogent   c. chronic   d. caustic

12. Sunshine laws in most states prohibit or restrict government groups from meeting _____.

   a. cogent   b. concise   c. clandestine   d. chronic

13. A strike by workers is a type of _____ designed to bring labor and employers to the bargaining table.

   a. coerce   b. cohere   c. condone   d. circumvent

14. Can you explain what causes the _____ of molecules in a chemical compound?

   a. collaborate   b. conjecture   c. coerce   d. cohere

15. "I have never been a _____ of sloth," Grandma said sternly to the two little boys sprawled on the couch watching TV.

   a. circumvent   b. conjecture   c. condone   d. collaborate

16. The people who score standardized tests of writing evaluate students' essays for clarity, _____, and the development of ideas.

   a. collaborate   b. condone   c. cohere   d. coerce

17. Do you suppose that the White Rabbit in Lewis Carroll's *Alice's Adventures in Wonderland* might have been _____ late for important dates?

   a. caustic   b. chronic   c. cogent   d. compatible

18. Because of the _____ of the route the taxi driver took, I ended up having to pay three times the usual fare.

   a. cogent   b. concise   c. complacent   d. circuitous

19. In a 1771 speech, the American patriot Samuel Adams warned colonists, "The necessity of the times, more than ever, calls for our utmost _____, deliberation, fortitude, and perseverance."

   a. circumspect   b. complacent   c. caustic   d. chronic

20. After she bought her new computer, Mia was dismayed to discover that _____ is a problem and that she might have to replace her printer.

   a. concise   b. compatible   c. complacent   d. cogent

Review

1. abdicate — 100. conjecture

Exercise I.   Syllabication and Pronunciation

Syllabicate the following words correctly, and place the major stress mark (') after the syllable that is accented when the word is pronounced. Two answers are correct in some instances.

1. acclimate   3. banal   5. chagrin
2. augur   4. bombastic   6. coerce

Exercise II.   Parts of Speech

Indicate the part of speech of each of the following words. In some cases, two answers are correct.

1. advocate   3. bicker   5. censure
2. atrophy   4. brash   6. conjecture

Exercise III.   Words Out of Context

In each of the following groups, select the lettered item that best expresses the meaning of the numbered word at the left.

1. abdicate   a. serve   b. retain   c. delete   d. beg
                   e. resign

2. appall   a. propose   b. determine   c. horrify
                   d. cover   e. attract

3. anarchy   a. chaos   b. hostility   c. support
                   d. ignorance   e. effort

4. boisterous   a. greedy   b. cowardly   c. ugly   d. noisy
                   e. lazy

5. bleak   a. mindless   b. fearless   c. aimless
                   d. timeless   e. cheerless

6. baffle   a. nurture   b. puzzle   c. aid   d. relish
                   e. conclude

7. captious   a. favorable   b. destitute   c. hypercritical
                   d. collective   e. clumsy

8. clandestine   a. opulent   b. sarcastic   c. furtive
                   d. vigilant   e. laudable

9. caustic   **a.** cutting   **b.** frivolous   **c.** occasional
                 d. indirect   **e.** lofty

10. cogent   **a.** loathsome   **b.** innocent   **c.** theoretical
                d. compelling   **e.** endless

Exercise IV.   Words in Phrases

In each of the following groups, select the lettered item that best expresses the meaning of the *italicized* word in the introductory phrase.

1. *adjourned* the meeting
   a. suggested   **b.** suspended   **c.** convened   **d.** arranged
   e. attended

2. *chronic* financial problems
   a. occasional   **b.** unexpected   **c.** severe   **d.** recurrent
   e. temporary

3. *badger* a witness
   a. call   **b.** find   **c.** harass   **d.** question   **e.** excuse

4. a *brusque* reply
   a. curt   **b.** puzzling   **c.** detailed   **d.** timely   **e.** written

5. a *complacent* attitude
   a. nasty   **b.** foolish   **c.** hostile   **d.** dangerous   **e.** smug

Exercise V.   Completing Sentences

Complete each of the following sentences by selecting the most appropriate word from the group of words given below. Use each word only once. Make any adjustments that are necessary to fit the words into the sentences properly.

asylum	boycott	concise
collaborate	affluent	bungle

1. Though I can occasionally afford some of life's more expensive luxuries, I'd hardly describe myself as _____.

2. "Usually I don't make a mess of things," I thought in dismay as I looked at the burned muffins, "but this time I've really _____ the job."

3. Traditionally, refugees from all sorts of oppression have sought _____ in the United States.

4. Since there isn't much space to write on a postcard, you must make your messages as _____ as possible.

5. When two famous dramatists _____ on the script for a new play, the result is likely to be extraordinary.

Exercise VI. Synonyms and Antonyms

Classify each of the following pairs of words as **S** for **synonyms** or **A** for **antonyms**.

1. hostile—belligerent
2. abhor—relish
3. augment—reduce
4. amnesty—pardon
5. bland—piquant

6. estrange—alienate
7. circuitous—roundabout
8. reckless—circumspect
9. affable—surly
10. deter—abet

Exercise VII. Framing Sentences

Use each of the following words in a short illustrative sentence of your own devising.

1. addiction
2. agile
3. boycott
4. buttress
5. cantankerous
6. charlatan

Exercise VIII. Related Forms

A. Give a **noun** form of each of the following words.

1. abstain
2. allege
3. cajole

B. Give a **verb** form of each of the following words.

1. authentic
2. confrontation
3. calumny

C. Give an **adjective** form of each of the following words.
1. apathy
2. bureaucracy
3. avarice

Exercise IX. Word Roundup

1. Explain the difference between the words in each of the following pairs.

   a. loathe—loath
   b. averse—adverse
   c. aesthetic—ascetic
   d. callow—callous
   e. allusion—illusion
   f. forbear—forebear

2. Explain what each of the following means.

   a. academic freedom
   b. halcyon days
   c. red tape
   d. living high off the hog

3. Explain the story behind each of the following expressions.

   a. Grundyism
   b. candidate

4. What principle of good writing and speaking is indicated by the term *coherence*? What are some of the characteristics of *incoherent* writing?

149

5. Give the singular form of the word *agenda.* Explain the fact that *agenda* itself may be used as a singular form.

Exercise X. Etymology

1. Give **three** English words that derive from the Latin root *ced* or *ceed.* What does this root mean?

2. What does the Greek prefix *a* or *an* mean? For each of the following definitions, supply an English word beginning with this prefix.

   a. shapeless or formless   **b.** of unknown authorship

3. How does the prefix *ad* change when it is added to a root beginning with a consonant? What is the technical name for this phenomenon?

4. Convert each of the following nouns or adjectives to a verb by adding the suffix *ize.* Make any spelling changes that are necessary. Then define the verb you have created.

   a. social   **b.** proselyte   **c.** maximum

5. Define each of the following words using the Germanic prefix *be,* and explain what function the prefix performs.

   a. bemoan   **b.** bewitch   **c.** besmirch

Exercise XI. Choosing the Right Meaning

Read each sentence carefully. Then underline the item that best completes the statement below the sentence.

1. During the late nineteenth and early twentieth centuries, millions of immigrants from western and eastern Europe sought (2) asylum in the United States. They fled from economic hardship, religious persecution, and political unrest. Many of (4) them sailed into New York Harbor, where they were welcomed by the Statue of Liberty, a gift from France. (6)

   The word **asylum** in line 3 means

   a. sanctuary   **c.** psychiatric hospital
   b. wealth   **d.** citizenship

2. The farm's owners seem to have mysteriously disappeared without making any provision for their animals. When neigh- (2) bors investigated after several days, they found the horses and cattle in abject condition. They fed and watered the ani- (4) mals and then notified the police.

   The word **abject** in line 4 means

   a. mean-spirited   **c.** wretched
   b. despicable   **d.** unhealthy

3. Voters overwhelmingly passed an amendment to the state constitution that mandates class size be decreased to a max- (2) imum of 25 students per classroom. But in a recent debate over the state's budget, one legislator denounced the plan as (4) purely academic. "Without a drastic raise in taxes," he claimed, "no funds are available to hire the necessary teach- (6) ers and build the new schools that the plan requires."

The word **academic** in line 5 means

a. scholarly   c. expensive
b. unrealistic   d. experimental

4. Abraham Lincoln may not have been an abolitionist, but he campaigned on his opposition to extending slavery into the (2) territories. By the time that Lincoln acceded to the presidency on March 4, 1861, seven states (South Carolina, Mississippi, (4) Florida, Alabama, Georgia, Louisiana, and Texas) had seceded from the Union. (6)

The words **acceded to** in line 3 mean

a. agreed to   c. campaigned for
b. balked at   d. entered the office of

5. In 1803 President Thomas Jefferson appointed his private secretary, Captain Meriwether Lewis, head of the expedition (2) to explore the Louisiana Territory and the West. Sacajawea, a Shoshone woman who accompanied the expedition, helped (4) Lewis and Clark acquire horses for their circuitous journey over the high Rocky Mountains to the land of westward- (6) flowing rivers and, finally, to the Pacific Ocean.

The word **circuitous** in line 5 means

a. long-winded   c. strenuous
b. winding   d. terrifying

6. Studies have shown that identical twins generally have a benign influence on each other's development and personali- (2) ties. As they grow, they maintain a strong bond of friendship and support each other's interests. Often, identical twins de- (4) velop similar—but not identical—personality traits.

The word **benign** in line 2 means

a. strong   c. gentle
b. harmful   d. wholesome

7. A tangram is a Chinese puzzle designed to baffle both adults and children. Tangrams are made by cutting a square into (2) seven smaller shapes (five triangles, a square, and a rhom- boid), that can then be arranged to create various geometric (4) shapes or designs.

The word **baffle** in line 1 means

a. mystify   c. thwart
b. challenge   d. annoy

8. Ansel Adams, an astute observer of nature, devoted his life to taking and developing black and white photographs of the (2) western and southwestern United States. His great love of nature is evident in his moving photographs—with their (4) stunning effects of light, clarity, and mist—taken in the Yosemite and High Sierra valleys. (6)

The word **astute** in line 1 means

a. perceptive   c. subtle
b. cunning   d. artistic

9. Choosing a topic for a research paper should not be arbitrary. Remember that you will spend upward of six weeks working (2) on your topic. That is why teachers recommend that you choose a subject that genuinely interests you. (4)

The word **arbitrary** in line 1 means

a. high-handed   c. random
b. compulsory   d. judgmental

10. Did you know that some household cleaners are caustic and therefore dangerous? Be careful to avoid combining bleach (2) with other cleaning agents, for example, because the combination may release gases that are extremely harmful if in- (4) haled.

The word **caustic** in line 1 means

a. sarcastic   c. poisonous
b. malodorous   d. corrosive

11. The push to have every child reading well by third grade continues to gain momentum. Reading experts advise that (2) families begin regularly reading aloud to children in infancy and that youngsters be encouraged to develop catholic (4) tastes in books and other reading matter.

The word **catholic** in line 4 means

a. religious   c. specialized
b. global   d. broad

12. In 1955 Rosa Parks triggered the Montgomery, Alabama, bus boycott by refusing to give up her seat on a bus to a (2) white man. In her autobiography, *Rosa Parks: My Story*, she is candid about her motivation. She wasn't old or physically (4) tired, she says. "The only tired I was, was tired of giving in."

The word **candid** in line 4 means

a. impromptu   c. impartial
b. forthright   d. biased

Lesson 11

---

101. **con·nois·seur**   *noun*   kŏn-ə-sûr'

[*connoisseur* (obsolete French), "expert"; from *connoistre* (Old French), "know"; from *co*, a form of *cum* (Latin), "thoroughly" + *(g)noscere* (Latin), "know"]

Definition: Someone with informed and discriminating judgment, especially in matters of art, literature, or taste.

Though the exhibition was by no means a popular success, it caused a sensation among **connoisseurs** and scholars.

I don't know anything about quiches or soufflés, but I'm a true **connoisseur** when it comes to pizza.

Synonyms: (*nouns*) expert, authority, specialist, pundit, savant, maven, devotee; judge, critic, arbiter; (*plural noun*) cognoscenti

Antonyms: (*nouns*) beginner, novice, neophyte, greenhorn, tenderfoot, tyro; amateur, dilettante

Usage Note:
Amateur and *dilettante* both refer to someone who studies or practices an art for his or her own amusement. *Dilettante* also suggests the idea of dabbling or not being very serious about the pursuit. A *connoisseur*, on the other hand, has sufficient knowledge or expertise to serve as a competent judge or critic.

102. **con·sen·sus**   *noun*   kən-sĕn'-səs

[*consensus* (Latin), "general agreement"; from *con*, a form of *cum* (Latin), "together" + *sentire, sensus* (Latin), "feel"]

Definition: Collective uniformity of opinion; general agreement in feeling or belief.

Though everyone in our club agreed that we had a problem, there was no group **consensus** on how to solve it.

Usage Note:
Adding the phrase "of opinion" to *consensus* is frowned upon by most authorities because the idea that these words express is already included in the meaning of *consensus*.

Synonyms: (*nouns*) unanimity, like-mindedness, concord, harmony, accord, unity, concurrence

Antonyms: (*nouns*) discord, disagreement, disunity, disharmony, dissent, conflict, diversity, dissidence

Related Phrases: in accord with, in unison, of the same mind

103. con-strue   *verb*   kən-strōō′
[*con*, a form of *cum* (Latin), "together" + *struere* (Latin), "heap up"]

Definition: To analyze, explain, interpret, or understand.

As you have already learned, the word *agenda* may be **construed** as either singular or plural.

"Am I to **construe** your silence as an admission of guilt?" Dad asked.

Related Forms: (*verb*) misconstrue; (*adjective*) construable; (*nouns*) construction, misconstruction

Synonyms: (*verbs*) deduce, infer, translate, gather, take to mean

Antonyms: (*verbs*) misinterpret, misunderstand

104. con-sum-mate   *adjective:* kən-sŭm′-ĭt   *verb:* kŏn′-sə-māt
[*con*, a form of *cum* (Latin), "together" + *summa* (Latin), "highest, supreme"]

Definition:
   a. (*adjective*) Complete or perfect in the highest degree.

     The soprano may lack the **consummate** artistry of a great singing actress such as Callas, but she is still a remarkable performer.

   b. (*verb*) To bring to completion or perfection.

     Though there are still a few minor details to iron out, we expect to **consummate** the deal sometime this week.

Related Forms: (*noun*) consummation; (*adverb*) consummately

Synonyms: (*adjectives*) superlative, supreme; transcendent, surpassing, matchless; finished, total; masterful, virtuoso; (*verbs*) clinch, conclude

Antonyms: (*adjectives*) mediocre, indifferent, run-of-the-mill, ordinary; inept, incompetent, inadequate; (*verbs*) begin, start, initiate, launch

105. co-pi-ous   *adjective*   kō′-pē-əs
[*copiosus* (Latin), "plentiful," from *copia* (Latin), "plenty"]

Definition: Large in number or quantity; full.

In no time at all, the guests reduced the **copious** supply of edibles to a mere memory.

A long epic poem such as Dante's *Divine Comedy* is equally the product of a **copious** mind and a fertile imagination.

Related Forms: (*nouns*) copiousness, copiosity; (*adverb*) copiously

Synonyms: (*adjectives*) abundant, plentiful, ample, bountiful, bounteous, profuse, lavish, numerous; extensive, comprehensive

Antonyms: (*adjectives*) meager, scanty, scarce, sparse; inadequate, insufficient; empty, vacant, vacuous, barren

Cornucopia

A Greek myth tells how Zeus, having been nursed in infancy by the nymph-goat Almathea, showed his gratitude by a gift of a miraculous horn. This horn, or *cornucopia* (Latin, *cornu,* "horn" + *copiae,* "of plenty") furnished the possessor with an inexhaustible supply of food and other good things. A horn overflowing with fruits and ears of grain has come to be used as an emblem of plenty in the decorative arts, as well as a general symbol of abundance and prosperity.

---

106. cor-pu-lent   *adjective*   kôr'-pyə-lĕnt
[*corpulentus* (Latin), "fat," from *corpus* (Latin), "body"]

Definition: Fat and bulky.

As I grew older and less active, I became decidedly more **corpulent**.

On paydays my wallet becomes pretty **corpulent**; the rest of the week it looks as if it's on a very stringent diet.

Related Forms: (*nouns*) corpulence, corpulency

Synonyms: (*adjectives*) chubby, plump, husky, burly, portly, stout, rotund, obese

Antonyms: (*adjectives*) lean, lanky, thin, wiry, scrawny, gaunt

---

107. cor-rob-o-rate   *verb*   kə'-rŏb-ə-rāt   *or*   kô-rŏb'-ô-rāt
[*corroborare, corroboratus* (Latin), "strengthen"; from *cor,* a form of *cum* (Latin), "thoroughly" + *robur, roboris* (Latin), "oak; strength"]

Definition: To confirm the truth or accuracy of.

The defendant's alibi may sound far-fetched, but highly reliable evidence **corroborates** every last word of it.

Only time can **corroborate** some predictions.

Related Forms: (*nouns*) corroboration, corroborator; (*adjectives*) corroborative, corroboratory

Synonyms: (*verbs*) verify, substantiate, support, back up, bear out

Antonyms: (*verbs*) contradict, refute, rebut, confute, discredit, impugn

108. coun-sel   *noun and verb*   kaun'-səl
[*conseil* (French), "advice," from *consilium* (Latin), "deliberation"]

Definition:

   a. (*noun*) Advice secured through consultation.

      At first I ignored my grandmother's advice, but as I grew older, I came to appreciate the wisdom of her **counsel**.

   b. (*noun*) An adviser, especially a legal adviser.

      Under a landmark Supreme Court ruling, every defendant in a criminal case is assured of representation by legal **counsel**.

   c. (*verb*) To advise or recommend as a course of action.

      "Before you make your final choice," my faculty adviser **counseled**, "visit each of the colleges to which you've applied."

Usage Note:

Do not confuse *counsel* with either *council* (a group assembled to give advice or exchange opinions) or *consul* (an official appointed to represent a government in a foreign country, especially in commercial matters).

Related Form: (*noun*) counselor

Phrases: keep one's own counsel, on advice of counsel, a camp counselor

Synonyms: (*nouns*) guidance, direction, recommendation; attorney, lawyer; (*verbs*) guide, instruct, urge, exhort, admonish, caution

109. cred-i-bil-i-ty   *noun*   krĕd-ə-bĭl'-ə-tē
[*credibilis* (Latin) "believable," from *credere* (Latin), "believe" + *abilis, abile* (Latin), "able to"]

Definition: The ability to inspire belief or trust.

"The secretary's public statements are often at odds with official pronouncements," the reporter observed. "This has seriously impaired his **credibility** as a reliable spokesman for the administration."

Related Forms: (*noun*) credibleness; (*adjective*) credible; (*adverb*) credibly

Usage Notes:

   a. Do not confuse *credibility*, which indicates the ability to inspire belief or trust, with *credence*, which indicates the belief or trust that has been inspired.

   b. Note too the difference between *credible*, which means "worthy of *belief*," and *creditable*, which means "worthy of *praise*."

   c. The phrase *credibility gap* refers to a general public skepticism about the truth or accuracy of official claims or statements.

Synonyms: (*nouns*) reliability, believability, plausibility, trustworthiness, dependability; (*adjective*) plausible

Antonyms: (*nouns*) unreliability, undependability

156

110. cri-te-ri-on   *noun*   krī-tîr'-ē-ən

[*kriterion* (Greek), "means of judging," from *krinein* (Greek), "judge"]

Definition: A standard or principle on which to base a judgment or decision.

Usefulness is not the only **criterion** for including words in this book, but it is the primary one.

Usage Note:

The plural of *criterion* is *criteria* (or sometimes *criterions*). Under no circumstances is the form ending in *a* acceptable as the singular.

Synonyms: (*nouns*) yardstick, touchstone, guideline, gauge, canon, rule

111. cru-cial   *adjective*   krōō'-shəl

[*crucial* (Old French), "cross-shaped," from *crux, crucis* (Latin), "cross"]

Definition: At a point that will determine the final outcome; of supreme importance.

"The next few months are **crucial**," President Harry S. Truman once said. "What we do now will affect our American way of life for decades to come."

Related Form: (*adverb*) crucially

Synonyms: (*adjectives*) critical, decisive, momentous, pivotal, vital

Antonyms: (*adjectives*) insignificant, unimportant, inconsequential

Related Phrases: the crux of the matter, reach the crisis point

112. cul-pa-ble   *adjective*   kŭl'-pə-bəl

[*culpabilis* (Latin), "blameworthy," from *culpa* (Latin), "guilt; fault"]

Definition: At fault; blameworthy.

"I should have kept a closer eye on the project," the supervisor confessed. "In this regard, I'm as **culpable** as those who actually botched the job."

Phrases: culpable stupidity, culpable neglect (or negligence)

Related Forms: (*nouns*) culpability, culpableness, culprit

Usage Note:

Culpable is stronger than *blameworthy* but less severe than *guilty*. As the example above indicates, it is usually reserved for a fault that is the result of an error of omission, lack of sound judgment, negligence, or ignorance, rather than actual criminal intent.

Synonyms: (*adjectives*) guilty, delinquent, peccant, wanting; blamable, censurable, reprehensible

Antonyms: (*adjectives*) innocent, blameless; laudable, commendable, meritorious, praiseworthy

113. cur-so-ry   *adjective*   kûr'-sə-rē
[*cursorius* (Late Latin), "pertaining to running," from *currere, cursus* (Latin), "run"]

Definition: Hasty and superficial.

"I was so pressed for time that I couldn't give the lengthy report more than a **cursory** reading," the busy executive confessed.

Phrases: a cursory examination, a cursory report, in a cursory fashion

Related Forms: (*noun*) cursoriness; (*adverb*) cursorily

Synonyms: (*adjectives*) hurried, perfunctory, quick, summary, careless, unmethodical, casual, slapdash

Antonyms: (*adjectives*) thorough, exhaustive, comprehensive, in-depth, systematic, painstaking, careful, meticulous

114. cur-tail   *verb*   kər-tāl'
[from obsolete English *to make a curtal of* (a *curtal* being a horse with shortened ears and tail); from *curtus* (Latin), "shortened"]

Definition: To shorten or reduce.

When problems arose at the office, I was forced to **curtail** my vacation and hurry back to the city.

Over the centuries, the powers of the British monarch have been greatly **curtailed**.

Related Form: (*noun*) curtailment

Synonyms: (*verbs*) abridge, abbreviate, truncate, lessen, diminish, cut short, cut back, dock, pare down, trim

Antonyms: (*verbs*) increase, enlarge, augment, amplify, expand, extend

115. cyn-i-cal   *adjective*   sĭn'-ĭ-kəl
[*kynikos* (Greek), "doglike, currish," from *kyon* (Greek), "dog"]

Definition: Inclined to doubt or deny the virtuousness or honesty of human motives; sneeringly bitter or negative.

"As you say, my view of the world may be far too rosy," I admitted. "On the other hand, yours is perhaps a bit too **cynical**."

Related Forms: (*nouns*) cynic, cynicism; (*adverb*) cynically

Synonyms: (*adjectives*) skeptical, suspicious, doubtful; pessimistic, misanthropic; derisive, scornful; caustic (Word 81), sardonic, acerbic

Antonyms: (*adjectives*) optimistic, sanguine, positive; naive, starry-eyed, romantic, idealistic

Related Phrase: view the world through rose-colored glasses

Diogenes of Sinope (*left*);
Alexander the Great (*above*)

Cynic

The Cynics were a group of ancient Greek philosophers who followed the teachings of Antisthenes of Athens (ca. 444–ca. 371 B.C.). Antisthenes, a pupil of Socrates, believed that virtue was the only good and that human happiness consisted in trying to be virtuous. In order to become virtuous, he argued, a person must reduce his or her dependence on the outside world. That meant living in poverty, scorning pleasure, and ignoring social conventions. As you can see, this was a high-minded but essentially negative program.

Of course, it wasn't long before the Cynics were sneering at people and their motives as well as at things. For instance, Diogenes of Sinope (ca. 412–323 B.C.), a pupil of Antisthenes, showed his contempt for worldly goods by living naked in a tub. He expressed his disdain for the average human being (and his or her motives) in an equally dramatic way. During the daytime, he went around Athens shining a lantern in people's faces and looking at them intently. When asked why he did this, he replied haughtily that he was "looking for an honest man."

Diogenes even sneered at Alexander the Great and his achievements. For instance, once Alexander asked Diogenes, "Can I do anything for you?" "Only get out of my sunshine!" Diogenes sarcastically replied.

It is from such contemptuous attitudes toward people and their motives that our modern words *cynic* and *cynical* take their meanings.

By the way, the ancient Greeks probably nicknamed these philosophers *Kynikoi* (that is, "doglike") because of the bad manners they displayed. The name was ironically appropriate because the gymnasium at which Antisthenes taught happened to be named the *Kynosarges*. To the Greeks, the first syllable of this name appeared to contain a form of the Greek word for *dog* (*kyon*).

Using the Words

Exercise I.   Syllabication and Pronunciation

Syllabicate the following words correctly, and place the major stress mark (') after the syllable that is accented when the word is pronounced. Two answers are correct in two instances.

1. connoisseur
2. consensus
3. consummate

4. corroborate
5. counsel
6. credibility

7. culpable
8. cursory
9. cynical

Exercise II.   Words Out of Context

In each of the following groups, select the item that best expresses the meaning of the numbered word at the left.

1. connoisseur   a. bystander   b. expert   c. foreigner   d. advocate   e. beginner

2. copious   a. some   b. few   c. none   d. one   e. many

3. counsel   a. advise   b. refuse   c. order   d. control   e. question

4. criterion   a. needle   b. thimble   c. pincushion   d. yardstick   e. scissors

5. culpable   a. in unison   b. on target   c. at fault   d. by heart   e. off guard

6. consummate   a. complete   b. plump   c. empty   d. reliable   e. mediocre

7. cursory   a. positive   b. different   c. innocent   d. hasty   e. abundant

Exercise III.   Completing Sentences

Complete each of the following sentences or pairs of sentences by selecting the most appropriate word from the group of words given below. Use each word only once. Make any adjustments that are necessary to fit the words into the sentences properly.

corpulent   consensus   corroborate

construe   cynical   credibility

connoisseur   curtail   crucial

1. The country is so deeply divided over the issue that no national _____ on how to handle the matter appears likely or even possible.

2. "The facts of the matter don't appear to _____ your suspicions," Grace said. "Can you offer any evidence to back up your ideas?"

3. The official's absurd excuses for covering up his involvement in the unsavory affair have completely destroyed his _____, even among his warmest supporters.

4. "I don't know what to make of their recent behavior," Jack admitted. "How should it be _____?"

5. Selling arms to both sides in a civil war strikes me as a heartless and _____ exploitation of an unfortunate situation.

6. "I realize that this decision is by no means inconsequential," Mom told me. "Still, I don't believe it is as _____ as you make out."

7. I'd describe some of my classmates as lean or lanky; others I'd call a bit _____.

8. Though her job responsibilities have been greatly enlarged this year, mine have by no means been _____.

Exercise IV.   Synonyms and Antonyms

Classify each of the following pairs of words as **S** for **synonyms** or **A** for **antonyms**.

1. disprove—corroborate
2. copious—plentiful
3. crucial—insignificant
4. unanimity—consensus
5. untrustworthiness—credibility
6. culpable—blameless
7. portly—corpulent
8. connoisseur—novice
9. cynical—starry-eyed
10. infer—construe
11. truncate—curtail
12. cursory—thorough
13. lawyer—counsel
14. consummate—clinch

Exercise V.   Word Roundup

1. What is the difference between a *dilettante* and *connoisseur*?

2. Why shouldn't the phrase *of opinion* be added to the word *consensus*?

3. What is the difference in meaning between *burly* and *husky*? *chubby* and *obese*?

4. Briefly explain the background behind the words *cornucopia* and *cynic*.

5. Tell the difference between the words in the following pairs.

   a. counsel—council
   b. counsel—consul
   c. credibility—credence
   d. credible—creditable

6. Give the plural of *criterion*. (Two forms are possible.)

7. Define each of the following words or phrases.

a. greenhorn
b. credibility gap
c. in unison

d. the crux of the matter
e. view the world through rose-colored glasses

Exercise VI.   Framing Sentences

A. Use each of the following words in an original illustrative sentence

1. connoisseur
2. consensus
3. construe

4. counsel
5. criterion
6. credibility

7. consummate
8. cursory
9. curtail

B. Give a **noun** form of each of these words, and use it in an illustrative sentence.

1. corpulent
2. corroborate
3. culpable

C. Give an **adverb** form of each of these words, and use it in an original sentence.

1. cynical
2. crucial
3. copious

Amy Tan

Amy Tan is one of the most successful Asian American writers working today. Born in Oakland, California, in 1952, the daughter of Chinese parents who had fled the communist revolution in their homeland, Amy Tan earned a degree in linguistics and then began a career as a business and marketing writer. At the same time she began to create language programs for developmentally impaired children. In 1987 she and her mother visited China to explore the people and places that had played so large a part in her mother's life. Her experiences in China were so powerful that she used them and her mother's life as the basis for her first novel, *The Joy Luck Club* (1989). Since then she has published several other novels and some children's books.

Dissecting the Words

Co, col, com, con, and **cor** are all combining forms of the Latin preposition **cum,** meaning "with," "together," or "completely." These elements appear in all the basic words studied in Lesson 10 and many of those studied in this lesson. Note how each is used.

a. **Co,** a shortened form of **com,** occurs before Latin words beginning with *h, gn,* or (usually) a vowel. It is also used to coin new words, in which case it may be attached to words beginning with other consonants.

coherent (*co,* "together" + *haerere,* "stick")—sticking together

cognizance (*co,* "completely" + *gnoscere,* "know")—conscious knowledge or recognition of something

coalesce (*co,* "together" + *alescere,* "grow")—to fuse or merge

coeducational (*co,* "together" + *educational*)—attended or participated in by both male and female students

cobelligerent (*co,* "with" + *belligerent*)—a partner in a war

b. **Col** is used before Latin words beginning with *l.*

colloquial (*col,* "together" + *loqui,* "speak")—acceptable only in familiar conversation

collusion (*col,* "together" + *ludere,* "play")—cooperation, usually secret, in some fraudulent or evil enterprise

c. **Com,** the basic combining form of **cum,** appears before Latin words beginning with *b, m, p,* and sometimes *i.*

combat (*com,* "together" + *battere,* "fight")—battle

commemorate (*com,* "completely" + *memmorare,* "mention, be mindful of")—to serve as a memorial of

commiserate (*com,* "together with" + *miserari, miseratus,* "pity")—to sympathize with; to feel pity or sorrow for

compete (*com,* "with" + *petere,* "strive")—to vie or contend with

d. **Con** is used before all consonants except *b, h, l, m, r,* and *w.*

contagious (*con,* "together" + *tangere,* "touch")—transmitted by direct or indirect contact

construct (*con,* "together" + *struere,* "pile up")—to build or erect

conjugal (*con,* "together" + *jugum,* "yoke")—relating to marriage

conform (*con,* "together" + *formare,* "shape")—to have the same form or character; to act in the same way

e. **Cor** is used before Latin words beginning with *r.*

corrode (*cor,* "completely" + *rodere,* "gnaw")—to dissolve or wear away by chemical action

correlate (*cor,* "together" + *relatus,* "carried back")—to show a logical relationship among different elements

Exercise

1. For each of the following definitions, give an English word that contains a form of the Latin preposition *cum.*
   a. work together
   b. meet together
   c. join together
   d. fall down completely
   e. unite into a compact mass
   f. existing at birth
   g. stick together
   h. agree together
   I. squeeze together
   j. destroy the virtue of

2. With or without the help of a dictionary, give the meanings of the component parts of the words listed below. Then define each word, and use it in a short illustrative sentence.
   a. coauthor
   b. commutation
   c. compatible
   d. corrugate
   e. coordinate
   f. commingle
   g. confederate
   h. coexistence
   I. compunction
   j. concurrent
   k. constrain
   l. contemplate

H. L. Mencken

H. L. Mencken (1880–1956) was one of the most colorful and influential figures in the history of American linguistics. Though Mencken was a working journalist and magazine editor all of his life, he found time to compile a monumental study of American English called *The American Language.* First published in 1919 and subsequently revised or expanded on several occasions, *The American Language* deals with all aspects of American English from its beginnings in the 17th century to developments in the 1930s and 1940s. The lively, often caustic style in which this and other works were written influenced such notable 20th-century American writers as Theodore Dreiser, Sinclair Lewis, and Sherwood Anderson. Indeed, the word *Menckenese,* coined to describe Mencken's pungent, vigorous style, has found a lasting place in our language.

Working with Context Clues

Sentence-Completion Exercises.   Today, practically every standardized vocabulary test contains at least one section involving sentence-completion exercises. A **sentence-completion** exercise (sometimes called a **cloze exercise**) asks a student to complete a sentence or group of sentences from which one or two words have been removed. The student is to do this by selecting one of the four or five possible answers that are supplied. Here is a sample sentence-completion exercise. See whether you can figure out which word belongs in the blank.

> Faithfully reading a weekly news magazine such as *Time* or *Newsweek* not only broadens my knowledge of current events but also _____ my vocabulary.
>
>   a. decreases   b. fragments   c. expands   d. demolishes   e. contains

Sentence-completion exercises test a student's ability to perceive a meaningful connection between the words in a sentence or between the sentences in a paragraph. They also test a student's knowledge of the meanings of specific words and the proper use of these words in an appropriate context. Thus, sentence-completion exercises are excellent tools for ascertaining a student's knowledge of the vocabulary of Modern English.

Of course, every sentence-completion exercise provides the student with enough information to make the correct choice without going beyond what is actually given. This is done through the use of context clues. As their name implies, **context clues** are verbal or logical hints that have been carefully sewn into the context that surrounds the blank for the missing word. Sometimes these hints are quite concrete—a word or a phrase that gives away the correct answer. Other times, they depend more on an appreciation of the whole situation that is outlined in the passage. In either case, context clues point the student unmistakably toward the correct choice. Here, for example, are the context clues in the sample sentence-completion exercise given above. They have been <u>underlined</u> so you can spot them easily.

> Faithfully reading a weekly news magazine such as *Time* or *Newsweek* <u>not</u> <u>only</u> <u>broadens</u> my knowledge of current events <u>but</u> <u>also</u> _____ my vocabulary.

Now can you figure out which of the five choices given above belongs in the blank? The answer, of course, is choice c, *expands*. Here's why.

If you look at the part of the sentence that follows the word *but,* you will realize that a verb is missing. This tells you that the kind of word you want is a verb.

Next you may notice that the sentence contains the phrase *not only . . . but also.* This is the type of conjunction that binds two parallel or similar parts of a sentence together. Accordingly, the verb that is missing after the words *but also* must mean something like the verb that follows the words *not only.* And what is the verb that follows *not only?* It is *broadens.*

Now you know that you need a verb that means more or less the same as *broadens.* And what is that verb? It is *expands,* which is the only one of the choices that means anything close to *broadens.*

As you can see, completing this type of exercise successfully boils down to a search for the context clues that point to the correct choice. This, in turn, involves knowing what general types of clues are usually employed in such exercises. These general types will be discussed in the "Working with Context Clues" sections of the next few lessons.

Exercise I

Three sample sentence-completion exercises are given below. The context clues that each contains have been underlined. Using these context clues as guideposts, choose the word that correctly completes each exercise.

1. Only one word can adequately describe the lawlessness that prevails when a government collapses: _____ .
   a. asylum   b. anarchy   c. avarice   d. bureaucracy
   e. confrontation

2. Criticism can be caring and constructive, but too often it is _____ and destructive.
   a. cogent   b. avid   c. caustic   d. banal   e. chronic

3. If you know little about art, consult a(n) _____ before paying a large sum of money for a painting.
   a. academic   b. agenda   c. charlatan   d. advocate
   e. connoisseur

Exercise II

Three more sample sentence-completion exercises are given below. The correct answer has been underlined in each case. Using the answer as a guidepost, underline the context clues that each of the samples contains.

1. When pupils are in a very _____ mood, teachers have to discipline them for their loud and rowdy behavior.
   a. copious   b. boisterous   c. bleak   d. clandestine
   e. ambivalent

2. Although politicians are not always open and accessible, they are usually _____ when campaigning for office.
   a. abject   b. concise   c. bland   d. affable   e. agile

3. If Congress wants to reduce federal government spending, it will have to _____ the expansion of already existing programs.
   a. curtail   b. abet   c. censor   d. coerce   e. accede

Enriching the Lesson

Exercise I.   The Greeks Had a Word for It

Even though you have probably never studied Greek, you may actually know some. That is because English has borrowed quite a few words and phrases with little or no change from Greek (allowing, of course, for the difference in alphabets). One of these items is *criterion*, studied in this lesson. Some others are listed below. With or without the aid of a dictionary, define each. Then choose any **five,** and for each compose a short illustrative sentence.

1. pathos	11. dilemma	21. dogma
2. aroma	12. climax	22. antithesis
3. plethora	13. diagnosis	23. catharsis
4. ethos	14. psyche	24. hubris
5. panacea	15. crisis	25. trauma
6. genesis	16. catastrophe	26. hypothesis
7. phenomenon	17. stigma	27. apotheosis
8. aegis	18. acme	28. charisma
9. hoi polloi	19. metamorphosis	29. iota
10. synopsis	20. nemesis	30. paralysis

Exercise II.   Linguistic Shortcuts

A. *Abbreviations.*   A good many abbreviations for Latin phrases commonly turn up in written English. Some of these items are listed below. With or without the help of a dictionary, define each, and give the full Latin phrase for which the abbreviation stands. Then, choose any **five** of the items, and use each in a short illustrative sentence.

1. etc.	7. op.cit.	13. ca. *or* c.
2. et al.	8. e.g.	14. A.D.
3. q.v.	9. i.e.	15. cf.
4. ibid.	10. N.B.	16. viz.
5. loc. cit.	11. A.M.	17. fl.
6. P.S.	12. sc.	18. vs.

B. *Acronyms.*   Another type of linguistic shortcut is called an acronym. **Acronyms** are pronounceable words that are made up of the initial letters (or sometimes syllables) of a multiword phrase. Since so many of our modern-day organizations, agencies, and products have fairly long formal names, acronyms are usually devised for them. This saves people the time and trouble of saying or writing the full name. For example, *NATO* (pronounced nā′-tō) is an acronym for the *N*orth *A*tlantic *T*reaty *O*rganization. Similarly, *Nabisco* (pronounced nə-bĭ′-skō) is an acronym for the *Na*tional *Bis*cuit *Co*mpany. Good acronyms become so common that soon everybody understands what is meant, and the long formal name may become quite scarce in everyday usage.

Below are listed a number of common acronyms. With or without the help of a dictionary, define each. Then give the phrase or formal name for which the acronym stands.

1. NASA	7. ASAP	13. SALT
2. CORE	8. NIMBY	14. radar
3. NOW	9. WASP	15. scuba
4. SEATO	10. AWOL	16. sonar
5. VISTA	11. ZIP code	17. laser
6. UNESCO	12. OPEC	18. ATM

Exercise III.   Philosophical and Religious Positions

The word cynical, studied in this lesson, suggests a philosophical position or a general attitude toward life. English is rich in such words. Some of them are listed below. With or without the aid of a dictionary, define each. Then choose any **five**, and use each in a short illustrative sentence.

1. materialist	11. romantic	21. skeptic
2. hedonist	12. stoic	22. monotheist
3. idealist	13. humanist	23. heretic
4. empiricist	14. egotist	24. altruist
5. atheist	15. mystic	25. racist
6. agnostic	16. optimist	26. pessimist
7. pragmatist	17. realist	27. latitudinarian
8. epicurean	18. egalitarian	28. utilitarian
9. freethinker	19. misogynist	29. fundamentalist
10. misanthrope	20. humanitarian	30. iconoclast

Exercise IV.   Expanding Your Word Power

The words listed below are not on the Basic Word List, but they were mentioned in passing in Lesson 11. All of them would make useful additions to your working vocabulary. Define each, give its etymology, list **two** synonyms and **two** antonyms (where possible), and use in a short illustrative sentence.

1. tyro	6. profuse	11. canon
2. discord	7. plausible	12. pivotal
3. deduce	8. gaunt	13. meticulous
4. derisive	9. rebut	14. abridge
5. initiate	10. admonish	15. acerbic

Lesson 12

---

116. **dap-per**   *adjective*   dăp'-ĕr
[*dapyr* (Middle English), "elegant," probably from *dapper* (Low German), "agile"]

Definition: Neatly and stylishly dressed.
I'd hardly call someone who always looks as though he's slept in his clothes a **dapper** dresser.

Related Form: (*adverb*) dapperly

Usage Note:
As the example given above suggests, *dapper* is normally reserved for *men*. Accordingly, a stylishly dressed *woman* would probably be called *chic* (pronounced shēk), not *dapper.*

Synonyms: (*adjectives*) natty, smart, spruce, stylish, chic

Antonyms: (*adjectives*) unkempt, sloppy, slovenly, shabby, seedy; dowdy, blousy, frowsy, frumpy

117. **de-fect**   *noun:* dē'-fĕkt   *verb:* dĭ-fĕkt'
[*deficere, defectus* (Latin), "fail; remove from"; from *de* (Latin), "away from" + *facere, factus* (Latin), "do; make"]

Definition:
a.   (*noun*) A flaw or shortcoming.
Members of Congress may draft new legislation to correct the **defects** in our tax laws.
b.   (*verb*) To desert one country, cause, or the like for another.
During the Cold War a good many Soviet artists and intellectuals **defected** to the West.

Related Forms: (*nouns*) defectiveness, defection, defector; (*adjective*) defective

Usage Notes:
a.   Something that is *defective* is faulty. For example, a piece of machinery or a copy of a book may be defective. Do not confuse the word with *deficient*, which means "lacking." A person may be deficient in good judgment, for instance.
b.   Someone who defects from one country or cause to another is called a *defector*, and the act of defecting is called a *defection.*

Synonyms: (*nouns*) blemish, fault, imperfection, weakness, failing, bug, kink; (*verbs*) abandon, forsake, bolt; repudiate, disown, abjure

169

118. **de-fer** *verb* di-fûr′

[*de* (Latin), "away" + *ferre* (Latin), "carry"]

Definition:

a. To put off or postpone.

Unfortunately, a person cannot **defer** payment of a debt indefinitely.

b. To yield courteously to the wishes or judgments of someone else.

It is usually a good idea to **defer** to the judgment of your elders in matters in which you are uncertain about what to do.

Related Forms: (*nouns*) deferment, deferral, deference; (*adjectives*) deferential, deferent

Usage Note:

The nouns *deferment* and *deferral* denote a temporary postponement of, or exemption from, something (for example, jury duty). *Deference* indicates a willing or courteous submission to another person's wishes or ideas, usually out of respect for the latter's age, wisdom, or experience. The adjectives *deferential* and *deferent* mean "respectful," as in "a deferential attitude."

Synonyms: (*verbs*) delay, table, shelve; bow (to), accede (to) (Word 8)

Antonyms: (*verbs*) expedite, facilitate, hasten; spurn, disdain, reject

Related Phrases: hold off on, put on ice, put on a back burner; give way to

119. **de-ject-ed** *adjective* dĭ-jĕk′-tĭd

[*dejicere, dejectus* (Latin), "cast down"; from *de* (Latin), "down" + *jacere, jactus* (Latin), "cast, throw"]

Definition: In very low spirits.

The whole school was very **dejected** after our team's unexpected loss of the championship.

Related Forms: (*noun*) dejection; (*verb*) deject; (*adverb*) dejectedly

Synonyms: (*adjectives*) sad, blue, depressed, gloomy, despondent, melancholy, morose, downcast, dispirited, disheartened

Antonyms: (*adjectives*) happy, merry, elated, exultant, jubilant

Related Phrases: on top of the world; down in the dumps

120. **de-lete** *verb* dĭ-lēt′

[*delere, deletus* (Latin), "wipe away"]

Definition: To strike out or remove.

When my article for the student newspaper ran a bit long, I **deleted** enough material to make it fit.

Related Form: (*noun*) deletion

Do not confuse the adjective *deleterious* with forms of the verb *delete*. *Deleterious* means "physically or morally harmful."

Synonyms: (*verbs*) cancel, expunge, omit, efface, excise

Antonyms: (*verbs*) retain, include; add, insert

121. de-lin-e-ate   *verb*   dĭ-lĭn'-ē-āt

[*delineare, delineatus* (Latin), "draw lines"; from *de* (Latin), "completely" + *linea* (Latin), "thread; line"]

Definition: To make an accurate line drawing or diagram of; to portray or describe in detail.

The artist's pen-and-pencil sketch not only **delineated** the model's features accurately but also captured something of her personality.

Few writers have J. D. Salinger's remarkable ability to **delineate** the emotions, aspirations, and troubled confusion of the average teenager.

Related Forms: (*nouns*) delineation, delineator

Usage Note:
As a technical term, *delineate* and *delineation* indicate a drawing or engraving that consists of lines, as opposed to one that employs shading or tints. Note too that both words stress fullness and accuracy of detail.

Synonyms: (*verbs*) picture, depict, set forth, sketch, etch

122. de-lin-quent   *adjective and noun*   dĭ-lĭng'-kwĕnt

[*delinquens, delinquentis* (Latin), "leaving completely undone"; from *de* (Latin), "completely" + *linquere* (Latin), "leave undone"]

Definition:
a. (*adjective*) Neglectful of a duty or obligation; seriously overdue.

Citizens who fail to vote out of indifference or laziness are **delinquent** in their civic duties.

"Pay your bills on time," Mom advised. "It's not a good idea to let any of your accounts become **delinquent**."

b. (*noun*) A person who fails to perform a duty; an offender.

The family court deals with juvenile **delinquents**, not adult offenders.

Related Form: (*noun*) delinquency

Synonyms: (*adjectives*) remiss, derelict, negligent; owing, outstanding, unsettled; (*nouns*) scofflaw; malefactor, wrongdoer

Antonyms: (*adjectives*) punctilious, scrupulous, dutiful, conscientious, meticulous; paid up

Related Phrases: dereliction of duty, in arrears

123. de·lude *verb* dĭ-lood'

[*deludere* (Latin), "play false"; from *de* (Latin), "away (*i.e.*, from the truth)" + *ludere* (Latin), "play"]

Definition: To mislead or deceive.

More than one Roman emperor **deluded** himself into believing that he was divine rather than mortal.

Related Forms: (*nouns*) deluder, delusion; (*adjectives*) deluded, delusive, delusory

Usage Note:

A *delusion* is a false belief that usually results from trickery, self-deception, or mental disease (*e.g.*, "*delusions* of grandeur"). Do not confuse the word with *illusion*, which indicates a mistaken impression based on faulty perceptions or wishful thinking (*e.g.*, "an optical *illusion*").

Professional magicians like the one shown in this photo are always devising new and exciting illusions with which to entertain their audiences.

Synonyms: (*verbs*) dupe, gull, cozen, hoodwink, trick, beguile

Related Phrases: a complete hoax, a clever scam, a con(fidence) game, a sting operation

124. de·mure *adjective* dĭ-myoor'

[*demore* (Old French), "quiet"; from *demorer* (Old French), "linger"; from *de* (Latin), "completely" + *morari* (Latin), "delay"]

Definition: Modest and reserved in dress, manner, or behavior.

The heroine of a popular action-adventure movie may be a far cry from the **demure** young women depicted in 19th-century novels.

The village is famous for its cozy thatched cottages and **demure** gardens.

Related Forms: (*noun*) demureness; (*adverb*) demurely

Usage Notes:

a. Frequently, *demure* is used disparagingly to indicate false or affected modesty. In this sense, it is a synonym of *coy*.

b. As the example given above indicates, *demure* is usually reserved for young women. Men who exhibit similar characteristics would probably be called *proper* or *staid*.

c. Do not confuse the adjective *demure* (with an *e* at the end) with the verb *demur* (without an a at the end), which means "take exception to" or "object to."

Synonyms: (*adjectives*) sedate, prim, decorous, seemly, staid; diffident, shy, self-effacing; coy

Antonyms: (*adjectives*) bold, forward, immodest; assertive, aggressive, jaunty, bumptious

Related Phrases: a wallflower, a shrinking violet

125. de-noue-ment   *noun*   dā-nōō-män'

[*dénouement* (French), "an untying"; from *dé* (French), "un-" + *nouer* (French), "tie"]

Definition: The point at which the plot of a novel or drama is finally resolved; the outcome or solution of a complex sequence of events.

In the **denouement** of a Victorian novel, vice is usually punished and virtue rewarded.

Their impulsive, often blundering behavior has entangled them in a series of complicated problems whose **denouement** is far from clear.

Synonyms: (*noun*) unraveling (of a plot), disentanglement, climax; final solution, final issue

126. des-ul-to-ry   *adjective*   děs'-əl-tô-rē

[*desultorius* (Latin), "relating to a jumper"; from *de* (Latin), "down" + *saltire* (Latin), "jump"]

Definition: Shifting from one thing to another without reason or purpose; haphazard or random.

The report on study habits indicated that fifteen minutes of concentrated effort produced better results than two hours of **desultory** labor.

Related Forms: (*noun*) desultoriness; (*adverb*) desultorily

Synonyms: (*adjectives*) fitful, erratic, spasmodic, intermittent; aimless, rambling; disconnected, unmethodical

Antonyms: (*adjectives*) constant, concentrated, steadfast; methodical, systematic, painstaking

Related Phrase: by fits and starts

127. de·vi·ate   *verb:* dē'-vē-āt   *noun:* dē'-vē-ĭt

[*deviare, deviatus* (Latin), "go off track"; from *de* (Latin), "away from" + *via* (Latin), "way, road"]

Definition:

   a. (*verb*) To move away from, especially what is considered normal, right, or acceptable.

      "I'm afraid I'll get lost," the driver said, "if I **deviate** from the route I was told to take."

      In any society, there are those who adhere to the accepted code of behavior and those who **deviate** from it.

   b. (*noun*) A person who differs markedly in behavior, belief, or attitude from what is accepted as normal or proper.

      Most societies not only frown upon but also proscribe the behavior of various kinds of nonconformists and **deviates**.

Related Forms: (*nouns*) deviation, deviator; (*adjective*) deviant

Synonyms: (*verbs*) diverge, veer, swerve, stray, wander, ramble, digress; (*nouns*) nonconformist, maverick, oddball, heretic

Antonyms: (*verbs*) conform to, stick to, abide by, adhere to; (*nouns*) conformist, traditionalist

Maverick

The word *maverick* is derived from Samuel A. Maverick (1803–1870), a Texas cattleman who refused to brand his calves in accordance with common procedure. At first, the word *maverick* was applied to an unbranded calf that had strayed from the herd and thus could not be readily identified and sent back where it belonged. Later, *maverick* came to mean an individual who does not follow the dictates of the majority, a political or social dissenter, one who refuses to conform to convention. Some synonyms for *maverick* follow: (*nouns*) loner, individualist, insurgent; (*adjectives*) heterodox, recalcitrant, refractory.

128. de-void   *adjective*   dĭ-void'

[*devoide* (Middle English), "rid of "; from *desvuidier* (Old French), "get rid of "; from *des* (Old French), "completely" + v*uidier* (Old French), "empty"]

Definition: Empty; lacking in.

"They are so smug and self-satisfied!" I remarked. "Rarely have I encountered people so completely **devoid** of any awareness of their own imperfections."

That slogan may sound impressive, but it is totally **devoid** of meaning.

Synonyms: (*adjectives*) destitute (of), bereft (of), wanting (in), deficient (in), barren (in)

Antonyms: (*adjectives*) replete (with), fraught (with), saturated (with), full (of), teeming (with), bursting (with), stuffed (with)

129. de-vout   *adjective*   dĭ-vout'

[*de* (Latin), "completely" + *vovere, votus* (Latin), "vow"]

Definition: Deeply religious, earnest, or sincere.

Although they make no great show of their religion, they are **devout** believers in the teachings of their faith.

For more than 50 years, her allegiance to the cause of human rights has been truly **devout**.

Related Forms: (*verb*) devote; (*nouns*) devoutness, devotion, devotee; (*adjectives*) devoted, devotional; (*adverb*) devoutly

Synonyms: (*adjectives*) pious, faithful; reverent; ardent, zealous

Antonyms: (*adjectives*) irreligious, unreligious, unfaithful; irreverent; lukewarm, tepid

130. dex-ter-ous   *adjective*   děk'-strəs

[*dexter* (Latin), "(on the) right; skillful"]

Definition: Skillful in using one's hands or mind; clever.

Professional jugglers are among the most **dexterous** people on the face of the earth.

Any potentially explosive situation requires extremely **dexterous** and sensitive handling by all the parties concerned.

Related Forms: (*nouns*) dexterity, dexterousness; (*adverb*) dexterously

Usage Note:
Dexterous is sometimes spelled *dextrous*, but this is not the preferred form of the word.

Synonyms: (*adjectives*) handy, adroit, deft, adept, proficient

Antonyms: (*adjectives*) awkward, clumsy, gauche, inept, maladroit

A debate in the House of Commons about 1905, showing the seating arrangement. Members of the party in power (here the Conservatives) sit to the right of the speaker (the man in the wig on the throne); members of the opposition (*i.e.*, those not in the government) sit to his left.

A Curious Case of Linguistic Prejudice

Dexterous is one of several words which show that English has a curious preference for the right side. This probably stems, at least in part, from the fact that right-handed people have always outnumbered left-handed ones.

A number of other common English words display the same prejudice. For example, *sinister*, which means "ominous" or "evil-looking," is simply the Latin word for "left." Similarly, *gauche*, which means "clumsy" or "boorish," is in fact just the French word for "left." Finally, *adroit*, which means "clever" or "skillful," comes from a French phrase meaning "to the right."

This preference for the right may even be connected with the origin of some of our most common political terms. In medieval times, the most important guest at a banquet was seated in the most favored spot. This was to the right of the host. When parliaments and similar legislative bodies began to appear in Europe, the practice was carried over into politics. Accordingly, the dominant political group (almost always the conservative element) was seated on the right of the official head of the legislature. Liberal and radical groups sat on his left.

From this arrangement modern English derives such terms as *the right* (the conservative or traditionalist element in any political party or country) and *the left* (the more liberal or radical element). The expressions *right wing*, meaning "conservative," and *leftist*, meaning "radical," also come from the same source. Variations on this theme include *rightist*, *right-winger*, *left wing*, and *left-winger*.

Using the Word

Exercise I.   Parts of Speech

Indicate the part of speech of each of the following words. In some cases, two answers are correct.

1. defer
2. demure
3. deviate
4. dexterous
5. defect
6. dapper
7. denouement
8. delinquent
9. delete

Exercise II.   Words in Phrases

In each of the following groups, select the item that best expresses the meaning of the *italicized* word in the introductory phrase.

1. *defer* a decision
   a. withdraw   b. overrule   c. confirm   d. postpone

2. in a very *dejected* frame of mind
   a. aggressive   b. gloomy   c. playful   d. bizarre

3. *delinquent* behavior
   a. callow   b. remiss   c. evasive   d. puzzling

4. in a very *demure* outfit
   a. flashy   b. odd   c. staid   d. elegant

5. *desultory* reading
   a. dull   b. careful   c. banal   d fitful

6. a truly *devout* follower of soap operas
   a. lukewarm   b. uninformed   c. ardent   d. sensitive

7. *deviate* from the straight and narrow
   a. veer   b. hale   c. infer   d. arise

Exercise III.   Completing Sentences

Complete each of the following sentences or pairs of sentences by selecting the most appropriate word from the group of words given below. Make any adjustments that are necessary to fit the words into the sentences properly.

dapper	delete	delinquent
delude	denouement	devoid
defect	dexterous	delineate

1. Though the idea looked good at first glance, I soon came to the conclusion that it was _____ of any real merit.

2. "The ending of this novel isn't very satisfactory," Paula observed. "The _____ just doesn't follow logically from the plot developments that lead up to it."

3. "How _____ you look!" Mom exclaimed as I descended the stairs in my newly acquired finery. "You'll be the best-dressed young man at the dance!"

4. "Describing a character's outward appearance isn't enough to make the figure come alive," my creative-writing teacher told me. "You must also _____ his or her inner thoughts, feelings, and motivations."

5. It takes fairly _____ manipulation of the control strings to make a marionette's movements look smooth and natural.

6. I shortened some of the overly long sentences in my essay by _____ a few unnecessary words from each.

7. No one is perfect, but that doesn't mean we should completely ignore all of a person's _____.

8. "There is no point in _____ myself that I am a great artist," Walt said. "I am only a competent copyist."

Exercise IV.   Synonyms and Antonyms

A. In each of the following groups, select the **two** words that are most nearly **synonyms**.

1. a. accede b. retain c. allude d. acquiesce e. reject

2. a. shabby b. remiss c. respectful d. jubilant
   e. negligent

3. a. mediocre b. final c. natty d. spruce e. constant

4. a. accelerate b. swerve c. elate d. infect e. veer

5. a. leave b. concern c. depict d. injure e. portray

Now, for each pair of synonyms that you have selected, supply a word from the Basic Word List for this lesson (Words 116–130) that means **the same** or **almost the same** thing.

B.   In each of the following, select the item that is most nearly **opposite** in meaning to the numbered word at the left.

1. delete   a. cancel b. harm c. encourage
                 d. insert e. construe

2. dexterous   a. clever b. scholarly c. inept
                 d. accurate e. bold

3. devoid   a. replete b. arbitrary c. wanting
                 d. bleak e. destitute

4. defect   **a.** forsake   **b.** elude   **c.** complete
                        d. sketch   **e.** adhere

5. desultory   **a.** sober   **b.** concentrated   **c.** expensive
                        d. merry   **e.** awkward

Exercise V.   Word Roundup

1. What is an *optical illusion?* Give an example of the phenomenon.

2. What is the difference between *devoted* and *addicted?* Use each in a sentence that clearly shows the difference.

3. In your own words, describe the kind of person indicated by each of the following phrases.

   a devoted mother   a devout Buddhist   a devotee of the arts

4. Explain the difference between the words in each of the following pairs.

   a. defective—deficient   **c.** delusion—illusion
   b. deferment—deference   **d.** demur—demure

5. What is a *leftist?* a *right-winger?* Explain the story behind these expressions.

6. Give **three** examples of words that indicate the preference English seems to have for the right side.

7. Explain the meaning of each of the following phrases.

   a. down in the dumps   **e.** a con artist
   b. on top of the world   **f.** dereliction of duty
   c. a complete hoax   **g.** in arrears
   d. a sting operation   **h.** by fits and starts

Exercise VI.   Framing Sentences

A. Use each of the following words in an original sentence.

1. dapper   4. delineate   7. denouement
2. delete   5. delinquent   8. desultory
3. delude   6. demure   9. devoid

B. Give a **noun** form of each of these words, and use it in an illustrative sentence.

1. dejected   2. dexterous   3. devout

C. Give an **adjective** form of each of these words, and use it in an illustrative sentence.

1. defect   2. defer   3. deviate

Completing Verbal Analogies

Analogy Question Type II   This is probably the most common type of analogy question used on standardized vocabulary tests. It looks more or less like this:

Type II

A   B

maple : tree =

a. acorn : oak
b. hen : rooster
c. iris : flower

d. shrub : lilac
e. tiger : ferocious

As you can see, in a Type-II analogy question, the student is given the two words in the key relationship (*A, B*). This pair of words is followed by five other pairs of words (*not* individual words!) labeled *a* through *e*. From this group, the student is to select the *pair of words* that will complete the analogy correctly.

Completing Type-II Analogies Correctly.   There are two basic steps in the correct completion of Type-II analogy questions.

Step 1.   Look at the two words in the key pair (*A, B*), and determine the relationship between them. This is the same procedure that was used to complete Type-I analogies (see page 70).

In the sample analogy question given above, the word *maple* denotes a particular kind of tree. In other words, a maple is an example of a tree. For convenience, this relationship can be expressed as "*A* is an example of *B*." This is the relationship that must appear on both sides of the equals sign if this particular analogy is to be correct.

A journalist at work on a story for a nightly news program. A job as a journalist of one type or another is an excellent career objective for someone who uses words well.

Step 2. Inspect the five choices given, and determine which illustrates the same relationship as the key pair of words.

In the example given above, only choice *c, iris : flower*, does this. An iris is an example of a flower, just as a maple is an example of a tree.

All the other choices do not illustrate the required relationship. An acorn is not an example of an oak, nor is a hen an example of a rooster. Similarly, a shrub is not an example of a lilac, though a lilac is an example of a shrub. In other words, the two components of choice *d* are given in the wrong order. Finally, both of the words in the key relationship (*A, B*) are nouns. Thus, *tiger : ferocious* is wrong because *ferocious* is an adjective, not a noun. Always remember to observe the parts of speech involved in the key relationship and the order in which its component parts appear. Doing this will help you eliminate many wrong choices quickly and efficiently.

Two Colons. On some standardized vocabulary tests (notably the Scholastic Assessment Test I), two colons (::) are used instead of the equals sign in the analogy questions. Thus, "maple : tree :: iris : flower" means exactly the same as "maple : tree = iris : flower." Both signs, of course, stand for the word *as.*

Exercise

The following items review what you have so far learned about analogy questions. Complete each.

Group A

1. **dexterous : clumsy** =
   a. copious : plentiful
   b. dapper : sloppy
   c. obese : cutpable
   d. devoid : lacking
   e. affluent : agile

2. **corpulence : portly** =
   a. corroboration : contradictory
   b. criterion : saturated
   c. denouement : virtuous
   d. consensus : unanimous
   e. desultoriness : methodical

3. **orange : sphere** =
   a. grapefruit : ellipse
   b. round : cylinder
   c. rug : area
   d. diameter : waist
   e. wheel : circle

4. **creditable : praiseworthy** =
   a. pivotal : crucial
   b. sanguine : cynical
   c. delinquent : consummate
   d. demure : forward
   e. sporadic : gaunt

5. **harmonious : discord** =
   a. skill : inept
   b. devout : sincerity
   c. cursory : thoroughness
   d. delusion : trickery
   e. deferential : respect

6. **deviate : stray ::**
   a. delete : include
   b. adhere : defect
   c. hasten : defer
   d. curtail : enlarge
   e. delineate : depict

7. **devotion : faithful ::**
   a. intoxication : sober
   b. warmth : bleak
   c. mistaken : illusion
   d. indigence : penniless
   e. complacence : quarrelsome

8. **covert : overt ::**
   a. verbose : laconic
   b. tactful : diplomatic
   c. stealthy : naive
   d. ephemeral : transitory
   e. frank : candid

9. **hammer : tool ::**
   a. singer : soprano
   b. horse : cow
   c. typewriter : machine
   d. continent : Asia
   e. trunk : branch

10. **ambivalent : certainty ::**
    a. plausible : reliability
    b. inane : substance
    c. pathos : feeling
    d. manifest : openness
    e. fretful : concern

Working with Context Clues

Handling Sentence-Completion Exercises Successfully. Study the following simple example of the kind of sentence-completion exercise that appears on standardized vocabulary tests:

When I told my landlord that I planned to _____ my apartment, he didn't seem too unhappy about my departure.

   a. clean   b. inspect   c. furnish   d. vacate   e. decorate

There are a number of simple steps involved in determining the answer to this or any other sentence-completion exercise you might encounter.

Step 1.   Read the sentence containing the blank carefully, and make sure you understand what it says.

In the example given above, the sentence says two things. First, it tells you that the speaker ("I") informed the landlord of something. Second, it indicates the landlord's reaction to this information.

Step 2.   Determine what you are to do, and where the clue to the correct answer is likely to be.

In the example given above, the part of the sentence indicating the landlord's reaction is complete. What you must do is finish the portion containing the speaker's initial statement.

This means that you must figure out what the speaker said *on the basis of* the landlord's reaction. Thus, the wording of this reaction is likely to contain the clue that you are looking for.

Step 3.   Isolate the clue.

In the example given above, look carefully at the landlord's reaction. It reads, "he didn't seem too unhappy about my departure."

Notice the words *about my departure*. These words don't tell you about the landlord's reaction; they tell you about what he was reacting to. In other words, they repeat or imply the gist of what the speaker ("I") said. This must have been something like "I'm moving out of the building" or "I'm giving up my apartment."

Now you know what the speaker initially said. You also know how to determine which word goes in the blank.

Step 4.   Look at the five items labeled *a* through *e*, and choose the correct answer.

In the example given above, only one of the five items has anything to do with the idea of leaving. It is choice *d, vacate*, which is, of course, the correct answer.

Step 5.   Insert your answer into the blank, and reread the completed sentence silently. Check carefully to see that the whole thing makes sense. If it doesn't, discard the answer you have chosen, and repeat steps 1–4.

Here is what the example given above looks like when the correct answer is in place:

> When I told the landlord that I planned to ___vacate___ my apartment, he didn't seem too unhappy about my departure.

Restatement Clues.   The example given above contains a clue that more or less *repeats* the meaning of the missing word. This type of clue is called a **restatement clue.** It is the simplest and most obvious kind of clue used in sentence-completion exercises. As the example also suggests, a restatement clue is often simply a *synonym* or *near-synonym* of the missing word. Sometimes, it may even give a short *definition* of it.

Exercise

Complete each of the following by selecting the word that makes the best sense in the sentence as a whole. Underline the clue or clues that led you to make this choice.

1. If you will agree to my price, I will _____ to your schedule.

    a. defect   b. cohere   c. accede   d. array   e. atone

2. A person with a(n) _____ attitude doubts that anyone is virtuous or honest.

    a. adverse   b. cynical   c. belligerent   d. bizarre
    e. complacent

3. I would like to look like those _____ male models wearing stylish clothes in the fashion magazines.

    a. affluent   b. desultory   c. dapper   d. bombastic
    e. brash

4. Judges are often willing to _____ a first offense but will not overlook any further breaking of the law.

    a. condone   b. abstain   c. assimilate   d. apprehend
    e. corroborate

5. The _____ of depressed people is so complete that they show no interest in any of their daily activities.

    a. attrition   b. consensus   c. credibility   d. blight
    e. apathy

Enriching the Lesson

Exercise I.   Borrowings from French

One of the words studied in this lesson is *denouement*, which English has borrowed more or less without change from French. A number of other French expressions that turn up in modern English are listed below. Define each. Then choose any **five**, and for each compose a short illustrative sentence.

1. ennui	11. macabre	21. sabotage
2. joie de vivre	12. nuance	22. de rigueur
3. mystique	13. tour de force	23. par excellence
4. fracas	14. nouveau riche	24. elite
5. éclat	15. charade	25. sortie
6. amour propre	16. repertoire	26. timbre
7. rapprochement	17. volte-face	27. mot juste
8. queue	18. suave	28. rapport
9. avant-garde	19. souvenir	29. sangfroid
10. pièce de résistance	20. verve	30. repartee

Exercise II.   Anemic Expressions

A great many inexact or meaningless expressions turn up in the speech and writing of what might be called "lazy thinkers." Some of these items are descriptive adjectives such as *lousy, swell,* and *fabulous.* Others are empty phrases such as *or whatever, or something,* and *you know.*

What's wrong with these weak or "anemic" expressions should be obvious. They are too inexact, too nonspecific, too fuzzy, to convey more than a vague impression of what the person using them has in mind.

Here's an example of a sentence containing such anemic expressions. Study it carefully

The special effects in that movie were *out of this world,* but the acting was *awful.*

This sentence doesn't say very much, does it? To be sure, it tells the reader how the person who wrote it felt about certain aspects of the movie. Still, it doesn't make the reasons for these feelings very clear. What, for example, do you suppose the writer means by "awful" acting? special effects that are "out of this world"?

The reader really can't tell because the wording of the sentence is too imprecise, too unfocused. Instead of using more specific words whose meanings are clear and unambiguous, the writer has chosen empty expressions that convey nothing more than generalized emotions. Thus, the reader is left to guess at what the writer really had in mind.

Now look at the same sentence when it has been reworded in a more precise and meaningful way.

> The special effects in that movie were *incredibly lifelike and convincing.* Unfortunately, the acting was *too wooden and stylized to make me believe that the characters were real human beings.*

Now the passage really tells the reader something not only about *how* the writer felt about the movie but also about *why.*

A number of sentences containing anemic expressions (printed in *italic* type) are given below. Substitute a more exact or meaningful expression for each italicized item. If you feel the sentence must be entirely rephrased in order to make it clearer, by all means rewrite it.

1. With a *terrific* quarterback, *dynamite* receivers, and a *super* defense, our team is sure to have a *fabulous* season.

2. Some of the paintings in the show were *gorgeous*; others were *blah*; still others were *just plain awful.*

3. Though I admit that his last novel was *pretty lousy*, I still think the man is a *fantastic* writer.

4. The food at the party was *heavenly: yummy* shrimp and lobster, a *lovely* salad, and a *swell* dessert.

5. Rose spent most of her vacation shopping, sightseeing, *etc.*

6. Even though the weather that day was *rotten*, we had a *great* time at the fair.

7. All their *neat* plans for improving the gym *or whatever* fell through at the last moment.

Exercise III.   Fused Phrases

The members of one group of English words were formed in a very curious way. Each is made up of a two- or three-word phrase that has been written as if it were one word. This phrase is usually of foreign origin, though in a number of cases it is just plain English. A good example of such "fused phrases" is the word *adroit*, which is simply a French phrase meaning "to the right" all run together.

Another is *alarm*, which comes from the Italian phrase *All'arme!*, meaning "To arms!"

Below are listed a number of other fused phrases used in present-day English. Define each. Then indicate the phrase from which the word comes, and translate it into English if it is of foreign origin.

1. debonair	7. nonplus	13. lagniappe
2. checkmate	8. metaphysics	14. puny
3. sinecure	9. akimbo	15. jeopardy
4. pedestal	10. apropos	16. orotund
5. legerdemain	11. pedigree	17. tantamount
6. namesake	12. vouchsafe	18. ado

Exercise IV. Expanding Your Word Power

The words listed below are not on the Basic Word List, but they were mentioned in passing in Lesson 12. All of them would make useful additions to your working vocabulary. Define each, give its etymology, list **two** synonyms and **two** antonyms (where possible), and use in a short illustrative sentence.

1. slovenly	6. hoodwink	11. intermittent
2. repudiate	7. jaunty	12. expunge
3. expedite	8. bumptious	13. digress
4. melancholy	9. systematic	14. tepid
5. scrupulous	10. dowdy	15. proficient

Related Forms in Context

Beneath each sentence below are four words introduced in Lesson 11 or 12. Review the related forms for these words, and choose the one that best completes the sentence. Write that related form in the space provided.

1. When the Wolf asked Red Riding Hood where she was going, she answered _____, "I'm on my way to visit my sick grandmother."

   a. consummate b. copious c. demure d. dapper

2. A pattern of _____ in paying your bills is likely to damage your credit rating.

   a. defect b. credible c. deviate d. delinquent

3. The panel of judges penalized the ice dancers for major _____ from the rules.

   a. delude b. deviate c. delineate d. curtail

4. Was it a military tribunal, a judge, or a jury that determined Aaron Burr's _____?

    a. culpable   b. cursory   c. dexterous   d. desultory

5. "Never look at a contract _____," the salesperson warned. "Be sure to read the fine print carefully."

    a. copious   b. consummate   c. dejected   d. cursory

6. As a _____ of French Impressionism and Claude Monet in particular, Kathleen journeyed to Monet's home and gardens at Giverny, France.

    a. consummate   b. devout   c. dexterous   d. cynical

7. James Watson and Francis Crick's work with DNA and the double helix provides _____ evidence of how species replicate themselves.

    a. defect   b. counsel   c. credibility   d. delinquent

8. In Shakespeare's *Othello*, the villainous Iago plots to have Othello _____ the meaning of his wife's lost handkerchief.

    a. construe   b. credibility   c. consensus   d. deviate

9. We admired the pizza chef's _____ as he tossed the dough high in the air, stretching it thinner with each throw.

    a. demure   b. dejected   c. corpulent   d. dexterous

10. Doctors warn Americans that their increasing _____ is a serious health threat because it is directly associated with a high risk of heart disease and stroke.

    a. copious   b. corpulent   c. cynic   d. demure

11. Although I had six weeks to complete my research paper, for the first month I worked on it only _____.

    a. copious   b. dapper   c. demure   d. desultory

12. The Bill of Rights, the first ten amendments to the U.S. Constitution, is a _____ of Americans' basic freedoms.

    a. delete   b. delude   c. delineate   d. deviate

13. From 1961 to 1989, _____ from East Germany risked their lives to scale the Berlin Wall in order to seek freedom in the West.

    a. counsel   b. connoisseur   c. defect   d. credibility

14. For many Olympic athletes, winning a medal is the _____ of their hopes, dreams, and years of discipline and hard work.

    a. consummate   b. corroborate   c. defer   d. delude

15. Do you think the ending of George Orwell's *Animal Farm* is evidence of the author's _____, or is he simply being realistic?

    a. copious b. culpable c. cursory d. cynical

16. Satellite photos provide definite _____ of environmentalists' predictions about the melting of polar ice caps.

    a. construe b. delude c. corroborate d. defer

17. Because of the budget constraints, the mayor had no choice but to announce the _____ of some city services deemed nonessential.

    a. corroborate b. consummate c. delineate d. curtail

18. Germaine, who has volunteered to become a peer _____, is attending the first of six training sessions.

    a. consensus b. credibility c. counsel d. delinquent

19. In China and Japan, the elderly are treated with great _____.

    a. delineate b. defer c. delude d. defect

20. The exhausted tennis player shook her opponent's hand but could not conceal her _____ at having failed to win the long, hard match.

    a. demure b. desultory c. devote d. dejected

2. "Don't expect them to do anything but _____ your abilities," my best friend warned me before my piano recital. "They never have a good word to say about anyone!"

3. "In 1900, there was a glaring _____ between the lifestyles of the haves and the have-nots of this country," the speaker said. "Fortunately, since then we have done much to close that appalling gap."

4. "I have some advice for our _____ coworkers in the shipping department," my supervisor said at the meeting. "Don't put off until tomorrow what you can do today!"

5. "At the end of the month, I found myself in _____ financial straits," Ed recalled bleakly. "Never before had I been in such an awful fix as far as money was concerned."

6. She is a _____ student whose hard work and dedication have been richly rewarded over the years.

7. "I believe it is wrong to _____ against people who are not exactly like ourselves," Sheila declared. "None of us should allow prejudice or bigotry to creep into our attitudes toward other human beings."

8. "Charlie Tompkins is much too _____ and easygoing to make an effective scoutmaster," Mr. Briggs remarked. "What we need is an energetic leader, not someone who can be led around by the nose with no trouble at all."

Exercise IV.   Synonyms and Antonyms

Classify each of the following pairs of words as **S** for **synonyms** and **A** for **antonyms**.

1. discourse—lecture
2. diligent—lazy
3. praise—disparage
4. discrimination—prejudice
5. discomfit—fluster
6. conceal—divulge
7. headstrong—docile
8. calamitous—dire
9. disparity—similarity
10. deception—duplicity
11. dilatory—prompt
12. mild—drastic
13. dormant—latent
14. distraught—composed

Exercise V.   Word Roundup

1. Explain what is meant by "a *discursive* writing style."

2. Explain the difference in meaning between the words in each of the following pairs.

    a. discomfit—discomfort   b. discriminating—discriminatory

3. Define the word *draconian*. What famous Greek lawgiver's name is embodied in this word? Why?

4. Explain the meaning of each of the following phrases.

a. go to seed
b. play a waiting game
c. work like a beaver
d. go public with
e. drag one's heels
f. run into the ground
g. plug security leaks
h. suspended animation

5. Explain what is meant by *a Judas kiss.*

6. In what famous 19th-century novel does the character called *the Artful Dodger* appear? Who is the author of this novel? What do you think the author was trying to suggest about the character by using this distinctive name?

Exercise VI. Framing Sentences

A. Use each of the following words in an original illustrative sentence.

1. dilatory
2. dire
3. dormant
4. distraught
5. divulge
6. duplicity

B. Give a **noun** form of each of these words, and use it in an illustrative sentence.

1. dilapidated
2. discomfit
3. disparage

C. Give an **adjective** form of each of these words, and use it in an illustrative sentence.

1. discourse
2. discriminate
3. disparity

D. Give an **adverb** form of each of these words, and use it in an illustrative sentence.

1. diligent
2. docile
3. drastic

Peter Mark Roget

Peter Mark Roget (1779–1869), an English physician with an "insatiable thirst for knowledge and an appetite for work," was the father of a new kind of word book called a *thesaurus*. Unlike a dictionary, the words in a thesaurus are neither defined nor alphabetically arranged. Instead, they are presented in groups according to related ideas. Roget also devised a slide rule, attempted to perfect a calculating machine, invented and solved difficult chess problems, and founded a society for the diffusion of knowledge.

Dissecting the Words

Prefixes

1. The Latin prefix **de** is found at the beginning of a good many common English words. Among them are *defer, defect,* and most of the other basic words studied in Lesson 12. **De** has two primary meanings:

a. It may mean "away," "off," or "down," as in these words:

depart (literally, "go away") — to leave or deviate from

decapitate (literally, "take the head off") — to cut off the head

devolve (literally, "roll down") — to pass or transfer from one person to another

depress (literally, "press down") — to lower physically; to cause a lowering of mood or spirit

despoil (literally, "carry away or plunder") — to plunder or rob of by force

deter (literally, "frighten away") — to prevent or discourage

b. It may have a negative force roughly like "not" or "un-," as in these words:

dethrone (literally, "unthrone") — to remove from the throne

debunk (literally, "take the bunk out of") — to expose the falseness of unsound or exaggerated claims

demerit (literally, "not a merit; an unmerit") — a black mark usually involving the loss of some privilege or right

destabilize (literally, "unstabilize") — to upset the stability of

2. The Latin prefix **dis** is related to **de**. It occurs at the beginning of a number of words studied in Lesson 13, including *disparity* and *discriminate.* As with **de**, the prefix **dis** has two basic meanings:

a. It may mean "away from" or "apart," as in these words:

dispel (*dis,* "away" + *pel,* "drive") — to scatter or dissipate

dislodge (*dis,* "apart" + *lodge,* "place") — to remove from a place that has been occupied up until then

b. It may have a negative force meaning roughly "not" or "lack of," as in these words:

dissimilar (*dis,* "not" + *similar*) — not similar or alike

disinclined (*dis,* "not" + *inclined*) — not inclined

disintegrate (literally, "make not whole") — to deteriorate or rot away

disfranchise (*dis,* "not" + *franchise*) — to take the right to vote away from

disorder (*dis,* "lack of" + *order*) — confusion; lack of order

Note that **dis** becomes **di** before the letters *f, g, l, m,* and *v,* and sometimes these letters double. For example:

$$dis + fer = \textbf{differ}$$

Root

The Latin root **cur** or **curs,** meaning "run," appears in one form or another in numerous English words. One of them is *discourse*, studied in this lesson. Here are a few other useful examples:

concur (literally, "run together") — to coincide; to agree

cursory — running over something hurriedly and superficially

curriculum — a course of study

precursor — a forerunner

discursive — passing from one subject to another in a rambling fashion

recur — to occur again

recourse — a turning to someone or something for help or protection

recurrent — happening again and again

concourse (literally, "a running together") — an assemblage; a place of meeting; an open space where several roads come together

courier (literally, "runner") — a messenger

Other words in which **cur(s)** appears include *excursion, occur, incur, current, currency,* and *course.*

Exercise

A. Complete the following activities relating to the prefixes *de* and *dis.*

1. Give the meaning of the following words containing the prefix *de*. Then choose any **five**, and for each compose a short illustrative sentence.

a. debar	e. denounce	i. deplete
b. demote	f. defer	j. depose
c. dejection	g. depreciate	k. decamp
d. delete	h. delinquent	l. decapitate

2. Define each of the following words, and show how its meaning is affected by the prefix *dis.*

a. disorganized	e. disqualify	i. disfranchise
b. disparity	f. discord	j. disinherit
c. dispraise	g. disenchant	k. disbar
d. disproportionate	h. disfigure	l. dismember

B. Now complete the following activities relating to the root *cur* or *curs.*

1. Give a synonym for each of the following words.

a. precursor	b. courier	c. discursive

2. With or without the aid of a dictionary, define the following words. Then use each in a short illustrative sentence.

a. recur	c. incur	e. recourse
b. excursion	d. recurrent	f. currency

Working with Context Clues

Review the "Working with Context Clues" section in Lesson 12 (pages 182–183) before you begin this section.

Guideposts to Restatement Clues. Sometimes the linking expressions present in a sentence-completion exercise can act as guideposts to the context clues you are looking for. In other words, these linking expressions can tip you off to the nature and location of the clue.

Let's look at the linking expressions that can do this for restatement clues. They include certain types of conjunctions (e.g., *and, or, both . . . and, not only . . . but also*), adverbs (e.g., *moreover, besides*), prepositional phrases (e.g., *in addition*), and related expressions (e.g., *that is*). Each in some way binds together two parallel or similar sentences or parts of a sentence. Usually, the clue is contained in one of these tied-together elements, and the blank appears in the other. The linking expression points to the clue by drawing your eye from the element containing the blank to the element to which it is tied. And as you already know, this is the element that probably contains the clue.

Study the following simple example of a sentence-completion exercise. It contains both a restatement clue and a linking expression that points to this clue.

> As both a hardworking businessman and an _____ community leader, Joseph X. Laurelli has done much to promote the well-being of those who live in this town.
>
> **a.** ignorant   **b.** ominous   **c.** energetic   **d.** ugly   **e.** apathetic

Notice that this sentence contains the phrase *both . . . and.* This is the type of conjunction that binds together parallel or similar parts of a sentence. In this case, it connects two parallel phrases, one of which contains the blank for the missing word.

A magazine editor prepares copy for a forthcoming issue. Working for a magazine or book publisher is an excellent career objective for someone who uses words well.

The presence of *both . . . and* in this situation tips you off to the type of clue you will find and its general location in the sentence. Since *both . . . and* connects parallel or similar sentence elements, you are probably going to find a restatement clue. Since, in this instance, it connects two parallel phrases, one of which contains the blank, you are probably going to find the clue in the other phrase, which is complete.

Look at the two phrases in question. They are "a hardworking businessman" and "an _____ community leader." Notice that each contains the indefinite article (*a, an*) and a noun (*businessman*) or noun phrase (*community leader*). Notice too that one of them contains an adjective (*hardworking*), but that the blank takes the place of a corresponding adjective in the other. This tells you that an adjective meaning something like *hardworking* is what goes in the blank.

Now look at the five words from which you are to choose the word that goes in the blank. Only one of them means anything even remotely like *hardworking*. It Is choice *c, energetic*. Clearly, this is the word that goes in the blank.

As you can see from this simple example, linking expressions can be very useful in dealing successfully with sentence-completion exercises.

Exercise

Complete each of the following by selecting the word that makes the best sense in the sentence (or group of sentences) as a whole. Underline the clue or clues that led you to make your choice.

1. A really good friend would never _____ information that was given in confidence. In addition, a good friend would never reveal anything that could hurt or embarrass someone he or she cared about.

   a. articulate   b. condone   c. divulge   d. corroborate
   e. delineate

2. Most of the new television programs that appear each fall are just like many others we've seen before, with _____ plots and boring characters.

   a. banal   b. original   c. blithe   d. avid   e. bleak

3. Parents should not permit children to _____ them into buying something they do not believe the children need, no matter how much the children coax and plead.

   a. augur   b. absolve   c. delude   d. cajole   e. coerce

4. Half-hour news programs give _____ accounts of the major stories but are too short to provide much depth.

   a. broad   b. copious   c. astute   d. agile   e. concise

5. Depriving Native Americans of their ancestral hunting grounds was a(n) _____, since this cruel policy destroyed their entire way of life.

   a. consensus   b. atrocity   c. anachronism   d. calumny
   e. affectation

6. A grandparent can be a(n) _____ figure who shows kindness and understanding to a lonely child.

   a. benign   b. demure   c. cranky   d. cynical   e. agile

7. I certainly looked a mess after romping with my five-year-old nephew. My shirttails were tangled, my hair was going in all directions, and my tie was _____.

   a. bizarre   b. askew   c. boisterous   d. dilapidated
   e. array

8. It is sometimes difficult for immigrants to adjust to the customs of their adopted country, but with time and patience they will _____ themselves to their new environment.

   a. construe   b. acclimate   c. apprehend   d. divulge
   e. endear

9. I know that she wanted me to give her an honest opinion about her performance. Still, I found it difficult to be _____ about her shortcomings.

   a. candid   b. benign   c. demure   d. brash   e. cogent

10. Although the gap between men's and women's pay has narrowed, a(n) _____ in the treatment of the sexes still exists.

   a. agenda   b. array   c. asylum   d. disparity   e. blight

Enriching the Lesson

Exercise I.   More Look-Alikes

As you know, English has a great many duos and even trios of words that look alike but mean quite different things. Some of these look-alikes were presented in Lesson 10 (page 143). Others are paired off below. With or without the aid of a dictionary, explain the difference in meaning between the members of each pair.

1. emulate—simulate	11. delegate—relegate
2. faint—feint	12. deprecate—depreciate
3. resemble—dissemble	13. allude—elude
4. discrete—discreet	14. envious—enviable
5. boor—bore	15. complaisant—complacent
6. manners—mannerisms	16. honorable—honorary
7. capital—capitol	17. authoritative—authoritarian
8. aesthetic—ascetic	18. imperial—imperious
9. amend—emend	19. allay—ally
10. solid—stolid	20. venal—venial

Now, choose any **five** of the pairs of words listed above. For each compose a set of **two** sentences, each of which illustrates the meaning of **one** of the words in the pair.

Exercise II. Biblical Expressions

One of the phrases mentioned in connection with *duplicity* (Word 145) in this lesson is *a Judas kiss*. As you know, this phrase derives from an incident related in the New Testament of the Bible. The Bible has given English many other words and phrases. Some of these expressions are listed below. With or without the aid of a dictionary or other reference book, define or explain each. Then choose any **five**, and for each compose a short illustrative sentence.

1. see the handwriting on the wall
2. a shibboleth
3. apocryphal
4. a doubting Thomas
5. separate the sheep from the goats (*or* the wheat from the chaff)
6. a jeremiad
7. hide one's light under a bushel
8. a Good Samaritan
9. the salt of the earth
10. a Jonah
11. serve two masters
12. reap the whirlwind
13. a behemoth
14. turn the other cheek
15. apocalyptic
16. cast one's bread upon the waters
17. antediluvian
18. the promised land
19. manna from heaven
20. cast pearls before swine

Exercise III. A Verbal Diversion

A good many expressions that occur in present-day English utilize the names of foreign peoples with whom Americans may or may not have come into contact. Most of these expressions employ the foreign name quite literally. For example, the *French* in *French fried potatoes* simply indicates that the potatoes have been fried in a manner that is (or at some point was considered to be) typical of French cooking.

A few of these expressions, however, have an extended or figurative meaning that is not immediately revealed by the name of the foreign people employed. Some examples are listed below. With or without the aid of a dictionary or other reference book, define or explain each. Then choose any **five**, and for each compose a short illustrative sentence.

1. a Dutch uncle
2. Indian summer
3. a bohemian
4. a Dutch treat *or* go Dutch
5. get your Irish up
6. vandalism
7. put a little English on the ball
8. a Scotch verdict
9. a Mexican standoff
10. French leave
11. get in Dutch with
12. Siamese twins
13. an Indian giver

Notice that some of the expressions listed above are not at all complimentary to the foreign peoples whose names appear in them. What do you think this says about the ways in which our language sometimes views foreigners?

Exercise IV.   Ricochet Words

A **ricochet word** (sometimes called a **reduplicate word**) is a word consisting of two elements that are almost identical in form—for example, *dillydally* or *hurdy-gurdy*. The two elements in a ricochet word usually differ from one another only in a single vowel (e.g., *chitchat)* or consonant (e.g., *namby-pamby*). Sometimes they are separated from each other by a hyphen (e.g., *hocus-pocus);* sometimes they are not (e.g., *hubbub*).

There are several hundred ricochet words in use in present-day English. Some of them are listed below. With or without the aid of a dictionary define each.

1. shilly-shally
2. willy-nilly
3. dillydally
4. wishy-washy
5. hoity-toity
6. harum-scarum
7. hanky-panky
8. mishmash
9. voodoo
10. hobnob
11. hocus-pocus
12. razzle-dazzle
13. flimflam
14. riffraff
15. claptrap
16. folderol
17. tittle-tattle
18. hubbub
19. hurdy-gurdy
20. hugger-mugger
21. hodgepodge
22. helter-skelter

Choose any **five** of the items given above, and for each compose a short illustrative sentence.

Exercise V.   Expanding Your Word Power

The words listed below are not on the Basic Word List, but they were mentioned in passing in Lesson 13. All of them would make useful additions to your working vocabulary. Define each, give its etymology, list **two** synonyms and **two** antonyms (where possible), and use in a short illustrative sentence.

1. decrepit
2. indefatigable
3. perfunctory
4. indolent
5. disconcert
6. treatise
7. perspicacity
8. bigotry
9. depreciate
10. parity
11. impassive
12. impart
13. tractable
14. feeble
15. chicanery

Lesson 14

146. eclectic — 160. enigma

---

146. **ec-lec-tic**   *adjective and noun*   ĕ-klĕk'-tĭk
[*eklektikos* (Greek), "picked out"; from *ek* (Greek), "out of" + *legein* (Greek), "choose"]

Definition:
a. (*adjective*) Choosing what seems best from various sources.

   Because of her **eclectic** teaching methods and "pick-and-choose" testing techniques, students enjoy Miss Curry's classes.

b. (*noun*) One whose opinions and beliefs are drawn from various sources.

   In a sense, St. Thomas Aquinas was an **eclectic** because he attempted to reconcile ancient Greek philosophy with Christian theology.

Phrases: an eclectic philosopher, an eclectic style of architecture

Related Form: (*noun*) eclecticism

Synonyms: (*adjectives*) selective, synthesized

Antonyms: (*adjectives*) uniform, monolithic

Related Phrase: all of a piece

147. **ef-fete**   *adjective*   ĕ-fēt' *or* ĭ-fēt'
[*effetus* (Latin), "worn out by childbearing"; from *ex* (Latin), "out" + *fetus* (Latin), "offspring"]

Definition: Worn out or exhausted; marked by weakness, self-indulgence or decadence.

   By late imperial times, centuries of soft living had turned the once hardy Roman people into an **effete** and indolent race.

Phrases: an effete snob, an effete aristocrat, an effete society

Related Form: (*noun*) effeteness

Usage Note:
When used of males, the word *effete* often carries with it a sense of effeminacy or unmanliness.

Synonyms: (*adjectives*) spent, burned-out; decadent; barren, sterile

Antonyms: (*adjectives*) vigorous, energetic, dynamic; productive, fertile, flourishing, prolific

Edward Gibbon

The English historian Edward Gibbon (1737–1794) was the author of the multivolume *Decline and Fall of the Roman Empire*, a monumental study of the material decay and moral decline that brought about the collapse of a great civilization and turned a vigorous people into an effete and indolent race. The work, which begins with events in the second century A.D., covers almost 1300 years of history. Despite harsh criticism from some quarters, the book won Gibbon immediate acclaim as a historian and is still one of the most widely read historical studies.

148. ef-fi-ca-cious   *adjective*   ĕf-ə-kā'-shəs
[*efficax, efficacis* (Latin), "effective"; from *ex* (Latin), "out" + *facere, factus* (Latin), "do"]

Definition: Capable of producing the desired effect.

After-school detention seems to be an **efficacious** solution to the problem of student lateness.

Related Forms: (*nouns*) efficacy, efficaciousness; (*adverb*) efficaciously

Synonyms: (*adjectives*) effective, effectual, efficient, powerful, potent

Antonyms: (*adjectives*) ineffective, ineffectual, inefficient, unserviceable, useless, inadequate

149. ef-fron-ter-y   *noun*   ĕ-frŭn'-tə-rē
[*effronterie* (French), "shamelessness"; from *effrons, effrontis* (Latin), "barefaced"; from *ex* (Latin), "out" + *frons, frontis* (Latin), "forehead"]

Definition: Shameless boldness.

"You mean to tell me," I exclaimed in surprise, "that you had the **effrontery** to ask for a raise when your productivity has really fallen off lately?"

Synonyms: (*nouns*) audacity, impertinence, temerity, gall, nerve, cheek, chutzpah, presumption

Antonyms: (*nouns*) timidity, shyness, meekness, modesty, diffidence

Related Phrase: barefaced audacity

150. **e-lic-it**   *verb*   ĭ-lĭs'-ĭt

[*elicere, elicitus* (Latin), "draw out"; from *ex* (Latin), "out of" + *lacere* (Latin), "draw"]

Definition: To draw out or call forth.

I was surprised that the mayor's appeal for help did not **elicit** more of a response than it did.

Occasionally, a teacher's question will **elicit** only a blank stare from the entire class.

Phrases: elicit a reaction, elicit the truth

Usage Note:

Do not confuse *elicit* with the adjective *illicit*, meaning "unlawful."

Synonyms: (*verbs*) evoke, prompt, extract, educe, produce

151. **e-lite**   *noun and adjective*   ĭ-lēt'   *or*   ā-lēt'

[*elite* (French), "choice"; from *ex* (Latin), "out" + *legere, lectus* (Latin), "pick"]

Definition:

a.   (*noun*) A highly select group of superior individuals.

Membership in the National Honor Society indicates that a young person belongs to this country's academic **elite**.

b.   (*adjective*) Select; superior.

Every army has one or two **elite** forces trained to handle especially difficult or dangerous assignments.

Related Forms: (*noun*) elitism; (*adjective*) elitist

A group of aristocrats, the elite of French society, attending a reception at Versailles during the reign of Napoleon III (1852–1870).

Usage Note:
Though *elite* is usually a favorable word, *elitist* and *elitism* are definitely not. These two words suggest undue pride in belonging to some supposedly superior group. They also imply an underlying belief in the domination of society by the people on top. Thus, they indicate attitudes that are usually considered antidemocratic and antilibertarian. For this reason, these words are distinctly pejorative in tone.

Synonyms: (*nouns*) privileged class, privileged few, aristocracy, nobility, upper crust, cream of the crop, crème de la crème; (*adjectives*) aristocratic, choice, exclusive, first-class, top-notch, top-drawer, A-one

Antonyms: (*nouns*) masses, common herd, proletariat, hoi polloi, rank and file, rabble, riffraff, dregs of society; (*adjective*) proletarian

152. **e-ma-ci-at-ed** *adjective* ē-mā'-shē-āt-ĭd
[*e* (Latin), "completely" + *maciare, maciatus* (Latin), "make lean"; from *macies* (Latin), "leanness"]

Definition: Wasted or reduced by starvation, disease, or the like.

The hollow eyes and shrunken cheeks of the **emaciated** children in the magazine ad were haunting reminders of our role in the fight against world hunger.

Nothing causes a checking account to look more **emaciated** than paying all the monthly bills.

Related Form: (*noun*) emaciation; (*verb*) emaciate

Synonyms: (*adjectives*) gaunt, haggard, shriveled, withered, skeletal, undernourished

Antonyms: (*adjectives*) fat, chubby, plump, corpulent, obese

153. **em-a-nate** *verb* ĕm'-ə-nāt
[*ex* (Latin), "out" + *manare, manatus* (Latin), "flow"]

Definition:
a. To flow out of.
   When Coach Casey gives his pregame pep talk, the enthusiasm that **emanates** from him sparks the whole team.
b. To send forth.
   Some radioactive substances can **emanate** dangerous radiation for many years.

Related Form: (*noun*) emanation

Synonyms: (*verbs*) flow from, proceed from, spring, originate, emerge; emit, project, give off, issue

Antonyms: (*verbs*) soak up, absorb, draw in, attract

154. em-bel-lish   *verb*   ĕm-bĕl'-ĭsh

[*embellir* (Old French), "beautify"; from *en* (Latin), "causing" + *bellus* (Latin), "beautiful"]

Definition: To decorate or enhance.

There is rarely a good reason to **embellish** the truth.

Medieval monks **embellished** the pages of the manuscripts they copied with all sorts of beautifully colored drawings called *illuminations*.

Related Form: (*noun*) embellishment

Usage Note:

Embellish is often used in the sense of adding fictitious details to a story or statement. When used in this way, the word is virtually a synonym of *fabricate* (Word 181). Thus, a story that has been *embellished* may be partially or totally untrue.

Synonyms: (*verbs*) adorn, dress up, spruce up, gussy up, garnish

Antonyms: (*verbs*) mar, deface, disfigure

155. em-i-nent   *adjective*   ĕm'-ə-nĕnt

[*eminens, eminentis* (Latin), "lofty"; from *ex* (Latin), "out" + *minere* (Latin), "stand; project"]

Definition:

a.   High in rank; distinguished.

Your best friend's father may be an **eminent** neurosurgeon.

Who would have suspected that such a soft-spoken, retiring woman was actually an **eminent** scientist with an international reputation?

b.   Outstanding; conspicuous.

Your mother may treat all her children with **eminent** fairness.

Tact and graciousness may be **eminent** among the sterling qualities you possess.

Related Forms: (*noun*) eminence; (*adverb*) eminently

Usage Notes:

a.   The legal expression *eminent domain* indicates the right of a government to take over private property for public use (after paying a reasonable compensation for it, of course).

b.   Do not confuse *eminent* with *imminent*, which means "threatening" or "impending."

c.   *Your Eminence* is the proper phrase to employ when addressing a cardinal of the Roman Catholic Church.

Synonyms: (*adjectives*) prominent, renowned, illustrious; notable, great, noteworthy; remarkable, marked

Antonyms: (*adjectives*) obscure, lowly, undistinguished; unremarkable

156. em·pa·thy   *noun*   ĕm'-pə-thē

[*empatheia* (Greek), "passion"; from *en* (Greek), "causing" + *pathos* (Greek), "suffering"]

Definition: A sympathetic understanding of, or identification with, the feelings, thoughts, and attitudes of someone or something else.

Ellen's volunteer work at the nursing home is motivated, not by a detached sense of duty, but by a genuine **empathy** for those who are lonely.

So strong is my **empathy** with the poems of Robert Frost that I often feel as though I could have written them myself.

Related Forms: (*adjectives*) empathic, empathetic; (*verb*) empathize

Synonyms: (*nouns*) sympathy, compassion

Antonyms: (*nouns*) insensitivity, callousness

Related Phrases: lack of understanding, lack of appreciation

157. em·u·late   *verb*   ĕm'-yə-lāt

[*aemulari, aemulatus* (Latin), "vie with, strive to be equal; be envious"]

Definition: To try to equal or excel the excellence of.

The old fable tells us to **emulate** the industry of the ant, so that we don't wind up empty-handed beggars like the improvident grasshopper.

Related Forms: (*nouns*) emulation, emulator

Synonyms: (*verbs*) imitate, match, rival, follow, mirror, take after

Related Phrases: follow in the footsteps of, follow the example of, model one's behavior on

158. en·clave   *noun*   ĕn'-klāv' *or* än'-klāv

[*enclave* (Old French), "enclosure"; from *in* (Latin), "in" + *clavis* (Latin), "key"]

Definition:

a.   A country or area lying wholly within the boundaries of another country or area.

Though a completely independent state, Vatican City is no more than a tiny **enclave** in the heart of the great Italian capital city of Rome.

b.   A separate group or community within a larger group or community.

"All of us had dedicated our lives to the arts," I recalled. "For that reason, we thought of ourselves as an **enclave** of culture in a society concerned only with making money and having fun."

Synonyms: (*nouns*) enclosure, precinct

159. en·dem·ic   *adjective*   ĕn-dĕm'-ĭk

[*endémique* (French), "endemic"; from *endem(i)os* (Greek), "dwelling in a place"; from *en* (Greek), "in" + *demos* (Greek), "people"]

Definition: Peculiar to a particular locality or group of people.

Lemurs are primates that are **endemic** to the island of Madagascar, which is located off the coast of Africa in the Indian Ocean.

Phrases: an endemic plant or animal, an endemic disorder

Related Forms: (*adjectives*) endemical

Usage Note:

Though the use of *endemic* is normally restricted to diseases and plant or animal life, the word may occasionally be used figuratively in other contexts. For example, a problem may be said to be endemic to a particular profession, or racism endemic to a particular area or group.

Synonyms: (*adjectives*) indigenous, native

Antonyms: (*adjectives*) alien, extraneous, foreign

An Enigmatic Creature

In classical mythology, the sphinx was a monster having the head of a woman, the body of a lion, and the wings of an eagle. This odd creature was said to crouch on a block of stone outside the Greek city Thebes, where she confronted travelers with a riddle intended to stump them. The traveler who could not answer the riddle was killed. When Oedipus, a famous figure in Greek mythology, solved the riddle, the sphinx promptly killed herself. The ancient Egyptians constructed a colossal figure of a recumbent sphinx near the pyramids of Gizah (*see photo*).

Our modern word *sphinx* derives from this creature out of Greek myth. Today, the word is sometimes used to indicate a person who habitually asks unsolvable riddles, is engaged in mysterious actions, always wears an enigmatic facial expression (the proverbial poker face), or deliberately answers questions evasively.

160. e-nig-ma   *noun*   ĭ-nĭg′-mə

[*ainigma* (Greek), "riddle"; from *ainos* (Greek), "tale; story"]

Definition:

   a. An intentionally obscure statement; a riddle.

      Sometimes crossword-puzzle clues contain puns, **enigmas**, and other kinds of brainteasers, rather than straightforward hints to the words that are wanted.

   b. Someone or something that is puzzling or mysterious.

      Her consistently strange and unpredictable behavior has caused many people to regard her as a complete **enigma**.

      The unexpected death of a young person is one of life's most perplexing **enigmas**, especially for those who are the same age as the deceased.

Related Forms: (*adjectives*) enigmatic, enigmatical

Synonyms: (*nouns*) mystery, puzzle, conundrum, dilemma, brainteaser, mind boggler

Related Phrases: a tough nut to crack, a complete question mark, terra incognita, a sealed (or closed) book

Using the Words

Exercise I.   Parts of Speech

Indicate the part of speech of each of the following words. In one case, two answers are correct.

1. endemic
2. enclave
3. emulate
4. empathy
5. enigma
6. effete
7. effrontery
8. elite
9. efficacious

Exercise II.   Words in Phrases

In each of the following groups, select the item that best expresses the meaning of the *italicized* word in the introductory phrase.

1. an *eclectic* style of architecture
   a. excellent   b. selective   c. efficacious   d. modern
   e. popular

2. an *effete* snob
   a. greedy   b. depressed   c. inventive   d. worn out
   e. outstanding

3. the *elite* of the entertainment world
   a. retired members   b. fans   c. rank and file   d. charlatans
   e. crème de la crème

4. a light *emanating* from the tunnel
   a. flashing   **b.** hurrying   **c.** blinking   **d.** radiating
   e. stolen

5. *endemic* to the North American continent
   a. related   **b.** averse   **c.** accustomed   **d.** extraneous
   e. native

6. *empathy* for her patient
   a. medical attention   **b.** compassion   **c.** fear   **d.** apathy
   e. financial support

7. a complete *enigma*
   a. puzzle   **b.** fool   **c.** success   **d.** failure   **e.** joke

8. an *eminent* historian
   a. elderly   **b.** obscure   **c.** renowned   **d.** retired   **e.** foreign

Exercise III.   Completing Sentences

Complete each of the following sentences or pairs of sentences by selecting the most appropriate word from the group of words given below. Use each word only once. Make any adjustments that are necessary to fit the words into the sentences properly.

emaciated	enclave	empathy
elicit	eminent	efficacious
effrontery	embellish	emulate

1. "I was really only on a fishing expedition," the D.A. remarked. "I never expected my innocent question to _____ such an incriminating statement from the witness."

2. Though several workable solutions to the landfill problem were suggested at the meeting, Mrs. Brown's appeared to be the most _____.

3. My dad lost so much weight during his recent illness that for a while he looked positively _____.

4. Paris fashions are so popular that profit-minded New York designers take pains to _____ them.

5. He had the _____ to ask me for a recommendation despite the fact that I had just fired him for gross inefficiency.

6. "I know Monaco is an independent country," I replied. "Still, as far as territory goes, it is nothing more than a tiny _____ in the southeast corner of France."

7. One of the candidates running for the Senate is an _____ educator with a national reputation. The other is an obscure used-car salesman from Missoula.

8. "Your hat is decorated enough already," Glenda remarked. "You don't need to _____ it any further."

Exercise IV. Synonyms and Antonyms

A. In each of the following groups, select the **two** words that are most nearly **synonyms**.

1. a. spent   b. vigorous   c. inclement   d. burnt-out
2. a. audacity   b. temerity   c. timidity   d. callousness
3. a. evoke   b. illicit   c. produce   d. echo
4. a. puzzle   b. enclosure   c. mind boggler   d. gall
5. a. sympathy   b. callousness   c. compassion   d. shyness

Now for each pair of synonyms that you have selected, supply a word from the Basic Word List in this lesson (Words 146–160) that means **the same** or **almost the same** thing.

B. In each of the following, select the item that is most nearly **opposite** in meaning to the numbered word at the left.

1. elite   a. hoi polloi   b. aristocracy   c. enclave
             d. affluence   e. modesty

2. emaciated   a. uniform   b. timid   c. corpulent
               d. haggard   e. barren

3. endemic   a. useless   b. native   c. fertile   d. alien
             e. puzzling

4. efficacious   a. selective   b. basic   c. exclusive
                 d. potent   e. ineffective

5. embellish   a. fabricate   b. adorn   c. deface   d. emerge
               e. imitate

Exercise V. Word Roundup

1. Explain the difference in meaning between the words in each of the following pairs:

   a. imminent—eminent   b. illicit—elicit

2. With or without the aid of a dictionary, explain the meaning of each of the following phrases:

   a. hoi polloi   d. upper crust   g. a sealed book
   b. terra incognita e. all of a piece   h. rank and file
   c. eminent domain   f. cream of the crop

3. Who should be addressed as *Your Eminence*?

4. With or without the aid of a dictionary, explain the story behind each of the following expressions:

   a. sphinx   b. a poker face

215

Exercise VI.   Framing Sentences

A. Use each of the following words in an original sentence.

1. eclectic
2. effete
3. elite
4. effrontery
5. endemic
6. elicit
7. enclave
8. empathize
9. enigmatic

B. Give a **noun** form of each of the following words, and use it in a short illustrative sentence.

1. embellish
2. emulate
3. eminent
4. emaciated
5. efficacious
6. emanate

Completing Verbal Analogies

"A Causes B."   Another word relationship that frequently appears in the analogy sections of standardized tests is "*A* necessarily causes *B*; *C* necessarily causes *D*." An example of an analogy question involving this relationship is given below. See if you can figure out the correct answer before you read the rest of this section.

starvation: emaciation ::
a. moderation : burliness
b. gluttony : obesity
c. fasting : corpulence
d. abstinence : stockiness
e. dieting : rotundity

The answer is *b. Starvation* will necessarily produce bodily *emaciation.* In the same way, *gluttony* (that is, excessive overeating) will necessarily lead to *obesity.*

None of the other choices offered exhibits the same cause-effect relationship involved in the key pair of words. *Moderation* in the consumption of food has nothing to do with *burliness* (choice *a*), nor does *abstinence* relate to *stockiness* (choice *d*). Similarly, *fasting* does not produce *corpulence* (choice *c*), and *dieting* does not lead to *rotundity* (choice *e*).

Notice, however, that two of the wrong choices exhibit a relationship that involves the *opposite* of the relationship that is wanted. *Fasting* certainly does not produce *corpulence,* but it may lead to *emaciation.* Similarly, *dieting* does not lead to *rotundity,* but *rotundity* may make a person want to go on a *diet.* These items were both purposely included to make the selection of the correct answer more difficult.

"A Will Make a Person B."   A closely related form of the word relationship "*A* necessarily causes *B*" can conveniently be expressed as "*A* will make a person *B*; *C* will make a person *D*." Here is an example of an analogy question involving this relationship. Study it carefully.

practice : proficient ::
a. interest : apathetic
b. experience : talented
c. study : knowledgeable
d. wealth : wise
e. famous : accomplishment

The answer is *c.* Continuous *practice* of a skill or art will make a person *proficient* at it. Similarly, continuous *study* of a subject will make a person *knowledgeable* about it.

None of the other choices exhibits this cause-effect relationship. *Interest* in something does not make a person *apathetic* about it (choice *a*). *Experience* does not make a person *talented* because talent tends to be inborn (choice *b*). The possession of *wealth* has nothing to do with how *wise* a person is (choice *d*). Finally, the two words in choice *e* come in the wrong order. In the key pair of words, the adjective (*proficient*) follows the noun (*practice*); in choice *e*, however, the adjective (*famous*) precedes the noun (*accomplishment*).

"A indicates the Extreme of B." Another common word relationship that appears on standardized vocabulary tests is "*A* indicates the extreme of *B*; *C* indicates the extreme of *D*." Here is an example of an analogy question involving this relationship. Study it carefully.

gigantic : large ::
a. cold : frigid
b. tepid : lukewarm
c. economical : frugal
d. tiny : small
e. drab : colorful

The answer is *d*. *Tiny* indicates that something is *very small*, just as *gigantic* indicates that it is *very large*.

None of the other choices exhibits this relationship. *Frigid* means *very cold*, but *cold* does not mean *very frigid* (choice *a*). Similarly, *frugal* means *very economical*, but *economical* does not mean *very frugal* (choice *c*). *Tepid* just means *lukewarm*, not *very lukewarm* (choice *c*). And finally, *drab* does not mean *very colorful*; it means the *opposite* of *colorful* (choice *e*).

Word Order. The comments just made about choices *a* and *c* point up an important consideration to bear in mind when answering analogy questions. It is this: Always make sure that the two words in the answer you select come *in the same order* as the two words in the key pair. If, for example, the key pair contains an adjective followed by a noun (or a strong word followed by a weak one), be certain that your answer also contains an adjective followed by a noun (or a strong word followed by a weak one). If not, you've made the wrong choice.

Teachers unfold the mysteries of computers and the Internet to groups of eager students. Teaching at any level is an excellent career goal for someone who uses words well.

Exercise I

Complete the following analogies based on the word relationships studied in this lesson.

1. **relish : like ::**
   a. upset : outrage
   b. cherish : loathe
   c. leave : depart
   d. deter : abet
   e. abhor : dislike

2. **liquor : intoxication ::**
   a. food : obesity
   b. color : candor
   c. noise : blandness
   d. water : aridity
   e. sun : pallor

3. **distraught : upset ::**
   a. bleak : rosy
   b. simple : austere
   c. gaunt : thin
   d. modest : demure
   e. irritation : peevish

4. **enigma : puzzlement ::**
   a. confrontation : belligerent
   b. discomfiture : chagrin
   c. bickering : empathy
   d. enclave : dejection
   e. calumny : devotion

5. **disappointment : cynical ::**
   a. hardship : blithe
   b. insult : dormant
   c. failure : dexterous
   d. irritation : peevish
   e. pressure : calm

Exercise II

Compose **two** complete analogies based on the word relationship "A necessarily causes B" (or the related relationship "A will make a person B"), and **two** based on "A indicates the extreme of B."

Exercise III

Complete the following analogies.

1. **dexterous : gauche** = circumspect :
   (*clandestine, complacent, cogent, compatible, incautious*)

2. **alienate : estrange** = augment :
   (*atone, augur, appall, increase, curtail*)

3. **dilatory : promptness** = distraught :
   (*composure, energy, money, backbone, honesty*)

4. **dormancy : inactive** = dilapidation :
   (*impartial, rundown, dissimilar, biased, manageable*)

5. **opulent : rich** = exhausted :
   (*energetic, lazy, tired, prosperous, untidy*)

Working with Context Clues

Contrast Clues. The second general type of context clue that you are likely to meet in the sentence-completion section of a standardized test may conveniently be called a **contrast clue**. As you already know, a restatement clue more or less repeats the meaning of the missing word. A contrast clue, on the other hand, provides an *antonym* for, or a phrase that means the *opposite* of, the word that is wanted.

Study the following example of a sentence-completion exercise carefully. It contains both a contrast clue and a linking expression that points to this clue.

"As you say, my view of the situation may be far too rosy," I admitted. "On the other hand, yours may be a bit too _____."

    a. optimistic **b.** scholarly **c.** pious **d.** concise **e.** bleak

Notice the presence of the phrase *On the other hand* at the beginning of the second sentence. This is the kind of linking expression that binds together two contrasting or dissimilar sentences or sentence elements. In this case, it connects two complete sentences.

Thus, the words *On the other hand* tell you that you are about to read a sentence that in some way contrasts with the preceding sentence. In other words, the phrase pretty much tells you what kind of clue you are likely to find. It is a contrast clue.

But the phrase *On the other hand* also tells you something else. It tells you where to look for the clue. Since the blank for the missing word follows (rather than precedes) the words *On the other hand,* you are likely to find your clue in the first sentence in the example.

Look at the first sentence. It tells you that the speaker ("I") has far too "rosy" a view of a particular situation. *Rosy,* of course, means "optimistic" or "confident." This implies that the person who is dealt with in the second sentence ("you") must have a view of the same situation that contrasts with the speaker's view. In other words, it must in some way be "unrosy." Now you know the sense of the missing word.

Now look at the five words from which you are to select the item that goes in the blank. Only one of them means anything like "unrosy" or "unoptimistic." It is choice *e, bleak,* which, as you learned in Lesson 7 (page 99), can mean "gloomy." This is clearly the missing word.

Exercise I

All the following sentence-completion exercises contain contrast clues. Complete each by selecting the word that makes the best sense in the sentence (or pair of sentences) as a whole. Underline the clue or clues that led you to make your choice.

1. "There is nothing bold about this character," the director said. "She is as _____ as a spring flower.

    a. effete **b.** delightful **c.** avid **d.** demure **e.** agile

2. Although it is easy to criticize the failings of people you dislike, it is much harder to _____ them for their good qualities.

    a. praise **b.** elicit **c.** condone **d.** abet **e.** compare

3. One child in a family can be very ＿＿＿＿＿ and easy to handle; while another sibling may be very troublesome and hard to manage.

   a. docile   b. diligent   c. boorish   d. affectionate   e. belligerent

4. I keep feeling responsible for our messy room, but my sister seems to ＿＿＿＿＿ responsibility for the mess.

   a. assume   b. claim   c. defer   d. abdicate   e. consider

5. Some household pets gain weight as they grow older; others, however, become ＿＿＿＿＿ with age and illness.

   a. chronic   b. demure   c. cantankerous   d. corpulent
   e. emaciated

Exercise II

The following exercise reviews everything that you have learned about sentence-completion questions and context clues to this point. Complete each item in the exercise by selecting the word that makes the best sense in the sentence (or pair of sentences) as a whole. Underline the clue or clues that led you to your choice.

1. I thought the meal was very ＿＿＿＿＿, but my companion found it very interesting and tasty.

   a. bland   b. eclectic   c. desultory   d. delicious   e. bizarre

2. Since our accountant advised us to put off buying a house until mortgage rates declined, we agreed to ＿＿＿＿＿ the purchase.

   a. abet   b. pursue   c. defer   d. expedite   e. conclude

3. The handiwork of one of the carpenters is extremely skillful and ＿＿＿＿＿; the other's is clumsy and awkward.

   a. captious   b. desultory   c. callous   d. dexterous   e. arbitrary

4, Although I find his argument ＿＿＿＿＿, I am not convinced he believes what he is saying so forcefully.

   a. captious   b. weak   c. dire   d. academic   e. cogent

5. When Edward VIII chose to ＿＿＿＿＿ the English throne, he did not realize he would have to give up most of his power and influence as well.

   a. abdicate   b. expel   c. secure   d. exalt   e. undo

Enriching the Lesson

Exercise I.   Our Latin Heritage

A number of the English words studied in this lesson (e.g., *efficacious*, *enclave*, *emulate*) are based on Latin originals. English is rich in such Latin borrowings. As a matter of fact, they make up a huge part of the vocabulary of present-day English.

A number of words and expressions borrowed or adapted from Latin (including medieval Latin) are listed below. With or without the aid of a dictionary, define each. Then choose any **five**, and for each compose a short illustrative sentence.

1. laborious	11. nugatory	21. lapse
2. unanimous	12. punitive	22. rapacious
3. magnanimous	13. obliterate	23. negotiate
4. puerile	14. ratify	24. superfluous
5. terminate	15. malevolent	25. provoke
6. mandate	16. nullify	26. quash
7. supersede	17. juxtapose	27. militate
8. raucous	18. regress	28. literate
9. nascent	19. minimal	29. notorious
10. jocose	20. malleable	30. reiterate

Exercise II.   "Extreme" Words

The adjective *emaciated*, studied in this lesson, indicates extreme thinness. Its opposite, *obese*, noted in the synonyms under *emaciated*, indicates extreme fatness. English is rich in such extreme expressions. Do the following exercise involving a few of them.

The words in column A refer to familiar emotions or traits of personality. The words in column B refer to the same emotions or traits but in a more extreme or intense sense. Match each word in column A with its related extreme word in column B.

Column A	*Column B*
1. glad	a. solemn
2. restrained	b. adore
3. dislike	c. immaculate
4. serious	d. elated
5. like	e. distraught
6. clean	f. chaotic
7. wise	g. sagacious
8. forceful	h. austere
9. disorderly	i. overbearing
10. perturbed	j. detest
11. well-off	k. outrage
12. offend	l. opulent

Exercise III.   Too Much of a Good Thing

The desire to excel is generally a healthy characteristic in a person. Experience, however, shows that it can easily go sour. Thus, under the "good" word *elite*, studied in this lesson, the negative words *elitist* and *elitism* also appear. Listed below are some other common English words that suggest a desire to be superior that is expressed in a negative or objectionable way. With or without the aid of a dictionary, define each. Then choose any **five**, and for each compose a short illustrative sentence.

1. snob	7. poseur	13. bumptious
2. moralistic	8. conceit	14. perfectionist
3. dogmatic	9. authoritarian	15. purist
4. sanctimonious	10. dilettante	16. self-righteous
5. labored	11. egocentric	17. narcissism
6. autocratic	12. preciosity	18. jingoism

Exercise IV.   Forms of Direct Address

Under *eminent*, a word studied in this lesson, it was noted that *Your Eminence* is the proper phrase to use when addressing a cardinal of the Roman Catholic Church. English has a few other such phrases. They are all used when addressing royalty or persons holding certain positions in the government, the church, or the legal system. Six of these phrases are listed below. With or without the aid of a dictionary, name the person or group of people to whom each is properly applied.

1. Your Excellency	3. Your Grace	5. Your Honor
2. Your Highness	4. Your Holiness	6. Your Majesty

Exercise V.   Expanding Your Word Power

The words listed below are not on the Basic Word List, but they were mentioned in passing in Lesson 14. All of them would make useful additions to your working vocabulary. Define each, give its etymology, list **two** synonyms and **two** antonyms (where possible), and use in a short illustrative sentence.

1. monolithic	6. diffidence	11. garnish
2. decadent	7. evoke	12. obscure
3. prolific	8. aristocratic	13. compassion
4. ineffectual	9. obese	14. indigenous
5. impertinence	10. originate	15. dilemma

Related Forms in Context

Beneath each sentence below are four words introduced in Lesson 13 or 14. Review the related forms for these words, and choose the one that best completes the sentence. Write that related form in the space provided.

1. The tour guide drew our attention to the _____ of the room's decor—Japanese prints, Classical Greek sculpture, Tiffany lamps, Navajo rugs, and Mission-style furniture.

   a. dilapidated   b. effete   c. eclectic   d. eminent

2. Before trying to feed an injured eagle or hawk, an avian wildlife rehabilitator needs to determine the bird's level of _____.

   a. dilatory   b. emaciated   c. distraught   d. dire

3. Comparing its past popularity with its currently dwindling numbers, the party functionaries bemoaned the sheer _____ of their movement today.

   a. effete   b. efficacious   c. dire   d. docile

4. The sixteenth-century French writer Montaigne, who developed the essay form, wrote short nonfiction pieces in a _____ style about topics that interested him.

   a. disparity   b. effrontery   c. duplicity   d. discourse

5. In Shakespeare's *King Lear*, the tragedy is set in motion when Lear's three daughters give _____ responses to their father's demand for an expression of their love.

   a. discourse   b. disparity   c. elite   d. enclave

6. If you stay up all night, skip breakfast, and neglect to read the questions carefully, you will _____ reduce your chances of doing well on the final exam.

   a. dilatory   b. diligent   c. docile   d. drastic

7. Eight days after the Nazis' _____ signing of a ten-year nonaggression pact with the Soviet Union, Germany invaded Poland on September 1, 1939.

   a. disparity   b. elite   c. duplicity   d. empathy

8. Ashley chose Samuel Taylor Coleridge's _____ poem "Kubla Khan" as the subject of her three-page essay of literary interpretation and analysis.

   a. duplicity   b. enigma   c. eclectic   d. enclave

9. While India was still a colony, Mohandas K. Gandhi led nonviolent protests—including marches, boycotts, and hunger strikes—against Britain's _____ rule.

   a. elite   b. enigma   c. disparity   d. discourse

10. Medical studies have proved the _____ and safety of immunization therapy for people who have shown extreme sensitivity to bee stings.

    a. efficacious   b. effete   c. eminent   d. elite

11. Our debaters were elated by the complete _____ of their opponents' team.

    a. divulge   b. emanate   c. discomfit   d. embellish

12. It was Miguel de Cervantes, not Benjamin Franklin, who first said, "_____ is the mother of good fortune."

    a. dilapidated   b. docile   c. dire   d. diligent

13. In order to carry out their work, food relief agencies try to get us to _____ with the plight of malnourished and starving people all over the world.

    a. disparity   b. elite   c. enigma   d. empathy

14. In 1972, Congress passed the Equal Rights Amendment aimed at ending _____ on the basis of sex, but the proposed amendment subsequently failed to be ratified by the required 38 states.

    a. divulge   b. discriminate   c. emulate   d. emanate

15. In physics class, our professor demonstrated the use of the Geiger counter, which measures the _____ of radiation from cosmic rays and radioactive substances.

    a. embellish   b. emulate   c. emanate   d. elicit

16. Newspaper reporters are supposed to write accurate, objective, factual reports without any _____ or subjective judgments.

    a. discomfit   b. discourse   c. emulate   d. embellish

17. Malaria, an infectious disease _____ to the tropics, is transmitted to humans by mosquitoes.

    a. eminent   b. endemic   c. efficacious   d. emaciated

18. After serving two terms in the House of Representatives, she is _____ qualified to run as a candidate for the U.S. Senate.

    a. drastic   b. eminent   c. diligent   d. dilatory

19. In Greek mythology, Apollo gives Cassandra the power to predict the future but then decrees that no one will believe her _____ prophecies.

    a. dire   b. dilapidated   c. endemic   d. dormant

20. By a large margin, voters defeated the candidate whose TV ad campaign depended solely on the _____ of his opponent.

    a. discriminate   b. divulge   c. disparage   d. emanate

Lesson 15

161. entice — 175. exigency

---

161. **en·tice**   *verb*   ĕn-tīs′

[*enticier* (Old French) "set on fire"; from *in* (Latin), "in" + *titio* (Latin), "firebrand"]

Definition: To lead on by arousing hope or desire.

Only the offer of a tremendous increase in salary could **entice** me into leaving my present job.

Related Forms: (*noun*) enticement; (*adjective*) enticing

Synonyms: (*verbs*) tempt, lure, allure, coax, inveigle, beguile, seduce

Antonyms: (*verbs*) repel, repulse, scare off, frighten away

Related Phrases: seductive charms, a beguiling manner, bait the hook, sweet-talk, soft-soap, rope into

---

162. **en·treat**   *verb*   ĕn-trēt′

[*entraitier* (Old French), "deal with; plead with"; from *en* (Old French), "in" + *traitier* (Old French), "deal, treat"]

Definition: To ask or petition earnestly.

The defense attorney **entreated** the jury to weigh *all* the evidence carefully and objectively before reaching a verdict.

Related Form: (*noun*) entreaty

Synonyms: (*verbs*) implore, beg, beseech, plead for, urge, importune, press for

Related Phrase: cap in hand

---

163. **en·vis·age**   *verb*   ĕn-vĭz′-ĭj

[*envisager* (French), "imagine"; from *en* (French), "in" + *visage* (French), "face"]

Definition: To have a mental image of something, especially when the thing does not yet exist; to conceive of.

I find it very difficult to **envisage** the kind of society that the Greek philosopher Plato once dreamt of creating.

From his writings it is clear that Thomas Jefferson **envisaged** an America made up of small independent farmers dedicated to hard work and egalitarian principles.

Synonyms: (*verbs*) envision, visualize, picture, imagine

164. ep·i·thet   *noun*   ĕp'-ə-thĕt

[*epitheton* (Greek), "an addition"; from *epi* (Greek), "on" + *tithenai* (Greek), "put, place"]

Definition:

a. A word or phrase used to describe or characterize someone or something. (The expression need not be derogatory.)

Some English kings, such as William the Conqueror and Richard the Lion-Hearted, are better known by their informal **epithets** than by their official titles.

To fill out a line of verse, Homer often employs a stock **epithet**— for example, "wine-dark" for the sea.

b. A term of abuse or contempt.

The irate motorist shouted a few choice **epithets** at the driver of the car that had cut him off.

Synonyms: (*nouns*) characterization, designation, appellation, label, nickname, moniker, handle; curse, oath, obscenity

Related Phrases: badmouth someone, hurl brickbats at, mudslinging

165. e·qua·nim·i·ty   *noun*   ē-kwə-nĭm'-ə-tē *or* ĕk-wə-nĭm'-ə-tē

[*aequanimitas* (Latin), "evenness of temper"; from *aequus* (Latin), "even; equal" + *animus* (Latin), "mind"]

Definition: Calmness or evenness of temper.

A true stoic, Abraham Lincoln tried to bear reverses of fortune with dignity and **equanimity**.

Synonyms: (*nouns*) composure, self-composure, placidity, tranquility, serenity, sangfroid, unexcitability, imperturbability, unflappability, self-possession, nonchalance

Antonyms: (*nouns*) excitability, fretfulness, agitation, distress, hysteria

Related Phrases: mental (or emotional) stability, presence of mind

166. eq·ui·ta·ble   *adjective*   ĕk'-wə-tə-bəl

[*equitable* (French), "fair, just"; from *equite* (Old French), "justice"; from *aequus* (Latin), "even, equal"]

Definition: Fair or just.

The owner of the company was satisfied that the distribution of raises and bonuses had been as **equitable** as possible.

Related Forms: (*adjective*) inequitable; (*adverb*) equitably; (*noun*) equity

Usage Note:

Do not confuse *equitable* with *equable*, which means "unvarying" or "tranquil."

Synonyms: (*adjectives*) impartial, unbiased, evenhanded

Antonyms: (*adjectives*) unfair, unjust, biased, partial; unreasonable, lopsided, one-sided, uneven

167. er·u·dite *adjective* ĕr'-yŏŏ-dīt *or* ĕr'-ŏŏ-dīt

[*erudire, eruditus* (Latin), "take the roughness out of, polish"; from *e* (Latin), "out of" + *rudis* (Latin), "rough, rude"]

Definition: Deeply learned, especially in a specialized area.

Lord Chesterfield once advised his son never to appear more **erudite** than the people he was with.

Last night Professor Maurice Lenkowski presented an **erudite**, yet entertaining, lecture on the early history of aviation in this country.

Related Forms: (*noun*) erudition; (*adverb*) eruditely

Synonyms: (*adjectives*) scholarly, profound, knowledgeable, informed

Antonyms: (*adjectives*) ignorant, uninformed

Related Phrases: a savant, a pundit, a maven, a walking encyclopedia, highbrow, an ignoramus, lowbrow

168. es·o·ter·ic *adjective* ĕs-ə-tĕr'-ĭk

[*esoterikos* (Greek), "inner"; from *eso* (Greek), "within"]

Definition:
  a. Understood by or intended for only a select few.

   Only the members of the executive committee know all the **esoteric** rites involved in the initiation ceremonies of our fraternity.

  b. Difficult to understand.

   "When those two computer programmers began to talk shop, the conversation became awfully **esoteric**," Molly remarked. "Yes," I replied, "I wasn't even sure that they were still speaking English!"

Related Form: (*adverb*) esoterically

Synonyms: (*adjectives*) occult, secret, confidential, private; mysterious abstruse, recondite, arcane, incomprehensible, unfathomable, cryptic, inscrutable, impenetrable

Antonyms: (*adjectives*) popular, exoteric; intelligible, accessible, crystal clear, comprehensible

Related Phrases: not for public consumption, insiders, privileged information

Usage Note:
The adjective *exoteric,* derived from the Greek word for "external," has a number of meanings, of which "less secret or confidential" (e.g., an *exoteric* rite") and "readily comprehensible" (e.g., an *exoteric* doctrine") are perhaps the most common.

169. eth·i·cal   *adjective*   ĕth'-ĭ-kəl

[*ethikos* (Greek), "moral"; from *ethos* (Greek), "custom, moral character"]

Definition: In accordance with accepted principles of right and wrong.

Although we cannot say outright that their sales techniques are illegal, we are prepared to argue that they are not **ethical**.

Related Forms: (*nouns*) ethicalness, ethicality, ethics, ethic, ethos; (*adjective*) unethical

Phrases: the Puritan work ethic, ethical drugs, the ethos of a people, the revolutionary ethos

Usage Notes:

a. *Ethics* is the branch of philosophy concerned with the general nature of morals and the specific moral choices facing the individual. It is also sometimes called *moral philosophy*.

b. An *ethic* is a principle of right or moral behavior or a set of such principles. The phrase *Puritan work ethic* refers to the fundamental belief in the value of hard work that was a basic part of the Puritan outlook on life.

c. An *ethos* is the set of fundamental attitudes, beliefs, and values that characterize a particular group or culture. Another word for this is *mores*, though today we would probably use *mind-set* instead. *Ethos* also indicates a governing principle or central idea, as in the phrase "the revolutionary *ethos*."

d. In such phrases as "*ethical* drugs," *ethical* indicates that the item is distributed solely through the medical profession.

Synonyms: (*adjectives*) moral, virtuous, honorable, decent, upright, honest, righteous, principled, correct, proper

Antonyms: (*adjectives*) unfair, unjust, immoral, unscrupulous, dishonorable, discreditable, unsportsmanlike, unprofessional

Related Phrases: fair play, a lack of principles, dirty pool, hit someone below the belt

170. eth·nic   *adjective*   ĕth'-nĭk

[*ethnikos* (Greek), "foreign"; from *ethnos* (Greek), "people, nation"]

Definition: Relating to a small but distinct social group within the population. (The group in question is usually distinguished from the rest of the population by its particular religious, racial, national, or cultural character.)

The population of a pluralistic society is made up of many different **ethnic** groups from many different parts of the world.

Phrases: ethnic food, ethnic pride, the ethnic vote

Related Forms: (*nouns*) ethnicity, ethnology

Usage Note:

Ethnic is sometimes used as a noun to indicate a member of a particular ethnic group. This usage, however, is decidedly informal.

An ethnologist at work in rural central India. *Ethnology* is the science that deals with the individual cultures that make up the human family and their socioeconomic systems. It also concerns itself with the factors that bring about cultural growth and change.

171. **eu-phe-mism**   *noun*   yōō'-fə-mĭz-əm

[*euphemismos* (Greek), "euphemism"; from *euphemia* (Greek), "use of good words"; from *eu* (Greek), "good, well" + *pheme* (Greek), "speech"]

Definition: The substitution of a relatively inoffensive term for one that is considered too harsh, unpleasant, or blunt.

If we know that a person has lied repeatedly, why don't we say so, instead of using **euphemisms** such as "stretched the truth"?

Related Form: (*adjective*) euphemistic

172. **ex-ac-er-bate**   *verb*   ĕg-zăs'-ĕr-bāt   *or*   ĕk-săs-ĕr-bāt

[*exacerbare, exacerbatus* (Latin), "make harsh"; from *ex* (Latin), "completely" + *acerbus* (Latin), "harsh, bitter"]

Definition: To increase the bitterness or severity of; to irritate.

His stubborn refusal to follow the doctor's orders has done nothing but **exacerbate** his already serious medical problems.

"I don't think the proposal will do much to alleviate our present economic woes," the senator remarked, "but it may **exacerbate** them."

Related Form: (*noun*) exacerbation

Synonyms: (*verbs*) aggravate, worsen, intensify

Antonyms: (*verbs*) lessen, moderate, temper, mitigate, mollify, allay, assuage, soothe, alleviate, palliate

Related Phrases: add fuel to the fire, stoke the flames, add insult to injury, rub salt in an open wound; pour oil on troubled waters

229

173. **ex·alt** *verb* ĕg-zôlt′ *or* ĭg-zôlt′

[*exaltare* (Latin), "lift up"; from *ex* (Latin), "out, up" + *altus* (Latin), "high"]

Definition: To elevate in power, position, character, or the like.

The Old Testament tells us that righteousness **exalts** a people but that evil debases it.

From truly humble beginnings, Cardinal Woolsey rose to one of the most **exalted** positions in English politics.

Related Forms: (*adjective*) exalted; (*noun*) exaltation

Usage Note:
Do not confuse *exalt* with *exult,* which means "rejoice" or "feel a sense of joy or satisfaction over some success."

Synonyms: (*verbs*) ennoble, uplift, upgrade

Antonyms: (*verbs*) debase, degrade, demote, humble, abase

174. **ex·em·pla·ry** *adjective* ĕg-zĕm′-plə-rē *or* ĭg-zĕm′-plə-rē

[*exemplaire* (Old French), "model"; from *exemplum* (Latin), "example"]

Definition:
a. Worthy of imitation.

The dean of students congratulated the members of the senior class on their **exemplary** behavior at the prom.

b. Serving as a model, illustration, or warning.

"I plan to mete out **exemplary** punishment to a few of the mutineers," the general said. "That, I believe, will induce the rest to return to their duty without further resistance."

Related Form: (*noun*) exemplar

Synonyms: (*adjectives*) model, sterling; commendable, meritorious, laudable; (*nouns*) paragon, epitome, archetype, prototype

Related Phrases: ne plus ultra, beau idéal

Exemplar

An exemplar is a model that is worthy of imitation. For example, in medieval times, Sir Galahad (*see illustration*) was the exemplar of the knightly virtues, especially purity and nobility. *Exemplar* is also used to indicate both the original or archetype of something and a typical representative of it.

230

175. ex-i-gen-cy   *noun*   ĕk'-sə-jən-sē

[*exigens* (Latin), "demanding"; from *exigere, exactus* (Latin), "drive out; demand"]

Definition: A state of urgency or a situation demanding immediate attention; the pressing needs caused by such a crisis.

"The **exigencies** of the situation demand that we curtail all unnecessary expenditures immediately," the chairman of the board announced yesterday.

Related Forms: (*noun*) exigence; (*adjective*) exigent; (*adverb*) exigently

Usage Note:
As the illustrative sentence given above suggests, *exigency* is frequently used in the plural with the meaning "pressing needs" or "urgent requirements."

Synonyms: (*nouns*) emergency, crisis; needs, demands, requirements

Related Phrases: in a tight fix, in hot water, a hot spot, a troubleshooter

Using the Words

Exercise I.   Syllabication and Pronunciation

Syllabicate the following words correctly, and place the major stress mark (') after the syllable that is accented when the word is pronounced.

1. esoteric	4. epithet	7. exigency
2. ethnic	5. erudite	8. entice
3. euphemism	6. exacerbate	9. ethical

Exercise II.   Words Out of Context

In each of the following groups, select the item that best expresses the meaning of the numbered word at the left.

1. entice   **a.** repel   **b.** tilt   **c.** force   **d.** exist   **e.** tempt

2. esoteric   **a.** intoxicated   **b.** agitated   **c.** unfair
               d. incomprehensible   **e.** interesting

3. envisage   **a.** feature   **b.** deceive   **c.** forget   **d.** offer
               e. visualize

4. ethical   **a.** morally correct   **b.** mildly amusing
              c. clearly wrong   **d.** emotionally stable
              e. deeply learned

5. exacerbate   **a.** alleviate   **b.** intensify   **c.** urge   **d.** imagine
                  e. humble

6. entreat   **a.** coddle   **b.** repulse   **c.** beg   **d.** downgrade
                       e. clarify

7. exalt   **a.** rejoice   **b.** uplift   **c.** question   **d.** pursue
                       e. upset

Exercise III.   Completing Sentences

Complete each of the following sentences or pairs of sentences by selecting the most appropriate word from the group of words given below. Use each word only once. Make any adjustments that are necessary to fit the words into the sentences properly.

exemplary	equitable	erudite
equanimity	euphemism	epithet
entice	exigencies	ethnic

1. "It is one thing to offer constructive criticism of me and my administration," the president remarked. "It is quite another to shower us with empty _____ and meaningless verbal abuse."

2. *Pass away* is a common _____ for *die*.

3. The _____ of an overloaded business schedule prevented my dad from taking his annual vacation last year.

4. "Emma is an _____ employee," the letter of recommendation read, "whose performance over the years might well serve as a model for any budding young executive."

5. Though Renaissance history is only a hobby with him, he is as _____ in the subject as any professional scholar.

6. Though I think of myself as an American, my family is of Polish origin, and I am proud of my _____ heritage.

7. "Someone who is wise will try to bear even the most appalling misfortune with _____," he observed. "Someone who is silly will be devastated by the slightest setback."

8. Joe seems satisfied that his present salary arrangements are _____, but I don't think they're at all fair.

Exercise IV.   Synonyms and Antonyms

Classify each of the following pairs of words as **S** for **synonyms** or **A** for **antonyms**.

1. ethical—immoral
2. alleviate—exacerbate
3. debase—exalt
4. implore—entreat
5. lure—entice

6. esoteric—abstruse
7. uninformed—erudite
8. equanimity—excitability
9. unfair—equitable
10. envisage—picture

Exercise V.   Word Roundup

1. With or without the aid of a dictionary, define each of the following colorful expressions.

   a. soft-soap
   b. bad-mouth someone
   c. hit below the belt
   d. mudslinging
   e. rub salt in an open wound
   f. pour oil on troubled waters
   g. ne plus ultra
   h. in hot water

2. Explain the difference between the items in each of the following word pairs.

   a. equitable—equable
   b. exalt—exult

3. What is a *savant?* a *pundit?* an *ignoramus?* What do *highbrow* and *lowbrow* mean?

4. What is *privileged information?* Who might *insiders* be?

5. Name a *hot spot* in the world today. What does a *troubleshooter* do?

6. Both *moniker* and *handle* are slang expressions. What do they mean?

7. Define or explain each of the following:

   a. the Puritan work ethic
   b. moral philosophy
   c. the ethos of a people
   d. ethical drugs

8. With what does the science of *ethnology* concern itself? What does an *ethnologist* do?

9. What does the phrase *a pluralistic society* mean? What relationship does it have to *a melting pot?*

10. What is a *paragon?* the *epitome* of gracious living?

11. Define the expression *beau idéal.* From what foreign language does it come?

Exercise VI.   Framing Sentences

A. Use each of the following words in an original sentence.

1. equanimity
2. equitable
3. envisage
4. ethical
5. epithet
6. esoteric
7. exemplary
8. exigency
9. exacerbate

B. Give a **noun** form of each of these words, and use it in a short illustrative sentence.

1. entreat
2. erudite
3. entice
4. ethnic

C. Give an **adjective** form of each of these words, and use it in a short illustrative sentence.

1. exalt
2. euphemism

Dissecting the Words

1. The Latin prefix **e**, **ex**, and its Greek counterpart, **ec**, **ex**, are among the most common word elements used in English. They appear in several words studied in Lessons 14 and 15, including *eclectic, elicit, effete,* and *exalt.*

   The primary meanings of **e**, **ec**, **ex** are "out (of)" and "away (from)." These meanings occur in the following common English words:

expel (*ex*, "out" + *pel*, "drive")—to drive out

erupt (*e*, "out" + *rupt*, "break")—to break out

eject (*e*, "out" + *ject*, "throw")—to throw out

expire (*ex*, "out" + *spir*, "breathe")—to breathe one's last; to come to an end

efface (*ex*, "out" or "away" + *face*)—to erase; to make indistinct by rubbing

excise (*ex*, "out" or "away" + *cise*, "cut")—to cut out or remove

exegesis (*ex*, "out" + *hegeisthai*, "lead")—a critical explanation, interpretation, or analysis, especially of a part of the Bible

expropriate (*ex*, "away from" + *proprius*, "one's own" + *ate*, "make")—to deprive of what is rightfully one's own, especially for public use

exorcise (*ex*, "away" + *horos*, "oath")—to expel an evil spirit by means of a spell or magical incantation

Note that in some words such as *efface*, *ex* becomes **ef** before an *f*.

Other meanings of *e*, *ex* include "up," as in *exalt* ("to lift up") and "completely," as in *efficacious* ("completely capable of producing the desired effect") and *execute* ("to perform completely").

Other common words containing the prefix *e*, *ec*, *ex* include *excavation, exhale, emigrate, excerpt* (all from Latin), and *eclipse* (from Greek).

Archaeologists excavating a Native American village on the Snake River in the state of Washington.

2. The formative prefix **en** occurs in several words studied in this lesson, including *envisage* (Word 163). This prefix comes from the Latin word element *in*. It is called *formative* because it serves to transform nouns and adjectives into verbs that take objects. For example, when *en* is prefixed to the noun *courage*, the result is the verb *encourage*, meaning "to inspire with courage." When it is attached to the adjective *noble*, it produces the verb *ennoble*, meaning "to make noble or elevate in dignity."

Note that *en* becomes **em** before the letters *b*, *p*, and sometimes *m*, as in the words *empower* and *emboss*.

Root

The Latin root **fac, fic, fact, fect,** all meaning "do" or "make," appeared in the word *efficacious* (Word 148). This root and its derivatives occur in countless common English words, including:

benefactor—one who does good

facile—easy to do

feat—a great deed

factual—pertaining to facts ("things done"); real

edifice—a building or structure

feasible—capable of being done; workable

facilitate—to help in getting something done

Other common words containing this root and its derivatives are *infect*, *effect*, *affect*, *perfect*, and *confection*.

Suffix

The Latin root *fac, fic, fact, fect* also gives English the suffix **fy**, which appears in such words as *clarify* and *exemplify*. Note that the attachment of *fy* to a root results in a word with a sense of action or performance. For example:

beautify—to make beautiful

amplify—(literally, "make large")—to enlarge

ratify—to make valid

pacify—to make quiet or set at peace

terrify—to make to feel terror

edify—to enlighten

codify—to arrange in a code; to systematize

magnify—to enlarge or increase

deify—to worship or revere as a god

glorify—to exalt, to make more glorious than is actually the case

rectify—to correct

villify—to defame or denigrate

falsify—to misrepresent; to counterfeit

signify—to mean or betoken

Exercise

A. With or without the aid of a dictionary, select the word that best answers the following questions relating to the prefix *e, ec, ex*.

1. Which of the following might be *eclipsed*?

    a. a luminary   b. a contingency   c. an extension

2. Which of the following might be *excised*?

    a. a mendicant   b. an abrogation   c. a paragraph

3. Which of the following might be *eclectic*?

    a. an encomium   b. an anthology   c. an ovation

4. Which of the following might be *effaced* by time?

    a. capitulations   b. recollections   c. denouements

B. With or without the aid of a dictionary, define each of the following words. Then show how the prefix *e, ec, ex* affects its overall meaning.

1. emanate
2. exegesis
3. elicit
4. efficacious
5. exacerbate
6. exalt

C. Attach the formative prefix *en* to each of the following nouns or adjectives, and define the resulting combination. Then choose any **five**, and for each compose a short illustrative sentence.

1. dear
2. shrine
3. feeble
4. crust
5. trap
6. compass
7. circle
8. gulf
9. vision
10. rich
11. throne
12. danger

D. With or without the aid of a dictionary, complete each of the following exercises relating to the root *fac, fic, fact, fect*.

1. Define each of the following English words containing a form of *fac*. Then choose any **five**, and for each compose a short illustrative sentence.

    a. facsimile
    b. edifice
    c. factotum
    d. feasible
    e. facilitate
    f. factor
    g. infection
    h. faction
    i. faculty
    j. feat
    k. benefactor
    l. facile

2. What is the difference in meaning between *affect* and *effect*? Use each in a short illustrative sentence.

3. The expressions *ipso facto* (Latin) and *fait accompli* (French) both stem from the Latin root *fac*. Explain what each means.

E. Form an English verb from each of the following English or Latin words by adding the suffix *fy*. Then define the resulting combination.

1. humid
2. pretty
3. null
4. identity
5. solid
6. person
7. verse
8. magnum ("great")
9. verus ("true")

Working with Context Clues

Review the "Working with Context Clues" section in Lesson 14 (page 219) before you begin the following material.

Guideposts to Contrast Clues. Just as some linking expressions act as guideposts to the presence and location of restatement clues in sentence-completion exercises, so other linking expressions signal contrast clues. One such expression, *on the other hand,* was examined in Lesson 14 (page 219). Others include certain conjunctions (e.g., *but, however, though, although, even though, still*), adverbs (e.g., *not, unfortunately*), prepositions (e.g., *despite*), prepositional phrases (e.g., *in spite of*), and similar contrasting expressions (e.g., *some . . . others*).

Each of these items in some way binds together two contrasting or dissimilar sentences or sentence elements. Usually, the clue is contained in one of these contrasting elements, and the blank appears in the other. The linking expression points to the contrast clue by making the reader keenly aware of the difference between the element containing the blank and the element to which it is tied.

Study the following example of a sentence-completion exercise carefully. It contains both a contrast clue and a linking expression that points to this clue.

"A person has to have a strong stomach to work in a funeral parlor or morgue," I observed. "Handling corpses is not a job for the _____."

a. enigmatic b. squeamish c. indigent d. ambitious e. callous

Read over the two sentences carefully. The first informs you that work in a funeral parlor or morgue requires persons with a certain kind of temperament. The second says that such work is *not* for people with another kind of temperament. You are to specify what the second kind of temperament is by filling in the blank.

Thus, the word *not* in the second sentence indicates that these two sentences present contrasting information. In other words, it is your guidepost to the type of clue that you are likely to find, and that is a contrast clue.

But the word *not* does something else as well. It tells you where to look for your contrast clue. Since the blank is in the same sentence as the word *not,* you are likely to find your clue in the other sentence.

Look at this sentence. It indicates that work in a funeral parlor or morgue is only for people who have strong stomachs. Clearly, the phrase "has to have a strong stomach" is your clue. If work in a funeral parlor or morgue requires people with strong stomachs, then such work is clearly *not* for people who *don't* have strong stomachs. Now you know the sense of the word that goes in the blank. It means, roughly, "without a strong stomach."

Now look at the five items from which you are to select the word that goes in the blank. Only one of them means anything like "without a strong stomach." It is choice *b, squeamish,* which means "easily nauseated, disgusted, or offended" or "overly sensitive." This is clearly the word that goes in the blank.

None of the other choices fits the situation as outlined above. Note, however, choice *e, callous,* which, as you know, means "insensitive"—the opposite of the word you are looking for. It was intentionally included to confuse you and make selecting the right answer more difficult.

Exercise I

The following sentence-completion exercises contain contrast clues and linking expressions that point to these clues. Complete each exercise by selecting the word that makes the best sense in the sentence (or pair of sentences) as a whole. Underline the clue or clues that led you to make your choice.

1. In an angry community, an obvious and massive police presence may _____ tensions and promote violence rather than soothe tempers and restore calm.

   a. curtail   b. consummate   c. defer   d. exacerbate
   e. condone

2. Some laid-off workers manage to keep their spirits up while looking for new jobs; on the other hand, others quickly become _____ after a few disappointing attempts to find employment.

   a. dejected   b. avid   c. hopeful   d. blithe   e. callous

3. A progressive income tax is supposed to be a(n) _____ system of financing government; however, in reality the middle class bears an unfair portion of the tax burden.

   a. efficient   b. equitable   c. productive   d. cogent
   e. concise

4. Good teachers praise their students' honest efforts rather than _____ them for failing to achieve perfection.

   a. cajole   b. abhor   c. censure   d. ignore   e. baffle

5. While receiving unemployment benefits, the unemployed are supposed to be making _____ efforts to find work, but often they are sitting home idle and unmotivated.

   a. chronic   b. attrition   c. equanimity   d. diligent
   e. clandestine

Exercise II

The following exercise reviews everything you have learned about sentence-completion questions and context clues to this point. Complete each item in the exercise by selecting the word that makes the best sense in the sentence (or pair of sentences) as a whole. Underline the clue or clues that led you to your choice.

1. Although scientific research has clearly explained the causes of many diseases, the precise cause of the common cold is still a matter of _____.

   a. conjecture   b. attrition   c. equanimity   d. diligence
   e. exigency

2. Journalists often reveal what they have been told off the record, but they refuse to _____ the names of their sources.

   a. delete   b. divulge   c. accede   d. conceal   e. disparage

3. It is easy for a hard-nosed politician to become _____ to the needs of ordinary citizens.

   a. sensitive   b. attuned   c. callous   d. attracted
   e. enslaved

4. The heads of postrevolutionary governments often choose to pardon former enemies in hopes that a policy of _____ will permit all parties to focus on the future.

   a. amnesty   b. revenge   c. trade   d. anger   e. bravado

5. I am blameless in the eyes of the law, but in my own heart, I know I am to some extent _____ in the matter.

   a. affable   b. free   c. tired   d. sick   e. culpable

Enriching the Lesson

Exercise I.   Words Ending in *(o)logy*

One of the items discussed in this lesson was the term *ethnology*. This term contains the element *logy*, which comes from the Greek word *logos*, meaning "word." *Logy* and its related form *ology* have several meanings, one of which is "the study of" or "the science of." This meaning appears in many scientific and philosophical terms used in present-day English. These include *biology*, the study of life, and *etymology*, the study of word origins.

Listed below are a number of other English words ending in *logy* or *ology*. Some of these words use these elements in their primary sense of "the science (study) of"; others employ them in different meanings. With or without the aid of a dictionary, define each of the words on the list. Then indicate what *logy* or *ology* means in that particular word.

1. ornithology	11. cosmology	21. philology
2. theology	12. penology	22. tautology
3. ecology	13. sociology	23. toxicology
4. physiology	14. astrology	24. ophthalmology
5. terminology	15. pathology	25. entomology
6. archaeology	16. trilogy	26. osteology
7. paleontology	17. geology	27. chronology
8. ontology	18. anthropology	28. tetralogy
9. teleology	19. phraseology	29. parasitology
10. psychology	20. mythology	30. methodology

Exercise II.   Euphemisms: Sugarcoating the Pill

If you called your overweight friends *fat*, they would undoubtedly be offended; if you called them *pleasantly plump*, they would probably smile and feel flattered. A discreet person who wishes to be candid and yet not have such frankness cause offense will often find it desirable to substitute a **euphemism** (Word 171) to sugarcoat the harsh facts.

Euphemisms were a fetish in the Victorian era. Propriety then decreed that one should avoid referring to certain parts of the body by their natural or common names. Little Nell might well have swooned at the mention of such "coarse" words as *belly* and *corsets*, or even *legs*. In writing, the epithet *damned* appeared as *d--d*.

The death of Little Nell, the heroine of Charles Dickens's novel *The Old Curiosity Shop* (1841).

Shakespeare's plays were published in bowdlerized editions, purged of words deemed to be obscene or unrefined and thus objectionable. Understandably, the adjective *Victorian* has become synonymous with prudishness and exaggerated genteelism.

Although we are much less likely than the Victorians to be squeamish about such matters, we are still given to verbal evasions of reality. For example, a clerical assistant in an office may try to enhance his job by calling himself a "junior executive."

This "word game" has spread into many other areas. Since the existence of poverty in our society is an unwelcome fact, we may choose to refer to poor people as "disadvantaged," or "underprivileged," or "in the lower-income brackets." Elderly people are "senior citizens." Charity has become "welfare assistance." A mistake in spelling may be presented as an "orthographic irregularity."

Governmental officials and military leaders are certainly not beyond retreating into euphemisms. A breakdown in services resulting from inefficiency has been called an "organizational disruption." A military retreat after a crushing defeat may be termed a "rearrangement of forces."

At this point, a word of warning is in order. Although we may laugh at such flabby and sometimes dishonest evasions of reality, we should also realize that there *are* occasions when euphemisms and genteelisms can serve a useful purpose. They may be used to spare the feelings of people under severe strain or to soften harsh or gross realities which for some reason we are not prepared to face at a given time. Certainly, no harm is done if euphemisms are used selectively and with good judgment under such circumstances to raise the level of courtesy and consideration for others. But the key word is *selectively*. If we use euphemisms indiscriminately in place of plain, homely words, our language may become at best overrefined and at worst obscure and even ludicrous.

A. Below are two lists of corresponding words or expressions. Those in Column A are "Euphemistic or Genteel"; in Column B, "Realistic or Natural." In what context or under what circumstances might each of these expressions be appropriately used? Give examples of such usage.

Column A *Euphemistic or Genteel*	Column B *Realistic or Natural*
perspire	sweat
odor	smell
expectorate	spit
cinema	movies
financially embarrassed	broke
exaggerate	lie
boutique	shop
retire for the night	go to bed
deceased	dead

B. Each of the following expressions is sometimes used euphemistically as a substitute for a more familiar, down-to-earth term. Give a blunt equivalent in each case.

1. mortician
2. protective custody
3. hair supplementation
4. billiard academy
5. gratuity

6. cocktail lounge
7. termination of employment
8. tonsorial parlor
9. weight control
10. pugilistic encounter

Exercise III.   Expanding Your Word Power

The words listed below are not on the Basic Word List, but they were mentioned in passing in Lesson 15. All of them would make useful additions to your working vocabulary. Define each, give its etymology, list **two** synonyms and **two** antonyms (where possible), and use in a short illustrative sentence.

1. inveigle
2. repel
3. importune
4. envision
5. designation

6. stability
7. literate
8. composure
9. confidential
10. allay

11. cryptic
12. crisis
13. abase
14. commendable
15. hysteria

Lesson 16

176. exodus — 190. fetish

---

176. ex·o·dus   *noun*   ĕk'-sə-dəs

[*exodos* (Greek), "a going out"; from *ex* (Greek), "out" + *hodos* (Greek), "road, way"]

Definition: A departure, usually of large numbers of people.

The massacre in Burundi in 1994 was the main cause of the hurried **exodus** of population from that African nation.

Large-scale building projects are likely to cause the **exodus** of wildlife from a previously undeveloped area.

Synonyms: (*nouns*) flight, escape, migration, emigration, hegira

Antonyms: (*nouns*) arrival, influx, immigration

Moses, by Michelangelo

Flight Words

In both Latin and English, the second book of the Old Testament of the Bible is called Exodus. It recounts the departure of the Israelites (under the leadership of Moses) from Egypt during the time of the pharaohs, about 1260 B.C. The word *exodus* is actually Greek in origin, but the title of the Old Testament book helped it come into English. This is just one of the ways in which the Bible has influenced the growth of our vocabulary. Refer to page 204 for other examples.

In Arabic, the prophet Mohammed's departure from Mecca in A.D. 622 is called "Al Hijrat," which means "The Flight." The event is important in the Muslim world because it is regarded as the beginning of the Muslim era. It has importance in the English-speaking world as well. That is because it gave modern English a new word for "flight" or "exodus." The word is **hegira**, which is pronounced hĭ-jī'-rə or hĕj'ər-ə.

177. ex-o-tic   *adjective*   ĕg-zŏt'-ĭk
[*exotikos* (Greek), "foreign"; from *exo* (Greek), "outside"]

Definition: Foreign; charmingly unfamiliar or strikingly unusual.
"Australia is a fascinating continent full of strange and **exotic** wildlife," my Canadian friend remarked.

Phrases: an exotic plant, exotic foods

Synonyms: (*adjectives*) alien; striking, extraordinary

Antonyms: (*adjectives*) native, indigenous, endemic; commonplace, familiar, ordinary

178. ex-pe-di-ent   *adjective and noun*   ĕk-spē'-dē-ĕnt
[*expediens, expedientis*, "freeing, disentangling"; from *ex* (Latin), "out of" + *pes, pedis* (Latin), "foot"]

Definition:
a.   (*adjective*) Advantageous to one's interest or purpose.
"In solving this problem, we cannot simply do whatever is **expedient**," I protested. "We must make sure that the course of action we adopt is also ethical."

b.   (*noun*) An emergency course of action; a means to an end.
"We can overcome our present financial problems in a number of ways," the personnel manager remarked. "Cutting back on the staff is by no means the only **expedient** open to us."

Related Forms: (*noun*) expediency; (*adjective*) inexpedient

Synonyms: (*adjectives*) convenient, opportune, timely, practical; (*nouns*) device, scheme, design, stratagem, maneuver, stopgap

Antonyms: (*adjectives*) disadvantageous, unserviceable, unsuitable

179. ex-ploit   *verb:* ĕk-sploit'   *noun:* ĕk'-sploit
[*exploit, explait* (Old French), "achievement"; from *ex* (Latin), "out" + *plicare* (Latin), "fold"]

Definition:
a.   (*verb*) To use to the greatest possible advantage, often selfishly.
Working conditions have come a long way since the "bad old days," when it was customary to **exploit** the labor of children.

b.   (*noun*) A brilliant or heroic deed.
Because he took such pride in his wartime **exploits**, we thought it fitting to bury my grandfather in his army uniform.

Related Forms: (*nouns*) exploitation, exploiter; (*adjective*) exploitable

Synonyms: (*verbs*) capitalize on; (*nouns*) feat, heroics, coup, tour de force, derring-do

Related Phrases: cash in on, make the most of, take advantage of

180. ex-pound   *verb*   ĕk-spound' *or* ĭk-spound'

[*espo(u)ndre* (Old French), "put forth"; from *ex* (Latin), "out" + *ponere* (Latin), "put, place"]

Definition: To explain in detail.

In an influential book published in 1936, the English economist J. M. Keynes **expounded** his epoch-making theory of the causes of economic collapse.

I spent most of the evening listening to her **expound** her views on all sorts of interesting topics.

Related Forms: (*nouns*) exposition, exponent; (*adjective*) expository

Synonyms: (*verbs*) clarify, elucidate, explicate, delineate (Word 121)

Antonyms: (*verbs*) summarize, abstract, synopsize

Related Phrases: air one's views, in a nutshell, a thumbnail sketch

Exposition and Expository Writing,

Basically, the word *exposition* refers to the setting forth of meaning or intent in a clear and intelligible way. Nonetheless, the word has several technical usages that are worth knowing about. For example, to musicians, *exposition* indicates the opening section of a sonata or fugue, where the various musical themes that will be developed are first introduced. To dramatists, the word indicates the part of a play where the chief characters and overall theme are first presented. And to producers of public entertainments, it indicates a public exhibition of recent artistic or industrial developments.

Expository writing is the technical term for the kind of writing that is designed to set forth ideas or describe people and events in straightforward intelligible English. This is essentially the kind of writing that is necessary in all sorts of everyday situations. For example, a book review, a newspaper article, a business letter, and a chapter in a textbook all involve expository writing of one kind or another. Students, of course, are familiar with expository writing from the compositions, reports, and term papers that they do for school courses.

181. fab-ri-cate   *verb*   făb'-rĭ-kāt

[*fabricari, fabricatus* (Latin), "make, build"]

Definition:
  a.   To assemble or construct from separate parts.

  Philosophers have been **fabricating** new theories of the universe for thousands of years.

  b.   To make up with the intention of deceiving.

  "I don't believe that your account of the incident has any basis in fact," Mom said. "I think you **fabricated** it in order to avoid my displeasure."

Related Forms: (*nouns*) fabrication, fabricator; (*verb*) prefabricate

Prefabricate refers to a manufacturing process in which standardized parts or sections are mass-produced for shipment and assembly elsewhere. Thus, a prefabricated house is constructed out of ready-made sections that were manufactured in another place.

Synonyms: (*verbs*) produce, devise, manufacture, concoct, contrive, come up with, cook up

Related Phrases: a trumped-up charge; coin an excuse; make up out of whole cloth

182. **fa-ce-tious** *adjective* fə-sē′-shəs

[*facetieux* (Old French), "joking"; from *facetia* (Latin), "joke, jest"]

Definition: Not meant seriously; playful or humorous.

"Be careful what you say to him," I warned my sister. "He is so sensitive that he takes even a **facetious** remark to heart."

I didn't pay any attention to what he said because I could see that he was being **facetious**.

Related Forms: (*noun*) facetiousness; (*adverb*) facetiously

Synonyms: (*adjectives*) waggish, whimsical, joking, comic, frivolous, droll

Antonyms: (*adjectives*) serious, grave, solemn, sober, earnest, humorless

Related Phrases: a tongue-in-cheek remark, joshing, kidding; for real

183. **fac·sim·i·le**   *noun and adjective*   făk-sĭm'-ə-lē

[*fac simile* (Latin), "make (it) the same"; from *facere* (Latin), "do, make" + *similis, simile* (Latin), "same"]

Definition:
a. (*noun*) An exact copy.

Art books often contain surprisingly accurate full-color **facsimiles** of the paintings they discuss.

b. (*adjective*) Reproduced exactly.

Usually, a photocopy is in every respect a **facsimile** copy of the original from which it was made.

Synonyms: (*nouns*) replica, reproduction, duplicate

Related Phrases: a carbon copy, a chip off the old block; a mirror image

184. **fal·la·cy**   *noun*   făl'-ə-sē

[*fallacia* (Latin), "deceit, trick"; from *fallere* (Latin), "deceive"]

Definition:
a. Faulty reasoning; an error in logic.

"It shouldn't be too hard to shoot holes in his argument," I observed. "After all, the **fallacies** it contains are as plain as day."

b. A false or mistaken notion.

It's a **fallacy** to assume that all redheaded people have quick tempers.

Related Forms: (*adjective*) fallacious; (*noun*) fallaciousness

Synonyms: (*nouns*) mistake, flaw, fault, defect (Word 117), solecism

185. **fath·om**   *noun and verb*   făth'-əm

[*faethm* (Old English), "the distance between two outstretched arms"]

Definition:
a. (*noun*) A unit of length roughly equal to six feet and used primarily in the measurement of marine depths.

It might be difficult to raise a famous wreck like the *Titanic* because its remains lie under hundreds of **fathoms** of water.

b. (*verb*) To get to the bottom of; to understand.

For as long as human beings have been able to think, they have attempted to **fathom** the mysteries of the universe.

Related Forms: (*adjectives*) fathomable, unfathomable, fathomless

Synonyms: (*verbs*) sound, plumb, probe, delve, penetrate; ferret out, root out; divine, grasp, comprehend

186. fat-u-ous   *adjective*   făch'-ōō-wəs
[*fatuus* (Latin), "silly, foolish"]

Definition: Unconsciously foolish, stupid, or absurd.

It was such a **fatuous** remark that I almost burst out laughing when I heard it.

Phrases: a fatuous expression on one's face, a fatuous monarch

Related Forms: (*nouns*) fatuousness, fatuity

Synonyms: (*adjectives*) inane, vacuous, vapid, nonsensical, laughable, silly, ridiculous, ludicrous; wacky, goofy

Antonyms: (*adjectives*) sensible, intelligent, perceptive; acute, incisive; judicious

187. fea-si-ble   *adjective*   fē'-zə-bəl
[*faisible* (Old French), "workable"; from *facere* (Latin), "do, make"]

Definition: Possible; both doable and workable.

"I would really like to invite everyone I know to my party," LeVar remarked. "Unfortunately, that idea just isn't **feasible** because my home is too small to hold all my friends."

Phrases: a feasible solution, a feasible plan, a feasible proposal

Related Forms: (*adjective*) unfeasible; (*nouns*) feasibility; feasibleness

Synonyms: (*adjectives*) practicable, practical, usable, realistic

Antonyms: (*adjectives*) impossible, unworkable, impracticable, impractical

Related Phrases: within the realm of possibility, out of the question

A Useful Distinction

Practicable indicates that something is capable of being done. *Practical* indicates that it is not only capable of being done but also sensible or worthwhile. Thus, it may be practicable to travel to and from the office by pogo stick, but the idea certainly doesn't sound practical.

Fetish

A *fetish* is an inanimate object that is believed to possess magical powers of some sort. Fetishes may be natural objects (for instance, an unusual stone) or man-made items (for example, a small carved image). Many peoples, both ancient and modern, have employed fetishes; and items thought to be fetishes of one kind or another have been found in prehistoric grave sites in many parts of the world. The use of fetishes is still fairly widespread today. Do you know someone who possesses a lucky rabbit's foot?

A group of Native American fetishes.

188. feign   *verb*   fān
[*feindre* (Old French), "pretend"; from *fingere* (Latin), "shape, form"]

Definition: To pretend or give a false appearance of.
"He wasn't really sick," I said. "He just **feigned** illness in order to get out of school early."

Phrases: feign sleep, feign authorship of, feign knowledge of

Related Forms: (*adjective*) feigned; (*noun*) feint

Synonyms: (*verbs*) fake, sham, simulate

Related Phrases: sail under false colors, pass oneself off as, pose as; a wolf in sheep's clothing, a humbug, an ignis fatuus; the real McCoy

189. fe-lic-i-tous   *adjective*   fĭ-lĭs'-ĭ-təs *or* fə-lĭs'-ə-təs
[*felicity* + *ous*; from *felicitas* (Latin), "happiness"; from *felix, felicis* (Latin), "happy"]

Definition: Agreeably suited to the purpose or occasion; aptly or gracefully expressed.
"I know you don't consider yourself much of a diplomat," Mom told me. "Still, I think you handled that very delicate problem in a truly **felicitous** manner."
"Perhaps the phrasing of your letter isn't particularly **felicitous**," I said, "but the sentiments you express are indeed appropriate."

Related Forms: (*nouns*) felicity, felicitousness; (*adverb*) felicitously; (*verb*) felicitate

Synonyms: (*adjectives*) appropriate, suitable, fitting, apropos, apposite, apt; graceful, agreeable, seemly, becoming; well chosen, well put

Antonyms: (*adjectives*) graceless, unseemly, unbecoming, unsuitable; awkward, inept

Related Phrases: to the point, on target, ad rem; wide of the mark

190. **fet-ish**　　　*noun*　　　fĕt'-ĭsh　*or*　fē'-tĭsh

[*feitiço* (Portuguese), "charm"; from *facere, factus* (Latin), "do, make"]

Definition:

   a. An object believed among primitive peoples to have magical powers.

   Down in the main square, a wrinkled old peasant woman sold charms and **fetishes** to ward off the evil eye.

   b. An object of unreasonably excessive attention or reverence.

   It is one thing to be concerned about discipline; it is quite another to make a **fetish** of it.

Synonyms:　(*nouns*) charm, amulet, talisman; fixation, obsession (Word 283), preoccupation; compulsion

Related Phrases:　an idée fixe; a hang-up; get a complex about; a monomaniac; a sacred cow

Using the Words

Exercise I.　Parts of Speech

Indicate the part of speech of each of the following words. In some cases, two answers are correct.

1. exotic
2. facsimile
3. expound
4. exploit
5. expedient
6. fabricate
7. fathom
8. exodus
9. feasible

Exercise II.　Words in Phrases

In each of the following groups select the item that best expresses the meaning of the *italicized* word in the introductory phrase.

1. *feign* illness
    a. cure　b. prevent　c. investigate　d. pretend　e. cause

2. *fatuous* comments
    a. perceptive　b. interesting　c. silly　d. appropriate
    e. surprising

3. a *felicitous* remark
    a. well-known　b. well-worn　c. well-heeled　d. well-fed
    e. well-chosen

4. *exotic* dishes
    a. delightfully unfamiliar　b. outrageously expensive
    c. unusually sweet　d. woefully inadequate
    e. moderately priced

5. will do whatever is *expedient*

   a. fashionable b. advantageous c. easy d. enjoyable
   e. correct

6. *expound* a theory

   a. attack b. demolish c. improve d. investigate
   e. explain

7. *facsimile* copies of the document

   a. secondhand b. forged c. newly discovered d. exact
   e. famous

Exercise III. Completing Sentences

Complete each of the following sentences or pairs of sentences by selecting the most appropriate word from the group of words given below. Use each word only once. Make any adjustments that are necessary to fit the words into the sentences properly.

fallacy	fabricate	feasible
fathom	facetious	feign
exodus	exploit	fetish

1. "He is not interested in solving this problem quickly and intelligently," I said. "He is only interested in _____ the difficulties it has created to his own advantage."

2. "Let's get out of here," Sy said after we'd been in the museum only ten minutes. "All these strange idols and _____ give me the creeps!"

3. In *The Art of the Possible,* Golda Meir suggests that politics and diplomacy have one thing in common. They are both concerned with what is _____ rather than with what is ideal.

4. Fortunately, we were able to _____ a replacement for the missing article from a few short press releases and some government statistics.

5. "I've puzzled about it for days," Mom told Dad, "but I still can't _____ the motives behind young Tom's strange behavior lately."

6. The blatant anti-Semitism of the Nazi regime was wholly responsible for the tremendous _____ of Jews from Germany in the 1930s.

7. "Your conclusion isn't valid," I remarked, "because the argument leading up to it contains an obvious _____."

8. "This is a serious conversation," Jane protested. "Why do you insist on disrupting it by constantly making _____ remarks?"

Exercise IV.   Synonyms and Antonyms

A. In each of the following groups, select the two words that are most nearly **synonyms**.

1. a. overwhelm   b. clarify   c. imagine   d. elucidate
    e. manufacture

2. a. devise   b. escape   c. concoct   d. stumble
    e. pretend

3. a. solution   b. duplicate   c. salary   d. problem
    e. copy

4. a. charm   b. hobby   c. guilt   d. profession   e. amulet

5. a. migrate   b. understand   c. comprehend   d. create
    e. summarize

Now, for each pair of synonyms, supply a word from the Basic Word List for this lesson (Words 176–190) that means the **same** or **almost the same** thing.

B. In each of the following, select the item that is most nearly **opposite** in meaning to the numbered word at the left.

1. fatuous   a. honest   b. brave   c. intelligent
                    d. wealthy   e. famous

2. feasible   a. unworkable   b. unknown   c. unseen
                    d. unfaithful   e. unavoidable

3. facetious   a. awkward   b. usable   c. ridiculous
                    d. commonplace   e. serious

4. exodus   a. scheme   b. arrival   c. flaw   d. lie
                    e. copy

5. exotic   a. convenient   b. sensible   c. mistaken
                    d. native   e. comic

Exercise V.   Word Roundup

1. Explain the difference between the words in each of the following pairs.

    a. feint—faint   b. practical—practicable

2. What is a *hegira*? From what foreign language does the word come, and to what historical event did it originally refer?

3. Define each of the following words.
    a. solecism   c. humbug   e. monomaniac
    b. coup   d. heroics   f. exposition

4. Explain the meaning of each of the following colorful phrases.
    a. in a nutshell   d. a carbon copy
    b. a tongue-in-cheek remark   e. a tour de force
    c. deeds of derring-do   f. an idée fixe

Exercise VI. Framing Sentences

A. Use each of the following words in an original sentence that clearly illustrates its meaning.

1. exodus	4. exploit	7. fatuous
2. exotic	5. expound	8. felicitous
3. expedient	6. facsimile	9. fetish

B. Give an **adjective** form of each of these words, and use it in an original sentence.

1. fallacy   2. feign   3. fathom

C. Give a **noun** form of each of these words, and use it in an original sentence.

1. feasible   2. fabricate   3. facetious

Completing Verbal Analogies

"*A Is Primarily Concerned with* B." Another word relationship that frequently appears in the analogy sections of standardized vocabulary tests is "*A* is primarily concerned with *B*; *C* is primarily concerned with *D*." Here is an example of an analogy question involving this relationship. Try to determine the correct answer before you go on to read the explanation of it.

veterinarian : animals =
   a. druggist : addicts
   b. psychology : mind
   c. disputes : arbitrator
   d. warden : prisoners
   e. theologian : angels

The answer is *d*. A *warden* is primarily concerned with *prisoners*, just as a *veterinarian* is primarily concerned with *animals*.
   None of the other choices exhibits the same relationship as the key pair of words. A *druggist* is not primarily concerned with *addicts* (choice *a*), nor is a *theologian* primarily concerned with *angels* (choice *e*). Though an *arbitrator* is certainly concerned with *disputes* (choice *c*), *disputes* are not concerned with *arbitrators*. In other words, the two items in the pair come in the wrong order. Finally, *psychology* is indeed concerned with the *mind* (choice *b*), but the items in the pair are not parallel to the items in the key pair. *Psychology* indicates a science, not a person (as *veterinarian* does), and *mind* indicates a human faculty, not a type of creature (as *animals* does). Both choices *b* and *c* were intentionally included to confuse the student and make the selection of the right answer more difficult.

"*A Is a Part of* B." Another word relationship that appears in the analogy sections of standardized tests is "*A* is a part of *B*; *C* is a part of *D*." Here is an example of an analogy question involving this relationship. Try to determine the correct answer before you read the explanation of it.

rung : ladder =
   a. cauldron : kettle
   b. saddle : stirrup
   c. apartment : room
   d. match : lighter
   e. step : staircase

The answer is *e*. A *step* is part of a *staircase*, just as a *rung* is part of a *ladder*.

None of the other choices exhibits the same relationship. A *cauldron* is not part of a *kettle* (choice *a*); it is a kind of kettle. In other words, the two words mean roughly the same thing. A *saddle* is not part of a *stirrup* (choice *b*), though a stirrup is part of a saddle. Similarly, an apartment is not part of a *room* (choice *c*), though a room is part of an apartment or may even be an apartment. In other words, the items in choices *b* and *c* come in the wrong order. Finally, a *match* is not part of a *lighter* (choice *d*), though it serves the same function as a lighter. In other words, these items are complementary, since they indicate two different ways of producing a flame.

Parallelism. In the explanation of the example under "A is primarily concerned with B," it was pointed out that the items in the answer you select should always be as parallel as possible to the items in the key pair. If they are not, you have probably made the wrong choice and should reconsider your answer.

Exercise I

Complete each of the following analogies based on the word relationships "A is primarily concerned with B" and "A is a part of B."

1. **chapter : novel =**
   a. pen : pencil
   b. dictionary : word
   c. essay : composition
   d. act : drama
   e. paragraph : sentence

2. **dentist : teeth =**
   a. ornithologist : ears
   b. surgeon : bruises
   c. ophthalmologist : eyes
   d. feet : chiropodist
   e. pharmacy : medicine

3. **deck : ship =**
   a. church : pew
   b. field : meadow
   c. chair : table
   d. bookcase : shelf
   e. floor : house

4. **legislator : lawmaking =**
   a. lawfulness : judge
   b. citizen : law-abiding
   c. criminal : lawbreaker
   d. lawsuit : attorney
   e. police officer : law enforcement

5. **astronomy : stars =**
   a. archaeologist : antiquities
   b. zoology : animals
   c. archery : buildings
   d. philatelist : coins
   e. insects : entomology

6. **county : state =**
   a. tree : forest
   b. hive : bee
   c. voyage : trip
   d. continent : peninsula
   e. mare : stallion

Exercise II.

Compose **two** complete analogies involving the word relationship "*A* is primarily concerned with *B*" and **two** involving "*A* is a part of *B*."

Exercise III

The following items review what you have so far learned about analogy questions. Complete each.

1. **augment : increase** :: horrify :
   (*arbitrate, appall, condone, atone, deviate*)

2. **circuitous : direct** :: skimpy :
   (*culpable, scant, devoid, copious, deferential*)

3. **failure : chagrin** :: success :
   (*disgust, puzzlement, elation, apathy, frustration*)

4. **cantankerous : affability** :: disgruntled :
   (*ability, wisdom, courage, honesty, contentment*)

5. **like : adore** :: dislike :
   (*loathe, lithe, lathe, loath, lath*)

Working with Context Clues

Inference Clues. The third general type of context clue you are likely to meet in the sentence-completion sections of standardized vocabulary tests is an **inference clue**. In an inference clue, the whole situation outlined in the sentence or pair of sentences suggests the sense of the word that goes in the blank. For that reason, the reader must *infer* the word that is wanted, often by recognizing familiar situations, drawing on past knowledge and experience, or applying simple logic. As you can see, an inference clue is a broader and more indirect type of hint than a restatement clue or a contrast clue.

Here is an example of a sentence-completion exercise that involves an inference clue. Try to determine the correct answer before you read the explanation of it given below.

Ninety-year-old Annie Blakeley's *The Lowing Herd Winds Slowly O'er the Lea* presents the reader with a touching picture of life in _____ Kansas at the turn of the 20th century.

   a. industrialized   b. rural   c. maritime   d. urban   e. colonial

The answer is *b. rural.* Here's why.

The position of the blank indicates that you are looking for a descriptive adjective. A quick check of the five choices you are offered confirms this impression. Now you know what you need.

But you know something else as well. The blank appears immediately before the word *Kansas*. This suggests that Kansas will be of some value in determining the word that goes in the blank.

Now read the entire sentence carefully to determine what else it offers in the way of clues to the correct choice. The sentence concerns the content of a novel or memoir by a woman who grew up in Kansas around 1900. This suggests that the title of the book will be of some help in ascertaining the correct choice. The sentence also suggests that the part of the country mentioned (Kansas) and the time frame indicated (at the turn of the 20th century) may be of some use.

Now you know where the clues are likely to be. Notice that an understanding of the sense of the sentence and the application of simple logic were the governing factors in isolating the probable clues.

Reread the title of the 90-year-old woman's book carefully. It evokes a picture that immediately eliminates three of the five choices as the correct answer.

And what is that picture? It is a picture of a herd of cows moving slowly through a meadow. *Low* means the same thing as *moo*, so you know you are dealing with a herd of cows. *Lea* is an old poetic word for *meadow*.

Now, in what sort of setting would you be likely to find a herd of cows crossing a meadow? Certainly not in an *industrialized* area (choice *a*) or an *urban* center (choice *d*) or even a *maritime* community (choice *c*). These three items are clearly wrong, and you are down to two possibilities because cows would be found in both a *rural* and a *colonial* setting (choices *b* and *e*).

To determine which of the two remaining possibilities is correct, think about each in regard to the part of the country mentioned (Kansas) and the time frame indicated (around 1900). Kansas was primarily an agricultural area at the turn of the century, so *rural* (choice *b*) seems to fit. However, Kansas was never one of the 13 colonies and by 1900 had long since become a full-fledged member of the Union. Clearly, *colonial* (choice *e*) won't work, so *rural* (choice *b*) must be the correct answer. And, of course, it is.

Notice that determining the correct answer to this sentence-completion exercise depended on a combination of utilizing the whole context, recognizing familiar situations, drawing on past knowledge, and applying simple logic. These are essentially the ingredients that go into the successful solution of the type of sentence-completion exercise that involves an inference clue.

Exercise I

The following sentence-completion exercises contain inference clues. Complete each by selecting the word that makes the best sense in the sentence (or pair of sentences) as a whole. Underline the clue or clues that led you to make your choice.

1. *Sanitary engineer* is an example of a(n) _____ for *janitor* or *garbage collector*.

   a. euphemism   b. criterion   c. qualification   d. epithet
   e. advertisement

2. As my polite request failed to _____ any response from my noisy neighbors, I decided to call the police.

   a. abet   b. buttress   c. curtail   d. stop   e. elicit

3. Self-help groups such as Narcotics Anonymous try to help people overcome their _____ to drugs.

   a. sensitivity   b. fetish   c. addiction   d. revulsion
   e. anathema

4. Only a truly _____ person could forgive a friend who deliberately spread lies about him and tried to ruin his reputation.

   a. benign   b. boisterous   c. felicitous   d. fatuous
   e. callous

5. Public officials who routinely tell half-truths to their constituents destroy their own _____.

   a. anachronism   b. equanimity   c. credibility   d. duplicity
   e. fallacy

Exercise II

The following exercises review everything you have learned about sentence-completion questions and context clues to this point. Complete each item in the exercise by selecting the word that makes the best sense in the sentence (or pair of sentences) as a whole. Underline the clue or clues that led you to make your choice.

1. Whenever I am in a lighthearted and carefree frame of mind, I find myself humming a _____ tune.

   a. banal   b. boisterous   c. blithe   d. belligerent
   e. bizarre

2. Many people cannot speak well before a large audience, but they can be surprisingly _____ when speaking in small, informal settings.

   a. effete   b. bland   c. elite   d. concise   e. articulate

3. Writers often complain that editors cut out important sections of their manuscripts without asking their permission to _____ the material.

   a. allude   b. delete   c. review   d. defer   e. deviate

4. In most corporations, you have to work hard to get ahead. Advancement goes to those who are most _____.

   a. efficacious   b. affable   c. diligent   d. erudite
   e. candid

5. The corporate president observed that although the financial officer's proposal would reduce some of the company's cash-flow problems, unfortunately it would also _____ others.

   a. exacerbate   b. circumvent   c. entice   d. atrophy
   e. delineate

Enriching the Lesson

Exercise I   Loan Words from Faraway Places

The inclusion of the word *exotic* in this lesson brings to mind the fact that some of the vocabulary of present-day English comes from very striking and unusual sources. Listed below are a number of these unusual loan words. With or without the aid of a dictionary, define each and tell where it comes from. Then choose any **five**, and for each compose an original sentence.

1. kowtow	8. taboo	15. juggernaut
2. amuck	9. loot	16. paradise
3. tycoon	10. mogul	17. mumbo jumbo
4. powwow	11. tariff	18. mufti
5. zombie	12. pariah	19. voodoo
6. thug	13. totem	20. nadir
7. boomerang	14. caucus	21. oasis

Exercise II.   The Language of Logic

One of the words studied in this lesson is *fallacy*, which is a technical term in the language of logic. Below are listed some other words and expressions used in the study of logic. With or without the aid of a dictionary, define each.

1. logic	6. induction
2. syllogism	7. deduction
3. major premise	8. valid
4. minor premise	9. invalid
5. conclusion	10. pathetic fallacy

Exercise III.   "Diehards"

This lesson includes the word *fathom*, which might be termed a "diehard" in the sense that it goes back, practically without change, to Old English. Old English, you will recall, represents the earliest stage of our language. It was used in England in the period before the Norman Conquest of 1066.

Diehards such as *fathom* make up an important and sizable segment of the vocabulary of present-day English. A few examples of other diehard expressions are listed below. With or without the aid of a dictionary, define each.

1. mirth	6. threat	11. quench
2. seethe	7. spurn	12. forbear
3. din	8. fret	13. mood
4. slough	9. mete (*verb*)	14. beckon
5. quell	10. swarthy	15. hurdle

Exercise IV.   The Language of the Mind

Fetish, studied in this lesson, is frequently used in connection with psychology, which is the science that deals with the workings of the mind and with human behavior. The 20th century witnessed major developments in the science of psychology, and for many years there has been great popular interest in it. As a result, many psychological terms have become part of everyday speech and writing.

Listed below are a number of terms and expressions drawn from the language of psychology. With or without the aid of a dictionary, define each.

1. neurotic	6. split personality	11. introvert
2. psychosomatic	7. maladjustment	12. extrovert
3. paranoid	8. psychic	13. schizophrenic
4. subconscious	9. complex	14. hypochondriac
5. extrasensory	10. psychotic	15. burnout

Exercise V.   Expanding Your Word Power

The words listed below are not on the Basic Word List, but they were mentioned in passing in Lesson 16. All of them would make useful additions to your working vocabulary. Define each, give its etymology, list **two** synonyms and **two** antonyms (where possible), and use in a short illustrative sentence.

1. influx	6. synopsis	11. replica
2. preoccupation	7. explicate	12. solecism
3. stratagem	8. devise	13. delve
4. talisman	9. earnest	14. simulate
5. feat	10. whimsical	15. apposite

Related Forms in Context

Beneath each sentence below are four words introduced in Lesson 15 or 16. Review the related forms for these words, and choose the one that best completes the sentence. Write that related form in the space provided.

1. For the most part Britain ignored the colonists' urgent _____ that they should not be taxed without being represented in Parliament.

   a. entice   b. exacerbate   c. entreat   d. exploit

2. The popular mystery novels of Dorothy L. Sayers display both the author's wit and her great _____.

   a. erudite   b. ethical   c. feasible   d. felicity

3. Homer's long narrative poem *The Iliad*, which recounts the deeds of heroes during the Trojan War, is a perfect _____ of the classical epic.

   a. equitable   b. ethical   c. expedient   d. exemplary

4. An ad hominem argument is a type of _____ reasoning that attacks an opponent's character and motives rather than debating the issue being discussed.

   a. fathom   b. fallacy   c. exigency   d. euphemism

5. Our Youth Center held a festival to celebrate the different _____ that make up our community.

   a. esoteric   b. ethnic   c. equitable   d. felicitous

6. Broken treaties and forcible relocations led to the _____ of relations between Native American tribes and the Bureau of Indian Affairs.

   a. entreat   b. exalt   c. fabricate   d. exacerbate

7. In order to lead a predator away from her vulnerable chicks, a mother bird may display a _____ injury such as a broken wing.

   a. entice   b. feign   c. envisage   d. expound

8. Thanks to the Hubble telescope, some of the mysteries of deep space are proving to be _____ at last.

   a. fathom   b. euphemism   c. exigency   d. fallacy

9. The leaves of the Venus's-flytrap give off a sweet-smelling nectar that acts as an _____ to insects to enter the plant's deadly trap.

   a. entreat   b. exalt   c. exploit   d. entice

10. The movement to pass federal child labor laws, designed to prevent the _____ of youngsters working in factories and mines, culminated in the passage of the Fair Labor Standards Act of 1938.

    a. exalt   b. exploit   c. expound   d. fabricate

11. Government and relief agencies agreed on the _____ of airlifting emergency supplies, personnel, and equipment to the villages that were buried by mudslides.

    a. fallacy   b. euphemism   c. expedient   d. equanimity

12. College applications usually require students to provide a sample of _____ or persuasive writing in response to a writing prompt.

    a. expound   b. exploit   c. entice   d. feign

13. The _____ of a commoner to the rank of lifetime peer is the prerogative of the British monarch.

    a. fabricate   b. entice   c. exacerbate   d. exalt

14. Instead of using the word *die*, many people prefer _____ terms and expressions such as "pass away" or "expire."

    a. epithet   b. euphemism   c. expedient   d. fallacy

15. The state's Department of Environmental Protection and county engineers published a detailed report on the _____ of restoring eroded beaches.

    a. fatuous   b. esoteric   c. ethnic   d. feasible

16. At the end of Shakespeare's comedy *Much Ado About Nothing*, two young couples are reunited and their friends and relatives rejoice in their _____.

    a. feasible   b. fatuous   c. facsimile   d. felicitous

17. Your local Better Business Bureau can tell you if the contractor you want to hire has been accused of _____ practices.

    a. ethnic   b. ethical   c. exemplary   d. esoteric

18. Some scholars write very _____ for a rarefied group of academic peers rather than for a wide audience.

    a. esoteric   b. erudite   c. felicitous   d. facetious

19. Here's an example of Mark Twain's wry _____: "Always do right. This will gratify some people, and astonish the rest."

    a. ethical   b. exotic   c. feasible   d. facetious

20. Through relentless cross-examination, the prosecution exposed the defendant's alibi as nothing more than a very clever _____.

    a. exploit   b. exalt   c. fabricate   d. feign

Lesson 17

191. fiasco — 205. futile

---

191. **fi-as-co**   *noun*   fē-ăs'-kō
[*fiasco* (Italian), "flask; failure"]

Definition: A complete failure.

In no time at all, poor management turned what should have been a surefire success into a **fiasco**.

Synonyms: (*nouns*) disaster, debacle, mess, bomb, flop

Antonyms: (*nouns*) triumph, success, hit

Related Phrases: go over like a lead balloon, a flash in the pan; a feather in one's cap, come off with flying colors

---

192. **fick-le**   *adjective*   fĭk'-əl
[*ficol* (Old English), "false, deceitful"]

Definition: Likely to change for no apparent reason; inconstant.

All during our stay on Cape Cod that memorable summer, the weather proved exceedingly **fickle**.

As many a clotheshorse has discovered, fashion can be a notoriously **fickle** mistress.

Related Forms: (*noun*) fickleness; (*adjective*) fickle-minded

Phrases: fickle weather, fickle fortune, fickle affections

Synonyms: (*adjectives*) changeable, capricious, unstable, mercurial, erratic, variable, flighty, fitful, volatile

Antonyms: (*adjectives*) steadfast, constant, immutable, steady

Related Phrase: blow hot and cold

---

193. **filch**   *verb*   fĭlch
[*filchen* (Middle English), "take as booty"; from *fylcian* (Old English), "draw up in battle array"; from *gefylce* (Old English), "band of men"]

Definition: To steal slyly, especially small things.

Two of the youngsters acted as decoys, while a third attempted to **filch** a couple of apples from the unguarded bin.

Synonyms: (*verbs*) pilfer, purloin, shoplift, pinch, rip off, snatch, heist, swipe

194. fi-nesse   *noun and verb*   fĭ-nĕs'

[*finesse* (French), "delicacy"; from *fin* (French), "fine"]

Definition:
 a. (*noun*) skill, delicacy, or subtlety in doing something or handling a situation.

   For over an hour, the two brilliant conversationalists traded verbal blows with all the **finesse** of expert fencers.

 b. (*verb*) To accomplish by subtle or skillful maneuvering.

   A clever operator may soon be able to **finesse** himself or herself into an important position in a business.

Synonyms: (*nouns*) artfulness, craftiness, shrewdness, adroitness, dexterity, facility, savoir faire, know-how, savvy; (*verbs*) maneuver, contrive, finagle, manipulate

In addition to its normal uses, *finesse* is a technical term in the card game bridge. As a bridge term, it refers to an attempt to take a trick with a low card while holding a much higher card in the same suit. The point of doing this is either to take the trick as cheaply as possible or to induce your opponent to play an intermediate card that you can then top.

195. fla-grant   *adjective*   flā'-grənt

[*flagrans, flagrantis* (Latin), "burning, blazing"; from *flagrare* (Latin), "burn"]

Definition: Extremely and deliberately conspicuous; glaring.

   Many people felt that the outcome of the trial constituted a **flagrant** miscarriage of justice.

Related Forms: (*nouns*) flagrancy, flagrance; (*adverb*) flagrantly

Synonyms: (*adjectives*) shocking, gross, rank, heinous (Word 222), atrocious, scandalous, disgraceful, brazen, egregious, arrant

Antonyms: (*adjectives*) negligible, insignificant, minor

Phrases: caught red-handed, in flagrante delicto

196. **flaunt** *verb* flônt

[Origin unknown; possibly akin to *flanta* (Norwegian), "gad about," and *flana* (Old Norse), "rush headlong"]

Definition: To show off in a conspicuous or offensive way.

Patriotism involves more than just **flaunting** the flag on the Fourth of July.

Synonyms: (*verbs*) display, parade, exhibit, sport, spotlight

Antonyms: (*verbs*) hide, conceal, screen, cover up; downplay, soft-pedal, de-emphasize

Related Phrase: draw attention to

197. **flout** *verb* flout

[*flouten* (Middle English), "play the flute"; from *flauter* (Old French), "play the flute," and *flaute* (Old French), "flute"]

Definition: To treat openly with scorn or contempt.

Many a monarch has been deposed for **flouting** the laws of the land.

Usage Note:
Be careful not to confuse *flout* with its look-alike *flaunt* (Word 196). Though these two words are sometimes considered to be synonyms in *nonstandard* English, they are quite different and should be kept separate.

Synonyms: (*verbs*) mock, scoff at, jeer at, deride, disparage, ridicule, sneer at, defy

Antonyms: (*verbs*) respect, observe, abide by; esteem, venerate, honor

Related Phrases: laugh up one's sleeve at, poke fun at

198. **fluc-tu-ate** *verb* flŭk'-chōo-āt

[*fluctuare, fluctuatus* (Latin), "move like a wave"; from *fluere* (Latin), "flow"]

Definition: To change continually from one position to another.

Since the moon lacks an atmosphere, temperatures on its surface **fluctuate** wildly.

Prices on the stock market may **fluctuate** on a day-to-day basis.

Related Forms: (*nouns*) fluctuation, flux

Phrases: fluctuating interest rates, fluctuating popularity

Synonyms: (*verbs*) waver, vacillate, oscillate, seesaw

Related Phrases: in a constant state of flux, ups and downs, ebb and flow, a checkered career

199. foi·ble   *noun*   foi'-bəl

[*foible* (obsolete French), "weak"]

Definition: A minor, often amusing, fault or weakness in character.

You may find your best friend's **foibles** extremely funny.

Usage Note:

When certain types of *foibles* become too pronounced, they may develop into *obsessions* (Word 283) or *phobias* (Word 301). For example, a concern for punctuality may become an obsession, or a dislike of cats a phobia.

Synonyms: (*nouns*) frailty, failing, flaw, defect (Word 117), shortcoming, idiosyncrasy, peculiarity, oddity, quirk, eccentricity, crotchet

Antonyms: (*nouns*) forte, strong point, long suit

200. fore·stall   *verb*   fôr-stôl'

[*foresteall* (Old English), "highway robbery"; from *fore* (Old English), "in front of" + *steall* (Old English), "position"]

Definition: To secure an advantage or prevent a loss by previous action.

English monarchs often **forestalled** the passage of legislation they did not like by simply adjourning Parliament.

Synonyms: (*verbs*) hinder, thwart (Word 376), frustrate, preclude, obviate, prevent, ward off, fend off, stave off, anticipate

Related Phrases: take precautionary measures, nip in the bud, cut off at the pass, steal a march on, beat to the draw, preventive medicine, a preemptive strike

201. for·mi·da·ble   *adjective*   fôr'-mǐ-də-bəl

[*formidabilis, formidabile* (Latin), "causing fear"; from *formido* (Latin), "terror, dread"]

Definition:

   a.   Arousing fear or admiration because of the unusual size or superiority of the thing involved.

     To the prehistoric inhabitants of Europe, Asia, and the Americas, large mountain ranges proved a **formidable** barrier to the spread of human populations.

   b.   Difficult to do because of the size of the job involved.

     The **formidable** task of cleaning up after a major hurricane or tornado cannot be accomplished without the help of all levels of government.

Phrases: a formidable opponent, a formidable intellect, a formidable memory, a formidable accomplishment

Related Forms: (*nouns*) formidability, formidableness

Synonyms: (*adjectives*) awesome, redoubtable, alarming, frightening, terrifying, horrifying; mind-boggling, impressive; huge, tremendous

Antonyms: (*adjectives*) unimpressive; inconsequential, insignificant, paltry, puny, negligible; simple, easy, undemanding

202. for-tu-i-tous   *adjective*   fôr-tōō'-ĭ-təs   *or*   fôr'-tyōō'-ĭ-təs

[*fortuitus* (Latin), "accidental"; from *fors, fortis* (Latin), "chance"]

Definition: Occurring by chance or accident.

Quite by chance I bumped into her on the street one day, and the results of that **fortuitous** meeting have changed the whole course of my life.

Related Forms: (*nouns*) fortuitousness, fortuity; (*adverb*) fortuitously

Usage Note:
Be careful not to confuse *fortuitous* with *fortunate. Fortuitous* means "accidental" or "happening by chance." The consequences of a *fortuitous* occurrence can be either fortunate or unfortunate, though the word tends to suggest that they are good rather than bad. *Fortunate*, on the other hand, simply means "lucky" or "happy," and the consequences of a fortunate development are always good. In other words, *fortuitous* refers to the way something happened, while *fortunate* refers to its results.

Synonyms: (*adjectives*) accidental, unplanned, inadvertent, casual, adventitious; unforeseen, unexpected, unanticipated

Antonyms: (*adjectives*) intentional, planned, deliberate, premeditated

Related Phrases: a fluke, a windfall, a chance occurrence

203. fru-gal   *adjective*   frōō'-gəl

[*frugalis* (Latin), "economical"; from *frux, frugis* (Latin), "fruit, produce"]

Definition:
a.   Thrifty or economical in the use of money.

"Inflation has really put a dent in my buying power this year," I thought. "If I'm going to make ends meet, I'll have to be more **frugal**."

b.   Involving little expense; meager.

Surprisingly, the **frugal** meal we got from the old peasant woman was more satisfying than many a banquet I'd attended.

Related Forms: (*nouns*) frugality, frugalness; (*adverb*) frugally

Synonyms: (*adjectives*) sparing, careful, prudent, provident; scanty, skimpy, paltry; stingy, parsimonious, penurious, niggardly, tightfisted, penny-pinching

Antonyms: (*adjectives*) lavish, extravagant, prodigal, improvident

Related Phrases: a skinflint, penny-wise and pound-foolish

204. ful-some   *adjective*   fŏŏl'-səm

[*fulsom* (Middle English), "loathsome"; from *full*, "excess" + *some*, "characterized by"]

Definition: Excessive and, for that reason, offensive to good taste and obviously insincere.

"We know you're trying to curry favor with the boss," the note read. "Still, must you greet every last one of his bright ideas with such **fulsome** and obvious flattery?"

Related Forms: (*noun*) fulsomeness; (*adverb*) fulsomely

Synonyms: (*adjectives*) inordinate, extravagant, gross, immoderate, overdone; repulsive, disgusting, nauseating, odious, loathsome; vulgar, crass, tasteless

Antonyms: (*adjectives*) modest, understated, muted, subdued, toned down, quiet

Related Phrases: ad nauseam, in poor taste

205. fu-tile   *adjective*   fyōō-təl   *or*   fyōō'-tĭl

[*futilis, futile* (Latin), "fragile; worthless"]

Definition: Incapable of producing the desired result; unsuccessful or ineffective.

Though the lifeguard made a heroic attempt to save the drowning woman's life, his efforts unfortunately proved **futile**.

Related Forms: (*nouns*) futility, futileness; (*adverb*) futilely

Synonyms: (*adjectives*) vain, fruitless, unavailing, idle, ineffectual, bootless, pointless, useless

Antonyms: (*adjectives*) effective, effectual, efficacious (Word 148), successful

Related Phrases: to no purpose, all for naught, carry coals to Newcastle

Carry Coals to Newcastle

The expression *carry coals to Newcastle* means "do something that is superfluous or unnecessary" or "supply something that is already abundant." Newcastle upon Tyne in northern England, the Newcastle of the expression, has long been the center of coal mining, so there is no need to import coal to the area.

Using the Words

Exercise I.   Syllabication and Pronunciation

Syllabicate the following words correctly, and place the major stress mark (') after the syllable that is accented when the word is pronounced.

1. fiasco
2. fickle
3. finesse
4. flagrant
5. frugal
6. fluctuate
7. foible
8. formidable
9. fortuitous

Exercise II.   Words Out of Context

In each of the following groups, select the item that best expresses the meaning of the numbered word at the left.

1. fickle   a. respectful   b. changeable   c. modest
               d. idle

2. flagrant   a. quiet   b. prudent   c. vain   d. gross

3. flaunt   a. show off   b. steal   c. frustrate   d. laugh at

4. flout   a. cover up   b. lavish   c. sneer at   d. waver

5. forestall   a. emphasize   b. observe   c. alarm
               d. prevent

6. fortuitous a. impressive   b. wasteful   c. accidental
               d. fruitless

7. fulsome   a. loathsome   b. generous   c. simple
               d. unstable

Exercise III.   Completing Sentences

Complete each of the following sentences by selecting the most appropriate word from the group of words given below. Use each word only once. Make any adjustments that are necessary to fit the words into the sentences properly.

finesse   frugal   fluctuate

futile   fiasco   forestall

foible   filching   formidable

1. Prices for consumer goods _____ in accordance with the ups and downs of the economy.

2. Though the young boxer doesn't look particularly impressive in his street clothes, he is a _____ opponent once he's in the ring.

3. I admire someone who can handle a delicate social situation with tact and _____.

4. Curiously, a play that "bombs" in London is a hit, while one that "bombs" on Broadway is a _____.

5. My personality isn't all of a piece; it's a mixture of strengths and weaknesses, fortes and _____.

6. She is a _____ homemaker who delights in comparison shopping and bargain hunting.

7. Someone who starts off _____ pennies may end up stealing millions.

8. The police recaptured one of the fugitives in a matter of hours, but their efforts to retake the other proved _____.

Exercise IV.   Synonyms and Antonyms

Classify each of the following pairs of words as **S** for **synonyms** or **A** for **antonyms**.

1. flagrant—glaring
2. shortcoming—foible
3. flaunt—conceal
4. formidable—awesome
5. success—fiasco
6. flout—respect
7. capricious—fickle
8. lavish—frugal
9. finesse—dexterity
10. effective—futile
11. fluctuate—vacillate
12. thwart—forestall
13. fortuitous—premeditated
14. pilfer—filch

Exercise V.   Word Roundup

1. Explain the difference between the items in each of the following pairs.

   a. flout—flaunt
   b. fortuitous—fortunate

2. With or without the aid of a dictionary, define each of the following colloquial or slang expressions.

   a. a heist
   b. to soft-pedal
   c. a windfall
   d. a fluke
   e. a skinflint
   f. a flop

3. With or without the aid of a dictionary, explain the meaning of each of the following colorful phrases.

   a. blow hot and cold
   b. caught red-handed
   c. laugh up one's sleeve at
   d. a checkered career
   e. go over like a lead balloon
   f. a person's long suit
   g. steal a march on
   h. carry coals to Newcastle
   i. a flash in the pan
   j. penny-wise and pound-foolish

4. Explain the meaning of the following Latin phrases commonly used in present-day English.

a. ad nauseam b. (in) flagrante delicto

5. Explain what *finesse* means in bridge.

Exercise VI.   Framing Sentences

A. Use each of the following words in an original illustrative sentence.

1. fiasco	4. flaunt	7. fortuitous
2. filch	5. flout	8. forestall
3. finesse	6. foible	9. fulsome

B. Give a **noun** form of each of the following words, and use it in an original illustrative sentence.

1. fickle	3. fluctuate	5. frugal
2. flagrant	4. formidable	6. futile

Dissecting the Words

Prefixes

1. The Old English prefix **fore**, meaning "before," "earlier," "in advance," or "in front of," appears in the word *forestall*, studied in this lesson. Following are some other common English words in which it occurs. In each case, note how the prefix contributes to the overall meaning of the word in which it appears.

forewarn (*fore*, "before" + *warn*)—to warn in advance

forecast (*fore*, "in advance" + *cast*)—to predict; a prediction

foresee (*fore*, "before" + *see*)—to see or know beforehand

forebear (*fore*, "before" + *bear* (Old English), "a being, person")—an ancestor

forebode (*fore*, "in advance" + *bode*)—to indicate the likelihood of; portend. (Note that *forebode* usually implies that what is coming is bad rather than good.)

foreshadow (*fore*, "beforehand" + *shadow*)—to indicate or suggest beforehand

Other common English words containing the prefix *fore* include *foretaste, forefather, foreword, forerunner,* and *foretell.*

2. Do not confuse the prefix *fore* with the Old English look-alike prefix **for** (without an *e*). *For* means "away, off" or "completely, utterly." It appears in a number of common English words, including:

forgo (*for*, "completely away" + *go*)—to abstain from completely; to do totally without *forlorn* (*for*, "completely" + *lorn*, "abandoned")—wretched and pitiful; nearly hopeless

forbear (*for*, "completely away" + *bear*)—to refrain completely from

forsake (*for*, "completely" + *sake*, "deny, reject")—to leave or desert completely

Other modern English words in which the prefix *for* appears are *forbid* and *forswear*.

Root

The Latin root **flu** or **fluct**, meaning "flow," is found in the word *fluctuate*, studied in this lesson. Here are some other common English words in which the root appears.

affluent (literally, "flowing toward")—wealthy, well-to-do

confluence (literally, "a flowing together")—the junction of two rivers

flux—a constant change or flow

fluent—easily flowing; effortless, polished, or graceful

influx (literally, "a flowing in")—the arrival of great numbers of something

superfluous (literally, "flowing over and above")—superabundant, excessive, extra. Noun: *superfluity*

mellifluous (literally, "flowing with honey")—very sweet and smooth; honeyed

Exercise

1. On the basis of your knowledge of the prefix *fore*, tell what each of the following compound words means:

   a. foreword   c. foremost   e. foresight
   b. forefront   d. foreshorten   f. forehand

2. With or without the aid of a dictionary, define each of the following words containing the prefix *for*. Explain how the prefix contributes to the overall meaning of the word.

   a. forlorn   b. forbearance   c. forswear

3. For each of the following definitions, supply an English word that contains either the prefix *fore* or the prefix *for*. In some instances, two answers are possible.

   a. an ancestor   c. predict   e. see beforehand
   b. do totally without   d. warn in advance   f. completely wretched

4. Define each of the following words, and use it in an original illustrative sentence.

   a. affluent   c. influx   e. fluent
   b. fusion   d. superfluous   f. influential

Working with Context Clues

Two-Word Omissions. So far you have been dealing with sentence-completion exercises containing only one blank. The sentence-completion sections of most standardized vocabulary tests, however, contain a good many items involving the omission of *two* words, not one. These two-word omissions work in exactly the same way as one-word omissions; they are just more challenging.

Study the following example of a typical two-word omission. Try to determine the correct answer before reading the explanation of it given below.

Florida Fats and the other _____ of McDuffy's Billiard Academy come from every walk of life. You are unlikely to find a more _____ crew assembled under any other roof in town.

a. quadrupeds . . . elegant   c. denizens . . . motley
b. employees . . . uniform   d. proprietors . . . aristocratic

The best way to begin dealing with this example is to determine the parts of speech of the missing words. From the position of the blanks, you seem to need a noun in the first and an adjective in the second.

Notice that the noun you need forms part of the subject of the first sentence. This suggests that it may form part of the subject of the entire passage. Accordingly, read the passage carefully to determine what it is about. It concerns the kind of people who can be found in a pool hall called McDuffy's Billiard Academy. This is confirmed by the phrase *crew assembled under any . . . roof* in the second sentence and the personal name *Florida Fats* in the first. Now you know that the noun you need means something like "customers" or possibly "employees."

Run your eye down the first item in each of the four lettered choices. Eliminate any choice that does not fit in with your conclusion about the meaning of the first missing word. Choices *b* and *c* seem to work. *Employees* (choice *b*) dovetails neatly with what you think may go in the first blank. So does *denizens* (choice *c*), which means "inhabitants" or "residents." Choices *a* and *d*, however, don't agree with your ideas, so they can be eliminated. A *quadruped* (choice *a*) is a four-legged animal, not a person; *proprietors* (choice *d*) indicates the owners of a business, not its customers or employees.

Though officially a "dead" language, Latin is still used in the modern world. For instance, carved over the entrance to the Amphitheater of Arlington National Cemetery in Virginia is the Roman poet Horace's simple but unforgettable line about patriotism, "It is satisfying and fitting to die for one's country."

Now you are down to two possibilities. However, you'll need more information before you can decide which of the two is correct. Accordingly, move on to consider the second blank, for which you need an adjective.

Notice that the missing adjective modifies the word *crew*. This suggests that it in some way describes the nature or character of the people who can be found at McDuffy's. Carefully reread the entire passage to determine what it has to say about this matter.

The passage says that the crew at McDuffy's *comes from every walk of life*. This suggests that the adjective you need means something like "extremely varied" or "richly diverse."

Run your eye over the second item in choices *b* and *c*, your two remaining possibilities for the correct answer. *Uniform* (choice *b*) does not agree with your conclusion about the meaning of the adjective you need, since the word means the opposite of *varied* or *diverse*. For that reason, it can be eliminated.

Motley in choice *c*, however, does fit, since it does mean "richly diverse" or "extremely varied." Choice *c*, therefore, must be the correct answer, and, of course, it is.

One final point: Notice that two-word omissions work on exactly the same kinds of context clues as one-word omissions. In the example given above, one of the hints was essentially a restatement clue since *crew* and *denizens* mean more or less the same thing. The other was an inference clue since *motley* is implied by the phrase *come from every walk of life*.

Exercise

Choose the pair of words that best complete the meaning of each of the following passages. Underline the clue or clues that led you to make your choice.

1. The anxious cast of young actors became _____ after several reviewers declared that their new play was a complete _____ which lacked any theatrical merit or entertainment value.

   a. affable . . . failure
   b. distraught . . . fiasco
   c. belligerent . . . surprise
   d. caustic . . . anachronism

2. We realized that the woman claiming to be a psychic was a complete _____ when she began to _____ a trance by suddenly falling to the floor and pretending to speak with spirits.

   a. anomaly . . . elicit
   b. fiasco . . . exploit
   c. harbinger . . . fabricate
   d. charlatan . . . feign

3. When the brilliant physicist talks to a group of nonscientists, he must adapt his _____ so that he can be understood by a lay audience far less _____ than he.

   a. discourse . . . erudite
   b. bravado . . . fulsome
   c. harangue . . . eminent
   d. temperament . . . academic

4. The foundations of democracy are threatened when a(n) _____ group of highly privileged citizens can _____ others with less power to accept the will of the wealthy and influential.

   a. facetious . . . delude   c. exotic . . . entreat
   b. ethnic . . . abet   d. elite . . . coerce

5. Because of the overlapping lines of authority in a large, impersonal organization, people working in a(n) _____ often fail to _____ their duties and then refuse to take responsibility for their mistakes.

   a. boycott . . . disparage   c. asylum . . . curtail
   b. bureaucracy . . . fulfill   d. enclave . . . assimilate

Enriching the Lesson

Exercise I.   Our Italian Heritage

This lesson includes *fiasco*, a word borrowed without change from Italian. Listed below are a number of other Italian words and phrases that are commonly used in present-day English. With or without the aid of a dictionary, define each expression as it is used in Modern English.

1. torso	8. quarantine	15. manifesto
2. imbroglio	9. libretto	16. solo
3. sotto voce	10. studio	17. scenario
4. vendetta	11. graffiti	18. vista
5. tempo	12. motto	19. cognoscenti
6. squadron	13. salvo	20. gala
7. prima donna	14. incognito	21. virtuoso

Exercise II.   Money Talks

The presence of *frugal* in this lesson brings to mind the fact that Modern English includes an impressive array of expressions relating to business, finance, and economics. A few of these items are listed below. With or without the aid of a dictionary or other reference book (*e.g.*, an economics textbook), define each.

1. depression	8. surplus	15. deficit
2. recession	9. monetary policy	16. monopoly
3. inflation	10. market economy	17. bull market
4. deflation	11. economic climate	18. national debt
5. boom	12. private sector	19. windfall profits
6. asset	13. free enterprise	20. liability
7. gross national product	14. medium of exchange	21. prime interest rate

Exercise III. A Verbal Diversion

Since sports and games play such an important role in our daily lives, it is only natural that many colorful terms and expressions have spilled over from the sports world into the everyday language. A few examples of this phenomenon are given below. With or without the aid of a dictionary, define or explain each. Then indicate the sport from which the expression comes.

1. pinch-hit for
2. put on a full-court press
3. par for the course
4. parry a blow
5. a gambit
6. have an ace up one's sleeve
7. kick off a campaign
8. a Monday morning quarterback
9. a goal-line stand
10. stymied
11. hotdog (*verb*)
12. a stalemate
13. a front-runner
14. showboating
15. a long shot
16. start out with two strikes against you

Exercise IV. Expanding Your Word Power

The words listed below are not on the Basic Word List, but they were mentioned in passing in Lesson 17. All of them would make useful additions to your working vocabulary. Define each, give its etymology, list **two** synonyms and **two** antonyms (where possible), and use in a short illustrative sentence.

1. debacle
2. erratic
3. steadfast
4. purloin
5. maneuver
6. egregious
7. defy
8. oscillate
9. forte
10. quirk
11. preclude
12. redoubtable
13. inadvertent
14. prodigal
15. inordinate

Lesson 18

---

206. gape   *verb*   gāp
[*gapa* (Old Norse), "open the mouth; stare"]

Definition: To stare openmouthed in amazement; to open wide.

Survivors **gaped** in disbelief at the destruction so quickly wrought by the tornado.

Scientists believe the huge crater that **gapes** in the Arizona desert was made by a meteorite crashing into the earth.

Related Forms: (*noun*) gap; (*adverb*) agape

Synonyms: (*verbs*) gawk (at); goggle (at), rubberneck, ogle; yawn

Antonyms: (*verbs*) purse (the lips), pucker (the mouth), furrow (the brow)

207. gar-ble   *verb*   gär'-bəl
[*garbellare* (Old Italian), "sift"; from *g(h)arbala* (Arabic), "he selected"; possibly from *cribellum* (Late Latin), "sieve"]

Definition: To distort in such a way as to make unintelligible.

The message was so badly **garbled** that I didn't even know who had called.

Phrases: a garbled quotation, garbled instructions

Synonyms: (*verbs*) scramble, jumble, confuse, mangle, mutilate, butcher, misrepresent, misquote, misreport

Related Phrases: take something out of context, get something wrong; get something straight, set the record straight

208. gloat   *verb*   glōt
[Origin uncertain; possibly *glotta* (Old Norse), "grin"]

Definition: To regard with excessive or malicious satisfaction.

A good winner doesn't **gloat** over victory, just as a good loser doesn't sulk over defeat.

Synonyms: (*verbs*) revel (in), delight (in), relish, crow (over), exult (in), glory (in)

Related Phrases: lord it over, rub it in

Mahouts always carry goads with them when training, caring for, and working with their elephants. Young elephants also learn to obey foot commands from their riders.

209. goad   *noun and verb*   gōd
[*gad* (Old English), "spearhead"]

Definition:
   a. (*noun*) A long pointed stick used for driving animals; anything that spurs a person on.

      Customarily, mahouts use short wooden **goads** to control and direct the movements of their huge charges.

      Simple financial necessity is often the **goad** that prompts a composer or painter to produce new material.

   b. (*verb*) To drive or urge on.

      Try as he might, he could not **goad** me into doing something that I knew in my heart was foolish.

Synonyms: (*nouns*) prod, spur, stimulus, incentive, inducement; gadfly; (*verbs*) prod, spur, propel, hound, impel, incite, provoke, egg on

Antonyms: (*nouns*) restraint, curb, check, deterrent; (*verbs*) restrain, curb, check, deter, impede

Related Phrases: needle someone, fire up an audience, whip up enthusiasm

210. graph·ic   *adjective*   grăf'-ĭk
[*graphikos* (Greek), "able to draw or paint"; from *graphein* (Greek), "draw, paint"]

Definition:
   a. Relating to a drawn or pictorial representation; visual.

      Messages posted on our refrigerator door have become quite eye-catching since my sister began majoring in **graphic** arts.

   b. Giving a clear and effective picture; vivid.

      The book contains a **graphic** and hair-raising account of the seizure of the U.S. embassy in Iran.

Related Forms: (*nouns*) graph, graphics; (*adverb*) graphically

Synonyms: (*adjectives*) pictorial, diagrammatic; striking, telling, lively, lifelike, realistic, true to life, picturesque

Antonyms: (*adjectives*) sketchy, vague; unrealistic; colorless, bloodless, anemic, pallid, bland

276

Graphs and Graphics

There is a whole family of terms and expressions related to the adjective *graphic*, studied in this lesson. For example, a *graph*, as you probably already know, is a line drawing or similar pictorial device used to represent numerical (or other abstract) relationships. The word is constantly used (both as a noun and as a verb) in mathematics and the other arts and sciences. For example, your math teacher may ask you to graph the equation $2x + y = 16$, or your history textbook may contain a graph showing unemployment in the United States during the Great Depression. Graphs, of course, are also widely used in business and other fields as convenient devices for representing abstract relationships in concrete and eye-catching ways.

A *graphic* (plural *graphics*) is similar to a graph but broader in meaning. To businesspeople and commercial artists, it indicates a picture, chart, or similar device that is designed to illustrate something. To computer experts, it refers to a diagram that the computer generates on the screen.

Graphics has several meanings. To architects and engineers, it refers to the art of making technical drawings according to strict mathematical rules. To commercial artists, it indicates the art of making graphic illustrations. And to computer experts, it is the capability of a network of linked databases to display pictures and other images as well as printed text on such systems as the Internet.

Finally, the *graphic arts* are any of the visual arts that involve applying lines to a two-dimensional surface. Thus, drawing, lettering, photography, and printing are all examples of the graphic arts.

A gratuity is a tip, usually in the form of money, given in thanks for a service. Waiters and waitresses (like the one shown in this photo) customarily receive gratuities in this country. In Europe and other parts of the world, a standard gratuity is often built into the bill.

211. gra·tu·i·tous   *adjective*   grə-tōō'-ĭ-təs *or* grə-tyōō'-ĭ-təs
[*gratuitus* (Latin), "given as a favor"; from *gratia* (Latin), "favor"]

Definition:
  a. Freely given; done without recompense.

> She gives people a great deal of **gratuitous** service, simply because she likes them.

  b. Uncalled-for; unjustified.

> After treating them so well, we were deeply offended by their **gratuitous** insults.

Related Forms: (*nouns*) gratuitousness, gratuity; (*adjective and adverb*) gratis; (*adverb*) gratuitously

Synonyms: (*adjectives*) free, complimentary, voluntary, unsolicited; unwarranted, unfounded, groundless, baseless

Related Phrases: on the house, free of charge, a freebie; foot the bill for

212. gre·ga·ri·ous   *adjective*   grĭ-gâr'-ē-əs
[*gregarius* (Latin), "belonging to a herd or flock"; from *grex, gregis* (Latin), "herd"]

Definition:
  a. Tending to form or move in a herd or other group; social.

> Many kinds of animals — sheep, for example — are naturally **gregarious**.

  b. Enjoying the company of others; sociable.

> Whether or not a person is **gregarious** is usually the result of how she or he was brought up.

Related Forms: (*noun*) gregariousness; (*adverb*) gregariously

Synonyms: (*adjectives*) outgoing, extroverted, friendly, companionable, affable, genial

Antonyms: (*adjectives*) antisocial, misanthropic, unsociable, unfriendly, withdrawn, reserved, detached, aloof, introverted

Related Phrases: esprit de corps, birds of a feather, a social butterfly; live in an ivory tower, a loner

213. **gri-mace**   *noun and verb*   grĭm'-ĭs *or* grĭ-mās'

[*grimache* (Old French), "grimace"; related to *grima* (Old English), "mask; fear" and ultimately of Germanic origin]

Definition:
  a. (*noun*) A twisted facial expression indicating pain, disgust, or disapproval.

   The **grimace** on her face told me more eloquently than words could have that she disapproved of my decision.

  b. (*verb*) To contort the features of the face in order to indicate pain, disgust, or disapproval.

   When the doctor jabbed me with that long needle, I involuntarily **grimaced** in pain.

Synonyms: (*nouns and verbs*) frown, scowl, glower, glare, wince

Antonyms: (*nouns and verbs*) smile, grin; (*verb*) beam

Related Phrases: make a (wry) face, make faces, screw up one's face; grin from ear to ear, grin like a Cheshire cat

---

214. **grope**   *verb*   grōp

[*grop(i)en* (Middle English), "grope"; from *grapian* (Old English), "grasp"]

Definition: To feel around uncertainly for.

When the lights suddenly went out, I **groped** my way down the stairs with the aid of a pocket lighter.

There was a momentary pause in the conversation as I **groped** for an answer to her unexpected question.

Phrases: grope for the telephone, grope for a clue

Synonyms: (*verbs*) fumble (for), poke around (for), hunt (for), cast about (for), fish around (for), look (for), flounder around (for)

Related Phrases: pick one's way through; send out a feeler, send up a trial balloon, see how the land lies, see which way the wind is blowing

---

215. **gru-el-ing**   *adjective*   grōō'-ə-lĭng

[Origin uncertain; possibly *gruel* (obsolete English), "punish" + *ing*]

Definition: Extremely demanding and exhausting.

With four minutes left to play, a glorious but **grueling** eighty-yard drive put the winning points on the board for the Rams.

Synonyms: (*adjectives*) taxing, draining, fatiguing, wearying, tiring, arduous, intense

Antonyms: (*adjectives*) easy, simple, enjoyable, relaxing, invigorating

216. grue-some   *adjective*   grōō'-səm
[*grue* (obsolete English), "shudder" + *some*, "characterized by"]

Definition: Causing great shock, horror, and repugnance.

The **gruesome** sight of maimed and burned bodies was enough to disillusion me forever about the so-called glories of war.

Phrases: a gruesome murder, the gruesome details

Related Forms: (*noun*) gruesomeness; (*adverb*) gruesomely

Synonyms: (*adjectives*) horrifying, horrible, monstrous, hideous, grisly, ghastly, macabre, grotesque, lurid

Antonyms: (*adjectives*) pleasant, lovely, delightful, agreeable, attractive, charming, engaging, pleasurable

217. gul-li-ble   *adjective*   gŭl'-ə-bəl
[*gull* (English), "cheat, dupe" + *ible*]

Definition: Easily cheated or deceived.

No matter how much protective legislation we pass, there will probably always be **gullible** consumers for swindlers and con artists to prey on.

Related Forms: (*noun*) gullibility; (*noun and verb*) gull

Synonyms: (*adjectives*) credulous, naive, ingenuous, unsuspecting, exploitable, trusting, unwary, green

Antonyms: (*adjectives*) skeptical, incredulous, dubious, wary, cautious, circumspect

Related Phrases: a patsy, a soft touch, a sitting duck, a pigeon; born yesterday, still wet behind the ears; pull the wool over someone's eyes, take someone for a ride; jive; caveat emptor

218. hag-gard   *adjective*   hăg'-ērd
[*haggard* (Old French), "wild," used of a female hawk in falconry]

Definition: Worn and exhausted from anxiety, disease, hunger, or fatigue.

As soon as I saw how **haggard** his face looked, I began to realize just how much he had been through recently.

Related Form: (*noun*) haggardness

Usage Note:
As the example above indicates, *haggard* usually refers to the face or facial expression. It suggests thinness, worry, or weariness and implies severe mental or physical distress.

Synonyms: (*adjectives*) careworn, drawn, gaunt, wasted, hollow eyed, drained, wan, cadaverous, pinched

Antonyms: (*adjectives*) rosy, florid, ruddy, rubicund, glowing, radiant

The Trojan Horse

The story of the Trojan Horse, as told in Homer's *Odyssey* and Virgil's *Aeneid*, is a classic example of guile and gullibility. The Greek army besieging Troy was unable to break into the city. The wily Greeks thereupon built a huge statue of a horse and left it outside the city walls. Armed Greek soldiers were concealed inside the hollow structure. Then the Greeks pretended to depart. The jubilant Trojans regarded the statue as a parting gift from a defeated foe and, despite warnings (the Trojan priest Laocoön remarked, "I fear the Greeks, even when bearing gifts"), dragged the "gift horse" into the city. At night the Greek soldiers crept out of the horse and opened the city's gates to their comrades. In this way, the city of Troy was taken.

219. **ha-rangue**   *noun and verb*   hə-răng′

[*harenga* (Medieval Latin), "public address"]

Definition:

a. (*noun*) A long, emotional public address designed to arouse strong feelings or spur the audience on to action; a similar piece of writing.

Suddenly a young man rushed onto the stage and began to deliver one of the most intemperate **harangues** I have ever heard.

b. (*verb*) To deliver a harangue.

It's a truly frightening experience to watch old film clips of Adolf Hitler **haranguing** his followers at the Nuremberg rallies of the 1930s.

Synonyms: (*nouns*) tirade, diatribe, philippic, denunciation; (*verbs*) rant, hold forth, pontificate

Related Phrases: rant and rave, get up on a soapbox, ride a hobbyhorse

220. har·bin·ger   *noun and verb*   här′-bĭn-jər

[*herbergere, herbengar* (Middle English), "person sent to prepare lodgings"; from *herberge* (Old French but of Germanic origin), "lodging." Originally, a harbinger was a servant or messenger sent on ahead to prepare lodging and entertainment for traveling royal or titled persons.]

Definition:
    a.   (*noun*) A forerunner.

       Wild geese flying south from Canada are **harbingers** of winter.

       The brutal conflict over Kansas and Nebraska in the 1850s turned out to be a modest **harbinger** of a much bloodier struggle in the 1860s.

    b.   (*verb*) To herald the approach of.

       To most people's minds, the appearance of crocuses **harbingers** the return of spring.

       I hope tonight's easy victory over Elk Grove **harbingers** success in our bid for the state basketball championship.

Synonyms: (*nouns*) precursor, herald; omen, sign, portent; (*verbs*) presage, foreshadow, prefigure, augur (Word 48), signal; usher in

Related Phrases: a point man, an advance man

Using the Words

Exercise I.   Parts of Speech

Indicate the part of speech of each of the following words. In some cases, two answers are correct.

1. gape
2. garble
3. goad
4. gratuitous
5. grimace
6. grope
7. gullible
8. harangue
9. harbinger

Exercise II.   Words in Phrases

In each of the following groups, select the item that best expresses the meaning of the *italicized* word in the introductory phrase.

1. *gratuitous* criticisms
    a. perceptive   b. unexpected   c. mindless   d. uncalled-for

2. a very *gregarious* young lady
    a. erudite   b. outgoing   c. beautiful   d. obese

3. the *gruesome* details
    a. vague   b. significant   c. horrible   d. minor

4. a *grueling* test
    a. surprise   b. written   c. brief   d. draining

5. *grope* for a name
   a. rush   b. call   c. send   d. fumble
6. a *haggard* expression
   a. careworn   b. felicitous   c. trite   d. foreign
7. *grimaced* in reply
   a. nodded   b. winked   c. scowled   d. laughed

Exercise III.   Completing Sentences

Complete each of the following sentences or pairs of sentences by selecting the most appropriate word from the group of words given below. Use each word only once. Make any adjustments that are necessary to fit the words into the sentences properly.

gloat	gaping	harbinger
graphic	haggard	gullible
harangue	goad	garbled

1. It made me dizzy to lean over the edge of the precipice and peer down into the _____ abyss below.

2. The report contained such a _____ and misleading account of my activities that at first I didn't recognize them.

3. Even though their crowing may embarrass you a little, your parents do have some right to _____ over your successes.

4. Fear and confusion may _____ a perfectly rational person into behaving in a most irrational way.

5. The article gave such a _____ description of the catastrophe that I could almost see it occurring before my eyes.

6. Only a thoroughly _____ person would be taken in by the absurd claims of some TV commercials.

7. "The man's no statesman," I declared. "He's a rabble-rouser who uses his official position as a soapbox from which to _____ a captive and reluctant audience."

8. In my family, opening day at the ballpark, not the advent of warmer weather, is the _____ of summer.

Exercise IV.   Synonyms and Antonyms

A. In each of the following groups, select the **two** words that are most nearly **synonyms**.

1. a. unwarranted   b. unplanned   c. uncontrolled
   d. unjustified   e. unnamed

2. a. rant   b. scramble   c. douse   d. spur   e. jumble

3. a. peasant   b. knight   c. herald   d. forerunner
   e. merchant

4. a. grisly   b. wary   c. ghastly   d. lazy   e. sketchy

5. a. chubby   b. gaunt   c. stately   d. radiant   e. cadaverous

Now, for each pair of synonyms you have selected, supply a word from the Basic Word List for this lesson (Words 206–220) that means **the same** or **almost the same** thing.

B. In each of the following, select the item that is most nearly **opposite** in meaning to the numbered word at the left.

1. goad   a. grin   b. mangle   c. rave   d. restrain
                 e. prod

2. gullible   a. energetic   b. disinterested   c. skeptical
                 d. friendly   e. frightening

3. grueling   a. fulfilling   b. undemanding   c. striking
                 d. unrewarding   e. fatiguing

4. gregarious   a. naive   b. genial   c. monstrous   d. aloof
                 e. ruddy

5. grimace   a. smile   b. yawn   c. cough   d. nod
                 e. scowl

Exercise V.   Framing Sentences

A. Use each of the following words in an original illustrative sentence.

1. gape   4. goad   7. grueling
2. garble   5. grimace   8. harangue
3. gloat   6. grope   9. harbinger

B. Give a **noun** form of each of the following words, and use it in an original illustrative sentence.

1. gullible   2. gregarious   3. haggard

C. Give an **adverb** form of each of the following words, and use it in an original illustrative sentence.

1. graphic   2. gruesome   3. gratuitous

Exercise VI.   Word Roundup

1. With or without the aid of a dictionary, explain what the following phrases mean.

   a. live in an ivory tower   d. wet behind the ears
   b. get up on a soapbox   e. see how the land lies
   c. pull the wool over   f. grin like a Cheshire
      someone's eyes   cat

2. With or without the aid of a dictionary, define each of the following colorful terms.

   a. rubberneck   c. social butterfly   e. freebie
   b. gadfly   d. sitting duck   f. birds of a feather

3. Explain what each of the following means.

   a. a graph   c. graphics
   b. a graphic   d. the graphic arts

4. Define the following foreign expressions used in present-day English.

   a. gratis   b. esprit de corps   c. caveat emptor

5. What is an *extrovert*? How does one differ from an *introvert*?

6. Recount the story of the Trojan Horse.

Completing Verbal Analogies

"If Something Is A, a Person Can B It." Another common word relationship that occurs in the analogy sections of standardized tests involves a state or action that is stipulated by the meaning of a given word. This relationship can be expressed in abstract terms as, "If something is *A*, a person can *B* it; if something is *C*, a person can *D* it."

Here is an example of an analogy question involving this relationship. Try to determine the correct answer before reading the explanation of it given below.

tangible : touch ::
   a. susceptible : doubt   d. pliant : enjoy
   b. affable : speak   e. mutable : show
   c. portable : carry

The answer is *c*. If something is *tangible*, a person can, *touch* it. Similarly, if something is *portable*, a person can *carry* it.

"If Something Is A, a Person Cannot B It." A related word relationship involves a state or action that is precluded by the meaning of a given word. This word relationship can be expressed in abstract terms as, "If something is *A*, a person cannot *B* it; if something is *C*, a person cannot *D* it."

Here is an example of an analogy involving this relationship. Try to figure out the correct answer before reading the explanation of it given below.

immutable : change ::
   a. insurgent : raise   d. inscrutable : see
   b. inadvertent : tame   e. indelible : erase
   c. irrevocable : examine

The answer is *e*. If something is *immutable*, a person cannot *change* it. Similarly, if something is *indelible*, a person cannot *erase* it.

One Final Note. The two word relationships examined in this section may apply to people as well as things. In that case, they may be expressed in abstract terms as "If someone is *A*, a person can(not) *B* him/her."

Exercise I

Complete each of the following analogies based on the word relationships "If something is *A*, a person can *B* it" and "If something is *A*, a person cannot *B* it."

1. **illegible : read** =
   a. invisible : see
   b. inaudible : taste
   c. innumerable : avoid
   d. immobile : touch
   e. inflammable : imagine

2. **edible : eat** =
   a. notable : forget
   b. feasible : scare
   c. pliable : bend
   d. execrable : relish
   e. stable : shift

3. **gullible : hoodwink** =
   a. reliable : mistrust
   b. affable : reject
   c. culpable : reward
   d. sensible : mislead
   e. tractable : control

4. **insuperable : overcome** =
   a. unquenchable : swallow
   b. invincible : choose
   c. inscrutable : raise
   d. indomitable : tame
   e. infallible : duplicate

Exercise II

Compose **one** complete analogy based on the word relationship "If something is *A*, a person can *B* it" and **one** based on the word relationship "If something is *A*, a person cannot *B* it."

Exercise III

The following items review what you have so far learned about analogy questions. Complete each.

1. **treachery : revulsion** :: courage :
   (*despair, horror, admiration, boredom, indifference*)

2. **poignant : sadden** :: droll :
   (*appall, enlighten, exhaust, puzzle, amuse*)

3. **nimble : ungainly** :: blithe :
   (*facetious, lithe, exotic, morose, gratuitous*)

4. **philosopher : truth** :: aesthete :
   (*beauty, research, money, fame, controversy*)

5. **prong : fork** :: spoke :
   (*headlight, wheel, pedal, handlebar, brake*)

6. **interest : absorption** :: joy :
   (*sadness, exultation, amazement, attention, apathy*)

286

7. **apple : fruit** :: potato :
   (*vegetable, mineral, animal, metal, product*)

8. **affluent : indigent** :: eminent :
   (*notable, genial, obscure, heinous, defective*)

9. **epigram : witty** :: cliché :
   (*prolix, hackneyed, piquant, rational, novel*)

10. **diminutive : puny** :: mammoth :
    (*specious, dapper, emaciated, gigantic, haggard*)

Working with Context Clues

More About Two-Word Omissions.   Study the following example of a typical two-word omission. Try to determine the correct answer before reading the explanation of it given below.

Though a(n) _____ master might deal kindly and generously with the slaves he owned, a cruel one would usually _____ his.

   a. brutal . . . exploit   c. humane . . . maltreat
   b. enlightened . . . coddle   d. affluent . . . emancipate

The answer is *c. humane . . . maltreat.* Here's why.

The word *though* at the beginning of the example should immediately suggest to you that the sentence will present contrasting information of some kind. It should also tip you off to the kind of clue you are likely to find—a contrast clue.

Bearing this in mind, read the sentence carefully to determine how the words that go in the blanks contribute to its meaning. The sentence does indeed present contrasting information. It says that one kind of master treated his slaves in one way, but another kind of master treated his differently. You are to supply an adjective that reveals the character of the first type of master and a verb that indicates how the second treated his slaves. To help you do this, you have been told how the first type of master behaved (*deal . . . generously*) and what the second was like (*cruel*).

You now have enough information to begin completing the sentence correctly. Accordingly, consider the first blank, for which you need an adjective that describes a person's character or personality. You know that the second type of master was cruel. This suggests that the first type was "uncruel"—that is, "kind." This conclusion is backed up by the statement that the first type treated his slaves *kindly and generously.*

Run your eye down the first item in each of the four lettered choices. Eliminate any choice that does not agree with your conclusion about the character of the first type of master. Choices *b* (*enlightened*) and *c* (*humane*) dovetail with it, so they can stay. Choice *a* (*brutal*), however, does not and can confidently be eliminated. Similarly, choice *d* (*affluent*) has nothing to do with kindness or cruelty, so it can be discarded as well.

Now you have reduced the likely possibilities for the correct answer to two. Still, you can't tell which is actually right without more help. Accordingly, turn to the second blank, for which you need a verb indicating behavior.

You know that the first type of master treats his slaves kindly and gener-ously. This suggests that the second type of master treats his *unkindly or meanly*. This conclusion, of course, also follows from the fact that the sec-ond type of master is known to be cruel.

In light of this new conclusion, consider the second item in choices *b* and *c*, your two remaining possibilities for the correct answer. Choice *b* reads *coddle*, which does not agree with your ideas about how the cruel master treated his slaves. *Coddle* means "treat too indulgently," not "treat badly." Accordingly, choice *b* can be eliminated.

Choice *c*, however, is *maltreat*, which fits in nicely with what you think belongs in the blank. Clearly, then, choice *c* is the correct answer simply because none of the other choices produces a sensible or meaning-ful statement when it is inserted into the sentence.

Exercise

Complete each of the following two-word omissions by selecting the pair of words that make the best sense in the passage as a whole. Underline the clue or clues that led you to make your choice.

1. If we wish to _____ the eventual exhaustion of our fossil fuel reserves, we must _____ the use of gas-guzzling vehicles now and conserve our fuel resources for the future.

   a. defer . . . exploit
   b. forestall . . . curtail
   c. advocate . . . avoid
   d. exacerbate . . . forbid

2. When people wish to avoid speaking directly about death, they often resort to a(n) _____ in order to _____ the discomfort which that subject causes.

   a. slogan . . . flout
   b. anomaly . . . decrease
   c. boycott . . . elude
   d. euphemism . . . circumvent

3. The purpose of tales that make a(n) _____ point is to encourage listeners to _____ in their personal lives the moral behavior reflected in the stories.

   a. obvious . . . disparage
   b. circuitous . . . imitate
   c. esoteric . . . condone
   d. ethical . . . emulate

4. In the _____ of Shakespeare's *Hamlet*, a(n) _____ pile of dead bodies including that of the title character, lies on the stage as the curtain closes.

   a. denouement . . . gruesome
   b. conclusion . . . devout
   c. ambience . . . graphic
   d. manuscript . . . bleak

5. Some self-satisfied criminals have had the _____ to _____ about their crimes in television interviews and then have been rewarded for their shamelessness.

   a. courage . . . cohere
   b. effrontery . . . gloat
   c. finesse . . . discourse
   d. duplicity . . . entreat

Enriching the Lesson

Exercise I. More Classical Contributions to English

The geography, history, and mythology of the classical world have contributed much to the richness and variety of modern English. Below are listed a few more examples of this remarkable heritage. Tell what each of the items means, and explain its connection with classical Greece or Rome. Then choose any **five** of the expressions, and for each compose an original illustrative sentence.

1. a mausoleum
2. an odyssey
3. chimerical
4. hector someone
5. a nestor
6. caught between Scylla and Charybdis
7. meander
8. a maecenas
9. a thespian
10. a nemesis
11. pile Pelion on Ossa
12. open a Pandora's box
13. a xanthippe
14. pander to
15. stentorian
16. a mentor
17. a platonic relationship
18. leave no stone unturned

Exercise II. Expressions Old and New

A. Below are listed a number of expressions that are frequently used in present-day English. With or without the aid of a dictionary, define each. Then choose any **three**, and for each compose an original illustrative sentence.

1. hit pay dirt
2. in the limelight
3. out of kilter
4. a Johnny-come-lately
5. buy a pig in a poke
6. the pecking order
7. moonlight as a cabbie
8. old hat
9. a backhanded compliment
10. wear one's heart on one's sleeve
11. swallow one's pride
12. jump the gun
13. reach for the moon
14. get wind of
15. open a can of worms
16. a bull in a china shop
17. roll out the red carpet
18. a rule of thumb
19. fly off the handle
20. keep one's nose to the grindstone

B. Below are listed ten expressions that you are likely to encounter in a newspaper or on radio or TV. None of them, probably, would have been used, or even understood, a few generations ago. With or without the aid of a dictionary, tell what each means. Then choose any **three**, and for each compose an original illustrative sentence.

1. keep one's options open
2. a counterculture
3. follow a game plan
4. make a value judgment
5. a polarized community
6. hands-on operations
7. a lifestyle
8. prime time
9. a ballpark estimate
10. a paraprofessional

Exercise III.   From the East to the West

Present-day English has been enriched by words from the many languages spoken from the Middle East to the islands in the Pacific Ocean. These loan words have come to us via many routes, including colonization, war, trade, travel, religion, philosophy, art, architecture, film and other mass media, and cuisine. Listed below are a number of these gifts from the East. With or without a dictionary, define each and tell where it comes from.

1. honcho	11. boomerang	21. sofa
2. aloha	12. caftan	22. raj
3. turban	13. lanai	23. guru
4. tulip	14. karaoke	24. shawl
5. kimono	15. curry	25. hula
6. billabong	16. khaki	26. tofu
7. genie	17. yogurt	27. yoga
8. pukka	18. rattan	28. lei
9. sahib	19. sari	
10. sushi	20. bonsai	

Exercise IV.   Expanding Your Word Power

The words listed below are not on the Basic Word List, but they were mentioned in passing in Lesson 18. All of them would make useful additions to your working vocabulary. Define each, give its etymology, list **two** synonyms and **two** antonyms (where possible), and use in a short illustrative sentence.

1. mutilate	6. anemic	11. florid
2. revel	7. introverted	12. diatribe
3. incentive	8. lurid	13. pontificate
4. incite	9. invigorate	14. gratuity
5. impede	10. dubious	15. portent

Related Forms in Context

Beneath each sentence below are four words introduced in Lesson 17 or 18. Review the related forms for these words, and choose the one that best completes the sentence. Write that related form in the space provided.

1. On December 16, 1773, a party of angry colonists disguised as Mohawk Indians _____ broke the law when they dumped tea into Boston Harbor to protest the British tax on tea.

   a. frugal   b. fortuitous   c. flagrant   d. graphic

2. What do you think is the income _____ between someone with a high school diploma and a person with a college degree?

   a. forestall   b. gape   c. gloat   d. garble

3. Undaunted by the _____ of the task of cleaning the filthy stables of King Augeas in a single day, Hercules simply diverted two rivers to run through the stables.

   a. fickle   b. frugal   c. fortuitous   d. formidable

4. Eyewitnesses must have stood _____ as they watched Daedalus and his son Icarus, the first people to fly on man-made wings, soar out over the sea.

   a. fluctuate   b. grope   c. gape   d. harangue

5. By the age of 30, Harriet Tubman realized the _____ of the dream of buying her own freedom and escaped to the North.

   a. gullible   b. gratuitous   c. futile   d. flagrant

6. In ninth grade, Jim did a study to determine if _____ in the U.S. stock market could be directly tied to national and international news.

   a. finesse   b. fluctuate   c. harbinger   d. forestall

7. After he kills Tybalt, Romeo exclaims, "O! I am Fortune's fool," bemoaning the _____ of fate.

   a. fickle   b. flagrant   c. gratuitous   d. gregarious

8. Modern chaos theory builds on Heraclitus's notion that every-thing in nature is in a constant state of _____.

   a. flout   b. harangue   c. forestall   d. fluctuate

9. For years Dennis lived _____ on his small salary so that he could save enough money to bring all of his family from Ireland to America.

   a. fulsome   b. futile   c. frugal   d. flagrant

10. Christopher Columbus discovered the New World quite _____, for he had set out to find a passage to India.

    a. futile   b. fortuitous   c. formidable   d. fulsome

11. Both Quakers and Shakers value a life of _____ and simplicity.

    a. flagrant   b. futile   c. gruesome   d. frugal

12. Although the two archrivals complimented each other _____, their mutual dislike was quite obvious.

    a. fulsome   b. graphic   c. fickle   d. fortuitous

13. Those who peddle potions and pills that promise eternal youth and vitality rely on the _____ of people looking for quick and easy remedies.

    a. haggard   b. fortuitous   c. gruesome   d. gullible

14. Dorothea Lange's photographs document the plight of rural Americans during the Great Depression, capturing the _____ and despair reflected in their faces.

    a. fickle   b. graphic   c. haggard   d. gratuitous

15. Waiters and waitresses generally receive a very small salary and depend for their livelihood on _____ that their customers leave them.

    a. fortuitous   b. gratuitous   c. graphic   d. flagrant

16. The fierce brushstrokes and turbulent sky of Vincent Van Gogh's *Wheat Field with Crows* _____ illustrate the artist's inner turmoil.

    a. graphic   b. gregarious   c. flagrant   d. frugal

17. Every year when our parents celebrate their anniversary, they tell us how grateful they are for the _____ of their improbable meeting so many years ago.

    a. futile   b. gregarious   c. fortuitous   d. formidable

18. Jane Goodall's studies of chimpanzees on the shore of Africa's Lake Tanganyika revealed new data about their social structure and _____.

    a. graphic   b. haggard   c. gratuitous   d. gregarious

19. The _____, which is based on statistics from the latest U.S. census, illustrates the diversity of country of origin among those who identified themselves as Hispanic.

    a. flagrant   b. formidable   c. graphic   d. gratuitous

20. When she offered ten dollars to the young man who'd stopped to change her tire, he smiled and said, "Thanks very much, but my help is _____."

    a. gullible   b. gratuitous   c. fickle   d. flagrant

Lesson 19

---

221. haugh·ty   *adjective*   hô'-tē
[*haut* (Old French), "high," from *altus* (Latin), "high"]

Definition: Scornfully superior and aloof.

I know I wasn't born with a silver spoon in my mouth, but that's no reason for a **haughty** salesclerk to treat me as if I had just crawled out of the woodwork.

Their **haughty** manner proclaimed more eloquently than words could have that they could never associate with an obscure nobody like me.

Phrases: a haughty aristocrat, a haughty manner

Related Forms: (*nouns*) haughtiness, hauteur; (*adverb*) haughtily

Synonyms: (*adjectives*) supercilious, disdainful, contemptuous, snooty, condescending, patronizing; proud, arrogant

Antonyms: (*adjectives*) modest, diffident, unassuming, unpretentious, meek; servile, fawning, obsequious (Word 282)

Related Phrases: as proud as a peacock, look down one's nose at, get up on one's high horse

222. hei·nous   *adjective*   hā'-nəs
[*haineus* (Old French), "hateful," from *haine* (Old French), "hatred"]

Definition: Grossly wicked or vile.

We found it hard to believe that our mild-mannered neighbor had actually committed the **heinous** crime of which he was accused.

For ancient Greeks and Romans, throwing away one's shield and fleeing from the battlefield was the most **heinous** act of cowardice a soldier could commit.

Phrases: a heinous offense, a heinous act of treason

Related Forms: (*noun*) heinousness; (*adverb*) heinously

Synonyms: (*adjectives*) diabolic, villainous, nefarious, monstrous, infamous; odious, reprehensible, abominable, loathsome, atrocious, despicable, abhorrent, execrable

Antonyms: (*adjectives*) laudable, commendable, meritorious, estimable, admirable

Related Phrases: moral turpitude, a venial sin, a mortal sin

223. ig·no·min·y   *noun*   ĭg'-nə-mĭn-ē
[*ignominia* (Latin), "removal of one's good name"; from *in* (Latin), "un-, not" + *nomen, nominis* (Latin), "name"]

Definition: Dishonor or disgrace usually resulting from some sort of shameful conduct.

He was indeed a changed young man after he had suffered the **ignominy** of expulsion from West Point for conduct unbecoming an officer and a gentleman.

Related Forms: (*adjective*) ignominious; (*adverb*) ignominiously

Synonyms: (*nouns*) humiliation, degradation; disrepute, opprobrium, odium, infamy, obloquy

Antonyms: (*nouns*) esteem, acclaim, honor, admiration, glory, fame

Related Phrases: be under a cloud, be in bad odor, a blot on the escutcheon

224. il·lic·it   *adjective*   ĭ-lĭs'-ĭt
[*ill*, a form of *in* (Latin), "not" + *licitus* (Latin), "allowed"]

Definition: Unlawful, illegal.

Each year, part of the American tax dollar goes toward stemming the flood of **illicit** narcotics pouring into the country.

Related Forms: (*noun*) illicitness; (*adverb*) illicitly; (*adjective*) licit

Synonyms: (*adjectives*) unauthorized, unsanctioned; banned, forbidden, proscribed, outlawed; under-the-counter, under-the-table

Antonyms: (*adjectives*) legal, lawful, authorized, sanctioned; permissible, admissible, allowable, legitimate

Related Phrases: contraband goods, the black market, get in by the back door, a wildcat strike, off limits; go by the book

225. im·mac·u·late   *adjective*   ĭ-măk'-yə-lĭt
[*im*, a form of *in* (Latin), "un-, not" + *maculatus* (Latin), "blemished"]

Definition: Entirely free of stain, blemish, fault, or error; spotless.

Despite the heat and dirt of a summer day in the city, my mother managed to keep her clothing absolutely **immaculate**.

He was a brilliant statesman whose record remained **immaculate** throughout a long career in public office.

Related Forms: (*noun*) immaculateness; (*adverb*) immaculately

Synonyms: (*adjectives*) unsoiled, unsullied, untarnished, undefiled; flawless, impeccable, unimpeachable, irreproachable

Antonyms: (*adjectives*) stained, spotted, blemished, sullied, tarnished

Related Phrases: spick-and-span, lily-white, simon-pure, pure as the driven snow

Police and U.S. Treasury agents close down a bar during Prohibition.

The Black Market

Black market is the popular term for the illegal sale and purchase of various kinds of commodities in violation of official restrictions, such as price controls and rationing. The expression is also applied to the place where such transactions are carried out. Today, there are black markets for a whole host of commodities ranging from automobiles and firearms to cigarettes and drugs. Black-market operations are also common in the exchange of foreign and domestic currency, especially in countries where the government has set the official exchange rate too high. During Prohibition in the United States (1920–1933), when the manufacture and sale of alcohol were illegal, *bootlegging* became a highly lucrative business. Bootlegging, which is the illegal sale of alcohol, was essentially a black-market operation under a different name.

226. im‑mu‑ni‑ty   *noun*   ĭ-myōō'-nĭ-tē

[*immunis* (Latin), "exempt from service"; from *in* (Latin), "not" + *munia* (Latin), "duty, tax"]

Definition: Exemption from something, especially a disease.

Many people are fortunate enough to possess a natural **immunity** to certain diseases.

Though we all long for security in life, none of us can acquire total **immunity** from the hazards and misfortunes of the human condition.

Related Forms: (*verb*) immunize; (*noun*) immunization; (*adjective*) immune

Phrases: immune from prosecution; immune to reason; the immunization procedure

Synonyms: (*nouns*) impunity, insusceptibility; freedom, exclusion, release, protection, safety; dispensation, amnesty

Related Phrases: handle with kid gloves, preferential treatment, with impunity, get off with a slap on the wrist, go scot-free

227. im·mu·ta·ble   *adjective*   ĭ-myōō'-tə-bəl

[*im*, a form of *in* (Latin), "not" + *mutare, mutatus* (Latin), "change" + *abilis, abile* (Latin), "able to"]

Definition: Not subject to change or modification.

"Our legal system is not an **immutable** institution," the chief justice observed. "Like all else, it grows, develops, and changes over time."

Despite a series of unforeseen setbacks and failures, her faith in her own abilities remained **immutable**.

Related Forms: (*nouns*) immutability, immutableness, mutability; (*adjective*) mutable; (*adverb*) immutably

Synonyms: (*adjectives*) unchangeable, changeless, constant, fixed, invariable, unalterable, permanent; resolute, steadfast, unwavering, inflexible, rigid

Antonyms: (*adjectives*) changeable, alterable, variable; fickle, erratic, capricious, mercurial

Related Phrases: as constant as the northern star, as solid as the Rock of Gibraltar; a house built on sand

228. im·passe   *noun*   ĭm'-păs

[*impasse* (French), "dead end"; from *in* (French), "not" + *passer, passé* (French), "pass"]

Definition: A deadlock or dead end.

"Since we have reached an **impasse** in these negotiations," the union official asked the representative of management, "why don't we adjourn for the night?"

Related Forms: (*adjective*) impassable; (*nouns*) impassability, impassableness

Synonyms: (*nouns*) stalemate, cul-de-sac, standstill, dilemma

Related Phrases: lead up a blind alley, paint oneself into a corner, in a fix, in a bind, a Catch-22, come to a screeching (grinding) halt, a standoff, on the horns of a dilemma

Catch-22

A *Catch-22* is a difficult problem for which the different solutions that seem to be possible are logically invalid. The expression comes from *Catch-22*, the title of a novel by American writer Joseph Heller (1923–1999) (*see photo*). The hero of *Catch-22* faces many such situations throughout the course of the novel.

229. **im-ped-i-ment**   *noun*   ĭm-pĕd′-ə-mĕnt

[*impedimentum* (Latin), "obstacle"; from *impedire* (Latin), "get under foot or in the way"; from *in* (Latin), "in (the way of)" + *pes, pedis* (Latin), "foot"]

Definition: A hindrance or obstruction.

Lack of computer literacy is a serious **impediment** to finding a good job in today's world.

Phrase: a speech impediment

Related Forms: (*verb*) impede; (*noun*) impedimenta

Synonyms: (*nouns*) encumbrance; obstacle, handicap, barrier, bar

Antonyms: (*nouns*) aid, help, assistance

Related Phrases: a stumbling block, a fly in the ointment, a bottleneck; without let or hindrance; pull oneself up by one's bootstraps

230. **im-per-vi-ous**   *adjective*   ĭm-pẽr′-vē-əs

[*im*, a form of *in* (Latin), "not" + *per* (Latin), "through" + *via* (Latin), "road, way"]

Definition: Incapable of being penetrated or affected.

Cloth raincoats are usually treated with chemicals to make them **impervious** to water.

You may know someone who is absolutely **impervious** to criticism.

Related Forms: (*noun*) imperviousness; (*adjective*) pervious

Synonyms: (*adjectives*) impenetrable, impermeable; unresponsive, unreceptive, unamenable, closed (to)

Antonyms: (*adjectives*) penetrable, permeable, responsive, receptive, amenable (to), open (to), susceptible (to)

Related Phrases: proof against, hermetically sealed, vacuum-packed; stonewall someone; a closed society, a closed mind

231. **im-pla-ca-ble**   *adjective*   ĭm-plăk′-ə-bəl

[*im*, a form of *in* (Latin), "not" + *placare* (Latin), "calm, soothe" + *abilis, abile* (Latin), "able to"]

Definition: Incapable of being pacified or appeased; inflexible.

An **implacable** foe of slavery, William Lloyd Garrison took an uncompromising stand in favor of its abolition as early as 1831.

Several eighteenth-century British judges were **implacably** heartless and mechanical in the administration of justice.

Phrases: an implacable disease, implacable wrath

Related Forms: (*nouns*) implacableness, implacability; (*adverb*) implacably

Synonyms: (*adjectives*) unappeasable, unrelenting, unforgiving, relentless, inexorable, remorseless, unbending, obdurate, adamant, merciless

Antonyms: (*adjectives*) conciliatory, compassionate, understanding, merciful, forbearing

232. im-plic-it   *adjective*   ĭm-plĭs'-ĭt

[*implicitus* (Latin), "entangled, involved"; from *in* (Latin), "in" + *plicare, plicatus* (Latin), "fold"]

Definition:

a. Understood, implied.

> In almost any contract, there are **implicit** duties and obligations which must be fulfilled even though they are not expressed in so many words.

b. Absolute, unquestioning.

> He is the type of officer who expects **implicit** obedience from the troops under his command. When he gives an order, he assumes that it will be carried out.

Related Forms: (*adverb*) implicitly; (*nouns*) implicitness, implication; (*verb*) imply

Synonyms: (*adjectives*) inferred, inherent; tacit, unspoken; complete, unqualified, unconditional

Antonyms: (*adjectives*) explicit, specific, express

Related Phrases: take something for granted, categorically deny something, on a person's express orders

233. im-pugn   *verb*   ĭm-pyo͞on'

[*in* (Latin), "against" + *pugnare* (Latin), "fight"]

Definition: To call into question; to cast doubt on.

> "Before you **impugn** the man's motives for doing what he did," I said, "you'd better make certain that you can back up your suspicions with hard evidence."

Phrases: impugn a person's veracity or honor, impugn a claim

Related Forms: (*nouns*) impugnment, impugnation; (*adjective*) impugnable

Synonyms: (*verbs*) question, query, challenge, deny, gainsay, dispute, malign

Antonyms: (*verbs*) vindicate, acquit, exonerate, exculpate; justify, rationalize; defend, champion, vouch for; affirm, verify, substantiate, confirm, corroborate

Related Phrases: cast aspersions on, run down, take exception to, badmouth someone, hurl brickbats at; backbiting; stick up for, an apologist

234. in-car-cer-ate   *verb*   ĭn-kär'-sə-rāt

[*incarcerare, incarceratus* (Latin), "imprison"; from *in* (Latin), "in" + *carcer* (Latin), "prison"]

Definition: To put in jail or otherwise confine.

In a democratic society such as ours, people may freely express their opinions without fear of being **incarcerated** for doing so.

In the Victorian era, fashionable ladies thought nothing of **incarcerating** their waists in tight corsets in order to achieve a chic hourglass figure.

Related Form: (*noun*) incarceration

Synonyms: (*verbs*) jail, imprison, intern; cage, immure, constrain, constrict

Antonyms: (*verbs*) liberate, emancipate, set free, release

Related Phrases: mew up, coop up, keep under lock and key, keep under wraps, a shut-in

235. in-cense   *verb*   ĭn-sĕns'

[*incendere, incensus* (Latin), "set on fire, enrage"; from *in* (Latin), "in, on" + *candere* (Latin), "glow"]

Definition: To make violently angry.

"You rarely give me cause to become angry," Dad said, "but this time your behavior has truly **incensed** me."

Related Form: (*adjective*) incendiary

Synonyms: (*verbs*) enrage, infuriate, enflame, provoke, incite

Antonyms: (*verbs*) soothe, calm, pacify, mollify, appease, placate

Related Phrases: see red, make one's blood boil, raise the hackles on one's neck, get under one's skin; a thorn in one's side.

(*Left*) A priest prepares incense for use during the Eucharist; (*right*) sticks of incense burning in a Buddhist temple. As a noun, *incense* (pronounced ĭn'-sĕns) indicates an aromatic gum or wood that produces a pleasant aroma when burned. Incense is often used in religious ceremonies to indicate the presence of God.

Using the Words

Exercise I. Syllabication and Pronunciation

Syllabicate the following words correctly, and place the major stress mark (') after the syllable that is accented when the word is pronounced.

1. heinous
2. ignominy
3. illicit
4. impediment
5. immunity
6. immutable
7. impugn
8. incarcerate
9. impasse

Exercise II. Words Out of Context

In each of the following groups, select the item that best expresses the meaning of the numbered word at the left.

1. illicit
   a. illiterate   b. illustrious   c. illegible
   d. illogical   e. illegal

2. immaculate
   a. harmless   b. spotless   c. timeless
   d. shameless   e. pointless

3. impasse
   a. solution   b. viewpoint   c. mistake
   d. deadlock   e. tunnel

4. implicit
   a. villainous   b. constant   c. implied
   d. legitimate   e. modest

5. impervious
   a. shocked by   b. closed to   c. fond of
   d. eager for   e. undecided about

6. implacable
   a. costly   b. outlawed   c. unspoken
   d. diabolic   e. relentless

7. incense
   a. enrage   b. puzzle   c. frighten
   d. bore   e. elate

Exercise III. Completing Sentences

Complete each of the following sentences by selecting the most appropriate word from the group of words given below. Use each word only once.

impugn	incarcerate	impediment
heinous	incense	immutable
immunity	ignominy	haughty

1. According to the Greek philosopher Heraclitus, the only _____ law of nature is, paradoxically, that everything changes.

2. Somehow or other, the convicted murderer managed to escape from the maximum-security prison in which he had been _____.

3. Once the leader's integrity had been _____, his authority began to be challenged as well.

4. It wasn't the misfortune of losing the tennis match that mortified me so much as the _____ of being defeated by a mere beginner.

5. Few crimes have been so monstrous and inhuman as Adolf Hitler's _____ scheme to exterminate millions of innocent people in grisly death camps.

6. With a sneer of contempt and a flick of his fingers, the _____ young man disdainfully dismissed both me and my suggestion from his mind.

7. No matter how carefully we try to protect ourselves, none of us ever achieves complete _____ from sickness and disease.

8. Fear of failure can often become a formidable _____ to success because it inhibits the mind and paralyzes the will.

Exercise IV. Synonyms and Antonyms

Classify each of the following pairs of words as **S** for **synonyms** or **A** for **antonyms**.

1. anger—incense
2. impervious—receptive
3. illicit—legal
4. immaculate—flawless
5. ignominy—disgrace
6. meek—haughty
7. heinous—loathsome

8. impediment—obstacle
9. fixed—immutable
10. defend—impugn
11. incarcerate—liberate
12. standstill—impasse
13. implacable—unrelenting
14. explicit—implicit

Exercise V. Word Roundup

1. With or without the aid of a dictionary, explain the difference in meaning between the words in each of the following pairs.

   a. illicit—elicit
   b. impugn—impute

   c. impassable—impassive
   d. venal—venial

2. With or without the aid of a dictionary, explain what each of the following expressions means.

   a. impedimenta
   b. an apologist
   c. a shut-in

   d. a bottleneck
   e. stonewall someone
   f. bad-mouth someone

3. With or without the aid of a dictionary, explain what each of the following colorful phrases means.

a. look down one's nose at   e. paint oneself into a corner
b. be under a cloud   f. go scot-free
c. go by the book   g. get up on one's high horse
d. see red   h. handle with kid gloves

4. Define each of the following, and explain where it came from.

a. a Catch-22   b. simon-pure

Exercise VI. Framing Sentences

A. Use each of the following words in an original sentence.

1. impugn   3. incense   5. implacable
2. impasse   4. immutable   6. impervious

B. Give a **noun** form of each of the following words, and use it in an original sentence.

1. incarcerate   2. heinous   3. haughty

C. Give a **verb** form related to each of the following words, and use it in an original sentence.

1. immunity   2. impediment   3. implicit

D. Give an **adverb** form of each of the following words, and use it in an original sentence.

1. illicit   2. immaculate   3. ignominy

Dissecting the Words

Prefixes

1. The Latin prefix **in** appears in a great many common English words. Basically, this prefix has two quite distinct meanings:

a. "Not," as in these words:

indefensible (*in*, "not" + *defensible*)—not capable of being defended, justified, or excused

invalidate (*in*, "not" + *validate*)—to nullify

inactivity (*in*, "not" + *activity*)—a lack of activity; idleness

inadvertently (*in*, "not" + *advertently*)—accidentally or unintentionally

When *in* has the meaning "not," it negates the sense of the word to which it is attached. In this regard, it functions in exactly the same way as the other negative prefixes used in modern English—*non*, *un*, and *a(n)*.

b. "In, into, within," as in these words:

incarnate (*in*, "into" + *caro, carnis* [Latin], "flesh")—to invest with bodily form and nature

inauguration (*in*, "in" + *augur*)—a formal beginning or introduction

incarcerate (*in*, "into" + *carcer* [Latin], "prison"]—to put in prison

Note: In a few English words, *in* acts as an intensive, with the general meaning "very" or "completely." This use of the prefix occurs, for example, in the word *incandescent*, which means "glowing very bright."

2. The prefix *in* has several variant forms which are used when the word to which *in* is attached begins with a particular consonant, as follows:

a. The form **ig** is used in a few English words starting with *n*. For example:

ignoble (*ig*, "not" + *noble*)—base or lowborn; dishonorable

ignore (*ig*, "not" + *gnarus* [Latin], "knowing, known")—to refuse to notice; to reject or throw out

b. The form **il** is used before words beginning with an *l*. For example:

illogical (*il*, "not" + *logical*)—not logical

illuminate (*il*, "in" + *lumen, luminis* [Latin], "light")—to light up. Noun: *illumination*

c. The form **im** is used before a word beginning with an *m* or a *p*. For example:

immoral (*im*, "not" + *moral*)—not in accord with the accepted moral code

immerse (*im*, "not" + *mergere, mersus* [Latin], "dip")—to submerge or absorb completely

impure (*im*, "not" + *pure*)—not pure

impede (*im*, "in" + *pes, pedis* [Latin], "foot")—to hinder or obstruct

d. The form **ir** is used before a word beginning with an *r*. For example:

irreverent (*ir*, "not" + *reverent*)—lacking in sufficient respect for

irrigate (*ir*, "in" + *rigare, rigatus* [Latin], "bring water")—to supply with water; to wash out with water or another fluid

Roots

1. The Latin word **via**, which appears in the word *impervious*, studied in this lesson, means "road" or "way." Other common English words in which *via* appears as a root element include:

viaduct (*via*, "road" + *ducere, ductus* (Latin], "lead")—a bridge supporting a road or railroad over a valley or another (rail)road

deviate (*de* [Latin], "away" + *via*, "road, way" + *ate*, an English verb-forming suffix)—to turn or move away from. Noun: *deviation*

devious (*de* [Latin], "away" + *via*, "road, way" + *ous*, "characterized by")—not straightforward; roundabout or shifty. Noun: *deviousness convey* (*cum* [Latin], "with" + *via*, "road, way")—to transmit or transport. Noun: *conveyance*—a vehicle; the act of transporting something

By itself, the Latin word *via* is used in English as a preposition with the meaning "by way of." For example, "I drove to Chicago *via* Buffalo."

2. The Latin root **nomin** means "name." It appears in a number of common English words, including *ignominy*, studied in this lesson. Other English words in which it is used are:

nominal (*nomen, nominis*, "name" + *alis* [Latin], "relating to")—existing in name only; insignificantly small

nominate (*nomen, nominis*, "name" + *ate*, an English verb-forming suffix) —to propose for some office, responsibility, or honor. Noun: *nomination*

denomination (*de* [Latin], "completely" + *nomen, nominis*, "name" + *ation* [Latin], "state or process of")—the name of a specific group or class; an organized religious group

misnomer (*minus* [Latin], "less, wrong" + *nomen, nominis*, "name")— an error in naming something; a name inappropriately applied to something

3. The parallel Greek word-building element usually appears in English as **onym** or **onomy**. Like *nomin*, these word elements mean "name." They appear in a number of very familiar English words, including *synonym*, *antonym*, and *homonym*. Other English words in which they are used are:

pseudonym (*pseudes* [Greek], "false" + *onoma, onyma*, [Greek], "name")— an assumed name

anonymous (*an* [Greek], "without" + *onoma, onyma*, [Greek], "name" + *ous* [Latin] "characterized by")—of unknown authorship. Noun: *anonymity*

onomatopoeia (*onoma, onyma*, [Greek], "name" + *poiein* [Greek], "make")— the formation of a word that imitates the sound of the thing it designates; for example, *hiss* or *buzz*

It is a little-known fact that Charlotte Bronte (1816–1855), the author of *Jane Eyre*, produced many of her works under the masculine pseudonym Currer Bell.

Exercise

1. For each of the following definitions, give an English word that contains the prefix *in* or one of its variants. Consult a dictionary if necessary.

    a. base or lowborn
    b. not capable of variation
    c. not able to be defended
    d. not in motion
    e. lacking sufficient respect
    f. not valid
    g. showing no emotion
    h. spotlessly clean
    i. not logical
    j. nullify

2. Change each of the following positive words to its negative form by adding the prefix *in* or one of its variants. Consult a dictionary if necessary.

    a. apt
    b. reversible
    c. excusable
    d. solvent
    e. contestible
    f. pious
    g. redeemable
    h. judicious
    i. reducible
    j. adequate

3. With or without the aid of a dictionary, define each of the following words and use it in a short illustrative sentence.

    a. nomenclature
    b. pseudonym
    c. nominate
    d. conveyance
    e. devious
    f. convoy
    g. deviate
    h. misnomer
    i. viaduct
    j. anonymity

Working with Context Clues

More About Two-Word Omissions. Carefully study the following example of a fairly difficult two-word omission. Try to determine the correct answer before you read the explanation of it given below.

> Because a medieval castle was primarily a fortress, it was built more for _____ than for _____.
>
> a. decoration . . . usefulness
> b. aggression . . . belligerence
> c. pageantry . . . protection
> d. defense . . . comfort

The correct answer is *d. defense . . . comfort,* as the following explanation clearly indicates.

Notice the brevity of the sentence contained in the example. It is only 17 words long. This suggests that some kind of inference clue will play a large part in determining the correct answer. Notice too the word *Because.* It suggests that you are dealing with a cause-and-effect relationship. Finally, notice the phrase *more for . . . than for* toward the end of the sentence. It indicates that two contrasting words go in the blanks.

Bearing these considerations in mind, reread the sentence carefully to find out what you are to do and how you can go about doing it. The sentence says that a medieval castle was by nature a certain type of build-

A view of the fortress at Carcassonne, France, one of the few surviving examples of a medieval walled city.

ing and that this defined the purpose it served. You are to explain what that purpose was based upon the information the sentence gives about the nature of a castle.

And what was the nature of a castle? The sentence says it was *primarily a fortress*. As you know, a fortress can be used for several purposes. It can serve as a refuge or as a prison or as a means of holding rebellious subjects in line. This suggests that the word that goes in the first blank means something like "protection" or "security" or some related idea.

Now run your eye down the first item in each of the four lettered choices. Eliminate any choice that does not conform to your conclusion about the general meaning of the word that goes in the first blank.

Choices *a* (*decoration*) and *c* (*pageantry*) do not agree with your conclusion, so they can safely be eliminated. Choices *b* (*aggression*) and *d* (*defense*), however, do, so you still have some thinking to do before you can make the correct choice.

At this point, recall what was said about the implication of the phrase *more for . . . than for*. It suggests that two *contrasting* words go in the blanks.

Accordingly, consider choices *b* and *d* from this angle. Choice *b* (*aggression . . . belligerence*) does not contain contrasting nouns, so it can be eliminated. Choice *d* (*defense . . . comfort*), however, does, so it must be the correct answer. And, of course, it is.

Exercise

Complete each of the following two-word omissions by selecting the pair of words that make the best sense in the passage as a whole. Underline the clue or clues that led you to make your choice.

1. After two difficult years in the White House, a few run-ins with the press, and several long, _____ battles with a stubborn Congress, it is no wonder that the president looks _____ and years older than when he took office.

   a. graphic . . . demure   c. diligent . . . emaciated
   b. grueling . . . haggard   d. gregarious . . . exotic

2. Clever advertisers continue to _____ supposedly sophisticated American consumers into believing the obvious _____ that cosmetics can confer youth and beauty on anyone.

   a. badger . . . effrontery
   b. cajole . . . epithet
   c. delude . . . fallacy
   d. coerce . . . calumny

3. Since the stock market is always rising and falling, investors who want to maintain their _____ must calmly stick with their investment strategy when stock prices _____ from day to day.

   a. equanimity . . . fluctuate
   b. bravado . . . augment
   c. finesse . . . deviate
   d. empathy . . . acclimate

4. The _____ monks who chose to _____ the *Book of Kells* with such beautiful decoration revealed not only their deep faith but also their superb artistry.

   a. eclectic . . . flaunt
   b. benign . . . array
   c. aesthetic . . . exalt
   d. devout . . . embellish

5. In 1955, when the black citizens of Montgomery, Alabama, defiantly refused to ride the segregated city buses, their _____ was meant to _____ local law and custom.

   a. anarchy . . . goad
   b. boycott . . . flout
   c. censure . . . exploit
   d. exodus . . . abet

Enriching the Lesson

Exercise I.   The Vocabulary of Social Change

Many expressions used today are associated with movements for social or cultural change. The words that make up these expressions have usually been around for a long time, but they are now being used in a sense that gives them a new significance and relevancy. This exercise is designed to help you improve your knowledge of a few of these terms.

A. *Causes Galore.*   Our national history in recent decades has been marked by many special causes and reform movements. The terms connected with a few of these movements are listed below. With or without the aid of a dictionary or other reference book, define each.

1. consumerism
2. environmentalism
3. urban renewal
4. feminism
5. multiculturalism
6. libertarianism
7. elitism
8. regionalism
9. animal rights

B. *The Struggle for Racial Equality.* Listed below are a number of terms and expressions associated with the struggle for racial equality. One of them, *lily-white*, was mentioned in passing in this lesson. With or without the aid of a dictionary or other reference book, define each.

1. racism
2. second-class citizen
3. black power
4. segregation
5. integration
6. racial profiling
7. stereotype
8. sit-in
9. lily-white
10. pluralism
11. redlining
12. equal opportunity

Exercise II.   The Heritage of Literature

A. *Contributions Old and New.* Modern English has borrowed a surprising number of words and phrases from the works of famous and not-so-famous authors. Two of these expressions, *Catch-22* and *simon-pure*, were mentioned in this lesson. A few more are listed below. With or without the aid of a dictionary or other reference book, define each. Then give the source of the expression.

1. quixotic
2. a Pollyanna
3. gargantuan
4. a Babbitt
5. braggadocio
6. a Scrooge
7. serendipity
8. a rodomontade
9. a quark
10. bite the hand that feeds you
11. a termagant
12. a yahoo
13. utopian
14. a ragamuffin
15. an Ugly Duckling

Sir Thomas More (1478–1535) was a great English statesman, humanist, and martyr. Which of the words listed in Part A of Exercise II on this page did he contribute to the English language?

B. *William Shakespeare.* The works of William Shakespeare (1564–1616) have had a remarkable impact on the English language, including its vocabulary. Listed below are a number of familiar expressions that all derive in one way or another from Shakespeare's plays. With or without the aid of a dictionary or other reference book, define each as it is used in present-day English. Then give the name of the play from which the expression comes.

1. salad days
2. a pound of flesh
3. the milk of human kindness
4. a benedict
5. the primrose path
6. sleep in Abraham's bosom
7. mum's the word
8. hoist by one's own petard

Exercise III.   A Verbal Diversion

One of the interesting English expressions mentioned in passing in this lesson was *see red*, meaning "become very angry." English has a number of other useful terms and expressions employing the adjective *red*. Some of them are listed below. With or without the aid of a dictionary, define or explain each. Then choose any **five** and for each compose an original illustrative sentence.

1. a red-letter day
2. a red herring
3. caught red-handed
4. a redneck
5. to paint the town red
6. in the red
7. to red-pencil
8. to roll out the red carpet
9. red tape
10. red flag

Exercise IV.   Expanding Your Word Power

The words listed below are not on the Basic Word List, but they were mentioned in passing, in one form or another, in Lesson 19. All of them would make useful additions to your working vocabulary. Define each, give its etymology, list **two** synonyms and **two** antonyms (where possible), and use in a short illustrative sentence.

1. condescend
2. nefarious
3. turpitude
4. sully
5. impunity
6. dispensation
7. unimpeachable
8. encumber
9. obdurate
10. gainsay
11. rationalize
12. constrain
13. acclaim
14. mollify
15. query

Lesson 20

236. **inception** — 250. **justify**

---

236. in·cep·tion   *noun*   ĭn-sĕp'-shən
[*inceptio, inceptionis* (Latin), "beginning"; from *incipere, inceptus* (Latin), "begin"; from *in* (Latin), "in, on" + *capere* (Latin), "take"]

Definition: The beginning of something.
"I have been an active member of our local bowling association," Grand-dad proudly boasted, "since its **inception** thirty years ago."
At the time of its **inception,** politicians always predict that great things will come of a new government program, but these high hopes are rarely fully realized.

Related Forms: (*adjective*) incipient; (*nouns*) incipience, incipiency

Synonyms: (*nouns*) commencement, inauguration, initiation, outset, kickoff, origin, onset, outbreak, debut, opening

Antonyms: (*nouns*) conclusion, finale, windup, finish, termination, close, completion, consummation, culmination, climax, denouement (Word 125)

Related Phrases: the opening gun, the starting lineup; from soup to nuts; the alpha and omega

237. in·di·gent   *adjective*   ĭn'-dĭ-jənt
[*indigens, indigentis* (Latin), "lacking, needing"]

Definition: Impoverished; needy.
The Wall Street Crash of 1929 left many a wealthy speculator as **indigent** as the proverbial church mouse.
Though the federal government does much to help those who are **indigent**, private charities play no little part in seeing to their welfare.

Related Form: (*noun*) indigence

Usage Note:
Be careful not to confuse *indigent* with either *indigenous*, meaning "native to," or *indignant*, meaning "irate" or "incensed."

Synonyms: (*adjectives*) destitute, impecunious, penniless, poverty-stricken

Antonyms: (*adjectives*) rich, wealthy, affluent (Word 17), well-to-do, well-off, well-heeled

Related Phrases: down in the heels, on the rocks, as poor as a church mouse; keep the wolf from the door, make ends meet, down and out

Thomas Alva Edison (1847–1931), the "Wizard of Menlo Park," was one of the most ingenious inventors ever produced by the United States.

238. in·gen·ious   *adjective*   ĭn-jēn′-yəs
[*ingenieux* (French), "clever"; from *ingenium* (Latin), "inborn talent"]

Definition: Showing remarkable originality, imagination, inventiveness, or skill; clever.

In 1793, Eli Whitney invented the cotton gin, an **ingenious** device for separating the seeds from the fiber quickly and easily.

Related Forms: (*nouns*) ingeniousness, ingenuity; (*adverb*) ingeniously

Usage Note:
Be careful not to confuse *ingenious* with *ingenuous* (note the first *u*), meaning "artless and unsophisticated" or "open and frank."

Synonyms: (*adjectives*) brilliant, inventive, creative, imaginative, talented; shrewd, cunning, crafty, astute; masterly, Daedalian

Antonyms: (*adjectives*) unimaginative, uninventive, unremarkable, unoriginal, pedestrian

239. in·her·ent   *adjective*   ĭn-hîr′-ĕnt
[*inhaerens, inhaerentis* (Latin), "sticking to"; from *in* (Latin), "in, on" + *haerere* (Latin), "stick, adhere"]

Definition: Existing as a natural or essential part of.

Most Americans firmly believe that the advantages **inherent** in a democratic form of government far outweigh the drawbacks that such a system usually entails.

Related Forms: (*adverb*) inherently; (*verb*) inhere; (*noun*) inherence

Synonyms: (*adjectives*) intrinsic, implicit, essential, internal, inner, fundamental, built-in, immanent, organic, natural, innate

Antonyms: (*adjectives*) extrinsic, external, extraneous, outside, foreign, alien; incidental, adventitious

Related Phrases: in the blood, to the manner born; a congenital defect

240. in-no-va-tion   *noun*   ĭn-ə-vā'-shən

[*innovare, innovatus* (Latin), "renew, alter"; from *in* (Latin), "completely" + *novus* (Latin), "new"]

Definition: Something new; a change.

In our eagerness to embrace whatever is new and modern, we must not assume that all **innovations** are necessarily practical and constructive.

Related Forms: (*noun*) innovator; (*verb*) innovate; (*adjective*) innovative

Usage Notes:

   a. Do not use the word *new* to qualify *innovation* because the word *new* is redundant.

   b. *Innovation* is often followed by the preposition *in*, as in the phrase "make innovations *in* the school curriculum."

Synonyms: (*nouns*) novelty, alteration, new wrinkle

Related Phrases: give something a new look, give something a face-lift; coin a word; cosmetic alterations, the avant-garde, a neologism

241. in-sti-gate   *verb*   ĭn'-stĭ-gāt

[*instigare, instigatus* (Latin), "spur on"]

Definition: To stir up or urge on.

Troublemakers in the crowd attempted to **instigate** a riot, but fortunately their efforts proved unsuccessful.

Related Forms: (*nouns*) instigation, instigator

Synonyms: (*verbs*) provoke, incite, foment, generate, touch off, start

Antonyms: (*verbs*) quell, quash, squelch, suppress, stop; allay, pacify

Related Phrases: put the kibosh on; an agent provocateur, a stormy petrel

242. in-su-per-a-ble   *adjective*   ĭn-sōō'-pêr-ə-bəl

[*insuperabilis, insuperabile* (Latin), "unconquerable" from *in* (Latin), "not" + *super-are* (Latin), "conquer" + *abilis, abile* (Latin), "able to"]

Definition: Incapable of being overcome.

"Much as I'd love to play shortstop for the Yanks, my age is an **insuperable** barrier to realizing any such dream," Granddad remarked.

Phrases: insuperable obstacles, insuperable difficulties

Related Forms: (*nouns*) insuperability, insuperableness

Synonyms: (*adjectives*) insurmountable, overwhelming, invincible, unconquerable, indomitable

Antonyms: (*adjectives*) surmountable, conquerable, vincible

243. in-ter-vene   *verb*   ĭn-tĕr-vēn′

[*intervenire* (Latin), "come between"; from *inter* (Latin), "between" + *venire* (Latin), "come"]

Definition: To come between; to involve oneself in.

A great many years **intervened** between the murder of the Russian imperial family and the discovery of their remains.

However benevolent your intentions, you may do more harm than good if you **intervene** in other people's quarrels.

Related Forms: (*nouns*) intervention, interventionism

Synonyms: (*verbs*) separate; interfere, meddle, intrude, interpose; kibitz

Related Phrases: an interloper; horn in on, poke one's nose into, put one's oar in, put one's two cents' worth in; in the interim; sandwiched in between

UN troops enter a town in Bosnia. During the early 1990s a multinational UN force was dispatched to the region to help put an end to a bloody civil war.

Interventionism

Interventionism is a term that is often used in discussions of international politics to describe the behavior of one country in regard to the other countries of the world, especially the smaller, weaker, and less stable ones. What the term indicates is the intentional policy of one sovereign nation of interfering in the domestic affairs of another sovereign nation. The implication, of course, is that such a policy is undertaken for purely selfish reasons or in order to achieve some advantage over one's enemies. Accordingly, the tone of the word is decidedly negative.

244. in-trep-id   *adjective*   ĭn-trĕp'-id

[*intrepidus* (Latin), "fearless"; from *in* (Latin), "not" + *trepidus* (Latin), "frightened, alarmed"]

Definition: Fearless and bold.

The rows of white gravestones in Arlington National Cemetery are poignant reminders of the **intrepid** men and women who gave their lives in defense of this country.

"In carrying out new programs," the legislator remarked, "we need people who are **intrepid** enough to take a few risks, even with their lives and reputations."

Related Forms: (*nouns*) intrepidity, intrepidness; (*adverb*) intrepidly

Synonyms: (*adjectives*) valiant, daring, courageous, gallant, gutsy, stouthearted, lionhearted, audacious, valorous, heroic

Antonyms: (*adjectives*) cowardly, craven, timorous, pusillanimous

245. in-veigh   *verb*   ĭn-vā'

[*invehere* (Latin), "carry in, attack"; from *in* (Latin), "in" + *vehere* (Latin),"carry"]

Definition: To protest bitterly or vehemently.

When the train ground to a halt yet again, one passenger began to **inveigh** angrily against the transit system and the people who ran it.

Related Form: (*noun*) invective

Usage Note:
Do not confuse *inveigh* with *inveigle,* which means "to obtain by flattery or deceit."

Synonyms: (*verbs*) rail against, fulminate against, denounce, berate, decry, lambaste

Antonyms: (*verbs*) praise, commend, extol, laud

Related Phrases: jump down someone's throat, give someone a tongue-lashing

246. i-ro-ny   *noun*   ī'-rə-nē

[*eironeia* (Greek), "pretended ignorance"; from *eirein* (Greek), "say"]

Definition: Incongruity between what might be expected and what actually happens.

It was one of life's little **ironies** that a man who had condemned so many others to the gallows should himself die by the noose.

Related Forms: (*adjectives*) ironic, ironical; (*adverb*) ironically

Synonyms: (*nouns*) contradiction, paradox

Related Phrases: a backhanded compliment, damn with faint praise

Mark Antony (Marlon Brando) delivers the funeral oration in the 1953 film version of Shakespeare's *Julius Caesar*.

Verbal and Dramatic Irony

Verbal irony refers to the use of words to convey the opposite of their literal meaning. For example, a person who uses expressions of praise in order to scold someone else is employing verbal irony. The device is frequently used to achieve a humorous, sarcastic, or dramatic effect. One of the most famous examples of the use of verbal irony to achieve a dramatic effect occurs in Shakespeare's *Julius Caesar*. In his funeral oration over Caesar's body, Mark Antony repeatedly characterizes Brutus and the other conspirators as "honorable men" who did Rome a service by murdering Caesar when, of course, he intends his audience to understand that they were quite the opposite.

Dramatic irony is a related device used in plays and similar material. The term indicates an incongruity between the significance of an action on the stage and the literal meaning of the words or speeches that accompany it. The audience, of course, perceives this incongruity, but the characters in the play do not. For example, Lady Macbeth's effusive greeting of King Duncan in Shakespeare's *Macbeth* is painfully ironic because the audience knows that she and her husband plan to murder the old monarch that night. King Duncan is unaware of this, so he takes the lady's words at face value and blithely walks into the trap. To Duncan, Lady Macbeth appears to be the quintessence of hospitality; to the audience, she is more like a spider luring a fly into its web.

247. jeop·ard·ize   *verb*   jĕp'-ẽr-dīz

[*jeu parti* (Old French), a game in which the chances of winning or losing are equal; from *jeu* (French), "game" + *parti* (French), "divided"]

Definition: To endanger.

High school students who settle for mediocre grades when they could be doing better are **jeopardizing** their chances of being accepted by the college of their choice.

Related Form: (*noun*) jeopardy

Usage Note:

The legal expression *double jeopardy* refers to putting a person on trial for the same crime twice. Under our system of law, this is of course illegal.

Synonyms: (*verbs*) risk, hazard, imperil, compromise, gamble with

Antonyms: (*verbs*) protect, shield, safeguard, defend; improve, better

Related Phrases: sail too near the wind, fly too close to the sun, tempt fate

248. jet·ti·son   *verb*   jĕt'-ĭ-sən *or* jĕt'-ĭ-zən

[*getteson(e)* (Old French), "a throwing overboard"; from *jacere, jactus* (Latin), "throw"]

Definition: To throw overboard; to discard.

The crew of the sinking freighter **jettisoned** most of the cargo in a desperate effort to keep the ship afloat.

In our eagerness to improve the quality of life in America, we should not be too quick to **jettison** old ideas simply because they are old.

Synonyms: (*verbs*) dump, throw out, junk, abandon, toss out

Antonyms: (*verbs*) conserve, preserve, keep, hold on to, retain

Related Phrases: flotsam and jetsam, give something the deep-six

249. ju·di·cious   *adjective*   jo͞o-dĭsh'-əs

[*judicieux* (French), "wise"; from *judicium* (Latin), "judgment"]

Definition: Having or exhibiting sound judgment.

Thanks to my broker's **judicious** advice, I refrained from making what turned out to be a very unsound investment.

Related Forms: (*noun*) judiciousness, (*adverb*) judiciously; (*adjective*) injudicious

Usage Note:

Be careful not to confuse the adjective *judicious,* meaning "having or showing sound judgment," with the related adjective *judicial.* The latter means "relating to a court, the administration of justice, or the office of a judge." For example, the *judicial* system is the court system.

316

Similarly, *judicial review* is the constitutional principle that gives the Supreme Court the right to cancel any legislative or executive act that the justices sitting on the Court consider unconstitutional.

Phrases: a judicious choice of words, a judicious mixture of elements

Synonyms: (*adjectives*) prudent, astute, discriminating, discerning, sagacious, sage, shrewd

Antonyms: unwise, imprudent, foolish, rash, unsound

250. **jus-ti-fy**   *verb*   jŭs'-tə-fī

[*justificare* (Latin), "do justice to"; from *justus* (Latin), "just" + *facere* (Latin), "do, make"]

Definition: To show to be just, right, valid, or free of blame.

"You may be able to **justify** your anger at Bill," I replied, "but you were quite wrong to hit him."

The excellent quality of the coat clearly **justifies** its high price.

Related Forms: (*adjective*) justifiable; (*adverb*) justifiably; (*nouns*) justification, justifiability, justifiableness

Synonyms: (*verbs*) defend, vindicate

Related Phrases: show just cause for, give good reasons for

Using the Words

Exercise I. Parts of Speech

Indicate the part of speech of each of the following words.

1. indigent
2. innovation
3. insuperable
4. intrepid
5. inveigh
6. irony
7. jettison
8. judicious
9. justify

Exercise II. Words in Phrases

In each of the following groups, select the item that best expresses the meaning of the *italicized* expression in the introductory phrase.

1. *jeopardize* one's chances of success
   a. insure   b. endanger   c. calculate   d. doubt
   e. enhance

2. a *judicious* choice of words
   a. surprising   b. silly   c. novel   d. painful   e. prudent

3. *inveigh against* injustice
   a. champion   b. ignore   c. denounce   d. report
   e. improve

4. an *ingenious* scheme to make money
   a. clever   b. unworkable   c. costly   d. problematic
   e. dangerous

5. full of *inherent* problems and defects
   a. built-in   b. minor   c. unexpected   d. knotty
   e. temporary

6. since its *inception*
   a. demise   b. graduation   c. marriage   d. inauguration
   e. dismissal

7. "*justify* the ways of God to man"
   a. criticize   b. divulge   c. vindicate   d. deplore
   e. conceal

Exercise III.   Completing Sentences

Complete each of the following sentences or pairs of sentences by selecting the most appropriate word from the group of words given below. Use each word only once.

intrepid	intervene	indigent
instigate	jettison	irony
innovation	inveigh	insuperable

1. The man's ragged clothing and emaciated body told me instantly that he was totally _____.

2. Often a(n) _____ that seems bold and inventive when it is first introduced is soon taken for granted.

3. "I will never concede defeat," I told myself, "no matter how _____ the odds against me appear to be."

4. The old adage "Don't throw the baby out with the bathwater" cautions us against inadvertently _____ the good with the bad.

5. There is an unmistakable _____ in the fact that the steps the dictator took to insure his own safety proved his undoing.

6. "It is one thing to be _____," my best friend observed when I tried to ride a horse I couldn't handle. "It is quite another to be foolhardy."

7. "Are you the troublemaker who _____ the food fight in the cafeteria today?" the principal asked me angrily.

8. Though I didn't start to write my report until two weeks after I had completed my research, I used the time that _____ to plan it out.

Exercise IV. Synonyms and Antonyms

A. In each of the following groups, select the **two** words that are most nearly **synonymous**.

1. a. clever   b. prominent   c. mature   d. inventive
2. a. baffle   b. provoke   c. foment   d. divulge
3. a. inaudible   b. insurmountable   c. inconceivable
   d. invincible
4. a. interfere   b. conclude   c. meddle   d. devise
5. a. abandon   b. discard   c. retain   d. increase

Now, for each pair of synonyms that you have selected, supply a word from the Basic Word List for this lesson (Words 236–250) that means **the same** or **almost the same** thing.

B. In each of the following, select the item that is most nearly **opposite** in meaning to the numbered word at the left.

1. judicious   a. illegal   b. wealthy   c. unwise   d. novel
   e. expert

2. inception   a. articulation   b. fabrication   c. inauguration
   d. collaboration   e. termination

3. indigent   a. dejected   b. coarse   c. blithe   d. eminent
   e. affluent

4. intrepid   a. slovenly   b. treacherous   c. ignorant
   d. cowardly   e. cruel

5. jeopardize   a. protect   b. yield   c. claim   d. delay
   e. encounter

Exercise V. Word Roundup

1. Explain the difference in meaning between the items in each of the following pairs of words.

   a. indigent—indigenous   c. ingenious—ingenuous
   b. inveigh—inveigle   d. judicious—judicial

2. With or without a dictionary, define each of the following French expressions commonly used in modern English.

   a. agent provocateur   b. tour de force   c. avant-garde

3. With or without the aid of a dictionary, explain what each of the following means.

   a. a backhanded compliment   c. a congenital defect
   b. cosmetic alterations   d. to the manner born

4. Define or explain the following legal expressions.

   a. judicial review   b. double jeopardy

5. Define each of the following colorful expressions.

   a. keep the wolf from the door

   b. jump down someone's throat

Exercise VI. Framing Sentences

A. Use each of the following words in an original sentence.

1. inception
2. indigent
3. insuperable
4. intrepid
5. inveigh
6. jettison

B. Give a **noun** form of each of the following words, and use it in a short illustrative sentence.

1. instigate
2. intervene
3. jeopardize

C. Give an **adjective** form of each of the following words, and use it in a short illustrative sentence.

1. innovation
2. irony
3. justify

D. Give an **adverb** form of each of the following words, and use it in a short illustrative sentence.

1. ingenious
2. judicious
3. inherent

Completing Verbal Analogies

"A *Is by Definition a Person Who* B*'s.*"   Another word relationship that frequently appears in the analogy questions on standardized vocabulary tests may be expressed as "*A* is by definition a person who *B*'s; *C* is by definition a person who *D*'s." Following is an example of an analogy question involving this relationship. Try to determine the correct answer before reading the explanation of it given below.

fugitive : flee =
a. critic : censor
b. spectator : observe
c. advertiser : conceal
d. doctor : operate
e. tyrant : prosecute

The answer is *b*. A *spectator* is by definition someone who *observes*, just as a *fugitive* is by definition someone who *flees*.

None of the other choices exhibits the same relationship as the key pair of words. A *critic* (choice *a*) may praise or censure, but he or she does not *censor*. Similarly, a *tyrant* (choice *e*) usually persecutes people, but he does not by definition *prosecute* them. (That is the job of someone like a district attorney.) Though a surgeon by definition *operates* on his or her patients, a *doctor* (choice *d*), the more general term for someone in the medical profession, is not by definition associated with such a procedure. (For choice *d* to be correct, it would have to read either *surgeon : operate* or *doctor : heal.*) Finally, an advertiser (choice *c*) makes a product or service more widely known; he or she does not *conceal* it.

Note: A related form of this word relationship may be expressed as "*A* is by definition someone who is *B*; *C* is by definition someone who is *D.*" For example, *hero : valorous = knight : chivalrous.*

"The Tone of A Is B." Another useful word relationship may be expressed as "The tone of *A* is *B*; the tone of *C* is *D*." Here is an example of an analogy question involving this relationship. Try to determine the correct answer before reading the explanation of it given below.

salubrious : favorable =
a. munificent : unfavorable
b. pernicious : favorable
c. deleterious : unfavorable
d. inimical : favorable
e. beneficial : unfavorable

The answer is *c*. The tone of *deleterious* is decidedly negative or *unfavorable*, just as the tone of *salubrious*, its antonym, is positive or *favorable*.

All of the other choices are clearly wrong. The tone of both *munificent* (choice *a*) and *beneficial* (choice *e*) is *favorable*, not unfavorable. Similarly, the tone of *pernicious* (choice *b*) and *inimical* (choice *d*) is *unfavorable*, not favorable.

Exercise I

Complete each of the following analogies based on the word relationships "*A* is a person who *B*'s" and "The tone of *A* is *B*."

1. **circumspect : favorable ::**
   a. opinionated : favorable
   b. rash : unfavorable
   c. cumbersome : favorable
   d. splendid : unfavorable
   e. erratic : favorable

2. **thief : steal ::**
   a. hoard : miser
   b. refugee : asylum
   c. researcher : investigator
   d. mendicant : beg
   e. monarch : usurp

3. **activist : militant ::**
   a. mourner : doleful
   b. proprietor : incessant
   c. accomplice : dominant
   d. peacemaker : belligerent
   e. coward : intrepid

4. **arbitrator : mediate ::**
   a. prophet : eavesdrop
   b. mason : slaughter
   c. parish : rector
   b. counselor : advise
   e. warden : prisoner

5. **murmur : low ::**
   a. mumble : clear
   b. jeer : gladden
   c. screech : piercing
   d. rasping : whine
   e. bellow : melodious

Exercise II

Compose **two** complete analogies based on the word relationship "*A* is by definition a person who *B*'s" and **two** based on "The tone of *A* is *B*." In your original analogies, use at least **two** words from the Basic Word List for Lessons 1–20 (Words 1–250).

The following items review what you have so far learned about analogy questions. Complete each.

1. **abet : encourage** = thwart :
   (connive, frustrate, abhor, forbear, defend)

2. **intrepid : craven** = laudable :
   (praiseworthy, illicit, reprehensible, timely, indigent)

3. **effrontery : audacious** = fickleness :
   (capricious, felicitous, adamant, fortuitous, haggard)

4. **haughty : humility** = effete :
   (duplicity, effrontery, credibility, equanimity, vitality)

5. **impervious : penetrate** = implacable :
   (grimace, justify, appease, impugn, filch)

Working with Context Clues

By now you have enough familiarity with the two-word omissions that appear on standardized tests to handle them without further guidance. Accordingly, the remaining "Working with Context Clues" sections of this book will concentrate on providing you with enough practice in dealing with two-word omissions for you to tackle those that actually appear on standardized tests with skill and confidence. In trying to apply the knowledge you now possess to practical situations, remember one important principle: Always isolate the context clues before you attempt to choose the right answer.

Exercise

Complete each of the following two-word omissions by selecting the pair of words that make the best sense in the passage as a whole. Underline the clue or clues that led you to make your choice.

1. Conservative politicians are sometimes accused by their liberal opponents of being _____ to the problems of poverty, but conservatives deny being unresponsive to the plight of the _____.

   a. dedicated . . . elite
   b. impervious . . . indigent
   c. adverse . . . belligerent
   d. ambivalent . . . frugal

2. In order not to _____ the safety of the community, a judge can refuse to grant bail and _____ a defendant when the judge believes the accused might cause harm if set free while on trial.

   a. jeopardize . . . incarcerate
   b. disparage . . . censure
   c. flout . . . absolve
   d. compromise . . . coerce

3. Some ambitious politicians will do whatever is _____ to get elected, even if that means they must abandon principles and _____ programs and policies that they once believed in and worked hard to achieve.

   a. crucial . . . justify
   b. fortuitous . . . exploit
   c. astute . . . bungle
   d. expedient . . . jettison

4. The shameful extent to which the federal government and the U.S. Army were willing to _____ the trust of the Native American peoples in the nineteenth century by repeatedly making and breaking treaties with them is a national _____.

   a. abuse . . . harbinger
   b. cajole . . . anomaly
   c. exploit . . . disgrace
   d. coerce . . . calumny

5. The nature of the crimes committed in the Nazi concentration camps was so _____ that it is hard to imagine any action redeeming enough to _____ for such terrible suffering.

   a. gratuitous . . . qualify
   b. flagrant . . . grope
   c. heinous . . . atone
   d. delinquent . . . abdicate

6. After hours of _____ debate, the exhausted senators were unable to resolve their differences and had to admit that they had reached a(n) _____.

   a. judicious . . . amnesty
   b. esoteric . . . boycott
   c. facetious . . . consensus
   d. grueling . . . impasse

7. Despite probing studies by many experts who are trying to _____ their meaning, the mysterious animal paintings on the caves of Altamira in northern Spain remain a(n) _____.

   a. fathom . . . enigma
   b. explain . . . fiasco
   c. divulge . . . conjecture
   d. elicit . . . irony

8. Due to the _____ efforts of courageous abolitionists, runaway slaves from the South were able to find shelter in a series of _____ way stations on their trek north to freedom on the secret Underground Railroad.

   a. frugal . . . convenient
   b. illicit . . . austere
   c. astute . . . exotic
   d. intrepid . . . clandestine

9. Some seasoned organizers of political demonstrations deliberately provoke a(n) _____ so they can use the face-to-face encounter to _____ the authorities into making themselves look bad.

   a. exigency . . . force
   b. confrontation . . . goad
   c. exodus . . . embarrass
   d. anecdote . . . harangue

10. The manufacturing sector of our economy is shrinking due to a continuing flight of capital investment abroad, resulting in _____ unemployment at home and obvious _____ in the number of domestic-made products.

   a. chronic . . . attrition
   b. temporary . . . growth
   c. implacable . . . duplicity
   d. arbitrary . . . apathy

Enriching the Lesson

Exercise I.   Coining Words

Coinage of English words goes on all the time. A new development occurs in politics, science, business, entertainment, or elsewhere. If current language has no suitable words to define or describe it, a new word will probably be devised, or an old word (or old words in combination) will be adapted to meet the need. If the coinage is vivid or picturesque or pointedly fitting, it catches on and may enjoy some degree of permanence.

Consider the word *conglomerate.* It is by no means a newcomer to English, having been used for centuries to refer to a certain type of rock composed of fragments. It *is* relatively new, however, in its application to a type of business combination that developed in the middle of the 20th century.

The nuclear age gave birth to the word *brinkmanship* (*brink* + *manship*), linguistically structured like *penmanship* and *sales-manship*, to describe a certain type of strategy used in international politics. It suggests the act of creating a potentially explosive situation and pushing it to the very brink of war in order to intimidate other nations and force them to make concessions.

In the 1950s, the novelist Jack Kerouac used the common word *beat* in a new phrase, *beat generation*, to identify members of the disillusioned generation following World War II who developed a new lifestyle of nonconformity and freewheeling self-expression and social criticism.

Some other more or less recent coinages include *take-home pay, astronaut, brainwash, telethon,* and *printout.*

Listed below are a number of coinages. Some are more or less recent. Others go farther back into the history of English. With or without the aid of a dictionary or other reference book, define each. Then choose any **five**, and for each compose a short illustrative sentence.

1. urbanologist
2. superstar
3. peacenik
4. telemarketing
5. debit card
6. environmentalist
7. astronaut
8. supersonic
9. brainwash
10. unisex
11. paraprofessional
12. cyberspace
13. programmer
14. brunch
15. quasar

During the 1950s, Jack Kerouac (1922–1969) was as much an "apostle" of the beat generation in prose as Allen Ginsberg was in poetry. A native of Lowell, Massachusetts, Kerouac roamed through the United States and Mexico for a number of years investigating the beatnik subculture. He published a series of novels that drew upon his travels and reflected his relentless pursuit of new experience and sensation. These include *The Town and the City* (1950), *On the Road* (1957), *The Dharma Bums* (1958), and *Big Sur* (1962).

16. virtual reality
17. biohazard
18. miniskirt
19. ecosystem
20. anchorperson
21. megalopolis
22. whistle-blower

23. prime time
24. play-off
25. motorcade
26. miniseries
27. fanzine
28. cheeseburger
29. soap opera

30. debrief
31. E-mail
32. camcorder
33. skateboard
34. litterbug
35. jet lag
36. camper

Exercise II. Expanding Your Word Power

The words listed below are not on the Basic Word List, but they were mentioned in one form or another in Lesson 20. All of them would make useful additions to your working vocabulary. Define each, give its etymology, list **two** synonyms and **two** antonyms (where possible), and use in a short illustrative sentence.

1. culmination
2. impecunious
3. immanent
4. adventitious
5. indomitable

6. fulminate
7. compromise
8. suppress
9. hazard
10. sagacious

11. vindicate
12. timorous
13. interpose
14. generate
15. conserve

Related Forms in Context

Beneath each sentence below are four words introduced in Lesson 19 or 20. Review the related forms for these words, and choose the one that best completes the sentence. Write that related form in the space provided.

1. Ella Fitzgerald, an _____ among jazz and blues singers, pioneered scat singing, a type of vocal improvisation without words.

   a. impasse   b. inception   c. impediment   d. innovation

2. It is _____ that the supposedly unsinkable SS *Titanic* sank on her maiden voyage after colliding with an iceberg.

   a. immunity   b. irony   c. innovation   d. inception

3. Sir Thomas Malory wrote most of *The Book of King Arthur and His Noble Knights of the Round Table* during his twenty-year _____ for violent crimes, including murder and robbery.

   a. impugn   b. instigate   c. incarcerate   d. intervene

4. When it came to planning King Duncan's murder, who do you think was the chief _____—Macbeth or Lady Macbeth?

   a. instigate   b. incense   c. intervene   d. jeopardize

5. During the Nuremburg trials of 1945–1946, concentration camp survivors testified to the _____ of the Nazis' crimes.

   a. inherent   b. impervious   c. implicit   d. heinous

6. "I know not what course others may take, but as for me, give me liberty or give me death!" cried Patrick Henry in his _____ speech to the Virginia Convention in March of 1775.

   a. impugn   b. incense   c. jeopardize   d. jettison

7. In December 1955, Rosa Parks _____ refused to give up her seat to a white man on a Montgomery, Alabama, municipal bus, touching off a year-long bus boycott led by Dr. Martin Luther King, Jr.

   a. incense   b. jeopardize   c. inveigh   d. justify

8. When they built the western leg of the transcontinental railroad, the mostly Chinese laborers tunneled through mountain ranges once thought to be _____.

   a. ignominy   b. impasse   c. innovation   d. immunity

9. On a number of occasions, _____ by U.N. multinational peacekeeping forces has been necessary in countries torn by civil war.

   a. incarcerate   b. instigate   c. intervene   d. inveigh

10. Despite his harsh _____ when our baseball crashed through his kitchen window, our softhearted neighbor tossed the ball back to us.

    a. instigate b. incense c. jeopardize d. inveigh

11. Queen Elizabeth I of England may have had a reputation for _____, but she was beloved by her people for the strong leadership she provided during her 44-year reign.

    a. haughty b. immaculate c. indigent d. impervious

12. Those who _____ copy and sell movies or recordings can be prosecuted for copyright infringement.

    a. haughty b. illicit c. implicit d. immutable

13. In both plants and animals, _____ cell membranes regulate the flow of materials into and out of the cell.

    a. immaculate b. implicit c. illicit d. impervious

14. Someone with an obsessive personality may perform mundane routines with an _____ that is startling to others.

    a. illicit b. implacable c. implicit d. heinous

15. _____ talented, the Austrian composer Wolfgang Amadeus Mozart was composing minuets at age five and his first symphony at age nine.

    a. indigent b. immutable c. implicit d. inherent

16. The Hoover Dam, which _____ the flow of the Colorado River at Black Canyon, provides hydroelectric power, water for irrigation and recreation, and flood control.

    a. inception b. impediment c. irony d. ignominy

17. Pediatricians recommend that children receive _____ for the following diseases: hepatitis B, diphtheria, whooping cough, tetanus, polio, measles, mumps, rubella, and chicken pox.

    a. ignominy b. innovation c. immunity d. impasse

18. Some historians believe that the _____ terms for German surrender in the 1919 Treaty of Versailles led directly to World War II.

    a. inception b. ignominy c. innovation d. impediment

19. As a child, what I admired most about Wonder Woman, the first female comic book superhero, was her _____.

    a. inherent b. immutable c. implicit d. intrepid

20. Wendy is sneezing and has a scratchy throat, sure signs of an _____ cold.

    a. inception b. innovation c. immunity d. impasse

Review

101. **connoisseur** — 250. **justify**

Exercise I.   Syllabication and Pronunciation

Syllabicate the following words correctly and place the major stress mark (') after the syllable that is accented when the word is pronounced. Two answers are correct in some instances.

1. construe
2. corroborate
3. defect
4. deviate
5. eclectic

6. emanate
7. esoteric
8. expedient
9. fetish
10. futile

11. grimace
12. gullible
13. harangue
14. inveigh
15. justify

Exercise II.   Parts of Speech

Indicate the part of speech of each of the following words. In some cases, two answers are correct.

1. consensus
2. consummate
3. counsel
4. curtail
5. dire

6. discourse
7. epithet
8. forestall
9. fickle
10. filch

11. finesse
12. heinous
13. impasse
14. impugn
15. irony

Exercise III.   Words Out of Context

In each of the following groups, select the lettered item that best expresses the meaning of the numbered word at the left.

1. devoid
   a. saturated   b. angry   c. empty
   d. foolish   e. clumsy

2. efficacious
   a. effective   b. inadequate   c. extravagant
   d. recent   e. lethargic

3. fabricate
   a. remove   b. concoct   c. conceal
   d. destroy   e. consider

4. facsimile
   a. oath   b. treachery   c. skill   d. duplicate
   e. fortune

5. garble
   a. distort   b. clarify   c. report   d. sing
   e. control

6. goad
   a. suppose   b. curb   c. investigate
   d. enjoy   e. prod

7. haggard
   a. sunny   b. wealthy   c. gaunt   d. fat

8. instigate   a. snoop   b. foment   c. explore   d. yawn
e. complain

9. illicit   a. invincible   b. illiterate   c. interminable
d. illegal   e. inflexible

10. jettison   a. beautify   b. discard   c. preserve   d. order

Exercise IV. Completing Sentences

Complete each of the following sentences by selecting the most appropriate word from the groups of words given below.

Group A

exacerbate	foibles	flagrant
grueling	criterion	deleted

1. Though I admire the candidate's strong points, I find his _____ laughable.

2. In my haste to cut my essay down to size, I accidentally _____ some essential information.

3. "Though the proposal will certainly solve some of our economic problems," the senator remarked, "it will unfortunately _____ others."

4. A 26-mile marathon is a(n) _____ test of any runner's strength and endurance, no matter how well prepared he or she may be.

5. Though the defense attorney was overjoyed by the outcome of the trial, the prosecutor branded it a(n) _____ miscarriage of justice.

Group B

fiasco	ethnic	innovation
jeopardize	gaped	dilatory

6. Having to pay a sizable fine on some overdue library books has taught me not to be so _____ in the future.

7. Many of the minority groups that have come to the United States have managed to preserve their _____ identities while at the same time becoming full-fledged Americans.

8. A combination of poor planning and bad luck turned what should have been a surefire success into an utter _____.

9. "Pursuing such a risky and ill-considered course of action now," I observed, "will surely _____ all that we have so far succeeded in achieving."

10. Observers on the shore _____ openmouthed in horror as the stricken vessel slowly sank beneath the turbulent waters of the storm-tossed sea.

329

Exercise V. Words in Phrases

In each of the following groups, select the item that means the same as the *italicized* word in the introductory phrase.

1. a *crucial* moment
   a. comical   b. pivotal   c. sad   d. boring   e. wasted

2. a group of *demure* young women
   a. bold   b. pretty   c. secretive   d. arrogant   e. modest

3. a *diligent* worker
   a. sedulous   b. new   c. pleasant   d. foreign
   e. bright

4. *fatuous* remarks
   a. perceptive   b. inane   c. amusing   d. brief   e. loud

5. *fluctuate* in popularity
   a. seesaw   b. continue   c. increase   d. remain
   e. decline

6. *elicit* a response
   a. make up   b. repeat   c. call forth   d. ignore
   e. strike out

7. *formidable* opposition to the proposal
   a. negligible   b. unexpected   c. reluctant   d. tremendous
   e. recent

8. *embellish* the facts
   a. investigate   b. report   c. conceal   d. reveal
   e. improve upon

9. the *gruesome* details
   a. relevant   b. horrible   c. minor   d. important
   e. unknown

10. all kinds of *ingenious* devices
    a. clever   b. unworkable   c. costly   d. practicable
    e. dangerous

Exercise VI. Related Forms

A. Give a **noun** form of each of the following words.

   1. cynical   3. ethical   5. haughty
   2. dormant   4. frugal   6. intervene

B. Give a **verb** form of each of these words.

   1. empathy   2. immunity   3. impediment

C. Give an **adjective** form of each of these words.

   1. enigma   2. fallacy   3. euphemism

D. Give an **adverb** form of each of these words.

   1. drastic   2. graphic   3. ignominy

Exercise VII. Synonyms and Antonyms

Classify each of the following pairs of words as **S** for **synonyms** or **A** for **antonyms**.

1. dapper—slovenly
2. dejected—crestfallen
3. corpulent—skinny
4. eminent—obscure
5. divulge—reveal

6. fathom—comprehend
7. feign—pretend
8. harbinger—forerunner
9. indigent—affluent
10. intrepid—timorous

Exercise VIII. Framing Sentences

Use each of the following words in a short illustrative sentence of your own devising.

1. cursory
2. copious
3. dexterous
4. disparage
5. emaciated

6. emulate
7. erudite
8. elite
9. feasible
10. gloat

11. gregarious
12. inception
13. incarcerate
14. innovation
15. judicious

Exercise IX. Word Roundup

1. Explain the difference between the words in each of the following pairs.

   a. flout—flaunt
   b. indigent—indigenous
   c. demur—demure
   d. credibility—credence
   e. discomfit—discomfort
   f. counsel—council
   g. exalt—exult
   h. feint—faint
   i. fortuitous—fortunate
   j. deferment—deference

2. Define each of the following terms.

   a. a skinflint
   b. a windfall
   c. a fluke
   d. to stonewall
   e. to rubberneck
   f. to soft-soap

3. Explain the meaning of each of the following colorful phrases.

   a. down in the dumps
   b. strike while the iron is hot
   c. pour oil on troubled waters
   d. paint oneself into a corner
   e. keep the wolf from one's door
   f. drag one's heels
   g. live in an ivory tower
   h. still wet behind the ears
   i. see red
   j. pull the wool over someone's eyes

4. Explain the meaning of each of the following foreign expressions used in present-day English, and tell what language it comes from.

   a. idée fixe
   b. hoi polloi
   c impedimenta
   d. esprit de corps
   e. ad nauseam
   f. tour de force

5. Explain why you would be *flattered* or *insulted* if you were described as each of the following:

   a. an ignoramus   c. a connoisseur   e. a patsy
   b. a greenhorn   d. a dapper Dan   f. a paragon

Exercise X. Etymology

1. For each of the following definitions, supply an English word that begins with the Latin prefix *co, col, com, con,* or *cor.*

   a. fight against   c. stick together   e. eat away
   b. fall down completely   d. build or erect   f. work together

2. Define each of the following words beginning with the Latin prefix *de* or the Latin prefix *dis.*

   a. dispel   c. depose   e. disinherit
   b. denounce   d. dismember   f. demerit

3. Form a verb from each of the following English words by adding the suffix *(i)fy.* Then define the resulting combination.

   a. null   c. identity   e. beauty
   b. person   d. solid   f. terror

4. List and define **three** English words containing the Latin root *flu* or *fluct.* What does this root mean?

5. Change each of the following positive words to its negative form by adding the Latin prefix *in* or one of its variants. Then define the resulting combination.

   a. reverent   c. moral   e. noble
   b. validate   d. logical   f. excusable

Exercise XI. Choosing the Right Meaning

Read each sentence carefully. Then underline the item that best completes the statement below the sentence.

1. The 9-1-1 telephone number for reporting dire emergencies had its origins in 1957, when an organization of fire chiefs recommended that there be a national, easy-to-remember phone number for reporting fires. Ten years later, the Federal Trade Commission and the American Telephone and Telegraph Company (AT&T) met to establish a universal emergency telephone number—9-1-1.   (2) (4) (6)

   The word **dire** in line 1 means

   a. gloomy   c. desperate
   b. unusual   d. suspicious

2. To Americans, the game of cricket, Britain's most popular sport, is decidedly esoteric compared with baseball. Cricket is played with a paddle-shaped bat and a hard leather ball.   (2)

332

Eleven players on each team come up to bat as a bowler throws (4)
the ball to the batsman in the middle of the field. The rules are
complicated, and a two-inning game may take several days to (6)
complete.

The word **esoteric** in line 2 means

a. antiquated   c. confidential
b. mysterious   d. humorous

3. When they framed the U.S. Constitution, the Founding Fathers
chose to defer dealing with the problem of slavery. It remained a (2)
festering issue, and there were bitter debates over the expansion
of slavery into the new territories. The Missouri Compromise, (4)
which admitted Maine (1820) and Missouri (1821) as states, was
an attempt to maintain the balance of slave and free states. (6)

The word **defer** in line 2 means

a. reject   c. investigate
b. accede to   d. postpone

4. In a radio broadcast on October 1, 1939, the year before he became prime minister of Britain, Winston Churchill noted the (2)
impossibility of predicting how the Soviet Union would act.
"I cannot forecast to you the action of Russia," Churchill said. (4)
"It is a riddle wrapped in a mystery inside an enigma."

The word **enigma** in line 5 means

a. obscure statement   c. devious player
b. dangerous game   d. something puzzling

5. An artist fabricates a collage by gluing found materials (such
as newspaper, wallpaper, magazine photos, ads, cloth, and (2)
string) onto a flat surface, creating a three-dimensional effect.
The artist may then use paint or pen and ink to add to the as- (4)
semblage. Pablo Picasso originated this new art form in 1912,
and it was soon taken up by other Cubist painters, most no- (6)
tably Georges Braque.

The word **fabricates** in line 1 means

a. creates   c. deceives
b. sketches   d. prints

6. Trapped in the cave of Cyclops, a man-eating one-eyed monster, the clever Odysseus blinds his formidable opponent. En- (2)
raged, Cyclops demands to know who blinded him, and the
wily Odysseus answers, "Noman." Then Odysseus devises a (4)
shrewd plan to free himself and his remaining men from the
monster's cave.

The word **formidable** in line 2 means

a. huge   c. terrifying
b. drunken   d. brutal

7. Among the Zuni people, animal fetishes carved from rock or
semiprecious stone represent the animal's spirit. A bear fetish, (2)
for example, is said to symbolize strength and health. Many
bear fetishes have small bundles of stones tied to their backs. (4)
These medicine bundles are offerings to the animal's spirit and
make the fetish more powerful.

The word **fetish** in line 2 means

a. obsession   c. talisman
b. sand painting   d. folk dance

8. Henry David Thoreau, the nineteenth-century American naturalist and writer, championed the frugal, simple life. For two   (2)
   years and two months, he lived alone in a house he built himself in the woods at Walden Pond near Concord, Massachu-   (4)
   setts, his birthplace. In *Walden*, the book he wrote about his
   thoughts and experiences there, he warns: "Beware of all   (6)
   enterprises that require new clothes."

The word **frugal** in line 2 means

a. stingy   c. rural
b. thrifty   d. natural

9. Shakespeare's *Hamlet* opens on an ominous, mysterious note.
   A ghost—looking very like the late King of Denmark—appears,   (2)
   and sorrow seems to emanate from this ghastly figure. The
   ghost appears and exits twice in the play's first scene. It   (4)
   seems about to speak when the cock crows, and it vanishes.

The words **emanate from** in line 3 mean

a. flow from   c. surround
b. send forth   d. draw in

10. In 1855, Walt Whitman self-published his revolutionary book
    of free verse, *Leaves of Grass*, and mailed copies to writers he   (2)
    admired. Ralph Waldo Emerson, the most eminent essayist
    and poet of his time, sent Whitman a congratulatory letter: "I   (4)
    find [in *Leaves of Grass*] incomparable things said incomparably
    well. . . . I greet you at the beginning of a great career. . . ."   (6)

The word **eminent** in line 3 means

a. conspicuous   c. distinguished
b. talented   d. original

11. Behavioral biologists study the social patterns and interactions
    of nonhuman primates, such as monkeys, chimpanzees, apes,   (2)
    and baboons. These gregarious animals live within a distinct
    structure, with identifiable patterns of interaction between—   (4)
    and among—the genders and between young and old.

The word **gregarious** in line 3 means

a. affable   c. social
b. territorial   d. living alone

12. There are several different types of color blindness, or color-
    vision deficiency. The most common type involves an inability   (2)
    to discriminate between red and green. Someone with this
    type of color blindness looks at a rainbow and sees red, or-   (4)
    ange, yellow, and green as a single color (yellow) and the other
    half of the rainbow as blue. Color blindness is genetic and   (6)
    almost twenty times more prevalent in men than in women.

The word **discriminate** in line 3 means

a. distinguish   c. treat prejudicially
b. carefully observe   d. treat fairly

Lesson 21

251. kudos — 265. medium

---

251. ku·dos   *noun*   kyoo′-dōs *or* koo′-dōz
[*kudos* (Greek), "fame, glory"; originally English university slang but popularized in the United States some years ago by *Time* magazine]

Definition: The prestige or acclaim that results from some noteworthy achievement or position.

An "unsung hero" is a person whose achievements have never been accorded the **kudos** they deserve.

Usage Note:
Since *kudos* is singular, it takes a singular verb. *Kudo* (without the *s*) is sometimes mistakenly used as the singular, but it is not considered correct.

Synonyms: (*nouns*) glory, honor, acclamation, credit, recognition, renown; accolade, plaudit

Antonyms: (*nouns*) odium, opprobrium, obloquy, contempt, disdain

Accolade

During the Middle Ages, an *accolade* was the ceremony in which a king or other overlord conferred knighthood upon a deserving subject. During part of this elaborate ceremony, usually conducted in the presence of the notables of the land, the king officially elevated the subject to the rank of knight by embracing him around (*ad* [Latin]) the neck (*collum* [Latin]) and tapping him lightly on the shoulder with the flat of a sword. The ceremony still survives in countries (*e.g.*, Great Britain) that have a titled nobility or where knighthood is customarily bestowed as an official token of thanks for outstanding personal service to the nation. It is from this connection with knighthood that the word *accolade* has now come to mean not only the formal bestowal of important honors and awards but also the simple granting of praise or approval.

Queen Elizabeth II makes a deserving subject a knight.

252. lack·a·dai·si·cal   *adjective*   lăk-ə-dā'-zĭ-kəl

[*lackaday* (obsolete English), "Woe is me," an archaic expression of sorrow or regret derived from *Alack* (= Woe) *the day*]

Definition: Sorely lacking in spirit, energy, or purpose.

"No matter how bright a youngster is," the child psychologist observed, "a **lackadaisical** attitude toward studying will result in poor grades."

Related Forms: (*noun*) lackadaisicalness; (*adverb*) lackadaisically

Synonyms: (*adjectives*) lethargic, listless, sluggish, torpid, indolent, lazy, supine, slothful; blasé, nonchalant, indifferent; perfunctory

Antonyms: (*adjectives*) energetic, vigorous, dynamic, spirited, animated

Related Phrases: a devil-may-care attitude, a fainéant administration, a drone

253. leg·a·cy   *noun*   lĕg'-ə-sē

[*legatia* (Medieval Latin), "office of deputy; bequest"; from *legare, legatus* (Latin), "send as a deputy; bequeath"]

Definition: Something left to a person in a will; something handed down from the past.

In her will, Grandmother left me a sizable cash **legacy,** which I have wisely used to further my education.

It is our duty to preserve and augment the **legacy** of freedom that we have received from earlier generations of Americans.

Synonyms: (*nouns*) bequest, inheritance, endowment; present, gift

Related Phrases: a family heirloom, a hand-me-down

254. li·a·bil·i·ty   *noun*   lī-ə-bĭl'-ə-tē

[*ligare, ligatus* (Latin), "tie, bind" + *abilis, abile* (Latin), "able to" + *itas, itatis* (Latin), "state or condition of"]

Definition:

a.   A debt or obligation, especially of a financial nature.

"When we balanced this company's assets against its **liabilities**," the executive remarked, "we found that we had turned a handsome profit this year."

b.   A hindrance or handicap.

Sometimes the traits of character that make people successful in the business world can prove to be **liabilities** in their personal lives.

My failure to learn how to type in high school later proved to be a **liability** when I applied for a secretarial position at a large Chicago firm.

Related Form: (*adjective*) liable

Synonyms: (*nouns*) indebtedness, debit, minus; disadvantage, drawback, obstacle

Antonyms: (*nouns*) asset, plus, advantage

Related Phrases: have an albatross around one's neck, have a cross to bear, have a millstone around one's neck, a stumbling block

255. li-bel   *noun and verb*   lī'-bəl
[*libellus* (Latin), "little book, petition"; from *liber* (Latin), "book"]

Definition:
a. (*noun*) A public statement or picture that damages a person by falsely impugning his or her character, motives, or actions or by unjustly exposing the person to public censure or ridicule.

"The laws of this land do not shield public figures from just criticism," the lawyer remarked, "but they do protect them against **libel**."

b. (*verb*) To slander publicly.

"Reliable witnesses can prove beyond the shadow of a doubt that the defendant has scurrilously **libeled** my client," the prosecutor told the jury.

Related Form: (*adjective*) libelous

Synonyms: (*nouns*) calumny, slander; (*verbs*) calumniate, defame, traduce, bad-mouth

Antonyms: (*verbs*) whitewash, gloss over, cover up

Related Phrases: hurl brickbats at, do a hatchet job on, drag someone's name through the mud; defamation of character; character assassination; a muckraker

256. lit-i-ga-tion   *noun*   lĭt-ĭ-gā'-shən
[*litigare, litigatus* (Latin), "sue"; from *lis, litis* (Latin), "lawsuit" + *agere, actus* (Latin), "bring, incite"]

Definition: Legal action; a lawsuit.

"You are perfectly free to take your case to court," the lawyer told her client, "but if you do, the matter may be tied up in **litigation** for years."

Related Forms: (*noun*) litigant; (*adjective*) litigious; (*verb*) litigate

Usage Notes:
a. *Litigation* usually indicates that a civil, as opposed to a criminal, action is involved.
b. *Litigious* means "given to engaging in lawsuits" or, more broadly, "quarrelsome, pugnacious."

Synonyms: (*noun*) legal proceedings

Related Phrases: initiate legal proceedings against, bring an action against, file suit against, press charges against, go to court over, bring to book

257. lu-cid   *adjective*   lōō'-sĭd
[*lucidus* (Latin), "clear, bright"; from *lucere* (Latin), "shine"]

Definition: Clear and intelligible to the understanding; mentally competent.

The speaker gave such a **lucid** explanation of the complicated medical procedure that even a nonprofessional like me could understand it.

Though George III was declared permanently insane in 1810, he occasionally had brief periods when he was quite **lucid**.

Related Forms: (*nouns*) lucidity, lucidness; (*adverb*) lucidly

Synonyms: (*adjectives*) crystal clear, understandable, comprehensible; sane, rational

Antonyms: (*adjectives*) unintelligible, confused, puzzling; ambiguous, equivocal; mad, insane, irrational

Related Phrase: (non) compos mentis

258. lu-cra-tive   *adjective*   lōō'-krə-tĭv
[*lucrativus* (Latin), "profitable"; from *lucrum* (Latin), "profit, gain"]

Definition: Profitable.

"Running a popular pizza parlor may not be the most elevated occupation in the world," he replied, "but it certainly is **lucrative**."

Elizabethan opposition to the growth of Spanish power in Europe and the Americas proved far more **lucrative** than originally anticipated.

Related Forms: (*nouns*) lucrativeness, lucre

Synonyms: (*adjectives*) gainful, remunerative, rewarding, worthwhile; productive, fruitful, advantageous

Antonyms: (*adjectives*) unprofitable, unrewarding, unremunerative; unproductive, barren

Related Phrase: the profit motive

259. lurk   *verb*   lûrk'
[*lurka* (Old Norse), "sneak away slowly"]

Definition: To sneak; to lie hidden or in wait.

The police officer stopped to question the seedy-looking man who had been **lurking** around the corner drugstore for hours.

Who would have imagined that such a subtle thought could **lurk** in that innocent-looking head!

Synonyms: (*verbs*) skulk, prowl, slink, loiter

Related Phrases: a prowler, a stalking-horse

Filthy Lucre

Lucre, meaning "monetary profit or gain," has a decidedly negative connotation, perhaps because its most common use occurs in the phrase *filthy lucre*, which is derived from the New Testament. In his first letter to his disciple Timothy, the apostle Paul mentions that a bishop should not be "greedy of filthy lucre" (1 Timothy 3:2). In this context, *filthy* means "sordid" or "dishonorable," and Paul is saying that a bishop should not be open to bribes and other questionable ways of acquiring money. Accordingly, the phrase *filthy lucre* has come to be a highly contemptuous synonym for "ill-gotten gains," though it is also sometimes applied to people who are simply overly interested in making and amassing money, whatever their means.

St. Paul

260. lush   *adjective*   lŭsh'
[*lusch* (Middle English), "lax, soft"]

Definition:
   a. Luxuriant, plentiful; luxurious, opulent.

   The **lush** vegetation of the Hawaiian Islands is home to countless species of exotic birds and other animals.

   The walls of medieval castles were covered with **lush** tapestries and other hangings to keep out drafts.

   b. Overelaborate or overripe.

   What a contrast between George Orwell's lean, understated prose and the **lush**, overblown style of some of his contemporaries!

Phrases: lush farmland, lush surroundings, a lush orchestral texture

Related Forms: (*noun*) lushness; (*adverb*) lushly

Synonyms: (*adjectives*) dense, thriving, flourishing, profuse, lavish, prodigal, extravagant; ornate, sumptuous

Antonyms: (*adjectives*) simple, restrained, spartan; bleak, barren

261. mal-a-prop-ism   *noun*   măl'-ə-prŏp-ĭz-əm

[*mal à propos* (French), "out of place, inappropriate"]

Definition: An unconscious and usually ludicrous misuse of a word.

In one of his typical **malapropisms**, my landlord informed me on the hottest day of the year that he didn't mind the heat so much as the humility.

Synonyms: (*nouns*) flub, gaffe, solecism

Related Phrases: a play on words, a pun, an Irish bull, a spoonerism

262. mal-ice   *noun*   măl'-ĭs

[*malitia* (Latin), "wickedness"; from *malus* (Latin), "bad, evil"]

Definition: A desire to cause harm or suffering; deep-seated ill will.

In a famous passage in his Second Inaugural Address (1865), Abraham Lincoln suggested that national unity could never be restored if the defeated South were treated with **malice** rather than magnanimity.

Phrase: malice aforethought

Related Forms: (*adjective*) malicious; (*noun*) maliciousness

Synonyms: (*nouns*) malevolence, spite, rancor, animosity, vindictiveness, malignity, enmity, resentment

Antonyms: (*nouns*) benevolence, beneficence, goodwill, generosity, charity, magnanimity

263. mam-moth   *noun and adjective*   măm'-əth

[*mammot* (Russian), "a mammoth"]

Definition:

a.   (*noun*) An extinct form of elephant; a giant or colossus.

During the Ice Age, woolly **mammoths** and other huge elephant-like creatures were common in much of North America.

According to legend, Paul Bunyan, America's most celebrated lumberjack, was a **mammoth** of a man whose proudest possession was a gigantic blue ox named Babe.

b.   (*adjective*) Gigantic.

The popular British singing group capped off its tour of the United States with a **mammoth** rock concert at Yankee Stadium.

Synonyms: (*nouns*) mastodon, behemoth; (*adjectives*) colossal, titanic, vast, gargantuan, enormous, monstrous, prodigious, stupendous

Antonyms: (*adjectives*) minute, minuscule, diminutive, Lilliputian, microscopic, tiny

The English actress Mary Boland as Mrs. Malaprop in Richard Brinsley Sheridan's comedy *The Rivals*.

Malapropisms, Irish Bulls, and Puns

The 18th-century Anglo-Irish playwright Richard Brinsley Sheridan (1751–1816) took the French phrase *mal à propos*, meaning "out of place" or "inappropriate," as the basis for the name of one of his most inspired comic creations, Mrs. Malaprop in *The Rivals* (1775). Mrs. Malaprop's most outstanding quality is her propensity to confuse words in a way that yields unintentionally comic effects. For example, she says, "I would have her instructed in geometry [*i.e.*, geography] that she might know something of the boundaries of contagious [*i.e.*, contiguous] countries" and "He is as headstrong as an allegory on the banks of the Nile." Such incongruous misusages, dubbed *malapropisms* in the lady's honor, are scattered like buckshot throughout *The Rivals*.

Movie mogul Sam Goldwyn achieved a certain amount of notoriety for his malapropisms. He was "credited" with such verbal gaffes as "A verbal agreement isn't worth the paper it's written on" and "I'll answer you with a definite maybe." Baseball great Yogi Berra had a similar gift for gaffes. He is credited with saying "If people don't want to come out to the ball park, nobody's going to stop them" and "When you come to a fork in the road, take it." This kind of self-contradictory statement is sometimes called an *Irish bull*.

Finally, it has been said that a *pun* (an intentionally comic play on words) is a "deliberate" or "controlled" malapropism. If you analyze a typical pun, you will see that this is true.

Larger Than Life

Modern English is rich in interesting expressions that indicate tremendous size. One of the most useful of these is *colossal*, which comes from the Greek word *kolossos* and its Latin equivalent, *colossus*. To the ancient Greeks and Romans, a kolossos or colossus was a gigantic statue. For example, the Colossus of Rhodes, one of the Seven Wonders of the World, was a gigantic statue erected about 280 B.C. by the inhabitants of Rhodes, an island republic off what is now southwest Turkey, to commemorate their deliverance from a siege. The statue, which represented the sun god Helios, the patron deity of the republic, was made entirely of bronze and rose to a height of 105 feet. It is from this connection with one of the most famous tourist attractions of the ancient world that we get our words *colossus*, meaning "anything of great size or impressiveness," and *colossal*, meaning "immense."

Our word *coliseum* also comes from the same source. It is a variant of the Latin word *Colosseum*, the name of the huge sports stadium that the Flavian emperors built in Rome about A.D. 80 (see photo). It is interesting to note, however, that many modern coliseums are not, strictly speaking, colosseums in the ancient sense because they are not open-air structures and were not primarily designed for sporting events.

Another useful expression relating to great size is *gargantuan*, which comes from the title of a famous novel by François Rabelais (c. 1483–1553), a French comic writer who lived during the Renaissance. Gargantua, the hero of this book, is described by Rabelais as a giant with enormous vitality and unlimited appetites. Accordingly, the English adjective *gargantuan* usually suggests an enormous capacity for food and pleasure, as in the phrase "a *gargantuan* appetite."

The 18th-century English satirist Jonathan Swift (1667–1745) also contributed two interesting "size" words to our vocabulary. Lemuel Gulliver, the hero of Swift's classic novel, *Gulliver's Travels*, visits the kingdom of Lilliput, where the inhabitants are only six inches tall and everything else is correspondingly small. On a later voyage, he travels to the land of Brobdingnag, where everything is gigantic. Swift's description of Gulliver's adventures in these two fantastic places was so memorable that soon the adjectives *Lilliputian*, meaning "extremely small in size or outlook," and *Brobdingnagian*, meaning "gigantic and correspondingly gross or boorish," had found permanent places in the vocabulary of English.

264. man-da-to-ry   *adjective*   măn'-də-tôr-ē

[*mandatum* (Latin), "command" + *orius* (Latin), "having the effect of"; from *manus* (Latin), "hand" + *dare, datus* (Latin), "give, place"]

Definition: Required, obligatory.

In this state, attendance at school is **mandatory** for children between the ages of six and seventeen.

Related Form: (*noun and verb*) mandate

Phrases: a mandatory life sentence, the mandate of the court, mandated services, a mandated territory, a writ of mandamus

Usage Notes:

a. In politics, the word *mandate* is sometimes used to express the authorization that the voters have presumably given to public officials by electing them. The following sentence illustrates this use of the word:

"The overwhelming victory I have won," the governor-elect said, "is a clear **mandate** to carry out my program."

b. After World War I, the League of Nations used the term *mandate* to describe a colonial territory that had been taken from one of the defeated belligerents and assigned to the administrative control of one of the victors. For example, Great Britain had a mandate over Palestine, which formerly belonged to the Turkish Empire. Under the UN, *trusteeship* is used for much the same arrangement.

Synonyms: (*adjectives*) compulsory, requisite; imperative

Antonyms: (*adjectives*) optional, discretionary, voluntary

Related Phrases: de rigueur, an elective course

265. me-di-um   *noun*   mē'-dē-əm

[*medium* (Latin), "the middle"; from *medius* (Latin), "middle"]

Definition: The means by which some goal is achieved or the person through whom it is realized.

Modern-day activists advocate strong political action as the most effective **medium** of social change.

Carlos was the **medium** through whom we made our views known to the student council.

Usage Notes:

a. Among those involved in the occult, a medium is a person who is believed to have the power to communicate with the dead.

b. The plural of *medium* is *media*. This plural form has come to be used to refer collectively to means of mass communication, particularly newspapers, radio, and television. Note: Since *media* is a plural form, it takes a *plural* verb, though some modern authorities sanction the use of the singular.

Synonyms: (*nouns*) agency, channel, vehicle

Using the Words

Exercise I. Syllabication and Pronunciation

Syllabicate the following words correctly, and place the major stress mark (') after the syllable that is accented when the word is pronounced.

1. kudos
2. lackadaisical
3. liability
4. lucid
5. lucrative
6. malice
7. mammoth
8. mandatory
9. medium

Exercise II. Words Out of Context

In each of the following groups, select the item that best expresses the meaning of the numbered word at the left.

1. kudos
   a. lawsuit b. glory c. agency
   d. calumny e. inheritance

2. lackadaisical
   a. obscure b. unrewarding c. energetic
   d. obligatory e. lethargic

3. lucrative
   a. daily b. intelligible c. eager
   d. profitable e. average

4. malice
   a. charity b. sensitivity c. animosity
   d. indifference e. idleness

5. liability
   a. refuge b. advantage c. environment
   d. commencement e. drawback

6. mammoth
   a. gigantic b. kindly c. optional
   d. shabby e. evil

7. libel
   a. murder b. slander c. famine
   d. chaos e. disaster

Exercise III. Completing Sentences

Complete each of the following sentences by selecting the most appropriate word from the group of words given below. Use each word only once.

lucid	legacy	mandatory
litigation	malapropism	lush
lurk	libel	medium

1. Deteriorating climatic conditions eventually transformed what had been a _____ tropical paradise into a barren and inhospitable wasteland.

2. Though slavery has long since passed from the scene, the _____ of guilt and fear it left behind still affects our national life.

3. Fortunately, we were able to avoid a great deal of costly _____ by settling the dispute out of court.

4. Though he worked in a variety of materials, stone was the _____ through which Michelangelo preferred to express his artistic ideas.

5. Her prose is as _____ and direct as mine is muddled and digressive.

6. Who can ever accurately predict what evil schemes _____ like sneak thieves in the dark recesses of a criminally insane person's mind?

7. The senator's command of English is so uncertain that his public utterances are full of bizarre _____ such as "make a bee dive for the door" and "the boy who cried, 'Woof'!"

8. Though high school students are no longer required to study Latin and Greek, English is still a _____ subject.

Exercise IV. Synonyms and Antonyms

Classify each of the following pairs of words as **S** for **synonyms** or **A** for **antonyms**.

1. lush—opulent
2. lackadaisical—energetic
3. libel—slander
4. skulk—lurk
5. liability—asset
6. channel—medium
7. litigation—lawsuit
8. lucrative—unprofitable
9. lucid—unintelligible
10. compulsory—mandatory
11. kudos—acclaim
12. benevolence—malice
13. legacy—bequest
14. diminutive—mammoth

Exercise V. Word Roundup

1. Give the plural of *medium*, explain how it is used in contemporary English, and use it in a short illustrative sentence.

2. Explain the story behind each of the following expressions.

   a. accolade
   b. filthy lucre
   c. Lilliputian
   d. gargantuan

3. With or without the aid of a dictionary, define each of the following.

   a. a drone
   b. a hand-me-down
   c. a muckraker
   d. a stalking-horse

4. What is a *mandate*?

5. With or without the aid of a dictionary, explain what each of the following means.

    a. an elective course   c. defamation of character
    b. a family heirloom   d. malice aforethought

6. With the help of a dictionary, define each of the following foreign phrases used in modern English.

    a. non compos mentis   b. de rigueur

7. Define each of the following expressions.

    a. a pun   c. an Irish bull
    b. a spoonerism   d. a malapropism

Exercise VI.   Framing Sentences

A. Use each of the following words in an original illustrative sentence.

1. kudos	3. lurk	5. mammoth
2. legacy	4. malapropism	6. medium

B. Give a **noun** form of each of the following words, and use it in an original illustrative sentence.

    1. lush   2. mandatory   3. lucrative

C. Give an **adjective** form of each of these words, and use it in an original illustrative sentence.

    1. litigation   2. libel   3. liability

D. Give an **adverb** form of each of these words, and use it in an original illustrative sentence.

    1. lucid   2. lush   3. lackadaisical

Dissecting the Words

Prefix

The Latin prefix **inter**, meaning "between" or "among," occurs in a great many English words, including *intervene* (Word 243). Here are a few other useful English words in which it appears:

interpose (*inter*, "between" + *ponere, positus* [Latin], "place")—to place between, to come between

interject (*inter*, "between" + *jacere, jactus* [Latin], "throw")—to thrust abruptly between. Noun: *interjection*

intermediary (*inter*, "between" + *medius* [Latin], "middle")—a go-between

interstice (*inter*, "between" + *sistere, status* [Latin], "cause to stand")—a space between two things *intersperse* (*inter,* "among" + *spargere, sparsus* [Latin], "scatter")—to scatter or distribute among other things

interrogate (*inter,* "between" + *rogare, rogatus* [Latin], "ask")—to question formally. Nouns: *interrogation* and *interrogator*

intersect (*inter,* "between" + *secare, sectus* [Latin], "cut")—to cut across or through. Noun: *intersection*

intercept (*inter,* "between" + *capere, captus* [Latin], "seize")—to stop or interrupt the intended progress of. Noun: *interception*

Do not confuse the prefix **inter** with the prefix **in** when the latter occurs before the syllable **ter**. For example, the word *interminable* begins with what looks like the prefix **inter** but is in fact the prefix **in** (meaning "not") followed by the word *terminable* (meaning "capable of being ended" or "having an end").

Roots

1.   The Latin and French roots **mal(e)** have a number of meanings: (*a*) "bad, badly"; (*b*) "evil, ill"; and (*c*) "abnormal, abnormally." These word elements occur in many common English words, including *malice,* studied in this lesson. For example:

malefactor (*male,* "evil" + *facere, factus* [Latin], "do")—a person who commits a crime or other offense

malevolent (*male,* "evil, ill" + *volens, volentis* [Latin], "wishing")—showing ill will; having an evil influence. Noun: *malevolence*

maladroit (*mal,* "ill, badly" + *adroit* [French], "skillful")—clumsy or inept

malodorous (*mal,* "badly" + *odor* [Latin], "smell")—foul smelling

malign (*mal,* "evil" + *gignere, genitus* [Latin], "bear, bring forth")—to speak evil or ill of

malaise (*mal,* "ill" + *aise* [French], "comfort, ease")—a vague, undefined feeling of illness or discomfort

malformation (*mal,* "abnormal" + *formation*)—an abnormal structure or formation

Other words that contain the word element **mal(e)** include *malcontent, malpractice, malfunction, malediction, malignant,* and *malnutrition.*

2.   The Latin word element **ben(e)** indicates the opposite of *mal(e);* that is, "good" or "well." It occurs in several useful English words, including *benign* (Word 57). Here are a few others in which it appears.

benefactor (*bene,* "good" + *facere, factus* [Latin], "do")—a person who confers some kind of good on another. Nouns: *benefactress, benefaction*

benediction (*bene,* "good, well" + *dicere, dictus* [Latin], "say")—a blessing

benevolent (*bene,* "good, well" + *volens, volentis* [Latin], "wishing")—kindly and generous. Noun: *benevolence*

benign (*bene,* "well" + *gignere, genitus* [Latin], "bear, bring forth")—gentle and mild; beneficial; not dangerous. Noun: *benignity*

Other words in which **ben(e)** appears include *benefit, beneficial, beneficiary, benefice, beneficent,* and *benignant.*

3. The Latin and Greek word element **gen** or **gene** has a number of meanings: (*a*) "give birth"; (*b*) "born" and; (*c*) "race or kind." Among the many words in which this element appears is *ingenious* (Word 238). Here are a few others.

genesis ([Greek], "beginning")—the origin of something. Adjective: *genetic*

generate (*genus* [Latin], "birth" + *ate* [from Latin -*atus*], "make")—to produce or bring into being. Noun: *generation*

genocide (*genos* [Greek], "race" + *caedere, caesus* [Latin], "kill")—the systematic destruction of a racial or cultural group

genealogy (*genea* [Greek], "family, kin" + *logy* [Greek], "study, science")— a record of the ancestry of a person or family; the study of family ancestry; lineage or descent. Adjective: *genealogical*

generic (*genus, generis* [Latin], "kind, sort")—characteristic of an entire group or class

progeny (*pro* [Latin], "forward" + *gignere, genitus* [Latin], "beget")— offspring, descendants

Other words in which **gen(e)** appears include *gentle, genteel, gentile, gender, general, generous, genre, congenial, heterogeneous, indigenous,* and *primogeniture.*

Exercise

1. Add the prefix *inter* to each of the following words. Then define the new word that results, and explain how *inter* contributes to its meaning.

   a. cede
   b. collegiate
   c. denominational
   d. lock
   e. marry
   f. national

2. With or without the aid of a dictionary, define each of the following words. Then choose any **five**, and for each compose a short illustrative sentence.

   a. intercession
   b. intermittent
   c. interloper
   d. interlude
   e. interval
   f. interpolate

3. For each of the following definitions, supply a word beginning with the root *mal(e)*. You may need to use a dictionary.

   a. a vague feeling of discomfort
   b. a lawbreaker
   c. foul smelling
   d. clumsy or inept
   e. to speak ill or evil of
   f. ill will or spite

4. For each of the following definitions, supply a word beginning with the root *ben(e)*. You may need to use a dictionary.

   a. a blessing
   b. gentle and mild
   c. an heir
   d. advantageous

5. With or without the aid of a dictionary, explain what each of the following words means.

a. engender   d. genus   g. genesis
b. degenerate   e. ingenuous   h. congenial
c. homogeneous   f. heterogeneous   i. progeny

Working with Context Clues

With or without the aid of a dictionary, complete each of the following two-word omissions by selecting the pair of words that make the best sense in the passage as a whole. Underline the clue or clues that led you to make your choice.

1. In order to reduce the ever-growing number of civil suits being filed each year in American courts, some legislators are calling for _____ ceilings on the amounts of money that juries can award plaintiffs. Their hope is that these legally binding limits will stem the tide of costly _____.

a. judicious . . . liability   c. lucid . . . arbitration
b. mandatory . . . litigation   d. reasonable . . . insurance

2. In today's technological marketplace, a lack of computer skills is a(n) _____ when searching for a job. However, it is not a(n) _____ drawback because it can be overcome by further education.

a. anomaly . . . implicit   c. ignominy . . . chronic
b. foible . . . graphic   d. liability . . . insuperable

3. Legitimate businesses may not be as _____ as _____ activities, such as gambling or drug selling, but the profits from a legal enterprise are far more secure than money made from criminal activity.

a. lucrative . . . illicit   c. feasible . . . callous
b. exotic . . . clandestine   d. frugal . . . unethical

4. In the aftermath of a(n) _____, such as flood or famine, in a developing country, there is an urgent need for sustained and systematic, rather than _____, relief efforts by the international community.

a. impasse . . . gratuitous   c. fiasco . . . austere
b. exigency . . . desultory   d. anathema . . . futile

5. A preacher who delivers a long emotional speech hoping that such a(n) _____ will spur the congregation into righteousness may discover that it is difficult to _____ people into being good with words alone.

a. legacy . . . coerce   c. harangue . . . goad
b. irony . . . deceive   d. argument . . . cajole

6. Public figures who sue for _____ must prove that those who spread lies about them are prompted by _____, not just mistaken or careless.

   a. fraud . . . bravado
   b. atrocity . . . jealousy
   c. libel . . . malice
   d. damages . . . apathy

7. The old adage "Money is the root of all evil" is a wise _____ against _____.

   a. anachronism . . . greed
   b. anecdote . . . malice
   c. appeal . . . empathy
   d. counsel . . . avarice

8. New ideas in art and politics tend to _____ from a(n) _____ such as Greenwich Village in New York or the Left Bank in Paris, where artists and intellectuals gather together to live and work. Often, the original source of these ideas is forgotten, and they are eventually accepted by the general public.

   a. emanate . . . enclave
   b. deviate . . . anomaly
   c. gape . . . legacy
   d. defect . . . aggregate

9. The instinct to nest in huge colonies is _____ in seabirds such as penguins and puffins. Such _____ behavior is inborn and helps these species to survive.

   a. boorish . . . implicit
   b. inherent . . . gregarious
   c. endemic . . . lucid
   d. widespread . . . gratuitous

10. Some writers passionately hate publicity and _____ the limelight, while others love to _____ their talents in front of any audience who will listen to them read from their works or talk about their lives.

    a. flout . . . disparage
    b. allude . . . censure
    c. court . . . array
    d. abhor . . . flaunt

Enriching the Lesson

Exercise I.   More Words from Literary Sources

A few useful expressions derived from the names or works of famous and not-so-famous authors are listed below. With or without the aid of a dictionary or other reference book, define each.

1. Machiavellian
2. a Lothario
3. namby-pamby
4. a Tartuffe
5. tilt at windmills
6. Rabelaisian
7. a Frankenstein
8. a pamphlet
9. a Sherlock
10. a Simon Legree
11. Barmecidal
12. Pecksniffery
13. euphuism
14. a Micawber
15. a panjandrum

Exercise II.   Russian Loan Words in English

In this lesson, you have studied a word derived from Russian: *mammoth* (Word 263). Listed below are a number of other English words that have been borrowed from Russian. With or without the aid of a dictionary, define each.

1. pogrom	4. ukase	7. czar
2. cossack	5. steppe	8. samovar
3. intelligentsia	6. tundra	9. dacha

Many Russian words that have made their way into English have to do with life under Communism in the USSR. This is scarcely surprising in view of the fact that Communism, whether perceived as a promise or a menace, was such an important factor in the politics and history of the twentieth century.

A few of the more common Russian words of this type are given below. With or without the aid of a dictionary, define each. Note, however, that you may have to consult an unabridged dictionary for some of them.

10. commissar	12. gulag	14. glasnost
11. perestroika	13. apparatchik	15. soviet
12. kulak	15. tovarish	18. kolkhoz

Exercise III.   Plurals in *A*

A number of useful English words form their plurals in the same way as *medium* (Word 265) does. A few of these items are listed below. With or without the aid of a dictionary, define each and give its plural form.

1. addendum	3. agendum	5. bacterium
2. erratum	4. datum	6. stratum

Exercise IV.   Expanding Your Word Power

The words listed below are not on the Basic Word List, but they were mentioned in one form or another in Lesson 21. All of them would make useful additions to your working vocabulary. Define each, give its etymology, list **two** synonyms and **two** antonyms (where possible), and use in a short illustrative sentence.

1. disdain	6. traduce	11. enmity
2. supine	7. rational	12. diminutive
3. equivocal	8. sumptuous	13. remuneration
4. endowment	9. skulk	14. imperative
5. liable	10. solecism	15. vehicle

Lesson 22

266. **mercenary** — 280. **nuance**

---

266. **mer-ce-nar-y**   *noun and adjective*   mûr'-sə-nêr-ē

[*mercenarius* (Latin), "hired, paid" from *merces* (Latin), "wages, salary"]

Definition:
   a. (*noun*) A hireling, especially a hired professional soldier.

   The Roman army of Republican times was essentially a citizen militia, though foreign **mercenaries** were sometimes used as auxiliary troops.

   b. (*adjective*) Motivated solely by a desire for material gain.

   Once the war had been won, the victors laid aside the high-minded ideals for which they had fought and became embroiled in a deplorably **mercenary** squabble over the spoils.

Related Form: (*noun*) mercenariness

Synonyms: (*nouns*) hired hand, freelancer, soldier of fortune, condottiere; (*adjectives*) greedy, avaricious, acquisitive, grasping, rapacious

Antonyms: (*adjectives*) altruistic, disinterested

---

267. **moot**   *adjective and verb*   mo͞ot

[*mot* (Old English), "a meeting for discussion"]

Definition:
   a. (*adjective*) Debatable and therefore unresolved.

   The seemingly incontestable right that a person has to direct his or her own life becomes a **moot** point when it interferes with the rights of others.

   b. (*verb*) To bring up for discussion.

   "I rejected the idea when it was first **mooted** years ago," the governor said, "and I haven't regretted my decision yet."

Phrases: a moot question, a moot court

Usage Note:
   A *moot court* is a mock court in which law students try hypothetical cases in order to obtain experience under fire.

Synonyms: (*adjectives*) arguable, disputable; questionable, doubtful; (*verbs*) broach, raise, pose, put forward

Antonyms: (*adjectives*) incontrovertible, indisputable, irrefutable

Related Phrases: a Gordian knot, a foregone conclusion

268. mo·rass   *noun*   mə-răs′ *or* mô-răs′

[*moeras* (Dutch), "marsh"; from *maresc, mareis* (Old French), "swamp"; of Germanic origin and related to *mersc, merisc* (Old English), "marsh"]

Definition: A swamp or bog; a confused or degrading situation that is difficult to get out of.

Heavy rains had transformed the unpaved road into a miniature **morass**, and we were soon up to our knees in mud.

"Our once-great city," the candidate complained, "is slowly sinking into a **morass** of waste, corruption, and decay."

Synonyms: (*nouns*) marsh, fen, quagmire

269. mot·ley   *noun and adjective*   mŏt′-lē

[Origin uncertain; perhaps from *mot* (Old English), "speck"]

Definition:
a. (*noun*) A kind of multicolored cloth; a garment made from this cloth, especially the costume worn by a court jester or clown.

Shakespeare's players were a versatile crew; even the great tragic actor Richard Burbage donned **motley** now and then.

b. (*adjective*) Multicolored; diverse or varied.

In no time at all, she turned a **motley** assortment of leftovers into an elegant and tasty dinner.

As W. S. Maugham once observed, the human personality is a **motley** collection of strengths and weaknesses, foibles and fortes.

Related Forms: (*adjective*) mottled; (*verb*) mottle

Synonyms: (*adjectives*) polychrome, polychromatic, piebald; variegated, heterogeneous, miscellaneous

Antonyms: (*adjectives*) monochrome, monochromatic; monolithic, homogeneous, uniform

Related Phrases: a pluralistic society, a diversified economy, a checkered career

270. mun·dane   *adjective*   mŭn-dān′ *or* mŭn′-dān

[*mundanus* (Latin), "relating to the world"; from *mundus* (Latin), "world"]

Definition: Worldly (as opposed to spiritual); humdrum or everyday.

"May I interrupt this esoteric discussion of interpersonal relationships," I asked, "and turn your attention to more **mundane** matters—like what's for dinner?"

Most people I know are too busy dealing with such **mundane** concerns as paying off the mortgage or meeting deadlines at the office to have much time for abstruse philosophical speculation.

Related Form: (*adverb*) mundanely

Synonyms: (*adjectives*) earthly, terrestrial; secular, temporal; material, physical; ordinary, prosaic, routine, commonplace, banal (Word 55)

Antonyms: (*adjectives*) celestial, heavenly, cosmic; unworldly, spiritual; metaphysical, transcendental; extraordinary, unique

Related Phrases: worldly goods, worldly wisdom; a man of the world

271. myr·i·ad   *adjective*   mîr′-ē-əd

[*myrias, myriadis* (Greek), "ten thousand"; from *myrios* (Greek), "countless"]

Definition: Countless, innumerable.

During the East Coast blackout of 1966, the **myriad** lights by which New York City is normally illuminated at night suddenly went out.

Can any one man or woman reasonably be expected to deal with the **myriad** problems and predicaments that now face a president of the United States?

Usage Note:
Occasionally, *myriad* is used in older writing as a noun—for example, in the phrases "a *myriad* of stars" and "a *myriad* of possibilities." In such cases, the word means "a vast number" or "a great multitude."

Synonyms: (*adjectives*) multitudinous, multifarious, manifold, infinite

Antonyms: (*adjectives*) finite, limited

272. nar·cis·sis·tic   *adjective*   när-sə-sĭs′-tĭk

[*Narcissus*, see caption on page 355 + *istic* (from Greek *istikos*), "like"]

Definition: Dominated by an excessive love or admiration of oneself.

"Is a constant need to admire oneself in the mirror a sign that someone is developing a **narcissistic** personality?" I asked.

Narcissistic tendencies can perhaps be excused as an inevitable phase in a teenager's struggle to achieve an identity, but they are alarming in an adult.

Related Forms: (*nouns*) narcissism, narcissist

354

Synonyms: *(adjectives)* egotistic(al), egoistic, egomaniacal, self-centered, conceited, vain

Antonyms: *(adjectives)* self-deprecating, self-deprecatory, self-critical, self-destructive

Related Phrase: amour propre

Narcissus and Narcissism

Narcissism is a psychological term derived from the ancient Greek mythological figure of Narcissus. Narcissus was a beautiful young man who steadfastly refused to fall in love with anyone, including the lovely mountain nymph Echo. As a punishment for this attitude, the gods made Narcissus fall in love with his own reflection in a mountain pool. Since he was unable to consummate this love, Narcissus pined away with grief. Eventually, he was transformed into the white or yellowish flower that we know by the name of narcissus. Echo, by the way, also pined away from unrequited love until all that was left of her was her voice, which, as you may suspect, was the first echo.

People who suffer from narcissism have exalted feelings of self-importance, personal success, and attractiveness. They generally feel a strong need to be the center of attention. They are dominated by fantasies of gaining great wealth and power, displaying dazzling creative talents, and achieving ideal love relationships. Of course, all people share symptoms of this type, but in the *narcissist* they become dominant to the point where reality blurs into fantasy. Accordingly, the narcissist is typically preoccupied with his or her own needs and feelings and shows little or no capacity to relate constructively and warmly to other people.

Adapted in part from *Psychology for You*, by Sol Gordon (New York: William H. Sadlier, Inc., 1983), page 59.

273. neb-u-lous   *adjective*   nĕb'-yə-ləs

[*nebulosus* (Latin), "cloudy, misty"; from *nebula* (Latin), "cloud"]

Definition: Hazy, vague, or indistinct.

Neither the police force nor the justice system can act on **nebulous** rumors and vague suspicions.

Physicians most always act with caution because the line between what is proper procedure and what is not is sometimes extremely **nebulous** and uncertain.

Phrases: a nebulous recollection of an event, nebulous fears and suspicions

Related Forms: (*nouns*) nebulousness, nebulosity, nebula

Synonyms: (*adjectives*) amorphous, opaque, shapeless, fuzzy, indefinite

Antonyms: (*adjectives*) clear, distinct, well-defined, unambiguous

Nebulae

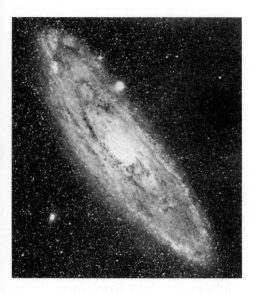

In astronomy, *nebula* (plural, *nebulae*) is the name given to a discrete mass of matter and gases that appears in the sky. Sometimes these formations are illuminated; sometimes they are not. They also have several different shapes. Some are cloudlike or spiral-shaped. Others are long, irregular veils or thin hazes stretched across the sky. Still others look something like planets because they consist of an outer envelope of gassy material completely surrounding a star. Though our galaxy, the Milky Way, contains a number of nebulae, other important examples of the formation can be found outside it. One nebula is even thought to be a separate galaxy of its own. This is the Great Spiral Nebula of Andromeda (*shown at the left*).

274. neg-li-gi-ble   *adjective*   nĕg'-lĭ-jə-bəl

[*neglegere* (Latin), "ignore" + *abilis, abile* (Latin), "able to"]

Definition: Too small to be significant.

Though the product does indeed contain a **negligible** amount of a harmful chemical, it poses absolutely no threat to anyone's health or longevity.

The effect of an unexpected downturn in the economy on a national election will probably be far from **negligible**.

Related Forms: (*nouns*) negligibility, negligibleness

Synonyms: (*adjectives*) insignificant, inconsequential, trivial, piddling, trifling, nugatory

Antonyms: (*adjectives*) significant, considerable; telling, meaningful; critical, crucial, pivotal

Related Phrases: small potatoes, trivia

275. nep·o·tism   *noun*   nĕp'-ə-tĭz-əm

[*nepotismo* (Italian), "favoritism to nephews"; from *nepote* (Italian), "nephew"; from *nepos, nepotis* (Latin), "nephew; descendant"]

Definition: Unwarranted favoritism shown to relatives or friends by someone in high office.

"If your brother-in-law is really the best available candidate for the job you have to offer," I told my boss, "no one will accuse you of **nepotism**."

Some **nepotism** is unavoidable in a small, family-run business such as a mom-and-pop candy store.

Related Forms: (*noun*) nepotist; (*adjectives*) nepotistic(al)

Synonyms: (*nouns*) partisanship, bias, partiality, patronage

Related Phrases: a client state, the spoils system; the merit system

Alexander VI

Cesare Borgia

During the Middle Ages and Renaissance, the rulers of the Roman Catholic Church were occasionally accused of showing special consideration for their nephews and other relatives when making appointments to high ecclesiastical office, such as the cardinalate. For example, Pope Alexander VI (1492–1503) was notorious for the blatant favoritism he showed to his relatives Cesare (1475–1507) and Lucrezia (1480–1519) Borgia.

276. no-mad-ic   *adjective*   nō-măd'-ĭk

[*nomas, nomados* (Greek), "wanderer in search of pasturage" (from *nemein* [Greek], "pasture") + *ikos* (Greek), "pertaining to"]

Definition: Wandering, roving.

About 5000 B.C., the peoples of the Near East began to make the transition from the **nomadic** existence of a hunter to the more settled life of a farmer.

Related Form: (*noun*) nomad

Phrase: urban nomads

Synonyms: (*adjectives*) itinerant, migratory, peripatetic

Antonyms: (*adjectives*) settled, fixed, stationary

Related Phrases: footloose and fancy-free; a fly-by-night operation, a roving reporter, a Peripatetic philosopher, a migrant farmworker; wanderlust

The Peripatetics

Aristotle

The *Peripatetic* school of ancient Greek philosophy owed its name in part to the unusual teaching habits of its founder, the famous philosopher Aristotle of Stagira (384–322 B.C.). Aristotle, a pupil of Plato, preferred to teach or lecture while walking about rather than while sitting or standing still. (His students, of course, would follow him as he moved around.) One of his favorite places for doing this kind of nomadic pedagogy was a covered walkway called the Peripatos ("Walkabout"), which formed part of a gymnasium in Athens called the Lykeion or Lyceum. Accordingly, the school of philosophy that Aristotle founded came to be called *peripatetikos*—that is, "the one founded in the Peripatos."

Initially, the members of the Peripatetic school were almost exclusively students or followers of Aristotle and his empirical approach to philosophy. These men spent most of their time writing commentaries on Aristotle's works, attempting to refine his philosophic system, or composing specialized treatises on the natural sciences. Later, however, some of the Peripatetics developed more independent lines of philosophic thought.

Urban Nomads

Pathetic reminders of our dim
nomadic past, bag ladies (like the one
in this photo) and other homeless persons now roam the streets of some of
our largest cities.

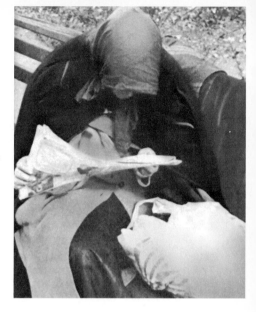

277. **nom·i·nal**   *adjective*   nŏm′-ə-nəl

[*nominalis* (Latin), "relating to a name"; from *nomen, nominis* (Latin), "name"]

Definition:
  a. Existing in name only.

> Since the prime minister actually directs the British government,
> the reigning monarch is really only the **nominal** head of state.

  b. Insignificantly small.

> Most government-funded medical centers charge only **nominal**
> fees so that even the poorest member of the community can afford
> their services.

Phrases: a nominal Christian, nominal representation on the board

Related Forms: (*adverb*) nominally; (*nouns*) nominalism, nominalist

Synonyms: (*adjectives*) titular; token, symbolic; trifling, inconsequential

Antonyms: (*adjectives*) real, actual; exorbitant, excessive

Related Phrase: a puppet ruler

278. **nos·tal·gia**   *noun*   nŏ-stăl′-jə *or* nə-stăl′-jə

[*nostos* (Greek), "a return home" + *algos* (Greek), "pain"; actually a learned
translation of *Heimweh* (German), "homesickness"]

Definition: A longing to return to a sentimentalized past; homesickness.

> Around Christmas, I always get a feeling of **nostalgia** for the days of my
> youth and the friends I grew up with.

Related Form: (*adjective*) nostalgic

Synonyms: (*nouns*) yearning, pining, hankering; wistfulness, sadness,
sentimentality, sorrow, regret; lonesomeness

279. **nov-ice** *noun* nŏv'-ĭs

[*novicius* (Medieval Latin), "probationary member of a religious order"; from *novus* (Latin), "new"]

Definition:
  a. A person who has just entered a religious order on a probationary basis.

  Many **novices** find their first days in a religious community difficult, but usually they become accustomed to the lifestyle relatively quickly.

  b. A beginner of any kind.

  Show jumping is an aspect of the art of horseback riding that an experienced rider can tackle, but not a **novice**.

  "He's such a consummate master of the art of politics that he makes even a seasoned veteran look like a **novice**," I remarked.

Related Form: (*noun*) novitiate

Usage Note:
  Occasionally *novice* is used as an adjective before another noun or a noun phrase—for example, "a *novice* swimmer."

Synonyms: (*nouns*) postulant; neophyte, tyro, fledgling, trainee, rookie, probationer, greenhorn, tenderfoot

Antonyms: (*nouns*) expert, pro, veteran, old hand, past master, virtuoso

Related Phrases: still wet behind the ears; a babe in the woods, a freshman senator; a black belt in karate

280. **nu-ance** *noun* n(y)ōo-äns' *or* n(y)ōo'-äns

[*nuance* (French), "shade, hue"; from *nubes* (Latin), "cloud"]

Definition: A slight or subtle variation in meaning, expression, tone, feeling, color, or the like.

  Two synonyms are never exactly alike because **nuances** of tone or applicability make each of the words unique.

  Music can sometimes express a **nuance** of mood or feeling that would be difficult to put into words.

  Her colorful outfit contained every imaginable **nuance** of red—from the palest pink to the deepest burgundy.

  We may hope that our friends will understand the **nuances** of feeling implied in our words, but we shouldn't expect them to be mind readers.

Synonyms: (*nouns*) subtlety, nicety, overtone, gradation, refinement, delicacy

Related Phrases: a fine point; read between the lines, read the small print

Using the Words

Exercise I. Parts of Speech

Indicate the part of speech of each of the following words. In some cases, two answers are correct.

1. mercenary
2. moot
3. motley
4. mundane
5. myriad
6. nebulous
7. nepotism
8. nominal
9. nuance

Exercise II. Words in Phrases

In each of the following groups, select the item that best expresses the meaning of the *italicized* word in the introductory phrase.

1. at a *nominal* cost to the consumer
   a. guaranteed   b. token   c. sizable   d. fair

2. *nebulous* plans
   a. radical   b. detailed   c. costly   d. vague

3. *mundane* pursuits
   a. commonplace   b. sensible   c. odd   d. interesting

4. a *motley* group
   a. snobbish   b. penniless   c. enthusiastic   d. diverse

5. for purely *mercenary* reasons
   a. practical   b. monetary   c. social   d. personal

6. *nuances* of tone and shading
   a. subtleties   b. theories   c. uses   d. problems

7. the *myriad* leaves on an oak
   a. edible   b. uniform   c. countless   d. colorful

Exercise III. Completing Sentences

Complete each of the following sentences by selecting the most appropriate word from the group of words given below. Use each word only once.

narcissistic	nepotism	nuance
novice	negligible	morass
nostalgia	nomadic	moot

1. Understandably, many of those who suffered through the hard economic times of the 1930s don't remember that particular era with much _____.

2. "Twenty-five dollars may be a _____ amount of money to you," I replied, "but it's sizable to me."

3. Whether or not Lincoln could have bound up the nation's wounds by being merciful is a _____ question simply because he was assassinated before he got the chance to try.

4. Since most people cannot resist sneaking a peek at their reflections in a plate-glass window, is it fair to say that human beings generally have a _____ streak in them?

5. Trying to work my way through the _____ of complicated paperwork involved in the project was like trying to swim through shark-infested custard.

6. "Once you have mastered the basics of the game and can play with some degree of skill and confidence," my instructor said, "you will cease to be a _____."

7. I chose the _____ life of a traveling salesperson simply because I felt too tied down by a nine-to-five office job.

8. "The appointment of your son to the job may have been based solely on merit," I told the mayor, "but your critics will surely see it as _____."

Exercise IV.   Synonyms and Antonyms

A. In each of the following groups, select the **two** words that are most nearly **synonymous**.

1. a. precipice   b. quagmire   c. grove   d. bog
2. a. conceited   b. affluent   c. vengeful   d. egotistic
3. a. prosaic   b. humdrum   c. gullible   d. slovenly
4. a. biased   b. infinite   c. hazy   d. vague
5. a. ace   b. greenhorn   c. tenderfoot   d. hillbilly

Now, for each pair of synonyms that you have selected, supply a word from the Basic Word List for this lesson (Words 266–280) that means **the same** or **almost the same** thing.

B. In each of the following, select the item that is most nearly **opposite** in meaning to the numbered word at the left.

1. moot   a. incredible   b. invaluable   c. interminable
             d. insoluble   e. indisputable

2. nomadic   a. pleasant   b. itinerant   c. awkward
             d. stationary   e. theatrical

3. motley   a. trite   b. uniform   c. charitable
             d. ambiguous   e. miscellaneous

4. nominal   a. exorbitant   b. genial   c. abject
             d. prompt   e. human

5. mercenary a. arduous   b. aggressive   c. altruistic
             d. arbitrary   e. ambitious

Exercise V.   Word Roundup

1. With or without the aid of a dictionary, explain the meaning of each of the following terms indicating kinds of people.

   a. a soldier of fortune
   b. a freelancer
   c. a puppet ruler
   d. a roving reporter
   e. a Peripatetic philosopher
   f. a man of the world
   g. a freshman senator
   h. an urban nomad
   i. a migrant farmworker
   j. a nominal Christian

2. With or without the aid of a dictionary, explain the meaning of each of the following expressions indicating things.

   a. a moot court
   b. a fly-by-night operation
   c. a client state
   d. a checkered career
   e. a diversified economy
   f. a pluralistic society

3. What is a *Gordian knot?* Tell the story behind the phrase.

4. With or without the aid of a dictionary, explain what each of the following foreign expressions means, and tell what language it comes from.

   a. condottiere   b. amour propre   c. wanderlust

5. With or without the aid of a dictionary, explain the meaning of each of the following colorful English expressions.

   a. wet behind the ears
   b. read between the lines
   c. small potatoes
   d. a babe in the woods

6. Tell the story of Echo and Narcissus. How does this story relate to the meaning of the psychological term *narcissism?* What is a *narcissist?*

7. What is *the spoils system? the merit system?* How do the two systems differ?

8. What is a *nebula?* In what science is this term used?

Exercise VI.   Framing Sentences

A. Use each of the following words in an original illustrative sentence.

1. mercenary
2. moot
3. morass
4. myriad
5. mundane
6. motley
7. nominal
8. novice
9. nuance

B. Give a **noun** form for each of the following words, and use it in an original illustrative sentence.

1. narcissistic   2. nomadic   3. negligible

C. Give an **adjective** form for each of these words, and use it in an original illustrative sentence.

1. nostalgia   2. nepotism   3. motley

Completing Verbal Analogies

By now you should be familiar enough with how verbal analogies work to handle them on your own. Accordingly, the remaining "Completing Verbal Analogies" sections of this book will concentrate on providing you with ample practice in dealing with them. That way, you will acquire the skill and confidence needed to tackle those that actually appear on standardized vocabulary tests. However, since many of the word relationships that you will meet, both in the remaining analogy sections in this book and on standardized tests, will be new to you, in the sense that you have not formally studied them, bear one important principle in mind: Always identify the relationship between the words in the key or given pair before you attempt to choose your answer.

Exercise

Complete each of the following analogies.

Group A

1. **momentous : trivial =**
   a. opportune : negligible
   b. year : decade
   c. temporary : ephemeral
   d. moot : nomadic
   e. significant :
      inconsequential

2. **ship : nautical =**
   a. subterranean : tunnel
   b. helicopter : lunar
   c. automobile : terrestrial
   d. horse : marine
   e. skateboard : celestial

3. **philatelist : stamps =**
   a. spendthrift : profits
   b. numismatist : coins
   c. charity : philanthropist
   d. speculation : philosopher
   e. astrologer : books

4. **behemoth : puny =**
   a. mammoth : massive
   b. gargantuan : carnivore
   c. mastodon : huge
   d. leviathan : minuscule
   e. colossus : gigantic

5. **cat : feline =**
   a. equine : horse
   b. cow : bovine
   c. rooster : hen
   d. dog : mongrel
   e. sheep : amphibian

Group B

1. **callow : experience ::**
   a. predatory : intelligence
   b. pensive : aplomb
   c. petulant : imagination
   d. self-esteem : narcissistic
   e. provincial :
      sophistication

2. **lax : stringent ::**
   a. circuitous : straight
   b. errant : nightly
   c. nominal : meritorious
   d. decadent : motley
   e. nebulous : hazy

3. **pickpocket : filch ::**
   a. cutthroat : deface
   b. spendthrift : hoard
   c. daredevil : lurk
   d. spoilsport : incarcerate
   e. scofflaw : flout

4. **avarice : grasping ::**
   a. humility : bare-knuckled
   b. liability : tightfisted
   c. nepotism : light-fingered
   d. generosity : openhanded
   e. nostalgia : double-jointed

5. **palace : opulence ::**
   a. mansion : austerity
   b. shack : affluence
   c. hovel : indigence
   d. cottage : luxury
   e. skyscraper : poverty

Working with Context Clues

Complete each of the following two-word omissions by selecting the pair of words that make the best sense in the passage as a whole. If necessary, consult a dictionary for the meaning of any word with which you are not familiar.

1. American democracy is in trouble if the only people running for office are either wealthy or motivated by a desire to become rich. The danger of such a situation is that the _____ may ignore the needs of the poor and the _____ may rob them.

   a. indigent . . . ambitious
   b. affluent . . . mercenary
   c. brash . . . delinquent
   d. erudite . . . gregarious

2. When a third of the members of a leader's inner circle are relatives, it is tempting to _____ the practice of _____ without any further solid evidence.

   a. allege . . . nepotism
   b. instigate . . . effrontery
   c. construe . . . euphemism
   d. delineate . . . demagoguery

3. When an ordinary citizen makes an embarrassing slip of the tongue, the effect is usually _____, but an ill-timed _____ by a candidate in a televised debate can have a serious impact on election results.

   a. facetious . . . remark
   b. brash . . . calumny
   c. grueling . . . accusation
   d. negligible . . . malapropism

4. When listening to old songs, I often find myself slipping into a confused state of joy and sadness that is hard to shake. I am not sure why I sink into such a(n) _____ of _____ at these times.

   a. morass . . . nostalgia
   b. ambience . . . despair
   c. legacy . . . apathy
   d. state . . . nuance

5. Children learn best when their parents are neither too quick to praise them nor too ready to _____ their efforts. _____ parents are too easily satisfied, and overly critical ones are too hard to please.

   a. exploit . . . Docile
   b. flout . . . Formidable
   c. condemn . . . Delinquent
   d. disparage . . . Complacent

6. When you _____ someone to give you a serious response to an important question and instead you are given a _____ reply, you are bound to be sorry you ever asked.

   a. cajole . . . brash
   b. entreat . . . facetious
   c. entice . . . candid
   d. goad . . . gratuitous

7. After a major earthquake, rescue workers are faced with an awesome challenge. Just removing the tons of debris is a(n) _____ task, and the huge effort may seem _____ when no survivors are found.

   a. gruesome . . . frugal
   b. formidable . . . futile
   c. insuperable . . . graphic
   d. grueling . . . fortuitous

8. If you invest cautiously and in a variety of investment vehicles, you should be able to ride out a major failure in the stock market. Investors who are _____ can usually avoid the huge losses that often accompany a Wall Street _____.

   a. prudent . . . bravado
   b. frugal . . . impasse
   c. circumspect . . . fiasco
   d. brash . . . collapse

9. When children are guilty of breaking the rules, they often make up stories to explain their _____ behavior. Usually, they give up this tendency to _____ excuses as they get older.

   a. brash . . . instigate
   b. heinous . . . gloat
   c. exemplary . . . alienate
   d. culpable . . . fabricate

10. The _____ bedouin are a tribe who move continually over the sands of Saudi Arabia, stopping occasionally at the _____ oases where the desert blooms.

   a. nomadic . . . lush
   b. formidable . . . blithe
   c. dilatory . . . exotic
   d. primitive . . . bleak

11. Sometimes when I am alone at night, I have horrible fears that _____ monsters _____ in the dark, waiting to pounce on me.

   a. implacable . . . toil
   b. intrepid . . . grope
   c. myriad . . . inveigh
   d. gruesome . . . lurk

Enriching the Lesson

Exercise I. Our German Heritage

Modern German has contributed a number of useful words to the vocabulary of present-day English. One such expression, *wanderlust,* was mentioned in passing in this lesson. A few others are listed below. With or without the aid of a dictionary, define each. Then choose any **three**, and for each compose a short illustrative sentence.

1. strafe
2. ersatz
3. leitmotif
4. wunderkind
5. blitz(krieg)
6. putsch
7. seminar
8. flak
9. kitsch

Exercise II. The Clothes We Wear

One of the meanings noted for the word *motley,* studied in this lesson, was "a kind of multicolored cloth" or "a garment made from this cloth." This brings to mind the fact that there is a great deal of interesting history involved in the names of some of our most familiar fabrics and articles of clothing.

Listed below are the names of some common fabrics or articles of wearing apparel. With or without the aid of a dictionary or other reference book, identify each, and explain where the name comes from.

1. raglan
2. jeans
3. knickerbockers
4. mackintosh
5. Levi's
6. muslin
7. madras
8. lisle
9. dungarees
10. Stetson
11. cardigan
12. denim
13. calico
14. oxfords
15. fedora

Exercise III. Words from the Sciences

One of the items mentioned in passing in this lesson was the term *nebula,* which comes from the science of astronomy. This brings to mind the fact that a good many scientific terms have been borrowed for use in a broad social sense. A few such expressions are listed below. With or without the aid of a dictionary, define each as it is used in the sciences and as it is used in more everyday situations. Then choose any **three**, and for each compose an original illustrative sentence.

1. catalyst
2. polarize
3. hybrid
4. eclipse
5. erosion
6. symbiosis
7. parasite
8. inertia
9. satellite

Exercise IV.   What's in a Name?

Listed below are a number of expressions for different kinds of names. With or without the aid of a dictionary, define each. Then choose any **four**, and for each compose an original illustrative sentence.

1. epithet
2. surname
3. alias
4. stage name
5. honorific
6. sobriquet
7. misnomer
8. appellation
9. moniker
10. toponym
11. pen name
12. nickname
13. pseudonym
14. patronymic
15. diminutive

Exercise V.   Number Words

Earlier in this lesson it was noted that *myriad* (Word 271) comes directly from the Greek term meaning "ten thousand." The English word, however, has lost this precise numerical denotation and is used to suggest (connote) the idea of "a very large number."

There are many other words in English derived from specific numbers. Some of them are listed below. Identify the number in each case. Then tell what the word means in present-day usage. In some cases, the original number meaning has been retained. In others, an entirely new meaning has been assumed. Try to account for the change. An unabridged dictionary will help.

1. millennium
2. quintet
3. decade
4. centurion
5. septuagenarian
6. bicentennial
7. trio
8. Pentecostal
9. trivial
10. unique
11. triumvirate
12. pentagon
13. trilogy
14. monolithic
15. decathlon
16. monogamy
17. monopoly
18. pentathlon
19. decimal
20. quadruped
21. decimate

Exercise VI.   Expanding Your Word Power

The words listed below are not on the Basic Word List, but they were mentioned in one form or another in Lesson 22. All of them would make useful additions to your working vocabulary. Define each, give its etymology, list **two** synonyms and **two** antonyms (where possible), and use in a short illustrative sentence.

1. altruistic
2. incontrovertible
3. fledgling
4. temporal
5. manifold
6. egotistical
7. opaque
8. finite
9. nugatory
10. patronage
11. itinerant
12. titular
13. partisanship
14. wistfulness
15. refinement

Related Forms in Context

Beneath each sentence below are four words introduced in Lesson 21 or 22. Review the related forms for these words, and choose the one that best completes the sentence. Write that related form in the space provided.

1. In *Brown v. Board of Education*, the landmark civil rights case, Brown, the _____, sued the Board of Education of Topeka, Kansas; and on May 17, 1954, the U.S. Supreme Court unanimously ruled the concept of "separate but equal" public schools unconstitutional.

   a. novice   **b.** litigation   **c.** mercenary   **d.** libel

2. The Ethics Committee is holding a hearing to determine whether the city manager's appointment of his second cousin by marriage is _____.

   a. libel   **b.** malice   **c.** nostalgia   **d.** nepotism

3. In "Pied Beauty," the English poet Gerard Manley Hopkins counters the traditional notion of beauty by celebrating all things that are _____.

   a. malice   **b.** motley   **c.** mercenary   **d.** novice

4. If the promised _____ of an investment scheme seems too good to be true, you would be wise to think twice before risking your life's savings on it.

   a. lucrative   **b.** lush   **c.** nebulous   **d.** negligible

5. In just a few paragraphs, a skillful columnist can _____ state her or his opinion and support it with convincing reasons and evidence.

   a. lackadaisical   **b.** lush   **c.** mundane   **d.** lucid

6. He moved through life _____, displaying little enthusiasm either for work or for play.

   a. lucrative   **b.** nominal   **c.** lackadaisical   **d.** mercenary

7. Determined to remain "the fairest of them all," the _____ queen disguises herself as an old woman and offers Snow White a poisoned apple.

   a. malapropism   **b.** motley   **c.** libel   **d.** malice

8. If someone falls and is injured on a sidewalk in front of your house, are you _____ for that person's medical expenses?

   a. liability   **b.** libel   **c.** litigation   **d.** nostalgia

9. In *A Christmas Carol*, Charles Dickens makes it clear that Ebenezer Scrooge's _____ prevents him from leading a happy, fulfilling life.

   a. lucrative   **b.** mercenary   **c.** lackadaisical   **d.** nominal

10. Many movie stars have sued tabloid newspapers for their _____ headlines and stories.

    a. mercenary b. liability c. libel d. motley

11. Although her voice was well past its prime, _____ fans cheered her renditions of her greatest hits.

    a. nostalgia b. nepotism c. malice d. litigation

12. Paul Gauguin's paintings of Tahiti are remarkable for the beauty of their composition and the _____ of their colors.

    a. mundane b. nominal c. lush d. mammoth

13. A candidate who wins an election by a landslide may be justified in believing that he or she has received a _____ from the voters.

    a. mercenary b. narcissistic c. mandatory d. nebulous

14. Although it is a thousand light years away, the bright _____ in the constellation Orion is visible to the naked eye.

    a. myriad b. nebulous c. narcissistic d. nomadic

15. Given the _____ of the differences between the performance ratings of the two automobiles, I will probably choose the one that looks sportier.

    a. mandatory b. lucid c. narcissistic d. negligible

16. I was surprised that she spoke so _____ of her travels to places that seem to me to be so exotic.

    a. mundane b. lucrative c. negligible d. nomadic

17. It may be said that _____ hold themselves in much higher esteem than anyone else does.

    a. motley b. lucrative c. nomadic d. narcissistic

18. Traditionally, the Inuit, like other _____, erected temporary shelters—igloos in winter, tents in summer—near their food source.

    a. narcissistic b. nominal c. nomadic d. mundane

19. Though the nine-year-old was _____ king of Egypt, all the real power rested with his advisors.

    a. mandatory b. nominal c. lucid d. mundane

20. Several candidates criticized the _____ of the frontrunner's plan for stimulating the nation's faltering economy.

    a. nominal b. nebulous c. mandatory d. lackadaisical

Lesson 23

---

281. **ob·scene**   *adjective*   ŏb-sēn' *or* əb-sēn'

[*obsc(a)enus* (Latin), "foul, repugnant"; perhaps from *ob* (Latin), "on account of" + *sc(a)enum* (Latin), "dirt, filth"]

Definition: Offensive to accepted standards of decency; repulsive.

Federal regulations forbid the use of **obscene** language in programs broadcast over the airwaves.

Concerned citizens may complain that the misuse of our national resources verges on the **obscene**.

Phrases: an obscene gesture, an obscene dance, an obscene picture

Related Forms: (*noun*) obscenity, (*adverb*) obscenely

Synonyms: (*adjectives*) indecent, lewd, salacious, smutty, bawdy, scatological, pornographic; risqué, suggestive; vulgar, crude, coarse; disgusting, abominable, reprehensible, loathsome

Antonyms: (*adjectives*) decent, refined, modest; laudable, meritorious

Related Phrases: an X-rated (or R-rated) film, an off-color joke

---

282. **ob·se·qui·ous**   *adjective*   ŏb-sē'-kwē-əs

[*ob* (Latin), "to, toward" + *sequi* (Latin), "follow, yield" + *osus* (Latin), "characterized by, full of"]

Definition: Excessively submissive to another person's wishes or ideas, often for purely self-interested reasons.

During imperial times, the Roman Senate was little more than a collection of **obsequious** yes-men, intent on preserving their own lives by gratifying the emperor's every whim.

At an autocrat's court, free speech is usually replaced by the **obsequious** twaddle of self-seeking toadies and flunkies.

Related Forms: (*nouns*) obsequiousness, obsequy; (*adverb*) obsequiously

Usage Note:
The noun *obsequy*, usually used in the plural, means "a funeral rite."

Synonyms: (*adjectives*) servile, fawning, subservient, groveling, mealymouthed, sycophantic, unctuous, compliant, deferential

Antonyms: (*adjectives*) independent; frank, candid, outspoken; self-assertive, aggressive, bumptious

Related Phrases: a yes-man, a rubber stamp; toe the line, knuckle under to

371

283. ob·ses·sion   *noun*   ŏb-sĕsh′-ən   *or*   əb-sĕsh′-ən

[*ob* (Latin), "in front of, before" + *sedere, sessus* (Latin), "sit"]

Definition: An irrational preoccupation with an idea or feeling that usually results in severe anxiety.

Fear of falling victim to some dread disease can become such an **obsession** that it actually drives a person into a nervous breakdown.

Related Forms: (*verb*) obsess; (*adjective*) obsessive

Phrases: obsessed by a sense of one's own importance, obsessed with an idea, an obsessive need for reassurance

Synonyms: (*nouns*) compulsion, fixation, mania, phobia, hang-up

Related Phrases: an idée fixe; have a one-track mind; have a bee in one's bonnet, have an ax to grind, ride a hobbyhorse; a perfectionist, a monomaniac, a paranoiac, a megalomaniac, a compulsive gambler

Have a Bee in One's Bonnet

The colloquial expression *have a bee in one's bonnet* means "have some fixed idea or obsession that other people find odd or eccentric."

284. ob·so·lete   *adjective*   ŏb-sə-lēt′   *or*   ŏb′-sə-lēt

[*obsolescere, obsoletus* (Latin), "grow old; wear out"]

Definition: No longer in use; outmoded.

"I'm interested in the present-day meaning of the word," I exclaimed, "not in one that has been **obsolete** for over 200 years!"

The automobile made many older forms of land transportation, such as the horse and buggy, **obsolete**.

Phrases: an obsolete expression, obsolete equipment, an obsolete idea

Related Forms: (*nouns*) obsolescence, obsoleteness; (*adjective*) obsolescent

Usage Note:

Be careful to distinguish between *obsolete*, which indicates that something has already become outmoded, and *obsolescent*, which indicates that it is still in the process of becoming antiquated.

Synonyms: (*adjectives*) old-fashioned, antiquated, dated, out-of-date, passé, old hat, superannuated; archaic, defunct, extinct

Antonyms: (*adjectives*) up-to-date, new, novel, fresh, newfangled, avant-garde, ultramodern

Related Phrases: behind the times, past one's prime; a discontinued model, a has-been, a thing of the past; au courant, dernier cri, still on the drawing board, hot off the presses

285. of-fi-cious   *adjective*   ə-fĭsh'-əs

[*officiosus* (Latin), "dutiful"; from *officium* (Latin), "duty, obligation"]

Definition: Excessively forward in offering unwanted or unnecessary help or advice; meddlesome.

"I'm not going to get this job done any faster," I objected, "just because you shout unnecessary instructions at me and otherwise make an **officious** nuisance of yourself."

Related Forms: (*noun*) officiousness; (*adverb*) officiously

Usage Note:
Be careful to distinguish between *officious* and *official,* which as an adjective means "authoritative" or "formal" and as a noun means "a person in authority." Of course, an official may be officious (annoyingly meddlesome), but the two words are not related in meaning.

Synonyms: (*adjectives*) intrusive; prying, nosy; forward, pushy, bossy; importunate

Related Phrases: a busybody, a gadfly, a self-appointed watchdog of the government

286. om-i-nous   *adjective*   ŏm'-ə-nəs

[*ominosus* (Latin), "ill-omened"; from *omen, ominis* (Latin), "sign, portent" + *osus* (Latin), "full of"]

Definition: Foreshadowing evil; menacing or threatening.

The **ominous** silence that greeted the proposal presented by one of the members clearly foretold the plan's eventual defeat.

If we had paid some attention to the **ominous** sounds coming from the engine, we would have not been so surprised when the car stopped dead in the middle of nowhere.

Phrases: an ominous pause, ominous clouds

Related Forms: (*nouns*) ominousness, omen; (*adverb*) ominously

Synonyms: (*adjectives*) portentous, ill-omened, foreboding, untoward, unpromising, sinister

Antonyms: (*adjectives*) lucky, happy, felicitous (Word 189), auspicious propitious

Related Phrase: a bird of ill omen

287. op-por-tune   *adjective*   ŏp-ẽr-tōōn′   *or*   ŏp-ẽr-tyōōn′

[*opportunus* (Latin), "suitable, favorable"; from the phrase *ob portum veniens* (Latin), "coming (*i.e.*, blowing) toward the harbor"; from *ob* (Latin), "to, toward" + *portus* (Latin), "harbor"]

Definition: Suitable, appropriate, or timely.

Someone with a natural sense of timing can usually select the most **opportune** moment to ask his or her boss for a raise.

Related Forms: (*nouns*) opportunity, opportunism, opportunist; (*adjectives*) inopportune, opportunistic

Usage Note:

An *opportunist* is a person who takes advantage of events to further his or her own purposes regardless of the principles involved. Similarly, *opportunism* is the policy or practice of letting circumstance, rather than principle, dictate a person's behavior or course of action.

Synonyms: (*adjectives*) convenient, seasonable, apt, fitting, propitious, fit, auspicious, advantageous

Antonyms: (*adjectives*) inappropriate, untimely, unsuitable, ill timed, inconvenient, inauspicious

Related Phrases: a timeserver, take time by the forelock

288. os-ten-si-ble   *adjective*   ŏ-stĕn′-sə-bəl

[*ostensibilis* (Medieval Latin), "apparent"; from *ostendere* (Latin), "to reveal; appear" + *abilis, abile* (Latin), "able to"]

Definition: Apparent or professed.

Though a commendable concern for the average wage earner's welfare was the **ostensible** reason for the candidate's proposal, I suspect that his real motives were more self-serving.

Related Form: (*adverb*) ostensibly

Synonyms: (*adjectives*) purported, alleged, avowed, nominal (Word 277), supposed, reputed, evident, manifest

Antonyms: (*adjectives*) true, real, actual, authentic (Word 50), genuine

289. os-tra-cize   *verb*   ŏs′-trə-sīz

[*ostrakizein* (Greek), "banish"; from *ostrakon* (Greek), "potsherd; shell"]

Definition: To banish or exclude from a group; to shun.

Once the details of his scandalous behavior became public knowledge, the entire community **ostracized** him.

Will the day ever come when Americans finally agree to **ostracize** industrial pollution of the environment once and for all?

Related Form: (*noun*) ostracism

374

Synonyms: (*verbs*) expel, exile; blacklist, blackball, snub; boycott (Word 67); bar, repudiate, reject; proscribe, outlaw

Antonyms: (*verbs*) accept, welcome, embrace; associate with

Related Phrases: give someone the cold shoulder, cut someone dead, drum out of the army, send someone to Coventry; a pariah

Ostraka from the marketplace in Athens. Among the names that appear on these broken bits of pottery are Aristeides and Themistokles.

Ostracism

In the ancient Greek city of Athens, it became customary to banish any citizen who was considered to be dangerous to the welfare of the state. Just who should be banished was decided by voting. On the day that the vote was taken, each citizen scratched the name of the person he wished to banish on a bit of broken pottery and deposited this curious ballot in one of the official voting urns set up for the purpose. These broken pieces of crockery were called *ostraka* (singular, *ostrakon*) in Greek. They were used as ballots because great numbers of them lay scattered about the marketplace (or *agora*), where the voting took place. Once all the ballots had been cast, the officials supervising the voting sorted them out. The man who received the largest number of votes was banished from Athenian territory, usually for a period of ten years. The voting was declared invalid, however, if fewer than 6000 votes (total) were cast.

The first *ostracism*, as the Greeks called this curious "unpopularity poll," took place in 487 B.C. and the last about 416 B.C. By the way, many famous Athenians, including Themistokles and Aristeides "the Just," two of Athens's greatest generals and statesmen, were the victims of ostracism, and no particular shame or disgrace was attached to it. In fact, ostracism became such a useful political tool that a number of other Greek city-states adopted it. In Syracuse, the institution was called *petalism* because the names were written on olive leaves (*petala*), not potsherds.

290. pan-de-mo-ni-um   *noun*   păn-də-mō'-nē-əm

[*pas, pan* (Greek), "all" + *daimon* (Greek), "spirit; deity." For further details, see the caption and illustration on page 377.]

Definition: General disorder, confusion, noise, and commotion.

When the verdict of the jury was announced, **pandemonium** broke loose in the courtroom.

The trading floor of the Commodities Exchange was a scene of unbelievable **pandemonium**, unlike anything I had ever witnessed before.

Related Form: (*adjective*) pandemoniac

Synonyms: (*nouns*) chaos, bedlam, turmoil, tumult, din, cacophony, hubbub, hullabaloo, ruckus, racket, rumpus

Antonyms: (*nouns*) order, silence, calm, tranquility, placidity, repose, peace

Related Phrases: raise a hue and cry, a three-ring circus, a brouhaha

291. par-a-dox   *noun*   păr'-ə-dŏks

[*paradoxos* (Greek), "incredible"; from *para* (Greek), "beyond" + *doxa* (Greek), "thought, opinion, expectation"]

Definition:

a. A seemingly self-contradictory statement that, on closer examination, proves worthy of belief.

At some time in our lives, all of us discover the truth of the ancient **paradox** that by giving freely to others, we gain more for ourselves.

b. Someone or something that is full of contradictions and inconsistencies.

That terrible instruments of war should in fact prove useful as guardians of the peace was one of the **paradoxes** of the Cold War.

Related Forms: (*adjective*) paradoxical; (*adverb*) paradoxically

Synonyms: (*nouns*) riddle, enigma, anomaly

Related Phrases: caught on the horns of a dilemma, a Gordian knot, an oxymoron, a contradiction in terms

Some Famous Paradoxes

Whosoever shall exalt himself shall be abased; and he that shall humble himself shall be exalted.

—The Bible

In this world there are only two tragedies. One is not getting what one wants, and the other is getting it.

—Oscar Wilde

Pandaemonium, by the 19th-century French illustrator Gustave Doré.

Pandemonium

The word *pandemonium* was originally coined by the English poet John Milton (1608–1674) as the name of the capital city of Hell, where much of the action of Milton's great epic poem *Paradise Lost* (1667) takes place. The following extract from this poem shows how Milton originally used the word and also how he spelled it:

> The rest were all
> Far to the inland retir'd, about the walls
> Of Pandaemonium, city and proud seat
> Of Lucifer. . . .
>
> *Paradise Lost*, X, 422–425

Milton also used the word as the name of the palace of Lucifer (or Satan), the ruler of Hell.

Later, the word came to mean Hell itself and, finally (now shorn of its capital letter and second *a*), any place that was like Hell—that is, any scene of wild commotion, general disorder, and noise. This more extended meaning is normally what the word denotes in present-day English.

292. par-a-phrase   *verb and noun*   păr'-ə-frāz

[*paraphrazein* (Greek), "restate"; from *para* (Greek), "alongside" + *phrazein* (Greek), "show, tell"]

Definition:
   a. (*verb*) To restate in other words or another form, often in order to clarify meaning or avoid difficulties.

      She didn't quote the passage verbatim; she **paraphrased** it.

   b. (*noun*) A restatement in other words or another form.

      Some of the most famous passages in Shakespeare's plays turn out to be loose **paraphrases** of Holinshed's *Chronicles* or North's translation of Plutarch.

Related Forms: (*adjective*) paraphrastic; (*noun*) paraphrasis

Usage Note:
Do not confuse the adjective *paraphrastic*, meaning "in the nature of a paraphrase," with the look-alike adjective *periphrastic*, which means "circumlocutory" or "roundabout."

Synonyms: (*verbs*) reword, rephrase; (*nouns*) rewording, rephrasing, free rendering, version

Antonyms: (*verbs*) quote, duplicate, reproduce; (*noun*) quotation

Related Phrase: a word-for-word (or literal) translation

293. pa-ro-chi-al   *adjective*   pə-rō'-kē-əl

[*parochia* (Latin), "parish" + *alis, ale* (Latin), "relating to"; from *paroikos* (Greek), "neighbor, Christian"; from *para* (Greek), "alongside" + *oikos* (Greek), "house"]

Definition:
   a. Located in, or supported by, a parish (a type of ecclesiastical district).

      The Roman Catholic Church maintains a system of **parochial** schools that provide students with religious instruction in addition to their regular academic education.

   b. Restricted in scope or range; narrow or limited.

      I found it hard to believe that a person who had read and traveled so extensively should have such a **parochial** outlook on life.

Related Form: (*noun*) parochialism

Usage Note:
When used of a school or school system, *parochial* is confined to establishments maintained by the Roman Catholic Church. Though other religious organizations certainly maintain schools of their own, these institutions are not normally referred to as parochial schools.

Synonyms: (*adjectives*) local, regional, district; narrow-minded, insular, provincial, hidebound, myopic

Antonyms: (*adjectives*) broad-minded, cosmopolitan, liberal

Related Phrase: wear blinders (or blinkers)

294. par-o-dy   *noun and verb*   păr'-ə-dē

[*paroidia* (Greek), "burlesque poem"; from *para* (Greek), "alongside; subsidiary to" + *oide* (Greek), "song, poem"]

Definition:

   a. (*noun*) A comic imitation of the style, form, or content of a serious piece of work.

      Satirical magazines often contain amusing **parodies** of popular movies and TV shows.

      MacBird is an amusing **parody** of Shakespeare's *Macbeth* set during the Johnson administration.

   b. (*noun*) A performance that is so bad as to constitute a mockery of the thing it is intended to represent.

      The famous show trials that Joseph Stalin mounted in the 1930s were little more than a **parody** of justice.

   c. (*verb*) To imitate in a mocking or unworthy way.

      Several popular entertainers are noted for their ability to **parody** the words and gestures of prominent Americans.

      The constitutions of some third world countries do little more than **parody** the principles of Western democracy.

Related Form: (*noun*) parodist

Synonyms: (*nouns*) spoof, takeoff, lampoon, caricature, burlesque, travesty, satire; (*verbs*) spoof, lampoon, satirize, mock, ridicule

Caricature

A *caricature* is a distorted representation of a person in which a characteristic physical feature, mannerism, or other peculiarity is exaggerated in order to produce a comic effect. Often certain physical features provide the focus of the caricature. Other times, the subject's style, attitudes, or ideas are the central feature, as the accompanying cartoon of Theodore Roosevelt reveals. By the way, a caricature need not be a drawing; it may also take the form of a written composition.

295. pen-sive   *adjective*   pĕn'-sĭv

[*pensif, pensive* (French), "thoughtful"; from *penser* (French), "think"; from *pensare* (Latin), "to weigh; ponder, consider"]

Definition: Immersed in deep, often melancholy, thought.

Usually Mary is overflowing with good cheer, but today she is rather **pensive** and withdrawn.

Related Forms: *(noun)* pensiveness; *(adverb)* pensively

Synonyms: *(adjectives)* meditative, reflective, contemplative, introspective; sad, melancholy, wistful, heavyhearted, mournful, doleful

Antonyms: *(adjectives)* lighthearted, blithe, cheerful, gay, mirthful, merry, jocund

Related Phrases: mull over, ruminate on, be lost in thought

Using the Words

Exercise I. Syllabication and Pronunciation

Syllabicate the following words correctly, and place the major stress mark (') after the syllable that is accented when the word is pronounced. Two answers are correct in one instance.

1. obsequious
2. obsolete
3. officious
4. ostensible
5. pandemonium
6. paradox
7. paraphrase
8. parochial
9. pensive

Exercise II. Words Out of Context

In each of the following groups, select the item that best expresses the meaning of the numbered word at the left.

1. obsequious   a. lively b. courteous c. deferential
d. vague e. profitable

2. obsolete   a. required b. insignificant c. daring
d. costly e. outmoded

3. officious   a. meddlesome b. changeable c. gigantic
d. exciting e. clever

4. ostensible   a. outrageous b. economical c. graphic
d. apparent e. luxurious

5. ostracize   a. steal b. shun c. seal d. sham
e. stun

6. paradox   a. enigma b. consensus c. anathema
d. kudos e. facsimile

7. paraphrase   a. recall   b. return   c. repulse   d. renew
                     e. restate

8. pensive   a. theoretical   b. crucial   c. disorderly
                     d. contemplative   e. foolhardy

Exercise III.   Completing Sentences

Complete each of the following sentences by selecting the most appropriate word from the group of words given below. Use each word only once. Make any adjustments that are necessary to fit the words into the sentences properly.

parody	pensive	ostracize
obsession	opportune	parochial
ominous	pandemonium	obscene

1. Today, films containing _____ language or nudity are usually given an "R" rating in order to alert potential viewers to the sensitive nature of the material presented.

2. Since I was desperately in need of funds, Mom's check arrived at a most _____ moment.

3. *Omlet, the Great Dane* is both an amusing _____ of Shakespeare's *Hamlet* and an irreverent commentary on American politics.

4. Some of my friends went to public school; others attended private or _____ schools.

5. Somehow or other, the speaker managed to make herself heard above the _____ that reigned in the convention hall.

6. It is one thing to be concerned about punctuality; it is quite another to allow it to become a(n) _____.

7. One look at the _____ black clouds rolling in from the west, and I knew we were in for a storm.

Exercise IV.   Synonyms and Antonyms

Classify each of the following pairs of words as **S** for **synonyms** or **A** for **antonyms**.

1. bedlam—pandemonium
2. fixation—obsession
3. ominous—auspicious
4. ostensible—alleged
5. newfangled—obsolete
6. parody—lampoon
7. paraphrase—quote
8. cosmopolitan—parochial
9. obscene—smutty
10. blithe—pensive
11. ostracize—blackball
12. opportune—timely

Exercise V.   Word Roundup

1. With or without the aid of a dictionary, explain what each of the following means.

   a. a yes-man
   b. a megalomaniac
   c. a monomaniac
   d. a has-been

   e. an opportunist
   f. a paranoiac
   g. a timeserver
   h. a perfectionist

2. With or without the aid of a dictionary, define each of the following colorful idiomatic expressions.

   a. raise a hue and cry
   b. knuckle under to
   c. wear blinders
   (or blinkers)

   d. give someone the
   cold shoulder
   e. take time by the forelock
   f. have a one-track mind

3. Explain what each of the following means. Consult a dictionary if necessary.

   a. a Gordian knot
   b. an off-color joke

   c. a rubber stamp
   d. an R-rated film

4. The following expressions have been borrowed from French. What does each mean?

   a. avant-garde   b. idée fixe   c. au courant

5. Explain the difference between the items in each of the following pairs of words.

   a. obsolete—obsolescent   b. officious—official

6. Explain the story behind the word *ostracize*. From what foreign language does it come? Name two famous statesmen who were subjected to ostracism.

Exercise VI.   Framing Sentences

A. Use each of the following words in an original illustrative sentence.

1. obsequious
2. obsolete
3. obsession

4. opportune
5. pandemonium
6. paraphrase

7. parochial
8. parody
9. pensive

B. Give a **noun** form of each of the following words, and use it in an original illustrative sentence.

1. obscene   2. ostracize   3. officious

C. Give an **adverb** form of each of the following words, and use it in an original illustrative sentence.

1. ostensible   2. paradox   3. ominous

Dissecting the Words

1. The Latin prefix **ob** occurs, in one form or another, in a great many common English words, including *obsequious, obsession,* and *obscene,* all of which were studied in this lesson. This prefix has a variety of meanings, depending upon how it is used in the word in which it appears. These meanings include:

a. "To, toward," as in these words:

objective (*ob*, "to, toward" + *jacere, jactus* [Latin], "throw")—(*noun*) an aim or goal; (*adjective*) real or actual; uninfluenced by personal feeling or prejudice

obverse (*ob*, "to, toward" + *vertere, versus* [Latin], "turn")—the part of something that is turned toward the viewer; the front

b. "Against, in opposition to," as in these words:

obstacle (*ob*, "against" + *stare, status* [Latin], "stand")—someone or something that is in a person's way

obloquy (*ob*, "against" + *loqui* [Latin], "speak")—abuse; the discredit resulting from such abuse

obstruct (*ob*, "against" + *struere, structus* [Latin], "pile up")—to block, hinder, or impede. Noun: *obstruction*

obtuse (*ob*, "against" + *tundere, tu(n)sus* [Latin], "beat")—dull or blunt

c. "In front of, before," as in these words:

obsess (*ob*, "in front of, before" + *sedere, sessus* [Latin], "sit")—to haunt, harass, or bedevil. Noun: *obsession* (Word 283)

obstetrics (*ob*, "in front of" + *stare, status* [Latin], "stand"; in Latin a midwife was called an *obstetrix,* literally, "a woman who stands before [the bed]")—the branch of medicine dealing with care of women before, during, and just after childbirth. Adjective: *obstetric.* Noun: *obstetrician*

d. "Down, over," as in this word:

obituary (*ob*, "down, over" + *ire, itus* [Latin], "go")—a death notice

e. "Out of, away from," as in this word:

obliterate (*ob*, "out of, away from" + *littera* [Latin], "letter" + *atus* [Latin], "make, do"; in Latin the verb for "delete" was *oblitterare*)—to do away with completely. Noun: *obliteration*

f. "Completely," as in these words:

obdurate (*ob*, "completely" + *durare, duratus* [Latin], "harden")—unyielding, inflexible, or intractable

obfuscate (*ob*, "completely" + *fuscare, fuscatus* [Latin], "darken")—to darken, muddy, or confuse. Noun: *obfuscation*

oblong (*ob*, "completely" + *longus* [Latin], "long")—having one dimension (length or width) much longer than the other

2. The prefix **ob** changes form, depending upon the first letter of the root to which it is attached. These changes include the following:

a. *Ob* becomes **o** before *m*, as in this word:

omit (*ob*, "away from" + *mittere, missus* [Latin], "send")—to leave out. Noun: *omission*

b. *Ob* becomes **oc** before *c*, as in these words:

occident (*ob*, "down" + *cadere, casus* [Latin], "fall, go")—the west (because that is where the sun sets). Adjective: *occidental*

occlude (*ob*, "completely" + *claudere, clausus* [Latin], "close")—to cause to close; to shut in, out, or off. Noun: *occlusion*

occult (*ob*, "completely" + *cul(t)*, a Latin root meaning "conceal")— secret, beyond the understanding of most people

c. *Ob* becomes **of** before an *f*, as in these words:

offend (*ob*, "against" + *-fendere, -fensus* [Latin], "strike")—to insult or outrage. Noun: *offense*. Adjective: *offensive*

offer (*ob*, "to, toward" + *ferre* [Latin], "bring")—to put forward or present. Noun: *offering*

Note, however, that *ob* remains unchanged in the word *obfuscate*, studied above.

d. *Ob* becomes **op** before *p*, as in these words:

oppose (*ob*, "against" + *ponere, positus* [Latin], "put")—to combat or resist. Nouns: *opposition, opponent*. Adjective: *opposite*

oppress (*ob*, "against" + *premere, pressus* [Latin], "press")—to weigh heavily on; to persecute. Adjective: *oppressive*

opprobrium (*ob*, "against" + *probum* [Latin], "reproach")—the disgrace that arises from shameful behavior. Adjective: *opprobrious*

3. The Greek prefix **par(a)** appears in a number of useful English words, including *paradox, paraphrase, parochial,* and *parody,* all of which were studied in this lesson. This prefix has a number of meanings, including:

a. "Alongside, by the side of, beside," as in these words:

parable (*parabola* [Greek], "comparison"; from *para*, "beside" + *ballein*, "throw")—a simple story of everyday life illustrating a moral or religious principle. Related noun: *parabola*

paradigm (*paradeigma* [Greek], "model; from *para*, "alongside" + *deiknynai*, "*show*, exhibit")—an example or model

paragon (*parakone* [Medieval Greek], "whetstone"; from *para*, "alongside" + *akonan*, "sharpen")—a model or pattern of excellence

paraprofessional (*para*, "alongside"+ *professional*)—a person who is not a member of a given profession but who helps those who are

parapsychology (*para*, "alongside" + *psychology*)—the study of phenomena that cannot be explained by known natural laws—for example, mental telepathy

Other words in which this meaning of *para* is used include *paraplegia, paragraph, parameter, parasite,* and *parenthesis.*

b. "Beyond," as in these words:

paralogism (*para*, "beyond" + *logos* [Greek], "logic")—faulty or illogical reasoning

paranoia (*paranoos* [Greek], "demented"; from *para*, "beyond" + *nous*, "mind")—a mental illness characterized by delusions of being persecuted or being greater than one is. Adjective: *paranoid*. Noun: *paranoiac*

paraphernalia (*para*, "beyond" + *pherne* [Greek], "dowry")—the gear or equipment used in some activity; one's personal belongings

c. "Wrongly, harmfully," as in this word:

paralysis (*paralyein* [Greek], "disable"; from *para*, "wrongfully" + *lyein*, "loosen, release")—loss or impairment of the ability to move or feel; a general stoppage of activity. Verb: *paralyze*

d. "Completely," as in this word:

paroxysm (*paroxysmos* [Greek], "irritation, stimulation"; from *para*, "completely, very" + *oxynein*, "whet, sharpen")—a sudden outburst of feeling or emotion (*e.g.*, laughter)

Note that in a few military words, such as *paratrooper*, the element *para* is not the Greek prefix but a shortened form of the word *parachute*.

Exercise

1. With or without the aid of a dictionary, define each of the following words containing the Latin prefix *ob*, and explain what the prefix means in that particular word. Then choose any **five** of the words, and for each compose an original illustrative sentence.

   a. obliterate
   b. oblong
   c. obloquy
   d. obviate
   e. obstruct
   f. obverse
   g. obituary
   h. obnoxious
   i. obsess
   j. obdurate
   k. obtuse
   l. obtrude

2. With or without the aid of a dictionary, define each of the following words containing the Greek prefix *para*, and explain what the prefix means in that particular word. Then choose any **five** of the words, and for each compose an original illustrative sentence.

   a. paranoid
   b. parabola
   c. paralyze
   d. parasite
   e. paraphernalia
   f. paroxysm
   g. parameter
   h. paraplegic
   i. paragon

3. Add the prefix *para* to each of the following English words, define the resulting combination, and explain how *para* has altered the meaning of the original word.

   a. military
   b. psychology
   c. medical
   d. professional

Working with Context Clues

Complete each of the following two-word omissions by selecting the pair of words that make the best sense in the passage as a whole. If necessary, consult a dictionary for the meaning of any word with which you are not familiar.

1. Rather than promptly paying his taxes, Greg is always _____. Every year he tries to put off the inevitable by asking the government to _____ the date on which he must submit his completed tax forms.

   a. demure . . . postpone
   b. frugal . . . confirm
   c. dilatory . . . defer
   d. diligent . . . arbitrate

2. It is irresponsible for a community leader to _____ a crowd that is already angry at a verdict it considers unjust. If a riot breaks out, the leader will bear some of the responsibility for the _____.

   a. ostracize . . . atrocity
   b. exploit . . . morass
   c. goad . . . duplicity
   d. incense . . . pandemonium

3. Few audiences today will welcome "Polish jokes" or any other type of humor that insults particular _____ groups. Such _____ remarks merely reveal the comic's prejudice and lack of imagination.

   a. ethnic . . . gratuitous
   b. elite . . . brash
   c. coherent . . . austere
   d. motley . . . opportune

4. When local politicians are elected to Congress, they are expected to balance the _____ concerns of their home district with a more _____ outlook that takes the good of the whole nation into account.

   a. dire . . . felicitous
   b. parochial . . . catholic
   c. pressing . . . narcissistic
   d. nominal . . . mercenary

5. After I glued the two halves of the antique vase back together, the _____ was no longer visible. In fact, to the naked eye, there was no _____ flaw to lower its resale value.

   a. impediment . . . fickle
   b. foible . . . gaping
   c. grimace . . . implicit
   d. defect . . . ostensible

6. All attempts to reword Shakespeare are _____ since any _____ of his poetry, no matter how polished, is arguably inferior to the original.

   a. futile . . . parody
   b. moot . . . paraphrase
   c. obsolete . . . translation
   d. nominal . . . attrition

7. It is hard to know who is more undesirable: a(n) _____ assistant who does far more than you ask or a(n) _____ one who does almost nothing at all.

   a. lucid . . . ominous
   b. haggard . . . fatuous
   c. officious . . . lackadaisical
   d. diligent . . . cynical

8. The conceited anchorman featured on several television comedies is a takeoff on one or more actual network anchors whose _____ personalities lend themselves to _____.

a. intrepid . . . irony
b. flagrant . . . cynicism
c. ominous . . . humor
d. narcissistic . . . parody

9. Alexander the Great was a(n) _____ foe of the Persians as long as they posed a threat to Greek security. Once he had _____ the danger by conquering them, however, he proved to be their most steadfast champion.

a. effete . . . exploited
b. implacable . . . forestalled
c. fulsome . . . exacerbated
d. boorish . . . curtailed

10. It is characteristic of narrow-minded groups to shun everyone who is unconventional. Such insecure people prefer to _____ those they consider _____ rather than try to understand anyone who is different from themselves.

a. ostracize . . . outlandish
b. exalt . . . banal
c. goad . . . implacable
d. forestall . . . motley

11. "I haven't had time to give your report more than a _____ glance," my boss told me. "However, I plan to _____ it carefully before we actually sit down to discuss it.

a. cursory . . . scrutinize
b. gratuitous . . . parody
c. nominal . . . libel
d. quick . . . disregard

Enriching the Lesson

Exercise I.   More of Our Greek Heritage

A number of the words studied in this lesson, including *ostracize* and *paradox*, are derived with very little change from Greek. Some other useful English words derived from Greek prototypes are listed below. With or without the aid of a dictionary, define each, and give its etymology. Then choose any **five** of the words, and for each compose an original illustrative sentence.

1. protagonist	11. polyglot	21. myth
2. spasmodic	12. toxic	22. heterogeneous
3. psychotic	13. xenophobic	23. lyric
4. tyrannical	14. phantasm	24. schism
5. polemic	15. litany	25. tragedy
6. lethargy	16. autochthonous	26. tautology
7. therapeutic	17. panoply	27. phlegmatic
8. mimic	18. metaphoric	28. kaleidoscope
9. rhetoric	19. mosaic	29. category
10. calisthenics	20. kinetic	30. periphery

Exercise II. Ecclesiastically Speaking

English is rich in words and phrases relating to the church or the clergy. One such expression, *parochial*, was studied in this lesson. A few others are listed below. With or without the aid of a dictionary or other reference book, define each, and give its etymology. Then choose any **five** of the items, and for each compose an original illustrative sentence.

1. sacrilege	6. pastoral	11. canonical
2. sacrament	7. liturgy	12. Pentecostal
3. prelate	8. ecumenical	13. theology
4. laity	9. diocese	14. rite
5. ecclesiastical	10. monastic	15. episcopal

Exercise III. Manias

A *mania* is an exaggerated or hampering obsession, a dominating preoccupation or craving that often leads to unbalanced or irrational behavior. The word *mania* forms part of many compound words that indicate particular kinds of behavior patterns. A few of these words are listed below. With or without the aid of a dictionary or other reference book, define each, and give its etymology.

1. pyromania	3. kleptomania	5. egomania
2. bibliomania	4. dipsomania	6. megalomania

Exercise IV. Expanding Your Word Power

The words listed below are not on the Basic Word List, but they were mentioned in passing, in one form or another, in Lesson 23. All of them would make useful additions to your working vocabulary. Define each, give its etymology, list **two** synonyms and **two** antonyms (where possible), and use in a short illustrative sentence.

1. salacious	6. omen	11. insular
2. unctuous	7. untimely	12. satire
3. compulsive	8. purport	13. duplicate
4. defunct	9. exile	14. portentous
5. intrusive	10. tumult	15. introspective

Lesson 24

296. **pe·remp·to·ry**   *adjective*   pə-rĕmp'-tə-rē
[*peremptorius* (Latin), "final"; from *per* (Latin), "completely" + *emere, emptus* (Latin), "buy, obtain" + *orius* (Latin), "characterized by"]

Definition:
  a. Having the nature of a command in that it does not allow discussion, contradiction, or refusal.

  Good supervisors soon learn that they can get more cooperation from those under them by making polite requests than by issuing **peremptory** orders.

  b. Determined, resolute.

  "Though we are always ready to settle our differences with other countries peacefully," the official said, "we are not afraid to make **peremptory** use of force when necessary."

  c. Offensively dictatorial.

  Though his manner is **peremptory** with those below him in the office hierarchy, it is obsequious with those higher up.

Related Forms: (*noun*) peremptoriness; (*adverb*) peremptorily

Synonyms: (*adjectives*) binding, obligatory, mandatory, prescriptive; categorical, unconditional, positive, emphatic, concerted; despotic, tyrannical, high-handed

Antonyms: (*adjectives*) tentative, contingent, provisional; irresolute, indecisive, hesitant; mild, unassuming, diffident

297. **per·jure**   *verb*   pēr'-jûr
[*per* (Latin), "harmfully, falsely" + *jurare* (Latin), "swear"]

Definition: To lie deliberately while under oath to tell the truth.

  Though there are minor inconsistencies in his testimony, there is no evidence that the witness actually **perjured** himself.

  I described my reaction to his performance at the recital as favorably as I could without actually **perjuring** myself.

Related Forms: (*nouns*) perjury, perjurer; (*adjective*) perjurious

Phrases: commit perjury, perjured testimony

Synonyms: (*verbs*) forswear, prevaricate

Related Phrases: bear false witness, give false testimony

298. per-me-ate   *verb*   pĕr'-mē-āt

[*permeare, permeatus* (Latin), "pass through"; from *per* (Latin), "through" + *meare, meatus* (Latin), "go, pass"]

Definition: To spread through; to penetrate.

Noxious fumes from the industrial accident so **permeated** the atmosphere that scores of people living nearby had to be evacuated from their homes.

During the days before Constantinople fell to the Turks in 1453, the mood of the besieged city was **permeated** by a sense of doom.

Related Forms: (*nouns*) permeation, permeability; (*adjectives*) permeable, impermeable

Synonyms: (*verbs*) pervade, infiltrate, diffuse, saturate, impregnate, imbue, filter into, seep through, soak through

Related Phrase: infiltrate enemy lines

299. per-ni-cious   *adjective*   pĕr-nish'-əs

[*perniciosus* (Latin), "destructive"; from *per* (Latin), "completely" + *nex, necis* (Latin), "violent death" + *osus* (Latin), "full of"]

Definition: Highly injurious or harmful.

Despite mounting medical evidence concerning the **pernicious** effects of fatty foods, many people categorically refuse to give up eating them on a daily basis.

Phrases: a pernicious influence, a pernicious practice

Related Forms: (*noun*) perniciousness; (*adverb*) perniciously

Synonyms: (*adjectives*) deleterious, detrimental, malignant, baneful, ruinous, destructive

Antonyms: (*adjectives*) wholesome, beneficial, salutary, salubrious

300. per-se-vere   *verb*   pĕr-sə-vîr'

[*perseverare* (Latin), "persist"; from *per* (Latin), "thoroughly" + *severus* (Latin), "serious, in earnest"]

Definition: To continue steadfastly despite obstacles or discouragment.

The old saying "If at first you don't succeed, try, try again" encourages us all to **persevere** in whatever we undertake.

Related Forms: (*noun*) perseverance; (*adjective*) persevering

Synonyms: (*verbs*) persist, endure

Antonyms: (*verbs*) quit, desist, give up on, abandon

Related Phrases: plug away at, stick something out, stop at nothing to achieve a goal, stick to one's guns; throw in the towel

301. pho·bi·a   *noun*   fō'-bē-ə

[*phobos* (Greek), "fear, flight" + *-ia* (Greek), "state of"]

Definition: An intense irrational fear of something; any strong aversion.

She attributed her pronounced **phobia** about dogs to the fact that she was nipped on the finger by an overly defensive collie when she was a child.

The legislator warned that we must not allow our natural concern for security to develop into an obsessive **phobia** about foreigners.

Related Form: (*adjective*) phobic

Usage Note:
Phobia often appears in compound words indicating particular kinds of fears or aversions. For example, *claustrophobia* (*claustrum* [Latin], "enclosed place" + *phobia*) is the proper term for an irrational fear of small, tightly enclosed places. The related word element *-phobe*, meaning "one who fears or dislikes," also appears in such words. For example, a *xenophobe* is a person who dislikes foreigners and all things relating to them. Note that *-phobe* is only used as a combining form, not as an independent word.

The Greek suffixes *-philia*, meaning "a liking or attraction for," and *-phil(e)* or *-philiac*, meaning "one who has a liking for or is attracted to," are the "antonyms" of *phobia* and *-phobe*. For example, a philosopher is someone who loves (*philos* [Greek], "loving, liking") wisdom (*sophia* [Greek], "wisdom"). Similarly, *necrophilia* is the technical name for a morbid attraction to dead bodies (*necros* [Greek], "corpse"). Note that *-philia*, *-phil(e)*, and *-philiac* are only used as combining forms, not independent words.

Synonyms: (*nouns*) dread (of), horror (of), aversion (to), distaste (for), abhorrence (of), antipathy (for), loathing (for)

Antonyms: (*nouns*) liking (for), taste (for), partiality (for), fondness (for), affinity (for), predilection (for)

Related Phrases: have a soft spot in one's heart for; have no stomach for

302. pla·gia·rism   *noun*   plā'-jə-rĭz-əm

[*plagiarius* (Latin), "kidnapper"; from *plaga* (Latin), "net"]

Definition: The use of another person's writings or ideas as one's own without acknowledging their source.

"No one is going to accuse you of **plagiarism**," the editor told the fledgling author, "just because a couple of paragraphs in a very long novel are vaguely reminiscent of Hemingway."

Far from being a retelling of one of O. Henry's best-loved short stories, as the author claims, the work is an outright **plagiarism**.

Related Forms: (*verb*) plagiarize; (*nouns*) plagiary, plagiarist, plagiarizer

Synonyms: (*nouns*) theft, piracy

Related Phrases: literary piracy, an infringement of copyright, a crib

303. **plain·tive**   *adjective*   plān'-tĭv

[*plaintif, plaintive* (Old French), "sorrowful"; from *plangere, planctus* (Latin), "lament"]

Definition: Sorrowful or melancholy; mournful.

She closed her recital with a **plaintive** little Scottish ditty entitled "The Exile's Lament."

The **plaintive** moaning of a distant foghorn accorded well with the regret I felt in my heart at leaving that fair city forever.

Related Forms: (*nouns*) plaint, plaintiveness; (*adverb*) plaintively

Phrases: the plaintive tones of an oboe, the plaintive cry of an orphan

Synonyms: (*adjectives*) doleful, dolorous, disconsolate, lachrymose, wistful, heartbroken, tearful, lugubrious

Antonyms: (*adjectives*) merry, jocund, cheerful, lighthearted

Related Phrase: shed crocodile tears

Jeremiad

In modern English, a long, involved lament is sometimes called a *jeremiad*. This word has an interesting origin. It is based on the name Jeremiah. Jeremiah (*c.* 628–586 B.C.), as you may recall, was one of the major prophets of the Old Testament and the author, among other things, of a book of moving poems mourning the destruction of Jerusalem by the Babylonians. As a result, Jeremiah became associated with the elegiac mood, and this in turn gave rise to the use of a word based on his name for any kind of lengthy lament or tale of woe.

Jeremiah

304. pleth-o-ra   *noun*   plĕth'-ə-rə

[*plethora* (Greek), "fullness"; from *plethein* (Greek), "be full"]

Definition: Superabundance or excess.

As usual, we got a **plethora** of advice about what to do but precious little help doing it.

Many Hollywood stars receive a **plethora** of fan mail every day.

Phrases: a plethora of ideas, a plethora of complaints, a plethora of food and drink

Synonyms: (*nouns*) profusion, welter, superfluity, glut, surplus, surfeit, deluge, avalanche

Antonyms: (*nouns*) scarcity, paucity, dearth, shortage, lack, want

Related Phrases: give something short shrift, a shortfall

In 1750, the poet Thomas Gray (1716–1771) published one of the most poignant poems in the English language, "Elegy Written in a Country Churchyard."

305. poign-ant   *adjective*   poin'-yənt

[*poignant,* present participle of *poindre* (Old French), "sting"; from *pungere* (Latin), "puncture, sting"]

Definition: Keenly touching or moving.

Though the play was essentially a comedy, it nevertheless contained a **poignant** moment or two.

Related Forms: (*nouns*) poignancy, poignance; (*adverb*) poignantly

Synonyms: (*adjectives*) heartbreaking, tender, heartrending, wistful, affecting, melancholy, elegiac, bittersweet

Antonyms: (*adjectives*) unaffecting; bland, vapid, insipid

306. pre·car·i·ous   *adjective*   prĭ-kâr′-ē-əs

[*precarius* (Latin), "dependent upon prayer or entreaty"; from *prex, precis* (Latin), "prayer, entreaty" + *arius* (Latin), "relating to"]

Definition: Dangerously insecure, unstable, or uncertain.

Some of the firefighters battled the blaze from a **precarious** perch atop a mobile crane called a *cherry picker.*

Even with the help of modern life-support systems, a premature baby's hold on life is often **precarious.**

Related Forms: (*noun*) precariousness; (*adverb*) precariously

Synonyms: (*adjectives*) perilous, hazardous, risky, treacherous; dubious, touch-and-go, ticklish, touchy, delicate

Antonyms: (*adjectives*) safe, secure, stable, firm, certain, impregnable

Related Phrases: skate on thin ice, walk a tightrope, hang by a thread, out on a limb, a sword of Damocles

307. pre·co·cious   *adjective*   prĭ-kō′-shəs

[*praecox, praecocis* (Latin), "ripening before its time"; from *prae* (Latin), "before" + *coquere, coctus* (Latin), "cook, boil"]

Definition: Developing unusually early.

Wolfgang Amadeus Mozart was a **precocious** youngster who wrote his first opera at the age of eleven.

Given the kinds of tools the Egyptians had to work with, raising the pyramids constituted an extraordinarily **precocious** feat of engineering.

Related Forms: (*nouns*) precociousness, precocity; (*adverb*) precociously

Phrases: at a precocious age, a precocious achievement

Synonyms: (*adjectives*) forward, gifted; advanced; premature

Antonyms: (*adjectives*) backward, retarded; underdeveloped; laggard

Related Phrases: a child prodigy; a late bloomer

308. pred·a·to·ry   *adjective*   prĕd′-ə-tô-rē

[*praedari, praedatus* (Latin), "plunder, pillage" + *orius* (Latin), "characterized by"; from *praeda* (Latin), "booty"]

Definition: Preying on, plundering, or piratical.

Though many other **predatory** creatures prefer to hunt at night, lions and leopards are active during the daytime.

Karl Marx viewed capitalists as an essentially **predatory** class of people because he felt that they lived off the labor of others.

Related Forms: (*nouns*) predator, predatoriness

Predators such as this mountain lion still inhabit the less settled areas of the western United States, where they prey on deer, horses, cattle, and other animals.

Synonyms: (*adjectives*) marauding, pillaging, looting; rapacious, voracious, avaricious, extortionate

Related Phrases: prey on, despoil the land of its resources, pirate a novel, cannibalize a manuscript; a harpy

309. **pre·lude** *noun* prā′-lo͞od *or* prĕl′-yo͞od
[*prae* (Latin), "before" + *ludere, lusus* (Latin), "play"]

Definition: An introductory piece of music; anything that precedes or introduces something else.

The **prelude** to the third act of Verdi's *La Traviata* is one of the most poignant pieces of music I have ever heard.

In the State Department's view, the unexpected concentration of troops along the border could be construed only as a **prelude** to invasion.

Synonyms: (*nouns*) overture, prologue, preface, curtain-raiser

Antonyms: (*nouns*) postlude, epilogue, aftermath, sequel

Related Phrases: lay the groundwork for, a dress rehearsal

310. pre·mise   *noun and verb*   prĕm'-ĭs
[*prae* (Latin), "before, ahead" + *mittere, missus* (Latin), "send"]

Definition:
  a. (*noun*) A statement upon which an argument is based or from which a conclusion is drawn.

  Your suggestion that you be given the lead in the school play is based on the totally unrealistic **premise** that you are the most talented actor available.

  b. (*verb*) To state or assume as the basis for something else; to offer in advance as an explanation of, or introduction to, something else.

  Much of the judge's thinking is **premised** on the proposition that, in the eyes of the law, all people are equal.

  "Let me **premise** my remarks tonight," the speaker said, "with a bit of personal history that will explain why I feel so strongly about certain subjects."

Usage Note:
  When used in the plural, *premise* also indicates a building or residence, including the land upon which it stands or that is immediately adjacent to it. This use of the word occurs in such phrases as "vacate the *premises*" and "on the *premises*."

Synonyms: (*nouns*) proposition, axiom, thesis, hypothesis, assumption; (*verbs*) preface, introduce; posit, predicate; presuppose

Using the Words

Exercise I.   Parts of Speech

Indicate the part of speech of each of the following words. In one case, two answers are correct.

1. peremptory
2. pernicious
3. plagiarism
4. plethora
5. poignant
6. precocious
7. predatory
8. prelude
9. premise

Exercise II.   Words in Phrases

In each of the following groups, select the item that best expresses the meaning of the *italicized* word in the introductory phrase.

1. a *peremptory* tone of voice
   a. hopeful   b. dictatorial   c. jubilant   d. discouraged

2. now *permeates* our system of justice
   a. makes better   b. investigates   c. spreads through
   d. ignores

3. a *pernicious* influence on society
   a. harmful   b. lasting   c. superficial   d. wholesome

4. *persevere* despite all obstacles
   a. die out   b. carry on   c. pull down   d. give up

5. the *plaintive* notes of an oboe
   a. merry   b. melodious   c. majestic   d. mournful

6. a *plethora* of problems
   a. shortage   b. creator   c. deluge   d. solver

7. *poignant* memories
   a. bittersweet   b. remarkable   c. vague   d. amusing

8. *predatory* bands of Vikings
   a. enormous   b. unexpected   c. friendly   d. piratical

Exercise III.   Completing Sentences

Complete each of the following sentences by selecting the most appropriate word from the group of words given below. Use each word only once. Make any adjustments that are necessary to fit the words into the sentences properly.

perjure	precarious	persevere
pernicious	precocious	prelude
premise	phobia	plagiarism

1. My most recent acquisition is a two-disc set of overtures and _____ to famous Italian operas.

2. "With a great team like the Islanders breathing down our necks," the Rangers' star goalie observed, "our hold on first place in the Eastern Conference can only be described as _____."

3. Over the years, her childhood fear of the dark developed into a serious and debilitating _____.

4. The judge instructed the jury to disregard the witness's testimony after the D.A. proved that the man had _____ himself while on the stand.

5. "Your conclusion is clearly invalid," I replied, "simply because it is based on a false _____."

6. She was a gifted youngster who started college at the _____ age of 15.

7. Though the United States subscribes to an international system of copyright laws designed to protect writers from _____ and other forms of literary piracy, China does not.

Exercise IV.   Synonyms and Antonyms

A. In each of the following groups, select the **two** words that are most nearly **synonyms**.

1. **a.** pervade   **b.** esteem   **c.** saturate   **d.** blemish   **e.** resolve
2. **a.** intelligence   **b.** reward   **c.** aversion   **d.** antipathy
   e. fondness
3. **a.** unassuming   **b.** piratical   **c.** sensible   **d.** tarnished
   e. plundering
4. **a.** treacherous   **b.** wistful   **c.** melancholy   **d.** feminine
   e. obvious
5. **a.** glut   **b.** request   **c.** scarcity   **d.** honor   **e.** profusion

Now, for each pair of synonyms you have selected, supply a word from the Basic Word List for this lesson (Words 296–310) that means **the same** or **almost the same** thing.

B. In each of the following, select the item that is most nearly **opposite** in meaning to the numbered word at the left.

1. persevere   **a.** cling   **b.** repair   **c.** quit   **d.** increase
   e. steal
2. plaintive   **a.** wooden   **b.** merry   **c.** puzzling   **d.** silent
   e. thoughtful
3. prelude   **a.** anathema   **b.** epilogue   **c.** facsimile
   d. euphemism   **e.** impasse
4. pernicious   **a.** wholesome   **b.** partial   **c.** ruinous
   d. shabby   **e.** tentative
5. precarious   **a.** delicate   **b.** envious   **c.** pompous
   d. illegal   **e.** secure

Exercise V.   Word Roundup

1. The expression *a peremptory challenge* is frequently used in the courtroom. What does it mean?
2. What is *claustrophobia*? a *xenophobe*?
3. Define a *jeremiad*. What is the origin of this word?
4. With or without the aid of a dictionary, define each of the following colorful idiomatic expressions.

   a. throw in the towel   **c.** skate on thin ice
   b. stick to one's guns   **d.** shed crocodile tears
5. With or without the aid of a dictionary, define each of the following useful terms.

   a. a child prodigy   **c.** a late bloomer
   b. a shortfall   **d.** a curtain-raiser

Exercise VI.   Framing Sentences

A. Use each of the following words in an original sentence.

1. peremptory	5. phobia	9. poignant
2. permeate	6. plagiarize	10. precocious
3. pernicious	7. plaintive	11. prelude
4. precarious	8. plethora	12. premise

B. Give a **noun** form of each of the following words, and use it in an original illustrative sentence.

1. persevere   2. predatory   3. perjure

Completing Verbal Analogies

Complete each of the following analogies.

Group A

1. **durable : long life ::**
    a. unison : great variety
    b. elite : great wisdom
    c. impecunious : great wealth
    d. prodigious : great size
    e. capricious : great reliability

2. **veer : away ::**
    a. inflate : down
    b. revert : back
    c. compress : apart
    d. proceed : sideways
    e. decline : forward

3. **rabbit : burrow ::**
    a. lion : den
    b. horse : lair
    c. nest : bird
    d. cow : bovine
    e. dog : manger

4. **kindle : extinguish ::**
    a. jeopardize : hazard
    b. instigate : repress
    c. parody : ostracize
    d. perjure : prevaricate
    e. allot : spare

5. **plod : slow ::**
    a. browse : fast
    b. dash : slow
    c. scurry : fast
    d. dawdle : fast
    e. sprint : slow

Group B

6. **fruitless : result =**
    a. heartless : skill
    b. tactless : merit
    c. value : priceless
    d. tireless : energy
    e. aimless : purpose

7. **sweater : attire =**
   a. sword : weapon
   b. horse : tether
   c. scavenger : jackal
   d. will : legacy
   e. mammoth : fetish

8. **thin : gaunt =**
   a. clear : cryptic
   b. lush : nebulous
   c. haughty : meek
   d. big : mammoth
   e. ominous : pensive

9. **officious : unfavorable =**
   a. obsequious : favorable
   b. astute : unfavorable
   c. precocious : favorable
   d. lucrative : unfavorable
   e. narcissistic : favorable

10. **scoff : contempt =**
    a. vex : enjoyment
    b. rue : sorrow
    c. happiness : elate
    d. lament : levity
    e. meditate : anger

Working with Context Clues

Complete each of the following two-word omissions by selecting the pair of words that make the best sense in the passage as a whole. If necessary, consult a dictionary for the meaning of any word with which you are not familiar. Underline the clue or clues that led you to choose your answer.

1. The prosecuting attorney did not provide many arguments to back up her plea for a guilty verdict, but those she did present were extremely well chosen. A larger but less _____ selection of arguments would probably have failed to _____ the verdict she was looking for.

   a. cogent . . . defer
   b. judicious . . . justify
   c. esoteric . . . elicit
   d. gratuitous . . . augur

2. An irrational fear can spread through an entire town as it did in Salem, Massachusetts. A similar _____ was able to _____ the whole nation in the 1950s, with Communists, not witches, as the source of the terror.

   a. phobia . . . permeate
   b. parody . . . instigate
   c. foible . . . penetrate
   d. nostalgia . . . jeopardize

3. You can be accused of stealing another writer's original ideas even if you put those ideas in your own words. Therefore, to avoid charges of _____, be sure you give credit to the source of any ideas that you _____ in your writing.

   a. duplicity . . . criticize
   b. effrontery . . . expound
   c. irony . . . embellish
   d. plagiarism . . . paraphrase

4. Since _____ animals must kill to live and since their victims escape them more often than not, they must _____ until they succeed in getting a meal.

   a. endemic . . . persist
   b. exotic . . . abstain
   c. predatory . . . persevere
   d. pernicious . . . entreat

5. Most experienced music teachers can distinguish an extraordinarily gifted _____ from an ordinary beginner by the speed and grace with which the _____ student learns.

   a. virtuoso . . . eminent
   b. veteran . . . erudite
   c. charlatan . . . fulsome
   d. novice . . . precocious

6. New styles in art and music often seem weird and baffling when they first appear, but what seems _____ initially may come to be seen as an exciting _____.

   a. ingenious . . . anachronism
   b. bizarre . . . innovation
   c. elite . . . medium
   d. graphic . . . harbinger

7. A person who relentlessly stalks another person and cannot control or stop the _____ is in the grip of a _____ fixation that may cause great harm.

   a. obsession . . . pernicious
   b. pandemonium . . . poignant
   c. nostalgia . . . chronic
   d. libel . . . gratuitous

8. If you are lost and alone in the bush, signs of lions or other _____ animals are bound to seem _____, since what greater evil could befall you than to become the prey of one of these hunters.

   a. predatory . . . ominous
   b. mercenary . . . gruesome
   c. mammoth . . . negligible
   d. exotic . . . felicitous

9. If you had committed a crime and wished to conceal it, you might be tempted to _____ yourself when giving testimony in a case against someone else. District attorneys sometimes offer protection from prosecution, in hopes that this _____ will induce witnesses to testify truthfully.

   a. parody . . . empathy
   b. flaunt . . . legacy
   c. protect . . . inception
   d. perjure . . . immunity

10. A warm, clear night is most suitable for stargazing. A cold, clear night is less _____ because although the sky provides a(n) _____ of stars, you cannot watch the abundant display in comfort for very long.

   a. fortuitous . . . nuance
   b. fulsome . . . array
   c. opportune . . . plethora
   d. bleak . . . myriad

Enriching the Lesson

Exercise I.   Common Phobias

It is a rare human being indeed who does not have some kind of personal anxiety or phobia. Listed below are the technical terms for a number of these peculiarities. With or without the aid of an unabridged dictionary or other reference book, define each and give its etymology. Then choose any **five**, and for each compose an original illustrative sentence.

1. ailurophobia
2. monophobia
3. hydrophobia
4. acrophobia
5. agoraphobia
6. xenophobia
7. gynephobia
8. nyctophobia
9. Anglophobia
10. bibliophobia
11. triskaidekaphobia
12. cynophobia
13. arachnophobia
14. keraunophobia
15. ophidiophobia

Exercise II.   Words Based on *Philos*

English has a group of words based on the Greek root **philos**, meaning "loving" or "dear." A number of these terms are listed below. With or without the aid of a dictionary, define each, and give its etymology.

1. philosophy
2. philatelist
3. Francophile
4. hemophilia
5. philanthropy
6. philology
7. philharmonic
8. discophile
9. Anglophile
10. philander

Exercise III.   A Verbal Diversion

Modern English contains a good many adjectives that refer to members of the animal kingdom. Some of these words are sometimes applied to individual human beings to indicate that they are the possessors of whatever characteristics are associated with that particular animal. A few of these adjectives are listed below. With or without the aid of a dictionary, define each, or name the animal to which it refers. Also give any figurative or extended meanings the word may have.

1. feline
2. canine
3. equine
4. bovine
5. leonine
6. vulpine
7. lupine
8. leporine
9. ovine
10. elephantine
11. porcine
12. pavonine
13. serpentine
14. ursine
15. simian
16. taurine
17. piscine
18. anserine

Exercise IV. Colorful Phrases

A number of colorful phrases usually employed in a figurative or metaphorical sense are listed below. With or without the aid of a dictionary or other reference book, define or explain each. Then choose any **five**, and for each compose an original illustrative sentence.

1. look a gift horse in the mouth
2. a dog in the manger
3. lose face
4. rob Peter to pay Paul
5. call someone on the carpet
6. rest on one's laurels
7. a snake in the grass
8. put all one's eggs in one basket
9. split hairs
10. pocket one's pride
11. pay through the nose for
12. fly off the handle
13. in a nutshell
14. live from hand to mouth
15. buy a pig in a poke
16. put something on a back burner

Exercise V. Expanding Your Word Power

The words listed below are not on the Basic Word List, but they were mentioned in one form or another in Lesson 24. All of them would make useful additions to your working vocabulary. Define each, give its etymology, list **two** synonyms and **two** antonyms (where possible), and use in a short illustrative sentence.

1. contingent
2. categorical
3. despotic
4. imbue
5. salubrious
6. desist
7. affinity
8. lugubrious
9. surfeit
10. elegiac
11. impregnable
12. pillage
13. aftermath
14. hypothesis
15. posit

Related Forms in Context

Beneath each sentence below are four words introduced in Lesson 23 or 24. Review the related forms for these words, and choose the one that best completes the sentence. Write that related form in the space provided.

1. According to Auguste Rodin, his sculpture of a man leaning his arm and head _____ on one knee represents the poet Dante planning his *Inferno*.

   a. ostensible   b. peremptory   c. pensive   d. precocious

2. Victims of leprosy, or Hansen's disease, were once forced to live in isolated colonies, thereby suffering _____ as well as the debilitating effects of their highly contagious disease.

   a. ostracize   b. permeate   c. paraphrase   d. perjure

3. In Act V, scene i, of *Macbeth*, the sleepwalking Lady Macbeth _____ about blood she cannot wash from her hands.

   a. pandemonium   b. plagiarism   c. parody   d. obsession

4. The general spoke _____, we thought, about the need to quadruple the size of the defense budget so that the nation could mobilize for peace.

   a. paraphrase   b. parody   c. paradox   d. pandemonium

5. Which, if any, of these electronic marvels do you consider _____: dial-up computer modems, fax machines, or audiocassette tapes?

   a. obsequious   b. obsolete   c. obscene   d. opportune

6. Although both defendants swore that the signature on the letter was theirs, the testimony of a handwriting expert convinced the jury that one of the defendants had committed _____.

   a. ostracize   b. paraphrase   c. parody   d. perjure

7. Rush says that he used to be _____ about flying in an airplane but that six months of group therapy completely cured him of his fears.

   a. plethora   b. plagiarism   c. phobia   d. paraphrase

8. To prevent her students from _____ an online research paper, Ms. Applegate requires them to turn in an outline and all of their prewriting notes.

   a. plagiarism   b. parody   c. paradox   d. obsession

9. The court jester, the only member of the court from whom the king did not demand total _____, literally lost his head when he went too far.

   a. obscene   b. obsolete   c. obsequious   d. officious

10. Although the upstream face of the Kangaroo Creek Dam in South Australia is constructed of _____ concrete, its downstream side is built from rockfill.

    a. perjure   b. persevere   c. paraphrase   d. permeate

11. In Act II, scene ii, of *Julius Caesar*, Caesar's wife begs him not to go to the Senate, for in her dream she has seen Caesar's statue gushing a fountain of blood—an evil _____ if ever there was one.

    a. obsequious   b. ominous   c. officious   d. parochial

12. The praying mantis is a(n) _____ that waits, so well camouflaged that it is practically invisible, for an insect to stray within its long reach.

    a. pernicious   b. predatory   c. peremptory   d. ominous

13. "We need to overcome our _____," proclaimed the mayor in her inauguration speech, "and make plans for the greater good of our tricounty area."

    a. pensive   b. plaintive   c. poignant   d. parochial

14. The consul _____ denied Wei Lan's request for a student visa despite the fact that he'd already been offered a scholarship to an American university.

    a. opportune   b. precarious   c. officious   d. peremptory

15. The young couple didn't mind the bride's mother's _____ about the wedding plans, for she clearly had a great need to be involved in all aspects of the event.

    a. officious   b. precarious   c. obsequious   d. obscene

16. Had he not been a confirmed _____, Jay Gatsby, in F. Scott Fitzgerald's *The Great Gatsby*, would probably not have been able to amass a fortune, coming as he did from such humble beginnings.

    a. obsolete   b. pernicious   c. opportune   d. ominous

17. To celebrate the birthdays of her friends, Maya, a talented _____, writes original lyrics for popular songs.

    a. paraphrase   b. parody   c. phobia   d. obsession

18. Rachel Carson started the environmental movement with the publication of *Silent Spring* (1962), which documents the _____ of chemicals such as DDT.

    a. pernicious   b. plaintive   c. poignant   d. precocious

19. Desperate with hunger, Oliver Twist walks up to the master, holds out his porridge bowl, and says _____, "Please, sir, I want some more."

    a. peremptory   b. pernicious   c. predatory   d. plaintive

20. Thanks to the _____ of British mathematician Alan Turing and a dedicated team of analysts, the Allies succeeded in cracking the Nazi's Enigma code.

    a. permeate   b. paraphrase   c. persevere   d. perjure

Lesson 25

---

311. pre-rog-a-tive   *noun*   prĭ-rŏg'-ə-tĭv
[*praerogativus* (Latin), "asked to vote first"; from *prae* (Latin), "before" + *rogare, rogatus* (Latin), "ask"]

Definition: A special right or privilege that belongs to a person or group by virtue of rank, position, or the like.

In republican Rome, election to the consulship came to be the special **prerogative** of a tiny group of noble families belonging to the senatorial order.

Synonyms: (*nouns*) perquisite, advantage, benefit, birthright

312. pro-bi-ty   *noun*   prō'-bə-tē
[*probitas* (Latin), "honesty, uprightness"; from *probus* (Latin), "honest, upright, virtuous" + *-itas, -itatis* (Latin), "state of"]

Definition: Unquestionable honesty or uprightness.

True **probity** is not just the absence of deceit; it is a positive passion for behaving honorably and speaking the truth.

"It is the **probity** of his financial dealings that has been called into question," I replied, "not their profitableness."

Synonyms: (*nouns*) integrity, rectitude, ethicality, righteousness, honorableness, decency

Antonyms: (*nouns*) unscrupulousness, underhandedness, shadiness, knavery, chicanery, skulduggery

Related Phrases: a man or woman of principle, moral fiber; sharp practice.

313. pro-cras-ti-nate   *verb*   prō-krăs'-tə-nāt
[*procrastinare, procrastinatus* (Latin), "put off until tomorrow"; from *pro* (Latin), "forward" + *cras* (Latin), "tomorrow"]

Definition: To delay action.

"We must do something about the problem now," the congresswoman declared. "The longer we **procrastinate**, the worse the situation will become."

Related Forms: (*nouns*) procrastination, procrastinator

Synonyms: (verbs) postpone, shilly-shally, dillydally, temporize, stall

Antonyms: (verbs and phrases) act (on), take action (on), settle, decide, dispose of, take care of

Related Phrases: play a waiting game, table (or shelve) a bill, put something on ice (or in cold storage), mark time, keep in a holding pattern, drag one's feet about, let something hang fire

314. pro·di·gious *adjective* prə-dĭj'-əs

[*prodigium* (Latin), "omen, ominous sign, enormity" + *osus* (Latin), "full of"]

Definition: Extraordinary in size or extent; marvelous.

Given the state of technology at the time, the raising of Stonehenge was a truly **prodigious** feat of engineering.

Lord Macaulay, the English historian and essayist, had such a **prodigious** memory that he had a clear recollection of every book he had ever read.

Phrases: a prodigious appetite, a prodigious effort

Related Forms: (nouns) prodigiousness, prodigy; (adverb) prodigiously

Synonyms: (adjectives) tremendous, stupendous, mammoth (Word 263), vast, gargantuan, immense, massive, enormous; phenomenal, fabulous, incredible, wondrous

Antonyms: (adjectives) puny, tiny, minute, trivial, minuscule, negligible, infinitesimal; unexceptional, undistinguished, unimpressive, mediocre

Related Phrases: a herculean task, a gargantuan appetite

315. pro·lif·er·ate *verb* prō-lĭf'-ə-rāt

[*proles, prolis* (Latin), "offspring" + *ferre* (Latin), "bear" + *ate*, English verb-forming suffix]

Definition: To increase rapidly in size or abundance.

The use of cellular phones has **proliferated** at a tremendous rate in recent years.

It was almost a law of ancient Roman historical writing that where the facts were few, fictions **proliferated**.

Though the Cold War is over, the United States and other countries are still trying to prevent the **proliferation** of nuclear armaments throughout the world.

Related Forms: (noun) proliferation; (adjective) prolific

Synonyms: (verbs) burgeon, snowball, mushroom, thrive, multiply, spread, prosper, flourish, expand, escalate, accelerate

Antonyms: (verbs) decline, diminish, wane, taper off, decrease, peter out, subside, dwindle

Clones and Cloning

The word *clone* (a derivative of the Greek *klon,* meaning "twig") comes from modern biological theory but has been popularized to a degree by both the social sciences and science fiction. A *clone* is a group of organisms (plants or animals) that come from a single parent and that receive exactly the same genetic makeup. Thus, all the members of the clone are, in effect, identical copies of one another. Indeed, they may be regarded, in a sense, as aspects of the same individual.

The production of clones, or *cloning,* was first limited to plants by such processes as grafting and budding. Hence the derivation from the word for "twig." However, during the 1960s and 1970s, scientists began to clone animals such as frogs and mice by physically splitting embryos. For example, a single mouse could be cloned into two or three identical mice.

For decades the possibility of cloning adult humans or animals remained largely in the realm of science fiction, but in the mid-1990s a team of Scottish researchers cloned a lamb from an adult sheep's tissue. The offspring, christened Dolly, was such an exact copy that she was, in essence, her mother's identical twin.

This ability to clone adult mammals opens many challenging possibilities, from producing organ replacements for transplant patients to propagating endangered animal species. It also presents a tremendous ethical problem.

316. **prom·ul·gate**   *verb*   prŏm'-əl-gāt

[*promulgare, promulgatus* (Latin), "publish"; possibly from *pro* (Latin), "before, in front of" + *vulgus* (Latin), "common people, crowd"]

Definition: To announce officially, as a law or decree.

What good will it do to **promulgate** new reforms if we lack the resources and the will to make them a reality?

Related Forms: (*nouns*) promulgation, promulgator

Synonyms: (*verbs*) proclaim, decree, broadcast, publish, disseminate

Antonyms: (*verbs*) conceal, keep secret

Related Phrases: issue a ukase, speak ex cathedra

317. **pro·pen·si·ty**   *noun*   prə-pĕn'-sə-tē

[*propendere, propensus* (Latin), "be inclined to" + *-itas, -itatis* (Latin), "state of"; from *pro* (Latin), "in the direction of" + *pendere* (Latin), "lean, hang"]

Definition: A natural tendency or inclination.

Someone who has a **propensity** for saying the wrong thing at the wrong time might be described as a victim of foot-in-mouth disease.

Synonyms: (*nouns*) penchant (for), proclivity (toward), capacity (for), predilection (for), bent (for), gift (for), genius (for), preference (for), fondness (for)

Antonyms: (*nouns*) aversion (to), repugnance (for), disinclination (to), antipathy (to); immunity (to)

Related Phrases: accident-prone, be allergic to something

318. **pro·pi·ti·ate**   *verb*   prō-pĭsh'-ē-āt

[*propitiare, propitiatus* (Latin), "appease"; from *propitius* (Latin), "favorable" + *-are, -atus* (Latin), a verb-forming suffix roughly meaning "make"]

Definition: To appease or pacify.

Before they set out, the hunters of the Ice Age performed ceremonies designed to **propitiate** the spirits of the animals they would slay.

Try as I might, I could not **propitiate** my wrathful father for having wrecked the family car.

Related Forms: (*nouns*) propitiation, propitiator; (*adjective*) propitiatory

Synonyms: (*verbs*) mollify, placate, conciliate

Antonyms: (*verbs*) antagonize, alienate (Word 21), exasperate, vex, anger, annoy, incense (Word 235)

Related Phrases: pour oil on troubled waters, hold out an olive branch, make one's peace with, defuse a situation, a scapegoat (Word 356)

319. pro-tract-ed   *adjective*   prō-trăk'-tĭd

[*protrahere, protractus* (Latin), "prolong, extend"; from *pro* (Latin), "forth, out" + *trahere, tractus* (Latin), "drag, draw"]

Definition: Extended or prolonged excessively.

Three great military blunders were responsible for turning World War I into a **protracted** struggle that neither side could win without outside help.

Related Forms: (*verb*) protract; (*nouns*) protraction, protractor

Synonyms: (*adjectives*) drawn-out, elongated; interminable, endless, long-winded

Antonyms: (*adjectives*) contracted, compressed, truncated, brief, foreshortened, curtailed

320. prow-ess   *noun*   prou'-ĭs

[*proesse* (Old French), "valor"; from *prou* (Old French), "brave"]

Definition: Superior courage, ability, or skill.

In World War I, Sergeant Alvin York of Tennessee received this country's highest decorations for his extraordinary feats of **prowess** on the battlefields of France.

Annie Oakley's **prowess** with a rifle became legendary, even in her own time.

Synonyms: (*nouns*) valor, gallantry, daring, bravery, intrepidity; mettle, pluck; expertise, facility, proficiency

Antonyms: (*nouns*) cowardice, timidity; incompetence, ineptitude

Related Phrases: feats of derring-do, a tour de force, a paladin

321. pseu-do-nym   *noun*   sōō'-də-nĭm

[*pseudonymos* (Greek), "having a false name"; from *pseudes* (Greek), "false" + *onyma, onoma* (Greek), "name"]

Definition: A fictitious name assumed by an author.

"Mark Twain," the **pseudonym** of Samuel Langhorne Clemens, is actually a Mississippi riverboat expression relating to the measurement of water depths.

Since the Victorians didn't think it proper for a lady to write novels, many women published their works under masculine **pseudonyms**.

Related Form: (*adjective*) pseudonymous

Synonyms: (*nouns and noun phrases*) pen name, nom de plume, nom de guerre, alias

George Sand

Mark Twain

Voltaire

George Eliot

Each of the famous authors pictured on this page wrote under a **pseudonym**. Find out their real names.

322. **purge**   *verb and noun*   pûrj

[*purgare* (Latin), "cleanse"; from *purus* (Latin), "pure" + *agere* (Latin), "lead, do, make"]

Definition:
  a. (*verb*) To cleanse or purify, especially to rid a group of undesirable elements.

   "The only way you can **purge** yourself of a charge of contempt," the judge admonished the refractory witness, "is to begin cooperating with this court."

   On the bloody "Night of the Long Knives," June 26, 1934, Adolf Hitler **purged** the Nazi Party of anyone who might threaten his position as absolute master of Germany.

  b. (*noun*) A medicine that cleanses; the elimination of undesirable elements from a group.

   Until relatively recent times, doctors frequently used strong **purges** designed to cure illness by removing impurities from the body.

   During the bloody **purges** of the 1930s, Josef Stalin liquidated all opposition to his rule, ideas, and methods.

Related Forms: (*nouns*) purgation, purgatory, purgative; (*adjective*) purgatorial; (*verb*) expurgate

Synonyms: (*verbs*) flush out; eject, expel, liquidate, exterminate, weed out; expiate, clear; (*nouns*) physic, laxative; pogrom

Related Phrases: wipe the slate clean, make a clean sweep of; a witch-hunt, a catharsis

Usage Note:
  A *pogrom* (from the Russian phrase meaning "like thunder") is an organized massacre or persecution of a minority group, especially the Jews.

323. **pu-sil-lan-i-mous**   *adjective*   pyo͞o-sə-lăn'-ə-məs

[*pusillus* (Latin), "very small or weak" + *animus* (Latin), "soul, spirit"]

Definition: Contemptibly cowardly or mean-spirited.

  Most people regarded the government's attempt to avert a war by buying off the aggressor as not only shameful but **pusillanimous** as well.

  He characterizes his behavior during the recent crisis as circumspect; I call it **pusillanimous**.

Related Forms: (*noun*) pusillanimity; (*adverb*) pusillanimously

Synonyms: (*adjectives*) timid, timorous, frightened, fearful, spineless, gutless, lily-livered, fainthearted

Antonyms: (*adjectives*) bold, daring, intrepid, courageous, spirited, dynamic, forceful

Related Phrases: afraid of one's own shadow; have spunk

A portrait of Dante Alighieri by Domenico di Michelino

Purgatory

In Roman Catholic theology, the term *Purgatory* indicates a temporary condition or state of the soul in the afterlife. It is in Purgatory that the souls of those who have died in grace and are eventually destined to enter Heaven are purged (through suffering) of whatever spiritual impurities still remain. The nature and length of this suffering varies, and the punishment is different from that of the souls in Hell. One of the most interesting descriptions of Purgatory is contained in the *Purgatorio* (Purgatory), which is the second part of the medieval Italian poet Dante Alighieri's long epic poem on salvation, *La Commedia Divina* (The Divine Comedy). It is from its connection with the theology of the afterlife that the modern English word *purgatory* (with a small *p*) has taken on the extended meaning of "any place or condition of prolonged misery and suffering."

324. quell   *verb*   kwĕl

[*cwellan* (Old English), "kill"]

Definition: To bring to an end, usually by force; to quiet or pacify.

When the handful of police officers who were on the scene were unable to **quell** the riot, reinforcements were called in.

A few kind words are often all it takes to **quell** a child's fears and soothe his or her anguished spirit.

Synonyms: (*verbs*) suppress, extinguish, subdue, stamp out, quash, squelch, crush, put down; silence, calm, allay, assuage

Antonyms: (*verbs*) instigate (Word 241), foment, provoke, incite, kindle; enflame, arouse, stir up

Related Phrases: put the kibosh on, incite to riot; an agent provocateur, a peacemaker

Pablo Picasso's famous depiction of
Don Quixote and Sancho Panza

325. quix-ot-ic   *adjective*   kwĭk-sŏt'-ĭk

[After Don Quixote, the main character in the Renaissance Spanish writer Miguel de Cervantes's famous novel of the same name]

Definition: High-minded but impractical.

The 1920s saw the passage of several important pieces of federal legislation, including a **quixotic** scheme to prohibit the sale and use of alcohol.

Related Form: (*adverb*) quixotically

Usage Note:
Quixotic has an alternate form, *quixotical,* but this is not the preferred form of the word.

Synonyms: (*adjectives*) idealistic, visionary, fanciful, unrealistic, utopian, chimerical

Antonyms: (*adjectives*) realistic, practical, down-to-earth

Related Phrases: have one's head in the clouds; a pie-in-the-sky proposal

Using the Word

Exercise I.   Syllabication and Pronunciation

Syllabicate the following words correctly, and place the major stress mark (') after the syllable that is accented when the word is pronounced.

1. prerogative
2. probity
3. proliferate
4. promulgate
5. propitiate
6. prowess
7. pseudonym
8. pusillanimous
9. quixotic

Exercise II. Words Out of Context

In each of the following groups, select the item that best expresses the meaning of the numbered word at the left.

1. probity
   a. blandness   b. knavery   c. skill
   d. integrity   e. hostility

2. prodigious
   a. immense   b. timely   c. offensive
   d. demure   e. eager

3. prowess
   a. prejudice   b. valor   c. arrogance
   d. courtesy   e. wisdom

4. promulgate
   a. disguise   b. contradict   c. foretell
   d. understand   e. proclaim

5. purge
   a. purify   b. mystify   c. edify
   d. sanctify   e. horrify

6. propitiate
   a. judge   b. bolster   c. pacify
   d. honor   e. investigate

7. pusillanimous
   a. rude   b. biased   c. expensive
   d. cowardly   e. ugly

8. quixotic
   a. practical but costly
   b. sensible but difficult
   c. inexpensive but worthless
   d. feasible but foolish
   e. high-minded but impractical

Exercise III. Completing Sentences

Complete each of the following sentences by selecting the most appropriate word from the group of words given below. Use each word only once. Make any adjustments that are necessary to fit the words into the sentences properly.

quell	proliferate	procrastinate
protracted	propensity	quixotic
prerogative	promulgate	pseudonym

1. The old adage "Don't put off until tomorrow what you can do today" warns all of us not to _____.

2. When she said that I "tended to view the world through rose-colored glasses," she simply meant that I had a _____ for looking on the bright side of things.

3. Though the insurrection ultimately proved unsuccessful, the government was hard-pressed to _____ it.

4. Though it was the _____ of the head of the Senate in ancient Rome to give his opinion first, no other special privilege seems to have attached to the office.

5. I wonder why Eric Blair (1903–1950) chose to publish his novels and essays under the _____ George Orwell.

6. As long as more and more Americans turn to home computers for entertainment, video games will continue to _____.

7. Mismanagement turned what should have been a quick and easy victory into a _____ struggle that ended in stalemate.

Exercise IV. Synonyms and Antonyms

Classify each of the following pairs of words as **S** for **synonyms** or **A** for **antonyms**.

1. promulgate—proclaim
2. propensity—aversion
3. utopian—quixotic
4. privilege—prerogative
5. stupendous—prodigious
6. prowess—intrepidity
7. intrepid—pusillanimous
8. liquidate—purge
9. procrastinate—act
10. multiply—proliferate
11. propitiate—appease
12. protracted—compressed
13. unscrupulousness—probity
14. squelch—quell

Exercise V. Word Roundup

1. With or without the aid of a dictionary, define each of the following foreign expressions used in present-day English, and tell what language it comes from.

   a. alias
   b. ex cathedra
   c. nom de plume
   d. agent provocateur
   e. nom de guerre
   f. tour de force

2. With or without the aid of a dictionary or other reference book, name the person who used each of the following *pseudonyms*.

   a. Mark Twain
   b. O. Henry
   c. Molière
   d. Voltaire
   e. George Eliot
   f. Saki

3. Explain the story behind each of the following interesting English words.

   a. chimerical
   b. bowdlerize
   c. quixotic

4. With or without the aid of a dictionary, define each of the following words.

   a. paladin
   b. clone
   c. scapegoat
   d. catharsis
   e. spunk
   f. protractor

5. With or without the aid of a dictionary, explain the meaning of each of the following phrases.

   a. a pie-in-the-sky proposal
   b. sharp practice
   c. table a bill
   d. a witch-hunt

Exercise VI. Framing Sentences

A. Use each of the following words in an original illustrative sentence.

1. prerogative
2. probity
3. propensity
4. protracted
5. prowess
6. pseudonym
7. purge
8. quell
9. quixotic

B. Give a **noun** form of each of the following words, and use it in an original illustrative sentence.

1. procrastinate
2. prodigious
3. proliferate
4. propitiate
5. promulgate
6. pusillanimous

Dissecting the Words

1. The Latin prefix **per** occurs in a great many common English words, including *peremptory* (Word 296), *perjure* (Word 297), and *permeate* (Word 298). As with many of the other word elements studied in this book, **per** has a number of meanings:

a. "Through" or "throughout," as in these words:

percolate (*per*, "through" + *colare, colatus* [Latin], "seep")—to seep or filter slowly through. Noun: *percolator*

perforate (*per*, "through" + *forare, foratus* [Latin], "bore")—to punch or pierce small holes in. Noun: *perforation*

perennial (*per*, "throughout" + *annus* [Latin], "year")—lasting throughout the year or through many years; recurring

permanent (*per*, "throughout" + *manens, manentis* [Latin], "remaining")—fixed, lasting, or unchanging. Noun: *permanence*

perambulate (*per*, "through" + *ambulare, ambulatus* [Latin], "walk")—to roam or stroll about, especially to inspect something.

pervade (*per*, "through" + *vadere* [Latin], "go")—to spread through. Adjective: *pervasive*

perspire (*per*, "through" + *spirare* [Latin], "breathe")—to sweat

perspicacious (*per*, "through" + *specere, spectus* [Latin], "look, see")—acutely perceptive. Noun: *perspicacity*

b. "Thoroughly" or "completely," as in these words:

perfect (*per*, "completely" + *facere, factus* [Latin], "do")—(*adjective*) complete or flawless; (*verb*) to bring to completion or perfection

permutation (*per*, "completely" + *mutare, mutatus* [Latin], "change")—a complete change or transformation

perpetrate (*per*, "completely" + *patrare, patratus* [Latin], "bring about or do with the authority of a father")—to carry out, perform, or commit. Nouns: *perpetration, perpetrator perplex* (*per*, "completely" + *plectere*, *plexus* [Latin], "weave, entwine")—to puzzle or bewilder. Noun: *perplexity*

pertinacious (*per*, "thoroughly" + *tenere* [Latin], "hold")—holding firmly to some purpose or belief despite all obstacles. Noun: *pertinacity*

perturb (*per*, "thoroughly" + *turbare* [Latin], "throw into disorder")—to disturb or upset greatly. Noun: *perturbation*

c. "Very," as in these words:

persist (*per*, "very" + *sistere* [Latin], "stand firm")—to continue; to hold firmly to some course or purpose. Noun: *persistence*. Adjective: *persistent*

perfervid (*per*, "very" + *fervidus* [Latin], "hot, seething, ardent")—extremely eager; impassioned or zealous

percussion (*per*, "very hard" + *quatere*, *quassus* [Latin], "strike")—the violent collision of two bodies or the sound that such a collision makes

d. "Away," as in these words:

perdition (*per*, "away" + *dare*, *datus* [Latin], "give")—eternal damnation; utter ruin

peregrination (*per*, "away" + *ager*, *agri* [Latin], "field")—a journey from place to place

perfidy (*per*, "away" + *fides* [Latin], "faith")—treachery. Adjective: *perfidious*

perish (*per*, "away" + *ire*, *itus* [Latin], "go")—to pass away, die, or disappear. Noun: *perishables*

Per also occurs as an independent word with the general meaning "by" in a number of phrases that modern English has borrowed from Latin, including:

per annum—annually	*per se*—by itself
per capita—by the head	*per diem*—by the day

2. The prefix **pre** (from Latin *prae*) occurs in a great many common English words, including *premise* (Word 310) and *prerogative*, studied in this lesson. **Pre** means "before, in front of, or ahead of in time, position, or importance," as these words show:

preamble (*prae*, "before" + *ambulare* [Latin], "walk")—an introductory statement or event

prearrange (*pre* + *arrange*)—to arrange ahead of time. Noun: *prearrangement*

precaution (*pre* + *caution*)—an action taken in advance to prevent a possible difficulty or danger. Adjective: *precautionary*

precede (*prae*, "before" + *cedere* [Latin], "go")—to come before in time or position. Nouns: *precedence*, *precedent*

preclude (*prae*, "before" + *claudere* [Latin], "close")—to prevent by previous action or by virtue of a previous situation

precursor (*prae*, "before" + *currere*, *curses* [Latin], "run")—a forerunner *predict* (*prae*, "before" + *dicere, dictus* [Latin], "say, tell")—to foretell or prophesy. Noun: *prediction*

predilection (*prae*, "before" + *diligere, dilectus* [Latin], "choose, prefer")—a preference

predominate (*prae*, "before" + *dominare, dominatus* [Latin], "rule over")—to prevail over or dominate totally. Adjective: *predominant*

preempt (*prae*, "before" + *emere, emptus* [Latin], "buy")—to gain possession of by advance action. Adjective: *preemptive*. Noun: *preemption*

preface (*prae*, "before" + *fari, fatus* [Latin], "speak")—(*noun*) an introductory statement or essay; (*verb*) to introduce

prehistoric (*pre* + *historic*)—belonging to the period before written history. Noun: *prehistory*

premature (*prae*, "before" + *maturus* [Latin], "ripe")—unexpectedly early in development; coming too soon

premeditate (*pre* + *meditate*)—to plan, arrange, or deliberate in advance. Noun: *premeditation*

premonition (*prae*, "before" + *monere, monitus* [Latin], "warn")—an advance warning or foreboding

preoccupy (*pre* + *occupy*)—to absorb completely or to the exclusion of all else. Noun: *preoccupation*

preponderate (*prae*, "before" + *ponderare, ponderatus* [Latin], "weigh")—to be greater in power, force, or importance than all others. Noun: *preponderance*. Adjective: *preponderant*

presage (*prae*, "before" + *sagire* [Latin], "perceive")—(*verb*) to warn of in advance; (*noun*) an omen or portent

presentiment (*prae*, "before" + *sentire* [Latin], "feel, perceive")—a premonition or foreboding

preside (*prae*, "before" + *sedere, sessus* [Latin], "sit")—to be head of or have authority over. Nouns: *president, presidency*

presume (*prae*, "before" + *sumere* [Latin], "take")—to suppose to be true, to take for granted; to be overbold. Adjectives: *presumptuous, presumptive*

prevail (*prae*, "before" + *valere* [Latin], "be strong")—to triumph over or win out against; to be in force, use, or effect. Adjective: *prevalent*

Note that **prae**, the Latin spelling of this prefix, is retained in a few words that relate to Roman history, notably *praetor* and *praenomen*.

3. The Latin prefix **pro** also occurs in numerous English words, including *procrastinate* and *propensity*, studied in this lesson. It, too, has a number of meanings:

a. "Forward," "forth," or "in public," as in these words:

proceed (*pro*, "forward" + *cedere* [Latin], "go")—to move forward or onward. Nouns: *proceedings, proceeds, process, procession, procedure*

proclaim (*pro*, "in public" + *clamare* [Latin], "cry out")—to announce or declare openly or officially. Noun: *proclamation*

The Chimaera

The *Chimaera* (from the Greek word *chimaira*, meaning "nanny goat") was a fabulous monster that, according to Homer, had the head of a lion, the body of a goat, and the tail of a dragon. It was the offspring of Typhon, the monstrous son of Gaea, and was born in Lycia in what is now southwest Turkey. (Typhon also fathered a number of other equally monstrous creatures, including Echidna, Cerberus, the Hydra, and the Sphinx.) The Chimaera was eventually killed by the Greek hero Bellerophon with the aid of his winged horse Pegasus. It is from this colorful creature out of Greek mythology that modern English gets the words *chimera* (pronounced kī-mîr'-ə), meaning "a wild and foolish fancy" or "a highly improbable and incongruous scheme," and *chimerical* (pronounced kī-mîr'-ə-kəl), meaning "given to unrealistic fantasies" or "wildly improbable."

produce (*pro*, "forth" + *ducere* [Latin], "lead")—(*verb*) to bring forth or yield; (*noun*) products, especially farm products. Adjective: *productive*

profess (*pro*, "in public" + *fateri, fassus* [Latin], "acknowledge")—to affirm openly; to claim. Nouns: *professor, profession*

profuse (*pro*, "forth" + *fundere, fu(n)sus* [Latin], "pour")—*plentiful, extravagant*. Noun: *profusion*

progress (*pro*, "forward" + *gradi, gressus* [Latin], "step, move")—(*noun*) forward movement; (*verb*) move forward. Noun: *progression*

promote (*pro*, "forward" + *movere, motus* [Latin], "move")—to raise or advance to a higher rank or degree; to contribute to the advancement or success of. Nouns: *promotion, promoter*

propel (*pro*, "forward" + *pellere* [Latin], "drive")—to cause to move forward. Nouns: *propulsion, propeller*

propose (*pro*, "forward" + *ponere, positus* [Latin], "put")—to put forward for consideration. Nouns: *proposal, proposition*

proscribe (*pro*, "in public" + *scribere* [Latin], "write")—to outlaw or condemn. Noun: *proscription*

b. "Away," as in these words:

prodigal (*pro*, "away" + *agere* [Latin], "drive" + *alis* [Latin], "relating to")—(*adjective*) recklessly wasteful; (*noun*) a spendthrift. Noun: *prodigality*

profligate (*pro*, "down and away" + *fligare, fligatus* [Latin], "strike")—dissolute, wasteful

c. "For" or "on behalf of," as in this word:

procure (*pro*, "on behalf of" + *curare* [Latin], "take care of")—to acquire or obtain, often for another person. Noun: *procurement*

d. "Before," as in this word:

profane (*pro*, "before, in front of" + *fanum* [Latin], "temple, sanctuary"; for the Romans, things done before [i.e., outside] a temple were neither sacred nor elevated)—(*adjective*) nonreligious, secular; vulgar, coarse; blasphemous; (*verb*) to treat with irreverence or otherwise abuse. Noun: *profanity*

e. "In favor of," as in this word:

prorevolutionary (*pro*, "in favor of" + *revolutionary*)—in favor of revolution

Pro also appears as an independent word with the general meaning "for" or "for the sake of" in a few phrases that English has borrowed from Latin, including:

pro forma—purely as a matter of form
pro tem(pore)—for the time being

4. The Greek prefix **pro**, meaning "in front of," "before," or "forward," also occurs in a few useful English words, including:

prologue (*pro*, "before" + *legein* [Greek], "say")—an introduction to a play; an introductory act or event

proboscis (*pro*, "in front" + *boskein* [Greek], "feed")—the long tubular nose of an elephant or similar animal

problem (*pro*, "forward" + *ballein* [Greek], "throw")—a difficulty. Adjective: *problematic(al)*

proem (*pro*, "before" + *oime* [Greek], "song")—a short introduction or preface

prognosis (*pro*, "before" + *gignoskein* [Greek], "know")—a prediction of the probable course or outcome of something. Verb: *prognosticate*

Exercise

1. With or without the aid of a dictionary, define each of the following words using the Latin prefix *per*, and explain what the prefix means in that particular word. Then choose any **three** of the words, and for each compose an illustrative sentence.

a. pervade   c. perpetrate   e. persist
b. perspicacious   d. pertinacious   f. perish

2. For each of the following definitions, supply an English word beginning with the Latin prefix *pre.*

   a. come before in time or position
   b. foretell or prophesy
   c. developing or occurring too early
   d. an advance warning or foreboding

3. With or without the aid of a dictionary, define each of the following words using the Latin prefix *pro*, and explain what the prefix means in that particular word. Then choose any **three** of the words, and for each compose an original illustrative sentence.

   a. proclaim   c. produce   e. profane
   b. propose   d. prodigal   f. pro-Marxist

4. For each of the following definitions, supply an English word beginning with the Greek prefix *pro.*

   a. the long tubular nose of an elephant
   b. the introductory scene of a play
   c. a difficulty or puzzle
   d. a prediction of the probable course or outcome of

5. Explain the meaning of each of the following Latin phrases commonly used in English. Then choose any **two**, and for each compose an original illustrative sentence. Consult a dictionary as necessary.

   a. per capita   c. per diem   e. pro forma
   b. per annum   d. per se   f. pro tem(pore)

Bowdlerize

In 1807 and 1818, an Englishman named Thomas Bowdler brought out editions of the works of Shakespeare in which "those words [were] omitted which [could not] with propriety be read aloud in a family." He called his edition *The Family Shakespeare.* Actually, much of the editing work on this project appears to have been done by Bowdler's sister Henrietta Maria (Harriet), but she didn't want her involvement in the matter made public "for propriety's sake." It is from the activities of Thomas Bowdler and his sister that modern English gets the verb *bowdlerize* (pronounced bōd'-lə-rīz), which means "expurgate or censor a literary work."

William Shakespeare

Working with Context Clues

Complete each of the following two-word omissions by selecting the pair of words that make the best sense in the passage as a whole. If necessary, consult a dictionary for the meaning of any word with which you are not familiar.

1. The reason contract negotiations usually drag on so long is that the parties put off talking about the major issue. If they did not _____ but tackled this issue first, the negotiations would not be so _____.

   a. arbitrate . . . cursory
   b. digress . . . poignant
   c. persevere . . . grueling
   d. procrastinate . . . protracted

2. The romantic _____ that children are essentially good and are corrupted by adult society is a _____ assumption that does not match reality.

   a. irony . . . nebulous
   b. fallacy . . . flagrant
   c. premise . . . quixotic
   d. paradox . . . pernicious

3. If you write a book revealing your friends' faults, use a(n) _____ rather than your own name, or be ready for anger from those whose _____ you've exposed.

   a. pseudonym . . . foibles
   c. anecdote . . . nuances
   b. medium . . . obsessions
   d. innovation . . . facsimiles

4. The ancients offered sacrifices to their _____ gods to soften their hard hearts. The people hoped that if they were able to _____ the gods, they could avoid misfortune.

   a. pensive . . . justify
   b. complacent . . . pacify
   c. immutable . . . envisage
   d. implacable . . . propitiate

5. What spiritual leaders such as Dr. Martin Luther King, Jr., leave after them is a _____ of _____ courage that young people can admire and imitate.

   a. phobia . . . futile
   b. legacy . . . exemplary
   c. prelude . . . prodigious
   d. plethora . . . dignified

6. Often the unspoken message of most advertising is that whoever buys the product will look or feel like the person in the ad. Since advertising does boost sales, many people must be _____ enough to believe this _____ promise.

   a. hopeful . . . obsequious
   b. rash . . . felicitous
   c. gullible . . . implicit
   d. effete . . . fatuous

7. Riot police are often called upon to _____ the violence that rabble-rousers _____ with no thought to the destruction they may be setting in motion.

   a. propitiate . . . suppress
   b. contain . . . exploit
   c. abet . . . expound
   d. quell . . . instigate

Enriching the Lesson

Exercise I.   Our Latin Heritage

A number of the English words studied in this lesson (e.g., *probity* and *pusillanimous*) are based on Latin originals. As you have already discovered in Lessons 9 (page 133) and 14 (page 221), English is rich in such Latin borrowings. A few more examples of this heritage are listed below. With or without the aid of a dictionary, define each of the items listed and give its etymology. Then choose any **five**, and for each compose an original illustrative sentence.

1. abjure	11. rabid	21. molest
2. juvenile	12. juncture	22. neutrality
3. latent	13. lethal	23. purport
4. opacity	14. magnate	24. enumerate
5. mendacious	15. luminous	25. mute
6. obtrude	16. nocturnal	26. putative
7. longevity	17. orifice	27. pulverize
8. oscillate	18. maturate	28. recluse
9. motivate	19. proxy	29. rancid
10. orbit	20. putrid	30. ordinance

Exercise II.   Verbal Pollution—the Ecology of Words

Recently, a national teachers' organization gave an award for obfuscation to a former press secretary of a national political figure. He was "honored" in this way for having sought to mislead the public over a period of years with garbled and spurious news releases. The citation hailed him as a master of dissembling whose specialty was not so much the outright misstatement of facts as the use of words to obscure the truth, give distorted impressions, and create unwarranted associations. In short, a sort of verbal pollution.

There is nothing unique about this. There are far too many examples of verbal pollution in the nation today, threatening our linguistic ecology. Euphemisms of various types are widely employed to disguise the true nature of what is happening, both here and abroad, in both civilian and military affairs. Never before has so much been obfuscated with such fogbanks of nebulous word fallout.

This is not to say the misuse of language is necessarily more rampant today than in earlier eras. Dissembling has always been with us. But technological advances, above all TV and the Internet, have greatly increased the potency of the communications media and have resulted in massive ecological disturbances in the area of language and understanding.

You know that TV announcers, especially in urban regions, give an air pollution index in connection with each weather report. It has been suggested that it might not be a bad idea to supplement this with a word pollution index to indicate just how badly our news sources are being fouled up by deliberate or inadvertent misuse of language.

Look for examples of deliberate misuse of words that threaten the wholesomeness of our verbal ecology. You may find them in statements of public figures, advertisements, speeches, publicity releases, newspaper editorials, columns, textbooks, classroom lectures, academic pronouncements, and many other sources. You may even find that you yourself are guilty of this kind of verbal pollution once in a while.

1. With or without the aid of a dictionary, define each of the following words as used in the preceding selection.

   a. obfuscation   f. unwarranted   k. nebulous
   b. spurious   g. distort   l. linguistic
   c. dissemble   h. unique   m. inadvertent
   d. pollution   i. potency   n. supplement
   e. ecology   j. fallout   o. civilian

2. Read each of the following examples of the art of dissembling in language, and then explain what is really being said.

   a. My previous statements are now inoperative.

   b. The downtrend in the economic indices may be reflected in a certain amount of drying up of employment opportunities.

   c. The inevitable tradeoff for needed industrial development may be a temporary raising of impurity levels in the atmosphere.

Exercise III. Expanding Your Word Power

The words listed below are not on the Basic Word List, but they were mentioned in one form or another in Lesson 25. All of them would make useful additions to your working vocabulary. Define each, give its etymology, list **two** synonyms and **two** antonyms (where possible), and use in a short illustrative sentence.

1. perquisite   6. disseminate   11. expurgate
2. skulduggery   7. proclivity   12. eject
3. temporize   8. rectitude   13. expiate
4. prodigy   9. truncate   14. quash
5. burgeon   10. mettle   15. utopian

Lesson 26

326. raze — 340. resilient

---

326. raze   *verb*   rāz
[*radere, rasus* (Latin), "scrape, shave"]

Definition: To level to the ground; to blot out or demolish.

The atomic bomb that was dropped on Hiroshima in 1945 **razed** almost every building in the city.

Before work on the new shopping mall could begin, a group of shabby old tenements occupying the site had to be **razed.**

Usage Note:
Be careful not to confuse *raze* with its look-alike, *raise,* which means "erect" or "lift up," the opposite of what *raze* means.

Synonyms: (*verbs*) flatten, gut, fell, obliterate, eradicate, efface, tear down, dismantle, knock down, devastate

Antonyms: (*verbs*) raise, erect, set up, build

Related Phrases: lay waste to, reduce to a pile of rubble

---

327. re-cal-ci-trant   *adjective and noun*   rĭ-kăl'-sĭ-trĕnt
[*recalcitrans, recalcitrantis* (Latin), "kicking backwards" (used of a horse); from *re* (Latin), "back(wards)" + *calx, calcis* (Latin), "heel"]

Definition:
   a.   (*adjective*) Stubbornly resistant to reason or authority.

Though a handful of **recalcitrant** delegates made a last-ditch effort to kill the bill, the measure was eventually passed.

   b.   (*noun*) A perverse or wayward person.

"Cell Block R," the warden explained, "houses a group of **recalcitrants** who have so far resisted every effort we have made to rehabilitate them."

Phrases: a recalcitrant child, a recalcitrant animal, a recalcitrant motor

Related Form: (*noun*) recalcitrance

Synonyms: (*adjectives*) obstinate, perverse, intractable, unyielding, contrary, rebellious, defiant, uncooperative, contumacious, pigheaded, ornery

Antonyms: (*adjectives*) compliant, complaisant, acquiescent, tractable, cooperative, docile, amenable, accommodating, willing

Related Phrases: be at odds with; a diehard, as stubborn as a mule

328. re-cant *verb* rĭ-kănt'

[*re* (Latin), "back" + *cantare* (Latin), "sing, chant"]

Definition: To withdraw formally or publicly.

The theory that the earth moves around the sun was so opposed to accepted thinking during the Renaissance that many a scientist of the time was forced to **recant** his belief in it.

Related Form: (*noun*) recantation

Synonyms: (*verbs*) disown, renounce, retract, repudiate, disavow, abjure

Antonyms: (*verbs*) affirm, reaffirm, aver; hold fast to, cleave to, adhere to

Related Phrase: eat one's words

329. re-cip-ro-cate *verb* rĭ-sĭp'-rə-kāt

[*reciprocare, reciprocatus* (Latin), "move back and forth"; possibly from *re* (Latin), "backward" + *pro* (Latin), "forward"]

Definition: To give in return for, or in response to, something already given.

Can you blame me for being bitter when a supposed friend **reciprocated** my confidence with betrayal and slander?

Phrases: reciprocal assistance, a reciprocal relationship

Related Forms: (*nouns*) reciprocation, reciprocity; (*adjective*) reciprocal

Usage Notes:

a. A *reciprocal trade agreement* is one in which two or more nations "swap" favors or concessions of more or less equal value. The principle involved in such an agreement is termed *reciprocity*.

b. In mathematics, a *reciprocal* is the quotient of a quantity divided into 1. For example, the reciprocal of 7 is $1/7$.

Synonyms: (*verbs*) exchange, repay, requite, reimburse, recompense, interchange

Related Phrases: tit for tat, pay back in kind

330. re-crim-i-na-tion *noun* rĭ-krĭm-ə-nā'-shən

[*re* (Latin), "back" + *crimen, criminis* (Latin), "charge, accusation" + *are, atus* (Latin), a verb-forming suffix roughly meaning "make"]

Definition: The act of answering one accusation with another; a bitter reply.

Although I have been deeply wounded by their totally unfounded accusations, I am not going to reply to them with ugly and pointless **recriminations**.

Related Forms: (*verb*) recriminate; (*adjective*) recriminatory

Synonyms: (*nouns*) countercharge, counteraccusation, retort

331. re·dun·dant   *adjective*   rĭ-dŭn'-dĕnt

[*redundans, redundantis* (Latin), "overflowing"; from *re* (Latin), "back" + *unda* (Latin), "wave")

Definition: Unnecessarily repetitive or superfluous; more than what is normally considered adequate or necessary.

In a way, the phrase "pizza pie" is **redundant** because, in Italian, *pizza* means "a type of pie."

Good writers soon learn to spot **redundant** words and phrases in their writing and to remove them.

Related Forms: (*nouns*) redundancy, redundance

Usage Note:

The English verb *redound* comes from the same Latin word elements as *redundant*, but the two words are not related in meaning. *Redundant*, as you know, means "repetitive"; *redound* means "have as a consequence" or "contribute to."

Synonyms: (*adjectives*) verbose, prolix, pleonastic, wordy, tautological; superabundant, excessive

Antonyms: (*adjectives*) succinct, laconic, terse; insufficient, scarce

The *principle of redundancy* is built into spacecraft, so that there are more than enough safeguards or backup systems to keep the machine operating if the main system goes out.

332. re-lent   *verb*   rĭ-lĕnt'

[*re* (Latin), "completely; very" + *lentare* (Latin), "soften"]

Definition: To become less harsh or severe; to let up or slacken.

At first I was determined to see justice done, but her eloquent appeal for compassion and understanding touched my heart, and I **relented**.

When the wind and rain finally **relented**, I went outside to inspect the damage the storm had done.

Related Forms: (*adjective*) relentless; (*noun*) relentlessness

Synonyms: (*verbs*) yield, moderate, soften

Antonyms: (*verbs*) harden, stiffen, be adamant

Related Phrase: temper the wind to the shorn lamb

333. rem-i-nis-cence   *noun*   rĕm-ə-nĭs'-ĕns

[*reminiscens, reminiscentis* (Latin), "remembering"; from *re* (Latin) + *mens, mentis* (Latin), "mind"]

Definition: The act of recalling the past; a memory.

Grandmother's **reminiscences** of her youth may seem trivial to an outsider, but as a family member, I know how precious they are to her.

Related Forms: (*adjective*) reminiscent; (*verb*) reminisce

Usage Notes:

a. The adjective *reminiscent*, meaning "suggestive," is normally followed by the preposition *of*. For example, the lyrics of a pop song may be *reminiscent of* one of Shakespeare's sonnets or a poem by John Keats.

b. The plural noun *reminiscences* is often used to indicate the narrated recollections that a person has published in book or essay form. These are also sometimes called *memoirs*.

Synonyms: (*nouns*) recollection, remembrance; memoir

Related Phrases: a flashback, dwell on the past, relive the past, total recall, déjà vu

Déjà Vu

"Somehow I had the feeling that I had been in that old house before and that I was familiar with many of its contents, even though I was well aware that I could not possibly have entered it on any previous occasion."

Many of us have had the kind of strange experience suggested by this statement. Psychologists refer to it by the term *déjà vu* (dā-zhä-vōō). This comes from French and means literally "already seen." The psychological reasons for such an illusion are not entirely clear and indeed may differ widely from one case to another.

Déjà vu is also used to characterize something (*e.g.*, a film) that is supposed to be original but is actually trite and reminiscent of other works.

334. re-morse   *noun*   rĭ-môrs'

[*re* (Latin), "back; very" + *mordere, morsus* (Latin), "bite"]

Definition: Anguish, self-reproach or bitter regret for wrongdoing.

Feeling **remorse** for your thoughtlessness cannot undo the harm you have done, but it may prevent you from doing the same thing again.

The great American poet Emily Dickinson once wrote that "**remorse** is memory awake."

Related Forms: (*adjectives*) remorseful, remorseless; (*nouns*) remorselessness; (*adverbs*) remorsefully, remorselessly

Synonyms: (*nouns*) regretfulness, shame, contrition, sorrow, repentance, penitence

Antonyms: (*nouns*) callousness, indifference, unconcern, impenitence

Related Phrases: wear sackcloth and ashes, a twinge (or pang) of conscience, the prick of conscience; have a heart of stone

Emily Dickinson

Emily Dickinson lived most of her life in Amherst, Massachusetts, where she was born in 1830. Her lawyer father raised her in the strict Puritan tradition that was characteristic of New England in the 19th century. After 1853, she gradually became a recluse, possibly as the result of an unhappy love affair. The secluded life that she led became her chief source of inspiration as a poet and resulted in over 1000 poems of great poignancy and beauty. Many of her brief, delicate lyrics, full of startling imagery, concern nature, love, death, and immortality. Only seven of them were published during her lifetime, and the extent of her literary output—sometimes scribbled on odd bits of paper or the backs of old envelopes—was not discovered until after her death. Indeed, her recognition as a poet of immense stature did not even begin until the publication of the first collected edition of her works four years after her death in 1886. Since that time, her remarkable achievement has exerted a tremendous influence on modern American writers. (For further details consult *Emily Dickinson: An Interpretive Biography* by T. H. Johnson.)

335. ren-e-gade   *noun and adjective*   rĕn'-ə-gād

[*renegado* (Spanish), "turncoat"; from *re* (Latin), "again; very" + *negare, negatus* (Latin), "deny"]

Definition:
a. (*noun*) A person who deserts one cause or group for another.

One of history's most celebrated **renegades** is a Roman emperor by the name of Julian, who gave up his Christian faith when he came to the imperial throne.

History no longer views Geronimo as a dangerous **renegade** but rather as a patriot committed to the preservation of his people and their way of life.

b. (*adjective*) Disloyal or traitorous.

The robber bands that roamed the French countryside during the Hundred Years' War were often led by **renegade** knights.

A group of **renegade** Southern Democrats, called *boll weevils* and *gypsy moths*, consistently supported Republican President Ronald Reagan against their own party.

Related Forms: (*verb*) renege

Synonyms: (*nouns*) turncoat, traitor, defector, deserter, apostate; (*adjectives*) recreant, perfidious

Antonyms: (*noun*) loyalist; (*adjectives*) loyal, staunch, true-blue, reliable

Related Phrases: a volte-face; do an about-face

Usage Note:
During the American Revolution the *Loyalists* (note the *L*), also called *Tories*, were the colonists who opposed independence and supported the British cause. Most of the Loyalists were large landowners, Crown officials, and members of the clergy, though other groups were also represented. The Loyalists were most numerous in the far South (Georgia and South Carolina) and in the Middle Atlantic region (New York and Pennsylvania). After the revolution was over, a great many Loyalists moved permanently to Canada, the West Indies, or England.

336. re-per-cus-sion   *noun*   rĕ-pĕr-kŭsh'-ən

[*re* (Latin), "back; very" + *per* (Latin), "through; very" + *cutere, cussus* (Latin), "strike (hard)"]

Definition: An indirect effect or result produced by an event or action.

The development of the computer has had far-reaching **repercussions** on the way people all over the world do business.

Even the slightest change in temperature can have profound **repercussions** on the ecosystem, just as the slightest change in the rate of inflation can have dire effects on the economy.

Synonyms: (*nouns*) aftereffect, aftermath, reverberation, backlash

337. re-plen-ish   *verb*   rĭ-plĕn'-ĭsh

[*re* (Latin), "back; very" + *plenus* (Latin), "full"]

Definition: To refill or provide a new supply of.

Just before I run out of my favorite snack food, I **replenish** my supply.

When I am most deeply discouraged, their optimism and confidence seem to **replenish** my faith in my own abilities.

Related Forms: (*nouns*) replenishment, repletion; (*adjective*) replete

Usage Notes:
   a.   The noun *repletion* indicates a state of excessive fullness.
   b.   The adjective *replete*, meaning "abundantly supplied," is followed by the preposition *with*—for example, an essay *replete with* glaring grammatical errors.

Synonyms: (*verbs*) restock, renew, replace

Antonyms: (*verbs*) deplete, use up, empty, exhaust

Related Phrase: devoid of

338. re-pris-al   *noun*   rĭ-prī'-zəl

[*reprisaille* (Medieval French), "retaliation"; from *reprehendere, reprehensus* (Latin), "seize, recover"]

Definition: Retaliation in kind for injuries received.

During the Cold War the Soviet Union would often expel an American diplomat in **reprisal** for our expulsion of one of theirs.

The Nazi occupiers of France usually replied to damage done by the resistance movement by taking **reprisals** on the civilian population of the country.

Synonyms: (*nouns*) retribution, requital, vengeance, revenge

Related Phrases: a vendetta; a quid pro quo; an eye for an eye, a tooth for a tooth; get a dose of one's own medicine

339. re-scind   *verb*   rĭ-sĭnd'

[*re* (Latin), "back; very" + *scindere* (Latin), "cut"]

Definition: To cancel or withdraw.

Congress has the power to **rescind** laws that prove ineffective or harmful to our national life.

When my boss saw that there was no practical way to carry out her orders, she **rescinded** them.

Phrases: rescind a contract, rescind an agreement, rescind a regulation

Related Forms: (*nouns*) rescindment, rescision

432

Synonyms: (*verbs*) revoke, repeal, retract, recall, abrogate, annul, nullify, countermand, invalidate

Antonyms: (*verbs*) affirm, confirm, enforce, endorse, uphold, ratify, underwrite

Related Phrase: null and void

340. re-sil-ient   *adjective*   rĭ-zĭl'-yĕnt

[*resiliens, resilientis* (Latin), "leaping back"; from *re* (Latin), "back" + *salire* (Latin), "jump, leap, spring"]

Definition:
  a. Springy or flexible; able to resume its original shape.
     Artificial turf is a tough but **resilient** material that is ideal for long-term use as a playing surface in professional sports.
  b. Able to recover quickly from sickness, change, or misfortune.
     Scarlett O'Hara's remarkable recovery from the disasters of the Civil War was chiefly due to her **resilient** spirit and indomitable will.

Related Forms: (*nouns*) resilience, resiliency

Synonyms: (*adjectives*) pliable, supple, malleable, buoyant

Antonyms: (*adjectives*) inflexible, rigid, stiff, obdurate, adamant

Related Phrase: roll with the punches

Using the Words

Exercise I. Parts of Speech

Indicate the part of speech of each of the following words. In some cases, two answers are correct.

1. recalcitrant	4. reminiscence	7. reprisal
2. recant	5. renegade	8. rescind
3. redundant	6. repercussion	9. resilient

Exercise II. Words in Phrases

In each of the following groups, select the item that best expresses the meaning of the *italicized* word in the introductory phrase.

1. a *recalcitrant* student
   a. foreign   b. brilliant   c. perverse   d. young   e. polite

2. *recant* his beliefs
   a. discuss   b. distort   c. disclose   d. discover   e. disavow

3. exchange *recriminations*
   a. pleasantries   b. countercharges   c. anecdotes   d. jokes
   e. addresses

4. when she finally *relented*
   a. yielded   b. arrived   c. complained   d. answered
   e. finished

5. felt no *remorse*
   a. loneliness   b. animosity   c. hunger   d. regret
   e. desire

6. a *renegade* politician
   a. fledgling   b. turncoat   c. freshman   d. veteran
   e. expert

7. the *repercussions* of an event
   a. memories   b. reports   c. details   d. causes   e. effects

8. *reprisal* for an attack
   a. retaliation   b. need   c. plan   d. occasion   e. weapon

Exercise III.   Completing Sentences

Complete each of the following sentences by selecting the most appropriate word from the group of words given below. Use each word only once. Make any adjustments that are necessary to fit the words into the sentences properly.

reciprocate	raze	recalcitrant
replenish	resilient	redundant
recrimination	rescind	reminiscence

1. As part of the mayor's urban renewal program, a group of run-down inner-city buildings was _____ and replaced by an ultramodern civic center.

2. To my mind, the name *Rio Grande River* is slightly _____ because the word *river* appears twice, once in English and once in Spanish.

3. About a week after the Elsons had me over for dinner, I _____ the kindness by inviting them to lunch.

4. When the legislators realized that the law they had passed simply couldn't be enforced, they _____ it.

5. Though we can replace some of the natural resources we have used up, we cannot _____ our dwindling supplies of fossil fuels.

6. As its name indicates, *Recollections of My Youth* contains the author's _____ of her girlhood and the people she grew up with.

7. People who are _____ are able to bounce back quickly and easily from unexpected failures or defeats.

Exercise IV.   Synonyms and Antonyms

A. In each of the following groups, select the **two** words that are most nearly **synonymous**.

1. a. defector   b. advocate   c. beggar   d. deserter
2. a. wordy   b. pleasant   c. verbose   d. relevant
3. a. reply   b. renounce   c. retract   d. report
4. a. proposal   b. hunch   c. recollection   d. memory
5. a. pride   b. contrition   c. stature   d. repentance

Now, for each pair of synonyms that you have selected, supply a word from the Basic Word List for this lesson (Words 326–340) that means **the same** or **almost the same** thing.

B. In each of the following groups, select the item that is most nearly **opposite** in meaning to the numbered word at the left.

1. replenish   a. exhaust   b. avoid   c. restock   d. contain
                   e. repel

2. raze   a. allay   b. consider   c. defer   d. smolder
                   e. erect

3. rescind   a. ravage   b. rival   c. ratify   d. ruffle
                   e. repudiate

4. recalcitrant   a. wordy   b. accommodating   c. gorgeous
                   d. affluent   e. knowledgeable

5. relent   a. collapse   b. wander   c. lend   d. stiffen
                   e. protrude

Exercise V.   Word Roundup

1. Explain the difference between *raze* and *raise*.
2. What is a *reciprocal trade agreement*?
3. Explain what is meant by the *principle of redundancy* as applied to space equipment.
4. Tell what preposition usually follows each of these words:
   a. replete   b. reminiscent
5. With or without the aid of a dictionary, define the following words.
   a. a diehard   c. overkill   e. apostate
   b. a Loyalist   d. reciprocity   f. a flashback

6. With or without the aid of a dictionary, explain what each of the following colorful expressions means.

   a. eat one's words
   b. be at odds with
   c. give tit for tat
   d. temper the wind to the shorn lamb

   e. wear sackcloth and ashes
   f. null and void
   g. roll with the punches
   h. lay waste to

7. With or without the aid of a dictionary, define each of the following foreign expressions used in present-day English, and tell what language it comes from.

   a. quid pro quo
   b. volte-face

   c. vendetta
   d. déjà vu

Exercise VI.   Framing Sentences

A. Use each of the following words in an original illustrative sentence.

1. raze
2. recrimination
3. recalcitrant
4. remorse
5. replenish
6. reprisal
7. renegade
8. repercussion
9. rescind

B. Give a **noun** form of each of the following words, and use it in an original illustrative sentence.

1. recant
2. resilient
3. redundant

C. Give an **adjective** form of each of the following words, and use it in an original illustrative sentence.

1. reciprocate
2. relent
3. reminiscence

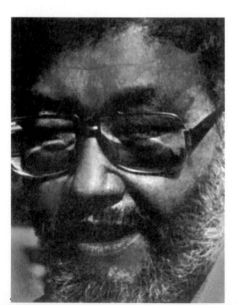

N. Scott Momaday

The noted Native American writer, painter, and teacher N. Scott Momaday is a member of the Kiowa tribe. His novels and poems present the oral traditions of his people in a contemporary idiom. His best-known work, *House Made of Dawn*, is a long prose poem about the land and those who love and value it. The book won the Pulitzer Prize for Literature in 1969.

Completing Verbal Analogies

Complete each of the following analogies.

1. **frugal : bountiful =**
   a. oblique : slanting
   b. timid : audacious
   c. churlish : expensive
   d. willful : garish
   e. resilient : flexible

2. **sequel : after =**
   a. residue : behind
   b. proximity : beneath
   c. avalanche : between
   d. intrigue : beyond
   e. postlude : before

3. **busybody : meddlesome =**
   a. grouch : genial
   b. advocate : perverse
   c. spendthrift : prodigal
   d. hero : coward
   e. faithful : renegade

4. **purge : oust =**
   a. pulverize : cement
   b. instill : remove
   c. bolster : delay
   d. reminisce : relent
   e. replenish : refill

5. **raze : down =**
   a. quell : up
   b. instigate : down
   c. erect : up
   d. exalt : down
   e. demolish : up

Group B

6. **hero : gallantry ::**
   a. bully : remorse
   b. prodigy : reprisal
   c. mendicant : levity
   d. renegade : disoyalty
   e. pusillanimous : coward

7. **rant : bombastic ::**
   a. exhort : dilatory
   b. whine : mellifluous
   c. inveigh : vitriolic
   d. champion : noncommittal
   e. poignant : melodrama

8. **bovine : sluggish ::**
   a. porcine : pig
   b. horse : equine
   c. feline : awkward
   d. mammoth : mastodon
   e. elephantine : huge

9. **reprehensible : condemnation ::**
   a. meritorious : approbation
   b. intrinsic : commiseration
   c. precocious : recrimination
   d. nominal : expiation
   e. elongation : protracted

10. **author : pseudonym ::**
    a. stage name : actress
    b. criminal : alias
    c. poet : playwright
    d. peasant : honorific
    e. nickname : sister

Working with Context Clues

Complete each of the following two-word omissions by selecting the pair of words that make the best sense in the passage as a whole. If necessary, consult a dictionary for the meaning of any word with which you are not familiar. Underline the clue or clues that led you to choose your answer.

1. An experienced worker doesn't normally have much trouble adapting to new methods or machinery; a _____, however, often has difficulty adjusting to _____ in the workplace.

   a. renegade . . . nuance
   b. veteran . . . reprisal
   c. novice . . . innovation
   d. charlatan . . . duplicity

2. Community groups have succeeded in cutting through government red tape and halting plans to _____ beautiful old buildings, proving that _____ can be defeated and architectural treasures saved from the bulldozer.

   a. buttress . . . consensus
   b. raze . . . bureaucracy
   c. embellish . . . litigation
   d. jeopardize . . . nostalgia

3. The earliest inhabitants of North America led _____ lives. Unlike farmers who stay in one place and accumulate large stores of food, these hunters had to be constantly on the move in order to _____ their small and ever-dwindling food supply.

   a. exotic . . . filch
   b. benign . . . enlarge
   c. precarious . . . purge
   d. nomadic . . . replenish

4. Characters such as George Eliot's Silas Marner _____ from all life's pleasures. They deprive themselves, not because they are _____, but because they refuse to spend the money they have.

   a. recant . . . pensive
   b. flinch . . . cantankerous
   c. abstain . . . indigent
   d. withdraw . . . desultory

5. "In your essay, you repeat the same words and phrases too often," the teacher said. "To trim the fat, you will need to _____ the _____ passages."

   a. delete . . . redundant
   b. rescind . . . felicitous
   c. purge . . . obscene
   d. finesse . . . circuitous

6. When sentimental old friends get together to talk about the past, one fond _____ usually leads to another; and before they know it, they are awash in _____ for the good old days.

   a. anecdote . . . empathy
   b. epithet . . . conjecture
   c. irony . . . parody
   d. reminiscence . . . nostalgia

7. The imagery in some contemporary poetry is so _____ that confused readers must _____ for the meaning of the vague language like a visitor searching for the light switch in a dark room.

   a. fatuous . . . search
   b. nebulous . . . grope
   c. esoteric . . . aspire
   d. cogent . . . advocate

8. In order to avoid being sued for _____, newspapers are often willing to admit in print that the statement in question is untrue. Usually when they agree to _____, the suit is dropped or settled.

   a. immunity . . . delete
   b. libel . . . recant
   c. ignominy . . . apologize
   d. reprisal . . . rescind

9. The heartbreaking _____ of parents who regret not spending enough time with their children is particularly _____ when it comes too late and the child has already developed serious problems.

   a. obsession . . . ominous
   b. remorse . . . poignant
   c. nostalgia . . . culpable
   d. empathy . . . flagrant

10. Our attempts to be _____ can backfire. One such _____ is an outburst of impulse buying if we put ourselves on an overly strict budget.

   a. frugal . . . repercussion
   b. affluent . . . effect
   c. judicious . . . exigency
   d. austere . . . propensity

Enriching the Lesson

Exercise I. Adjectives Derived from Proper Names

If a poet or dramatist were described as *Shakespearean*, you would certainly interpret this as a very high compliment. It suggests immediately all the qualities that we associate with Shakespeare—vivid characterization, insight into human motivation, evocative use of language, and so forth. In short, the name *Shakespeare* carries so many clearly understood associations that it can serve as a useful adjective.

There are a good many other names, drawn from various cultures and different periods of history, that have been converted into adjectives. In each case, of course, the adjective suggests the qualities and accomplishments for which a particular person is famous. The words are commonly, but not always, used in a favorable or complimentary sense.

Terms of this type can be a useful part of your vocabulary. You are bound to run across some of them in your reading, and you can often introduce them into your own speech and writing to express forcefully a particular aspect of meaning that you have in mind.

Each of the words listed below is derived directly from the name of a famous person. In each case, identify the person whose name is involved. Incidentally, some of these forms may not appear in your dictionary. In that case, you may want to refer to an encyclopedia or other reference work to pin down the source of the word and the person to whom it refers.

1. Byronic	8. Kafkaesque	15. Napoleonic
2. Keynesian	9. Jeffersonian	16. Socratic
3. Chaucerian	10. Elizabethan	17. Freudian
4. Joycean	11. Platonic	18. Machiavellian
5. Marxist	12. Thomistic	19. Shavian
6. Aristotelian	13. Dickensian	20. Darwinian
7. Edwardian	14. Mosaic	21. Rabelaisian

Drawing by Ed Fisher; © 1975 *The New Yorker* Magazine, Inc.

"Ho, ho, ho! Ah, Monsieur Rabelais, there's just no word to describe that earthy humor of yours."

Exercise II.   Our Celtic Heritage

Modern English contains a number of expressions drawn from Irish, Welsh, and Scottish Gaelic, the chief modern representatives of the Celtic branch of the Indo-European family of languages. A few of these items are listed below. With or without the aid of a dictionary, define each.

1. shamrock	4. clan	7. plaid
2. banshee	5. brogue	8. slogan
3. crag	6. leprechaun	9. bog

Exercise III.   Thanks to the French

Hundreds of the expressions used in Modern English are of French origin. You have already met some of these items in Lessons 3 and 12 and elsewhere in this book. A few more are listed below. With or without the aid of a dictionary, define each. Then choose any **five**, and for each compose an original illustrative sentence.

1. communiqué
2. etiquette
3. morale
4. protégé
5. entrée

6. vis-à-vis
7. flair
8. plateau
9. reservoir
10. encore

11. penchant
12. genre
13. ensemble
14. tête-à-tête
15. liaison

Exercise IV.   Expanding Your Word Power

The words listed below are not on the Basic Word List, but they were mentioned, in one form or another, in Lesson 26. All of them would make useful additions to your working vocabulary. Define each, give its etymology, list **two** synonyms and **two** antonyms (where possible), and use in a short illustrative sentence.

1. dismantle
2. devastate
3. contumacious
4. verbose
5. requite

6. retort
7. tautological
8. contrition
9. memoir
10. buoyant

11. deplete
12. backlash
13. underwrite
14. malleable
15. apostate

Related Forms in Context

Beneath each sentence below are four words introduced in Lesson 25 or 26. Review the related forms for these words, and choose the one that best completes the sentence. Write that related form in the space provided.

1. The district attorney was known for the _____ with which he prosecuted members of organized crime.

    a. replenish   b. reciprocate   c. relent   d. recant

2. The _____ of the temperamental chess champion, who refused to play his matches in the presence of an audience, delayed the start of the tournament for two days.

    a. renegade   b. remorse   c. recalcitrant   d. purge

3. Under the old motion picture Production Code, censors could demand that scenes deemed offensive to moral standards be _____ from a film.

    a. propitiate   b. promulgate   c. proliferate   d. purge

4. For her science paper, Sondra plans to research the _____ of the hoof-and-mouth disease that ravaged Britain's cattle and sheep.

   a. proliferate   b. promulgate   c. propitiate   d. procrastinate

5. Captain Ahab in Melville's *Moby Dick* pursues the great white whale _____, without regard for the safety of his crew.

   a. reminiscence   b. remorse   c. purge   d. recrimination

6. Some screenwriters who were blacklisted during the McCarthy era created _____ identities in order to continue to work.

   a. pseudonym   b. recrimination   c. reminiscence   d. remorse

7. Juneteenth, the holiday that celebrates the end of slavery, dates back to June 19, 1865, when Union soldiers rode into Galveston, Texas, and announced the _____—more than two years earlier—of the Emancipation Proclamation.

   a. propitiate   b. proliferate   c. promulgate   d. purge

8. John's research paper is due next week, but he is the world's worst _____ and has not begun writing it yet.

   a. proliferate   b. promulgate   c. propitiate   d. procrastinate

9. No 20th-century artist could rival Pablo Picasso (1881–1973) for the _____ of his output and its astonishing variety.

   a. quixotic   b. prodigious   c. protracted   d. redundant

10. The movie I just saw runs for more than three and a half hours, and I think the director chose to _____ many scenes unnecessarily.

   a. prodigious   b. protracted   c. resilient   d. renegade

11. Once you sign a contract, you will not be able to _____ on the agreement; so always read carefully before you sign anything.

   a. renegade   b. recrimination   c. reminiscence   d. probity

12. Some automobiles and vans now come _____ with a television and DVD player for backseat passengers' viewing pleasure.

   a. recant   b. reciprocate   c. relent   d. replenish

13. The purpose of the Twenty-first Amendment (1933) was the _____ of the Eighteenth Amendment (1919), which had prohibited the manufacture and sale of alcoholic beverages.

   a. replenish   b. reciprocate   c. rescind   d. relent

14. In Stephen Crane's classic novel of the Civil War, *The Red Badge of Courage*, do you think it is _____ or simply fear that motivates the hero to flee from his first battle?

   a. prodigious   b. protracted   c. resilient   d. pusillanimous

15. When I was a child, family get-togethers began with a feast prepared by Grandma and ended with _____ remarks as relatives rehashed old grievances.

    a. purge   b. recrimination   c. renegade   d. prerogative

16. In both writing and public speaking, it is acceptable to use repetition sparingly for emphasis, but it is best to avoid _____.

    a. redundant   b. recalcitrant   c. pusillanimous   d. resilient

17. In *Jane Eyre* by Charlotte Brontë, Jane's _____ and strength of character enable her to overcome her very unhappy childhood.

    a. prodigious   b. protracted   c. resilient   d. redundant

18. Galileo (1564–1642), the great Italian astronomer and physicist, was forced into a _____ of his statements that Earth revolves around the Sun.

    a. procrastinate   b. recant   c. relent   d. reciprocate

19. The purpose of a _____ trade agreement between two countries is to reduce tariffs on goods imported and exported between the trading partners.

    a. promulgate   b. purge   c. replenish   d. reciprocate

20. The latest fashions from the major design houses in Milan and Paris seem _____ of popular fashions during the early 1960s.

    a. repercussion   b. pseudonym   c. recrimination
    d. reminiscence

Lesson 27

341. reticent — 355. satellite

---

341. ret-i-cent   *adjective*   rĕt'-ĭ-sənt

[*reticens, reticentis* (Latin), "keeping silent"; from *re* (Latin), "very; completely" + *tacere, tacitus* (Latin), "keep silent"]

Definition: Disinclined to speak out; reserved or restrained.

Though he is usually willing to talk about a wide range of general subjects, he is curiously **reticent** about his personal life.

I've always felt that a person who is **reticent** about his or her private life may have something to hide.

Understandably, diplomats must be **reticent** people, simply because what they say publicly may adversely affect delicate and complicated negotiations.

Related Forms: (*noun*) reticence

Synonyms: (*adjectives*) taciturn, tight-lipped, uncommunicative, close-mouthed, hesitant

Antonyms: (*adjectives*) voluble, prolix, garrulous, loquacious, talkative

Related Phrases: mum's the word; run off at the mouth

---

342. re-tri-bu-tion   *noun*   rĕt-rə-byōō'-shən

[*re* (Latin), "back" + *tribuere, tributus* (Latin), "pay" + *tio, tionis* (Latin), a noun-forming suffix roughly meaning "state or act of"]

Definition: Just payment for something else, especially a punishment.

Most ancient peoples looked upon plagues, famines, and other natural disasters as forms of divine **retribution** for human sin.

"I believe you all know just what kind of **retribution** you can expect if you willingly collaborate with the enemy," the leader of the resistance movement warned the crowd.

"Can any society that thinks of justice exclusively in terms of **retribution** be considered 'enlightened'?" the lawyer asked.

Related Forms: (*adjectives*) retributive, retributory

Phrases: retributive justice, in retribution for

Synonyms: (*nouns*) requital, recompense, redress, compensation, satisfaction, retaliation, reprisal (Word 338), restitution, vengeance, revenge

Related Phrase: one's just deserts

444

The Four Horsemen of the Apocalypse

In the Book of Revelations (sometimes called the Apocalypse) in the New Testament, St. John the Divine describes four horsemen who issue from four seals on a closed book. These figures are usually interpreted as forms of divine retribution for human sin. They consist of pestilence (on a white horse), war (on a red horse), famine (on a black horse), and death (on a "pale" horse). Though the calamities represented by this grisly group appear regularly throughout history as the result of natural or man-made causes, St. John regards them as the instruments of God's judgment on a wayward and iniquitous human race. In the 1920s, the phrase "the four horsemen (of the Apocalypse)" was applied to a group of invincible Notre Dame football players who exacted the appropriate revenge on any opponent that attempted to score against the Fighting Irish. The Spanish novelist Vicente Blasco Ibáñez (1867–1928) called his most famous novel *The Four Horsemen of the Apocalypse* (*Los cuatro jinetes del Apocalipsis*, 1916).

The Four Horsemen of the Apocalypse by Albrecht Dürer.

---

343. **ret-ro-ac-tive**   *adjective*   rĕt-rō-ăk'-tĭv

[*retro* (Latin), "back" + *agere, actus* (Latin), "drive, lead"]

Definition: Applying or referring to a period prior to enactment.

Though I didn't actually receive my salary increase until the middle of February, it was **retroactive** to the first of the year.

Phrases: a retroactive order, a retroactive law, a retroactive tax hike

Related Form: (*adverb*) retroactively

Synonym: (*adjective*) retrospective

Related Phrases: an ex post facto law, an a priori argument

Usage Notes:

a. An *ex post facto law* is one that imposes a punishment on an action that was not punishable or illegal at the time it was committed. Such laws are, of course, unconstitutional in the United States.

b. An *a priori argument* is one in which the conclusion is deduced from a theory or hypothesis that has been stated in advance, rather than from experiment, experience, or fact.

344. re-ver-ber-ate   *verb*   rĭ-vûr'-bə-rāt

[*re* (Latin), "back; again" + *verberare, verberatus* (Latin), "whip, lash"; from *verber* (Latin), "a whip"]

Definition: To echo over and over again; to resound.

The majestic chords of the organ **reverberated** from the walls of the cathedral as the funeral cortege began its slow journey down the center aisle.

Lincoln's call for volunteers to fight to preserve the Union **reverberated** through the Northern states.

Related Forms: (*noun*) reverberation; (*adjective*) reverberant

Synonyms: (*verbs*) rebound, recoil, ricochet, bounce back, snap back; resonate, rumble, boom, thunder

Related Phrase: the recoil of a rifle

345. re-vere   *verb*   rĭ-vîr'

[*re* (Latin), "very; completely" + *vereri* (Latin), "respect"]

Definition: To hold in great awe, esteem, or respect.

People of all ages, races, and backgrounds **revere** the memory of Dr. Martin Luther King, Jr., and his fight for human dignity.

Even though the old man was in no way related to the little orphan, she **revered** him as a father.

People **revered** the old sage for the wisdom of his advice and the probity of his behavior.

Related Forms: (*noun*) reverence; (*adjectives*) reverent, reverential

Usage Note:
Reverend (with a capital *R*) is regularly used to address a Protestant minister or priest. *Rev.* is the usual abbreviation of the word.

Synonyms: (*verbs*) venerate, cherish, idolize, esteem, admire, honor

Antonyms: (*verbs*) ridicule, revile, execrate, disparage, belittle, denigrate

Related Phrases: hero worship, put someone on a pedestal

346. rit-u-al   *noun*   rĭch'-ōō-əl

[*ritus* (Latin), "ceremony" + *alis, ale* (Latin), "pertaining to; like"]

Definition: A prescribed form or order for some kind of ceremony; something that is regularly and faithfully practiced.

Much of the religion of the ancient Romans involved carrying out elaborate **rituals** designed to propitiate the gods and elicit their support.

Pledging allegiance to the flag can become an empty **ritual** if we fail to think of the meaning behind the words and gestures involved in it.

The coronation of Queen Elizabeth II at Westminster Abbey, June 2, 1953. The crowning of an English monarch is an impressive ritual full of pomp and pageantry.

Related Forms: (*nouns*) rite, ritualism; (*adjective*) ritualistic; (*adverb*) ritually

Usage Note:
Ritual is sometimes used as an adjective. In that case, it means "ceremonial" or "having the nature of a ritual." Examples of this use of the word include "pay a *ritual* call on a sick aunt" and "a *ritual* dance."

Synonyms: (*nouns*) liturgy, ceremony, formalities, service, ceremonial

Related Phrase: stand on ceremony

347. **ru‧di‧ment** *noun* rōō'-də-měnt
[*rudimentum* (Latin), "beginning, first attempt"; from *rudis* (Latin), "rough, raw"]

Definition: A basic principle, element, or skill.

Any good teacher will tell you that you must master the **rudiments** of a subject before you can proceed to its fine points.

Anyone who has the slightest acquaintance with the **rudiments** of economics will see that we cannot solve our financial problems simply by borrowing more and more money.

Related Forms: (*adjectives*) rudimentary, rudimental

Synonyms: (*nouns*) basics, fundamentals, ABCs, first principles

Related Phrases: a primer, in an embryonic stage of development

348. ru·mi·nate   *verb*   rōō'-mə-nāt

[*ruminare, ruminatus* (Latin), "chew the cud; ponder"; from *rumen, ruminis* (Latin), "gullet, stomach"]

Definition:
   a. To chew cud. (In this sense, the word is applied to cows and other ruminants.)

   The barn was full of dairy cows contentedly **ruminating** in their stalls.

   b. To ponder at length; to turn over in one's mind.

   In the corner of the garden stood a copy of Rodin's great statue of *The Thinker*, forever **ruminating** on the problems of the world.

Related Forms: (*adjective*) ruminative; (*noun and adjective*) ruminant

Ruminant

A *ruminant* is an animal that chews a cud, which is a wad of partially digested food that has been regurgitated into the mouth. Sheep, goats, cattle, oxen, deer (*e.g.*, the whitetail buck shown at the right), camels, and giraffes are all ruminants.

Synonyms: (*verbs*) masticate; mull over, reflect upon, deliberate, muse on, cogitate

Related Phrase: put on one's thinking cap

349. ruse   *noun*   rōōz

[*ruse* (Old French), "trick, stratagem"; ultimately from *recusare* (Latin), "reject"]

Definition: An action or device designed to confuse or mislead.

After ten long years of fruitless fighting, the Greeks finally captured Troy by resorting to a **ruse**.

Many a wily criminal has been trapped by an even more clever **ruse**.

Synonyms: (*nouns*) stratagem, ploy, subterfuge, artifice, gimmick, trick

Related Phrase: a red herring

350. sab·o·tage   *verb and noun*   săb'-ə-täzh

[*saboter* (French), "throw a wooden shoe into; botch"; from *sabot* (French), "a kind of wooden shoe." Supposedly, disgruntled French and Belgian factory workers threw their wooden shoes into the machinery owned by the company they worked for in order to cause damage and delay.]

Definition:

   a. (*verb*) To hamper, injure, or destroy maliciously or stealthily.

      Members of the resistance movement tried unsuccessfully to **sabotage** an enemy munitions factory outside their native town.

      Sensing that they would be left out in the cold if the two nations actually signed a peace treaty, the extremists on both sides did everything they could to **sabotage** the negotiations.

   b. (*noun*) Malicious damage, destruction, or hindrance of something.

      The inhabitants of that country could express their opposition to the ruthless military regime under which they lived only through **sabotage** and subversion.

Related Form: (*noun*) saboteur

Synonyms: (*verbs*) subvert, undermine, disrupt, hamstring, wreck, damage; (*nouns*) subversion, treachery

Related Phrases: throw a monkey wrench into the works, stab someone in the back, gum up the works, fifth column, a job action

Fifth Column

The term *fifth column* originated during the Spanish Civil War in the 1930s. In 1936, the insurgent (rebel) forces had an army composed of four distinct columns or units driving on Madrid (*below*). The insurgent commander, General Emilio Mola, predicted victory because, he said, he had a "fifth column" of secret sympathizers within the city, ready to engage in espionage and sabotage against the defenders. Today, the term *fifth column* is used to indicate a subversive or traitorous element within any type of organization.

351. sac·ri·le·gious   *adjective*   săk-rə-lē′-jəs   *or*   sak-rə-lĭ′-jəs

[*sacrilegus* (Latin), "one who steals sacred things"; from *sacer* (Latin), "holy, sacred" + *legere* (Latin), "gather"]

Definition: Wickedly disrespectful of sacred or revered things.

In 17th-century New England it was considered **sacrilegious** to read any book but the Bible on Sunday.

In the eyes of most Americans, those who burn or deface our flag are guilty of an intolerably **sacrilegious** act.

Related Forms: (*noun*) sacrilege; (*adverb*) sacrilegiously

Usage Note:

Sacrilege indicates the criminal abuse or misuse of something that is considered holy or sacred. Since the tone of the word is very strong, *sacrilege* is normally reserved for actions that are really reprehensible— for example, desecrating a cemetery or vandalizing a house of worship. Nonetheless, the word is occasionally used in a light or semihumorous context. For example, "he regarded my attempt to sit in his favorite chair as tantamount to *sacrilege*."

Synonyms: (*adjectives*) impious, blasphemous, ungodly, unholy, wicked, sinful, immoral, reprobate, irreverent, iconoclastic

Antonyms: (*adjectives*) pious, reverent, godly, devout

Related Phrases: accused of blasphemy, blaspheme (against), a blasphemer, an iconoclast

352. sa·li·ent   *noun and adjective*   sā′-lē-ĕnt   *or*   sā′-lyĕnt

[*saliens, salientis* (Latin), "jumping, leaping"; from *salire, saltus* (Latin), "jump, leap"]

Definition:

a.   (*noun*) An outward projection in a military position; anything that protrudes beyond its surroundings.

The long Allied struggle to push back the **salient** that the Nazis had created in Belgium in 1944 is popularly known as the Battle of the Bulge.

Peninsulas can be defined as **salients** of land protruding into the sea.

b.   (*adjective*) Prominent or conspicuous.

The newspaper article contained a brief synopsis of the **salient** points in the president's address.

Huge chalk cliffs projecting into the sea are the **salient** feature of the landscape around Dover.

Fair-mindedness is probably the most **salient** quality of her personality.

Phrases: a salient trait, the salient details

Related Forms: (*noun*) salience; (*adverb*) saliently; (*verb*) sally

Synonyms: (*nouns*) protuberance, protrusion, bulge, bump; (*adjectives*) outstanding, noticeable, striking, pronounced

Antonyms: (*nouns*) dent, depression, trough, cavity, hole, dip; (*adjectives*) inconspicuous, unobtrusive

Related Phrases: in high relief; keep a low profile

353. sanc-ti-mo-ni-ous *adjective* săngk-tə-mō'-nē-əs
[*sanctimonia* (Latin), "holiness"; from *sanctus* [Latin], "holy"]

Definition: Making a great but insincere show of being holy or righteous, usually for the purpose of impressing others.

    The **sanctimonious** manner in which they flaunt their faith makes me suspect that, deep down, they aren't very religious.

    I have always admired that woman because she is high-minded without being **sanctimonious** and tenderhearted without being sentimental.

Related Forms: (*noun*) sanctimony; (*adverb*) sanctimoniously

Synonyms: (*adjectives*) hypocritical, pietistic, self-righteous, canting, pompous, insincere, holier-than-thou, simon-pure

Antonyms: (*adjectives*) heartfelt, sincere

Related Phrases: a stuffed shirt, a Tartuffe

354. san-guine *adjective* săng'-gwĭn
[*sanguineus* (Latin), "bloody; blood-red"; from *sanguis* (Latin), "blood"]

Definition:
   a. Reddish or ruddy.

    My uncle was a large man with a **sanguine** complexion that radiated good health and good cheer.

   b. Cheerfully confident or optimistic.

    "Given the depressed state of the economy," I replied, "your **sanguine** assessment of this company's future doesn't appear to be very realistic."

Related Forms: (*nouns*) sanguinity, sanguineness; (*adverb*) sanguinely

Usage Note:
Be careful not to confuse *sanguine* with *sanguinary*, which means "bloodthirsty" or "murderous."

Synonyms: (*adjectives*) rosy, rubicund; florid, flushed, glowing; buoyant, sunny, bright, hopeful

Antonyms: (*adjectives*) pale, pallid, wan; pessimistic, despondent, bleak (Word 61), gloomy, glum

Related Phrases: a Pollyanna; a prophet of doom, a Cassandra

355. sat-el-lite   *noun and adjective*   săt'-əl-īt

[*satelles, satellitis* (Latin), "attendant"; possibly from *satnal* (Etruscan), "guard"]

Definition:

   a. (*noun*) A natural or artificial body revolving around a celestial body of larger size.

      Earth has only one natural **satellite**, the Moon.

      Man-made **satellites** positioned above the Atlantic and Pacific oceans make a global system of telecommunications possible.

   b. (*noun*) A country that is under the domination or influence of a larger or more powerful country.

      Although nominally independent, a number of Eastern European countries became **satellites** of the Soviet Union at the end of World War II.

   c. (*adjective*) Dependent.

      Multinational corporations consisting of a number of **satellite** companies under the direct control of the parent organization exert a tremendous influence on today's economy.

Synonyms: (*nouns*) spacecraft; appendage, protectorate, client; (*adjectives*) subordinate, subject

Antonyms: (*nouns*) hegemony, dominion; (*adjectives*) dominant, parent, predominant, principal, governing

Related Phrases: a sphere of influence, a client state; a mother country, a parent organization

Rudolfo Anaya

Born in 1927, Rudolfo Anaya is both a professor at the University of New Mexico and a noted writer of novels, plays, and short stories that comment on and interpret the Hispanic way of life in the Southwest. In such novels as *Bless Me, Ultima* he weaves together folktales and questions of religious belief to produce a memorable picture of the Hispanic experience in contemporary America.

Using the Words

Exercise I.   Syllabication and Pronunciation

Syllabicate the following words correctly, and place the major stress mark (') after the syllable that is stressed when the word is pronounced.

1. reticent	4. ritual	7. sacrilegious
2. retroactive	5. ruminate	8. sanctimonious
3. reverberate	6. sabotage	9. satellite

Exercise II.   Words Out of Context

In each of the following groups, select the item that best expresses the meaning of the numbered word at the left.

1. reticent   a. colorful   b. needy   c. fortunate
   d. tremendous   e. reserved

2. reverberate   a. honor   b. recall   c. echo   d. question
   e. ponder

3. ritual   a. garment   b. ceremony   c. weapon
   d. development   e. profession

4. sabotage   a. consider   b. forecast   c. scorn
   d. wreck   e. improve

5. sacrilegious a. judicious   b. obscure   c. impious
   d. stubborn   e. garish

6. salient   a. elaborate   b. workable   c. prominent
   d. unexpected   e. costly

7. sanguine   a. optimistic   b. wordy   c. useful
   d. treacherous   e. bleak

8. satellite   a. utensil   b. principle   c. texture
   d. appendage   e. focus

Exercise III.   Completing Sentences

Complete each of the following sentences by selecting the most appropriate word from the group of words given below.

revere	retroactive	reverberate
sanctimonious	satellite	ruminate
retribution	rudiment	ruse

1. A novice swimmer is someone who is just learning the _____ of the sport.

2. Though the man was scorned and laughed at in his own lifetime, he is greatly _____ today.

3. Since the general couldn't take the enemy town by direct assault, he tried to capture it by a _____.

4. Though ordinary Greeks didn't give the nature of reality a second thought, professional philosophers like Plato and Aristotle spent their lives _____ on the matter.

5. Knowing what I do about repression in the People's Republic of China, I found Beijing's criticisms of excessive government regulation in the United States offensively _____.

6. My rent didn't actually go up until March, but the increase was _____ to the first of the year.

7. Though many of his contemporaries looked upon the destruction of Pompeii as an act of divine _____, Pliny the Elder saw it as a purely natural phenomenon unconnected with questions of reward and punishment.

Exercise IV.   Synonyms and Antonyms

Classify each of the following pairs of words as **S** for **synonyms** or **A** for **antonyms**.

1. undermine—sabotage
2. revere—revile
3. ponder—ruminate
4. reverberate—resound
5. sacrilegious—reverent
6. sanctimonious—self-righteous
7. retribution—reprisal
8. subject—satellite
9. fundamentals—rudiments
10. reticent—talkative
11. ritual—rite
12. ruse—stratagem
13. pessimistic—sanguine
14. salient—inconspicuous

Exercise V.   Word Roundup

1. Explain the difference in meaning between *sanguine* and *sanguinary*.

2. To whom is the title *Reverend* properly applied?

3. What kind of animal is referred to as a *ruminant*? Give two examples of animals that are ruminants.

4. With or without the aid of a dictionary, explain what each of the following means:

   a. an iconoclast
   b. a saboteur
   c. a stuffed shirt
   d. a fifth column

5. With or without the aid of a dictionary, explain the meaning of the following phrases:

   a. an ex post facto law
   b. an a priori argument

c. hero worship
d. a primer
e. a red herring

f. a job action
g. a client state
h. a sphere of influence

6. With or without the aid of a dictionary, explain what each of the following colorful expressions means:

a. run off at the mouth
b. stand on ceremony

c. keep a low profile
d. stab someone in the back

Exercise VI. Framing Sentences

A. Use each of the following words in an original illustrative sentence.

1. retroactive
2. ritual
3. ruminate

4. ruse
5. sabotage
6. salient

7. sanctimonious
8. sanguine
9. satellite

B. Give a **noun** form of each of the following words, and use it in an original illustrative sentence.

1. reticent
2. reverberate
3. sacrilegious

C. Give an **adjective** form of each of these words, and use it in an original illustrative sentence.

1. rudiment
2. revere
3. retribution

Dissecting the Words

Prefixes

1. The Latin prefix **re** appears in a great many common English words, including *revere* and *reticent*, studied in this lesson. This prefix has a number of different meanings, depending upon how it is used in the word in which it appears. These meanings include:

a. "Back, backward(s)," or "behind," as in these words:

revert (*re*, "back" + *vertere*, *versus* [Latin], "turn")—to return to a previous condition, subject, or practice. Noun: *reversion*

recede (*re*, "back" + *cedere*, *cessus* [Latin], "go")—to move back. Noun: *recession*

retract (*re*, "back" + *trahere*, *tractus* [Latin], "draw, drag")—to take back something that has been said, offered, or published. Noun: *retraction*

remain (*re*, "back" + *manere*, *mansus* [Latin], "stay")—to continue without change. Noun: *remainder*

relinquish (*re*, "behind" + *linquere* [Latin], "leave")—to give up or yield *relic* (*re*, "behind" + *linquere* [Latin], "leave")—something that has survived the passage of time; an artifact of the past

b. "Again" or "repeatedly," as in these words:

redo (*re*, "again" + *do*)—to do over

revive (*re*, "again" + *vivere, victus* [Latin], "live")—to impart new life to. Noun: *revival*

c. "Very" or "completely," as in this word:

revile (*re*, "very, completely" + *vilis, vile* [Latin], "vile")—to denounce or scorn

Occasionally **re** appears as **red**, especially before a vowel. This happens, for example, in the following word:

redeem (*red*, "back; again" + *emere, emptus* [Latin], "buy")—to rescue or recover. Noun: *redemption*

2. The Latin prefix **retro** is related to **re**. Like **re**, it means "back, backward(s), or behind." It appears in the following useful English words:

retrocede (*retro*, "back" + *cedere, cessus* [Latin], "go")—to go back or recede. Noun: *retrocession*

retrograde (*retro*, "back, backwards" + *gradi, gressus* [Latin], "walk, step")—moving backwards; reverting to an earlier condition; inverted or reversed; contrary or opposed to

retrogress (*retro*, "back, backwards" + *gradi, gressus* [Latin], "walk, step")—to move or go backwards; to return to an earlier, inferior, or less complicated state. Noun: *retrogression*. Adjective: *retrogressive*

retrospect (*retro*, "back" + *specere, spectus* [Latin], "look")—a survey or review of the past. Adjective: *retrospective*

retroversion (*retro*, "back" + *vertere, versus* [Latin], "turn")—a turning or tilting backwards

Roots

1. The Latin root **sacr** or **secr**, meaning "holy" or "sacred," appears in a a number of useful English words, including *sacrilegious*, studied in this lesson. For example:

consecrate (*con*, a form of *cum* [Latin], "very; completely" + *sacrare, sacratus* [Latin], "make holy")—to set apart as holy. Noun: *consecration*

desecrate (*de* [Latin], "away from; un-" + *sacrare, sacratus* [Latin], "make holy")—to abuse or violate the sanctity of. Noun: *desecration*

sacrament (*sacramentum* [Latin], "a holy oath or binding obligation")—one of the seven sacred rites of the Christian church; a religious rite or observance; a sacred symbol or bond. Adjective: *sacramental*

sacristy (*sacristia* [Latin], "holy place")—a room in a church for housing sacred vessels and vestments

sacrifice (*sacer, sacri* [Latin], "holy, sacred" + *facere, factus* [Latin], "make")—(*verb*) to offer to a deity as homage or in atonement for sin; to forfeit something of value for something else of greater value; (*noun*) an offering to a deity; the forfeiture of something valuable for something else of greater value. Adjective: *sacrificial*

2. The Latin root **sanct** is related to **sacr** or **sect**. It also means "holy" or "sacred." Here are a few common words in which this root appears.

sanctify (*sanctus* [Latin], "holy" + *facere, factus* [Latin], "make")—to consecrate; to give religious approval to

sanctity (*sanctus* [Latin], "holy" + *itas, itatis* [Latin], "state of")—holiness, godliness, or saintliness

sanctuary (*sanctuarium* [Latin], "a holy place")—the most holy part of a sacred place; a place of asylum or refuge

sanction (*sanctio, sanctionis* [Latin], "an ordaining")—(*verb*) to authorize or approve; (*noun*) authorization or approval; a measure adopted to coerce a nation or other entity into observing the law

Note the following word in which both **sacr** and **sanct** appear:

sacrosanct—sacred and inviolable

Sacrosanct may sometimes be used ironically to suggest an undeserved immunity from questioning or attack. For example, a person may say that a particular way of doing a job at his or her office is *sacrosanct*.

Exercise

1. With or without the aid of a dictionary, define each of the following words, and explain what the prefix *re* means in that particular word.

   a. reactionary   c. recompense   e. retrench
   b. revive   d. revere   f. relinquish

2. For each of the following definitions, supply an English word using the prefix *retro*. Two answers are correct in some instances.

   a. a review of the past   c. moving backwards
   b. return to an earlier state   d. a turning or tilting backwards

3. With or without the aid of a dictionary, define each of the following words using the root *sacr* or *secr*. Then choose any three, and for each compose an original illustrative sentence.

   a. desecrate   c. sacrifice   e. sacrilegious
   b. consecrate   d. sacrament   f. sacristy

4. For each of the following definitions, supply an English word employing the Latin root *sanct*. Then use each in an original illustrative sentence.

   a. authorize   b. refuge   c. holiness

5. With or without the aid of a dictionary, explain what each of the following means.

   a. a sacrifice hit   c. a sacred cow
   b. an inner sanctum

Working with Context Clues

Complete each of the following two-word omissions by selecting the pair of words that make the best sense in the passage as a whole. If necessary, consult a dictionary for the meaning of any word with which you are unfamiliar. Underline the clue or clues that led you to choose your answer.

1. The judge's public _____ of the way the prosecution was handling its case resounded throughout the courtroom and no doubt the condemnation will _____ in the newspapers tomorrow.

    a. reprisal . . . appear
    b. parody . . . relent
    c. censure . . . reverberate
    d. litigation . . . cohere

2. The people of ancient Greece esteemed the physical bravery and skill of superheroes such as Hercules just as we _____ the extraordinary _____ of celebrity athletes such as Joe DiMaggio.

    a. emulate . . . effrontery
    b. flaunt . . . empathy
    c. disparage . . . finesse
    d. revere . . . prowess

3, The signers of the peace treaty fear that _____ elements within their own ranks may try to betray the agreement and destroy the peace. Therefore, they are making joint plans to deal with such _____ if and when it occurs.

    a. effete . . . chagrin
    b. cynical . . . effrontery
    c. pernicious . . . prowess
    d. renegade . . . sabotage

4. A common ploy of pickpockets is to jostle or bump into you so they can _____ your wallet from your pockets or snatch your purse. Another _____ is to distract you by asking a question or creating a scene.

    a. filch . . . ruse
    b. explore . . . recrimination
    c. grope . . . enigma
    d. raze . . . propensity

5. Dieting, especially crash diets, will not necessarily make you look thinner and more glowing. On the contrary, the more _____ you get, the more drawn and _____ you may look.

    a. immaculate . . . pale
    b. emaciated . . . haggard
    c. diligent . . . austere
    d. corpulent . . . gruesome

6. Some people have an inclination to talk happily about their good fortune, while others are _____ to share good news. Perhaps the latter's _____ to keep their happiness to themselves is out of fear of losing it.

    a. distraught . . . obsession
    b. ambivalent . . . reluctance
    c. reticent . . . propensity
    d. eager . . . tendency

7. Since the copy of the Declaration of Independence that we possess is merely a(n) _____ and not the real thing, we cannot expect to sell it for as much money as a(n) _____ document would bring.

   a. facsimile . . . authentic   **c.** aggregate . . . elite
   b. enigma . . . antique   **d.** anomaly . . . copious

8. Public execution is a(n) _____ example of punishment for crimes against the community. Such glaring _____ is designed to discourage others from committing similar offenses.

   a. obscene . . . ritual   **c.** flagrant . . . retribution
   b. sanguine . . . ignominy   **d.** heinous . . . nepotism

9. It is the _____ of a family to arrange the funeral service for a loved one who dies. No one should try to take away their right to the kind of _____ that will give them comfort.

   a. nuance . . . remorse   **c.** effrontery . . . legacy
   b. privilege . . . equanimity   **d.** prerogative . . . ritual

10. I did not _____ in the dispute between my two sisters because I thought that outside interference would _____ rather than lessen the tensions between them.

   a. intervene . . . exacerbate   **c.** abdicate . . . augment
   b. participate . . . justify   **d.** arbitrate . . . impugn

Enriching the Lesson

Exercise I. Myth and Ritual

In this lesson, we have studied *ritual* (Word 346), meaning a prescribed way of doing things in order to satisfy some standard of a religious, intellectual, or emotional nature. Students of society and of literature have emphasized that the rituals practiced by any group of people are closely tied up with their *myths*.

The word *myth* (from the Greek *mythos*, "tale or story") is a word with many levels of meaning that has found new applications in recent years. In the most familiar and traditional sense, the word refers to an anonymous (usually ancient) story reflecting primitive beliefs and purporting to explain the mysteries of the natural universe. Thus, we have myths of the creation of the world, of the origin of a particular group of people, of heroes and gods, of cosmic catastrophes and miraculous redemptions.

The word *myth* is sometimes used in a rather pejorative sense. It suggests a belief that many people accept but that has no basis in fact and may lead to wrong and harmful judgments. Thus, we may say that writers such as James Baldwin and Ralph Ellison have devoted themselves to shattering racist *myths* about African Americans.

This has provided the basis for the word *demythologize*, which means "to strip away an accretion of legend and sentiment and to get to the hard facts underneath." We speak of historians who have sought to *demythologize* such revered figures as Thomas Jefferson and John F. Kennedy. (Of course, there is always the danger that the demythologizer, in seeking to be rigorously critical and scientific, may be propagating new myths.)

In more recent theory, a *myth* is thought of, not as a sort of harmless (or harmful) fairy tale, but rather as a symbolic projection of a people's collective values. It is a way of expressing, in a communal or instinctive fashion, how a group of people feels about life and what its ultimate values are. The rituals associated with the myth—whether religious, patriotic, aesthetic, or whatever—are a means of expressing group loyalty and acceptance of a common body of tradition.

A myth, in this extended meaning, may be embodied in a work of art that strikes some very deep chord in the collective consciousness of the group. In this sense, Hamlet, Oedipus, Captain Ahab, and Moby Dick are all *mythic* figures embodied in literary creations. Whether or not they are *literally* true is beside the point. They are *mythically* true.

A sociologist might define a myth as the imaginative interpretation of social reality. In other words, it is a way of looking at the experience of the group and of making it satisfying and familiar in common human terms. It may have great value in promoting a feeling of solidarity and in helping the group to defend itself and to survive. Indeed, it has been said that there is no successful and long-lasting grouping of human beings that does not have its accepted mythology.

The psychologist Carl Jung, a colleague and then a rival of Sigmund Freud, built his interpretation of human nature and behavior on myths. The accepted myths of the group, as Jung saw it, represent *archetypes* of the human psyche or mind. An *archetype* in this sense is a basic pattern or theme of life experience to which special details may be added to make a story. There is, for example, the archetype of the struggle between a hero and a monster, which may represent symbolically man's never-ending fight against the hostile forces of nature that seek to destroy him. Virtually all cultures of which we have any knowledge seem to possess some variation of this mythical archetype.

Modern anthropologists (*anthropology* is the "science of man") undertake, among other things, the comparative study of the mythologies of different societal groups. Much attention is given to the mythologies of primitive (that is, technologically underdeveloped) groups and to the rituals connected with them. However, anthropologists such as Margaret Mead have been quick to emphasize that the mythological traditions of such peoples are not necessarily more fanciful or childlike than the mythologies of people who consider themselves highly developed.

A. The preceding discussion contained some form of all of the following words. With or without the aid of a dictionary, define each.

1. traditional	11. projection	21. prescribed
2. purport	12. ultimate	22. propagate
3. cosmic	13. aesthetic	23. extended
4. catastrophe	14. colleague	24. collective
5. redemption	15. solidarity	25. symbolic
6. accretion	16. societal	26. primitive
7. demythologize	17. fanciful	27. embody
8. rigorous	18. anthropology	28. comparative
9. anonymous	19. archetype	29. psyche
10. communal	20. racist	30. technological

B. With or without the aid of an encyclopedia, dictionary, or other reference book, identify each of the following mythic figures.

1. Balder (Norse)	6. Marduk (Babylonian)
2. Quetzalcoatl (Mexican)	7. Prometheus (Greek)
3. Osiris (Egyptian)	8. Romulus (Roman)
4. Cú Chulainn (Irish)	9. Paul Bunyan (American)
5. Shiva (Hindu)	10. Siegfried (German)

Exercise II.   A Verbal Diversion

The inclusion of *reticent* in this lesson brings to mind the fact that modern English contains a good many compound adjectives that involve parts of the human body. A few of these items are listed below. With or without the aid of a dictionary, define each. Then choose any **five**, and for each compose an original illustrative sentence.

1. silver-tongued	6. openhanded	11. light-fingered
2. tight-lipped	7. thin-skinned	12. tightfisted
3. hard-nosed	8. sharp-tongued	13. light-headed
4. flat-footed	9. closemouthed	14. wide-eyed
5. hotheaded	10. open-faced	15. hot-blooded

Exercise III.   Expanding Your Word Power

The words listed below are not on the Basic Word List, but they were mentioned, in one form or another, in Lesson 27. All of them would make useful additions to your working vocabulary. Define each, give its etymology, list **two** synonyms and **two** antonyms (where possible), and use in a short illustrative sentence.

1. prolix	6. liturgy	11. reprobate
2. cogitate	7. embryonic	12. cant
3. retaliation	8. ploy	13. hypocritical
4. retrospective	9. hamstring	14. wan
5. recoil	10. blaspheme	15. hegemony

Lesson 28

---

356. scape-goat   *noun*   skāp'-gōt

[*(e)scape* + *goat*; an English translation of *ez-ozel* (Hebrew), "goat that escapes." from the allusion in Leviticus 16:8 to a goat that was let loose to perish in the wilderness after the Jewish High Priest had symbolically placed the sins of the Jewish people on its head]

Definition: Someone or something that is innocently made to bear the blame or punishment for the sins or misdeeds of others.

"I can understand why *you* don't want to take the blame for this fiasco," I said, "but why are you trying to make *me* the **scapegoat**?"

Making the Jews the **scapegoat** for the ills of Germany was part and parcel of Hitler's malevolent scheme to become master of Europe.

Synonyms: (*nouns*) victim, butt, target, patsy

Related Phrases: a whipping boy, a fall guy; pin the blame on; a witch-hunt

357. schism   *noun*   sĭz'-əm   *or*   skĭz'-əm

[*schisma* (Greek), "cleft, division"; from *schizein* (Greek), "split"]

Definition: A split or division within the ranks of an organization.

The split in the Roman Catholic Church that lasted from 1378 to 1417 is usually referred to as the "Great **Schism**."

The 20th century witnessed an ever widening **schism** between popular and so-called serious music.

Related Form: (*noun and adjective*) schismatic

Synonyms: (*nouns*) breach, break, cleft, rupture, rift, cleavage

Antonyms: (*nouns*) merger, fusion, union, amalgamation

Related Phrases: a falling-out among friends, a splinter group, a separatist movement; a fusion ticket

358. scru-ti-nize   *verb*   skrōō'-tĭ-nīz

[*scrutinium* (Latin), "search" (from *scrutari* [Latin], "search closely") + *ize*]

Definition: To examine closely or critically.

I reread my essay carefully, **scrutinizing** it for errors that I had overlooked before.

Related Forms: (*noun*) scrutiny; (*adjective*) inscrutable

Synonyms: (*verbs*) peruse, study, inspect, pore over; critique

Antonyms: (*verbs*) gloss over, skip over, scan

Related Phrases: eyeball something; give something a lick and a promise

359. sec-u-lar   *adjective*   sĕk'-yə-lər

[*saecularis, saeculare* (Latin), "coming once in an age"; from *saeculum* (Latin), "lifetime, age, century"]

Definition: Not religious; pertaining to worldly (as opposed to spiritual) matters; pertaining to the state.

The program presented at last night's concert contained a fine blend of sacred and **secular** music.

It should come as no surprise to anyone that members of the clergy have **secular** concerns and interests just like everyone else.

During the Middle Ages, a person convicted of a crime in a religious court was sometimes handed over to the **secular** authorities for punishment.

Phrases: secular studies, the secular clergy, secular humanism

Related Forms: (*verb*) secularize; (*nouns*) secularism, secularization

Synonyms: (*adjectives*) temporal, civil, mundane (Word 270)

Antonyms: (*adjectives*) sacred, divine; spiritual; ecclesiastical, religious

The Secular Games

In ancient Rome, gladiatorial shows, chariot races (like the one from the film *Ben Hur* shown below), and other sporting events honoring the gods were given at irregular intervals. These entertainments, which lasted three days, were called the *secular games*, principally because they were supposed to be celebrated only once in a person's lifetime (*saeculum* in Latin). Theatrical entertainments, banquets, and the recitation of hymns specially composed for the occasion were also featured. One of these hymns has come down to us from antiquity. It is the "Secular Hymn" (*Carmen Saeculare*) composed by the Roman poet Quintus Horatius Flaccus (better known as Horace) for the secular games given by the Emperor Augustus about 17 B.C.

360. se-nile   *adjective*   sē'-nīl *or* sĕn'-īl

[*senilis, senile* (Latin), "relating to an old man"; from *senex, senis* (Latin), "old; old man"]

Definition: Showing the signs of old age, especially advanced mental or physical deterioration.

"I may be getting on in years," Granddad said at his retirement party, "but I'm not **senile** yet."

By A.D. 450, the once vigorous Roman Empire had become decidedly **senile**.

Related Forms: (*nouns*) senility, senescence; (*adjective*) senescent

Usage Notes:

  a. *Senescent* and *senescence* indicate that someone or something is in the process of becoming old; *senile*, on the other hand, indicates that he, she, or it has already reached that stage.

  b. *Senile dementia* is the technical term for the abnormally rapid deterioration of the mental and emotional faculties that sometimes comes with advanced age.

Synonyms: (*adjectives*) aged, decrepit, doddering, feebleminded, infirm, superannuated, obsolescent

Antonyms: (*adjectives*) youthful, adolescent, juvenile, infantile

Related Phrase: the science of gerontology

361. sol-ace   *noun and verb*   sŏl'-ĭs

[*solacium* (Latin), "comfort"; from *solari* (Latin), "console"]

Definition:

  a. (*noun*) Comfort or consolation in sorrow, distress, or misfortune.

While waiting to be executed for treason, the Roman statesman Boethius sought **solace** from personal misfortune in the composition of one of the world's greatest spiritual works, *The Consolation of Philosophy*.

It is the duty of a friend to offer congratulations in times of triumph, encouragement in times of trial, and **solace** in times of distress.

  b. (*verb*) To comfort or console.

In his or her own way, each person who attended the funeral tried to **solace** the grieving widow.

Related Phrase: give solace to

Synonyms: (*nouns*) succor, sympathy, commiseration, condolence, cheer; (*verbs*) succor, soothe, reassure

Antonyms: (*verbs*) vex, aggravate, badger, worry, upset, alarm

Related Phrases: give someone a boost (*or* a lift), a letter of condolence; cold comfort

464

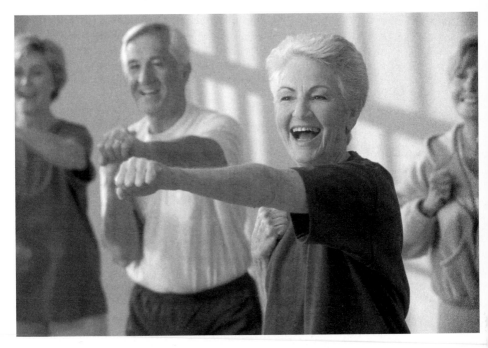

A group of seniors keeping in tip-top condition.

Some Seniors You Should Know

The English word *senior* comes from the same Latin root as *senile*. Modern English contains a good many useful expressions involving the word *senior*. For instance, a *senior citizen* is a person who has reached or gone beyond the age when many people retire from their jobs. In some places a *senior high school* is a high school that comprises grades 10 through 12. It is the counterpart of a *junior high school*, which consists of grades 7 through 9. A *senior* is a student in his or her last year of high school or college or a person who is over the retirement age. *Seniority* indicates a privileged status attained by virtue of long service in a company, institution, or other organization. The privileges that seniority brings include preferential treatment in regard to promotions and choice of work shift. The phrase *seniority rule* refers to the custom by which members of Congress choose their committee assignments according to their length of service in the House or Senate. By the way, the word *senate* is also related to *senile*. Originally, it referred to a group of old men who acted as the advisers to a king or other ruler. Now, of course, it is used of the highest lawmaking body in the land, regardless of the age or sex of its members. *Senatorial courtesy* refers to the custom of refusing to confirm a presidential appointment when both senators from the prospective appointee's state or the senior senator in the president's party oppose the idea.

362. sor-did   *adjective*   sôr′-dĭd

[*sordidus* (Latin), "filthy"; from *sordere* (Latin), "be filthy" and *sordes, sordis* (Latin), "filth"]

Definition:
a. Filthy and mean.

Despite the great wealth and abundance this country has to offer, some Americans still live and die in **sordid** and depressing slum conditions.

b. Morally degrading or reprehensible.

The country was dumbfounded as, little by little, the **sordid** details of the scandal came to light.

Disgusted with what he considered the **sordid** materialism of his countrymen, the French painter Paul Gauguin fled to Tahiti to live close to nature.

Phrases: a sordid crime, sordid motives

Related Form: (*noun*) sordidness

Synonyms: (*adjectives*) foul, wretched, gross, sleazy, squalid; vile, shameful, dishonorable; crass

Antonyms: (*adjectives*) splendid, opulent, luxurious; admirable, meritorious, praiseworthy; noble, lofty

Related Phrases: a slumlord, urban blight

363. stam-i-na   *noun*   stăm′-ĭ-nə *or* stăm′-ə-nə

[*stamina,* the plural of *stamen, staminis* (Latin), "thread, fiber." Originally, the *stamina* were believed to be the threads of life spun by the Fates at a person's birth. These determined how long a person would live and, by extension, how much staying power he or she had.]

Definition: Endurance; the moral or physical strength required to withstand hardships or overcome obstacles.

A runner needs a great deal of determination, as well as remarkable physical **stamina**, to complete a 26-mile marathon.

Do you think that present-day Americans display the same amount of mental, moral, and physical **stamina** as the early pioneers?

I agree that the candidate is a brilliant person, but I'm not sure that he has the **stamina** to serve effectively in the most trying job in the world.

Synonyms: (*nouns*) fortitude, perseverance, guts, grit, mettle, staying power, energy, vitality

Antonyms: (*nouns*) weakness, infirmity, debility, frailty, fragility, lack of strength, impotence

Related Phrases: intestinal fortitude; run out of steam

The Fates

In Greek mythology, the Fates (*Moirai*) were three sisters who were believed to determine a person's life span by spinning and cutting a slender thread that represented time. (This thread was called a *stamen* in Latin.) Clotho ("Spinner") spun the thread, Lachesis ("Allotter") measured it, and Atropos ("Inflexible") cut it. The Romans called these divinities the *Parcae*, and they are known as the *Norns* in Norse myth. One of the most interesting representations of the Norns occurs in the prologue to Richard Wagner's great music drama, *Twilight of the Gods* (*Götterdämmerung*), which was first performed in Germany in 1876.

The Three Fates by Francesco Salviati

---

364. ster-e-o-type   *noun and verb*   stĕr′-ē-ə-tīp   *or*   stîr′-ē-ə-tīp
[*stéréotype* (French), "a kind of plate used in printing"]

Definition:
   a. (*noun*) A conventional, usually oversimplified, conception or representation of something.

   > Though we all have a tendency to think in **stereotypes**, it would be a mistake to base our behavior on such simplistic notions.

   > In recent years, the women's movement has done much to demolish the sexist **stereotypes** of a bygone age.

   b. (*verb*) To force into a uniform, and usually oversimplified, mold; to develop a fixed and unvarying idea about.

   > Some popular shows of TV's golden age tended to **stereotype** the average American family and its component members.

   > During a war people are easily beguiled into **stereotyping** the enemy as somehow subhuman.

Related Forms: (*adjectives*) stereotypic(al), stereotyped

Synonyms: (*noun*) cliché; (*verbs*) classify, generalize about, typecast, pigeonhole, categorize

Related Phrase: force of habit

467

365. stig·ma·tize   *verb*   stĭg'-mə-tīz

[*stigmatizein* (Greek), "brand, mark"; from *stigma, stigmata* (Greek), "mark, brand, tattoo"]

Definition: To brand or characterize as blemished or disgraceful.

Stigmatized as a traitor by his fellow Americans, Benedict Arnold spent the last years of his life in exile in England.

Related Forms: (*nouns*) stigma, stigmata, astigmatism; (*adjective*) stigmatic

Usage Notes:

a. A *stigma* is a mark or token of infamy, disgrace, or reproach. For example, Edgar Allan Poe bore the *stigma* of having been expelled from West Point.

b. *Astigmatism* is a condition in which the eye does not focus properly. Glasses can usually correct this problem.

Synonyms: (*verbs*) denounce, condemn, decry, discredit, disparage, belittle; label, impute

Antonyms: (*verbs*) whitewash; compliment, extol

Stigmata

In Roman Catholicism, the term *stigmata* (the plural of *stigma*) is used to designate the impressions or marks that the Crown of Thorns and the nails left on the body of Christ during His crucifixion. Devout Roman Catholics believe that replicas of these marks have by divine favor appeared miraculously on the bodies of certain saintly men and women, including St. Francis of Assisi, on whose body the stigmata are said to have been impressed by a seraph with six wings.

366. stip·u·late   *verb*   stĭp′-yə-lāt

[*stipulari*, *stipulatus* (Latin), "make a specific demand for some condition in an agreement"]

Definition: To specify or demand as a condition for agreement; to guarantee or affirm.

One of the clauses in the contract **stipulates** that the agreement may be canceled if the price of oil drops below a certain level.

The lawyer for the defense **stipulated** that her client had employed the witness as a private investigator on numerous occasions.

Phrases: stipulate a price, stipulate the manner of payment

Related Form: (*noun*) stipulation

Synonyms: (*verbs*) require, contract, provide for

Related Phrases: a proviso, a must, a sine qua non; with no strings attached

367. strat·e·gy   *noun*   străt′-ə-jē

[*strategia* (Greek), "generalship"; from *strategos* (Greek), "general"; from *stratos* (Greek), "army" + *agein* (Greek), "lead"]

Definition:
   a.   An overall plan of action designed to achieve a specific goal.

"The **strategy** by which we hope to win this war," the general said, "employs guerrilla tactics and avoids set battles."

Only a person with a broad knowledge of politics, social conditions, and popular attitudes throughout the country can effectively plan the **strategy** of a presidential campaign.

   b.   The science of planning and directing such an operation.

Among the subjects I studied at West Point were **strategy** and tactics.

Related Forms: (*nouns*) strategist, stratagem; (*adjective*) strategic

Phrases: a strategic withdrawal, at strategic points; strategic bombing

Usage Notes:
   a.   *Strategy* is sometimes used as an adjective—for example, in the phrase "a *strategy* meeting."

   b.   Do not confuse *strategy* with *stratagem*. A *stratagem* is a specific scheme or device employed to gain some advantage over an opponent. In other words, it is a *tactic*. *Strategy*, on the other hand, refers to the broad, overall plan of operation.

   c.   The use of *strategy* is not confined to military operations; the word may properly be applied to business, politics, sports, or other areas of life in which planning is essential.

Synonyms: (*nouns*) plan, blueprint, program, policy, approach, scenario

Related Phrases: a game plan; operational tactics; the science of logistics

469

368. stri-dent   *adjective*   strīd′-ĕnt

[*stridens, stridentis* (Latin), "loud and harsh"; from *stridere* (Latin), "make a loud, harsh noise"]

Definition: Loud and harsh in sound.

On the corner a man shouting at the top of his lungs in a very **strident** voice was haranguing a throng of idle passersby.

As election day got closer and closer, the tone of his political oratory became more and more **strident**.

Related Forms: (*nouns*) stridence, stridency; (*adverb*) stridently

Synonyms: (*adjectives*) grating, shrill, raucous, dissonant, cacophonous, jarring

Antonyms: (*adjectives*) mellifluous, euphonious, melodious, dulcet

369. sur-veil-lance   *noun*   sər-vā′-ləns

[*sur* (French), "over, on" + *veiller* (French), "watch" + *ance* (French), "state or act of"]

Definition: Close observation of a person or group considered suspicious; a continuous watch for the purpose of direction or control.

Throughout the period that the mobster thought he had gone undetected, he was actually under close **surveillance** by the FBI.

The disputed territory was kept under strict UN **surveillance** until peace was restored to the area.

Observers on the ground keep close **surveillance** on air traffic at a busy international airport by means of various electronic devices, including radar.

Synonyms: (*nouns*) watch, monitoring, supervision, vigilance

Related Phrases: a stakeout, tail (*or* put a tail on) a suspect, keep tabs (*or* an eye) on, industrial espionage

370. syn-drome   *noun*   sĭn′-drōm

[*syndrome* (Greek), "combination"; from *syn* (Greek), "together" + *dramein* (Greek), "run"]

Definition: A group of traits, symptoms, or signs that collectively characterize a disease or social condition.

A temperature, a sore throat, and a general feeling of overwhelming fatigue are characteristic of the mononucleosis **syndrome**.

The conference sought to develop effective strategies to combat the **syndrome** of drug abuse, violence, and crime that afflicts our society.

Synonym: (*noun*) complex

Using the Words

Exercise I.   Parts of Speech

Indicate the part of speech of each of the following words. In some cases, two answers are correct.

1. schism
2. scrutinize
3. senile
4. solace
5. stamina
6. stereotype
7. strident
8. surveillance
9. syndrome

Exercise II.   Words in Phrases

In each of the following groups, select the item that best expresses the meaning of the *italicized* word in the introductory phrase.

1. a *schism* in the ranks
   a. traitor   b. movement   c. spy   d. split

2. *scrutinized* the report
   a. ignored   b. examined   c. delivered   d. questioned

3. *secular* pursuits
   a. religious   b. scholarly   c. typical   d. worldly

4. slowly becoming *senile*
   a. feebleminded   b. tight-lipped   c. ironclad   d. openhanded

5. sought *solace* in her scholarly activities
   a. payment   b. glory   c. knowledge   d. comfort

6. *sordid* motives
   a. unclear   b. shameful   c. puzzling   d. lofty

7. has no *stamina*
   a. money   b. evidence   c. staying power   d. job

8. a *strident* voice
   a. shrill   b. soft   c. clear   d. deep

Exercise III.   Completing Sentences

Complete each of the following sentences by selecting the appropriate word from the group of words given below.

stipulate	syndrome	scapegoat
strident	strategy	stereotype
stigmatize	sordid	surveillance

1. One of the clauses in the contract _____ that employees are to be allowed ten sick days a year.

2. The courts have placed strict limits on secret monitoring of telephone conversations and other forms of electronic _____.

3. He is clever at devising temporary measures to prevent his company from going bankrupt, but he seems incapable of developing a long-term financial _____.

4. "Instead of looking for a _____ to saddle with the blame for this mess," I asked, "why don't you admit your own responsibility for it?"

5. "Though the official must, of course, bear the burden of guilt for what he has done," Angela observed, "we should not allow his misdeeds to _____ innocent members of his family."

6. The fact that we throw away so much edible food is evidence of the _____ of wastefulness that seems to afflict modern American life.

7. Though we tend to regard racial and ethnic _____ as relatively modern phenomena, we should not forget that the ancient world thought in such clichés as well.

Exercise IV.   Synonyms and Antonyms

A. In each of the following groups, select the **two** words that are most nearly **synonymous**.

1. a. brand   b. reply   c. intrude   d. condemn

2. a. consider   b. inspect   c. examine   d. support

3. a. plan   b. blueprint   c. essay   d. novel

4. a. modern   b. sleazy   c. affluent   d. squalid

5. a. endurance   b. fortitude   c. memory   d. plight

   Now, for each pair of synonyms you have selected, supply a word from the Basic Word List for this lesson (Words 356–370) that means the **same** or **almost the same** thing.

B. In each of the following, select the item that is most nearly **opposite** in meaning to the numbered word at the left.

1. secular   a. financial   b. scientific   c. athletic
              d. political   e. sacred

2. senile   a. lush   b. wealthy   c. abrupt   d. youthful
              e. kindly

3. strident   a. mellifluous   b. obscure   c. hurried
              d. docile   e. raucous

4. schism   a. crusade   b. development   c. fusion
              d. rupture   e. prologue

5. solace   a. pay   b. upset   c. study   d. answer   e. burn

Exercise V. Word Roundup

1. Give the origin of the word *scapegoat.*

2. With what is each of the following sciences concerned?

   a. gerontology   b. logistics

3. Explain the difference in meaning between the words in each of the following pairs:

   a. senile—senescent   b. obsolete—obsolescent

4. Name the Fates, and explain how they were thought to determine a person's life span.

5. With or without the aid of a dictionary, define each of the following expressions:

   a. a whipping boy   d. a slumlord
   b. a splinter group   e. a game plan
   c. a senior citizen   f. a stakeout

6. With or without the aid of a dictionary, explain what each of the following terms means:

   a. seniority   c. astigmatism
   b. merger   d. industrial espionage

7. With or without the aid of a dictionary, define each of the following foreign expressions used in present-day English, and tell what language it comes from.

   a. sine qua non   b. scenario   c. proviso

8. With or without the aid of a dictionary or other reference book, explain what is meant by each of the following colorful phrases:

   a. to pigeonhole something   c. to eyeball something
   b. to give something a lick   d. to put a tail on
      and a promise   someone

Exercise VI. Framing Sentences

A. Use each of the following words in an original illustrative sentence.

1. scapegoat   3. solace   5. surveillance
2. secular   4. stamina   6. syndrome

B. Give a **noun** form of each of the following words, and use it in an original illustrative sentence.

1. scrutinize   3. sordid   5. stipulate
2. senile   4. stigmatize   6. strident

C. Give an **adjective** form of each of the following words, and use it in an original illustrative sentence.

1. schism   2. stereotype   3. strategy

Completing Verbal Analogies

Complete each of the following analogies.

1. **gibberish : meaning ::**
   a. bombast : padding
   b. clarity : exhortation
   c. innuendo : subtlety
   d. drivel : substance
   e. stamina : endurance

2. **vitriolic : acid ::**
   a. petulant : wine
   b. decadent : water
   c. unctuous : oil
   d. sordid : milk
   e. secular : soda

3. **expurgate : censor ::**
   a. persevere : lie
   b. embezzle : steal
   c. desecrate : cheat
   d. award : rob
   e. solace : murder

4. **dapper : slovenly ::**
   a. shrewd : astute
   b. quixotic : feasibility
   c. coward : pusillanimous
   d. mellifluous : strident
   e. precarious : perch

5. **hypocrite : sanctimonious ::**
   a. showoff : ostentatious
   b. glutton : abstinent
   c. avarice : miser
   d. drunkard : winsome
   e. infantile : senile

Group B

6. **egregious : mountain =**
   a. punctilious : pigsty
   b. grandiose : foxhole
   c. dispassionate : toadstool
   d. precocious : mousetrap
   e. inconsequential : molehill

7. **asymmetrical : balance =**
   a. anomalous : function
   b. frog : amphibian
   c. satellite : autonomous
   d. amorphous : shape
   e. axiom : theorem

8. **dowdy : appearance =**
   a. abstemious : background
   b. gauche : behavior
   c. sedentary : age
   d. debonair : build
   e. prodigious : color

9. **fox : fur =**
   a. giraffe : gist
   b. monkey : simian
   c. ruminant : gnu
   d. parrot : plumage
   e. colt : foal

Working with Context Clues

Complete each of the following two-word omissions by selecting the pair of words that make the best sense in the passage as a whole. If necessary, consult a dictionary for the meaning of any word with which you are not familiar. Underline the clue or clues that led you to choose your answer.

1. We can go ahead with our _____ to gain new club members if we can get the approval of the board. Otherwise, our plan of action must remain _____ until a new board is elected, and that is not scheduled to occur for at least another year and a half.

   a. innovation . . . active
   b. premise . . . nominal
   c. propensity . . . strident
   d. strategy . . . dormant

2. Some advertisers make their ads loud and insistent in the hope that the _____ tone will cause resistant consumers to _____ and buy their products, even if they really do not need them.

   a. strident . . . relent
   b. facetious . . . recant
   c. felicitous . . . grope
   d. affected . . . bicker

3. If your general attitude toward other people is so hostile and off-putting that you _____ everyone you meet, you had better think about why you are so _____.

   a. goad . . . obsequious
   b. impugn . . . benign
   c. alienate . . . belligerent
   d. stigmatize . . . cynical

4. A _____ is an oversimplified label that is used to discredit entire groups of people and to _____ individuals simply because they are members of a particular group.

   a. stereotype . . . stigmatize
   b. euphemism . . . censure
   c. paradox . . . exploit
   d. scapegoat . . . libel

5. Some senators _____ against a proposal in committee; but when it comes to the floor, they no longer protest but turn _____ and go along with the majority.

   a. inveigh . . . docile
   b. stipulate . . . reticent
   c. harangue . . . belligerent
   d. array . . . askew

6. Younger patients are more likely to recover quickly from surgery. Older patients are less _____ and may lack the _____ to endure a long operation.

   a. blithe . . . equanimity
   b. resilient . . . stamina
   c. implacable . . . bravado
   d. circumspect . . . courage

Enriching the Lesson

Exercise I.   Fairness in Language

One of the basic complaints of supporters of the women's movement was that sexist attitudes that tended to belittle and degrade women were embedded in our language. They called attention, for example, to issues such as the following:

- The use of the masculine pronoun in contexts that should apply to women fully as much as to men—for example, "Each of us should do *his* best to serve *his* community." Did this imply that men were the pivotal figures in society and that the role of women was inferior or inconsequential? Perhaps there was no such idea in the mind of the speaker or writer, but it may still have been true that the constant use of this kind of expression reflected and reinforced sexist attitudes, if only on an unconscious level. It was argued that English, unlike some other languages, doesn't have an equivalent for *he* and *his* that applies to both sexes and that we must accept this linguistic peculiarity. The answer was that one can usually get around the snag with just a little ingenuity—for example, "All of us should do *our* best to serve *our* community."

- The use of *Mrs.* and *Miss* as terms of address for married and un-married women, respectively. The term *Mr.* applies to men, whether married or not. Did this imply that a woman had no real identity aside from her marital status—that is, her relationship to men? Supporters of the women's movement recommended the title *Ms.* for all women, and this form is now in common use.

- The use of such expressions as *chairman, congressman, foreman, spokesman,* and *anchorman* to indicate positions of authority and importance. It was often said that the *man* part of such terms is simply a convention of language, with no sexist intent. However, feminists asserted that such expressions derived from a period when male dominance was taken for granted and that it was time to root them out. Suggested substitutes, such as *congressperson* and *chairperson,* seemed strange at first to some people. However, with continued use, such gender-neutral terms became the norm.

- The tendency to specify the sex of a doctor, lawyer, or some other professional person who happened to be a woman—for example, "I am being treated by a lady dentist." Would anyone say, "I am being treated by a man dentist"? Or (even more ridiculous) by a "gentleman dentist"? Surely sex was irrelevant to professional qualifications, and the specification that a dentist was a woman was male-oriented and patronizing, if not insulting. Incidentally the use of *lady* was frowned upon by many feminists because it suggested a delicate and sheltered creature, probably of the upper classes, who must be kept apart from the gross realities of real life. The more down-to-earth term *woman*—the exact equivalent of *man*—was much preferred.

Not everyone fully accepted such criticisms of our language habits. However, it is hard to deny that there were conventions of English usage that reflected a male-dominated society and that it was high time to make some changes that reflected the status and attitudes of women.

Listed below are some words and phrases commonly used in connection with the women's movement. Define each.

1. sexism	9. stigma	17. denigrate
2. feminism	10. male chauvinism	18. conformity
3. stereotype	11. glass ceiling	19. liberation
4. feminine mystique	12. consciousness-raising	20. male supremacy
5. conventions	13. grievance	21. dependence
6. mommy track	14. fulfillment	22. domestic
7. discrimination	15. identity	23. pink collar
8. equal rights	16. career-oriented	24. confrontation

Exercise II.   "Sound" Words

This lesson includes the word *strident*, which refers to sound. A number of other useful "sound" words are listed below. With or without the aid of a dictionary, define each, and give its etymology. Then choose any **five**, and for each compose an original illustrative sentence.

1. vociferate	6. sibilant	11. purl
2. rasping	7. shrill	12. dulcet
3. sonorous	8. tremulous	13. snarl
4. bleat	9. keen (*verb*)	14. discordant
5. quaver	10. stentorian	15. clangorous

Exercise III.   Expanding Your Word Power

The words listed below are not on the Basic Word List, but they were mentioned, in one form or another, in Lesson 28. All of them would make useful additions to your working vocabulary. Define each, give its etymology, list **two** synonyms and **two** antonyms (where possible), and use in a short illustrative sentence.

1. cleft	6. succor	11. scan
2. fusion	7. squalid	12. vigilance
3. critique	8. debility	13. euphonious
4. scrutiny	9. categorize	14. monitor
5. superannuated	10. denounce	15. civil

Related Forms in Context

Beneath each sentence below are four words introduced in Lesson 27 or 28. Review the related forms for these words, and choose the one that best completes the sentence. Write that related form in the space provided.

1. Those who vandalize houses of worship or damage holy objects are guilty of _____.

   a. retroactive   b. sanctimonious   c. sanguine   d. sacrilegious

2. After killing his brother Abel, Cain bore a _____ (the "mark of Cain") that identified him as a social outcast and a murderer.

   a. stereotype   b. stipulate   c. stigmatize   d. scrutinize

3. The eponymous heroine of the novel *Pollyanna* faces every trial that life has to offer her with remarkable _____.

   a. sanguine   b. sacrilegious   c. secular   d. salient

4. I find the _____ of television ads so grating that I hit the mute button on my remote or leave the room during commercial breaks.

   a. senile   b. sanctimonious   c. strident   d. salient

5. The 1960 television documentary *Harvest of Shame* focused public attention on the _____ of the conditions in which migrant farmworkers were forced to live.

   a. sordid   b. sanguine   c. senile   d. sanctimonious

6. The Old Testament prophet railed against his people's increasing _____ and their abandonment of traditional ways.

   a. sordid   b. senile   c. secular   d. strident

7. The great American poet Emily Dickinson, known for her _____ and shyness, gave vent to her feelings in gemlike poems of great emotional power.

   a. reticent   b. retroactive   c. senile   d. sordid

8. Tsunamis, gigantic sea waves that can be 100 feet high, are caused by _____ from underwater earthquakes or volcanic eruptions.

   a. revere   b. ruminate   c. stipulate   d. reverberate

9. A totally _____ facial expression, revealing not a hint of emotion, is a great asset to someone who plays poker or other card games.

   a. reverberate   b. sabotage   c. scrutinize   d. stigmatize

10. All Social Security recipients have been notified that their cost-of-living increase will be effective _____ from January 1.

    a. salient   b. retroactive   c. santimonious   d. strident

11. Do you think the old king's madness at the end of *King Lear* is caused by _____, or are we meant to view it as a tragic consequence of his actions in Act I, scene i?

    a. senile   b. sanguine   c. reticent   d. secular

12. In the earliest movies, African American actors were restricted to playing racially _____ roles; but in the 1920s and 1930s pioneering African American filmmakers began to cast black actors in starring roles in Westerns, mysteries, comedies, and musicals.

    a. stipulate   b. stereotype   c. ruminate   d. revere

13. Every Friday at sundown, Jews begin the Sabbath by _____ reciting blessings over candles, wine, and bread.

    a. salient   b. strategy   c. ritual   d. rudiment

14. When it comes to planning and executing football plays, Miles, the sophomore quarterback, has proved to be the best _____ the team has had in years.

    a. stereotype   b. schism   c. strategy   d. stamina

15. The navy sometimes uses specially trained dolphins to detect man-made objects, such as mines, that _____ have planted in a harbor.

    a. retribution   b. schism   c. sabotage   d. strategy

16. Tecumseh, chief of the Shawnee Nation, expressed his _____ for the earth when he said, "The earth is my mother—and on her bosom I will recline."

    a. solace   b. stereotype   c. reverberate   d. revere

17. The human appendix is a _____ organ that serves no useful purpose and that may become inflamed and have to be removed.

    a. ritual   b. rudiment   c. salient   d. schism

18. From time to time in the history of all the world's great religions, serious differences of opinion have led to the formation of _____ cults.

    a. scapegoat   b. retribution   c. strategy   d. schism

19. In Dante Alighieri's "Inferno," the first part of *The Divine Comedy*, sinners suffer _____ justice, with punishments especially appropriate to their sins on earth.

    a. rudiment   b. retribution   c. ritual   d. syndrome

20. Some authors of whodunits give _____ to intricately constructed plots, but others emphasize complexity of character.

    a. sanctimonious   b. secular   c. salient   d. strident

Lesson 29

---

371. tac-it   *adjective*   tăs′-ĭt
[*tacitus* (Latin), "silent" ; from *tacere* (Latin), "be silent"]

Definition: Unspoken; implied or inferred.

Her friendly smile of recognition was a **tacit** invitation to join the little group of admirers surrounding her.

When my proposal was returned without comment of any kind, I took it as **tacit** approval to proceed.

"Don't you think that anybody who neglects to vote is in a way giving **tacit** support to the enemies of democracy?" she asked.

Though we were still angry with each other, we had a **tacit** agreement not to let our feelings show while our parents were present.

Phrases: a tacit assumption, tacit consent, a tacit warning, a tacit arrangement

Related Forms: (*noun*) tacitness; (*adverb*) tacitly

Synonyms: (*adjectives*) understood, implicit, wordless, unexpressed, unvoiced

Antonyms: (*adjectives*) explicit, express, expressed, specific

Related Phrase: a silent partner

372. tac-i-turn   *adjective*   tăs′-ə-tûrn
[*taciturnus* (Latin), "silent"; from *tacere, tacitus* (Latin), "be silent"]

Definition: Habitually untalkative.

My uncle is a **taciturn** man who rarely utters more than a word or two at a time.

Some of my friends are as talkative as magpies; others are definitely on the **taciturn** side.

Jim is such a **taciturn** fellow that I sometimes forget he is even in the room.

Related Forms: (*noun*) taciturnity; (*adverb*) taciturnly

Synonyms: (*adjectives*) closemouthed, tight-lipped, laconic, reserved, uncommunicative, reticent (Word 341)

Antonyms: (*adjectives*) talkative, loquacious, garrulous, prolix, voluble

Related Phrases: economy of words, give someone the silent treatment, a silent butler

373. tan·gi·ble   *adjective*   tăn'-jə-bəl
[*tangibilis, tangibile* (Late Latin), "able to be touched"; from *tangere* (Latin), "touch"]

Definition: Capable of being touched; real or concrete.

"I need to see **tangible** proof of your identity, such as a driver's license or passport," the postal clerk said, "before I can give you this registered letter."

One **tangible** result of the administration's economic policy was a slow but steady decline in the annual rate of inflation.

Phrases: a tangible reward, a tangible benefit, a tangible gain, tangible assets

Related Forms: (*nouns*) tangibility, tangibleness; (*adverb*) tangibly; (*adjective*) intangible

Usage Notes:
   a.   The legal term *tangible assets* refers to possessions that are capable of being valued in money or can be turned into cash. Similarly, the related term *tangibles* indicates material assets or property.

   b.   *Intangible* means "not capable of being perceived, identified, or defined precisely." In other words, something that is intangible is *elusive*. The plural noun *intangibles* refers to things that cannot be perceived or identified, especially what cannot be perceived by the senses. For example, a person's influence on the course of events is an intangible.

Synonyms: (*adjectives*) perceptible, discernible, palpable; material, actual, physical, solid

Antonyms: (*adjectives*) imperceptible, insubstantial, immaterial, untouchable; nebulous, hazy, vague

374. ten·a·ble   *adjective*   tĕn'-ə-bəl
[*tenable* (Old French), "capable of being held"; from *tenere* (Latin), "hold"]

Definition: Capable of being defended or maintained.

When the general realized that his forward positions were no longer **tenable**, he ordered an immediate withdrawal to more defensible ground.

Modern scientific research has shown that many 19th-century theories about the origins of language are no longer **tenable**.

Phrases: a tenable argument, a tenable idea, a tenable assumption

Related Forms: (*nouns*) tenableness, tenability; (*adverb*) tenably; (*adjective*) untenable

Synonyms: (*adjectives*) defensible, defendable, maintainable; irrefutable, incontestable, unassailable; plausible, believable, credible

Antonyms: (*adjectives*) indefensible, insupportable, unmaintainable; flawed, faulty; specious, implausible, questionable

375. ten-ta-tive   *adjective*   tĕn'-tə-tĭv

[*tentativus* (Medieval Latin), "provisional"; from *tentare, tentatus* (Latin), "try, attempt"]

Definition: In the nature of an experiment or trial; uncertain.

"We have made **tentative** plans to go to the shore next weekend," Randy reported, "but we will call off the trip if the weather turns bad."

A sort of **tentative**, almost apologetic smile spread over his face when I told him that I wasn't angry at him for making a first-class mess of the project.

Phrases: a tentative arrangement, tentative acceptance, a tentative schedule

Related Forms: (*noun*) tentativeness; (*adverb*) tentatively

Usage Note:
Occasionally *tentative* is used as a noun with the meaning "an experiment."

Synonyms: (*adjectives*) provisional, contingent, probationary, interim; experimental, exploratory; hesitant, unsure, doubtful; iffy

Antonyms: (*adjectives*) definite, settled, certain, finalized

Related Phrases: send up a trial balloon, a pilot program, subject to change, contingency plans, buy something on approval; finalize one's plans

376. thwart   *verb*   thwôrt

[*thwerr, thwert* (Old Norse), "oblique; across"]

Definition: To block or frustrate.

Those who dared attempt to **thwart** the bizzare schemes of the mad Roman emperor Caligula often paid for their actions with their lives and those of their families.

Our opponents' alert defense **thwarted** our efforts to score on a surprise end sweep.

"Watching too much TV has a tendency to **thwart** the natural growth of a child's reading abilities," the noted educator remarked.

Related Form: (*preposition*) athwart

Usage Note:
Athwart is an old preposition that means "across" or "crosswise." It sometimes occurs in older writing or literature—for example, in the phrase "a log lying *athwart* my path."

Synonyms: (*verbs*) foil, baffle (Word 54), neutralize, defeat, stymie, cripple; impede, inhibit

Antonyms: (*verbs*) promote, aid, help, abet (Word 2), encourage, advance, foster

Related Phrases: short-circuit something, nip something in the bud, take the wind out of someone's sails, clip someone's wings

482

377. tran·quil *adjective* trăn'-kwĭl
[*tranquillus* (Latin), "quiet"]

Definition: Peaceful and quiet; free of mental agitation.

After years of living amid the noise and hubbub of the city, we were delighted to discover the **tranquil** atmosphere of that sleepy country town.

At first I was almost hysterical with rage; but as I grew more **tranquil**, I began to perceive that the situation was not as bad as it seemed.

"Now that I have retired from the storms and stresses of the political arena," the ex-senator remarked, "my heart has become as **tranquil** as a country churchyard on an autumn afternoon."

Related Forms: (*nouns*) tranquility, tranquilness, tranquilizer; (*verb*) tranquilize

Phrase: domestic tranquility

Usage Note:
A *tranquilizer* is a drug that lessens anxiety or tension in a person or animal.

Synonyms: (*adjectives*) calm, serene, placid; cool, composed, self-possessed, unexcited, unperturbed; impassive, dispassionate

Antonyms: (*adjectives*) turbulent (Word 380), tumultuous, stormy, tempestuous, raucous; distraught, agitated, troubled, upset

Related Phrase: keep one's cool

378. trau·mat·ic *adjective* trô-măt'-ĭk *or* trou-măt'-ĭk
[*trauma* (Greek), "wound" + *ikos* (Greek), "relating to"]

Definition: So shocking as to produce a lasting psychological effect.

"Being lost in the woods for almost a day," Fred recalled, "was one of the most **traumatic** experiences of my childhood."

The sudden death or assassination of a great political leader usually has a **traumatic** effect on his or her followers.

The aftermath of the Civil War was probably as **traumatic** for most Southerners, black and white, as the war itself had been.

Related Forms: (*nouns*) trauma, traumatism; (*verb*) traumatize

Usage Note:
In medicine, *trauma* indicates a wound produced by sudden physical injury. In psychology, it refers to an emotional shock that produces substantial and lasting psychological damage. The plural of the word is either *traumas* or *traumata*.

Synonyms: (*adjectives*) shocking, paralyzing, jolting

Antonyms: (*adjectives*) beneficial, salutary, salubrious; uplifting, inspirational

379. trench-ant   *adjective*   trĕn'-chĕnt
[*trenchant* (Old French), "cutting"; from *trenchier* (Old French), "cut"]

Definition: Perceptive and forceful; cutting.

Dorothy Parker once dismissed an actress's performance of a certain role with the **trenchant** comment that she had run "the gamut of emotions from A to B."

Today's newspaper contains one of the most **trenchant** letters to the editor I have ever read.

Phrases: a trenchant reply, a trenchant pen, a trenchant imagination, a trenchant argument, a trenchant writer

Related Forms: (*noun*) trenchancy; (*adverb*) trenchantly

Synonyms: (*adjectives*) incisive, keen, acute; effective, cogent; caustic, mordant, biting

Antonyms: (*adjectives*) bland, pallid; obtuse, vacuous, vapid, inane

380. tur-bu-lent   *adjective*   tûr'-byə-lĕnt
[*turbulentus* (Latin), "stormy"; from *turba* (Latin), "turmoil, confusion"]

Definition: Violently agitated or disturbed; restless or unruly.

During a storm the normally calm waters of the lake become so **turbulent** that a small boat may easily founder.

He is well informed and has many interesting ideas, but his **turbulent** nature infuriates the people around him.

The years between 1789 and 1815 were a **turbulent** era in the history of Europe.

Related Forms: (*noun*) turbulence; (*adverb*) turbulently

Usage Note:
Do not confuse *turbulent* with the related adjective *turbid*, which means "muddy," "unclear," or "confused."

Synonyms: (*adjectives*) stormy, troubled, tumultuous, tempestuous

Antonyms: (*adjectives*) calm, peaceful, placid, tranquil (Word 377)

381. u-biq-ui-tous   *adjective*   yōō-bik'-wə-təs
[*ubiquitas* (Latin), "state of being everywhere"; from *ubique* (Latin), "everywhere"]

Definition: Being or seeming to be everywhere.

"I almost get the impression that Harry is **ubiquitous**," Roseann remarked. "No matter where or when there's a party, Harry's present."

Nowadays absolutely nothing seems to escape the **ubiquitous** eye of the closed-circuit surveillance camera.

Related Forms: (*nouns*) ubiquity, ubiquitousness

An airplane experiences turbulence during an electrical storm. The word *turbulence* is often used by pilots and other people connected with airplanes to indicate a highly irregular atmospheric condition produced by rapid changes in the speed and direction of the wind and the presence of up and down air currents.

Synonyms: (*adjectives*) omnipresent, pervasive, universal, ever-present

Antonyms: (*adjectives*) rare, scarce

Related Phrases: in short supply, as scarce as hen's teeth

382. **ur-bane** *adjective* ûr-bān′
[*urbanus* (Latin), "belonging to a city; refined"; from *urbs, urbis* (Latin), "city"]

Definition: Refined, elegant, and sophisticated in manner or style.

The American novelist Edith Wharton (1862–1937) usually wrote about the **urbane** gentlemen and elegant ladies who made up New York's social elite in the last quarter of the 19th century.

If these negotiations are to be successful, we need less emotionalism and more of the calm, **urbane** manner of a diplomat.

Related Forms: (*noun*) urbanity; (*adverb*) urbanely

Usage Note:
Be careful not to confuse *urbane* with its look-alike *urban*, which means "relating to, or characteristic of, the city." Synonyms of *urban* include *metropolitan* and *citified.*

Synonyms: (*adjectives*) suave, cosmopolitan, polished, genteel, smooth, bland, courtly, well-bred

Antonyms: (*adjectives*) crude, boorish, rude, discourteous, ill-bred, gauche

383. u-surp   *verb*   yōō-sûrp′   *or*   yōō-zûrp′

[*usurpare* (Latin), "take possession of something simply by using or occupying it"; from *usu* (Latin), "by use" + *rapere, raptus* (Latin), "seize"]

Definition: To seize a power, office, function, or the like without any legal right to do so.

In 1399, the Duke of Hereford **usurped** the English throne and set in motion a train of events that led to civil war 56 years later.

The legislators resisted the governor's attempts to **usurp** powers specifically granted to them by the state constitution.

I was decidedly miffed when my archrival attempted to **usurp** my place in my true love's heart.

Related Forms: (*nouns*) usurpation, usurper

Synonyms: (*verbs*) expropriate, arrogate; encroach, infringe; supplant, supersede

Related Phrases: a coup d'état, steal someone's thunder, steal the show, upstage someone, make inroads into

---

384. va-ga-ry   *noun*   vā′-gər-ē   *or*   və-gâr′-ē

[*vagari* (Latin), "wander"; from *vagus* (Latin), "meandering"]

Definition: A bizarre or eccentric idea, action, or condition.

Any decision to drop out of school and travel around the country is far too serious to be dismissed as a mere adolescent **vagary**.

Making a success of a small business connected with one of our beaches is unavoidably dependent on the **vagaries** of the weather.

"Say what you will," Steve remarked, "there's just no accounting for the **vagaries** of fashion."

Synonyms: (*nouns*) whim, caprice, peculiarity, quirk, crotchet, oddity, eccentricity

Related Phrases: a passing fancy, maggots in the brain, a fad, without rhyme or reason

---

385. ve-nal   *adjective*   vē′-nəl

[*venalis* (Latin), "for sale"]

Definition: Open to, or marked by, bribery or corruption.

Although President Ulysses S. Grant was personally incorruptible, he surrounded himself with **venal** politicians and financiers whose scandalous dealings rocked the nation.

Gaius Verres, governor of Sicily between 73 and 71 B.C., headed up one of the most **venal** and extortionate administrations ever imposed on a Roman province.

Related Form: (*noun*) venality

Usage Note:
Do not confuse *venal* with *venial* (note the *i*), which means "not serious enough to merit severe criticism" or "pardonable." For example, theologians speak of "a *venial* (minor) sin."

Synonyms: (*adjectives*) corruptible, bribable, mercenary (Word 266)

Antonyms: (*adjectives*) incorruptible, scrupulous, honest, upright

Phrases: on the take, grease someone's palm

Using the Words

Exercise I. Syllabication and Pronunciation

Syllabicate the following words correctly, and place the major stress mark (') after the syllable that is accented when the word is pronounced. Two answers are correct in one instance.

1. taciturn
2. tangible
3. tentative
4. traumatic
5. turbulent
6. ubiquitous
7. urbane
8. vagary
9. venal

Exercise II. Words Out of Context

In each of the following groups, select the item that best expresses the meaning of the numbered word at the left.

1. tacit
   a. laconic b. implicit c. general
   d. valuable e. doubtful

2. taciturn
   a. unprofitable b. unspoken c. unlikely
   d. uncommunicative e. unfortunate

3. tenable
   a. calm b. worthless c. experimental
   d. biting e. defendable

4. traumatic
   a. banal b. wealthy c. shocking
   d. faithful e. reliable

5. trenchant
   a. incisive b. specific c. muddy
   d. provisional e. inane

6. turbulent
   a. sunny b. cool c. humid d. rainy
   e. stormy

7. urbane
   a. prominent b. final c. suave
   d. affluent e. metropolitan

8. venal
   a. minor b. corruptible c. raucous
   d. sharp e. beneficial

Exercise III.   Completing Sentences

Complete each of the following sentences by selecting the most appropriate word from the group of words given below.

thwart	tentative	tranquil
tangible	vagary	traumatic
ubiquitous	venal	usurp

1. Camels may be a rare sight in the United States, but in the Sahara they are _____.

2. Farmers don't lead _____ lives, free of cares and worries; they are involved in a tough and competitive business.

3. "Since my vacation plans were only _____ anyway," the busy executive remarked, "I didn't mind changing them at the last minute."

4. Far from abetting his starry-eyed scheme to run off and join a traveling circus, I did everything in my power to _____ it.

5. The plot of the novel concerns an evil nobleman's attempt to murder a young king and _____ his throne.

6. Since stock prices fluctuate for all kinds of unexpected reasons, it is often difficult to account for the _____ of the market.

7. Though recent political polls indicate that support for candidate X has declined considerably, they also show that candidate Y has made _____ gains in popularity.

Exercise IV.   Synonyms and Antonyms

Classify each of the following pairs of words as **S** for **synonyms** or **A** for **antonyms**.

1. thwart—foil
2. trenchant—obtuse
3. usurp—seize
4. incorruptible—venal
5. loquacious—taciturn
6. defensible—tenable
7. tentative—provisional
8. tempestuous—tranquil
9. traumatic—paralyzing
10. boorish—urbane
11. quirk—vagary
12. tacit—explicit
13. tangible—concrete
14. turbulent—placid

Exercise V.   Word Roundup

1. Explain the difference between the words in each of the following pairs.

    a. venal—venial

    b. urban—urbane

2. Define each of the following foreign expressions used in present-day English and tell what language it comes from.

   a. gauche   b. coup d'état

3. With or without the aid of the dictionary, explain what each of the following means.

   a. a silent partner   e. tangible assets
   b. a silent butler   f. contingency plans
   c. a pilot program   g. maggots in the brain
   d. a tranquilizer   h. domestic tranquility

4. With or without the aid of a dictionary, explain what each of the following colorful expressions means.

   a. upstage someone   e. nip in the bud
   b. on the take   f. buy on approval
   c. keep one's cool   g. give someone the silent
   d. send up a trial balloon   treatment

Exercise VI.   Framing Sentences

A. Use each of the following words in an original illustrative sentence.

   1. tacit   4. tentative   7. trenchant
   2. tangible   5. tranquil   8. ubiquitous
   3. tenable   6. thwart   9. vagary

B. Give a **noun** form of each of the following words, and use it in an original illustrative sentence.

   1. taciturn   3. turbulent   5. usurp
   2. traumatic   4. urbane   6. venal

Dissecting the Words

Prefix

The Latin prefix **sub** or one of its variants appears in a great many common English words, including *subvert*, mentioned in Lesson 7. This prefix has a number of meanings, including:

a. "Under, below, or beneath," as in these words:

   subbasement—a story or floor below the main basement of a building

   subjugate—(sub +*jugum* [Latin], "yoke")—to conquer or subdue. Noun: *subjugation*

   subliminal (sub + *limen, liminis* [Latin], "threshold")—below the level of conscious perception. Noun: *sublimation*

   submerge (sub + *mergere* [Latin], "plunge")—to thrust fully under, or cover with, water; to hide from view

subordinate (*sub* + *ordinare, ordinatus* [Latin], "arrange in order")—
(*adjective*) secondary; (*noun*) a person who is inferior in rank or status to another person; (*verb*) to make inferior to. Noun: *subordination*

subpoena (Latin for "under penalty")—(*noun*) a legal document requiring a person to appear in a court to give testimony; (*verb*) to order or serve such a document

substratum (*sub* + *sternere, stratus* [Latin], "lie flat")—an underlying layer; the foundation or groundwork for something

subsume (*sub* + *sumere* [Latin], "take up")—to place in a more comprehensive category or under a more general heading

b. "Secondary in rank," as in these words:

subcommittee—a subordinate committee composed of some of the members of a larger committee

subculture—a distinct cultural group within the main culture

subdivide—to divide a part of something into smaller parts. Noun: *subdivision*

sublet—to rent property from someone who is himself or herself renting it from the owner

c. "Away" or "after," as in these words:

subdue (*sub*, "away" + *ducere, ductus* [Latin], "lead")—to conquer or defeat

subsequent (*sub*, "after" + *sequens, sequentis* [Latin], "following")—coming after something in time or position

d. "Down," as in these words:

subside (*sub* + *sidere* [Latin], "settle")—to sink, decrease, or abate

subsidy (*sub* + *sidere* [Latin], "settle")—financial assistance. Verb: *subsidize*

e. "Up from under," as in this word:

subsist (*sub* + *sistere* [Latin], "cause to stand")—to live or exist. (Note that this verb is often followed by the prepositions *on* or *by*.) Noun: *subsistance*

f. "Secretly," as in this word:

suborn (*sub* + *ornare* [Latin], "equip")—to induce a person to commit a wrong or illegal act. Noun: *subornation*

g. "Somewhat less than," as in these words:

subhuman—not fully human

subtropical—relating to areas adjacent to the tropics

Note that **sub** becomes **suc, suf, sug, sum, sup,** or **sur** before *c, f, g, m, p,* or *r,* respectively. **Sub** also sometimes becomes **sus** before *c, p,* or *t.* The process by which this happens is called *assimilation* (see page 57). Here are a few words illustrating these changes:

succumb (*sub*, "under" + *cumbere, cubitus* [Latin], "to lie under, give way, yield")—to yield or submit to; to give in to *suffice* (*sub*, "under" + *facere* [Latin], "do, make")—to meet present needs; to be equal to the intended task or function

suggest (*sub*, "underneath" + *gerere*, *gestus* [Latin], "carry")—to offer for consideration. Adjective: *suggestive*

summon (*sub*, "secretly" + *monere* [Latin], "warn, remind")—to send for or request. Noun: *summons*

supplant (*sub*, "up from under" + *planta* [Latin], "sole of the foot")—to take the place of; to oust

surreptitious (*sub*, "secretly" + *rapere* [Latin], "seize")—performed in secret or by stealth

susceptible (*sub*, "up from under" + *capere*, *captus* [Latin], "take")—readily subject to or influenced by. Noun: *susceptibility*

suspend (*sub*, "up from under" + *pendere* [Latin], "hang")—to hang up; to bar temporarily from a privilege or position

sustain (*sub*, "up from under" + *tenere* [Latin], "hold")—to maintain, support, or prolong; to affirm the validity of. Noun: *sustenance*

Roots

1. The Latin root **ten** (also spelled **tain** and **tin**) means "hold." It is used in a number of common English words, including *tenable*, studied in this lesson. Here are a few more useful words in which it appears:

retain (*re* [Latin], "back" + *tenere* [Latin], "hold")—to keep or hold back; to keep in mind or remember. Adjective: *retentive*. Noun: *retention*

maintain (*manu* [Latin], "by hand" + *tenere* [Latin], "hold")—to carry on or continue; to preserve or keep up. Noun: *maintenance*

sustenance (*sub* [Latin], "up from under" + *tenere* [Latin], "hold")—support for life or health, especially food or a means of livelihood

tenacity (*tenacitas* [Latin], "perseverance")—persistence or perseverance. Adjective: *tenacious*

pertinent (*per* [Latin], "thoroughly" + *tenens*, *tenentis* [Latin], "holding") —relevant. Noun: *pertinency*. Verb: *pertain*

detain (*de* [Latin], "away" + *tenere* [Latin], "hold")—to delay; to hold in custody. Noun: *detention*

tenet (literally "he, she, or it holds")—a belief or doctrine held by a person or group

2. The Latin root **tang**, **tact**, meaning "touch," is the source of the word *tangible*, studied in this lesson. Other useful English words in which this root appears are given below. As these words indicate, **tang**, **tact** has a number of variant forms, including **tig**, **tag**, **ting**, and **tain**.

tact (*tactus* [Latin], "sense of touch")—the ability to do or say the kindest or most appropriate thing. Adjectives: *tactful*, *tactless*

tactile (*tactus* [Latin], "sense of touch" + *ilis*, *ile* [Latin], "pertaining to") —perceptible to the sense of touch; used for feeling

tangent (*tangens*, *tangentis* [Latin], "touching")—a line touching but not intersecting another line. Phrase: *go off at* (or *on*) *a tangent tangential*—merely touching or only superficially connected with

contiguous (*cum* [Latin], "with" + *tangere* [Latin], "touch")—having the same edge or boundary as something else; adjacent. Noun: *contiguity*

contingent (*cum* [Latin], "with" + *tangens, tangentis* [Latin], "touching")—dependent on events or developments that have not yet occurred; possible. (Note that this adjective is often followed by the prepositions *on* or *upon*.) Noun: *contingency*

contagious (*cum* [Latin], "with" + *tangere* [Latin], "touch")—transmitted by direct contact. Noun: *contagion*

attain (*ad* [Latin], "to, as far as" + *tangere* [Latin], "touch, reach")—to gain, reach, or accomplish. Noun: *attainment*

Exercise

1. With or without the aid of a dictionary, define the following words using the Latin prefix *sub*, and explain what the prefix means in each.

   a. subjugate   d. subsist   g. subtitle
   b. subsequent   e. suborn   h. subsidy
   c. subdivide   f. subpoena   i. subhuman

2. With or without the aid of a dictionary, explain the meaning of each of the following phrases involving an *italicized* word derived from the Latin root *ten*.

   a. a *retentive* memory   c. have *tenure*
   b. a *tenacious* grip   d. a *retainer* fee

3. With or without the aid of a dictionary, define each of the following words using the Latin root *tang, tact* (or one of its variants).

   a. tactful   d. tactile   g. contiguous
   b. attainment   e. tangential   h. intangibles
   c. contagious   f. contingency   i. tactless

Walter W. Skeat

To Walter W. Skeat (1853–1912) goes the credit for creating a general interest in linguistics in both England and the United States. In 1878, Skeat became Professor of Anglo-Saxon at Cambridge, a post he retained for the rest of his life. His most important work was probably *The Etymological Dictionary of the English Language*, which first appeared in 1882. It has been said that Skeat contributed more to a sound knowledge of English linguistics than any other scholar of his time.

Working with Context Clues

Complete each of the following two-word omissions by selecting the pair of words that make the best sense in the passage as a whole. Underline the clue or clues.

1. Most dictators don't speak reasonably or calmly to their people; instead they _____ them. Far from creating a(n) _____ atmosphere, the dictator's words and manner usually instill fear and anxiety.

   a. instigate . . . urbane
   b. revere . . . turbulent
   c. harangue . . . tranquil
   d. deceive . . . blithe

2. Novels such as George Orwell's famous fable *1984*, written in 1949, dramatized the fear that an ever-present and prying central government, the _____ Big Brother, would _____ every aspect of a citizen's life.

   a. sordid . . . sabotage
   b. ubiquitous . . . scrutinize
   c. implacable . . . flaunt
   d. fatuous . . . exploit

3. I really appreciate the _____ that my grandmother left me in her will, and I intend to honor her _____ wish that I look after my younger brother, even though she never made this request explicitly.

   a. kudos . . . poignant
   b. retribution . . . strident
   c. propensity . . . mundane
   d. legacy . . . tacit

4. Many men who served in World War I suffered from a(n) _____ that was then called *shell shock*. Their symptoms were a result of the _____ events they experienced in the deadly trenches of France.

   a. anomaly . . . benign
   b. stereotype . . . drastic
   c. obsession . . . pernicious
   d. syndrome . . . traumatic

5. After the fall of Communism, corruption and lawlessness spread rapidly in Russia. In this _____ atmosphere, many ordinary citizens felt free to _____ the law.

   a. venal . . . flout
   b. secular . . . rescind
   c. precarious . . . revere
   d. mundane . . . thwart

6. Although there is often no _____ monitoring of security at many ATM sites, there is usually hidden electronic _____ by video camera.

   a. efficient . . . repercussion
   b. prodigious . . . medium
   c. ostensible . . . surveillance
   d. protracted . . . confrontation

7. In times of trouble or loss, a comforting phone call from a friend can be a very concrete source of _____. At such times, we need _____ signs that we are loved.

   a. solace . . . tangible
   b. remorse . . . ostensible
   c. empathy . . . esoteric
   d. anarchy . . . fulsome

8. In order to avoid a ———————— between the conservatives and the liberals, the party leader proposed a ——————— agreement that he firmly believed would buy time and avoid a lasting split.

   a. boycott . . . strategic   **c.** scapegoat . . . feasible
   b. schism . . . tentative   **d.** recrimination . . . graphic

9. When developing a marketing plan, executives want a _____ that will not only promote sales of their products but will also _____ their competitors' plans.

   a. paradox . . . stipulate   **c.** consensus . . . abet
   b. strategy . . . thwart   **d.** discourse . . . discomfit

10. Although my uncle was a(n) _____ man who spoke very little in company, he was a(n) _____ letter writer, often producing as many as ten lengthy letters a day. Curiously, most of these letters were addressed to friends and acquaintances with whom he would rarely share more than a word or two in public.

   a. urbane . . . agile   **c.** affable . . . diligent
   b. tranquil . . . dilatory   **d.** taciturn . . . prolific

Enriching the Lesson

Exercise I.   Is There a Doctor in the House?

The word *trauma*, discussed in this lesson, now has a wide range of applications, but its first use was in medical science. This is just one example of how medical terminology yields words of general application to enrich and enlarge the vocabulary resources of English. A few other words of this type are listed below. With or without the aid of a dictionary, define each, and give its etymology.

1. diagnosis	6. convalescence	11. fatal
2. symptom	7. psychosomatic	12. prognosis
3. therapy	8. organic	13. inoculate
4. pathology	9. epidemic	14. hysteria
5. aggravate	10. debilitate	15. cancerous

Now complete each of the following sentences by selecting the right word from the list of words given above.

1. My point is that if we borrow money to meet our immediate obligations, we will only _____ our long-range problems.

2. His style of oratory, which you evidently admire so much, seems to depend on building up emotion to the point of _____.

3. The crisis has been overcome; the immediate danger is past. Now begins the long period of _____.

4. It is our collective task in the years ahead to clear the social organism of the _____ growth of racial, ethnic, and religious prejudice.

5. This neighborhood has been going downhill rapidly, and it shows all the _____ of developing into a full-fledged slum.

6. It is difficult to predict how such a simple and isolated society will react to a(n) _____ of ideas and resources from the outside world.

Exercise II. Some Tricky Words

Some English words are very deceptive. They seem to mean one thing but actually mean something else. Anyone, therefore, trying to guess at their proper meaning on the basis of their appearance is likely to go far afield.

Below is a list of such tricky words that merit your close attention. First indicate what you think each of these words means, based on the way it looks. Then, with or without the aid of a dictionary, define each. Finally, choose any **five** of the words, and for each compose an original illustrative sentence.

1. scarify	6. fulsome	11. adventitious
2. histrionic	7. enjoin	12. momentum
3. quizzical	8. officious	13. egress
4. noisome	9. contentious	14. bombination
5. querulous	10. meretricious	15. irenic

Exercise III. Expanding Your Word Power

The words listed below are not on the Basic Word List, but they were mentioned in passing in one form or another, in Lesson 29. All of them would make useful additions to your working vocabulary. Define each, give its etymology, list **two** synonyms and **two** antonyms (where possible), and use in an original illustrative sentence.

1. provisional	6. neutralize	11. omnipresent
2. voluble	7. serene	12. cosmopolitan
3. palpable	8. raucous	13. arrogate
4. irrefutable	9. inspiration	14. crotchet
5. interim	10. mordant	15. upright

Lesson 30

---

386. ve-neer   *noun and verb*   və-nēr'

[*Furnier* (German), "veneer"; from *fournir* (French), "furnish"]

Definition:

a. (*noun*) A thin layer of fine material put on the surface of something in order to make it more attractive or cover defects; a deceptively attractive outward appearance.

The table was made of inexpensive pine that had been covered with a thin **veneer** of fine walnut.

Beneath the **veneer** of kindness and concern, I recognized the amoral opportunist I had known so long ago.

b. (*verb*) To cover something with a veneer of fine material.

Aluminum siding is one of the most popular materials with which Americans **veneer** their houses.

Synonyms: (*nouns*) facing, facade, coating, gloss, sheen, overlay, varnish, lacquer, glaze; (*verbs*) overlay, laminate, whitewash, glaze, gild; mask, screen

Related Phrases: a false facade, a false front

387. ven-er-a-ble   *adjective*   věn'-ēr-ə-bəl

[*venerabilis, venerabile* (Latin), "revered"; from *venerari, veneratus* (Latin), "revere" + *abilis, abile* (Latin), "able to"]

Definition: Worthy of reverence or respect because of character, position, age, or religious or historical associations.

Though he had retired from public life many years before, the **venerable** old statesman was still consulted on matters of national concern.

I am glad to see that yet another **venerable** old building in this city has been declared a landmark.

"The **venerable** oak trees that line the broad avenue to the big house," the guide said, "have seen a good deal of Southern history played out beneath them."

Related Forms: (*nouns*) venerableness, venerability, veneration; (*verb*) venerate

Usage Note:

Venerable is used as a title of respect for anyone who has achieved the first degree of sainthood in the Roman Catholic Church—for example, the *Venerable* Bede.

Synonyms: (*adjectives*) time-honored, revered, esteemed, august, eminent, hallowed, hoary

Antonyms: (*adjectives*) spurned, scorned, reviled

Related Phrases: as old as the hills, hallowed ground, hallowed halls, an elder statesman

The Venerable Bede

One of the most important historians of the Old English period was a Benedictine monk whom we now call the Venerable Bede (672?–735). Bede spent the whole of his adult life in the monasteries of Wearmouth and Jarrow in northern England. One of the most learned men of his time, he wrote treatises on all sorts of theological, historical, and scientific subjects. His most famous work is *The Ecclesiastical History of the English Nation*. Originally written in Latin but soon translated into Old English, this book contains a full and reliable account of the growth of Christianity in England and the flowering of Anglo-Saxon culture. It is still an indispensable source for the history of England between 597 and 731. Bede was named a Doctor of the Church in 1899.

388. ve-rac-i-ty   *noun*   və-răs'-ə-tē

[*veracitas* (Medieval Latin), "truth"; from *verus* (Latin), "true"]

Definition: Habitual adherence to the truth; accuracy.

My judgment may be open to question, but I have told you the facts as I know them, so you have no reason to doubt my **veracity**.

The 18th-century English poet Thomas Gray once wrote that any fool could compose a valuable book if he would only put down what he had heard or seen with **veracity**.

Phrases: unshakable veracity, the veracity of a witness

Related Forms: (*adjective*) veracious; (*noun*) veraciousness

Synonyms: (*nouns*) truthfulness, honesty, integrity, reliability, credibility; authenticity, genuineness

Antonyms: (*nouns*) dishonesty, falsity, spuriousness, deceptiveness; untrustworthiness

Related Phrase: in vino veritas

389. ver-sa-tile   *adjective*   vûr'-sə-təl *or* vûr'-sə-tīl

[*versatilis, versatile* (Latin), "revolving"; from *versare* (Latin), "turn" + *abilis, abile* (Latin), "able to"]

Definition: Capable of doing many things or serving many functions.

A truly **versatile** actor or actress is at home in many different types of theater, from tragedy and drama to comedy and farce.

"This company produces a **versatile** line of products designed for a wide range of uses in the home and office," the president of the corporation boasted.

Phrases: a versatile player, a versatile speaker, a versatile painter, a versatile garment, a versatile material

Related Forms: (*nouns*) versatility, versatileness

Synonyms: (*adjectives*) all-around, all-purpose, many-sided, multipurpose; flexible, adaptable, resourceful

Antonyms: (*adjectives*) single-purpose; unadaptable, unresourceful

Related Phrases: all-purpose flour, an all-around athlete, all-purpose wear, a utility infielder

390. ve-to   *noun and verb*   vē'-tō

[*veto* (Latin), "I forbid"; from *vetare* (Latin), "forbid"]

Definition:

a.   (*noun*) The right or power of the chief executive to reject measures approved by the legislative body; any authoritative prohibition.

"Even if the legislation is approved by both houses of Congress," the senator observed, "a presidential **veto** is sure to prevent it from becoming law."

The principal's **veto** put a quick end to student council plans to eliminate the school dress code.

b.   (*verb*) To prevent a bill from becoming law by exercising the right of veto; to prohibit or reject.

Though the British monarch still possesses the power to **veto** bills passed by Parliament, no king or queen has actually exercised the right since the reign of Queen Anne (1702–1714).

I had planned to travel across the country this summer, but my parents **vetoed** the idea.

Phrases: a pocket veto, the veto power, a veto message

Synonyms: (*nouns*) rejection, refusal, interdiction; (*verbs*) kill, quash, turn down, forbid, interdict, rule out

Antonyms: (*nouns*) approval, consent, sanction; (*verbs*) approve, ratify, sanction

Related Phrases: turn thumbs down to, say nix to; give something one's blessing, give something the green light (*or* go-ahead)

An American president signs a bill into law. The president has the right to veto legislation passed by Congress and return it (with a statement of his or her objections) to the house in which it originated. The bill can then be repassed over the president's veto by a two-thirds vote of both houses of Congress.

391. **vie** *verb* vī

[*envier* (Old French), "challenge"; from *invitare* (Latin), "invite"]

Definition: To struggle for superiority with; to contend with.

Having recovered from a crushing defeat in World War II, Japan went on to **vie** with the world's leading manufacturing countries for dominance in the electronics and automobile markets.

Three teams are now **vying** with one another for possession of first place in the American League East.

Synonyms: (*verbs*) compete, contest

Related Phrases: neck and neck; nolo contendere

392. **vin-dic-tive** *adjective* vĭn-dĭk'-tĭv

[*vindicta* (Latin), "vengeance" + *ivus*, a Latin suffix roughly meaning "tending toward" or "performing"]

Definition: Inclined to seek revenge; intended to inflict pain or harm.

Though I am by no means a **vindictive** person, I sometimes find it very difficult not to retaliate for a particularly nasty insult.

Related Forms: (*noun*) vindictiveness; (*adverb*) vindictively

Synonyms: (*adjectives*) vengeful, revengeful, retaliatory, malevolent, spiteful, hostile

Antonyms: (*adjectives*) magnanimous, forgiving, conciliatory

Related Phrases: bear a grudge; bury the hatchet, let bygones be bygones

393. vi·ti·ate   *verb*   vĭsh'-ē-āt

[*vitiare, vitiatus* (Latin), "injure"; from *vitium* (Latin), "defect, flaw"]

Definition: To impair the quality, force, or value of; to debase.

Even though the effect of the article was somewhat **vitiated** by erroneous statistics and garbled quotations, the point it was making was sound.

"Be careful," the elder statesman told the would-be presidential candidate. "Every time you make a wrong choice or take a questionable stand, you **vitiate** your influence in the party."

Related Form: (*noun*) vitiation

Synonyms: (*verbs*) mar, poison, taint, contaminate, reduce, lower, lessen, weaken, depreciate, dilute, tarnish

Antonyms: (*verbs*) strengthen, buttress (Word 73), bolster, reinforce, promote, brace

Related Phrase: feet of clay

Feet of Clay

One of the most interesting expressions that present-day English has derived from the Bible is *feet of clay*. The expression comes from the Old Testament Book of Daniel. Nebuchadnezzar II, the conqueror-king of Babylon from 605 to 562 B.C., was troubled by a bad dream in which he saw a statue of himself. The Bible describes this statue as follows: "This image's head was of fine gold, its chest and arms of silver, its stomach and thighs of brass, its legs of iron, and its feet partly of iron and partly of clay." In the dream, a stone thrown by some unseen supernatural force (*i.e.,* God) hits the feet of the statue and causes it to collapse and smash to smithereens on the pavement. Daniel explains that this is a vision of the eventual destruction of Nebuchadnezzar's kingdom as the result of some fatal flaw (the feet of clay) in one of his successors. By extension, the expression *feet of clay* has now come to mean "*any* fatal personal flaw that proves to be a person's undoing."

394. vol-a-tile   *adjective*   vŏl'-ə-təl

[*volare, volatus* (Latin), "fly" + *ilis, ile* (Latin), "tending to"]

Definition:
    a. Evaporating readily at normal temperatures or pressure levels.

       Gases such as argon and helium are not very active chemically, but ammonia is extremely **volatile**.

    b. Changeable and potentially explosive.

       "I feel as though we're sitting on a powder keg," the diplomat confessed in reference to the **volatile** situation in that troubled area of the world.

       I think that "having a short fuse" aptly describes his **volatile** temperament.

Related Forms: (*nouns*) volatility, volatileness

Synonyms: (*adjectives*) volcanic, heated, supercharged; mercurial, erratic

Antonyms: (*adjectives*) stable, static, constant, settled; stagnant, torpid, sluggish, inert, quiescent, dormant; phlegmatic

Related Phrases: a short fuse, a hot spot

---

395. wane   *verb and noun*   wān

[*wanen* (Middle English), "decrease"; from *wanian* (Old English), "diminish"]

Definition:
    a. (*verb*) To decrease gradually in size, extent, power, or intensity.

       During the 19th century it was literally true that the sun did not set nor the full moon **wane** on the British Empire.

       As their infatuation with one another **waned**, they found themselves making excuses for not getting together as often as before.

    b. (*noun*) A gradual decline or decrease.

       "If the president's popularity continues on the **wane**," the senator remarked, "he may well lose the next election."

Usage Note:
Be careful not to confuse the verb *wane* with the adjective *wan* (pronounced wŏn), which means "pale or colorless." Two other words with which *wane* is sometimes confused are *wain* (a large heavy cart used in farming) and *vane* (a device for showing the direction of the wind).

Synonyms: (*verbs*) slacken, subside, dim, diminish, abate, taper off, ebb, fade, peter out, dwindle; (*nouns*) diminution, weakening, falloff, fading

Antonyms: (*verbs*) wax, increase, intensify, grow, swell, mushroom, expand, augment; (*nouns*) increase, augmentation, growth, expansion, increment, addition, accretion

Related Phrases: an ebb tide, a recessional

396. **wrath** *noun* răth

[*wraeththu* (Old English), "anger"; from *wrath* (Old English), "angry"]

Definition: Intense anger.

"My father's **wrath** will know no bounds when he sees the damage I have done to the family car," Shelly moaned.

In a blistering tirade, the old prophet called down the **wrath** of God on those who had offended against His laws.

The easternmost tip of Cuba was the first populated area to feel the **wrath** of the hurricane.

Related Forms: (*adjective*) wrathful; (*noun*) wrathfulness

Usage Note:
Be careful not to confuse the noun *wrath* with its look-alike *wraith* (pronounced răth), which means "a specter or apparition."

Synonyms: (*nouns*) rage, fury, indignation, ire, choler, spleen

Antonyms: (*nouns*) favor, blessing, approval, pleasure

Related Phrase: in high dudgeon

397. **yoke** *noun and verb* yōk

[*geoc* (Old English), "yoke"]

Definition:
a. (*noun*) A wooden frame joining a pair of oxen or other draft animals together at the neck; any form or symbol of bondage or subjection.

The barn had been turned into a museum of all kinds of old-fashioned implements and devices used in farming, including flails, **yokes**, and other interesting items.

In 1776, the 13 American colonies cast off their **yoke** of subjection and declared themselves free and independent of Great Britain.

b. (*verb*) To join or bond together.

Many of the pioneers crossed the Great Plains in Conestoga wagons drawn by pairs of oxen **yoked** together at the neck.

A remarkable collaboration in the composition of light operas and other kinds of musical entertainments has forever **yoked** the names *Gilbert* and *Sullivan.*

Phrases: a yoke of oxen, the yoke of oppression

Usage Note:
In the phrase *a yoke of oxen*, sometimes encountered in older literature, the word *yoke* means "pair."

Synonyms: (*nouns*) harness, collar, oxbow; (*verbs*) hitch, link, harness, couple, unite

Antonyms: (*verbs*) sunder, separate, disconnect, dissociate, detach, split, divide

Conestoga wagons drawn by yokes of oxen brought the early pioneers into the fertile farmlands of the Great Plains.

398. **zany**   *noun and adjective*   zā'-nē

[*zanni* (Italian), "buffoon," a variant of *Gianni* (Italian), "Johnny," the pet form of *Giovanni* (Italian), "John," the name of the clownish servant in early Italian comedies]

Definition:
 a.   (*noun*) A comical person given to outlandish behavior; a buffoon.

It disturbed me to watch a person of such taste and intelligence assuming the role of a vulgar **zany**.

 b.   (*adjective*) Ludicrously comic, bizarre, or absurd.

I still enjoy watching the **zany** antics of old-time movie clowns such as the Marx Brothers or Abbott and Costello.

Whenever a party starts to get dull, you can count on their **zany** behavior to liven things up.

Related Form: (*noun*) zaniness

Synonyms: (*nouns*) clown, fool, prankster; (*adjectives*) ridiculous, laughable, hilarious, ludicrous, inane; wacky, goofy, loony

Antonyms: (*adjectives*) sensible, serious, proper, staid, sober

Related Phrases: play the fool; high jinks; a straight man

503

399. zeal   *noun*   zēl

[*zelos* (Greek), "fervor, enthusiasm"]

Definition: Enthusiastic devotion to something; fervor.

"In our **zeal** to improve the quality of life in the United States," the speaker declared, "let us not blindly discard old ideas and institutions simply because they are old."

Related Forms: (*nouns*) zealot, zealotry; (*adjective*) zealous; (*adverb*) zealously

Synonyms: (*nouns*) ardor, gusto, eagerness, passion, intensity, alacrity, vigor, enthusiasm, relish, keenness, rapture, ecstasy

Antonyms: (*nouns*) apathy (Word 32), indifference, listlessness, unconcern, nonchalance

Related Phrase: gung ho

Masada

Zealot

The Zealots were a group of fervently devout Jews who organized themselves into a sort of political party or action group during the reign of Herod the Great, King of Judaea (37–4 B.C.). They derived their name from their unswerving devotion to orthodox Judaism as prescribed by the Torah, the scroll containing the first five books of the Bible. (The Torah was used for instruction during services at a synagogue.) The Zealots opposed the secularizing tendencies of Herod and other contemporary Jewish leaders. They also detested the Romans, who controlled Palestine at the time, and frequently caused minor revolts and other problems for them. After a large-scale Jewish revolt was put down in A.D. 70, a group of Zealots fled to Masada, a fortress atop an impregnable rock formation overlooking the Dead Sea. There they held out against the Romans for several years. When the Romans were on the point of taking the place, the Zealots chose to kill themselves rather than submit to the hated foreign overlords. It is from the activities of this 1st-century religious group that present-day English has derived the word *zealot*, meaning "anyone excessively or fanatically committed to some cause, idea, or belief."

400. **ze-nith**   *noun*   zē'-nĭth

[*zenit* (Old Spanish), "apex"; from *samt ar-ra's* (Arabic), "way over the head"]

Definition:
  a. The point of a celestial sphere that is directly above the observer and vertically opposite the extreme point below.

> We knew that it was close to noon because the sun was almost at its **zenith.**

  b. The highest point or state of something.

> Historians agree that Rome reached the **zenith** of her power during the reigns of the "Five Good Emperors" in the 2nd century of the Christian era.

> "If I am indeed at the **zenith** of my creative powers now," the world-famous author ruefully thought to himself, "there is no place for me to go from here but down."

Synonyms: (*nouns*) summit, apex, apogee, peak, acme, culmination, climax, pinnacle

Antonyms: (*nouns*) nadir, perigee

Using the Words

Exercise I.   Parts of Speech

Indicate the part of speech of each of the following words. In some cases, two answers are correct.

1. veneer	4. veto	7. volatile
2. veracity	5. vie	8. wane
3. versatile	6. vindictive	9. zany

Exercise II.   Words in Phrases

In each of the following, select the item that best expresses the meaning of the *italicized* word in the introductory phrase.

1. a *veneer* of respectability
   facade b. wealth c. goal d. lack e. history

2. a *vindictive* attitude
   a. puzzling b. foolish c. healthy d. modern
   e. spiteful

3. a very *volatile* situation
   a. heartwarming b. explosive c. curious d. ordinary
   e. stable

4. *vitiate* the effect of the speech
   a. analyze b. confirm c. impair d. measure
   e. assess

5. a *yoke* around their necks
   a. jewel   b. oxbow   c. medal   d. sign   e. scarf

6. a *zany* thing to do
   a. sensible   b. costly   c. sad   d. ridiculous   e. thoughtful

7. the *zeal* of her followers
   a. fervor   b. age   c. intelligence   d. background
   e. number

Exercise III.   Completing Sentences

Complete each of the following sentences by selecting the appropriate word from the group of words given below. Use each word only once.

zenith	vie	veracity
veto	venerable	yoke
wane	versatile	wrath

1. Toward the end of his life the champion wrestler's fabulous strength _____ to the point where he could hardly walk.

2. All through high school, Laura and Peter _____ energetically for first place in their class.

3. "Only a trial in a court of law can establish the _____ of the charges leveled at my client," the lawyer remarked.

4. A utility infielder has to be a _____ player because he is a jack-of-all-trades on the baseball diamond.

5. Though Spain had been at the _____ of her power during the 16th century, the 17th century saw the beginning of a long, slow decline in the country's fortunes.

6. The school I went to was a _____ old institution with a long and cherished history of outstanding accomplishment in the field of secondary education.

7. The countless religious ceremonies that the ancient Romans performed during the year were designed to gain the favor of the gods and turn away their _____.

8. "The president is still trying to decide whether to sign or _____ that bill," the aide reported.

Exercise IV.   Synonyms and Antonyms

A.   In each of the following groups, select the **two** words that are most nearly **synonymous**.

1. a. hallowed   b. emaciated   c. revered   d. dilapidated

2. a. equitable   b. flexible   c. culpable   d. adaptable

3. a. complain b. compete c. contend d. confer
4. a. mar b. collect c. repeal d. impair
5. a. rage b. fury c. terror d. delight

Now, for each pair of synonyms you have selected, supply a word from the Basic Word List for this lesson (Words 386–400) that means **the same** or **almost the same** thing.

B. In each of the following, select the item that is most nearly **opposite** in meaning to the numbered word at the left.

1. veto
    a. boycott b. sanction c. permeate
    d. compete e. rescind

2. veracity
    a. antiquity b. immunity c. sincerity
    d. equanimity e. falsity

3. wane
    a. buff b. polish c. wax d. varnish
    e. glaze

4. zany
    a. obvious b. weird c. expensive d. sensible
    e. ruthless

5. zenith
    a. nadir b. anathema c. kudos d. plethora
    e. consensus

Exercise V. Word Roundup

1. Explain the difference in meaning between the words in each of the following pairs:

    a. wan—wane b. wrath—wraith

2. What is *a pocket veto?*

3. Who were the *Zealots,* and how are they connected with the present-day meaning of the word *zealot?*

4. With or without the aid of a dictionary or other reference book, define each of the following:

    a. a hot spot d. an ebb tide
    b. a recessional e. a short fuse
    c. high jinks f. an elder statesman

5. With or without the aid of a dictionary or other reference book, explain what each of the following means:

    a. in high dudgeon b. neck and neck c. gung ho

6. With or without the aid of a dictionary or other reference book, explain the meaning of each of the following colorful expressions:

    a. bear a grudge against d. play the fool
    b. turn thumbs down to e. feet of clay
    c. bury the hatchet f. give something the green light

Exercise VI.   Framing Sentences

A. Use each of the following words in an original sentence.

1. veneer	4. vie	7. yoke
2. venerable	5. vitiate	8. zany
3. veto	6. wane	9. zealous

B. Give a **noun** form of each of these words, and use it in an original illustrative sentence.

1. versatile   2. vindictive   3. volatile

C. Give an **adjective** form of each of these words, and use it in an original illustrative sentence.

1. veracity   2. wrath   3. zeal

Completing Verbal Analogies

Complete the following analogies.

Group A

1. **lawyer : legal** =
   a. nautical : naval
   b. policeman : criminal
   c. athlete : intellectual
   d. chef : culinary
   e. wraith : wrath

2. **deluge : water** =
   a. avalanche : wind
   b. holocaust : fire
   c. hurricane : ice
   d. snow : tornado
   e. blizzard : air

3. **sponge : impervious** =
   a. glass : brittle
   b. wall : rigid
   c. umbrella : porous
   d. belt : pliable
   e. circuitous : detour

4. **sword : brandish** =
   a. string : kite
   b. flag : wave
   c. inflate : deflate
   d. airplane : train
   e. unfurl : banner

5. **malevolent : unfavorable** =
   a. deft : favorable
   b. undaunted : unfavorable
   c. unfavorable : officious
   d. ominous : favorable
   e. scrupulous : unfavorable

Group B

6. **pinnacle : high ::**
   a. strait : wide
   b. plateau : steep
   c. haven : level
   d. abyss : deep
   e. flat : mountain

7. **bear : hibernate ::**
   a. horse : mare
   b. yoke : ox
   c. scavenger : jackal
   d. cow : ruminate
   e. camel : giraffe

8. **fathom : depth ::**
   a. width : meter
   b. bushel : height
   c. knot : speed
   d. inch : yard
   e. length : breadth

9. **small : infinitesimal ::**
   a. large : small
   b. poor : beggar
   c. big : colossal
   d. wide : deep
   e. mansion : opulent

10. **poignant : sadden ::**
   a. nondescript : whet
   b. droll : amuse
   c. frighten : zany
   d. comfort : solace
   e. innocuous : appall

Working with Context Clues

Complete each of the following two-word omissions by selecting the pair of words that make the best sense in the passage as a whole. If necessary, consult a dictionary for the meaning of any word with which you are not familiar. Underline the clue or clues that led you to choose your answer.

1. On the surface, some actors may appear very breezy and _____ but behind the carefree _____, they may actually be so insecure that they must always pretend to be someone other than who they are.

   a. blithe . . . veneer
   b. bland . . . affectation
   c. effete . . . effrontery
   d. benign . . . duplicity

2. In their summations, the prosecuting and defense attorneys _____ for the minds of the jury. They compete to make their final arguments as _____ as possible, hoping to compel the jury to come up with a verdict in favor of their client through the force of their reasoning and evidence.

   a. vie . . . trenchant
   b. collaborate . . . cogent
   c. persevere . . . nebulous
   d. ruminate . . . sanguine

3. In Shakespeare's plays, there is often a parallel between what is happening in nature and in society. For example, the heavens grow _____ when the social order is disturbed by ambitious upstarts who are trying to _____ legitimate authority.

   a. tranquil . . . justify
   b. lucid . . . discomfit
   c. bleak . . . circumvent
   d. turbulent . . . usurp

4. One aftereffect of parents losing their tempers is that children learn fear but not self-control. Parents who wish to avoid that unfortunate _____ should try to control their own _____.

   a. irony . . . zeal
   b. repercussion . . . wrath
   c. nuance . . . prowess
   d. exigency . . . malice

5. In their eagerness to appear upright and moral, some politicians come across as _____, especially when their new-found-piety begins to _____ right after election day.

   a. fatuous . . . augment
   b. boorish . . . deviate
   c. sanctimonious . . . wane
   d. fulsome . . . fluctuate

6. Some Communists were so fired up with enthusiasm for their atheistic doctrine that they destroyed church property and mistreated members of the clergy. It was their revolutionary _____ that led them to commit such _____ acts.

   a. obsession . . . predatory
   b. reprisal . . . brash
   c. zeal . . . sacrilegious
   d. addiction . . . volatile

7. A jury would probably doubt the _____ of a witness who had been convicted of lying under oath. They might reason that a person willing to _____ himself once was capable of lying again.

   a. plagiarism . . . embarrass
   b. veracity . . . perjure
   c. duplicity . . . censure
   d. equanimity . . . curtail

8. Those who ponder endlessly over every decision are bound to _____ their energy and sap their ability to act. Their tendency to _____ paralyzes rather than empowers them.

   a. flaunt . . . defer
   b. propitiate . . . persevere
   c. vitiate . . . ruminate
   d. usurp . . . relent

9. A(n) _____ personality such as Shakespeare's Iago never lets go of an injury or an insult until he retaliates, and often the _____ is more harmful and cruel than the original injury.

   a. eminent . . . repercussion
   b. vindictive . . . reprisal
   c. exemplary . . . bravado
   d. formidable . . . malice

10. It is a basic legal principle that one party to a contract cannot cancel its provisions. On the contrary, all parties must agree to _____ the terms of a contract before this _____ of contract law can be set aside.

   a. rescind . . . rudiment
   b. arbitrate . . . vagary
   c. stipulate . . . strategy
   d. promulgate . . . yoke

Enriching the Lesson

Exercise I.   Misusing Words: A Look Back

In earlier lessons we have referred to various ways of using language that are usually considered weak or ineffective, even if they are not flatly wrong. These language flaws may be classified under the following headings:

Clichés (= **C**)
Malapropisms (= **M**)
Euphemisms (= **E**)
Inappropriate Connotation (= **I**)
Gobbledygook (= **G**)

At this point, you will do well to review the sections in which these concepts are analyzed and illustrated. You will note that most of these flaws are matters of *degree*. For example, it would be extremely difficult to avoid clichés entirely, and there is no point in attempting to do so; but a piece of writing that is saturated with clichés is likely to be weak, boring, and even ridiculous. Similarly, a limited amount of euphemism in speech or writing may serve a good purpose; but beyond a certain point, it almost always turns sour.

When you are confident that you have refreshed your recollection of these ideas, do the following exercise.

Each of the following sentences illustrates one of the language flaws listed above. Apply the correct identifying letter in each case. Then try your hand at rephrasing each statement in more acceptable form. (In some cases, you may be able to fit a sentence into more than one category. This really doesn't make too much difference, as long as you see what has gone wrong.)

1. *From a furniture store advertisement:* We sell the cheapest furniture in town.

2. *Sign in government office:* Illumination by electrical facilities is hereby required to be extinguished on these premises promptly upon the termination of daily activities prior to the vacating of the area.

3. We were all required to take cover during the stimulated air raid.

4. What a terrific bed! No sooner had I hit the hay than I was in the arms of Morpheus, and I slept like a top all night.

5. Alaska and Rhode Island are respectfully the largest and smallest of the 50 states.

6. He is world famous as an interpreter of Bach's music and as an organ freak.

7. Receiving the full weight of the enemy attack, the troops of the 5th Division broke and scampered to the rear at full speed.

8. It is the established policy of this company to extend full cooperation to its employees in assisting them to qualify for more responsible positions within the existing organizational framework of the enterprise.

9. When I saw that the doors were open, I made a bee dive for the exit.

10. The Nazis attempted to solve their minority problems by a policy of selective elimination of population elements considered undesirable.

11. Dr. Bellman is considered an outstanding maven in the field of cancer research.

12. With her exquisite features, magnificent eyes, flawless complexion, and long, golden hair, she was perhaps the cutest girl I have ever seen.

13. Having made every mistake in the book, I found myself behind the well-known eight ball and was in the depths of despair.

14. Is it any wonder that the country is in trouble when the administration has flaunted all the laws of sound financial management!

15. We worked like dogs to make our social function a rousing success.

16. At this point in time, we hope to finalize the agreement, with full confidence that profits will be maximized and that the bottom line will be a source of satisfaction to all concerned.

17. Our gridiron heroes looked none the worse for wear after a grueling workout in preparation for the annual classic against State.

Exercise II.   Expanding Your Word Power

The words listed below are not on the Basic Word List, but they were mentioned in passing, in one form or another, in Lesson 30. All of them would make useful additions to your working vocabulary. Define each, give its etymology, list **two** synonyms and **two** antonyms (where possible), and use in an original illustrative sentence.

1. facade	6. ire	11. dilute
2. august	7. spiteful	12. nadir
3. deceptive	8. taint	13. hoary
4. resourceful	9. static	14. detach
5. interdict	10. increment	15. ecstasy

Related Forms in Context

Beneath each sentence below are four words introduced in Lesson 29 or 30. Review the related forms for these words, and choose the one that best completes the sentence. Write that related form in the space provided.

1. In Greek mythology, Cerberus, a three-headed dog with a serpent's tail, _____ guards the gate of the Underworld to keep out all who have not yet died.

   a. veracity   b. zany   c. zeal   d. zenith

2. It is difficult to have a lengthy conversation with Len because his _____ often makes others feel uncomfortable.

   a. tacit   b. taciturn   c. traumatic   d. trenchant

3. The boy had cried "Wolf!" so many times when there was no wolf that the townspeople, doubting his _____, ignored his cries when the wolf finally did appear.

   a. vagary   b. wrath   c. zeal   d. veracity

4. We howled at the _____ of the Marx Brothers' 1935 comedy *A Night at the Opera*, especially the scene in which dozens of people crammed into a tiny stateroom.

   a. wrath   b. zeal   c. zany   d. veracity

5. Cindy's letter to the editor is a _____ protest against the city council's cancellation of after-school tutoring and sports at the community center.

   a. veto   b. wrath   c. zany   d. vagary

6. The naturalist shot a _____ dart deep into the grizzly bear's shoulder so that the sedated animal could be transported by truck far from the populated areas of the park.

   a. tranquil   b. tangible   c. tenable   d. tentative

7. With just a slight nod of his head, the man wearing the red tie _____ indicated to the auctioneer that he was raising his bid.

   a. tacit   b. tangible   c. trenchant   d. venerable

8. Leora was so _____ by being taken on a roller coaster when she was a small child that she still refuses to go on any amusement park rides.

   a. ubiquitous   b. tranquil   c. traumatic   d. vindictive

9. My friend and I _____ plan to go out to dinner once a month.

   a. tangible   b. tentative   c. taciturn   d. trenchant

10. After only a dozen moves, Larry could see that White's position was _____ and predicted that White would resign in two moves.

    a. tacit   b. tangible   c. vindictive   d. tenable

11. The flyer says: "Anyone with information leading to the return of a female golden retriever answering to the name of Lady will be thanked from the bottom of our hearts and _____ rewarded, too."

    a. taciturn   b. turbulent   c. tangible   d. trenchant

12. In *As You Like It*, Shakespeare _____ summarizes the human life cycle—for women as well as men—in Jacques's speech about "the seven ages of man."

    a. trenchant   b. ubiquitous   c. venal   d. volatile

13. Because everyone feared the captain's _____, no one dared to disobey his orders.

    a. volatile   b. venerable   c. vindictive   d. versatile

14. Pilots know that wind shear—changes in the wind's speed or direction (or both) where cold and warm air meet—is a major cause of _____ during flight.

    a. taciturn   b. tangible   c. turbulent   d. versatile

15. The _____ of fast-food, gas, and retail chains makes every commercial street and shopping mall in America look basically the same.

    a. volatile   b. ubiquitous   c. venerable   d. trenchant

16. Dave's love of Chinese cooking led him to a lifelong _____ of Chinese art, literature, movies, and music.

    a. venerable   b. tranquil   c. tentative   d. tangible

17. Dressed in his finest, with Judy Garland on his arm, Fred Astaire _____ tips his hat to elegantly clad passersby in the finale of the classic movie *Easter Parade*.

    a. turbulent   b. trenchant   c. tacit   d. urbane

18. Switch-hitters, who can bat both right- and left-handed, are greatly valued for their _____ and their ability to hit against right- and left-handed pitchers.

    a. tangible   b. turbulent   c. venerable   d. versatile

19. In the final scene, the _____ places the crown on his head and slowly ascends the steps to the throne.

    a. thwart   b. usurp   c. vitiate   d. vie

20. Since the Hindenburg disaster in 1937, hydrogen has not been used to fill blimps and other lighter-than-air craft because of its extreme _____.

    a. vindictive   b. venerable   c. ubiquitous   d. volatile

Review

Exercise I.   Syllabication and Pronunciation

Syllabicate the following words correctly, and place the major stress mark (') after the syllable that is accented when the word is pronounced.

1. legacy
2. mercenary
3. nepotism
4. ostensible
5. permeate
6. precocious
7. propitiate
8. redundant
9. resilient
10. retribution
11. stereotype
12. taciturn
13. tentative
14. venerable
15. veto

Exercise II.   Parts of Speech

Indicate the part of speech of each of the following words. In some cases, two answers are correct.

1. libel
2. mammoth
3. morass
4. narcissistic
5. paraphrase
6. parody
7. peremptory
8. pusillanimous
9. recant
10. remorse
11. sacrilegious
12. satellite
13. surveillance
14. tacit
15. yoke

Exercise III.   Words Out of Context

In each of the following groups, select the lettered item that best expresses the meaning of the numbered word at the left.

1. kudos   a. lawsuit   b. glory   c. agency   d. falsehood
                  e. inheritance

2. nebulous   a. tasty   b. crazy   c. lazy   d. hazy   e. daisy

3. obscene   a. foolhardy   b. crucial   c. outmoded
                  d. frugal   e. smutty

4. plaintive   a. majestic   b. malicious   c. melodious
                  d. merry   e. mournful

5. prowess   a. wisdom   b. significance   c. valor
                  d. arrogance   e. terror

6. rescind   a. repeal   b. repeat   c. repel   d. reply
                  e. reprove

7. ruse   a. fiasco   b. impasse   c. exodus
                d. stratagem   e. enigma

8. solace   a. interest   b. comfort   c. schedule
                d. report   e. ally

9. trenchant   a. experimental   b. profitable   c. fortunate
                d. hazardous   e. incisive

10. vie   a. complete   b. complain   c. compete
                d. compose   e. comply

Exercise IV.   Words in Phrases

In each of the following groups, select the lettered item that best expresses the meaning of the *italicized* word in the introductory phrase.

1. a *lucrative* business venture
   a. reprehensible   b. profitable   c. risky   d. clandestine
   e. expensive

2. *nomadic* tribes
   a. primitive   b. indigent   c. numerous   d. superstitious
   e. wandering

3. an *ominous* development
   a. disturbing   b. recent   c. puzzling   d. sudden
   e. pleasing

4. a *pernicious* influence
   a. pivotal   b. salubrious   c. curious   d. detrimental
   e. welcome

5. *promulgate* a law
   a. retract   b. support   c. announce   d. oppose
   e. amend

6. a group of *renegade* Republicans
   a. loyal   b. elderly   c. turncoat   d. eminent   e. junior

7. a *sanctimonious* pronouncement
   a. pie-in-the-sky   b. holier-than-thou   c. devil-may-care
   d. fly-by-night   e. hand-me-down

8. *scrutinize* a report
   a. write   b. suggest   c. ignore   d. type   e. study

9. *tangible* evidence
   a. hidden   b. questionable   c. new   d. fabricated
   e. concrete

10. a *vindictive* attitude
    a. retaliatory   b. benign   c. disinterested   d. strange
    e. foolish

Exercise V. Completing Sentences

Complete each of the following sentences or pairs of sentences by selecting the most appropriate word from the group of words given below. Use each word only once. Make any adjustments that are necessary to fit the words into the sentences properly.

Group A

relent	procrastinate	negligible
pensive	scapegoat	phobia

1. "Why are you so _____ today?" I asked. "Do you have something weighing on your mind?"

2. "Don't postpone your research until the last minute," my professor cautioned me. "Students who _____ usually can't get their term papers done on time."

3. "Though I'm perfectly willing to take the blame for my own mistakes," I replied angrily, "I'm not about to let you make me the _____ for yours."

4. By then the hurricane had pretty much blown itself out, and damage in the area was _____.

5. Over the years, her childhood fear of heights developed into a serious and debilitating _____.

Group B

stamina	volatile	lush
usurp	reminisce	pandemonium

6. It is hard to believe that such a bleak and barren wasteland had once been a(n) _____ tropical paradise.

7. In an interesting article called "Strolling Down Memory Lane," a world-famous actress _____ about life in the theater over 50 years ago.

8. The kind of physical, mental, and emotional _____ a runner needs to complete a 26-mile marathon can justly be called "true grit."

9. In Shakespeare's *Richard III*, the villainous Duke of Gloucester has his royal nephews murdered in the Tower of London and then _____ the throne.

10. "We're sitting on a volcano that is ready to erupt," the official remarked in reference to the _____ situation in that turbulent part of the world.

Exercise VI.   Synonyms and Antonyms

Classify each of the following pairs of words as **S** for **synonyms** or **A** for **antonyms**.

1. lackadaisical—energetic
2. nominal—token
3. fixation—obsession
4. prelude—aftermath
5. quell—foment
6. undermine—sabotage
7. raze—erect
8. schism—rift
9. pervasive—ubiquitous
10. zenith—nadir

Exercise VII.   Framing Sentences

Use each of the following words in an original illustrative sentence.

1. mandatory
2. motley
3. novice
4. opportune
5. poignant
6. purge
7. replenish
8. ritual
9. salient
10. strident
11. sordid
12. thwart
13. vagary
14. veneer
15. zeal

Exercise VIII.   Related Forms

A. Give a **noun** form of each of the following words.

1. perjure
2. prodigious
3. reciprocate
4. predatory
5. ostracize
6. versatile

B. Give a **verb** form of each of the following words.

1. plagiarism
2. tranquil
3. traumatic

C. Give an **adjective** form of each of the following words.

1. rudiment
2. strategy
3. nostalgia

D. Give an **adverb** form of each of the following words.

1. mundane
2. paradox
3. lucid

Exercise IX.   Word Roundup

1. Explain the difference between the words in each of the following pairs.

   a. obsolete—obsolescent
   b. officious—official
   c. senile—senescent
   d. venal—venial
   e. urban—urbane
   f. turbid—turbulent
   g. wrath—wraith
   h. wan—wane

2. Define each of the following.

   a. a muckraker
   b. a drone
   c. a timeserver
   d. a clone
   e. a has-been
   f. a slumlord

3. Explain the meaning of each of the following expressions.

   a. a whipping boy   f. a splinter group
   b. an elective course   g. sphere of influence
   c. maggots in the brain   h. feet of clay
   d. a hand-me-down   i. urban nomads
   e. hero worship   j. tangible assets

4. Explain what each of the following colorful phrases means.

   a. wet behind the ears   f. shed crocodile tears
   b. eat one's words   g. throw in the towel
   c. bury the hatchet   h. put a tail on someone
   d. keep a low profile   i. in high dudgeon
   e. send up a trial balloon   j. give someone the cold shoulder

5. Define each of the following foreign expressions used in present-day English, and tell what language it comes from.

   a. idée fixe   d. scenario   g. amour propre
   b. vendetta   e. wanderlust   h. coup d'état
   c. non compos mentis   f. sine qua non   i. quid pro quo

6. Explain the story behind each of the following.

   a. Lilliputian   c. fifth column   e. chimerical
   b. gargantuan   d. quixotic   f. zealot

Exercise X. Etymology

1. Define each of the following words utilizing the Latin prefix *inter*.

   a. intercede   c. interlude   e. intercept
   b. interact   d. interloper   f. interim

2. Define each of the following words utilizing the Latin prefix *ob*, and explain what the prefix means in that particular word.

   a. obverse   c. obtuse   e. obsess
   b. obituary   d. obliterate   f. obdurate

3. Define each of the following expressions utilizing the Latin preposition *per*.

   a. per annum   b. per capita   c. per se

4. For each of the following definitions, supply an English word using the Latin root *sanct*.

   a. authorize   b. refuge   c. holiness

5. Define each of the following words utilizing the Latin root *tang, tact* or one of its variants.

   a. tactful   c. tangential   e. contiguous
   b. contagious   d. attainment   f. contingency

Exercise XI. Choosing the Right Meaning

Read each sentence carefully. Then underline the item that best completes the statement below the sentence.

1. After examining the defendant, the court-appointed psychiatrist testified that she believes the boy is lucid and capable of standing trial. The defendant's attorneys argue that he is a minor and has no idea that he committed a serious crime. It will be up to the judge to decide.   (2)   (4)

   The word **lucid** in line 2 means

   a. understandable   c. honest
   b. sane   d. reliable

2. In Fort Myers on the west coast of Florida, you can tour Thomas Edison's winter home and visit his laboratory. His lush gardens contain exotic species of tropical trees, including an enormous banyan tree more than 390 feet in diameter.   (2)   (4)

   The word **lush** in line 2 means

   a. flourishing   c. enormous
   b. overripe   d. scientific

3. The many museums that make up the Smithsonian Institution do not charge even a nominal admission fee. Some of the Smithsonian's most popular sites are the National Museum of African Art, the National Air and Space Museum, the National Portrait Gallery, and the Arthur M. Sackler Gallery.   (2)   (4)

   The word **nominal** in line 2 means

   a. membership   c. titular
   b. monthly   d. token

4. Baseball season opened on April 5, and the Swallows proceeded to lose six straight games—three of them shutouts. Pestered relentlessly by reporters, the coach held a press conference after the sixth loss. "I'm extremely sanguine about our team's chances of catching up and pulling ahead," he assured the skeptical journalists.   (2)   (4)

   The word **sanguine** in line 4 means

   a. optimistic   c. concerned
   b. pessimistic   d. ruddy

5. Go is a board game invented in China about 2000 B.C. Like chess, Go is an intellectually demanding "battle game" that requires strategy. Two players start with an empty board on which there is a 19-by-19 grid. Each player attempts to acquire territory by placing his or her stones at the intersections of the grid lines to surround empty spaces and to capture the opponent's stones. The player with the most territory wins the game.   (2)   (4)   (6)

   The word **strategy** in line 3 means

   a. the science of planning   c. great intelligence
   b. a plan of action   d. great skill

6. When the dictator fled, the situation in the tiny nation became extremely volatile. There was no established line of succession, and analysts feared that the many factions vying for power would bring the nation to the brink of civil war. (2) (4)

The word **volatile** in line 2 means

a. dangerous
b. anarchic
c. evaporating readily
d. potentially explosive

7. The curator's selection of objects for the exhibit of Northwest Coast American Indian art is quite parochial. Among the objects on display are Tlingit ceremonial shirts and baskets, Haida slate carvings, Salish blankets woven from mountain goat's wool and vegetable fibers, and painted wooden face masks from various tribes. (2) (4) (6)

The word **parochial** in line 2 means

a. supported by a parish
b. narrow in scope
c. eclectic
d. eye-opening

8. In the process of choosing jurors for a trial, each side has a certain number of peremptory challenges. That is, after questioning members of the jury pool, attorneys for the defendant and for the prosecution can each eliminate a number of jurors without giving cause—that is, a specific reason—based on a hunch that the potential jurors would be prejudiced against their case. (2) (4) (6)

The word **peremptory** in line 2 means

a. tyrannical
b. tentative
c. binding
d. resolute

9. Photos transmitted from weather satellites allow forecasters to make accurate long-range predictions. Such images are especially important when scientists are tracking hurricanes. You can see images of various views of Earth online at the home page of the Geostationary Satellite Server, a division of the National Oceanic and Atmospheric Administration (NOAA). (2) (4) (6)

The word **satellites** in line 1 means

a. protectorates
b. companies
c. subordinates
d. spacecraft

10. Before clocks were invented, people measured time with sundials. The principle of a sundial is simple: The sun at its zenith casts no shadow. From sunrise to sunset, time is indicated by the extent and direction of a shadow on a flat surface marked with hours. The earliest known sundial, a flat stone with an L-shaped bar, is Egyptian and dates from the 8th century B.C. (2) (4) (6)

The word **zenith** in line 3 means

a. highest point directly overhead
b. closest point to an observer
c. height of fame
d. brightest moment

Cumulative Review

1. abdicate — 400. zenith

Exercise I.   Syllabication and Pronounciation

Syllabicate each of the following words properly, and place the major stress mark (') after the syllable that is accented when the word is pronounced. In one case, two answers are correct.

1. academic	11. credibility	21. lucrative
2. aggregate	12. deviate	22. nostalgia
3. anecdote	13. duplicity	23. ostensible
4. anomaly	14. eminent	24. precarious
5. atrocity	15. epithet	25. procrastinate
6. bizarre	16. feasible	26. reprisal
7. bravado	17. formidable	27. sacrilegious
8. cantankerous	18. gregarious	28. stipulate
9. circuitous	19. heinous	29. vagary
10. confrontation	20. intervene	30. vindictive

Exercise II.   Parts of Speech

Indicate the part of speech of each of the following words. In many cases, two answers are correct.

1. abject	11. consummate	21. mammoth
2. advocate	12. delinquent	22. mercenary
3. anachronism	13. discourse	23. obsequious
4. array	14. eclectic	24. premise
5. atrophy	15. esoteric	25. prowess
6. benign	16. expedient	26. renegade
7. boorish	17. finesse	27. salient
8. buttress	18. harangue	28. stereotype
9. censor	19. incarcerate	29. taciturn
10. compatible	20. jettison	30. yoke

Exercise III.   Words Out of Context

In each of the following groups, select the lettered item that best expresses the meaning of the numbered word at the left.

1. abet   a. deplore   b. conclude   c. assist   d. refine
    e. hamper

2. agenda   a. failure   b. battle   c. omen   d. environment
    e. schedule

3. anarchy   a. chaos   b. poverty   c. throwback   d. prejudice
    e. curse

4. apprehend   a. accuse   b. catch   c. protect   d. invade
    e. release

5. augment   a. increase   b. scorn   c. curtail   d. expiate
      e. compensate

6. bicker   a. esteem   b. measure   c. provide   d. relax
      e. squabble

7. boisterous   a. bloated   b. dismal   c. friendly   d. rowdy
      e. suspicious

8. candid   a. learned   b. costly   c. frank   d. sour
      e. tactful

9. charlatan   a. officer   b. employee   c. fraud   d. baker
      e. relative

10. condone   a. point at   b. flinch at   c. aim at   d. rail at
      e. wink at

11. culpable   a. in unison   b. at fault   c. off guard
      d. on target   e. by heart

12. devout   a. casual   b. ignorant   c. eccentric   d. ardent
      e. polite

13. dormant   a. inactive   b. cursory   c. frantic   d. decrepit
      e. obedient

14. emaciated   a. gaunt   b. gigantic   c. gleeful   d. gingerly
      e. gracious

15. exacerbate   a. alleviate   b. incur   c. intensify   d. confuse
      e. humble

16. feign   a. cure   b. pretend   c. honor   d. cause
      e. investigate

17. fiasco   a. development   b. effect   c. reason   d. attempt
      e. failure

18. garble   a. distort   b. revise   c. allow   d. concede
      e. embellish

19. impasse   a. solution   b. tunnel   c. error   d. deadlock
      e. viewpoint

20. ingenious   a. expensive   b. modern   c. frank   d. clever
      e. dangerous

21. mandatory   a. grasping   b. lethargic   c. required
      d. masculine   e. profitable

22. moot   a. debatable   b. snobbish   c. radical   d. diverse
      e. monetary

23. parody   a. saloon   b. monsoon   c. pontoon   d. lampoon
      e. dragoon

24. pernicious   a. welcome   b. eternal   c. fragile   d. economical
      e. harmful

25. prerogative   a. privilege   b. facility   c. antipathy
      d. circumstance   e. requirement

26. rescind   a. reply   b. repeal   c. reprove   d. repel
      e. repeat

27. retribution   a. hostility   b. discord   c. pestilence
                     d. vengeance   e. calamity

28. senile   a. openhanded   b. tight-lipped   c. feebleminded
                     d. hot-blooded   e. thin-skinned

29. ubiquitous   a. incisive   b. omnipresent   c. vacuous
                     d. provisional   e. specific

30. veracity   a. endurance   b. wisdom   c. truthfulness
                     d. determination   e. agility

Exercise IV.   Completing Sentences

Complete each of the following sentences by selecting the most appropriate word from the groups of words given below. Make any adjustments that are necessary to fit the words into the sentences properly.

Group A

distraught	accede	ignominy
incense	pseudonym	brash

1. Though most of the committee readily _____ to my request for additional funds, a few members stubbornly refused to countenance the unexpected expenditure.

2. "He is a(n)_____ young man," the general observed sourly, "whose reckless and precipitate actions almost cost us the battle."

3. Though one of the women received the news of the accident with remarkable composure, the other became _____ with grief and worry.

4. Most writers publish their works under their own names, but a few prefer to use _____.

5. I could tell from the loud voices and angry words issuing from my boss's office that something had really _____ him.

Group B

cajole	innovation	inherent
enigma	affluent	replenish

6. The fact that I have grown up in a(n) _____ suburb does not mean that I am unaware of conditions in the inner-city slums.

7. Though we all desire to improve life in the United States, we should not blindly accept every _____ that comes along simply because it is new.

8. A little sweet talk is usually a surefire means of _____ someone into doing what you want done.

9. When I realized that we were running out of potato chips, I made a hurried trip to the corner grocery store to _____ our supply.

10. Just who is being described in Sir Edward Elgar's _____ Variations puzzled music lovers for many years.

Group C

| euphemism | sabotage | ethnic |
| anathema | caustic | lurk |

11. He is so malicious that if he cannot control the organization, he may try to _____ or otherwise hinder its operations.

12. After the nightmarish experience I had in the park last fall, I began to imagine muggers and purse snatchers _____ behind every tree or bush I passed.

13. When he said, "One man's meat is another man's poison," he simply meant that what one person likes may be _____ to somebody else.

14. In order to spare the feelings of relatives, funeral directors usually resort to _____ such as "the loved one" or "the dear departed" when speaking of the person who has died.

15. She has a sharp tongue and a(n) _____ wit that she uses with great skill and imagination in her televised movie reviews.

Group D

| collaborate | arbitrate | fathom |
| myriad | surveillance | secular |

16. When the contract negotiations broke down, both labor and management agreed to call in an impartial third party to _____ the dispute.

17. One of the verses in a Shakespearean song about the sea begins, "Full _____ five thy father lies; Of his bones are coral made."

18. For almost 20 years, Gilbert and Sullivan _____ on a series of world-famous light operas, including *H.M.S. Pinafore* and *The Yeoman of the Guard.*

19. The facets of the human personality are as _____ as the stars in a summer sky or the grains of sand on a tropical beach.

20. Though members of the clergy must devote most of their time to their clerical duties, they are usually able to pursue _____ interests that have little or no bearing on their profession.

Group E

| obsession | construe | fortuitous |
| connoisseur | traumatic | augur |

21. Although he had been looking forward to retirement, he found the change in his lifestyle a disturbing, even a(n) _____ experience.

22. I have no objection to a person having a keen interest in bridge, but I am afraid that the game has become almost a(n) _____ with you.

23. When Albert Einstein remarked that God does not play dice with the world, he meant that developments in nature are not purely _____.

24. Since I didn't know how to _____ her unexpected remark, I asked my best friend what he made of it.

25. We might describe a promising development as something that _____ well for success or victory in the future.

Group F

harbinger	grope	venerable
phobia	devoid	baffle

26. What began as a mere distaste for subway travel has developed into a full-blown _____ that makes even a short trip an agonizing experience.

27. That school is a _____ institution that has seen generations of students pass through its hallowed portals.

28. The proposal may look good at first glance; but if you study it carefully, you will see that it is _____ of any real merit.

29. Suddenly awakened by the insistent ringing of the telephone, I _____ around sleepily for the receiver.

30. Ordinary detectives may be _____ by a particularly ingenious crime, but the redoubtable Hercule Poirot is never stumped.

Exercise V. Words in Phrases

In each of the following groups, select the lettered item that best expresses the meaning of the *italicized* word in the introductory phrase.

1. completely *absolved* the defendant
   a. ignored   b. convicted   c. reproached   d. arrested
   e. acquitted

2. *adjourned* the meeting
   a. planned   b. suspended   c. attended   d. approved   e. opened

3. their *ambivalent* attitude
   a. scholarly   b. laudable   c. narrow-minded   d. contradictory
   e. discourteous

4. an *articulate* proponent of the plan
   a. long-standing   b. unexpected   c. well-known   d. eloquent
   e. self-appointed

5. seek *asylum* in the United States
   a. justice   b. refuge   c. wealth   d. fame   e. revenge

6. motivated solely by *avarice*
   a. hatred   b. fear   c. greed   d. ambition   e. jealousy

7. a *brusque* reply
   a. curt   b. pompous   c. interesting   d. amusing   e. silly

8. an outright *calumny*
   a. joke   b. disaster   c. blunder   d. refusal   e. falsehood

9. *clandestine* meetings
   a. unexpected   b. welcome   c. noisy   d. secret   e. important

10. an interesting *conjecture*
    a. fact   b. development   c. guess   d. book   e. history

11. my *corpulent* uncle
    a. portly   b. elderly   c. stately   d. wealthy   e. surly

12. *defer* a decision
    a. withdraw   b. overrule   c. ignore   d. confirm   e. postpone

13. *diligent* students
    a. recalcitrant   b. indolent   c. knowledgeable   d. indefatigable
    e. talented

14. the *elite* of the entertainment world
    a. retired members   b. fans   c. rank and file   d. has-beens
    e. cream of the crop

15. bore the news with *equanimity*
    a. assistance   b. composure   c. indifference   d. reluctance
    e. hysteria

16. *expound* a theory
    a. attack   b. verify   c. explain   d. demolish   e. ignore

17. *filch* an apple
    a. steal   b. polish   c. eat   d. grow   e. buy

18. a *grueling* race
    a. downhill   b. contested   c. brief   d. draining   e. surprising

19. *impugned* my motives
    a. cash doubt on   b. threw light on   c. paid attention to
    d. gave evidence of   e. took comfort in

20. "*justify* the ways of God to man"
    a. criticize   b. vindicate   c. divulge   d. deplore   e. report

21. a *lucid* account
    a. muddled   b. long   c. funny   d. brief   e. clear

22. at a *nominal* cost to the consumer
    a. guaranteed   b. legal   c. token   d. sizable   e. fair

23. in a *pensive* mood
    a. puzzling   b. thoughtful   c. elated   d. friendly   e. obstinate

24. a *peremptory* tone of voice
    a. hopeful   b. dictatorial   c. jubilant   d. discouraged
    e. plaintive

25. *promulgate* a law
    a. announce   b. oppose   c. circumvent   d. advocate   e. propose

26. felt no *remorse*
    a. loneliness   b. animosity   c. hunger   d. regret   e. desire

27. became a mere *satellite* of Alexander's empire
    a. enemy   b. friend   c. aim   d. protectorate   e. citizen

28. *scrutinize* the faces on the platform
    a. ignore   b. examine   c. draw   d. memorize   e. remember

29. *tangible* results
    a. insignificant   b. costly   c. unexpected   d. negative
    e. concrete

30. the *volatile* situation in that part of the world
   a. heartwarming   b. curious   c. explosive   d. tranquil
   e. recent

Exercise VI.   Synonyms and Antonyms

Classify each of the following pairs of words as **S** for **synonyms** or **A** for **antonyms**.

1. abhor—relish
2. amiable—affable
3. alienate—estrange
4. apathy—enthusiasm
5. astute—obtuse
6. belligerent—hostile
7. boycott—patronize
8. catholic—parochial
9. habitual—chronic
10. complacent—smug
11. truncate—curtail
12. dapper—slovenly
13. praise—disparage
14. endemic—native
15. ignorant—erudite

16. exploit—feat
17. fluctuate—vacillate
18. smile—grimace
19. explicit—implicit
20. inception—inauguration
21. liability—asset
22. nebulous—vague
23. bedlam—pandemonium
24. plaintive—mournful
25. quell—foment
26. raze—erect
27. ruse—stratagem
28. strident—mellifluous
29. foil—thwart
30. nadir—zenith

Exercise VII.   Related Forms

A. Give a **noun** form of each of the following words.

1. abdicate
2. agile
3. allege
4. banal
5. bombastic
6. corroborate
7. emulate
8. entice
9. futile
10. jeopardize
11. nomadic
12. prodigious
13. redundant
14. usurp
15. versatile

B. Give an **adjective** form of each of the following words.

1. coerce
2. bureaucracy
3. defect
4. disparity
5. rudiment
6. strategy

C. Give an **adverb** form of each of the following words.

1. arbitrary
2. circumspect
3. facetious
4. graphic
5. tenable
6. paradox

D. Give a **verb** form of each of the following words.

1. authentic
2. impediment
3. plagiarism

Exercise VIII.   Look-Alikes

Explain the difference in meaning between the words in each of the following pairs.

1. loath—loathe
2. averse—adverse
3. aesthetic—ascetic
4. callous—callow
5. forbear—forebear
6. flout—flaunt

7.	indigent—indigenous	10.	exalt—exult	13.	urban—urbane
8.	demur—demure	11.	official—officious	14.	venal—venial
9.	discomfit—discomfort	12.	turbid—turbulent	15.	wan—wane

Exercise IX.   Framing Sentences

Compose an original illustrative sentence for each of the following words.

Group A

1.	abstain	6.	crucial	11.	lackadaisical
2.	amnesty	7.	divulge	12.	ominous
3.	austere	8.	ethical	13.	purge
4.	bleak	9.	foible	14.	revere
5.	censure	10.	immunity	15.	tranquil

Group B

16.	affectation	21.	delineate	26.	motley
17.	appall	22.	effrontery	27.	perjure
18.	avid	23.	exodus	28.	reciprocate
19.	bungle	24.	goad	29.	scapegoat
20.	concise	25.	judicious	30.	veto

Exercise X.   Word Roundup

1. Define each of the following words.

a.	teetotaler	f.	windfall	k.	timeserver
b.	academician	g.	rubberneck	l.	has-been
c.	claptrap	h.	fluke	m.	clone
d.	aesthete	i.	dilettante	n.	gadfly
e.	mannerism	j.	greenhorn	o.	muckraker

2. Explain what each of the following phrases means.

a.	academic freedom	f.	Judas kiss
b.	halcyon days	g.	mirror image
c.	red tape	h.	hero worship
d.	devil's advocate	i.	feet of clay
e.	credibility gap	j.	splinter group

3. Explain what each of the following colorful idioms means.

a.	living high off the hog	f.	live in an ivory tower
b.	rest on one's laurels	g.	pour oil on troubled waters
c.	put on airs	h.	bury the hatchet
d.	see red	i.	throw in the towel
e.	paint oneself into a corner	j.	shed crocodile tears

4. Explain the story behind each of the following words.

   | a. | boycott | c. | jeremiad | e. | quixotic |
   | b. | Comstockery | d. | malapropism | f. | zealot |

5. Explain the meaning of each of the following foreign expressions used in present-day English, and tell what language it comes from.

a.	milieu	d.	vendetta
b.	impedimenta	e.	coup d'état
c.	tour de force	f.	quid pro quo

Exercise XI. Choosing the Right Meaning

Read each sentence carefully. Then underline the item that best completes the statement below the sentence.

1. An economics professor who appears on a weekly talk show claims that many people do not fully apprehend the gravity of the current situation. Inflation is rising along with business inventories, and, she warns, we may be on the brink of a global recession. (2) (4)

   The word **apprehend** in line 2 means

   a. capture
   b. fear
   c. comprehend
   d. anticipate

2. Be sure to keep all caustic substances, such as lye, in tightly sealed containers in locked cabinets. Young children, who are naturally curious, can be severely injured by coming in contact with these substances. (2)

   The word **caustic** in line 1 means

   a. hazardous
   b. sardonic
   c. corrosive
   d. cleansing

3. This pie chart, a graphic representation of statistics from the U.S. Census Bureau, shows that in 1992, 40 percent of American females age seven and older participated in some form of aerobic exercise. Of these, about 32 percent ran, and about 32 percent played basketball. (2) (4)

   The word **graphic** in line 1 means

   a. realistic
   b. vivid
   c. factual
   d. visual

4. Women in the United States did not obtain the right to vote until 1920. But advocates of woman suffrage both here and in England had for decades protested unequal treatment of women. No women, they insisted, should be discriminated against because of her sex. (2) (4)

   The words **discriminated against** in line 4 mean

   a. differentiated
   b. treated unfairly
   c. criticized
   d. isolated

5. Cattle, sheep, and other animals that ruminate exhale a sizable quantity of methane gas and thereby contribute to global warming. Scientists are researching ways to reduce ruminants' methane emissions by improving the kinds of feed given to livestock. (2) (4)

   The word **ruminate** in line 1 means

   a. contract diseases
   b. chew cud
   c. ponder at length
   d. roam freely

6. Betty Comden and Adolph Green collaborated for six decades, producing the lyrics and screenplays for several of Hollywood's best-loved musical comedies. Their many successes include *On the Town* (1949), *Singin' in the Rain* (1952), and *Bells Are Ringing* (1960). (2) (4)

   The word **collaborated** in line 1 means

   a. teamed up
   b. acted in
   c. conspired
   d. wrote

7. The course will cover works by the twentieth-century Argentine essayist, short story writer, and poet Jorge Luis Borges. Many of (2) Borges's fictional pieces are esoteric fantasies or allegories, but he has also written detective stories. (4)

The word **esoteric** in line 3 means

a. secret   c. famous
b. popular   d. cryptic

8. After an unusually harsh winter, spring proved to be disappointingly erratic. A string of warm and sunny April days was followed by over- (2) cast skies and bleak, snowy weather.

The word **bleak** in line 3 means

a. sunny   c. barren
b. changeable   d. cold and gloomy

9. Woods Hole, Massachusetts, on the southwestern tip of Cape Cod, is home to a prestigious enclave of marine scientists. Founded in 1930, (2) the Woods Hole Oceanographic Institution sponsors research and education in many fields, including applied ocean physics and engi- (4) neering, marine chemistry, biology, geology, geophysics, deep ocean exploration, and ocean and climate change. (6)

The word **enclave** in line 2 means

a. separate community   c. fenced-in enclosure
b. country within a country   d. academy

10. In many states, drivers must prove that they have liability insurance before they can obtain or renew their motor vehicle registration or dri- (2) ver's license or obtain their vehicle safety inspection. Individual state laws mandate the minimum dollar amounts of liability coverage. (4)

The word **liability** in line 1 means

a. hindrance or handicap   c. safety
b. financial obligation   d. medical

11. Hot pepper and curry powder give mulligatawny soup its name, for *mulligatawny* comes from the Tamil words that mean "pepper water." (2) The soup, which is far from bland, is a popular Anglo-Indian recipe from eastern India. (4)

The word **bland** in line 3 means

a. boring   c. mild
b. spicy   d. exciting

12. In Stephen Vincent Benét's short story "The Devil and Daniel Webster," a fictional New Hampshire farmer named Jabez Stone pleads (2) with Webster, a real-life statesman and orator, to act as his counsel. Stone explains that ten years earlier he had sold his soul to the devil (4) and that now the devil has come to collect it.

The word **counsel** in line 3 means

a. guidance   c. friend
b. protector   d. lawyer

13. Some county-wide services (such as parks, libraries, and schools) are gratuitous to all residents, paid for by taxes. For other services (such (2) as garbage pickup and water), property owners pay the county directly.

The word **gratuitous** in line 2 means

a. unjustified   c. free
b. expensive   d. available

14. Hansel and Gretel carefully leave a trail of breadcrumbs to mark their circuitous journey through the woods. When it's time to find their way (2) home, they discover that birds have eaten their markers and they are lost. Soon they find themselves standing before a gingerbread house (4) decorated with candy.

The word **circuitous** in line 2 means

a. roundabout   c. dark and dangerous
b. long-winded   d. steep and rocky

15. Louise Erdrich's poem "Indian Boarding School" alludes to efforts by the Federal Bureau of Indian Affairs to assimilate Native Americans into the (2) mainstream culture. Starting in the 1870s, children from all tribes were pressured into attending boarding schools far from their homes. Once at (4) the schools, they were prohibited from practicing any tribal rituals or speaking their native languages; only English was allowed. (6)

The word **assimilate** in line 2 means

a. integrate   c. digest
b. separate   d. educate

16. During the Battle of Chancellorsville in May 1863, Union forces out-numbered Confederates two to one. Nevertheless, General Robert E. (2) Lee discomfited Major General Joseph Hooker's Union forces in a fierce battle that lasted several days. The toll was grim. More than (4) 1,700 Confederate soldiers died and over 9,200 were wounded, while Union forces lost more than 1,600 dead and nearly 9,700 wounded. (6)

The word **discomfited** in line 3 means

a. soundly defeated   c. embarrassed
b. confused   d. angered

17. The United Nations Commission on Human Rights issued a resolution asking the tiny nation to allow U.N. monitors to investigate the treat- (2) ment of those who openly protested the current regime. Implicit in this resolution was a criticism of the harsh crackdown on political (4) dissidents.

The word **implicit** in line 3 means

a. unconditional   c. emphasized
b. directly stated   d. implied

18. Children can be exceedingly resilient. During the prolonged bombing of London during World War II, for example, most of the children who (2) were sent for safety to strangers' homes in towns outside London ad-justed to their new circumstances despite being uprooted from their (4) family, friends, and homes.

The word **resilient** in line 1 means

a. able to resume original shape   c. able to remain cheerful
b. able to recover quickly   d. unable to make changes easily

19. The sun's ultraviolet rays can cause several types of skin cancer, pre- (2)
mature wrinkles, and other signs of aging. Therefore, dermatologists
recommend that when you are out in the sun, you should apply sun-
screen liberally and frequently, especially if you have a sanguine or (4)
pale complexion.

The word **sanguine** in line 4 means

a. optimistic   c. freckled
b. dark   d. ruddy

20. Here's a paradox with overtones of Washington Irving's story, "Rip Van
Winkle." Imagine that an astronaut has been in space for 25 years, (2)
always traveling near the speed of light. When the astronaut returns
to Earth, his family and friends will have aged 25 years, but the as- (4)
tronaut will not have aged as much. Can you explain why?

The word **paradox** in line 1 means

a. anomaly   c. riddle
b. scientific fact   d. humorous imitation

21. Voter apathy is a serious problem in the United States. Every year an
alarming number of registered voters do not bother to vote, even in pres- (2)
idential elections. Some nonvoters profess a blithe attitude toward governmental matters. Others claim they are too busy to vote. Still others (4)
say that they don't vote as a protest against the choice of candidates.

The word **blithe** in line 3 means

a. jolly   c. blasé
b. ambivalent   d. gloomy

22. You and a friend can take an online test to see how compatible you
are. Among other topics, the test asks about the way you like to spend (2)
your free time, your attitude toward neatness, your spending habits,
your ambitions, your dislikes, and your fears. (4)

The word **compatible** in line 1 means

a. consistent   c. well-adjusted
b. inconsistent   d. like-minded

23. In a long-running comedy, three actors perform *The Complete Works
of William Shakespeare (Abridged)* in just under 97 minutes. There is (2)
a parody of *Hamlet*, of course, during which the actors present *Hamlet* backward. (4)

The word **parody** in line 3 means

a. take-off   c. condensation
b. mockery   d. serious analysis

24. In Greek mythology, Orpheus journeys to the Underworld—a
formidable undertaking—to find and recover his beloved wife Eury- (2)
dice. Impressed by Orpheus's great devotion, Hades promises Orpheus that his wife will be restored to him on one condition: He must (4)
not look back at her until they reach the land of the living. But, alas,
Orpheus turns around to see if Eurydice is behind him, and she van- (6)
ishes forever.

The word **formidable** in line 2 means

a. tremendous   c. terrifying
b. courageous   d. misguided

Index

The words that make up the Basic Word List are included in this Index and are printed in **boldface** type. The number following each of these words indicates the page on which the word is first introduced. Exercises and review materials in which these words also appear are not cited.

Photo Credits